Exam 70-646: Pro: Windows Serve
Server Administrator (2ⁿᵈ Edition)

D0690910

Exam Objectives   The exam objectives listed here are current as of this book's publication date. Exam objectives are subject to change at any time without prior notice and at Microsoft's sole discretion. Please visit the Microsoft Learning Web site for the most current listing of exam objectives: *http://www.microsoft.com/learning/en/us/Exam .aspx?ID=70-646.*

![Microsoft]

MCITP Self-Paced Training Kit (Exam 70-646): Windows Server® 2008 Server Administrator (2nd Edition)

Orin Thomas
Ian McLean

PUBLISHED BY
Microsoft Press
A Division of Microsoft Corporation
One Microsoft Way
Redmond, Washington 98052-6399

Library of Congress Control Number: 2011929711
ISBN: 978-0-7356-4909-5

2 3 4 5 6 7 8 9 10 11 QG 6 5 4 3 2 1

Printed and bound in the United States of America.

First Printing

Microsoft Press books are available through booksellers and distributors worldwide. If you need support related to this book, email Microsoft Press Book Support at mspinput@microsoft.com. Please tell us what you think of this book at http://www.microsoft.com/learning/booksurvey.

Acquisitions Editor: Jeff Koch
Developmental Editor: Karen Szall
Project Editor: Rosemary Caperton
Editorial Production: Christian Holdener, S4Carlisle Publishing Services
Technical Reviewer: Mitch Tulloch; Technical Review services provided by Content Master, a member of CM Group, Ltd.
Copyeditor: Sue McClung
Indexer: Jean Skipp
Cover: Twist Creative • Seattle

[2011-09-30]

This book is dedicated to my second grandchild, who is due to be born in early September 2011 and is currently known as Bump – also to Bump's Mummy and Daddy, Harjit and Drew, and of course to Bump's sister Freya, who is almost four and a big girl now.

—IAN MCLEAN

To the awesome team at DDLS Melbourne, hope that we work together again soon!

—ORIN THOMAS

Contents at a Glance

Contents

What do you think of this book? We want to hear from you!

Microsoft is interested in hearing your feedback so we can continually improve our
books and learning resources for you. To participate in a brief online survey, please visit:

www.microsoft.com/learning/booksurvey/

Chapter 9   Remote Access and Network Access Protection   433

Chapter 10   Provision Data and Plan Storage   473

What do you think of this book? We want to hear from you!

Microsoft is interested in hearing your feedback so we can continually improve our books and learning resources for you. To participate in a brief online survey, please visit:

www.microsoft.com/learning/booksurvey/

Introduction

This training kit is designed for server and domain administrators who have two to three years of experience managing Windows servers and infrastructure in an environment that typically supports 250 to 5,000 (or even more) users in three or more physical locations and has three or more domain controllers. You will likely be responsible for supporting network services and resources such as messaging, database servers, file and print servers, a proxy server, a firewall, the Internet, an intranet, remote access, and clients. You also will be responsible for implementing connectivity requirements, such as connecting branch offices and individual users in remote locations to the corporate network and connecting corporate networks to the Internet.

The material covered in this training kit and on Exam 70-646 relates to the technologies in a Windows Server 2008 or Windows Server 2008 R2 network that support distributed access to web content, media, operating systems, and applications. The topics in this training kit cover what you need to know for the exam as described on the Skills Measured tab for the exam, which is available at

http://www.microsoft.com/learning/en/us/exam.aspx?ID=70-647&locale=en-us

By using this training kit, you will learn how to do the following:

- Plan and implement the deployment of servers running Windows Server 2008 and Windows Server 2008 R2
- Plan and implement the management of servers running Windows Server 2008 and Windows Server 2008 R2
- Monitor, maintain, and optimize servers
- Plan application and data provisioning
- Plan and implement high-availability strategies and ensure business continuity

Refer to the objective mapping page in the front of this book to see where each exam objective is covered in the book.

System Requirements

The following are the minimum system requirements that your computer needs to meet to complete the practice exercises in this book and to run the companion CD. To minimize the time and expense of configuring physical computers for this training kit, it's recommended that you use Hyper-V, which is a feature of Windows Server 2008 and Windows Server 2008 R2. You can use third-party virtualization products, but the practice setup instructions in the book are written on the assumption that you are using Hyper-V.

Hardware Requirements

It is possible to complete almost all the practice exercises in this book using virtual machines rather than real server hardware. The system requirements for Windows Server 2008 R2 are listed on the following Web page:
http://www.microsoft.com/windowsserver2008/en/us/system-requirements.aspx.

If you intend to implement several virtual machines on the same computer (which is recommended), a higher specification will enhance your user experience. In particular, a computer with 8 GB of RAM and 150 GB of free disk space can host all the virtual machines specified for all the practice exercises in this book.

Software Requirements

The following software is required to complete all the practices:

- Windows Server 2008 R2 Enterprise edition
- Windows 7 Enterprise or Ultimate edition

You can obtain evaluation versions of the Windows Server 2008 R2 Enterprise edition and Windows 7 Enterprise edition from the Microsoft Download Center at the following address: *http://www.microsoft.com/Downloads/Search.aspx.*

Preparing the Computers Running Windows Server 2008 R2 Enterprise Edition

Detailed instructions for installing Windows Server 2008 R2 and installing and configuring the domain controller and member server running Windows Server 2008 R2 Enterprise edition are given in Appendix A, "Setup Instructions for Windows Server 2008 R2." The required server roles are added in the practice exercises in subsequent chapters.

Practice Setup Instructions

The exercises in this training kit require a minimum of two computers or virtual machines, as follows:

- One server running Windows Server 2008 R2 Enterprise, configured as a domain controller
- One server running Windows Server 2008 R2 Enterprise, configured as a member server

If you want to carry out all the practices and suggested practices in Chapter 4, "Group Policy Strategies," you need an additional client running Windows 7 Enterprise or Ultimate edition. All these computers can be virtual machines. You also need a second hard disk (internal or external) that is connected to your domain controller to carry out the practices in Chapter 13, "Backup and Recovery." If you are using virtual machines, this can be a virtual hard disk.

All computers must be connected physically to the same network. We recommend that you use an isolated network that is not part of your production network to do the practice exercises in this book. To minimize the time and expense of configuring physical computers, we recommend that you use virtual machines. To run computers as virtual machines on a server running Windows Server 2008 or Windows Server 2008 R2, you need to install the Hyper-V server role. Alternatively, you can use supported third-party virtual machine products.

Using the CD

The companion CD included with this training kit contains the following:

- **Practice tests** You can reinforce your understanding of how to configure Windows Server 2008 R2 by using electronic practice tests that you customize to meet your needs from the pool of Lesson Review questions in this book. Alternatively, you can practice for the 70-646 certification exam by using tests created from a pool of 200 realistic exam questions, which give you many opportunities to take practice exams to ensure that you are prepared.

- **An eBook** An electronic version (eBook) of this book is included so that you do not always have to carry the printed book with you. The eBook is in Portable Document Format (PDF), and you can view it by using Adobe Acrobat or Adobe Reader.

How to Install the Practice Tests

To install the practice test software from the companion CD to your hard disk, perform the following steps:

1. Insert the companion CD into your CD-ROM drive and accept the license agreement. The CD menu appears.

> *NOTE* **IF THE CD MENU DOES NOT APPEAR**
>
> If the CD menu or the license agreement does not appear, AutoRun might be disabled on your computer. Refer to the Readme.txt file on the CD-ROM for alternate installation instructions.

2. Click Practice Tests and follow the instructions on the screen.

How to Use the Practice Tests

To start the practice test software, follow these steps:

1. Click Start, All Programs, and then Microsoft Press Training Kit Exam Prep. A window appears that shows all the Microsoft Press training kit exam prep suites that are installed on your computer.

2. Double-click the lesson review or practice test that you want to use.

> **NOTE LESSON REVIEWS VS. PRACTICE TESTS**
>
> Select the (70-646) Windows Server 2008 R2 Server Administrator *lesson review* to use the questions from the "Lesson Review" sections of this book. Select the (70-646) Windows Server 2008 R2 Server Administrator *practice test* to use a pool of 300 questions similar to those that appear on the 70-646 certification exam.

Lesson Review Options

When you start a lesson review, the Custom Mode dialog box appears so that you can configure your test. You can click OK to accept the defaults or you can customize the number of questions you want, how the practice test software works, which exam objectives you want the questions to relate to, and whether you want your lesson review to be timed. If you are retaking a test, you can select whether you want to see all the questions again or only the questions you missed or did not answer.

After you click OK, your lesson review starts.

-   To take the test, answer the questions and use the Next, Previous, and Go To buttons to move from question to question.

-   After you answer an individual question, if you want to see which answers are correct—along with an explanation of each correct answer—click Explanation.

-   If you prefer to wait until the end of the test to see how you did, answer all the questions and then click Score Test. You will see a summary of the exam objectives that you chose and the percentage of questions that you got right, both overall and per objective. You can print a copy of your test, review your answers, or retake the test.

Practice Test Options

When you start a practice test, you choose whether to take the test in Certification Mode, Study Mode, or Custom Mode, which are as follows:

-   **Certification Mode**   This mode closely resembles the experience of taking a certification exam. The test has a set number of questions, it is timed, and you cannot pause and restart the timer.

- **Study Mode** This mode creates an untimed test, in which you can review the correct answer and the explanations for all the answer choices after you answer each question.
- **Custom Mode** This mode gives you full control over the test options so that you can customize them as you like.

The user interface when you are taking the test is basically the same in all the modes, but with different options enabled or disabled depending on the mode. The main options are discussed in the previous section, "Lesson Review Options."

When you review your answer to an individual practice test question, a "References" section is provided, which lists where in the training kit you can find the information that relates to that question and provides links to other sources of information. After you click Test Results to score your entire practice test, you can click the Learning Plan tab to see a list of references for every objective.

How to Uninstall the Practice Tests

To uninstall the practice test software for a training kit, use the Program And Features option in the Control Panel.

> **NOTE   COMPANION CONTENT FOR DIGITAL BOOK READERS**
>
> If you bought a digital edition of this book, you can enjoy select content from the print edition's companion CD. Visit *http://go.microsoft.com/FWLink/?Linkid=219765* to get your downloadable content.

Acknowledgments

The authors' names appear on the cover of a book, but we are only two members of a much larger team. First of all, thanks to Jeff Koch, for allowing us to update the first edition of this book, and to Karen Szall, our developmental editor. During the writing process, we worked most closely with Rosemary Caperton and Susan McClung. Rosemary and Sue, thanks for your patience with us and for making this a great book. Mitch Tulloch was our technical reviewer, and he was far more committed to the project than any reviewer we've worked with in the past. We would also like to thank Christian Holdener, of S4Carlisle Publishing Services, for his invaluable assistance in orchestrating the diverse actors in the enterprise of putting this book together. Each of our editors contributed significantly to this book, and we hope to work with them all in the future.

Support & Feedback

The following sections provide information on errata, book support, feedback, and contact information.

Errata & Book Support

We've made every effort to ensure the accuracy of this book and its companion content. Any errors that have been reported since this book was published are listed on our Microsoft Press site at oreilly.com:

http://go.microsoft.com/FWLink/?Linkid=219763

If you find an error that is not already listed, you can report it to us through the same page.

If you need additional support, please email Microsoft Press Book Support at *mspinput@ microsoft.com*.

Please note that product support for Microsoft software is not offered through the addresses above.

We Want to Hear from You

At Microsoft Press, your satisfaction is our top priority, and your feedback our most valuable asset. Please tell us what you think of this book at:

http://www.microsoft.com/learning/booksurvey

The survey is short, and we read every one of your comments and ideas. Thanks in advance for your input!

Stay in Touch

Let us keep the conversation going! We are on Twitter: *http://twitter.com/MicrosoftPress*

Preparing for the Exam

M icrosoft certification exams are a great way to build your resume and let the world know about your level of expertise. Certification exams validate your on-the-job experience and product knowledge. While there is no substitution for on-the-job experience, preparation through study and hands-on practice can help you prepare for the exam. We recommend that you round out your exam preparation plan by using a combination of available study materials and courses. For example, you might use the Training Kit and another study guide for your "at home" preparation, and take a Microsoft Official Curriculum course for the classroom experience. Choose the combination that you think works best for you.

Microsoft
C E R T I F I E D
Technology
Specialist

CHAPTER 1

Installing, Upgrading, and Deploying Windows Server 2008 R2

This chapter is about planning the deployment of Windows Server 2008 and Windows Server 2008 R2. Throughout the text, we will use the name "Windows Server 2008 R2" to describe the product. However, unless explicitly stated otherwise, the information provided will apply to both the Windows Server 2008 and Windows Server 2008 R2 operating systems. In Lesson 1, "Planning Installation and Upgrade," you will learn which edition of Windows Server 2008 R2 is most appropriate for a given set of roles, the differences in licensing between editions of the software, advice on whether to perform a physical or virtual deployment, and what you need to take into account when upgrading a computer from Windows Server 2003. In Lesson 2, "Automated Server Deployment," you will learn about automated deployment options, from creating and using unattended installation files to scheduling the deployment of multiple Windows Server 2008 R2 operating systems using Windows Deployment Services and System Center Configuration Manager 2007 R3.

> **IMPORTANT**
>
> ### Have you read page xxix?
>
> It contains valuable information regarding the skills you need to pass the exam.

Exam objectives in this chapter:

- Plan server installations and upgrades.
- Plan for automated server deployment.

Lessons in this chapter:

Before You Begin

To complete the exercises in the chapter, you must do the following:

- Acquire access to a computer with at least 32 gigabytes (GB) of unpartitioned disk drive space, 512 megabytes (MB) of RAM, and an x64 1.3-gigahertz (GHz) or faster processor. The practice exercises in this book were designed with the assumption that the computer that you are using is not connected directly or indirectly to the Internet, but is connected to a network with a private Internet Protocol (IP) address.
- Download the evaluation version of Windows Server 2008 R2 Enterprise edition from the Microsoft Download Center (*http://www.microsoft.com/Downloads/*).

No additional configuration is required for this chapter.

 **REAL WORLD**

Orin Thomas

It takes time for organizations to change to a new server operating system. Unlike a consumer operating system, where there is a flurry of people buying it on the day of release, it takes time for organizations to come around to deploying a new server operating system. This is primarily because server operating systems tend to host very important services, and when you are dealing with very important services, there is something to be said for taking the approach of the tortoise rather than that of the hare.

When it comes to server deployment, you should take a similarly measured approach. Getting server deployment right is important. A decade ago, when disk drives were much smaller, it was easy to deploy yourself into a corner by not taking careful account of how much space was available on the volume that hosted the operating system files. If you weren't careful, you could find that it was impossible to install new software on the server even though the server had a significant amount of disk space on another volume. This was because the installer for the software that you were deploying insisted on placing its program files on the already-close-to-capacity volume hosting the operating system files.

Today, one of the biggest decisions you will make will be whether to deploy the operating system on a virtual host or a physical chassis. Deploying to a physical chassis is generally more expensive because you are sure to have to devote a new license to the deployment, and you also have to provide the hardware. Deploying to a virtual host might allow you to use an existing virtual license and save you the cost of a chassis, but it also might introduce performance problems for other hosts on the same Hyper-V server. Of course, that being said, today it is at least possible to migrate from physical to virtual and back relatively seamlessly given the right tools—something that was a bit more difficult to do with an old computer running Microsoft Windows NT 4.0 Server that had run out of disk space on the volume hosting the operating system files.

Lesson 1: Planning Installation and Upgrade

This lesson covers the various editions of Windows Server 2008 R2 and the roles that they are designed to meet. You will learn about Server Core, which is a version of Windows Server administered entirely from the command line. You will learn about the Windows Server 2008 installation and upgrade process, the differences in licensing between editions, and whether you should perform a physical or virtual deployment.

After this lesson, you will be able to:

- Plan for the installation of or upgrade to Windows Server 2008 or Windows Server 2008 R2.
- Determine which edition of Windows Server is appropriate for a specific set of circumstances.
- Understand licensing considerations.
- Determine whether a physical or virtual deployment is appropriate.

Estimated lesson time: 60 minutes

The Differences Between Windows Server 2008 and Windows Server 2008 R2

The updated 70-646 exam deals with both the Windows Server 2008 and Windows Server 2008 R2 operating systems. Where there is a difference between these products, such as whether Hyper-V supports dynamic allocation of memory or whether Remote Desktop Protocol (RDP) supports RemoteFX, an exam question will clearly indicate that Windows Server 2008 R2 is the operating system being used. Where differences exist in this book, such as where Terminal Services in 2008 is labeled as Remote Desktop Services in Windows Server 2008 R2, the text and exam will use the Windows Server 2008 R2 terminology, but it will also mention the Windows Server 2008 terminology. For example, a question on Remote Desktop Services may look as follows:

> You are in the process of planning the deployment of Remote Desktop Services (known as Terminal Services in Windows Server 2008) at several sites across several domains in your organization's Active Directory forest. You want to configure a licensing server so that all Remote Desktop Services servers are able to obtain licenses centrally. Which of the following Remote Desktop Services license server options should you configure?

Some of the key differences between these operating system versions are as follows:

- Windows Server 2008 R2 does not support x86 processors. Windows Server 2008 R2 supports both x64 and IA64 processor architectures. Windows Server 2008 supports all three processor types.

- Windows Server 2008 R2 comes with a Foundation edition, while Windows Server 2008 does not.

- Terminal Services has been renamed Remote Desktop Services in Windows Server 2008 R2.

- Windows Server 2008 R2 includes new features such as the Active Directory Recycle Bin, Hyper-V Dynamic Memory, managed service accounts, AppLocker, DirectAccess, BranchCache, IIS 7.5, and support for Certificate Services in the Server Core installation option of Windows Server 2008 R2.

> **MORE INFO** **DIFFERENCES BETWEEN WINDOWS SERVER 2008 AND WINDOWS SERVER 2008 R2**
>
> For a list of all the differences, including some of the minor ones, consult the following document on Microsoft's website: *http://www.microsoft.com/windowsserver2008/en/us/whats-new.aspx*.

Selecting the Right Edition

Windows Server 2008 R2 comes in several different editions, each appropriate for a specific role. One edition and configuration is appropriate for a branch office file server; another edition and configuration is appropriate for a head office's Microsoft Exchange Server 2010 mailbox server that supports Database Availability Groups. On top of these different editions, there are different versions of most editions for different processor architectures, as well as the ability to install the stripped-down Server Core version of each edition. In the following pages, you will learn how all of these options fit into different deployment plans and how you can assess a set of requirements to determine which edition of Windows Server 2008 R2 best meets a particular set of needs.

> **MORE INFO** **FEATURE COMPARISON BY EDITION**
>
> To learn more about the roles supported by each edition of Windows Server 2008 R2, navigate to the following page on Microsoft's website: *http://www.microsoft.com/windowsserver2008/en/us/r2-compare-roles.aspx*.
>
> To learn more about the features supported by each edition of Windows Server 2008 R2, navigate to the following page on Microsoft's website: *http://www.microsoft.com/windowsserver2008/en/us/r2-differentiated-features.aspx*.

Windows Server 2008 R2 Standard Edition

Windows Server 2008 R2 Standard edition is the version of the software that is targeted at the small to medium-sized business. This edition of Windows Server 2008 R2 is the one that you will choose to deploy most often to support Windows Server 2008 R2 roles in your environment. The following Windows Server 2008 R2 Standard edition properties differ from other editions of the software:

- Supports a maximum of 32 GB of RAM. Supports up to 4 physical processors (sockets)
- Licensed for the host plus one virtual machine
- Does not support failover clustering
- Does not support Active Directory Federation Services (AD FS)
- Is limited to 250 incoming Routing and Remote Access or Remote Desktop Gateway connections
- Does not support all the features of the Active Directory Certificate Services (AD CS) role

When planning the deployment of servers, you are likely to select the Standard edition of Windows Server 2008 to fill the roles of domain controller, application server, DNS server, DHCP server, file server, and print server. Although these services are vital to your organization's network infrastructure, they do not require the increased features present in the Enterprise and Datacenter editions of the operating system. You should use Windows Server 2008 R2 Standard edition in your deployment plans unless Enterprise edition features, such as failover clustering or AD FS, are required to meet your goals.

Windows Server 2008 R2 Enterprise Edition

Windows Server 2008 R2 Enterprise edition is the version of the operating system targeted at large businesses. Plan to deploy this version of Windows Server 2008 R2 on servers that will run applications such as Exchange Server 2010 if you want to implement Database Availability Groups or Microsoft SQL Server failover clustering. These products require the extra processing power, RAM, and features, such as failover clustering, that Enterprise edition supports. When planning deployments, consider Windows Server 2008 R2 Enterprise edition in situations that require the following technologies that are unavailable in Windows Server 2008 R2 Standard edition:

- Supports a maximum of 2 terabytes (TB) of RAM and 8 sockets
- Licensed for the host plus 4 virtual machines
- Supports failover clustering
- Supports AD FS
- Supports all AD CS features

When planning deployments, you are likely to use Enterprise edition in conjunction with Windows Server 2008 R2 Standard edition. Standard edition will meet most of your organization's requirements, and it will be necessary to plan the deployment of the Enterprise edition only when a server has unusual requirements, such as needing to be a part of a failover cluster or needing exceptional processing or memory capacity.

Windows Server 2008 R2 Datacenter Edition

The Datacenter edition of Windows Server is aimed directly at very large businesses. The key reason to deploy the Datacenter edition of Windows Server 2008 R2 instead of Enterprise edition is that Datacenter edition allows unlimited virtual machine rights. Windows Server 2008

R2 Datacenter edition is likely to be the best choice for organizations that use virtualization to consolidate existing servers or simply require significant hardware capacity for application servers. Windows Server 2008 R2 Datacenter edition has the following properties:

- Supports a maximum of 2 TB of RAM and 64 sockets
- Licensed for the host and an unlimited number of virtual machines
- Supports all roles and features

Windows Web Server 2008 R2

Windows Web Server 2008 R2 is designed to function specifically as a Web application server. Other roles, such as Windows Deployment Server and Active Directory Domain Services (AD DS), are not supported on Windows Web Server 2008 R2. You deploy this server role either on a screened subnet to support a website viewable to external hosts or as an intranet server. As appropriate given its stripped-down role, Windows Web Server 2008 R2 does not support the high-powered hardware configurations that other editions of Windows Server 2008 R2 do. Windows Web Server 2008 R2 has the following properties:

- Supports a maximum of 32 GB of RAM and 4 sockets in symmetric multiprocessing (SMP) configuration

You should plan to deploy Windows Web Server 2008 R2 in the Server Core configuration, which minimizes its attack surface, something that is very important on a server that interacts with hosts external to your network environment. You should plan to deploy the full version of Windows Web Server 2008 R2 only if your organization's web applications rely on features that are not available in the Server Core version of Windows Web Server 2008 R2. Unlike the Server Core version of Windows Web Server 2008, Windows Web Server 2008 R2 supports a greater amount of Internet Information Services (IIS) functionality.

Windows Server 2008 R2 for Itanium-Based Systems

Windows Server 2008 R2 for Itanium-Based Systems is designed for the Intel Itanium 64-bit processor architecture, which is different from the x64 architecture that you will find in chips such as the Intel Core i7 or AMD Turion series of processors. This is the only edition of Windows Server 2008 R2 that you can install on an Itanium-based computer and requires an Itanium 2 processor. Both application server and Web server functionality are provided by Windows Server 2008 R2 for Itanium-based systems. Other server roles, such as virtualization and Windows Deployment Services (WDS), are not available. Up to 64 processors in SMP configuration and 2 TB of RAM are supported on Windows Server 2008 R2 for Itanium-Based Systems. Windows Server 2008 R2 for Itanium-Based Systems will be the last iteration of the Windows Server product line to support the Itanium processor architecture.

> **MORE INFO   ITANIUM EDITION**
>
> To learn more about Windows Server 2008 R2 for Itanium-Based Systems, consult the following article on Microsoft's website: *http://www.microsoft.com/windowsserver2008/en/us/2008-IA.aspx*.

Foundation Edition

The Foundation edition of Windows Server 2008 R2 is aimed at organizations with 15 users or fewer. The server can be configured as a domain controller, but it will enter reduced functionality mode in the event that more than 15 user accounts are present within AD DS. The Foundation edition of Windows Server 2008 R2 supports AD RMS, IIS 7.5, NAP, Remote Desktop, and WDS, but it doesn't support features such as Hyper-V, failover clustering, and its ability to function as a BranchCache server. This edition of Windows Server 2008 R2 is not addressed directly by the 70-646 exam, but it is included in this discussion for the sake of completeness.

> **MORE INFO   WINDOWS SERVER 2008 R2 FOUNDATION**
>
> To learn more about Windows Server 2008 R2 Foundation edition, consult the following page on Microsoft's website: *http://www.microsoft.com/windowsserver2008/en/us/ foundation.aspx.*

HPC Server

The HPC Server edition of Windows Server 2008 R2 is aimed at organizations that need high-performance calculations performed in a distributed manner. For example, financial organizations that want to perform analysis on large data sets stored in Microsoft Excel spreadsheets can use Windows HPC Server 2008 R2 as a distributed computing platform. The 70-646 exam does not address Windows HPC Server 2008 R2 directly, but the edition is included in this discussion for the sake of completeness.

> **MORE INFO   WINDOWS HPC SERVER 2008 R2**
>
> A real-world example of how HPC Server 2008 R2 was used in a research laboratory to perform scientific calculations is provided in the following TechNet magazine article: *http://technet.microsoft.com/en-us/magazine/2009.04.hpc.aspx.*

Server Core Installation Option

Server Core is a stripped-down installation option of Windows Server 2008 R2. Rather than providing a full desktop, you manage Windows Server 2008 R2 from the command shell, as shown in Figure 1-1. You can manage a computer running Server Core remotely by connecting through a Microsoft Management Console (MMC). You can also establish a Remote Desktop Protocol (RDP) session to a computer running Server Core, although you will need to use the command shell to perform administrative duties once connected. You can use management consoles to administer a computer running Server Core remotely, and you can run Windows PowerShell commands against a computer running Server Core if Windows Remote Management (WinRM) has been configured properly.

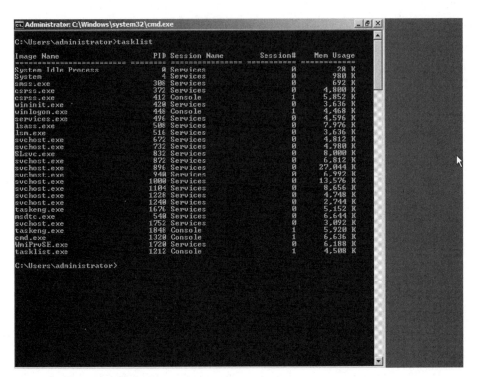

FIGURE 1-1 Server core desktop

Using the Server Core installation option of Windows Server 2008 R2 has the following benefits:

- **Reduced update requirements.** A computer running only a small number of components to meet a specialized role also needs fewer updates. For example, security updates related to Windows Internet Explorer are not relevant to computers running a Server Core installation option of Windows Server 2008 R2. The fact that there are fewer relevant updates means that you will reboot the server less frequently.

- **Reduced attack surface.** Fewer component binaries are installed, which reduces the number of components that might be attacked by someone attempting to compromise the computer.

- **Lower hardware requirements.** Because so much has been stripped out of the Server Core installation option of Windows Server 2008 R2, you can run Server Core on a computer that would exhibit performance bottlenecks running a traditional full installation. A benefit of this is that it allows organizations to use older hardware, such as hardware purchased to run Microsoft Windows 2000 Server as a platform for a Windows Server 2008 R2 installation.

When you purchase a license for a particular edition of Windows Server 2008 R2, you have the option of installing the Full option or the scaled-down Server Core installation option of the operating system. Either way, the license for the product will cost the same amount.

If you license a particular edition, you can install that edition in either its Full or Server Core option, as shown in Figure 1-2. The Foundation edition of Windows Server 2008 R2 does not support the Server Core option.

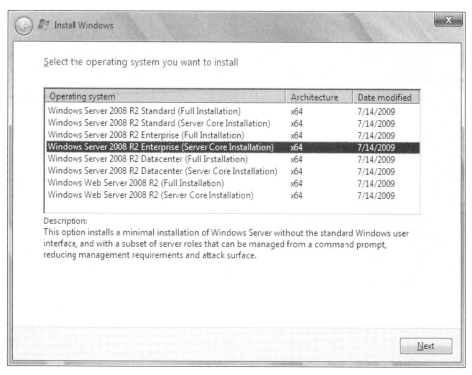

FIGURE 1-2 Installation options.

Windows Server 2008 R2 versions of Server Core support PowerShell V2. You can run PowerShell V2 commands remotely against computers running Windows Server 2008 R2 in the Server Core configuration. It is also possible to run Windows Script Host scripts on a Server Core installation, just as it is possible to run the same scripts on fully featured installations of Windows Server 2008 R2.

As shown in Figure 1-3, you can run several important tools graphically on a Server Core installation, including Registry Editor and Notepad. It is also possible to open the Time And Date item and International Settings items from Control Panel using the commands control timedate.cpl and control intl.cpl.

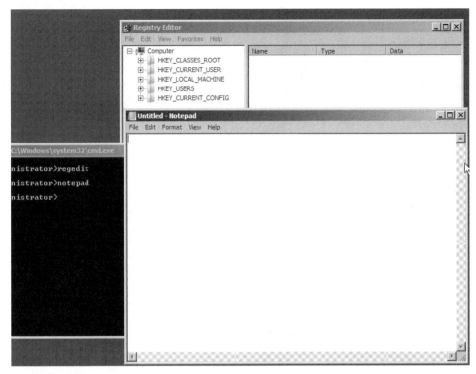

FIGURE 1-3 Registry Editor and Notepad are available in Server Core

Two more important commands are `oclist.exe` and `ocsetup.exe`. `Oclist.exe` provides a list of all server roles that are currently installed on the server and what roles are available to install. Figure 1-4 shows the list of features installed by default on a Server Core installation of Windows Server 2008 R2 Enterprise edition. You can add and remove these features using the `ocsetup.exe` command. For example, to install the Web Services (IIS) role, issue the command `ocsetup.exe IIS-WebServerRole`. It is important to note that the role name is case-sensitive. The command `ocsetup.exe /uninstall IIS-WebServerRole` is used to remove the Web Services (IIS) role, although it is necessary to ensure that all the role's services are shut down prior to attempting this.

When considering Server Core as a deployment option, consider the following factors:

- It is not possible to upgrade a computer running the Server Core installation option of a specific edition to the Full option.

- It is not possible to upgrade a computer running Windows Server 2003 to a Server Core installation of Windows Server 2008 R2.

- Some roles, such as AD FS, Network Policy and Access Services, and WDS, are not available on Server Core.

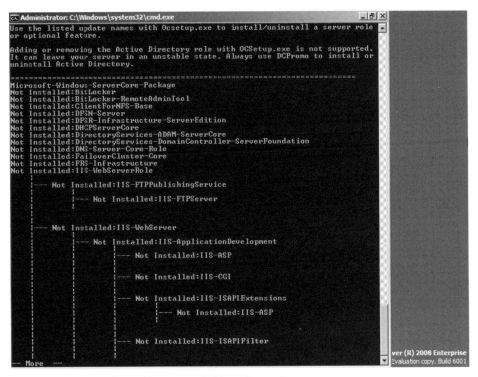

FIGURE 1-4 Viewing roles and features available on Server Core

Physical Versus Virtual Deployment

An important consideration when deciding on how you will deploy Windows Server 2008 R2 is whether you will deploy it virtually or physically. Traditionally, administrators have used physical hardware as the deployment platform for servers at head and branch office locations. For example, if your branch office requires a DNS server, a DHCP server, a domain controller, an IIS server, and a file server, you would deploy several physical servers to host these roles. In some cases, you might co-locate roles, such as having the DHCP, DNS, and domain controller roles on the same server. If you factor availability and redundancy into your deployment calculation, you may end up deploying more server chassis.

As an alternative, you might choose to simplify things by creating a Hyper-V failover cluster using two physical servers and virtual machines stored on a storage area network (SAN). By taking advantage of included virtual licenses, you could reduce your expenditure on server licenses, as well as reduce hardware expenses by deploying two chassis with Windows Server 2008 R2 installed on them to serve as Hyper-V cluster nodes. If one cluster node fails, the virtual machines would fail over, to be hosted on the other node until such time as the failed node was returned to operational status.

There are no hard-and-fast rules when it comes to saying that one type of deployment must always be physical and another type virtual. When considering physical against virtual deployments, take into account the following factors:

- Enterprise edition includes licenses for four virtual machines. This means that you can have the host and four virtual machines on one physical machine.

- Datacenter edition includes licenses for an unlimited number of virtual machines. This means that you can have the host and an unlimited number of virtual machines so long as they are hosted on the same physical machine. In this case, the only limitation is the resources on the host platform.

- Computers that have intensive workloads may be poor choices for virtual machines because other virtual machines on the same host must share the same resources with them. If you have a virtual machine that is consuming an extraordinary amount of the host platform's processor, network, or disk resources, this will necessarily place pressure on the resources available to other virtual machines hosted on the platform.

- A virtual deployment can simplify the process of assigning administrative permissions. Rather than being concerned about users performing tasks outside their designated job responsibilities when they log onto a server that they need to manage, you can isolate the server role as a virtual machine—for example, if you need IIS 7.5 and an SQL Server 2008 R2 deployment, but the administrators of one service should not have permissions over the other. Although it is possible to separate the two sets of users through diligent assignment of permissions, it may be simpler to enable IIS 7.5 on one virtual machine and SQL Server 2008 R2 on the other and host them off the same platform.

Installing Windows Server 2008 R2

Installing Windows Server 2008 R2 in a traditional manner is straightforward. The main thing to remember is that your server needs to meet the minimum hardware requirements and that if you are installing any edition of Windows Server 2008 R2 except the Itanium edition, the hardware or virtualization platform on which you are installing needs to have a processor that supports the x64 architecture. To perform installation, complete the following steps:

1. Boot off the installation media.
2. Select your language options.
3. Choose which edition and installation option (Full or Server Core) you want to install.
4. Accept the license terms.

5. Choose between an Upgrade or a Custom installation. Most of the time, you will choose a Custom installation because this is the option that allows a new installation.

6. Choose where you want to install the operating system. The operating system will now install.

7. Provide a password for the local Administrator account.

Unlike previous versions of Windows Server operating systems, you do not need to enter a product key during installation. You only need to provide a product key prior to performing activation. You will learn more about activation later in this chapter.

> **NOTE   DO NOT INSTANTLY ACTIVATE**
>
> It is a good idea to use part of the activation grace period to let the server settle, ensuring that nothing drastic needs to change, such as upgrading the processor or RAM (which would normally lead to a reactivation) before the server undergoes the activation process. You can also use the command slmgr.vbs -rearm to reset the activation clock up to three times. So remember to wait, ensure that the server does not require further hardware upgrades, and then perform activation.

If the computer on which you want to install Windows Server 2008 R2 does not have a DVD-ROM drive, you can use one of the following alternatives:

- You can configure the computer to boot from a USB flash device that hosts the Windows Server installation files. As the data transfer speeds of USB flash devices are often faster than the speed of optical media drives, this method of deployment, once configured, is often the fastest available.

- If the computer has a Preboot Execution Environment (PXE)–capable network card, you can configure WDS, covered in detail in Lesson 2, as a method of deploying Windows Server 2008 R2 over the network. In large environments, you are more likely to rely on automated deployment methods than the traditional media-based installation.

- You can boot using a USB flash device configured with the Windows Preinstallation Environment (Windows PE). You can then connect to and use operating system files hosted on a network share to perform a network installation. Although it is possible to perform an installation this way, it is simpler if you are configuring a USB flash device to include the Windows Server installation files.

> **MORE INFO   WINDOWS PE**
>
> To learn more about Windows PE, consult the following TechNet webpage: *http://technet.microsoft.com/en-us/library/dd799308(WS.10).aspx.*

Upgrading from Windows Server 2003

Some organizations will want to upgrade their existing computers running Windows Server 2003 to Windows Server 2008 or Windows Server 2008 R2. You perform upgrades using the same media that you use to perform a normal installation. Organizations choose to perform upgrades because the upgrade process is simpler than migrating applications and data to a new platform. When planning upgrades, consider the following:

- You cannot upgrade an x86 version to an x64 version.
- If you have an x86 version of Windows Server 2003, you'll only be able to upgrade it to an x86 version of Windows Server 2008.
- You can upgrade to an equivalent edition if the processor architecture is the same.
- You can upgrade from Standard edition to Enterprise edition so long as the processor architecture is the same.
- You can upgrade to Datacenter edition only if the previous operating system is running Datacenter edition and the processor architecture is the same.
- You cannot upgrade from Windows Server 2003 to any Server Core installation option of Windows Server 2008 or Windows Server 2008 R2.
- You can upgrade from a Server Core installation option of Windows Server 2008 to a Server Core installation option of Windows Server 2008 R2 so long as the processor architecture is x64.
- To upgrade from Windows Server 2003 to Windows Server 2008 requires that at least Service Pack 1 is installed on the Windows Server 2003 host.

From a planning perspective, it is not always clear whether you should perform an upgrade or back up an existing server, format the hard disk drive, install Windows Server 2008 R2, and then restore the data and reinstall any applications. Virtualization makes this decision trickier because it is possible to perform a physical-to-virtual conversion, wipe the original host, perform a clean install of Windows Server 2008 R2, install Hyper-V, and then host the original server as a virtual machine on the new installation of Windows Server 2008 R2.

Organizations use upgrades when the transition is simple, such as upgrading a computer that functions as a Windows Server 2003 domain controller to a Windows Server 2008 R2 domain controller. When a server has a more complex role, such as a server hosting a large SQL Server 2008 instance, you need to weigh your options carefully. If you need to do a lot of post-installation custom configuration for the roles that the server hosts, performing the upgrade can be significantly quicker. Because you need to perform a full backup prior to performing any upgrade or in-place migration anyway, you should attempt the upgrade first and then look at other options, including rolling back to the original configuration if the upgrade goes awry. Rollback scenarios are covered in more depth in Lesson 2 in the section entitled "Rollback Preparation."

> **NOTE ITANIUM**
>
> Although Itanium is a 64-bit architecture, it is not the same as the x64 architecture. You cannot upgrade from or to an Itanium version of Windows Server 2008 R2 unless your existing version of Windows is the Itanium edition of Windows Server 2003 or Windows Server 2008.

Prior to initiating the upgrade process, the Windows Server 2008 R2 installation routine will perform a compatibility check, presenting findings in a compatibility report.

The compatibility report will attempt to advise you of any problems that might occur if the upgrade commences. It is important to note that the compatibility report can only inform you of problems of which Microsoft is aware. If the computer that you are going to upgrade has an unusual hardware or application configuration, the compatibility check might not flag the problem, and you will be unaware of it until you encounter it directly. If you are running custom software, you may want to test it in a development environment before attempting to upgrade a production server.

To ensure that the compatibility check is as accurate as possible, you should ensure that Windows Server 2008 R2 is able to retrieve the most up-to-date installation files when you are queried about retrieving updated installation files at the beginning of the upgrade process. Another important factor to note is that upgrades require significantly more disk space than direct installs, and you should ensure that at least 30 GB are free on the volume that hosts the operating system before attempting an upgrade. Contingency plans for the upgrade process are covered in more detail in Lesson 2.

Lesson Summary

- Windows Server 2008 and Windows Server 2008 R2 come in Standard, Enterprise, Datacenter, Web Server, and Itanium editions. The Enterprise and Datacenter editions support failover clustering, AD FS, and more powerful hardware configurations. Windows Server 2008 R2 also comes in HPC and Foundation editions.

- Standard edition includes one virtual license, Enterprise edition includes four virtual licenses, and Datacenter edition includes unlimited virtual licenses.

- Windows Server 2008 R2 can be installed only on 64-bit processors.

- Server Core is an installation option that allows Windows Server 2008 R2 to be deployed with a smaller attack surface and smaller hardware footprint than the Full installation option.

- You cannot upgrade a 32-bit version of Windows Server 2003 to a 64-bit version of Windows Server 2008 or to Windows Server 2008 R2. You cannot upgrade a 32-bit version of Windows Server 2008 to Windows Server 2008 R2.

Lesson Review

You can use the following questions to test your knowledge of the information in Lesson 1, "Planning Installation and Upgrades." The questions are also available on the Companion Media if you prefer to review them in electronic form.

> **NOTE ANSWERS**
>
> Answers to these questions and explanations of why each answer choice is correct or incorrect are located in the "Answers" section at the end of the book.

1. Your organization has a computer that has Windows Server 2003 R2 x64 Standard edition installed. This computer functions as an intranet server. Which of the following upgrade paths is possible for this computer?

   A. Windows Server 2008 R2 Datacenter edition

   B. Windows Web Server 2008 R2

   C. Windows Server 2008 R2 Enterprise edition

   D. Windows Server 2008 x86 Standard edition

   E. Windows Server 2008 x64 Standard edition (Server Core)

2. Your organization has a computer with an x64 architecture processor that has Windows Server 2003 R2 (x86) Standard edition operating system installed. Which of the following versions of Windows Server 2008 or Windows Server 2008 R2 can this computer be upgraded to?

   A. Windows Server 2008 (x86) Standard edition

   B. Windows Server 2008 R2 Standard edition

   C. Windows Server 2008 (x86) Datacenter edition

   D. Windows Server 2008 R2 Enterprise edition

3. Which of the following services or roles is supported on a computer running the Server Core version of Windows Server 2008 R2 Enterprise edition?

   A. Active Directory Domain Services

   B. Active Directory Rights Management Services

   C. Active Directory Federation Services

   D. Windows Deployment Services

4. How many virtual machine licenses are included with a Windows Server 2008 R2 Enterprise edition license?

   A. One

   B. Two

   C. Four

   D. Unlimited

5. Which edition of Windows Server 2008 R2 would you choose if you wanted to deploy an Exchange Server 2010 mailbox server with the Database Availability Group feature? The Database Availability Group feature requires that the failover clustering feature be available.

   A. Windows Web Server 2008 R2

   B. Windows Server 2008 R2 Standard edition

   C. Windows Server 2008 R2 Enterprise edition

   D. Windows Server 2008 R2 Foundation edition

Lesson 2: Automated Server Deployment

As an experienced systems administrator, you probably have server deployment down to a fine art. You have probably performed this process so often that you could do it with your eyes closed. In this lesson, you will learn what tools you can use to create Extensible Markup Language (XML) answer files for the Windows Server 2008 R2 installation process and how to install and configure WDS, a service that allows you to send operating system images to compatible clients over the network.

> **After this lesson, you will be able to:**
> - Create and use an unattended XML file to install Windows Server 2008 R2.
> - Schedule the deployment of Windows Server 2008 R2 using operating systems and WDS.
>
> **Estimated lesson time: 40 minutes**

Windows Server 2008 R2 Answer Files

An answer file allows you to set specific setup options such as how to partition hard disk drives, the location of the Windows Server 2008 R2 image that is to be installed, and the product key. The Windows Server 2008 R2 answer file is usually called Autounattended.xml. This is the file name that the Windows Server 2008 R2 installation process automatically looks for on the local and attached media during setup in an attempt to initiate an unattended installation.

Windows Server 2008 R2 answer file uses XML format. As an administrator, you will almost always create this file using the Windows System Image Manager (Windows SIM) tool. The Windows SIM tool is included with the Windows Automated Installation Kit (Windows AIK or WAIK), which you can obtain from the Microsoft Download Center or download from the Microsoft Deployment Toolkit (MDT) Deployment Workbench. Although you can create an answer file using a text editor, the complex XML syntax of the unattended installation file makes the Windows AIK tools a more efficient use of your time. Another benefit of the Windows SIM tool is that it allows you to verify that an unattended answer file actually produces the desired result.

To create an answer file using the Windows SIM, perform the following steps:

1. Start the Windows SIM. This application can be downloaded as an update to the MDT, which can be downloaded from Microsoft's website (*http://technet.microsoft.com/en-us/solutionaccelerators/dd407791.aspx*).

2. Copy the file \Sources\Install.wim from the Windows Server 2008 R2 installation media to a temporary directory on the computer running Windows Server 2008 R2 on which you have installed the Windows AIK component of MDT 2010.

3. Click the File menu, and then click Select Windows Image. Navigate to the temporary directory where you copied Install.wim and select the file. This file contains all editions and versions of Windows Server 2008 R2 that can be installed from the installation media.

4. You will be prompted to select an image in the Windows Image file. Select Server Enterprise, or the image that you want to create an answer file for, and then click OK.

5. When prompted to create a catalog file, click Yes. When prompted by the User Account Control dialog box, click Continue. The Catalog file will be created.

6. From the File menu, select New Answer File.

7. By selecting the appropriate component in the Windows Image, you can configure the properties for that component. Figure 1-5 shows the configuration settings that allow the computer being installed to join the domain contoso.internal automatically with the specified set of credentials.

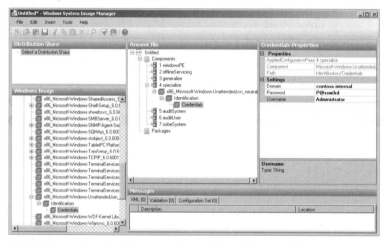

FIGURE 1-5 Creating the Autounattended.xml file in Windows SIM

8. When the answer file is saved, it is validated automatically against the operating system image that has been loaded.

MORE INFO   **UNATTENDED FILES**

For more information on the creation and configuration of unattended installation files, consult the Unattended Windows Setup Reference, which is accessible from the Help menu in Windows SIM.

Running an Unattended Installation

Traditionally, unattended installations used floppy diskettes that contained the unattended text file. Most modern server hardware does not include a floppy disk drive, so—as mentioned earlier—the Windows Server 2008 R2 setup routine will check all the server's local volumes automatically for a file called Autounattended.xml. This automatic check also includes any removable USB memory devices attached to the computer.

If the installation will use setup files located on a network share, it will be necessary to boot into Windows PE, connect to the network share, and then issue the command **setup.exe /unattend:x:\autounattended.xml** (where *x:* is the path of the Autounattended.xml file). In the section entitled "Windows Deployment Services," which comes next in this lesson, you will learn how to use unattended answer files with WDS.

 Quick Check

- Which tool should you use to generate an unattended XML answer file?

Quick Check Answer

- Windows SIM.

Windows Deployment Services

WDS is a role you can add to a computer running Windows Server 2008 R2 that allows remote deployment of the Windows Server 2008 R2, Windows Server 2008, Windows 7, and Windows Vista operating systems.

WDS requires that a client have a PXE-compliant network card. If a client does not, you will need to use another method—such as creating a bootable image that can detect the WDS server—to perform a remote installation. The process works when the computer with the PXE-based network card starts and then locates the WDS server. If the client is authorized and multicast transmissions have been configured, the client will begin the setup process automatically. Unicast transmissions, which are less efficient when multiple clients are involved, are enabled once an operating system image is installed. If an Autounattended.xml answer file has not been installed on the WDS server, this installation will proceed normally, requiring input from the administrator. The only difference between a WDS-based installation and a normal installation is that the server appears to be starting from the Windows Server 2008 R2 installation media over the network rather than starting from the media located in a local DVD-ROM drive.

WDS can be installed on a computer running Windows Server 2008 R2 only under the following conditions:

- The computer on which WDS is deployed is a member of an AD DS domain. A DNS server is required, although this is implied by the existence of the domain.
- An authorized DHCP server is present on the network.
- An NTFS partition is available for storing operating system images.

You cannot deploy WDS on a computer running a Server Core edition of Windows Server 2008 R2. After you install WDS, you need to configure it before it can be activated. You can do this by using the Windows Deployment Services Configuration Wizard, which is covered in the practice at the end of this lesson, or by using the Wdsutil.exe command-line utility.

If the WDS server is collocated with the DHCP server, it is necessary to configure WDS not to listen on port 67. If you do not do this, WDS and DHCP will have a conflict. It is also important to configure the WDS server to add option tag 60, as shown in Figure 1-6, so that PXE clients are able to detect the presence of a WDS server.

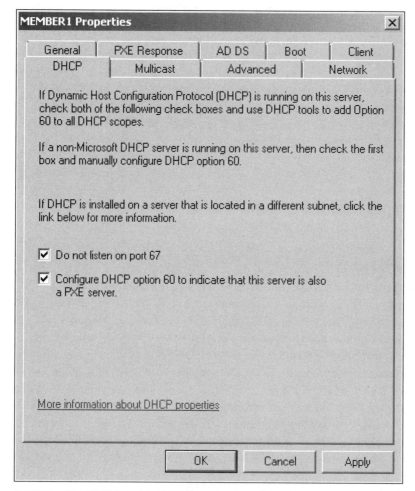

FIGURE 1-6 The DHCP tab of the WDS server settings dialog box

The Client tab of a WDS server's properties, shown in Figure 1-7, allows you to specify an unattended installation file for each specific architecture. If the Autounattended.xml file is not specified for the architecture of Windows Server 2008 R2 that you are installing, the installation will require the normal amount of manual input.

> **MORE INFO** **ADVANCED UNATTENDED INSTALLATIONS**
>
> To learn more about configuring WDS for unattended installations, consult the following TechNet article: *http://technet.microsoft.com/en-us/library/cc771508(WS.10).aspx.*

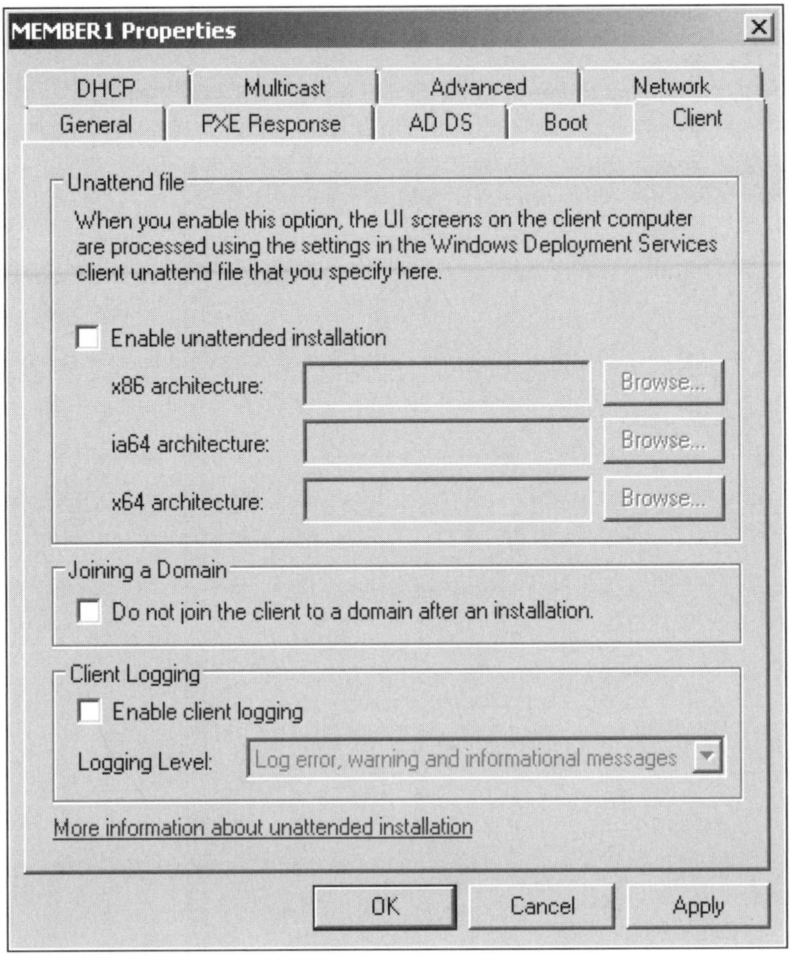

FIGURE 1-7 You can specify default unattended installation files on the WDS server

Some network environments will have services such as teleconferencing and videocasting that already use IP addresses in the multicast range. You can use the Network Settings tab, shown in Figure 1-8, to configure the multicast IP address range used by WDS and the User Datagram Protocol (UDP) ports that will be used by the multicast server. You can also configure transfer settings on this tab so that clients at different speeds get a different multicast session. The ability to separate clients into different settings means that the whole deployment transmission will not be slowed down by one computer with a sluggish network card.

You can also configure the PXE response policy by configuring the WDS server settings. The first setting to configure is the PXE Response Delay. You configure this setting when you want to specify the order in which WDS servers respond to PXE requests. You can configure three PXE response settings:

- **Do Not Respond To Any Client Computer.** WDS does not respond to PXE requests.

- **Respond Only To Known Client Computers.** This option is used if clients have been prestaged in AD DS.
- **Respond To All (Known And Unknown) Client Computers.** This setting has an additional option allowing for administrators to approve unknown clients manually.

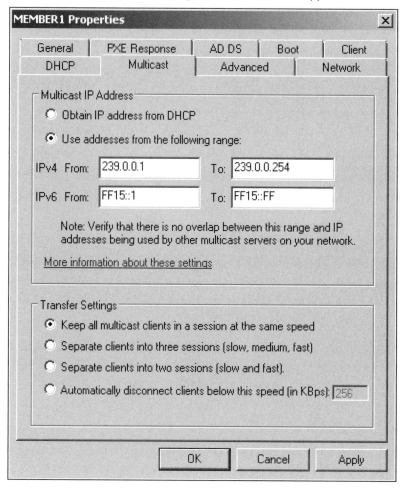

FIGURE 1-8 Configuring the multicast IP address

Multicast, Scheduled, and Automatic Deployment

Multicast allows organizations to use their network bandwidth more efficiently, allowing an operating system image to be transmitted over the network once to multiple installation clients. For example, if you are deploying 20 computers running Windows Server 2008 R2, you save significant bandwidth in transmitting one installation image across the network (approximately 1.5 GB of data) compared to transmitting all 20 (approximately 60 GB of data). Multicast deployment is supported only in network environments where the routers support multicast transmissions.

You can also schedule deployments. This allows the transmission of installation image data to occur at a predetermined time. For example, you could configure deployment to occur during off-peak hours, when the transmission of a significant amount of data would have little impact on a network's day-to-day operation. Alternatively, you can configure a scheduled multicast to occur when specific numbers of clients are ready to receive an image. You can also combine these settings. For example, Figure 1-9 shows a multicast transmission that will occur at 3:00 A.M. if 10 clients are ready to receive the image. When you combine WDS with an unattended installation file, you can turn on a set of computers prior to leaving the office for an evening and come back the next day to find that each has been installed and configured automatically, during the overnight lull in network activity. An auto-cast means that a multicast transmission will start as soon as a client requests an install image. Auto-casts are most often used for one-time deployments rather than large-scale deployments, where scheduled casts are more appropriate.

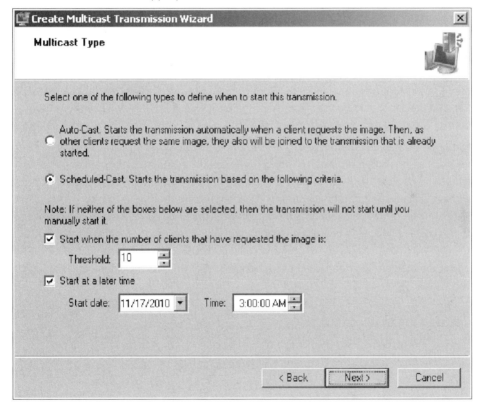

FIGURE 1-9 Configuring a multicast transmission

EXAM TIP

Remember that a deployment scheduled to occur in the middle of the night needs an answer file; otherwise, the deployment process will stall when administrator input is required.

WDS Images

WDS uses two different types of images: install images and boot images. Install images are the operating system images that will be deployed to computers running Windows Server 2008 R2, Windows Server 2008, Windows 7, or Windows Vista. A default installation image named Install.wim is located in the \Sources directory of the installation DVD. If you are using WDS to deploy Windows 7 to computers with different processor architectures, it will be necessary to add separate installation images for each architecture to the WDS server. Architecture-specific images can be found on the architecture-specific installation media; for example, the Itanium image is located on the Itanium installation media, and the x64 default installation image is located on the x64 installation media. Although it is possible to create custom images, it is necessary to have only one image per processor architecture. For example, deploying Windows Server 2008 R2 Enterprise edition x64 to a computer with two x64 processors and to a computer with eight x64 processors in SMP configuration only requires access to the default x64 installation image.

Boot images are used to start a client computer prior to the installation of the operating system image. When a computer starts off a boot image over the network, a menu is presented that displays the possible images that can be deployed to the computer from the WDS server. The Windows Server 2008 R2 Boot.wim file allows for advanced deployment options, and this file should be used instead of the Boot.wim file that is available from other sources.

In addition to the basic boot image, there are two separate types of additional boot images that can be configured for use with WDS. The capture image is a boot image that starts the WDS capture utility. This utility is used with a reference computer, prepared with the Sysprep utility, as a method of capturing the reference computer's image for deployment with WDS. The second type of additional boot image is the discover image. Discover images are used to deploy images to computers that are not PXE-enabled or on networks that don't allow PXE. These images are written to CD, DVD, or USB media and the computer is started off the media rather than off the PXE network card, which is the traditional method of using WDS.

> *MORE INFO* **MANAGING IMAGES**
>
> For more information on how to manage WDS images, consult the following TechNet article: *http://technet.microsoft.com/en-us/library/cc770460.aspx.*

WDS and Product Activation

Although product activation does not need to occur during the actual installation process, administrators considering using WDS to automate deployment should also consider using volume activation to automate activation. Volume activation provides a simple centralized method that systems administrators can use to activate large numbers of deployed servers. Volume activation allows for two types of keys and three methods of activation. The key types are the Multiple Activation Key (MAK) and the Key Management Services (KMS).

MAKs allow activation of a specific number of computers. Each successful activation depletes the activation pool. For example, a MAK key that has 100 activations allows for the activation of 100 computers. The MAK can use the MAK Proxy Activation and the MAK Independent Activation activation methods. MAK Proxy Activation uses a centralized activation request on behalf of multiple products using a single connection to Microsoft's activation servers. You perform MAK Proxy Activation using the Volume Activation Management Tool (VAMT). MAK Independent Activation requires that each computer activates individually against Microsoft's activation servers.

> **MORE INFO** **VOLUME ACTIVATION MANAGEMENT TOOL**
>
> To learn more about the VAMT, consult the following article on TechNet:
> *http://technet.microsoft.com/en-us/library/cc770460.aspx.*

Key Management Service (KMS) keys allow for computers to be activated in a managed environment without requiring individual connections to Microsoft. Computers activate against the KMS server rather than against Microsoft's activation servers. KMS has the following properties:

- You need to have five computers running Windows Server 2008 R2 or Windows Server 2008 before you can use KMS. Alternatively, you can have 25 computers running a client operating system such as Windows 7 or Windows Vista.

- To install KMS, obtain a KMS key from Microsoft and then install it on a computer running Windows Server 2008 R2. Once the computer activates, either directly or over the phone, it functions as a KMS server. Although you can install KMS on a computer running Windows 7, you won't be able to use this computer to activate computers running Windows Server 2008 R2.

- The same KMS key can be installed on up to six computers in your environment. You can reactivate each of these six computers up to nine times.

- All computers activated by KMS servers must be able to contact the KMS server every 180 days. If this threshold is not met, the computers enter reduced functionality mode.

- The KMS server needs to activate only once. The exception to this is if you change the KMS server's hardware substantially and you trigger a reactivation.

KMS and MAK can be used in conjunction with one another. The number of computers, how often they connect to the network, and whether there is Internet connectivity determines which solution you should deploy. You should deploy MAK if substantial numbers of computers do not connect to the network for more than 180 days. If there is no Internet connectivity and more than 5 servers or 25 clients, KMS should be deployed. If there is no Internet connectivity and less than 5 servers or 25 computers, you will need to use MAK and the VAMT to perform proxy activation. Proxy activation allows you to collect activation data from computers that are on a network that is not connected to the Internet, to export that data to a client that is connected to the Internet, to perform the activation, and then to export the activation information back to the computers on the non-connected network.

Rollback Preparation

In the best of all worlds, each upgrade works flawlessly, bringing increased functionality, stability, and performance to the computer that has been upgraded. In reality, you will find the best approach to take as a systems administrator is to assume that Murphy's Law is always in effect: Anything that can go wrong probably will. Prior to upgrading a computer from Windows Server 2003 to Windows Server 2008 R2, you should have a rollback plan in place in case something goes dramatically wrong.

Rollback is often necessary when a server's functionality is compromised by the upgrade. For example, a custom application may be deployed on a computer running Windows Server 2003 that is rendered nonfunctional by upgrading to Windows Server 2008 R2. If the custom application is critical to a business's function, you will need to roll back to Windows Server 2003 so that the application can continue to be used.

During the upgrade process, you can roll back to the existing Windows Server 2003 installation. However, after a successful logon has occurred, the upgrade cannot be rolled back. The drawback of this situation is that often you will not be aware of problems with an upgrade until after successful logon occurs. The only way to roll back is to format the hard disk drive and restore the Windows Server 2003 backups that you took prior to attempting the upgrade. An alternative to formatting the hard disk drive and restoring Windows Server 2003 is to deploy Windows Server 2003 through the virtualization feature of Windows Server 2008 R2.

Prior to upgrading a computer from Windows Server 2003 to Windows Server 2008 R2, take the following precautions:

- Perform an Automated System Recovery (ASR) Backup of the computer running Windows Server 2003.
- Perform a full backup of all data, including system state data.
- Have a plan to roll the upgrade back if something goes wrong.

If you need to remove Windows Server 2008 R2 from a computer that has been upgraded from Windows Server 2003, the quickest way to restore the prior functionality is to apply the Windows Server 2003 ASR backup, restore the system state and user data, and then reinstall all extra applications.

Lesson Summary

- A Windows Server 2008 R2 answer file allows an administrator to automate some or all of the installation process by providing information to the setup routine on the components and configuration settings that are necessary for the installation of Windows Server 2008 R2.
- The answer file, typically called Autounattend.xml, is created using Windows SIM, a component of Windows AIK.

- You can store answer files on a removable USB memory device, where they will be detected automatically by the Windows Server 2008 R2 setup routine. Alternatively, they can be located on a network share and called if a network setup is started from within Windows PE.

- You can use WDS to deploy Windows Server 2008 R2 operating system images to PXE clients using multicast transmissions. The advantage of a multicast transmission is that the image data is transmitted only once over the network, minimizing bandwidth use.

- You can schedule multicast transmissions to occur at particular times, when a particular number of clients have connected to the WDS server, or a combination of both. It is also possible to create an auto-cast, which begins automatically.

- If the WDS server also hosts the DHCP Server service, you must configure WDS to listen on a separate port and to configure DHCP option tag 60 for all scopes.

- Volume activation allows for the use of two types of activation keys. The MAK is a single key that can be used to activate multiple computers. This can occur on a per computer basis or through an MAK proxy. The Key Management Service (KMS) key requires a minimum of 5 servers or 25 clients that need to connect to the KMS server every 180 days.

Lesson Review

You can use the following questions to test your knowledge of the information in Lesson 2, "Automated Server Deployment." The questions are also available on the Companion Media if you prefer to review them in electronic form.

> **NOTE ANSWERS**
>
> Answers to these questions and explanations of why each answer choice is correct or incorrect are located in the "Answers" section at the end of the book.

1. You have just installed Windows Server 2008 R2 on a computer on which you intend to deploy the WDS server role. Which of the following requirements must be met prior to installing the WDS server role? (Each answer presents part of the solution. Choose three.)

   A. The computer must be made a member of an AD DS domain.

   B. An authorized DHCP server must be present in the network environment.

   C. A DNS server must be present in the network environment.

   D. The Application Server role must be installed on the computer running Windows Server 2008.

2. Which of the following environments allows you to initiate an unattended installation?

   A. Windows PE

   B. Windows NT Boot Disk

   C. MS DOS Boot Disk

   D. Windows Server 2008 Installation Media

3. You have just deployed the WDS server role on a computer that functions as a domain controller, DHCP server, and DNS server. When you try to start a server with a PXE network card, you are unable to connect to the PXE server on WDS. Which of the following should you do to try to resolve this issue?

   A. Configure the DHCP settings in the WDS server properties.

   B. Configure DHCP settings on the DHCP Server console.

   C. Configure DNS settings on the DNS Server console.

   D. Configure the client settings in the WDS server properties.

4. You have configured a multicast transmission in WDS to start at 7:00 P.M. on Friday night as soon as 10 clients are ready to receive the image. Your WDS server is located in a server room downstairs, and the 10 computers on which you are going to install Windows Server 2008 R2 are located in the staging room, next to your fourth-floor office. The server room and the rest of the building are on separate subnets. DNS and DHCP in your environment are hosted on a different server to the WDS server. You have configured the WDS server with an appropriate unattended installation file. You stay at the office to verify that the deployment starts correctly, but you find that it does not. Which of the following changes will be necessary before you can get this method of deployment to function?

   A. Update DNS zones to ensure that they are AD DS–integrated.

   B. Configure a special IPv6 DHCP scope for PXE clients.

   C. Configure a special IPv6 DHCP scope for PXE clients.

   D. Replace the router with one that supports multicast.

5. You have 15 Windows Server 2008 server images to deploy to clients using WDS. All servers need to be configured in an almost-identical manner. None of the servers has floppy disk drives or optical media drives. How can you configure WDS such that the amount of manual intervention required for the installation of these servers is minimized?

   A. Place an unattended XML file on a shared folder.

   B. Configure the properties of the multicast transmission within WDS.

   C. Configure an unattended XML file within the WDS server's properties.

   D. Place an unattended XML file on a removable USB device and connect it to each server.

Installing and Configuring Windows Server 2008 R2 and the WDS Role

In this practice, you will install Windows Server 2008 R2 on a computer, configure this computer as a domain controller, configure the WDS role, import operating system images from the Windows Server 2008 R2 installation media, and configure a multicast transmission to deploy these operating system images to appropriately configured PXE clients.

EXERCISE 1 Install Windows Server 2008 R2 Enterprise Edition

In this exercise, you perform the installation and initial configuration of Windows Server 2008 R2. You start with a clean hardware setup, install the operating system, and then configure the server to function as a domain controller in a new Windows Server 2008 R2 domain. You do all the configurations using the Administrator account. You will perform later exercises using the Kim_Akers user account. To complete this exercise, perform the following steps:

1. Start the computer or virtual machine on which you will install the operating system from the Windows Server 2008 R2 Enterprise edition installation media that you have downloaded from the Microsoft Download Center at *http://www.microsoft.com/Downloads/Search.aspx*.

2. On the Install Windows page, select your language, time and currency format, and keyboard or input method, and click Next.

3. Click Install Now. On the Select The Operating System You Want To Install page, click Windows Server 2008 R2 Enterprise (Full Installation), and then click Next.

4. On the Please Read The License Terms page, review the license, and then select the I Accept The License Terms check box. Click Next.

5. On the Which Type Of Installation Do You Want? page, click Custom (Advanced).

6. On the Where Do You Want To Install Windows? page, click Next.

7. The installation process will begin. This process may take up to 20 minutes, depending on the speed of the hardware upon which you are installing the operating system. The computer will restart twice automatically during this period.

8. You will be asked to change the password prior to logging on for the first time. This is where you set the password for the Administrator account. Click OK, enter the password **Pa$$w0rd** twice in the dialog box, and then press Enter. Click OK when you are informed that your password has been changed and you will be logged on.

9. Open an elevated command prompt and issue the following commands:

   ```
   Netsh interface ipv4 set address "Local Area Connection" static 10.10.0.10
   Netdom renamecomputer %computername% /newname:VAN-DC1
   ```

10. Restart the computer and log back on using the Administrator account

11. Click Start. In the Search Programs and Files text box, type the following:

    ```
    Dcpromo
    ```

12. When the Active Directory Domain Services Installation Wizard starts, click Next twice.

13. On the Choose A Deployment Configuration page, choose Create A New Domain In A New Forest and then click Next.

14. On the Name The Forest Root Domain page, enter **Adatum.com**, and then click Next.

15. On the Set Forest Functional Level page, set the Forest Functional Level to Windows Server 2008 R2 and then click Next.

16. On the Additional Domain Controller Options page, ensure that the DNS Server option is checked, and then click Next. When presented with the warning that the delegation for the DNS server cannot be created, click Yes when asked if you want to continue.

17. Accept the default settings for the Database, Log Files, and SYSVOL locations and click Next.

18. In the Directory Services Restore Mode Administrator Password dialog box, enter the password **Pa$$w0rd** twice and then click Next.

19. On the Summary page, click Next to begin the installation of Active Directory Domain Services on computer VAN-DC1. When the wizard completes, click Finish. When prompted, click Restart Now to reboot computer VAN-DC1.

EXERCISE 2 Preparing for the Installation of the WDS Server Role

In this short exercise, you perform several housekeeping exercises that will prepare the server for the installation of the WDS server role. This includes the installation of the DHCP Server service and the creation of a user account that has limited, but not complete, administrative rights. This user account mirrors the IT professionals whose job role intersects with the types of tasks tested on the 70-646 exam. This account has administrative rights but is not a member of the Schema Admins or Enterprise Admins group. To complete this exercise, perform the following steps:

1. Log on to the domain controller VAN-DC1 using the Administrator account.

2. Open Active Directory Users And Computers from the Administrative Tools menu.

3. In the Users container, create a new user account called **Kim_Akers**. Assign Kim's user account the password **Pa$$w0rd** and set the password to never expire.

> *NOTE* **FOR TRAINING KIT CONVENIENCE ONLY**
>
> In a real-world environment, you should ensure that administrator accounts have the same password expiration policy as all other user accounts.

4. Add the Kim Akers user account to the Domain Admins security group. Do not add the Kim Akers user account to any other administrative group at this time.

5. Log off server VAN-DC1 and log back on using the Kim_Akers account.

6. If the Server Manager console does not open automatically, open it using the shortcut pinned to the Taskbar or from Administrative Tools in the Start menu.

7. Right-click the Roles node and then click Add Roles. This will start the Add Roles Wizard.

8. On the Before You Begin page, click Next.

9. On the Select Server Roles page, select DHCP Server and then click Next.

10. On the Introduction To DHCP Server page, click Next.

11. On the Network Connection Bindings page, select the interface 10.10.0.10 as the one that will accept DHCP requests and click Next.

12. On the IPv4 DNS Settings page, ensure that the figures match those displayed in Figure 1-10. Click Validate and then click Next.

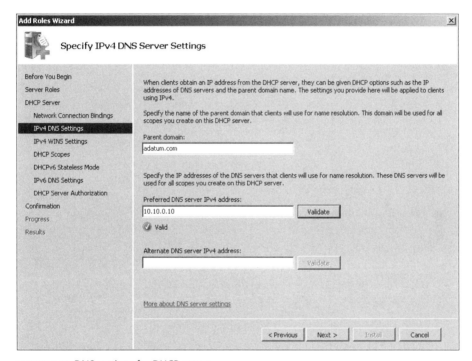

FIGURE 1-10 DNS settings for DHCP server

13. On the IPv4 WINS Settings page, accept the defaults and click Next.

14. On the DHCP Scopes page, click Add.

15. In the Add Scope dialog box, add entries so that it appears as shown in Figure 1-11. Click OK twice, and then click Next.

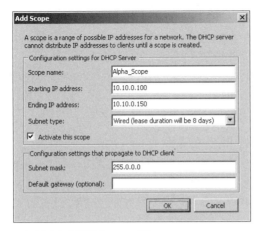

FIGURE 1-11 DHCP Scope settings.

16. Review the default DHCPv6 Stateless Mode settings and then click Next.

17. Review the default DHCP IPv6 DNS Server settings and then click Next.

18. Verify that the Use Current Credentials setting is selected and that the User Name is set to ADATUM\kim_akers. Click Next and then, on the Confirmation page, click Install. The installation of the DHCP Server role will begin.

19. When the DHCP Server role has been installed, click Close to close the Add Roles Wizard.

EXERCISE 3 Installing the WDS Server Role and Adding Image Files

In this exercise, you install the WDS server role and add image files from the Windows Server 2008 R2 installation media. You should ensure that the Windows Server 2008 R2 installation media is located in your computer's DVD-ROM drive. To complete this exercise, perform the following steps:

1. If the Server Roles console is open, open it using the shortcut pinned to the Taskbar or from Administrative Tools in the Start menu.

2. Right-click the Roles node, and then click Add Roles.

3. If you are presented with the Before You Begin page of the Add Roles Wizard, click Next; otherwise, proceed to step 4.

4. On the Select Server Roles page, select the Windows Deployment Services role and then click Next.

5. Review the Things To Note section of the Overview Of Windows Deployment Services page, and then click Next.

6. On the Select Role Services page, ensure that both the Deployment Server and Transport Server role services are selected. Click Next, and then click Install. The installation of WDS will begin. When the installation completes, click Close.

7. From the Administrative Tools menu, select Windows Deployment Services.

8. In the Windows Deployment Services console, expand the Servers node, right-click VAN-DC1.adatum.com, and then click Configure Server. This will start the Windows Deployment Services Configuration Wizard. Click Next.

9. Accept the default Remote Installation Folder Location of C:\RemoteInstall and then click Next.

10. On the System Volume Warning, note the recommendation that the remote installation folder should be placed on a volume different than that of the system volume and click Yes.

11. Ensure that the Do Not Listen On Port 67 and Configure DHCP Option 60 To "PXEClient" options are selected, and then click Next.

12. On the PXE Server Initial Settings page, select the Respond Only To Known Client Computers option and click Finish.

13. On the Configuration Complete page, ensure that the Add Images To The Windows Deployment Server Now option is selected, and click Finish.

> **NOTE** **INSTALLATION MEDIA REQUIRED**
>
> Ensure that the Windows Server 2008 R2 installation media are present in the computer's DVD drive prior to attempting step 17. The images will require approximately 3 GB of disk space.

14. In the Windows Image Files Location dialog box, click Browse and navigate to the Sources directory on the DVD drive. Click OK and then click Next.

15. On the Image Group page, verify that the Create A New Image Group option is selected and that the new image group name will be ImageGroup1. Click Next.

16. In the Review Settings dialog box, verify that 1 boot image and 8 install images will be transferred to the server, and then click Next. Images now will be transferred from the Windows Server 2008 R2 installation media to the C:\RemoteInstall folder.

17. When the images have been transferred to the server, click Finish.

18. In the Windows Deployment Services console, right-click the Multicast Transmissions node, and then select Create Multicast Transmission.

19. On the Transmission Name page, type **TestAlpha** and click Next.

20. On the Select Image page, verify that ImageGroup1 is selected, and then click Next.

21. On the Multicast Type page, ensure that Scheduled-Cast is selected. Select the Start Automatically When The Number Of Clients Ready To Receive This Image Is option. Set the threshold value to 10. Click Next and then click Finish.

22. Close the Windows Deployment Services console and then shut down the computer.

Chapter Review

To further practice and reinforce the skills you learned in this chapter, you can perform the following tasks:

- Review the chapter summary.
- Review the list of key terms introduced in this chapter.
- Complete the case scenarios. These scenarios set up real-world situations involving the topics of this chapter and ask you to create a solution.
- Complete the suggested practices.
- Take a practice test.

Chapter Summary

- Determining which edition of Windows Server 2008 R2 is appropriate requires understanding needs such as hardware requirements, clustering requirements, and what roles the server will need to provide.
- Windows Server 2008 R2 traditionally is deployed by using DVD-ROM installation media. You can also use Windows PE to boot into an environment with a network share containing the Windows Server 2008 installation files, although this is generally only done when a PXE network adapter is not available and WDS cannot be used.
- Windows Server 2008 answer files are usually called Autounattended.xml and are generated using the Windows SIM, a tool available in the Windows AIK. You can configure WDS to use Autounattended.xml to automate the installation process.
- WDS allows operating system images to be deployed to multiple computers with PXE network cards using scheduled multicast transmissions. Multicast transmissions minimize the amount of bandwidth used, and scheduling allows for the disruption of operating system image transmission to occur during periods of low network utilization.

Key Terms

The following terms were introduced in this chapter. Do you know what they mean?

- boot partition
- Dynamic Host Configuration Protocol (DHCP)
- multicast
- Preboot Execution Environment (PXE)
- system partition
- Windows Preinstallation Environment (Windows PE)

Case Scenarios

In the following case scenarios, you will apply what you have learned about planning server installs and upgrades. You can find answers to these questions in the "Answers" section at the end of this book.

Case Scenario 1: Contoso's Migration to Windows Server 2008

Contoso is in the process of moving its network infrastructure to Windows Server 2008 R2 from Windows Server 2003 under the direction of Windows Server 2008 R2 Enterprise administrators. In several of the situations involved in the migration plan, the staff at Contoso want your advice on the specifics of implementation. The situations in which they wish to ask your opinion include the following:

1. Five of Contoso's branch office servers will be updated so that they are running the Server Core installation option of Windows Server 2008 R2 Standard edition. These servers currently are running Windows Server 2003 x64 Standard edition. Each server has a 2-GHz Core 2 Duo processor, 4 GB of RAM, and 1 TB of free hard disk space. What plans would you make to meet this goal?

2. Which edition of Windows Server 2008 R2 would be most appropriate to deploy on the Contoso screened subnet, given that the only functionality the server requires is hosting the corporate website?

3. You intend to host a large number of virtual machines running Windows Server 2008 R2 on a server with significant hardware resources. Which edition of Windows Server 2008 R2 should you choose so that you minimize the number of extra licenses that will need to be purchased?

Case Scenario 2: Tailspin Toys Automates Windows Server 2008 Deployment

Tailspin Toys is a toy aircraft manufacturer with an aging network infrastructure. Determined to modernize, Tailspin Toys will be deploying a significant number of computers running Windows Server 2008 R2 as a part of a comprehensive IT infrastructure upgrade. You have been brought in as a consultant by Tailspin Toys to help plan the deployment of all these new servers.

1. The physical infrastructure of the Tailspin Toys network is almost a decade old. Which important part of the infrastructure might have to be upgraded or replaced prior to attempting to deploy Windows Server 2008 R2 using multicast transmissions?

2. If the server that will host the WDS role also hosts the DHCP Server role, what steps need to be taken?

3. You have 10 servers that you want to use WDS to install. You are concerned that the multicast transmission will begin before you have all 10 servers ready, and you want to avoid multiple transmissions. What steps can you take to ensure that this does not occur?

Suggested Practices

To help you successfully master the exam objectives presented in this chapter, complete the following tasks.

Plan Server Installations and Upgrades

If you have the available hardware or virtual machine capacity and you want to investigate automated server deployment further, perform the following practices based on what you have learned in this chapter:

- Practice 1: Install the Server Core option of Windows Server 2008 R2 on another computer.
- Practice 2: Add the Server Core installation to the domain created in the practice exercise. Add the IIS Server role to the Server Core installation.

Plan for Automated Server Deployment

If you have the available hardware or virtual machine capacity and you want to investigate automated server deployment further, perform the following practices based on what you have learned in this chapter:

- Practice 1: Download and install the Windows AIK from Microsoft's website.
- Practice 2: Use Windows SIM, a component of the Windows AIK, to create a custom image based on one of the Windows Server 2008 R2 installation images.
- Practice 3: Use the Windows SIM, a component of the Windows AIK, to create an answer file for the installation of Windows Server 2008 R2.

Take a Practice Test

The practice tests on this book's Companion Media offer many options. For example, you can test yourself on just one exam objective, or you can test yourself on all of the 70-646 certification exam content. You can set up the test so that it closely simulates the experience of taking a certification exam, or you can set it up in study mode so that you can look at the correct answers and explanations after you answer each question.

> **MORE INFO**   **PRACTICE TESTS**
>
> For details about all of the practice test options available, see the section "How to Use the Practice Tests" in this book's Introduction.

CHAPTER 2

Infrastructure Services Planning

As a senior administrator responsible for a multiple-site network, you will be (or possibly already are) responsible for the overall IT environment and architecture within your organization. You will be required to plan infrastructure design and implement global configuration changes. You should already be an experienced IT professional with administrative experience in Windows Server 2008 R2, Windows Server 2008, or other Windows Server operating systems.

As an experienced professional, you will almost certainly be familiar with name resolution and Internet Protocol version 4 (IPv4) addressing. You are probably also familiar with the format of Internet Protocol version 6 (IPv6) addresses, but you might not be fully aware of the various IPv6 address types and IPv4-to-IPv6 transition strategies. You should be familiar with name resolution, particularly the Domain Name System (DNS), but you might not have configured an IPv6 DNS reverse lookup zone. This chapter builds upon your current knowledge and gives you the skills required to extend your expertise to plan for and configure multi-site networks.

Exam objectives in this chapter

- Plan infrastructure services server roles.

Lessons in this chapter:

Before You Begin

To complete the exercises in the practice session in this chapter, you need to have done the following:

- Installed a Windows Server 2008 R2 Enterprise server called VAN-DC1, configured as a domain controller in the Adatum.com domain as described in Appendix A, "Setup Instructions for Windows Server 2008 R2."

- Installed a Windows Server 2008 R2 Enterprise server called VAN-SRV1, configured as a member server in the Adatum.com domain as specified in Appendix A. This server can act as a client of the domain controller and is referred to as "the client" in this chapter.

- Created a user account in the Adatum.com domain with the user name Kim Akers and password Pa$$w0rd, and added this account to the Domain Admins, Enterprise Admins, and Schema Admins groups. If you are not sure whether you know how to add a user account to a security group, open Active Directory Users And Computers and access the Help files.

- We recommend that you use an isolated network that is not part of your production network to do the practice exercises in this book. Internet access is not required for the exercises, and you do not need to configure a default gateway. To minimize the time and expense of configuring physical computers, we recommend you use virtual machines. You can create virtual machines using the Hyper-V server role, for example.

 REAL WORLD

Ian McLean

Do you remember the millennium bug?

In 1999, the world of networking was in turmoil (according to press reports, anyway). It seemed that on the stroke of midnight, as the new millennium began, computers would explode, airplanes would fly backwards, and other cataclysmic events would occur because of a long-ago error in programming that would fail to recognize the year 2000.

Networking professionals knew that problems could occur, especially in older, 4-bit microprocessors. But we'd had plenty of notice about the situation, and a lot of clever people had been working very hard to minimize its effects. Most of us predicted (correctly) that nothing big was about to happen as 2000 dawned. Unfortunately, we had something else to worry about. You see, the world of networking was in a real turmoil.

It was predicted that by April 2000, there would be no more IPv4 addresses to be allocated. IPv6 was around, and the IPv6 Internet (then called the 6Bone) existed. However, they were not widely used. Some professional network engineers were displaying signs of a most unprofessional panic. A cynical old author called Ian McLean was negotiating a book about IPv6.

The book was never written, which was just as well because it wouldn't have sold. Suddenly, Network Address Translation (NAT) and private networks became popular. Organizations clamoring for hundreds of public addresses found they could cope perfectly well with two. The use of Classless Interdomain Routing (CIDR) enabled the Internet Assigned Numbers Authority (IANA) to claw back IP addresses from organizations that had been allocated 65,000 of them in a Class B network but had only used 1,000. The problem had been solved.

Well, actually, it hadn't. It had been masked, but it still exists today. IPv4 address space remains under threat of depletion, and IPv4 header structure is still causing problems with Internet routers. Automatic Private IP Addressing (APIPA) allocates only nonroutable internal addresses, and we rely heavily on Dynamic Host Configuration Protocol (DHCP). All that has happened is we have bought some time for the clean, calm transition that's happening now. By default "Internet Protocol" had always meant IPv4; now, it means IPv6. Modern server and client operating systems use IPv6.

"What was IPv4, Daddy?"

"Well, once upon a time . . ."

Lesson 1: Planning IPv6

As an experienced IT professional, you should be aware that the private IP address ranges are 10.0.0.0/8, 172.16.0.0/12, and 192.168.0.0/16, and that the Automatic Private IP Addressing (APIPA) range is 169.254.0.0/16. You should know that NAT typically lets you use a relatively small number of public IP addresses to enable Internet access to many internal clients with private IP addresses. You should be able to identify Class A, B, and C networks, but be aware that most modern network design uses CIDR. You should know that Class D addresses (224.0.0.0/4) are used for multicasting.

You should know that DHCP can allocate IPv4 addresses, subnet masks, default gateways, Domain Name System (DNS) and Windows Internet Naming Service (WINS) servers, and many other settings, and that APIPA can configure IPv4 addresses automatically for use in an isolated private network. You should be aware that three DHCP infrastructure models exist: the centralized DHCP infrastructure model, the decentralized DHCP infrastructure model, and the combined DHCP infrastructure model. You should know that DHCP works with DNS so that Host and (if appropriate) pointer (PTR) records are added to DNS zones when DHCP allocates IP addresses.

Many books have been written that describe IPv4 and DHCP configuration, and it is not the purpose of this lesson to repeat this information. You might be somewhat less familiar with the IPv6 infrastructure, the types of IPv6 address, the operation of DHCP version 6 (DHCPv6), and how to set up a DHCPv6 scope. You also need to be aware of IPv4-to-IPv6 transition strategy and Ipv4 and IPv6 interoperability, particularly the use of Teredo addresses. This lesson looks at IPv6, DHCPv6, transition strategy, and interoperability.

> **After this lesson, you will be able to:**
> - Identify the various types of IPv6 addresses and explain their use.
> - Identify IPv6 addresses that can be routed on the IPv4 Internet.
> - Recommend an appropriate IPv4-to-IPv6 transition strategy.
> - Implement IPv4 and IPv6 interoperability.
> - Use IPv6 tools.
> - Configure DHCPv6 scopes.
>
> **Estimated lesson time: 35 minutes**

Analyzing the IPv6 Address Structure

The extremely large (2^{128}) IPv6 address space allows for multiple levels of subnetting and address allocation between the Internet backbone and individual subnets within an organization. This allows us to allocate not one but several unique IPv6 addresses to a network entity, with each address being used for a different purpose.

IPv6 provides addresses that are equivalent to IPv4 address types and others that are unique to IPv6. A node can have several IPv6 addresses, each of which has its own unique purpose. This section describes the IPv6 address syntax and the various classes of IPv6 address.

IPv6 Address Syntax

The IPv6 128-bit address is divided into 16-bit blocks, and each 16-bit block is converted to a 4-digit hexadecimal number. Colons are used as separators. This representation is called *colon-hexadecimal*.

Global unicast IPv6 addresses are equivalent to IPv4 public unicast addresses. To illustrate IPv6 address syntax, consider the following IPv6 global unicast address:

21cd:0053:0000:0000:03ad:003f:af37:8d62

IPv6 representation can be simplified by removing the leading zeros within each 16-bit block. However, each block must have at least a single digit. With leading zero suppression, the address representation becomes

21cd:53:0:0:3ad:3f:af37:8d62

A contiguous sequence of 16-bit blocks set to 0 in the colon-hexadecimal format can be compressed to ::. Thus, the previous example address could be written as

21cd:53::3ad:3f:af37:8d62

Some types of addresses contain long sequences of zeros and thus provide good examples of when to use this notation. For example, the multicast address ff05:0:0:0:0:0:0:2 can be compressed to ff05::2.

IPv6 Address Prefixes

The prefix is the part of the address that indicates either the bits that have fixed values or the network identifier bits. IPv6 prefixes are expressed in the same way as CIDR IPv4 notation, or slash notation. For example, 21cd:53::/64 is the subnet on which the address 21cd:53::23ad:3f:af37:8d62 is located. In this case, the first 64 bits of the address are the network prefix. An IPv6 subnet prefix (or subnet ID) is assigned to a single link. Multiple subnet IDs can be assigned to the same link. This technique is called *multinetting*.

> **NOTE IP SUBNET MASKS**
>
> IPv6 does not use dotted decimal notation in subnet masks. Only prefix length notation is supported in IPv6. IPv4 dotted decimal subnet mask representation (such as 255.255.255.0) has no direct equivalent.

IPv6 Address Types

The three types of IPv6 address are unicast, multicast, and anycast.

- **Unicast** Identifies a single interface within the scope of the unicast address type. Packets addressed to a unicast address are delivered to a single interface. RFC 2373 allows multiple interfaces to use the same address, provided that these interfaces appear as a single interface to the IPv6 implementation on the host. This accommodates load-balancing systems.

- **Multicast** Identifies multiple interfaces. Packets addressed to a multicast address are delivered to all interfaces that are identified by the address.

- **Anycast** Identifies multiple interfaces. Packets addressed to an anycast address are delivered to the nearest interface identified by the address. The nearest interface is the closest in terms of routing distance, or number of hops. An anycast address is used for one-to-one-of-many communication, with delivery to a single interface.

> *MORE INFO* **IPV6 ADDRESSING ARCHITECTURE**
>
> For more information about IPv6 address structure and architecture, see RFC 2373 at *http://www.ietf.org/rfc/rfc2373.txt*.

> *NOTE* **INTERFACES AND NODES**
>
> IPv6 addresses identify interfaces rather than nodes. A node is identified by any unicast address that is assigned to one of its interfaces.

IPv6 Unicast Addresses

IPv6 supports the following types of unicast address:

- Global
- Link-local
- Site-local
- Special
- Network Service Access Point (NSAP) and Internetwork Packet Exchange (IPX) mapped addresses

GLOBAL UNICAST ADDRESSES

Global unicast addresses are the IPv6 equivalent of IPv4 public addresses and are globally routable and reachable on the IPv6 Internet. These addresses can be aggregated to produce an efficient routing infrastructure and are therefore sometimes known as *aggregatable global unicast addresses*. An aggregatable global unicast address is unique across the entire IPv6 Internet. (The region over which an IP address is unique is called the *scope* of the address.)

The Format Prefix (FP) of a global unicast address is held in the three most significant bits, which are always 001. The next 13 bits are allocated by the IANA and are known as the Top Level Aggregator (TLA). IANA allocates TLAs to local Internet registries, which in turn allocate individual TLAs to large Internet Service Providers (ISPs). The next 8 bits of the address are reserved for future expansion.

The next 24 bits of the address contain the Next Level Aggregator (NLA). This identifies a specific customer site. The NLA enables an ISP to create multiple levels of addressing hierarchy within a network. The next 16 bits contain the Site Level Aggregator (SLA), which is used to organize addressing and routing for downstream ISPs and to identify sites or subnets within a site.

The next 64 bits identify the interface within a subnet. This is the 64-bit Extended Unique Identifier (EUI-64) address, as defined by the Institute of Electrical and Electronics Engineers (IEEE). EUI-64 addresses are either assigned directly to network adapter cards or derived from the 48-bit media access control (MAC) address of a network adapter, as defined by the IEEE 802 standard. Put simply, the interface identity is provided by the network adapter hardware.

To summarize, the FP, TLA, reserved bits, and NLA identify the public topology; the SLA identifies the site topology; and the interface ID identifies the interface. Figure 2-1 illustrates the structure of an aggregatable global unicast address.

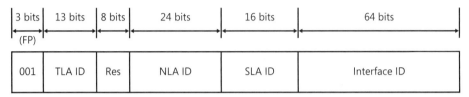

FIGURE 2-1 Global unicast address structure

> **MORE INFO** **GLOBAL UNICAST ADDRESS FORMAT**
>
> For more information about aggregatable global unicast addresses, see RFC 2374 at *http://www.ietf.org/rfc/rfc2374.txt*.

EXAM TIP

For the exam, you need to know that an aggregatable global unicast address is the IPv6 equivalent of an IPv4 public unicast address. You should be able to identify a global unicast address from the value of its three most significant bits. Knowing the various components of the address helps you understand how IPv6 addressing works, but the exam is unlikely to test this knowledge in the depth of detail provided by the RFCs.

LINK-LOCAL ADDRESSES

Link-local IPv6 addresses are equivalent to IPv4 addresses that are autoconfigured through APIPA and use the 169.254.0.0/16 prefix. You can identify a link-local address by the FP of 1111 1110 10, which is followed by 54 zeros (link-local addresses always begin with *fe8*). Nodes use link-local addresses when communicating with neighboring nodes on the same link. The scope of a link-local address is the local link. A link-local address is required for ND and is always configured automatically, even if no other unicast address is allocated.

Figure 2-2 shows a link-local address configured on an interface on the VAN-DC1 domain controller. No global addresses exist in the configuration because domain controllers are never exposed directly to the Internet. The IPv6 addresses on your test computer will probably be different.

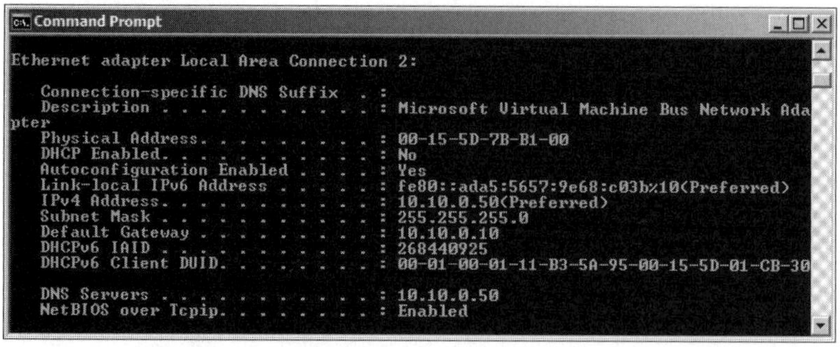

FIGURE 2-2 IPv6 addresses on computer interfaces

SITE-LOCAL ADDRESSES

Site-local IPv6 addresses are currently being deprecated, but a replacement for them has yet to be agreed upon and they remain widely used in enterprise environments, so you still need to know about them. These addresses are equivalent to the IPv4 private address space (10.0.0.0/8, 172.16.0.0/12, and 192.168.0.0/16). Private intranets that do not have a direct, routed connection to the IPv6 Internet can use site-local addresses without conflicting with aggregatable global unicast addresses. The scope of a site-local address is the site (or organization internetwork).

Site-local addresses can be allocated by using stateful address configuration, such as from a DHCPv6 scope. A host uses stateful address configuration when it receives router advertisement messages that do not include address prefixes. A host will also use a stateful address configuration protocol when no routers are present on the local link.

Site-local addresses can also be configured through stateless address configuration. This is based on router advertisement messages that include stateless address prefixes and require that hosts do not use a stateful address configuration protocol.

Alternatively, address configuration can use a combination of stateless and stateful configuration. This occurs when router advertisement messages include stateless address prefixes but require that hosts use a stateful address configuration protocol.

> ***NOTE*** **SMALL BRANCH OFFICES**
>
> In small branch offices with very few computers, you should consider whether using DHCP and DHCPv6 over slow or unreliable network connections is an appropriate choice. It may not be worthwhile configuring a DHCP server in such sites, and manual configuration may be the more appropriate option.

Site-local addresses begin with *fec0*, followed by 32 zeros and then by a 16-bit subnet identifier that you can use to create subnets within your organization. The 64-bit Interface ID field identifies a specific interface on a subnet.

MORE INFO **REPLACEMENT FOR SITE-LOCAL ADDRESSES**

If you want to research the proposed replacement for site-local addresses, see
http://www.ietf.org/rfc/rfc4291.txt.

Link-Local and Site-Local Addresses

You can implement IPv6 connectivity between hosts on an isolated subnet by using link-local addresses. However, you cannot assign link-local addresses to router interfaces (default gateways), and you cannot route from one subnet to another if only link-local addresses are used. DNS servers cannot use only link-local addresses. If you use a link-local address, you need to specify its interface ID—that is, the number after the % symbol at the end of the address, as shown previously in Figure 2-2. Link-local addresses are not registered dynamically in Windows Server 2008 and Windows Server 2008 R2 DNS.

For these reasons, site-local addresses are typically used on the subnets of a private network to implement IPv6 connectivity over the network (until such time as a replacement is agreed upon). If every device on the network has its own global address (a stated aim of IPv6 implementation), global addresses can route between internal subnets, to peripheral zones, and to the Internet.

SPECIAL ADDRESSES

Two special IPv6 addresses exist—the unspecified address and the loopback address. The unspecified address 0:0:0:0:0:0:0:0 (or ::) is used to indicate the absence of an address and is equivalent to the IPv4 unspecified address 0.0.0.0. It is typically used as a source address for packets attempting to verify whether a tentative address is unique. It is never assigned to an interface or used as a destination address. The loopback address 0:0:0:0:0:0:0:1 (or ::1) is used to identify a loopback interface and is equivalent to the IPv4 loopback address 127.0.0.1.

NSAP AND IPX ADDRESSES

NSAP addresses are identifying labels for network endpoints used in Open Systems Interconnection (OSI) networking. They are used to specify a piece of equipment connected to an Asynchronous Transfer Mode (ATM) network. IPX is no longer widely used because modern Novell Netware networks support Transmission Control Protocol/Internet Protocol (TCP/IP). IPv6 addresses with an FP of 0000001 map to NSAP addresses. IPv6 addresses with an FP of 0000010 map to IPX addresses.

EXAM TIP

The 70-646 exam is unlikely to include questions about NSAP or IPX mapping.

IPv6 Multicast Addresses

IPv6 multicast addresses enable an IPv6 packet to be sent to a number of hosts, all of which have the same multicast address. They have an FP of 11111111 (they always start with *ff*). Subsequent fields specify flags, scope, and group ID, as shown in Figure 2-3.

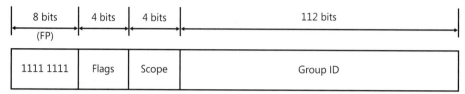

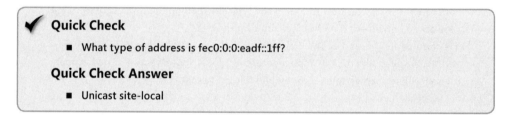

FIGURE 2-3 Multicast address structure

The *flags* field holds the flag settings. Currently the only flag defined is the Transient (T) flag, which uses the low-order field bit. If this flag is set to 0, the multicast address is well known—in other words, it is assigned permanently and has been allocated by IANA. If the flag is set to 1, the multicast address is transient.

> ✔ **Quick Check**
> - What type of address is fec0:0:0:eadf::1ff?
>
> **Quick Check Answer**
> - Unicast site-local

The scope field indicates the scope of the IPv6 internetwork for which the multicast traffic is intended. Routers use the multicast scope, together with information provided by multicast routing protocols, to determine whether multicast traffic can be forwarded. For example, traffic with the multicast address ff02::2 has a link-local scope and is never forwarded beyond the local link. Table 2-1 lists the assigned scope field values.

TABLE 2-1 Scope Field Values

VALUE	SCOPE
0	Reserved
1	Node-local scope
2	Link-local scope
5	Site-local scope
8	Organization-local scope
e	Global scope
f	Reserved

The group ID represents the multicast group and is unique within the scope. Permanently assigned group IDs are independent of the scope. Transient group IDs are relevant only to a specific scope. Multicast addresses from ff01:: through ff0f:: are reserved, well-known addresses.

In theory, 2^{112} group IDs are available. In practice, because of the way that IPv6 multicast addresses are mapped to Ethernet multicast MAC addresses, RFC 2373, "IP Version 6 Addressing Architecture," recommends assigning the group ID from the low-order 32 bits of the IPv6 multicast address and setting the remaining original group ID bits to zero. In this way, each group ID maps to a unique Ethernet multicast MAC address.

> **MORE INFO**   **ASSIGNING GROUP IDS**
>
> For more information about assigning group IDs, see *http://www.ietf.org/rfc/rfc2373.txt*.

IPv4-to-IPv6 Compatibility and Transition to IPv6

This section discusses the transition from IPv4 to IPv6 and why this has advantages for your organization. However, IPv4 and IPv6 are likely to coexist in most organizations, and the transition from IPv4 to IPv6 is typically gradual. Therefore, this section also discusses IPv4-to-IPv6 compatibility.

IPv6 was designed to overcome the limitations of IPv4. IPv6 has the following advantages over its predecessor:

- **Increased Address Space**   In retrospect, the 32-bit structure that IPv4 uses was not sufficient for an addressing structure. IPv6 offers 128 bits. This gives enough addresses for every device that requires a unique public IPv6 address. In addition, the 64-bit host portion (interface ID) of an IPv6 address can be generated automatically from the network adapter hardware.

- **Automatic Address Configuration**   Typically, IPv4 is configured either manually or by using DHCP. Automatic configuration (autoconfiguration) through APIPA is available for isolated subnets that are not routed to other networks. IPv6 deals with the need for simpler and more automatic address configuration by supporting both stateful and stateless address configuration. Stateful configuration uses DHCPv6. If stateless address configuration is used, hosts on a link automatically configure themselves with IPv6 addresses for the link and (optionally) with addresses that are derived from prefixes advertised by local routers. You can also configure stateless DHCPv6 configuration that does not assign addresses to hosts but can assign settings to (for example) DNS servers whose domain names are not included in the router advertisements.

- **Network-Level Security**   Private communication over the Internet requires encryption to protect data from being viewed or modified in transit. Internet Protocol Security (IPsec) provides this facility, but its use is optional in IPv4. IPv6 makes IPsec mandatory. This provides a standards-based solution for network security needs and improves interoperability among different IPv6 implementations.

- **Real-Time Data Delivery**   Quality of Service (QoS) exists in IPv4, and bandwidth can be guaranteed for real-time traffic (such as video and audio transmissions) over a network. However, IPv4 real-time traffic support relies on the Type of Service (ToS) field and the identification of the payload, typically using a User Datagram Protocol (UDP) or Transmission Control Protocol (TCP) port. The IPv4 ToS field has limited functionality, and payload identification using a TCP and UDP port is not possible when an IPv4 packet payload is encrypted. Payload identification is included in the Flow Label field of the IPv6 header, so payload encryption does not affect QoS operation.

- **Routing Table Size**   The IPv6 global addresses used on the IPv6 Internet are designed to create an efficient, hierarchical, and summarizable routing infrastructure based on the common occurrence of multiple levels of ISPs. On the IPv6 Internet, backbone routers have greatly reduced routing tables that use route aggregation and correspond to the routing infrastructure of top-level aggregators.

- **Header Size and Extension Headers**   IPv4 and IPv6 headers are not compatible, and a host or router must use both IPv4 and IPv6 implementations to recognize and process both header formats. Therefore, the IPv6 header was designed to be as small as was practical. Nonessential and optional fields are moved to extension headers placed after the IPv6 header. As a result, the IPv6 header is only twice as large as the IPv4 header, and the size of IPv6 extension headers is constrained only by the size of the IPv6 packet.

- **Removal of Broadcast Traffic**   IPv4 relies on Address Resolution Protocol (ARP) broadcasts to resolve IP addresses to the MAC addresses of the network interface cards (NICs). Broadcasts increase network traffic and are inefficient because every host processes them. The Neighbor Discovery (ND) protocol for IPv6 uses a series of Internet Control Message Protocol for IPv6 (ICMPv6) messages that manage the interaction of nodes on the same link (neighboring nodes). ND replaces ARP broadcasts, ICMPv4 Router Discovery, and ICMPv4 Redirect messages with efficient multicast and unicast ND messages.

Route Aggregation

Route aggregation provides for routing of traffic for networks with smaller prefixes to networks with larger prefixes. In other words, it permits a number of contiguous address blocks to be combined and summarized as a larger address block. Route aggregation reduces the number of advertised routes on large networks. When an ISP breaks its network into smaller subnets to provide service to smaller providers, it needs to advertise the route only to its main supernet for traffic to be sent to smaller providers.

Route aggregation is used when the large ISP has a continuous range of IP addresses to manage. IP addresses (IPv4 or IPv6) that are capable of summarization are termed *aggregatable addresses*.

Implementing IPv4-to-IPv6 Compatibility

In addition to the various types of addresses described earlier in this lesson, IPv6 provides the following types of compatibility addresses to aid migration from IPv4 to IPv6 and to implement transition technologies.

IPV4-COMPATIBLE ADDRESS

The IPv4-compatible address 0:0:0:0:0:0:w.x.y.z (or ::w.x.y.z) is used by dual stack nodes that are communicating with IPv6 over an IPv4 infrastructure. The last four octets (w.x.y.z) represent the dotted decimal representation of an IPv4 address. Dual stack nodes are nodes with both IPv4 and IPv6 protocols. When the IPv4-compatible address is used as an IPv6 destination, the IPv6 traffic is encapsulated with an IPv4 header and sent to the destination using the IPv4 infrastructure automatically.

> **NOTE** **IPV4-COMPATIBLE ADDRESSES ARE NOW DEPRECATED**
>
> Current IPv6 transition mechanisms no longer use IPv4-compatible addresses. New or updated implementations are not required to support this address type. You should be aware of this address type because you might come across it in existing compatibility schemes, but you should not implement IPv4-compatible addresses in current designs.

> **MORE INFO** **DEPRECATING IPV4-COMPATIBLE ADDRESSES**
>
> For more information about deprecating IPv4-compatible addresses, see *http://www.ietf.org/rfc/rfc4291.txt*.

IPV4-MAPPED ADDRESS

The IPv4-mapped address 0:0:0:0:0:ffff:w.x.y.z (or ::ffff:w.x.y.z) is used to represent an IPv4-only node to an IPv6 node, and hence to map IPv4 devices that are not compatible with IPv6 into the IPv6 address space. The IPv4-mapped address is never used as the source or destination address of an IPv6 packet.

TEREDO ADDRESS

A Teredo address consists of a 32-bit Teredo prefix. In Windows Server 2008 and Windows Server 2008 R2 (as well as Windows Vista and Windows 7), this is 2001::/32. The prefix is followed by the IPv4 (32-bit) public address of the Teredo server that assisted in the configuration of the address. The next 16 bits are reserved for Teredo flags. Currently, only the highest-ordered flag bit is defined. This is the cone flag, and it is set when the NAT connected to the Internet is a cone NAT.

> **NOTE** **TEREDO IN WINDOWS XP AND WINDOWS SERVER 2003**
>
> In Windows XP and Windows Server 2003, the Teredo prefix was originally 3ffe:831f::/32. Computers running Windows XP and Windows Server 2003 use the 2001::/32 Teredo prefix when updated with Microsoft Security Bulletin MS06-064.

The next 16 bits store an obscured version of the external UDP port that corresponds to all Teredo traffic for the Teredo client interface. When a Teredo client sends its initial packet to a Teredo server, NAT maps the source UDP port of the packet to a different, external UDP port. All Teredo traffic for the host interface uses the same external, mapped UDP port. The value representing this external port is masked or obscured by exclusive ORing (XORing) it with 0xffff. Obscuring the external port prevents NATs from translating it within the payload of packets being forwarded.

The final 32 bits store an obscured version of the external IPv4 address that corresponds to all Teredo traffic for the Teredo client interface. The external address is obscured by XORing it with 0xffffffff. As with the UDP port, this prevents NATs from translating the external IPv4 address within the payload of packets being forwarded.

The external address is obscured by XORing the external address with 0xffffffff. For example, the obscured version of the public IPv4 address 131.107.0.1 in colon-hexadecimal format is 7c94:fffe. (131.107.0.1 equals 0x836b0001, and 0x836b0001 XOR 0xffffffff equals 0x7c94fffe.) Obscuring the external address prevents NATs from translating it within the payload of the packets being forwarded.

For example, Northwind Traders currently implements the following IPv4 private networks at its headquarters and branch offices:

- Headquarters: 10.0.100.0 /24
- Branch 1: 10.0.0.0 /24
- Branch 2: 10.0.10.0 /24
- Branch 3: 10.0.20.0 /24

The company wants to establish IPv6 communication between Teredo clients and other Teredo clients, and between Teredo clients and IPv6-only hosts. The presence of Teredo servers on the IPv4 Internet enables this communication to take place. A Teredo server is an IPv6/IPv4 node connected to both the IPv4 Internet and the IPv6 Internet that supports a Teredo tunneling interface. The Teredo addresses of the Northwind Traders networks depend on a number of factors, such as the port and type of NAT server used, but they could, for example, be the following:

- Headquarters: 2001::ce49:7601:e866:efff:f5ff:9bfe through 2001::0a0a:64fe:e866:efff:f5ff:9b01
- Branch 1: 2001:: ce49:7601:e866:efff:f5ff:fffe through 2001::0a0a:0afe:e866:efff:f5ff:ff01
- Branch 2: 2001:: ce49:7601:e866:efff:f5ff:f5fe through 2001::0a0a:14fe:e866:efff:f5ff:f501
- Branch 3: 2001:: ce49:7601:e866:efff:f5ff:ebfe through 2001::0a0a:1efe:e866:efff:f5ff:ebfe

Note that, for example, 10.0.100.1 is the equivalent of 0a00:6401, and 0a00:6401 XORed with ffff:ffff is f5ff:9bfe.

Cone NATs

Cone NATs can be full-cone, restricted-cone, or port-restricted-cone. In a full-cone NAT, all requests from the same internal IP address and port are mapped to the same external IP address and port, and any external host can send a packet to the internal host by sending a packet to the mapped external address.

In a restricted-cone NAT, all requests from the same internal IP address and port are mapped to the same external IP address and port, but an external host can send a packet to the internal host if the internal host had previously sent a packet to the external host.

In a port-restricted-cone NAT, the restriction includes port numbers. An external host with a specified IP address and source port can send a packet to an internal host only if the internal host had previously sent a packet to that IP address and port.

ISATAP ADDRESSES

IPv6 can use an ISATAP address to communicate between two nodes over an IPv4 intranet. An ISATAP address starts with a 64-bit unicast link-local, site-local, global, or 6to4 global prefix. The next 32 bits are the ISATAP identifier 0:5efe. The final 32 bits hold the IPv4 address in either dotted decimal or hexadecimal notation. An ISATAP address can incorporate either a public or a private IPv4 address.

For example, the ISATAP address fe80::5efe:w.x.y.z address has a link-local prefix; the fec0::1111:0:5efe:w.x.y.z address has a site-local prefix; the 3ffe:1a05:510:1111:0:5efe:w.x.y.z address has a global prefix; and the 2002:9d36:1:2:0:5efe:w.x.y.z address has a 6to4 global prefix. In all cases w.x.y.z represents an IPv4 address.

By default Windows Server 2008 and Windows Server 2008 R2 automatically configure the ISATAP address fe80::5efe:w.x.y.z for each IPv4 address that is assigned to a node. This link-local ISATAP address allows two hosts to communicate over an IPv4 network by using each other's ISATAP address.

You can implement IPv6-to-IPv4 configuration by using the IPv6 tools netsh interface ipv6 6to4, netsh interface ipv6 isatap, and netsh interface ipv6 add v6v4tunnel. For example, to create an IPv6-in-IPv4 tunnel between the local address 10.0.0.11 and the remote address 192.168.123.116 on an interface named *Remote,* you would enter:

```
netsh interface ipv6 add v6v4tunnel "Remote" 10.0.0.11 192.168.123.116.
```

You can also configure the appropriate compatibility addresses manually by using the `netsh interface ipv6 set address` command or the TCP/IPv6 graphical user interface (GUI) as described in the next section of this lesson.

> **NOTE 6TO4CFG**
>
> Windows Server 2008 and Windows Server 2008 R2 do not support the 6to4cfg tool.

Planning an IPv4-to-IPv6 Transition Strategy

No specific time frame is mandated for IPv4-to-IPv6 transition. As a senior administrator, one of your decisions is whether to be an early adopter, taking immediate advantage of IPv6 enhancements such as addressing and stronger security, or wait and take advantage of the experience of others. Both are valid strategies.

However, you do need to find out whether your upstream ISPs support IPv6, and whether the networking hardware in your organization (or the several organizations in your enterprise) also support the protocol. The most straightforward transition method, called dual stack, requires that both IPv4 and IPv6 be supported. By the same token, do not delay the decision to transition to IPv6 for too long. If you wait until the IPv4 address space is fully depleted, dual stack will no longer be available, and you (and the users you support) will find the transition process much more traumatic.

Currently, the underlying assumption in transition planning is that an existing IPv4 infrastructure is available and that your most immediate requirement is to transport IPv6 packets over existing IPv4 networks so that isolated IPv6 network islands do not occur. As more networks make the transition, the requirement will change to transporting IPv4 packets over IPv6 infrastructures to support older IPv4 applications and avoid isolated IPv4 islands.

Because no single strategy fits all situations, several transition strategies and technologies exist. RFC 4213, "Basic Transition Mechanisms for Hosts and Routers," describes the key elements of these transition technologies, such as dual stack and configured tunneling. The RFC also defines a number of node types based upon their protocol support, including older systems that support only IPv4, future systems that will support only IPv6, and the dual node, which implements both IPv6 and IPv4.

> **MORE INFO IPV4-TO-IPV6 TRANSITION**
>
> For more information about basic transition mechanisms, see RFC 4213 at *http://www.ietf.org/rfc/rfc4213.txt* and download the white paper "IPv6 Transition Technologies" from *http://technet.microsoft.com/en-us/library/bb726951.aspx*.

DUAL STACK TRANSITION

Dual stack (also known as a *dual IP layer*) is arguably the most straightforward approach to transition. It assumes that hosts and routers provide support for both protocols and can send and receive both IPv4 and IPv6 packets. Thus, a dual stack node can interoperate with an IPv4 device by using IPv4 packets and interoperate with an IPv6 device by using IPv6 packets. It can also operate in one of the following three modes:

- With only the IPv4 stack enabled
- With only the IPv6 stack enabled
- With both IPv4 and IPv6 stacks enabled

Because a dual stack node supports both protocols, you can configure it with both IPv4 32-bit addresses and IPv6 128-bit addresses. For example, it can use DHCP to acquire its IPv4 addresses and stateless autoconfiguration or DHCPv6 to acquire its IPv6 addresses. Current IPv6 implementations are typically dual stack. An IPv6-only product would have very few communication partners.

CONFIGURED TUNNELING TRANSITION

If a configured tunneling transition strategy is employed, the existing IPv4 routing infrastructure remains functional, but it also carries IPv6 traffic while the IPv6 routing infrastructure is under development. A *tunnel* is a bidirectional, point-to-point link between two network endpoints. Data passes through a tunnel using encapsulation, in which the IPv6 packet is carried inside an IPv4 packet. The encapsulating IPv4 header is created at the tunnel entry point and removed at the tunnel exit point. The tunnel endpoint addresses are determined from configuration information that is stored at the encapsulating endpoint.

Configured tunnels are also called *explicit tunnels*. You can configure them as router-to-router, host-to-router, host-to-host, or router-to-host, but they are most likely to be used in a router-to-router configuration. The configured tunnel can be managed by a *tunnel broker*. A tunnel broker is a dedicated server that manages tunnel requests coming from users, as described in RFC 3053, "IPv6 Tunnel Broker."

> **MORE INFO   TUNNEL BROKER**
>
> For more information about tunnel broker, see RFC 3053 at *http://www.ietf.org/rfc/rfc3053.txt*.

AUTOMATIC TUNNELING

RFC 2893, "Transition Mechanisms for IPv6 Hosts and Routers" (which subsequently was replaced by RFC 4213), describes automatic tunneling. This allows IPv4/IPv6 nodes to communicate over an IPv4 routing infrastructure without using preconfigured tunnels. The nodes that perform automatic tunneling are assigned a special type of address called an IPv4-compatible address, described later in this lesson, which carries the 32-bit IPv4 address within a 128-bit IPv6 address format. The IPv4address can be extracted automatically from the IPv6 address.

6TO4

RFC 3056, "Connection of IPv6 Domains via IPv4 Clouds," describes the 6to4 tunneling scheme. 6to4 tunneling allows IPv6 sites to communicate with each other via an IPv4 network without using explicit tunnels, and to communicate with native IPv6 domains via relay routers. This strategy treats the IPv4 Internet as a single data link.

TEREDO

RFC 4380, "Teredo: Tunneling IPv6 over UDP Through Network Address Translations (NATs)," describes Teredo, which is an enhancement to the 6to4 method and is supported by Windows Server 2008 and Windows Server 2008 R2. Teredo enables nodes that are located behind an IPv4 NAT device to obtain IPv6 connectivity by using UDP to tunnel packets. Teredo requires the use of server and relay elements to assist with path connectivity. Teredo address structure was discussed earlier in this lesson.

INTRA-SITE AUTOMATIC TUNNELING ADDRESSING PROTOCOL

RFC 4214, "Intra-Site Automatic Tunnel Addressing Protocol (ISATAP)," defines ISATAP, which connects IPv6 hosts and routers over an IPv4 network using a process that views the IPv4 network as a link layer for IPv6, and views other nodes on the network as potential IPv6 hosts or routers. This creates a host-to-host, host-to-router, or router-to-host automatic tunnel.

Using IPv6 Tools

Windows Server 2008 and Windows Server 2008 R2 provide tools that let you configure IPv6 interfaces and check IPv6 connectivity and routing. Tools also exist that implement and check IPv4-to-IPv6 compatibility.

In Windows Server 2008 and Windows Server 2008 R2, the standard command-line tools, such as ping, ipconfig, pathping, tracert, netstat, and route, have full IPv6 functionality. For example, Figure 2-4 shows the `ping` command used to check connectivity with a link-local IPv6 address on a test network. The IPv6 addresses on your test network will be different. Note that if you were pinging from one host to another you would also need to include the interface ID, such as `ping fe80::ada5:5657:9e68:c03b%10`. Interface IDs are discussed later in this lesson.

FIGURE 2-4 Pinging an IPv6 address

> ### NOTE PING6
>
> The ping6 command-line tool is not supported in Windows Server 2008 or Windows Server 2008 R2.

Tools specific to IPv6 are provided in the netsh (network shell) command structure. For example, the `netsh interface ipv6 show neighbors` command shows the IPv6 interfaces of all hosts on the local subnet. You use this command in the practice later in this lesson, after you have configured IPv6 connectivity on a subnet.

Verifying IPv6 Configuration and Connectivity

If you are troubleshooting connectivity problems or merely want to check your configuration, arguably the most useful tool—and certainly one of the most used—is ipconfig. The ipconfig /all tool displays both IPv4 and IPv6 configuration.

If you want to display the configuration of only the IPv6 interfaces on the local computer, you can use the `netsh interface ipv6 show address` command. Figure 2-5 shows the output of this command run on the VAN-DC1 computer. Note the % character followed by a number after each IPv6 address. This is the interface ID, which identifies the interface that is configured with the IPv6 address. In addition, note that the site-local address still exists, but it is displayed as deprecated, as discussed earlier in this lesson.

FIGURE 2-5 Displaying IPv6 addresses and interface IDs

If you are administering an enterprise network with a number of sites, you also need to know site IDs. You can obtain a site ID by using the command netsh interface ipv6 show address level=verbose. The output from this command is shown in Figure 2-6.

FIGURE 2-6 Displaying IPv6 addresses and site IDs

Configuring IPv6 Interfaces

Typically, most IPv6 addresses are configured through autoconfiguration or DHCPv6. However, if you need to configure an IPv6 address manually, you can use the netsh interface ipv6 set address command, as in this example:

```
netsh interface ipv6 set address "local area connection 2" fec0:0:0:fffe::2.
```

You need to run the Command Prompt as an administrator to use this command. In Windows Server 2008 and Windows Server 2008 R2 (as well as in Windows Vista and Windows 7), you can also configure IPv6 addresses manually from the properties of the TCP/IPv6 GUI. Figure 2-7 shows this configuration.

FIGURE 2-7 Configuring an IPv6 address through a GUI

The advantage of using the TCP/IPv6 GUI is that you can specify the IPv6 addresses of one or more DNS servers in addition to specifying the interface address. If, however, you choose to use Command Line Interface (CLI) commands, the command to add IPv6 addresses of DNS servers is `netsh interface ipv6 add dnsserver`, as in this example:

```
netsh interface ipv6 add dnsserver "local area connection 2" fec0:0:0:fffe::1.
```

To change the properties of IPv6 interfaces (but not their configuration), use the `netsh interface ipv6 set interface` command, as in this example:

```
netsh interface ipv6 set interface "local area connection 2" forwarding=enabled.
```

You need to run the Command Prompt as an administrator to use the `netsh interface ipv6 add` and `netsh interface ipv6 set` commands.

> ### ✔ Quick Check
> - What `netsh` command lists site IDs?
>
> ### Quick Check Answer
> - `netsh interface ipv6 show address level=verbose`

Verifying IPv6 Connectivity

To verify connectivity on a local network, your first step should be to flush the neighbor cache, which stores recently resolved link-layer addresses and might give a false result if you are checking changes that involve address resolution. You can check the contents of the neighbor cache by using the command netsh interface ipv6 show neighbors. The command netsh interface ipv6 delete neighbors flushes the cache. Figure 2-8 shows these two commands. You need to run the Command Prompt as an administrator to use the netsh tool.

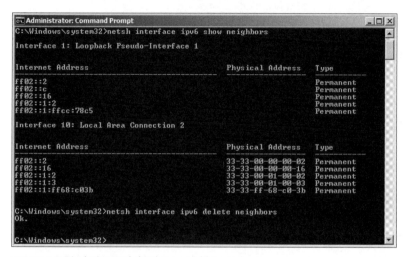

FIGURE 2-8 Displaying and clearing a neighbor cache

You can test connectivity to a local host on your subnet and to your default gateway by using the ping command. You can add the interface ID to the IPv6 interface address to ensure that the address is configured on the correct interface. Figure 2-4, earlier in this lesson, shows the result of a ping command using an IPv6 address.

To check connectivity to a host on a remote network, your first task should be to check and clear the destination cache, which stores next-hop IPv6 addresses for destinations. You can display the current contents of the destination cache by using the netsh interface ipv6 show destinationcache command. To flush the destination cache, use the netsh interface ipv6 delete destinationcache command. You need to run the Command Prompt as an administrator to use this command.

Your next step is to check connectivity to the default router interface on your local subnet. This is your default gateway. You can identify the IPv6 address of your default router interface by using the ipconfig, netsh interface ipv6 show routes, or route print command. You can also specify the zone ID, which is the interface ID for the default gateway on the interface on which you want the ICMPv6 Echo Request messages to be sent. When you have ensured that you can reach the default gateway on your local subnet, ping the remote host by its IPv6 address. Note that you cannot ping a remote host (or a router interface) by its link-local IPv6 address because link-local addresses are not routable.

If you can connect to the default gateway but cannot reach the remote destination address, trace the route to the remote destination by using the `tracert -d` command followed by the destination IPv6 address. The `-d` command-line switch prevents the tracert tool from performing a DNS reverse query on router interfaces in the routing path. This speeds up the display of the routing path. If you want more information about the routers in the path, and particularly if you want to verify router reliability, use the `pathping -d` command, again followed by the destination IPv6 address.

 Quick Check

- What `netsh` command could you use to identify the IPv6 address of your default router interface?

Quick Check Answer

- `netsh interface ipv6 show route`

Troubleshooting Connectivity

As an experienced administrator, you know that if you cannot connect to a remote host, you (or, more probably, a more junior member of your team) first want to check the various hardware connections (wired and wireless) in your organization and ensure that all network devices are up and running. If these basic checks do not find the problem, the Internet Protocol Security (IPsec) configuration might not be configured properly, or firewall problems (such as incorrectly configured packet filters) might exist.

You can use the IP Security Policies Management Microsoft Management Console (MMC) snap-in to check and configure IPsec policies and the Windows Firewall With Advanced Security snap-in to check and configure IPv6-based packet filters.

Note that you can use the IP Security Policy snap-in to create IPsec policies that are applied to computers running Windows Vista and Windows Server 2008, but this snap-in does not use new security algorithms and other new features available in Windows 7 and Windows Server 2008 R2. To create IPsec policies for these computers, use the Windows Firewall With Advanced Security snap-in. However, you need to take care when doing this because the Windows Firewall With Advanced Security snap-in does not create policies that you can apply to earlier versions of Windows.

Figures 2-9 and 2-10 show these tools.

> **_MORE INFO_ USING THE IP SECURITY POLICIES MANAGEMENT SNAP-IN AND THE WINDOWS FIREWALL WITH ADVANCED SECURITY SNAP-IN**
>
> For more information about which of these snap-ins you should use in a specific situation, see _http://technet.microsoft.com/en-us/library/cc730656(WS.10).aspx_.

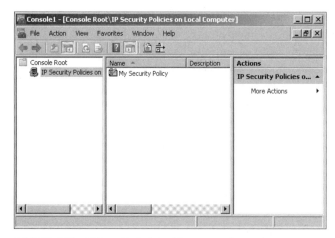

FIGURE 2-9 The IP Security Policies Management snap-in

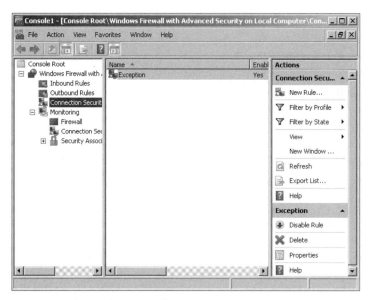

FIGURE 2-10 The Windows Firewall With Advanced Security snap-in

NOTE **IPSEC6**

The IPSec6 tool is not implemented in Windows Server 2008 or Windows Server 2008 R2.

You might be unable to reach a local or remote destination because of incorrect or missing routes in the local IPv6 routing table. You can use the `route print`, `netstat -r`, or `netsh interface ipv6 show route` command to view the local IPv6 routing table and verify that you have a route corresponding to your local subnet and to your default gateway. Note that the `netstat -r` command displays both IPv4 and IPv6 routing tables.

If you have multiple default routes with the same metric, you might need to modify your IPv6 router configurations so that the default route with the lowest metric uses the interface that connects to the network with the largest number of subnets. You can use the `netsh interface ipv6 set route` command to modify an existing route. To add a route to the IPv6 routing table, use the `netsh interface ipv6 add route` command. The `netsh interface ipv6 delete route` command removes an existing route. You need to run the Command Prompt as an administrator to use these commands.

If you can access a local or remote host by IPv4 address but not by host name, you might have a DNS problem. Tools to configure, check, and debug DNS, include dnscmd, ipconfig, netsh interface ipv6 show dnsservers, netsh interface ipv6 add dnsserver, nslookup, and the TCP/IPv6 GUI. Lesson 2 of this chapter, "Planning DNS," discusses these tools.

Verifying IPv6-based TCP Connections

If the telnet client tool is installed, you can verify that a TCP connection can be established to a TCP port by entering the `telnet` command followed by the destination IPv6 address and the TCP port number, as in this example: `telnet fec0:0:0:fffe::1 80`. If telnet successfully creates a TCP connection, the `telnet>` prompt appears, and you can type telnet commands. If the tool cannot create a connection, it will return an error message.

> **MORE INFO INSTALLING THE TELNET CLIENT**
>
> For more information about telnet, including how to install the telnet client, search Windows Server 2008 Help or Windows Server 2008 R2 Help for "Telnet: frequently asked questions."

Configuring Clients Through DHCPv6

You can choose stateless or stateful configuration when configuring hosts by using DHCPv6. Stateless configuration does not generate a host address—which is instead autoconfigured—but it can, for example, specify the address of a DNS server. Stateful configuration specifies host addresses.

Whether you choose stateful or stateless configuration, you can assign the IPv6 addresses of DNS servers through the DNS Recursive Name Server DHCPv6 option (option 0023). If you choose stateful configuration, the IPv6 addresses of DNS servers can be configured as a scope option, so different scopes could have different DNS servers. Scope options override server options for that scope. This is the preferred method of configuring DNS server IPv6 addresses, which are not configured through router discovery.

With DHCPv6, an IPv6 host can receive subnet prefixes and other configuration parameters. A common use of DHCPv6 for Windows-based IPv6 hosts is to configure the IPv6 addresses of DNS servers automatically.

Currently, when you configure an IPv6 scope, you specify the 64-bit prefix. By default, DHCPv6 can allocate host addresses from the entire 64-bit range for that prefix. This allows for

IPv6 host addresses that are configured through adapter hardware. You can specify exclusion ranges, so if you wanted to allocate only host addresses in the range fec0::0:0:0:1 through fec0::0:0:0:fffe, you would exclude addresses fec0::0:0:1:1 through fec0::ffff:ffff:ffff:fffe.

Several DHCPv6 options exist. Arguably, the most useful option specifies the DNS server. Other options are concerned with compatibility with other systems that support IPv6, such as the UNIX Network Integration Service (NIS).

DHCPv6 is similar to DHCP in many respects. For example, scope options override server options, and DHCPv6 requests and acknowledgements can pass through BOOTP-enabled routers and Layer-3 switches (almost all modern routers and switches act as DHCP relay agents) so that a DHCPv6 server can configure clients on a remote subnet.

EXAM TIP

If you want to configure a server running Windows Server 2008 or Windows Server 2008 R2 as a DHCP relay agent, you need to install the Routing and Remote Access Services (RRAS) role service.

As with DHCP, you can implement the 80:20 rule so that a DHCPv6 server is configured with a scope for its own subnet that contains 80 percent of the available addresses for that subnet, and a second scope for a remote subnet that contains 20 percent of the available addresses for that subnet. A similarly configured DHCPv6 server on the remote subnet provides failover. If either server fails, the hosts on both subnets still receive their configurations.

For example, the Melbourne office network of Tailspin Toys has two private virtual local area networks (VLANs) that have been allocated the following site-local networks:

- VLAN1: fec0:0:0:aaaa::1 through fec0:0:0:aaaa::fffe
- VLAN2: fec0:0:0:aaab::1 through fec0:0:0:aaab::fffe

Exceptions are defined so that IPv6 addresses on the VLANs can be statically allocated to servers. In this case, you could implement the 80:20 rule by configuring the following DHCPv6 scopes on the DHCP server on VLAN1:

- fec0:0:0:aaaa::1 through fec0:0:0:aaaa::cccb
- fec0:0:0:aaab::cccc through fec0:0:0:aaab::fffe

You would then configure the following DHCPv6 scopes in the DHCP server on VLAN2:

- fec0:0:0:aaab::1 through fec0:0:0:aaab::cccb
- fec0:0:0:aaaa::cccc through fec0:0:0:aaaa::fffe

DHCP servers (especially DHCP servers that host 20-percent scopes) are excellent candidates for virtualization because they experience only limited I/O activity. In addition, you can deploy this role on Server Core. This technique is particularly applicable to more complex networks.

NOTE   VIRTUAL DNS SERVERS

Like DHCP servers, DNS servers—particularly secondary DNS servers—are good candidates for virtualization.

For example, Trey Research is a single-site organization, but it has five buildings within its site, connected by fiber-optic links to a Layer-3 switch configured to allocate a VLAN to each building. VLAN1, allocated to the main office, supports the majority of the company's computers. VLAN3 supports most of the remainder. VLAN2, VLAN4, and VLAN5 each support only a few computers.

In this case, you can configure the DHCP server on VLAN1 to host 80 percent of the VLAN1 address range. You can configure a virtual DHCP server on the same VLAN to host 20 percent of the VLAN2 through VLAN5 address ranges. On VLAN3, you can configure a DHCP server to host the 80-percent ranges for VLAN2 through VLAN5 and a virtual server to host the 20-percent range for VLAN1. If either server fails, hosts on all the VLANs can continue to receive their configurations through DHCP.

> *NOTE* **THE 80:20 RULE**
>
> The 80:20 rule is typically implemented within a site because a wide area network (WAN) link (with routers over which you have no control) might not pass DHCP traffic. In general, if you implement DHCP failover by using the 80:20 rule, you need at least two DHCP servers per site.

Planning an IPv6 Network

Configuring IPv6 and implementing IPv6 are relatively straightforward. Planning an IPv6 network, however, is rather more complex. Every scenario has unique features, but in general, you might want to deploy IPv6 in conjunction with an existing IPv4 network. You might have applications that require IPv6, although your network is principally IPv4. You might want to design a new network or restructure a current one so that it is primarily IPv6. You could be designing a network for a large multinational company with multiple sites and thousands of users, or for a small organization with a head office and a single branch office.

Whatever the scenario, you will need to maintain interoperability with older functions and with IPv4. Even in a new IPv6 network, it is unlikely that you can ignore IPv4 completely—at least for now.

Analyzing Hardware Requirements

An early step in the design process will be to identify and analyze the required network infrastructure components. Hardware components could include the following:

- Routers
- Layer-3 switches
- Printers
- Faxes
- Firewalls
- Intrusion-detection equipment

- Hardware load balancers
- Load-balancing server clusters
- Virtual private network (VPN) entry and exit points
- Servers and services
- Network interconnect hardware
- Intelligent NICs

This list is not exclusive, and you might need to consider other hardware devices depending upon the scenario. Which of these hardware devices store, display, or allow the input of IP addresses? Can all the necessary hardware be upgraded to work with IPv6? If not, what are the workarounds? If you need to replace hardware, is there a budget and a time frame for hardware refresh?

Analyzing Software and Application Requirements

From the software and applications viewpoint, network management is the area most likely to be affected by the version of IP used, although some line-of-business (LOB) applications could also be affected. You might need to consider the IPv6 operation and compatibility of the following components:

- Network infrastructure management, such as WINS
- Network management systems, such as systems based on Simple Network Management Protocol (SNMP)
- Performance management systems
- High-level network management applications (typically third-party applications)
- Configuration management, such as DHCP and DHCPv6
- Security policy management and enforcement
- LOB applications
- Transition tools

Consideration of transition tools implies the requirement—except in a new IPv6 network—of determining the transition strategy that you want to deploy. Transition strategies were discussed earlier in this lesson and depend largely on the planned scenario and whether both IPv4 and IPv6 stacks are available. If some older components of your network do not support IPv6, you need to consider how to support them while transitioning is in progress, and whether you will continue to support them in a dual stack when transitioning is complete. You need to ensure interoperability between IPv4 and IPv6 components.

Your first step in configuration management may be to decide whether to use stateful or stateless configuration. With IPv6, it is possible to have every component on your network configured with its own global unicast address. Security is implemented by firewalls, virus filters, spam filters, IP filtering, and all the standard security methods. IPSec provides end-to-end encryption. You can configure peripheral zones in IPv6 networks as you can in IPv4 networks. DHCPv6 in stateless mode can configure options—for example, DNS servers—that are not configured through router discovery. In either case, you need to ensure that your provider is IPv6-compliant and obtain a range of IPv6 addresses.

Integrating DHCP with NAP

You can further increase security on your network by integrating DHCP and DHCPv6 with Network Access Protection (NAP). NAP provides policy enforcement components that help ensure that computers connecting to or communicating on a network comply with administrator-defined requirements for system health and limiting the access of computers that do not meet these requirements to a restricted network. The restricted network contains the resources needed to update computers so that they meet the health requirements. When you integrate DHCP with NAP, a computer must be compliant to obtain an unlimited-access IP address configuration from a DHCP server. Network access for noncompliant computers is limited through an IP address configuration that allows access only to a restricted network. DHCP enforcement ensures health policy requirements every time a DHCP client attempts to lease or renew an IP address configuration. DHCP enforcement also actively monitors the health status of the NAP client and renews the IP address configuration for access only to the restricted network if the client becomes noncompliant.

When planning DHCP integration with NAP, you must decide whether DHCP NAP enforcement will be enabled on all DHCP scopes, selected DHCP scopes, or no DHCP scopes at all. In addition, you must configure which NAP profile to use for DHCP NAP enforcement. Last, you must determine how a DHCP server will behave when the Network Policy Server (NPS) is unreachable. A DHCP server can be configured to allow full access, allow restricted access, or drop client packets when the NPS server is unreachable.

> *MORE INFO*   **NAP**
>
> To learn more about NAP, see *http://technet.microsoft.com/ en-us/network/bb545879.aspx*.

You may decide that exposing the global unicast addresses of all your network components to the IPv6 Internet represents a security risk. This is a matter of debate in the networking community and outside the scope of this book. If you do make that decision, you can choose to implement site-local IPv6 addresses on your internal subnets, assuming your NAT servers support IPv6. You can choose stateful configuration by DHCPv6. Assuming that your routers or Layer-3 switches can pass DHCP traffic, you can follow the 80:20 rule across your subnets or VLANs to ensure that configuration still occurs even if a DHCP server is down.

When you have made the basic decisions about network infrastructure and transitioning strategy and have discovered whether your current network (or proposed new network) is capable of supporting IPv6, you then need to address other requirements and considerations. For example, unless you are implementing a new IPv6 network, you need to ensure that the IPv4 infrastructure is not disrupted during the transition. With this requirement in mind, it may not be feasible to deploy IPv6 on all parts of your network immediately.

On the other hand, if your only requirement is to deploy a set of specified IPv6 applications (such as peer-to-peer communication), your IPv6 deployment might be limited to the minimum required to operate this set of applications.

Documenting Requirements

Your next step is to determine and document exactly what is required. For example, you might need to address the following questions:

- Is external connectivity (to the IPv6 Internet, for example) required?
- Does the organization have one site or several sites? If the latter, what are the geographical locations of the sites, and how is information currently passed securely between them?
- What is the current IPv4 structure of the internetwork?
- What IPv6 address assignment plan is available from the provider?
- What IPv6 services does the provider offer?
- How should prefix allocation be delegated in the enterprise?
- Are site-external and site-internal IPv6 routing protocols required? If so, which ones?
- Does the enterprise currently use an external data center? (For example, are servers located at the provider?)
- Is IPv6 available using the same access links as IPv4?
- Which applications need to support IPv6, and can they be upgraded to do so? Will these applications need to support both IPv4 and IPv6?
- Do the enterprise platforms support both IPv4 and IPv6? Is IPv6 installed by default on server and client platforms?
- Is NAT v4-v6 available, and do the applications have any issues with using it?
- Do the applications need globally routable IP addresses?
- Will multicast and anycast addresses be used?

You also need to analyze and document the working patterns and support structure within the organization. You need to obtain the following information:

- Who takes ownership of the network? For example, is network support in-house or outsourced?
- Does a detailed asset management database exist?
- Does the organization support home workers? If so, how?
- Is IPv6 network mobility used or required for IPv6?
- What is the enterprise's policy for geographical numbering?
- Do separate sites in the enterprise have different providers?
- What is the current IPv4 QoS policy (assuming that you are not designing a new IPv6-only network)? Will this change when IPv6 is implemented?
- What proposals are in place for training technical staff in the use of IPv6?

Documenting and analyzing this information will take a lot of time. However, without this documentation, you will not know the precise requirements for IPv6 implementation, and the project will take much longer and result in a less satisfactory outcome. When you have gathered the information, you can plan the tasks that you and your team need to perform and the requirements for each. You will have a better idea of the time and cost of the project, and whether it should be implemented in stages.

Your next step is to draw up and implement a project plan. Project planning is beyond the scope of this book. However, you would be wise to heed a word of warning: Do not ignore what might seem to be peripheral or non-time-critical activities. Training your technical staff is a good example of such a task. Every part of the final plan is important, and unless every aspect is implemented, the result will be less than optimal. In the worst case, the project can fail completely because of an unconsidered component.

> **MORE INFO**   **IPV6 NETWORK SCENARIOS**
>
> For more information about IPv6 planning and specific scenario examples, see RFC 4057, "IPv6 Enterprise Network Scenarios," at *http://www.ietf.org/rfc/rfc4057*.

Lesson Summary

- IPv6 supports unicast, multicast, and anycast addresses. Unicast addresses can be global, site-local, link-local, or special. IPX- and NSAP-mapped addresses are also supported.
- IPv6 is fully supported in Windows Server 2008 and Windows Server 2008 R2 and addresses problems that are associated with IPv4, such as lack of address space.
- IPv6 is designed to be backward-compatible, and IPv4-compatible addresses can be specified. Transitioning strategies include dual stack, configured tunneling, automatic tunneling, 6to4, Teredo, and ISATAP.

- IPv6 addresses can be configured through stateful (DHCPv6) and stateless (autoconfiguration) methods. DHCPv6 can also be used statelessly to configure DNS servers while hosts are autoconfigured.

- Tools to configure and troubleshoot IPv6 include ping, ipconfig, tracert, pathping, and netsh. You can also configure IPv6 by using the TCP/IPv6 Properties GUI.

Lesson Review

You can use the following questions to test your knowledge of the information in Lesson 1, "Planning IPv6." The questions are also available on the Companion Media if you prefer to review them in electronic form.

NOTE ANSWERS

Answers to these questions and explanations of why each answer choice is correct or incorrect are located in the "Answers" section at the end of the book.

1. What type of IPv6 address is the equivalent of a public unicast IPv4 address?
   - **A.** Site-local
   - **B.** Global
   - **C.** Link-local
   - **D.** Special

2. A node has a link-local IPv6 address fe80::6b:28c:16a7:d43a. What is its corresponding solicited-node address?
   - **A.** ff02::1:ffa7:d43a
   - **B.** ff02::1:ff00:0:16a7:d43a
   - **C.** fec0::1:ff a7:d43a
   - **D.** fec0::1:ff00:0:16a7:d43a

3. Which protocol uses ICMPv6 messages to manage the interaction of neighboring nodes?
   - **A.** ARP
   - **B.** EUI-64
   - **C.** DHCPv6
   - **D.** ND

4. Which IPv6-to-IPv4 transition strategy uses preconfigured tunnels and encapsulates an IPv6 packet within an IPv4 packet?
   - **A.** Configured tunneling
   - **B.** Dual stack

C. ISATAP

D. Teredo

5. What command lets you configure an IPv6 address manually on a specified interface?

    A. `netsh interface ipv6 show address`

    B. `netsh interface ipv6 add address`

    C. `netsh interface ipv6 set interface`

    D. `netsh interface ipv6 set address`

6. Trey Research is an innovative research organization that prides itself on being at the forefront of technology. The company currently has 82 client PCs, all running Windows 7 Enterprise edition. All its servers—including its domain controllers—have recently been upgraded to Windows Server 2008 R2 Enterprise edition. Trey's site consists of two buildings linked by a fiber-optic cable. Each building has its own VLAN, and Trey's peripheral zone is on a separate VLAN. All Trey's clients receive their IPv4 configurations through DHCP, and the 80:20 rule is used to implement failover if a DHCP server goes down. All servers and router interfaces are configured manually, as are the company's network printers and network projectors. Trey has a Class C public IPv4 allocation and sees no need to implement NAT. It uses a network management system based on SNMP. It uses a number of high-level graphics applications in addition to business software and the Microsoft Office 2010 suite. The company wants to introduce IPv6 configuration and access the IPv6 Internet. It has verified that its provider and all of its network hardware fully support IPv6. Which of the following are likely to form part of Trey's IPv6 implementation plan? (Each answer forms part of the solution. Choose four.)

    A. Trey is likely to adopt a dual-stack transition strategy.

    B. Trey is likely to adopt a configured-tunneling transition strategy.

    C. Trey is likely to configure its internal network hosts with site-local unicast addresses.

    D. Trey is likely to configure its internal network hosts with global unicast addresses.

    E. Trey needs to ensure that its servers and clients support IPv6.

    F. Trey needs to ensure that its network projectors and network printers support IPv6.

    G. Trey needs to ensure that its network management system is compatible with IPv6.

    H. Trey needs to ensure that its graphic applications are compatible with IPv6.

Lesson 2: Planning DNS

As an experienced administrator, you will have worked with DNS and with Microsoft Dynamic DNS (DDNS). You should also be familiar with Network Basic Input/Output System (NetBIOS) names, the NetBIOS Extended User Interface (NetBEUI), and WINS. It is not, therefore, the purpose of this lesson to explain the basic operation of these features, but rather to look at Windows Server 2008 and Windows Server 2008 R2 enhancements to them (particularly to DNS) and to discuss the planning of a name resolution infrastructure across an enterprise network.

One of the first planning decisions you may need to make is whether to use WINS to resolve NetBIOS names. When Microsoft introduced DDNS, it was seen as a replacement to WINS, but WINS is still in use in many networks and is supported in Windows Server 2008 and Windows Server 2008 R2. However, IPv6 does not support WINS. Microsoft describes WINS as approaching obsolescence and introduces the GlobalNames DNS zone to provide single-label name resolution for large enterprise networks that do not deploy WINS. If you do not use WINS, you can consider disabling NetBIOS over TCP/IP (NetBT) on your network.

When planning a DNS infrastructure, you need to decide when to use Active Directory Domain Services (AD DS)–integrated, standard primary, secondary, stub, reverse lookup, and GlobalNames DNS zones. You need to plan DNS forwarding and decide when to use conditional forwarding, which is especially relevant to the enterprise environment where you can have multiple AD DS forests in the same intranetwork. Enterprise networks are also likely to include, or need to integrate with, non-Microsoft DNS servers, and you need to know how Microsoft DNS interoperates with, for example, Berkeley Internet Daemon (BIND) servers. Windows Server 2008 and Windows Server 2008 R2 (as well as Windows Vista and Windows 7) support IPv6 by default, and you need to understand and use the IPv6 records in DNS. Setting up a reverse lookup IPv6 DNS zone can best be described as a "tricky" procedure and is one of the exercises in the practice later in this chapter.

> **After this lesson, you will be able to:**
> - Consider Windows Server 2008 and Windows Server 2008 R2 DNS features when planning your name resolution infrastructure.
> - Identify Windows Server 2008 and Windows Server 2008 R2 enhancements to DNS and use these in your planning process.
> - Configure static IPv6 DNS records.
> - Configure an IPv6 reverse lookup zone.
> - Administer DNS using the MMC snap-in and command-line tools.
>
> **Estimated lesson time: 45 minutes**

Planning Windows Server 2008 and Windows Server 2008 R2 DNS

DNS resolves IP host names to IP addresses and can also resolve IP addresses to host names in reverse lookup DNS zones. Name resolution is important for IPv4 because IPv4 addresses are difficult to remember and we mostly use host names or fully qualified domain names (FQDNs)—for example, in Internet addresses such as *www.litware.com*. Remembering IPv6 addresses is almost impossible and name resolution is even more important on the IPv6 section of the World Wide Web (the IPv6 Internet). This section covers the enhancements to DNS introduced in Windows Server 2008 and Windows Server 2008 R2 and how DNS deals with IPv6 addresses.

The Windows Server 2008 and Windows Server 2008 R2 DNS Server roles retain the features introduced by Windows Server 2003 DNS, including dynamic configuration and incremental zone transfer, and introduce several new features and significant enhancements.

Windows Server 2008 and Windows Server 2008 R2 DNS in a Windows-based network support AD DS. If you install the AD DS role on a server or run the dcpromo command, and a DNS server that meets AD DS requirements cannot be located, you can install and configure a DNS server and, by default, create an AD DS–integrated DNS zone automatically. Typically, this happens when you are installing the first domain controller in a forest.

A partition is a data container in AD DS that holds data for replication. You can store DNS zone data in either the domain or the application directory partition of AD DS, and you can specify which partition should store the zone. This choice defines the set of domain controllers to which that zone's data is replicated. DNS replication takes place between all domain controllers specified in the replication scope of a DNS application directory partition.

Microsoft recommends that you use the Windows Server 2008 DNS Server service, although other types of DNS server can support AD DS deployment. Partitions help to ensure that only updates to DNS zones are replicated to other DNS servers. Incremental zone transfer is discussed later in this lesson.

EXAM TIP

As an experienced network professional, you should be familiar with master and subordinate name servers, primary and secondary name servers, and when a name server is authoritative. In the 70-646 exam, you are likely to be tested on infrastructure planning considerations rather than on single-site setup. For example, if you are specifying the DNS servers used by clients via DHCP, would you specify that branch office computers use branch office DNS as the primary and the head office DNS as the secondary? Bear in mind that local DNS is typically primary and authoritative.

Windows Server 2008 and Windows Server 2008 R2 DNS Compliance

The DNS Server role in Windows Server 2008 and Windows Server 2008 R2 complies with all RFCs that define and standardize the DNS protocol. It uses standard DNS data file and resource record formats and can work successfully with most other DNS server implementations, such as DNS implementations that use the BIND software. Windows Server 2008 DNS and Windows Server 2008 R2 DNS are fully compliant with the dynamic update protocol defined in RFC 2136.

Configuring Windows Server 2008 and Windows Server 2008 R2 DNS

Close integration with other Windows services, including AD DS, WINS (if enabled), and DHCP and DHCPv6, ensures that Windows Server 2008 DDNS requires little or no manual configuration. Computers that run the DNS Client service register their host names and IPv4 and IPv6 addresses (although not link-local IPv6 addresses) dynamically. You can configure the DNS Server and DNS Client services to perform secure dynamic updates. This ensures that only authenticated users with the appropriate rights can update resource records on the DNS server. Figure 2-11 shows a zone being configured to allow only secure dynamic updates.

FIGURE 2-11 Allowing only secure dynamic updates

> **MORE INFO** **DEPLOYING SECURE DNS**
>
> For more information about deploying secure DNS, see *http://technet.microsoft.com/ en-us/library/cc772661(WS.10).aspx.*

> **NOTE** **SECURE DYNAMIC UPDATES**
>
> Secure dynamic updates are available only for zones that are integrated with AD DS.

Using Stub Zones

A stub zone is a zone copy that contains only the resource records necessary to identify the authoritative DNS servers for that zone. Stub zones ensure that DNS servers hosting parent zones can determine authoritative DNS servers for child zones, thus helping to maintain efficient DNS name resolution. Figure 2-12 shows a stub zone specified in the New Zone Wizard.

You can use stub zones when name servers in the target zone are in transition—for example, if part of or all the company network is undergoing IP address transition and resolution of names is problematic. For example Contoso, Ltd. recently acquired the sales organization Litware, Inc. Contoso has a Windows Server 2008 R2 domain. Litware has a Windows 2000 Server mixed-mode domain and, for historical reasons, uses stand-alone Microsoft Windows NT 4.0 DNS servers and BIND servers for name resolution. Contoso has decided that the Litware name will no longer be used and the Litware organization will instead be the Contoso sales division, with a subdomain sales.contoso.com. You are currently planning to configure the new sales.contoso.com subdomain with a new name resolution and an IP addressing structure that complies with Contoso's policy.

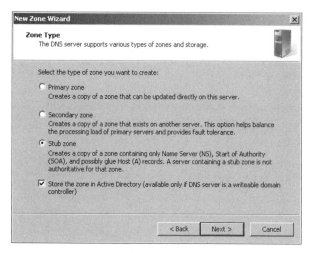

FIGURE 2-12 Creating a stub zone

In this case, your plan would include a stub zone in the Contoso AD DS domain contoso.com that contains resource records that identify the authoritative DNS servers for the sales.contoso.com subdomain. As the sales.contoso.com domain is implemented and the names and IP addresses of its DNS servers change, the stub zone in the contoso.com domain can be updated easily.

Stub zones are typically used to hold the records for DNS servers in delegated zones. In this case, a name server (NS) record in the parent zone lists the name server that is authoritative for the delegated zone. For example, the name server for the contoso.com zone can delegate authority for the sales.contoso.com zone to a DNS server in that delegated zone. You can use stub zones to keep delegated zone information current, improve name resolution, and simplify DNS administration.

> **NOTE   DELEGATION AND GLUE RECORDS IN WINDOWS SERVER 2008 AND WINDOWS SERVER 2008 R2**
>
> The DNS Server role in Windows Server 2008 and Windows Server 2008 R2 automatically adds delegation and glue records when you delegate a subdomain. Delegated name servers are listed by name rather than by IP address. Thus, a resolving name server needs to find out the IP address of the server to which it has been referred and must issue another DNS request to do so. This can introduce a circular dependency, in which a name server accesses an NS record that refers to itself. To prevent this from happening, the name server providing the delegation can provide the IP address of the next name server. This record is called a *glue record*.

DNS Forwarding

DNS servers to which other DNS servers forward requests are known as *forwarders*. If a DNS server does not have an entry in its database for the remote host specified in a client request, it can return the address of a DNS server more likely to have that information to the client, or it can query the other DNS server itself. This process takes place recursively until either the client computer receives the IP address or the DNS server establishes that the queried name cannot be resolved.

The Windows 2008 DNS Server service uses *conditional forwarders* to extend the standard forwarder configuration. A conditional forwarder is a DNS server that forwards DNS queries according to the DNS domain name in the query. For example, you can configure a DNS server to forward all the queries that it receives for names ending with *adatum.com* to the IP address of one or more specified DNS servers that are authoritative for the adatum.com domain. This feature is particularly useful on enterprise extranets, where several organizations and domains access the same private internetwork.

EXAM TIP

In Windows Server 2008 and Windows Server 2008 R2, conditional forwarding entries can be stored in AD DS and configured to replicate to all DNS servers in the forest, all DNS servers in the domain, or all domain controllers in the domain.

Figure 2-13 shows the dialog box used to create a conditional forwarder. You cannot configure this on your test network unless you set up more than one DNS server.

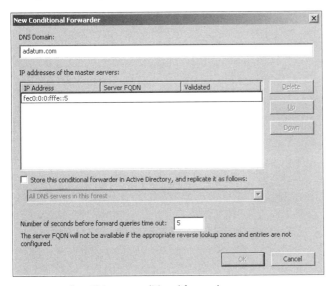

FIGURE 2-13 Specifying a conditional forwarder

Zone Replication

Windows Server 2008 and Windows Server 2008 R2 DNS zones are replicated between DNS servers for failover and to improve DNS name resolution efficiency. Zone transfers implement zone replication and synchronization. If you add a new DNS server to the network and configure it as a secondary DNS server for an existing zone, it performs a full zone transfer to obtain a read-only copy of resource records for the zone. Any further changes to the authoritative zone are replicated to the secondary zone. Windows Server 2003 introduced incremental zone replication, which replicates only changes to the authoritative zone. Windows Server 2008 and Windows Server 2008 R2 support this functionality. Prior to Windows Server 2003, a full zone transfer was required to replicate any changes in the authoritative DNS zone to the secondary DNS server. Incremental transfer enables a secondary server to pull only those zone changes that it needs to synchronize its copy of the zone with its source zone, which can be either a primary or secondary copy of the zone that is maintained by another DNS server.

You can allow zone transfers to any DNS server, to specified DNS servers only, and to DNS servers listed on the Name Servers tab (any server that has registered an NS record). Figure 2-14 shows a DNS zone configured to allow zone transfers to DNS servers listed on the Name Servers tab.

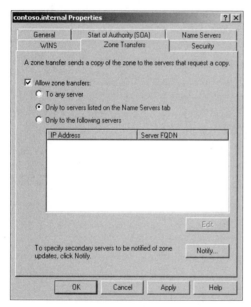

FIGURE 2-14 Configuring zone transfer

DNS Records

As an experienced network professional, you should be familiar with standard DNS record types, such as IPv4 host (A), SOA, PTR, CNAME, NS, MX, SRV, and so on. You might use other DNS record types, such as Andrew File System Database (AFSDB) and Asynchronous Transfer Mode (ATM) address, if you are configuring compatibility with non-Windows DNS systems. Figure 2-15 shows some of the record types available in Windows Server 2008 and Windows Server 2008 R2 DNS. If you need to create an IPv6 record for a client that cannot register itself with AD DS, you need to create an AAAA (quad-A) record manually.

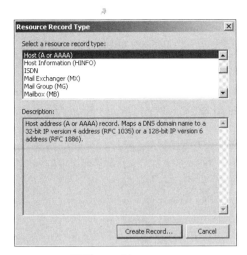

FIGURE 2-15 DNS record types

Administering DNS

You can use the DNS Manager MMC snap-in GUI to manage and configure the DNS Server service. Windows Server 2008 and Windows Server 2008 R2 also provide configuration wizards for performing common server administration tasks. Figure 2-16 shows the DNS Manager tool and also displays IPv4 and IPv6 host records dynamically registered in DNS.

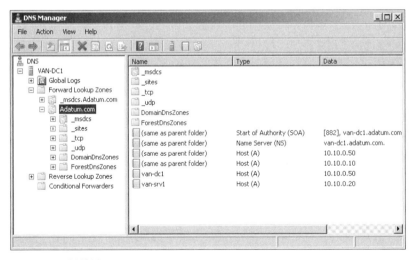

FIGURE 2-16 DNS Manager

Windows Server 2008 and Windows Server 2008 R2 provide command-line tools that help you better manage and support DNS servers and clients on your network. You can use the dnscmd tool to configure and administer both IPv4 and IPv6 records and to create reverse lookup zones. Figure 2-17 lists the command-line switches that you can use with this tool. Typically, you need to run the Command Prompt as an administrator to use the dnscmd tool.

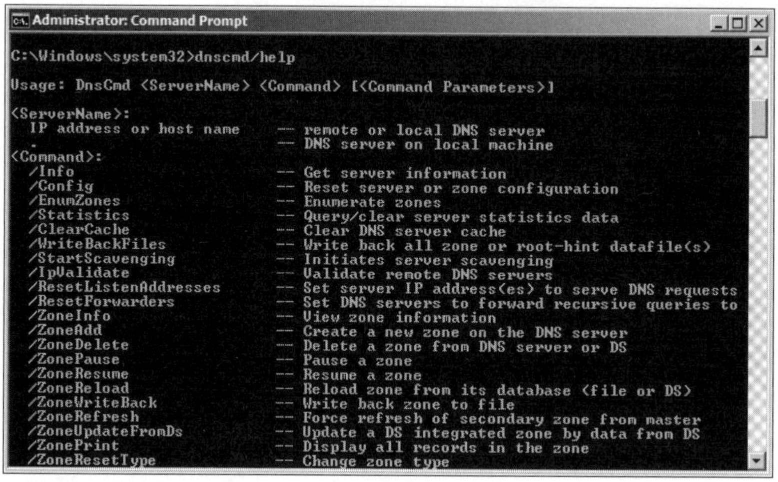

FIGURE 2-17 The dnscmd tool

You can use the `ipconfig` command to view interface adapter configurations. You can also release IPv4 and IPv6 configurations by using `ipconfig /release` and `ipconfig /release6`, respectively. Similarly, you can renew configurations with `ipconfig /renew` and `ipconfig /renew6`. Although an ordinary user can use `ipconfig` and `ipconfig /all` to view IP configuration, you typically need to run the Command Prompt as an administrator to use the other switches provided with the ipconfig tool.

If a client sends a request to a DNS server and the remote host name cannot be resolved, the DNS cache on the client stores the information that the resolution failed. This is known as *negative caching,* and it is designed to prevent clients from continually accessing DNS servers and attempting to resolve unresolvable host names. However, the disadvantage of using negative caching is that if the remote host name cannot be resolved because of a server problem and that problem is subsequently repaired, the client cannot obtain resolution for that host name until the information that it is not resolvable is cleared from the cache. In this situation, you can use `ipconfig /flushdns` on the client to clear the cache immediately. Typically, the cache is refreshed every 15 minutes, so this problem will fix itself even if you are not around to issue the command.

A new client on a network takes some time to register with dynamic DNS. You can speed up this process by using the `ipconfig /registerdns` command. You can display DNS information by using the `ipconfig /displaydns` command. The `ipconfig` commands that display information can be run without elevated privileges, but the commands that configure interfaces, release configuration, flush the cache, or register the client require you to run the Command Prompt as an administrator. Figure 2-18 shows the command-line switches available with the `ipconfig` command.

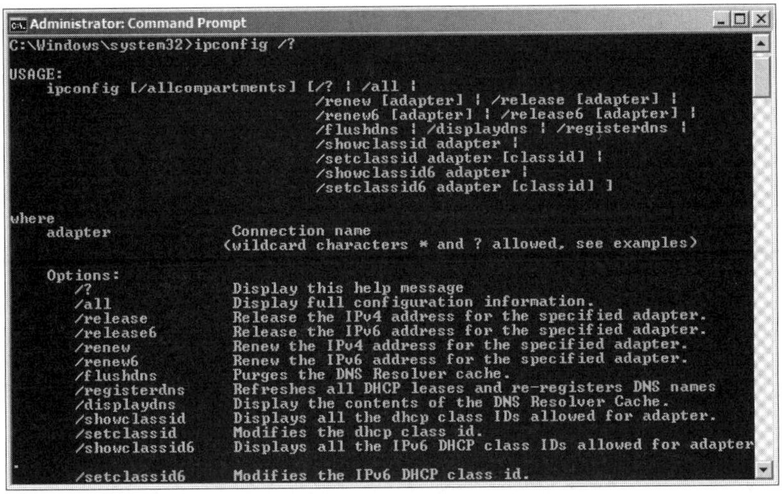

FIGURE 2-18 The ipconfig tool

✔ **Quick Check**

1. What CLI tool can you use to create reverse lookup zones?

2. What CLI commands release and renew nonstatic IPv6 configurations?

Quick Check Answers

1. dnscmd

2. ipconfig /release6 and ipconfig /renew6

If a client cannot obtain remote host name resolution from a DNS server and you have used the ping command to ensure that you have network connectivity between the server and the host, you can use nslookup to check whether the server is providing a DNS service. If, for example, you enter the nslookup VAN-DC1 command from the VAN-SRV1 client on your test network, this tests connectivity to the VAN-DC1.adatum.com server. You can issue the command nslookup adatum.com from the same client, and it will return the IPv4 addresses of DNS servers on the adatum.com domain.

If you enter nslookup on VAN-SRV1 and then enter ls –d adatum.com at the nslookup> prompt, this lists all the DNS records in the adatum.com domain, as shown in Figure 2-19.

NOTE *NSLOOKUP LS ID <DOMAIN>*

The nslookup ls –d <domain> command does not work unless you have enabled zone transfer (see Figure 2-14, earlier in this lesson), even if you run it on a DNS server that hosts the domain. If you cannot get this to work, try selecting To Any Server on the Zone Transfers tab, but be aware that doing so compromises your security.

```
Command Prompt - nslookup
> ls -d adatum.com
[UnKnown]
 adatum.com.                    SOA    van-dc1.adatum.com hostmaster.adatum.com.
 (882 900 600 86400 3600)
 adatum.com.                    A      10.10.0.50
 adatum.com.                    A      10.10.0.10
 adatum.com.                    NS     van-dc1.adatum.com
 _msdcs                         NS     van-dc1.adatum.com
 _gc._tcp.Default-First-Site-Name._sites SRV     priority=0, weight=100, port=326
8, van-dc1.adatum.com
 _kerberos._tcp.Default-First-Site-Name._sites SRV     priority=0, weight=100, po
rt=88, van-dc1.adatum.com
 _ldap._tcp.Default-First-Site-Name._sites SRV     priority=0, weight=100, port=3
89, van-dc1.adatum.com
 _gc._tcp                       SRV    priority=0, weight=100, port=3268, van-dc
1.adatum.com
 _kerberos._tcp                 SRV    priority=0, weight=100, port=88, van-dc1.
adatum.com
 _kpasswd._tcp                  SRV    priority=0, weight=100, port=464, van-dc1
.adatum.com
 _ldap._tcp                     SRV    priority=0, weight=100, port=389, van-dc1
.adatum.com
 _kerberos._udp                 SRV    priority=0, weight=100, port=88, van-dc1.
adatum.com
 _kpasswd._udp                  SRV    priority=0, weight=100, port=464, van-dc1
.adatum.com
 DomainDnsZones                 A      10.10.0.50
 DomainDnsZones                 A      10.10.0.10
 _ldap._tcp.Default-First-Site-Name._sites.DomainDnsZones SRV     priority=0, wei
ght=100, port=389, van-dc1.adatum.com
 _ldap._tcp.DomainDnsZones      SRV    priority=0, weight=100, port=389, van-dc1
.adatum.com
 ForestDnsZones                 A      10.10.0.50
 ForestDnsZones                 A      10.10.0.10
 _ldap._tcp.Default-First-Site-Name._sites.ForestDnsZones SRV     priority=0, wei
ght=100, port=389, van-dc1.adatum.com
 _ldap._tcp.ForestDnsZones      SRV    priority=0, weight=100, port=389, van-dc1
.adatum.com
 van-dc1                        A      10.10.0.50
```

FIGURE 2-19 DNS records in the adatum.com domain

A list of `nslookup` commands is shown in Figure 2-20.

```
Command Prompt - nslookup
Commands:   (identifiers are shown in uppercase, [] means optional)
NAME            - print info about the host/domain NAME using default server
NAME1 NAME2     - as above, but use NAME2 as server
help or ?       - print info on common commands
set OPTION      - set an option
    all                 - print options, current server and host
    [no]debug           - print debugging information
    [no]d2              - print exhaustive debugging information
    [no]defname         - append domain name to each query
    [no]recurse         - ask for recursive answer to query
    [no]search          - use domain search list
    [no]vc              - always use a virtual circuit
    domain=NAME         - set default domain name to NAME
    srchlist=N1[/N2/.../N6] - set domain to N1 and search list to N1,N2, etc.
    root=NAME           - set root server to NAME
    retry=X             - set number of retries to X
    timeout=X           - set initial time-out interval to X seconds
    type=X              - set query type (ex. A,AAAA,A+AAAA,ANY,CNAME,MX,NS,PTR,
SOA,SRV)
    querytype=X         - same as type
    class=X             - set query class (ex. IN (Internet), ANY)
    [no]msxfr           - use MS fast zone transfer
    ixfrver=X           - current version to use in IXFR transfer request
server NAME     - set default server to NAME, using current default server
lserver NAME    - set default server to NAME, using initial server
root            - set current default server to the root
ls [opt] DOMAIN [> FILE] - list addresses in DOMAIN (optional: output to FILE)
    -a          -  list canonical names and aliases
    -d          -  list all records
    -t TYPE     -  list records of the given RFC record type (ex. A,CNAME,MX,NS,
PTR etc.)
view FILE           - sort an 'ls' output file and view it with pg
exit            - exit the program
```

FIGURE 2-20 `Nslookup` commands

The `netsh interface ipv6 show dnsservers` command displays IPv6 DNS configurations and also indicates which DNS server addresses are statically configured.

Using New DNS Features and Enhancements

The Windows Server 2008 DNS Server role provides the following new or enhanced features:

- **Support for read-only domain controllers (RODCs)** The Windows Server 2008 DNS Server role provides primary read-only zones on RODCs. A DNS zone on an RODC is authoritative, but it is not updated dynamically whenever a new network entity (client, server, network printer, or network projector) is added to the domain. If a network entity is added on the same site as an RODC, the RODC can pull its corresponding DNS records from a writable domain controller, provided the writable domain controller is configured to allow this. This enables name resolution to be performed locally on a site rather than over a WAN.

> **MORE INFO   RODCS**
>
> For more information about RODCs, go to *http://technet.microsoft.com/en-us/library/cc772234(WS.10).aspx*.

- **Background zone loading** Loading DNS zone data is a background operation in Windows Server 2008 and Windows Server 2008 R2. If you need to restart a DNS server that hosts one or more large DNS zones that are stored in AD DS, the server is able to respond to client queries more quickly because it does not need to wait until all zone data is loaded.
- **Global single names** The GlobalNames DNS zone provides single-label name resolution for large enterprise networks that do not deploy WINS. This zone is used when it is impractical to use DNS name suffixes to provide single-label name resolution.
- **IPv6 support** The Windows Server 2008 DNS Server role fully supports IPv6 addresses. It implements AAAA and IP6 records and supports IPv6 reverse lookup zones.

Supporting RODCs

An RODC provides a shadow copy of a domain controller and cannot be configured directly. This makes it less vulnerable to attack. Microsoft advises using RODCs in locations where you cannot guarantee the physical security of a domain controller. You can delegate RODC configuration to non-administrative accounts and do not need to have domain or enterprise administrators working at branch offices.

Windows Server 2008 and Windows Server 2008 R2 support primary read-only authoritative zones (sometimes called *branch office zones*). When a Windows Server 2008 or Windows Server 2008 R2 server is configured as an RODC, it replicates a read-only copy of all AD DS partitions that DNS uses, including the domain partition, ForestDNSZones, and DomainDNSZones. A user with the appropriate permissions can view the contents of a primary read-only zone but cannot change its contents. The contents of a read-only zone in an RODC change only when the DNS zone on the master domain controller changes and the master domain controller is configured to allow the RODC to pull these changes.

Background Zone Loading

In a large organization with large Windows Server 2003 (or earlier) zones that store DNS data in AD DS, restarting a DNS server can take considerable time. The DNS server needs to retrieve zone data from AD DS and is unavailable to service client requests while this is happening.

In Windows Server 2008 and Windows Server 2008 R2, DNS addresses this situation through background zone loading. A Windows Server 2008 or Windows Server 2008 R2 DNS server loads zone data from AD DS in the background, and it can respond almost immediately to client requests when it restarts instead of waiting until its zones are fully loaded. Also, because zone data is stored in AD DS rather than in a file, that data can be accessed asynchronously and immediately when a query is received. File-based zone data can be accessed only through a sequential file read, and it takes longer to access than data in AD DS.

When the DNS server starts, it identifies all zones to be loaded, loads root hints from files or AD DS storage, loads any file-backed zones, and starts to respond to queries and remote procedure calls (RPCs) while using background processes (additional processor threads) to load zones that are stored in AD DS.

If a DNS client requests data for a host in a zone that has already been loaded, the DNS server responds as required. If the request is for information that has not yet been loaded into memory, the DNS server reads the required data from AD DS so that the request can be met.

When you are planning your name resolution infrastructure, you should have more than one DNS server servicing name resolution requests. Typically, all domain controllers (writable and RODC) in an AD DS domain host AD DS–integrated DNS zones. Both AD DS–integrated and standard primary zones can use secondary zones for load sharing and failover. Secondary DNS servers are good candidates for virtualization. If a primary server is rebooting, DNS requests are normally answered by other AD DS–integrated DNS servers or by secondary servers. The effect of background loading in this situation is that a rebooted DNS server comes online more quickly to share the load of satisfying client requests.

 Quick Check

- What DNS record enables a host name to be resolved to an IPv6 address?

Quick Check Answer

- AAAA

Using the GlobalNames DNS Zone for Single-Label Name Resolution

WINS uses NetBT, which Microsoft describes as approaching obsolescence and is not supported by IPv6. Nevertheless, NetBT provides static, global records with single-label names and is still widely used. Windows Server 2008 DNS introduced the GlobalNames zone to hold single-label names and provide support for older networks that previously used WINS for NetBIOS name resolution. Windows Server 2008 R2 uses the GlobalNames zone for the same purpose.

Typically, the replication scope of this zone is the entire forest, which ensures that the zone can provide single-label names that are unique in the forest. The GlobalNames zone also supports single-label name resolution throughout an organization that contains multiple forests—provided that you use Service Location (SRV) resource records to publish the GlobalNames zone location. This enables organizations to disable WINS and NetBT, which will probably not be supported in future Windows Server releases. You need to keep this in mind when planning changes in your name resolution structure and deciding whether to retain WINS. If you can disable NetBT, this reduces the attack surface of your servers and makes them less vulnerable to malicious users.

The GlobalNames zone provides single-label name resolution for a limited set of host names, which typically are centrally managed corporate servers and websites, and is not used for peer-to-peer name resolution. Client workstation name resolution and dynamic updates are not supported. Instead, GlobalNames zone holds CNAME resource records to map a single-label name to an FQDN. In networks that are currently using WINS, the GlobalNames zone usually contains resource records for centrally managed names that are already statically configured on the WINS server.

Microsoft recommends that you integrate the GlobalNames zone with AD DS and that you configure each authoritative DNS server with a local copy of the GlobalNames zone. This provides maximum performance and scalability. AD DS integration of the GlobalNames zone is required to support deployment of the GlobalNames zone across multiple forests.

> **NOTE   ENABLING A DNS SERVER TO SUPPORT GLOBALNAMES ZONES**
>
> The */config* switch in the dnscmd command-line tool enables a DNS server to support GlobalNames zones.

 EXAM TIP

Unlike WINS, GlobalNames zone functionality does not permit host name entries to be registered dynamically. All host name entries in the GlobalNames zone must be created manually.

Planning WINS Replication for Older Networks

You may need to support older networks, such as Windows NT 4.0 domains. Therefore, you need to know how to support WINS and include it in your planning and design process. The major planning and design decision that you need to make when planning WINS services concerns which WINS replication topology to use. You might not have looked at WINS for some time, and therefore this section includes some basic information as a review.

WINS database replication occurs whenever the WINS database changes on any WINS server, such as when a NetBIOS name is released. WINS replication enables a WINS server to resolve NetBIOS names of hosts registered with other WINS servers. To replicate database entries, each WINS server must be configured as either a pull or a push partner with at least one other WINS server.

A *push partner* sends a message to its pull partners notifying them when its WINS database has changed. When a WINS server's pull partners respond to the message with a replication request, the WINS server pushes a copy of its new database entries to its pull partners. A *pull partner* is a WINS server that requests new database entries from its push partners by requesting entries with a higher version number than the entries it received during the last replication.

Push replication occurs when a specified number of updates to the WINS database have occurred, and it works best when you have fast links between your WINS servers that can support a high bandwidth. You can configure pull replication to occur at specific intervals, and you can control the replication traffic by adjusting the bandwidth. Pull replication is used between sites connected by slow WAN links. To replicate database entries in both directions configures each server to be both a push partner and a pull partner. Every WINS server must be both a push partner and a pull partner (but not necessarily with each other) for the replication to complete.

EXAM TIP

Push replication occurs when a specified number of updated WINS database entries is reached. Pull replication can be configured to occur at specific intervals.

How you plan your WINS replication topology primarily depends on the network topology and disaster recovery requirements in your organization. The following WINS replication topologies are available:

- **Centralized WINS topology** This topology uses a single centralized high availability WINS server or WINS server cluster. Centralized WINS topology simplifies deployment and maintenance. No server-to-server replication overhead exists, and all clients are configured with the same WINS server address. Fault tolerance can be achieved by using clustering. If, however, the shared cluster database is corrupted, it needs to be restored from backup. No WINS replication occurs in this topology. Centralized WINS topology does not provide WINS database fault tolerance.

- **Full-mesh WINS topology** This topology is a distributed WINS design with multiple WINS servers or clusters deployed across the enterprise. You need to plan WINS replication to ensure synchronization of the WINS database between all WINS servers. All WINS servers replicate with all other WINS servers. You can configure replication manually or through use of the WINS autodiscovery (automatic partner configuration) feature. In a full-mesh WINS topology, some clients can be configured to use one WINS server as the primary, and the remaining clients can use another WINS server, which allows you to implement load balancing. Full-mesh WINS topology is typically used when the network topology consists of multiple data centers and remote offices. Each WINS server replicates with every other WINS server in this topology, which causes a significant amount of network traffic. This topology can introduce security risks and requires more management and support than other technologies. The full-mesh WINS topology is illustrated in Figure 2-21.

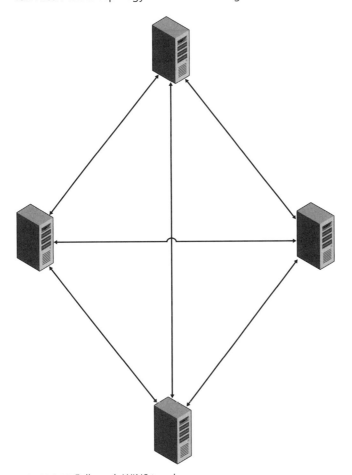

FIGURE 2-21 Full-mesh WINS topology

- **Ring WINS topology** This topology is a distributed WINS design in which each WINS server replicates with a specific neighboring partner, forming a circle. This topology needs to be created manually because relationships between each server must be determined and configured by a WINS administrator. A ring WINS topology is easier to maintain than a full-mesh WINS topology, and you can provision for load balancing by distributing your clients across WINS servers. However, troubleshooting is more difficult in a ring WINS topology, and the convergence time, which is the time it takes for a database change to replicate to all WINS servers, is longer because updates are passed sequentially from server to server. The ring WINS topology is illustrated in Figure 2-22.

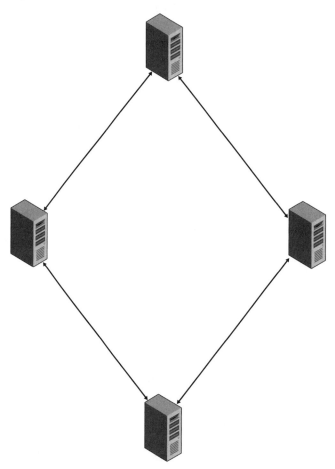

FIGURE 2-22 Ring WINS topology

- **Hub-and-spoke WINS topology** This topology is a distributed WINS design in which a central WINS server is designated as the hub and additional WINS servers replicate with the hub only in the site where they are located. A hub-and-spoke WINS topology provides for efficient convergence, simple management, and allows you to provision for load balancing. It is typically used when the network topology consists of a central data center and multiple remote offices or branch offices. The central data center typically provides name resolution for the majority of the computers on the network, and the branch offices provide name resolution for local computers. The hub-and-spoke WINS topology is illustrated in Figure 2-23.

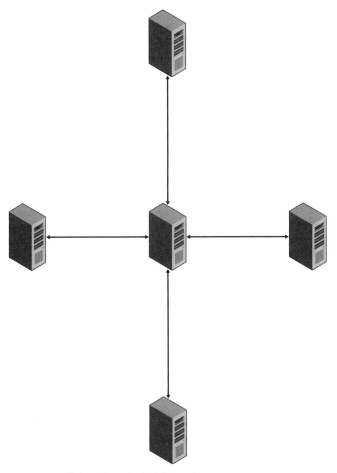

FIGURE 2-23 Hub-and-spoke WINS topology

When you have planned your WINS replication topology, you can determine the number of WINS servers required. This depends on the number of clients that need WINS name resolution services and on the available bandwidth for client name queries and registrations and server-to-server replication between sites. As a guideline, there should be one WINS server for every 10,000 clients, with a minimum of two WINS servers to provide redundancy in sites that require highly available WINS services.

Supporting IPv6 Addresses

Windows Server 2008 DNS and Windows Server 2008 R2 DNS support IPv6 addresses as fully as they support IPv4 addresses. IPv6 addresses register dynamically, and you can create an AAAA record for any computer on the network whose operating system does not support dynamic registration. You can also create IPv6 reverse lookup zones. You configure an AAAA record and create an IPv6 reverse lookup zone in the practice later in this chapter.

> **MORE INFO** **IPV6 REVERSE LOOKUP ZONES**
>
> For more information about IPv6 reverse lookup zones and additional information about a wide range of IPv6 topics, see *http://www.microsoft.com/technet/network/ipv6/ipv6faq.mspx.*

The dnscmd command-line tool accepts addresses in both IPv4 and IPv6 format. Windows Server 2008 and Windows Server 2008 R2 DNS servers can send recursive queries to IPv6-only servers, and a DNS server forwarder list can contain both IPv4 and IPv6 addresses. DHCP clients can register IPv6 addresses in addition to (or instead of) IPv4 addresses. Windows Server 2008 and Windows Server 2008 R2 DNS servers support the ip6.arpa domain namespace for reverse mapping.

> **Quick Check**
>
> - What feature in Windows Server 2008 DNS and Windows Server 2008 DNS helps organizations phase out WINS and NetBT?
>
> **Quick Check Answer**
>
> - The GlobalNames zone

Planning a DNS Infrastructure

As a network professional, you will almost certainly know that in a dynamic DNS system, most hosts and servers register their host (A) records automatically, and you can configure DHCP to create DNS records when it allocates configurations. Compared to older static DNS, where records needed to be added manually (unless DNS was integrated with WINS), DDNS requires very little manual configuration. You have probably created IPv4 reverse lookup zones. In the practice later in this chapter, you create an IPv6 reverse lookup zone.

However, you might not have experience planning a DNS infrastructure. As you advance in your chosen profession, you will discover that planning takes up much of your time. You therefore need to consider the process of planning a DNS infrastructure.

Planning a DNS Namespace

Planning and defining a DNS namespace is typically a task for a senior administrator. You need to know the options available so that you can plan and implement enterprise-level decisions more efficiently.

If you use a DNS namespace only for internal purposes, the name does not need to conform to the standard defined in RFC 1123, "Requirements for Internet Hosts—Application and Support," RFC 2181, "Clarifications to the DNS Specification," and the character set specified in RFC2044, "UTF-8, A Transformation Format of Unicode and ISO 10646." For example, a namespace such as contoso.internal could be used internally.

However, when you specify a corporate namespace to be used on the Internet, it needs to be registered with the appropriate authority and conform to the relevant RFC standards. Examples of corporate namespaces are treyresearch.com and tailspintoys.co.uk. Most organizations have both a private and a public network. You can implement the DNS infrastructure by using one of the following schemes:

- Use separate namespaces for your external and internal namespaces, such as tailspintoys.com and tailspintoys.private. This improves security by isolating the two namespaces from each other and preventing internal resources from being exposed directly to the Internet. Zone transfers do not need to be performed between the two namespaces, and the existing DNS namespace remains unchanged.

- Use a corporate namespace for both the internal and external (Internet) portions of your network. This configuration is straightforward to implement and provides access to both internal and external resources. However, you need to ensure that the appropriate records are being stored on the internal and external DNS servers and that the security of your internal network is protected.

> **NOTE   INTERNAL USERS NEEDING TO ACCESS EXTERNAL RESOURCES**
>
> Using a single corporate namespace presents a challenge when internal users require name resolution for publically accessible resources, because the external DNS zone is not configured to resolve internal resources. This challenge can be overcome by duplicating the external zone on internal DNS servers for clients to resolve resources. You can also configure split DNS, which is discussed later in this lesson.

> **EXAM TIP**
>
> Using the same namespace internally and externally requires duplicating the external zone on internal DNS servers for clients to resolve external resources.

- Use delegated namespaces to identify your organization's internal network. For example, Trey Research could have the public namespace treyresearch.com and the private namespace intranet.treyresearch.com. This fits neatly with AD DS structure and is implemented easily if you use AD DS–integrated DNS. You need to ensure that internal clients can resolve external namespace addresses, but external clients cannot resolve internal namespace addresses. All internal domain data is isolated in the domain tree and requires its own DNS server infrastructure. An internal DNS server will forward requests for an external namespace address to an external DNS server. The disadvantage of namespace delegation is that FQDNs can become quite long. The maximum length of an FQDN is 255 bytes. FQDNs for domain controllers are limited to 155 bytes.

AD DS–integrated DNS provides several advantages and should always be considered as an option when you are planning you organization's DNS structure. Not the least of these advantages is that DNS zone information is replicated automatically with other AS DS information through distributed file system replication (DFSR). You can implement RODCs that hold authoritative read-only DNS zones and provide secure local name resolution in branch offices where the physical security of servers cannot be guaranteed. You can implement secondary DNS zones on Windows DNS or BIND servers that need not be part of the AD DS structure. For example, DNS servers on peripheral zones are frequently stand-alone servers.

How you implement AD DS on your network plays a critical role in determining how domains should be created and nested within each other. Your zone structure typically mirrors your AD DS domain structure, although this is not compulsory. You can create delegated zones easily. For example, you could use engineering.tailspintoys.com rather than tailspintoys.com/engineering.

You can partition your DNS namespace by geographical location, by department, or by both. For example, if Tailspin Toys has several locations but only a single Human Resources department located at central office, you could use the namespace hr.tailspintoys.com. If Contoso, Ltd. has a main office in Denver and manufacturing facilities in Boston and Dallas, you could configure namespaces denver.contosos.com, boston.contoso.com, and dallas. contoso.com. You can combine both systems, such as maintenance.dallas.contoso.com. If you are concerned that the design implements too many hierarchical levels, you can choose instead to use AD DS organizational units (OUs), such as dallas.contoso.com/maintenance.

Using Split DNS

In a split DNS infrastructure, you create two zones on two separate name servers for the same domain. The zones have the same name, such as contoso.com. Internal network clients use one of the zones, and external network clients use the other. You require at least two name servers because a single name server cannot host two different zones with the same name.

The zone used by external clients resolves host names to public IP addresses. For example, the zone database on the external zone for contoso.com could contain the DNS records shown in Table 2-2.

TABLE 2-2 DNS Records for the External Contoso.com Zone

HOST NAME	RECORD TYPE	RESOLVES TO
www	A	207.46.232.182
ftp	A	207.46.232.184
mail	A	207.46.232.186
-	MX	mail.corp.net

The zone used by internal clients resolves host names to private IP addresses and provides aliases for the external host names. The zone database on the internal zone for contoso.com could contain the DNS records shown in Table 2-3.

TABLE 2-3 DNS Records for the Internal Contoso.com Zone

HOST NAME	RECORD TYPE	RESOLVES TO
www	CNAME	webserver.corp.net
ftp	CNAME	ftpserver.corp.net
mail	CNAME	exchange.corp.net
exchange	A	10.0.0.25
webserver	A	10.0.0.27
ftpserver	A	10.0.0.29

When external network clients resolve the name www.contoso.com, they obtain the external IP address of the web server, 207.46.232.182, which is required. External network clients should not receive the private IP address of the server on the internal network.

When internal network clients access www.contoso.com, they connect to the server webserver using the internal, private IP address 10.0.0.27. The CNAME record for www resolves to the Host (A) record of webserver.contoso.com, and requests are forwarded to 10.0.0.27. You also need to configure the Internet Security and Acceleration (ISA) server on your network to support split DNS, but ISA server configuration is beyond the scope of this book.

Planning DNS Forwarding

A DNS forwarder accepts forwarded recursive lookups from another DNS server and then resolves the request for that DNS server. For example, a local DNS server can forward DNS queries to a central DNS server that is authoritative for an internal DNS zone. If the forwarding server does not receive a valid resolution from the server to which it forwards the request, it attempts to resolve the request itself unless it is a subordinate server. Subordinate servers do not try to resolve a resolution request if they do not receive a valid response to a forwarded DNS request. Typically, subordinate servers are used in conjunction with secure Internet connections.

Windows Server 2003 introduced conditional forwarding, described earlier in this lesson, which can be used in Windows Server 2008 and Windows Server 2008 R2. You should plan to use conditional forwarders if, for example, you want requests made for internal name resolution to be forwarded to a master DNS server that stores internal DNS zones, and you want name resolution requests for Internet domains to be sent to the Internet, where they can be satisfied through recursion. You can also use conditional forwarding on an extranet where resolution requests that specify domains in the extranet can be sent to DNS servers authoritative for the DNS zone corresponding to the domain; and requests for the resolution of names external to the extranet can be sent to the Internet for recursive resolution.

EXAM TIP

Forwarding DNS requests requires that the DNS server be capable of making recursive queries. Exam answers that suggest that you should configure forwarding and disable recursion can be discarded as incorrect.

A typical DNS forwarding scenario could specify a DNS server that is permitted to forward queries to DNS servers outside the corporate firewall. This implementation allows the firewall to be configured to allow DNS traffic only from this specific DNS server, and to allow only valid replies back to the DNS server to enter the protected network. By using this approach, all other DNS traffic—both inbound and outbound—can be dropped at the firewall. This improves the overall security of the network and the DNS service.

Planning the Zone Type

AD DS networks typically use AD DS–integrated zones for internal name resolution. In this case, DNS zone information is held on writable domain controllers in the domain (usually all the writable domain controllers). This gives the advantages of DFSR, failover if one domain controller goes down, and increased availability through a multimaster arrangement. Standard primary zones installed on Windows stand-alone servers can be used where a writable DNS server is required but access to the AD DS database is seen as a security risk, such as in peripheral zones. RODCs can be used where you want the advantages of AD DS–integrated DNS but cannot guarantee the physical security of your servers, such as in branch offices.

Both AD DS–integrated and standard primary zones can provide zone information to standard secondary DNS zones. In Windows Server 2008 and Windows Server 2008 R2 networks, secondary DNS zones can be implemented on member servers, stand-alone servers, and RODCs. Locating a secondary DNS server at a remote location can improve the speed of name resolution at that location significantly. Secondary zone servers increase redundancy by providing name resolution even if the primary zone server is unresponsive, and they reduce the load on primary servers by distributing name resolution requests among more DNS servers. A secondary zone server does not need to be part of the AD DS domain (except in the case of RODCs), and you can install secondary zones on non-Windows servers. You can configure secondary zone servers on virtual machines.

As a network professional, you have probably configured the aging and scavenging settings for DNS records, configured dynamic updates, specified zone replication scopes, and configured zone transfers. However, it is one thing knowing how to configure these settings. It is quite another to plan your zones and decide what the optimum settings are for your name resolution structure. This is a job for the senior administrator.

 Quick Check

- What type of record in a stub zone can prevent circular dependency by ensuring that the name server providing the delegation can provide the IP address of the next name server?

Quick Check Answer

- A glue record

If large numbers of stale resource records remain in zones, they take up server disk space and cause unnecessarily long zone transfers. DNS servers that load zones containing stale resource records risk using outdated information to answer client queries, potentially causing name resolution problems. DNS servers and zones can be configured to scavenge stale resource records within a period of time. In environments where resource records can become stale, you need to ensure that you enable the scavenging of these records.

The design of aging and scavenging settings is dependent on your name resolution traffic and upon how often your network changes. A network that is reasonably stable with few stations being added or removed can probably be configured with long aging settings and less frequent scavenging cycles than a more dynamic environment can. Frequent scavenging and short aging periods can increase your network traffic.

DNS zones can also be configured to allow or disallow dynamic updates, although it is unusual for dynamic updates to be disallowed in modern networks. AD DS–integrated zones can also be configured to allow secure dynamic updates only. Secure dynamic updates, discussed earlier in this lesson, are strongly recommended because they ensure that only authorized changes are made to DNS data.

EXAM TIP

Only AD DS–integrated zones support secure dynamic updates.

When you plan the replication scope of AD DS–integrated zones, you need to decide whether the zone should be replicated to all DNS servers in the forest, all DNS servers in the domain (the default), or all domain controllers in the domain. If you need to broaden the replication scope, you can configure the zone to replicate to all DNS servers in the forest. Replicating to all domain controllers in the domain is recommended only if you have Windows 2000 Server domain controllers in your environment.

You can configure the primary name server, the refresh interval, and the minimum default Time-To-Live (TTL) values for zone resource records in the zone's Start of Authority (SOA) record. The TTL controls the minimum amount of time that clients, including other DNS servers, cache resource records for the zone. If your environment is dynamic with frequent IP address changes, you should plan to configure the minimum TTL to a low value, such as one day.

When planning DNS zones, you need to specify whether zone transfers are permitted, and if so, to which servers. You can configure zone transfers to any server, to the name servers listed on the Name Servers tab or the zone, or to a specific list of name servers.

Planning Root Hints

When you install a Windows Server 2008 or Windows Server 2008 R2 DNS server that has access to the Internet, the server is configured with a list of root servers automatically. If a DNS server receives a query for a DNS zone for which it is not authoritative, the server will send a query to one of the root servers that initiates a series of queries until the name is resolved. You can use root hints to prepare servers that are authoritative for non-root zones so that they can discover authoritative servers that manage domains at a higher level or in other subtrees of the DNS domain namespace.

Root hints are essential for servers that are authoritative at lower levels of the namespace when locating and finding other servers. By default, the DNS Server service implements root hints by using a file named cache.dns that normally contains the NS and A resource records for the Internet root servers. If, however, you are using the DNS Server service on a private network, you should plan to edit or replace this file with similar records that point to your own internal root DNS servers.

Planning to Integrate AD DS with an Existing DNS Infrastructure

Many large, multiple-site organizations already use one or more BIND servers. BIND provides name resolution for UNIX systems or Internet name resolution for internal users. In this case, Windows AD DS–integrated DNS needs to interoperate with the BIND DNS infrastructure.

Two options are available within the Windows Server 2008 and Windows Server 2008 R2 DNS infrastructures:

- You can use the existing DNS infrastructure to host the DNS zone for AD DS. Potentially, this reduces hardware requirements and administrative effort. However, this option can also mean that the DNS infrastructure is supported by a different team than that which supports AD DS. As an enterprise administrator, one of your tasks is to rationalize your support organization, and you or your line manager might find this option unacceptable.

- You can deploy Windows Server 2008 or Windows Server 2008 R2 DNS and use forwarders to integrate both DNS infrastructures. This can give you more flexibility for DNS infrastructure design, DNS namespace design, and DNS administration modeling. Windows-based DNS is required for AD DS–integrated zones and you can use forwarders to provide interoperability between Windows Server 2008 or Windows Server 2008 R2 DNS infrastructure and the existing DNS infrastructure. Windows Server 2008 and Windows Server 2008 R2 DNS servers can forward any DNS queries for records hosted on the existing DNS infrastructure to the existing DNS servers.

Figure 2-24 depicts the forwarding of DNS queries between a Windows Server 2008 DNS infrastructure and a BIND DNS infrastructure.

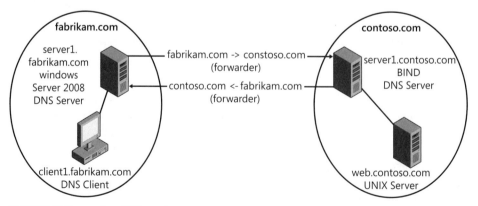

FIGURE 2-24 Forwarding DNS queries

For example, Contoso, Ltd. has an existing BIND-based DNS infrastructure with a DNS domain name of contoso.com. Contoso plans to deploy a new Windows Server 2008 R2 DNS infrastructure for AD DS with a DNS domain name of sales.contoso.com. A conditional forwarding entry for contoso.com has been created on the Windows Server 2008 R2 DNS server in the sales.contoso.com domain. A conditional forwarding entry for sales.contoso.com has been created on a BIND-based DNS server in the contoso.com domain.

When a client in the sales.contoso.com domain needs to access a UNIX web server in the contoso.com domain, it first queries its primary DNS server in the sales.contoso.com domain. This server is not authoritative for the contoso.com zone, but it does have a conditional forwarding entry for the contoso.com zone. Through the conditional forwarding entry on its DNS server in the sales.contoso.com domain, it contacts the BIND-based DNS server in the contoso.com domain to retrieve the name resolution for web.contoso.com.

Planning the GlobalNames Zone

To plan your GlobalNames zone design, you need to understand the deployment scenarios in which a GlobalNames zone can be configured. You can deploy a GlobalNames zone in a single-forest environment or a multiple-forest environment. A single-forest deployment of a GlobalNames zone allows single-label name resolution through DNS using a single AD DS–integrated GlobalNames zone. A multiple-forest deployment of a GlobalNames zone allows single-label name resolution through DNS using an AD DS–integrated GlobalNames zone for each forest within the multiple-forest environment.

You can adapt a single-forest GlobalNames zone deployment to meet an assortment of single-label name resolution requirements in the following ways:

- **All domains and clients in a forest**   Microsoft recommends this scenario for organizations that have a single forest and a small number of domains. Single-label name resolution is provided to all domain-joined clients in the forest. In this scenario, you need to ensure that all authoritative DNS servers in the forest are Windows Server 2008 or Windows Server 2008 R2 domain controllers. You then need to create an AD DS–integrated GlobalNames zone on one DNS server in the forest and replicate this to all domain controllers in the forest that are DNS servers. You then add CNAME records for single-label names pointing to the FQDN of the resource servers.

- **A multiple-forest GlobalNames zone**   This deployment scenario is recommended for companies that have multiple domains and multiple forests. You can customize a multiple-forest DNS server to meet diverse single-label name resolution requirements for all domains and clients in all forests by ensuring that all authoritative DNS servers in the forest are Windows Server 2008 or Windows Server 2008 R2 DNS servers installed on domain controllers. You also need to ensure that GlobalNames zone functionality has been enabled on each DNS server in the forest. You create an AD DS–integrated GlobalNames zone on one DNS server in a forest and replicate the GlobalNames zone to all domain controllers in the forest that are DNS servers. You then add CNAME records for single-label names pointing to the FQDN of the resource servers. In each of the other forests, you add SRV resource records pointing to each remote domain controller DNS server that hosts a local copy of the GlobalNames zone to the forest-wide __msdcs zone.

- **A selected set of DNS Servers hosts the GlobalNames zone**   Microsoft recommends this deployment scenario for companies that have multiple domains and multiple forests but want to limit the GlobalNames zone to a selected set of DNS servers. This deployment scenario provides single-label name resolution to all client computers in the forests.

- **Selected domains across a multiple forest**   Microsoft recommends this deployment when you want to deploy a GlobalNames zone in a multiple-forest environment in a set of selected domains as a pilot program.

Lesson Review

You can use the following questions to test your knowledge of the information in Lesson 2, "Planning DNS." The questions are also available on the Companion Media if you prefer to review them in electronic form.

> **NOTE   ANSWERS**
>
> Answers to these questions and explanations of why each answer choice is correct or incorrect are located in the "Answers" section at the end of the book.

1. You want to create an IPv6 reverse lookup zone that holds PTR records for hosts with IPv6 addresses in the fec0::eefd/64 subnet. Your DNS server is called DEN-DC1, and it is also a domain controller. DNS on your domain is AD DS–integrated. You use Remote Desktop to connect to DEN-DC1 and run the Command Prompt as an administrator. What command do you enter to create the reverse lookup zone?

    A. `dnscmd den-dc1 /ZoneAdd d.f.e.e.0.0.0.0.0.0.0.0.0.0.c.e.f.ip6.arpa /Primary`

    B. `dnscmd den-dc1 /ZoneAdd d.f.e.e.0.0.0.0.0.0.0.0.0.0.c.e.f.ip6.arpa /DsPrimary`

    C. `dnscmd den-dc1 /ZoneAdd d.f.e.e.0.0.0.0.0.0.0.0.0.0.c.e.f.in-addr.arpa /Primary`

    D. `dnscmd den-dc1 /ZoneAdd fec0::eefd/64.ip6.arpa /DsPrimary`

2. You want to list all the DNS records in the adatum.internal domain. You connect to the DNS server Edinburgh.adatum.internal by using Remote Desktop and open the Command Prompt. You enter **nslookup**. At the `nslookup>` prompt, you enter **ls –d adatum.internal**. An error message tells you that zone data cannot be loaded to that computer. You know that all the DNS records in the domain exist on Edinburgh. Why are they not displayed?

    A. You have not configured the adatum.internal forward lookup zone to allow zone transfers.

    B. You need to run the Command Prompt as an administrator to use nslookup.

C. You should have entered **nslookup ls –d adatum.internal** directly from the Command Prompt. You cannot use the ls function from the `nslookup>` prompt.

D. You need to log on to the DNS server interactively to use nslookup. You cannot use it over a Remote Desktop connection.

3. A user tries to access the company internal website from a client but cannot do so because of a network problem. You fix the network problem, but the user still cannot reach the website, although she can reach other websites. Users on other clients have no problem reaching the internal website. How can you quickly resolve the situation?

A. Create a static host record for your local web server in DNS.

B. Run `ipconfig /flushdns` on the primary DNS server.

C. Run `ipconfig /registerdns` on the user's computer.

D. Run `ipconfig /flushdns` on the user's computer.

4. Which WINS topology uses a distributed WINS design with multiple WINS servers or clusters deployed across the enterprise and each server or cluster replicating with every other server or cluster?

A. Centralized WINS topology

B. Full-mesh WINS topology

C. Ring WINS topology

D. Hub-and-spoke WINS topology

Lesson Summary

- The DNS Server role in Windows Server 2008 and Windows Server 2008 R2 complies with all current standards and can work successfully with most other DNS server implementations.

- Windows Server 2008 DNS and Windows Server 2008 R2 DNS are dynamic and typically require very little static configuration. You can use the DNS Manager GUI or CLI tools such as dnscmd, nslookup, ipconfig, and netsh to configure and manage DNS.

- Windows Server 2008 DNS and Windows Server 2008 R2 DNS functions include background zone loading, support for RODCs, and the GlobalNames DNS zone. Windows Server 2008 DNS and Windows Server 2008 R2 DNS fully support IPv6 forward lookup and reverse lookup zones.

- WINS resolves NetBIOS names to IP addresses. Windows Server 2008 and Windows Server 2008 R2 support WINS to provide support for older networks. The GlobalNames DNS zone provides single-label name resolution for large enterprise networks that do not deploy WINS.

PRACTICE Configuring IPv6

In this practice, you configure a static IPv6 configuration on the VAN-DC1 domain controller. You then create an ISATAP address and, if you want, enable an ISATAP router as well.

EXERCISE 1 Configure IPv6 on the VAN-DC1 Computer

In this exercise, you configure IPv6 on the VAN-DC1 domain controller. Typically, a senior administrator would not configure IPv6 on a single computer because this is not a high-level task. However, you are asked to do so in this instance because this enables you to create a reverse lookup IPv6 zone and a PTR record for the VAN-DC1 computer in subsequent exercises. The exercise asks you to log on interactively to the domain controller. If you want to make this more realistic, you can instead log on to the VAN-SRV1 client and connect to the domain controller through Remote Desktop.

1. Log on to the VAN-DC1 domain controller with the Kim Akers account.
2. Click Network And Internet on the Control Panel. Under Network And Sharing Center, click View Network Status And Tasks.
3. Click Change Adapter Settings in the resulting dialog box (on the left side near the top).
4. Right-click the network connection to your private network and click Properties.
5. Select Internet Protocol Version 6 (TCP/IPv6) and click Properties.
6. Select Use The Following IPv6Address and type the static, site-local IPv6 address **fec0:0:0:fffe::a** in the IPv6 Address box.
7. Click the Subnet Prefix Length box. The value 64 should be entered automatically.
8. Ensure that Use The Following DNS Addresses is selected, and then type the address **fec0:0:0:fffe::a** in the Preferred DNS Server box. Note that a default gateway is not specified because your isolated test network is not being configured to access other networks.
9. If your domain controller is running Windows Server 2008 R2, check the Validate Settings On Exit check box. The Properties dialog box should look similar to Figure 2-25.

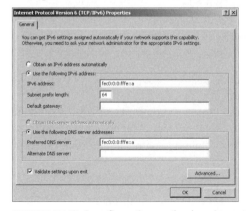

FIGURE 2-25 IPv6 configuration on the domain controller

10. Click OK. Close the Local Area Connections Properties dialog box.

11. Close the Network Connections dialog box.

12. Close Network And Sharing Center.

EXERCISE 2 Creating an ISATAP Address

IPv6 uses an ISATAP address to communicate between two nodes over an IPv4 intranet. In this exercise, you create an ISATAP address that starts with the 64-bit unicast site-local prefix *fec0:0:0:fffe*. The next 32 bits are the ISATAP identifier *0:5efe*. The final 32 bits hold the IPv4 address 10.10.0.50 in dotted decimal notation. You should complete Exercise 1 before doing this exercise.

1. If necessary, log on to the VAN-DC1 domain controller with the Kim Akers account.

2. Click Start. Right-click Command Prompt. Click Run As Administrator.

3. Click Yes to clear the User Account Control (UAC) dialog box.

4. Enter the following command:

   `netsh`

5. At the Netsh> prompt, enter the following command:

   `interface`

6. At the Netsh interface> prompt, enter the following command:

   `ipv6`

7. At the Netsh interface ipv6> prompt, enter the following command:

   `add address "isatap" fec0:0:0:fffe:0:5efe:10.10.0.50`

8. At the Netsh interface ipv6> prompt, enter the following command:

   `exit`

9. Enter the following command:

   `ipconfig /all`

Your screen should show a configuration similar to that in Figure 2-26. Note that the address of the ISATAP adapter is not displayed because no ISATAP connection currently exists.

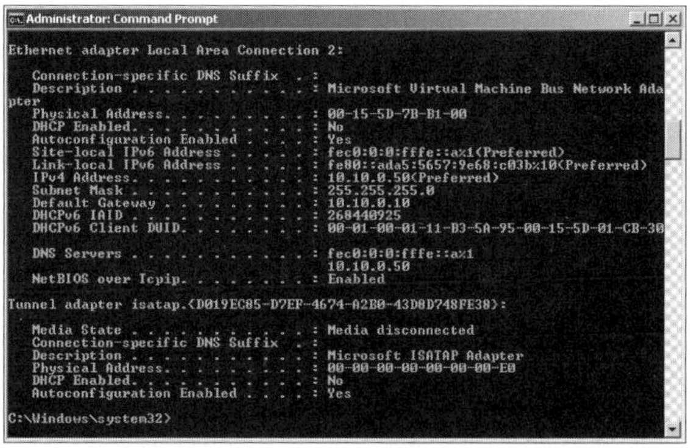

FIGURE 2-26 Displaying the IPv4 and IPv6 configuration on a network connection

EXERCISE 3   Enabling an ISATAP Router (optional)

If you are configuring ISATAP connections on a production network, you need to enable ISATAP routing. This optional exercise has no effect on your current small test setup, but it is included to demonstrate how you would enable ISATAP routing on a larger network.

1. If necessary, log on to the VAN-DC1 domain controller with the Kim Akers account.
2. If the Command Prompt console is not already running in Administrator mode, click Start. Right-click Command Prompt. Click Run As Administrator, and click Yes to clear the User Account Control (UAC) dialog box.
3. Enter the following command:

   ```
   netsh interface ipv6 isatap set router isatap enabled
   ```

   This command returns the message "Ok" when it completes satisfactorily. You can specify the name of a router in the command and specify the resolution interval in minutes.

PRACTICE   Configuring DNS

In this practice, you configure a static AAAA record and an IPv6 reverse lookup zone. You create a PTR record in the reverse lookup zone for the VAN-DC1 computer.

EXERCISE 1   Configuring an AAAA Record

The stand-alone server DEN-SRV1 has an operating system that cannot register in Windows Server 2008 R2 DNS. You therefore need to create a manual AAAA record for this server. Its IPv6 address is fec0:0:0:fffe::aa. Note that you can create an AAAA record for this server even though it does not currently exist on your network.

1. If necessary, log on to the VAN-DC1 domain controller with the Kim Akers account.
2. In Administrative Tools, click DNS to open DNS Manager.
3. If a User Access Control (UAC) dialog box appears, click Yes.
4. In DNS Manager, expand Forward Lookup Zones. Right-click Adatum.com and select New Host (A or AAAA).
5. Enter the server name and IPv6 address as shown in Figure 2-27. Ensure that the Create Associated Pointer (PTR) Record check box is not selected.
6. Click Add Host. Click OK to clear the DNS message box.
7. Click Done. Ensure that the new record exists in DNS Manager.
8. Close DNS Manager.

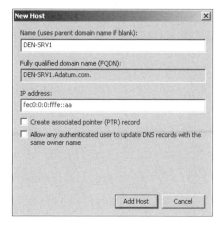

FIGURE 2-27 Specifying a DNS host record

EXERCISE 2   Configuring a Reverse Lookup IPv6 Zone

In this exercise, you create an IPv6 reverse lookup zone for all site-local IPv6 addresses—that is, addresses starting with *fec0*. You then create a PTR record in the zone. Note that in IPv6, reverse lookup zone addresses are entered as reverse-order 4-bit nibbles, so *fec0* becomes *0.c.e.f*. You need to complete Exercise 1 before you carry out this exercise.

1. If necessary, log on to the domain controller with the Kim Akers account.

2. Click Start. Right-click Command Prompt and select Run As Administrator.

3. If a UAC dialog box appears, click Yes.

4. Enter the following command:

   ```
   dnscmd VAN-DC1 /ZoneAdd 0.c.e.f.ip6.arpa /DsPrimary
   ```

   Figure 2-28 shows that the zone was created successfully. Close the Command Prompt.

FIGURE 2-28 Creating an IPv6 reverse lookup zone

5. Open DNS Manager by clicking DNS in Administrative Tools. If a UAC dialog box appears, click Yes.

6. Expand Forward Lookup Zones. Click adatum.com.

7. Right-click the AAAA record for VAN-DC1 and then click Properties.

8. Select the Update Associated Pointer (PTR) Record check box as shown in Figure 2-29. Click OK.

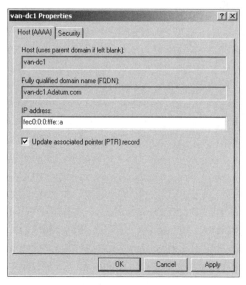

FIGURE 2-29 Creating a PTR record

9. Expand Reverse Lookup Zones and select 0.c.e.f.ip6.arpa. Ensure that the PTR record for VAN-DC1 exists, as shown in Figure 2-30. If you don't see it, try selecting Refresh from the Action menu of DNS Manager.

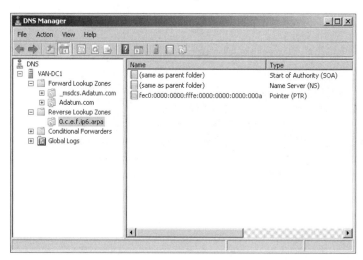

FIGURE 2-30 The PTR record for VAN-DC1.

10. Log off from the domain controller.

Chapter Review

To further practice and reinforce the skills you learned in this chapter, you can perform the following tasks:

- Review the chapter summary.
- Review the list of key terms introduced in this chapter.
- Complete the case scenarios. These scenarios set up real-world situations involving the topics in this chapter and ask you to create a solution.
- Complete the suggested practices.
- Take a practice test.

Chapter Summary

- IPv6 is fully supported in Windows Server 2008 and Windows Server 2008 R2, and is installed by default. It supports unicast, multicast, and anycast addresses. It is backward-compatible with IPv4 and offers a selection of transitioning strategies.
- IPv6 addresses can be configured through stateful and stateless configuration. Both GUI and CLI tools are available to configure IPv6 and check network connectivity.
- Windows Server 2008 DNS and Windows Server 2008 R2 DNS fully support IPv6, in addition to offering several new and enhanced features. It conforms to all current standards. GUI and CLI tools are available to configure DNS and check DNS functionality.

Key Terms

The following terms were introduced in this chapter. Do you know what they mean?

- Address space
- Anycast address
- BootP-enabled
- Forward lookup zone
- Multicast address
- Reverse lookup zone
- Route aggregation
- Scope
- Unicast address

Case Scenarios

In the following case scenarios, you will apply what you have learned in this chapter. You can find answers to these questions in the "Answers" section at the end of this book.

Case Scenario 1: Implementing IPv6 Connectivity

You are a senior network administrator at Wingtip Toys. Your company intranetwork consists of two subnets with contiguous private IPv4 networks configured as VLANs connected to a Level-3 switch. Wingtip Toys accesses its ISP and the Internet through a dual-homed ISA server that provides NAT and firewall services and connects through a peripheral zone to a hardware firewall, and hence to its ISP. The company wants to implement IPv6 connectivity. All of the network hardware supports IPv6, as does the ISP. Answer the following questions:

1. What options are available for the type of unicast address used on the subnets?
2. Given that the Wingtip Toys network can support both IPv4 and IPv6, what is the most straightforward transition strategy?
3. You decide to use stateful configuration to allocate IPv6 configuration on the two subnets. How should you configure your DHCPv6 servers to provide failover protection?

Case Scenario 2: Configuring DNS

You administer the Windows Server 2008 R2 AD DS network at Blue Yonder Airlines. When the company upgraded to Windows Server 2008 R2, it also introduced AD DS–integrated DNS, although two BIND servers are still used as secondary DNS servers. Answer the following questions:

1. Blue Yonder has set up wireless hotspots for the convenience of its customers. However, management is concerned that attackers might attempt to register their computers in the company's DNS. How can you protect against this?
2. Your boss is aware of the need to replicate DNS zones to the two stand-alone BIND servers. She is concerned that an attacker might attempt to replicate DNS zone information to an unauthorized server, thus exposing the names and IP addresses of company computers. What precautions can you take to help counter such an attack?
3. For additional security, Blue Yonder uses RODCs at its branch locations. Management is concerned that DNS zone information on these computers is kept up to date. What information can you provide?
4. Blue Yonder wants to use an application that needs to resolve IPv6 addresses to host names. How do you implement this functionality?

Suggested Practices

To help you successfully master the exam objectives presented in this chapter, complete the following tasks.

Configure IPv6 Connectivity

Carry out all the practices in this section.

Investigate Netsh Commands

- The `netsh` command structure provides you with many powerful commands. In particular, use the help function in the Command Prompt to investigate the `netsh interface ipv6 set`, `netsh interface ipv6 add`, and `netsh interface ipv6 show` commands. Also, investigate the `netsh dhcp` commands.

Find Out More About DHCPv6 Scope and Server Options

- You should have installed the DHCP Server role in Chapter 1—if not, install it. Use the DHCP administrative tool to list the DHCP scope and server options. Access Windows Server 2008 or Windows Server 2008 R2 Help and the Internet to find out more about these options. In the process, you should learn something about NIS networks. Although the 70-646 exam objectives do not cover NIS, you should know what it is as a network professional.

Test DHCPv6 Address Allocation

- Configure the client VAN-SRV1 to obtain its IPv6 configuration automatically. Ensure that the DHCPv6 scope you have configured provides configuration for this computer, and that the host IPv6 address configured falls outside the range fec0:0:0:fffe::1 through fec0:0:0:fffe::ff.

Configure DNS

Do both practices in this section.

Use the Command Prompt Tools

- It would take an entire book to do justice to the nslookup, dnscmd, ipconfig, and netsh tools. The only way to become familiar with these tools is to use them.

Configure IPv6 Reverse Lookup Zones

- This procedure was described in Lesson 2. Specifying IPv6 reverse lookup zones in DNS can be an error-prone procedure because of the way the prefixes are specified. You will become comfortable with this notation only through practice.

Take a Practice Test

The practice tests on this book's Companion Media offer many options. For example, you can test yourself on just one exam objective, or you can test yourself on all the 70-646 certification exam content. You can set up the test so that it closely simulates the experience of taking a certification exam, or you can set it up in study mode so that you can look at the correct answers and explanations after you answer each question.

> **MORE INFO** **PRACTICE TESTS**
>
> For details about all the practice test options available, see the "How to Use the Practice Tests" section in this book's Introduction.

CHAPTER 3

Planning Core Active Directory Infrastructure

This chapter looks at Active Directory, specifically Active Directory Domain Services (AD DS) and Active Directory Certificate Services (AD CS). It discusses the new features and enhancements introduced by Windows Server 2008 and Windows Server 2008 R2, and how Certificate Services are implemented in Active Directory. The focus of the chapter is planning rather than implementation. You will learn how to use graphical user interface (GUI) and command-line tools, but the most important consideration is not how you make configuration changes, but why and when. As you progress in your chosen career, you will spend more and more time planning rather than configuring.

Exam objectives in this chapter:
- Plan infrastructure services and server roles.

Lessons in this chapter:

Before You Begin

To complete the exercises in the practice in this chapter, you need to have done the following:

- Installed a Windows Server 2008 R2 Enterprise server called VAN-DC1 and configured as a domain controller in the adatum.com domain, as described in Exercise 1 of Appendix A, "Setup Instructions for Windows Server 2008 R2."
- Installed the Group Policy Management feature on VAN-DC1 if this is not already installed—note that the Group Policy Management Console (GPMC) should have been installed automatically when you promoted VAN-DC1 to a domain controller.

- Installed a Windows Server 2008 R2 Enterprise server called VAN-SRV1 and configured as a member server in the adatum.com domain, as specified in Exercise 2 of Appendix A. This server can act as a client machine of the domain controller and is referred to as "the client" in this chapter.

- Created a user account in the adatum.com domain with the user name Kim Akers and password Pa$$w0rd, and added this account to the Domain Admins, Enterprise Admins, and Schema Admins groups. This procedure is described in Exercise 1 of Appendix A.

- Created a user account in the adatum.com domain with the user name Don Hall and password Pa$$w0rd, and added this account to the Backup Operators group (to enable Don Hall to log on interactively to a domain controller).

- We recommend that you use an isolated network that is not part of your production network to do the practice exercises in this book. Internet access is not required for the exercises, and you do not need to configure a default gateway. To minimize the time and expense of configuring physical computers, we recommend that you use virtual machines. For example, you can create virtual machines using the Hyper-V server role.

 REAL WORLD

Ian McLean

Active Directory has been around for some time. As a network professional, you will be familiar with most Active Directory domain administration tasks and with tools such as Active Directory Users and Computers (ADUC) that let you carry them out. Even relatively unsophisticated corporate users might have heard of Active Directory, and they know that if they forget their passwords or need permissions to a folder, an administrator will do something magical in the directory.

However, you might sometimes be called on to explain "this Active Directory thing" to users with little knowledge of, or interest in, the technical aspects of networking. These users are typically managers who can't see why all computers in the organization can't just be linked to each other (and some may even have heard of workgroups) and why you need domain controllers and other servers that, as far as they are concerned, don't actually do anything.

I find that a good way to explain a directory structure is to use the analogy of a library. A "flat" storage system, such as that implemented by the Security Accounts Management (SAM) database in Microsoft Windows NT 4, is the equivalent of storing all the books in a heap on the floor. If a reader wants to read a particular book, she needs to look at them one at a time until the book is found. A directory structure, on the other hand, is the equivalent of having the books on bookcase shelves, in alphabetical order by author name, and the bookcases themselves located in designated parts of the library.

Thus, if I wanted to find a history book, I would look in nonfiction, find the history bookcases, and easily locate the volume. In a large library, the bookcases could be further subdivided into (for example) ancient history, U.S. history, European history, and so on.

Even more efficiently, I could consult the library index and find exactly which shelf has a book I'm looking for. I could look at a map of the library layout and determine the physical location of that shelf. This is (approximately) the function of the Active Directory schema. You could extend the analogy to describe rooms in the library that hold specialist materials (organizational units, or OUs). Specialist researchers would sit in these rooms and read the books located there. You could have access policies for the specialist rooms that differ from those that apply to the main library. You could have a person that controls access to materials within a specific room but has no authority in other rooms or in the main library.

Finally, and most significantly, an ordered library, like an ordered directory structure, can have defined and centrally controlled security policies. In the free-for-all heap of books on the floor, anyone can access any book, write on the flyleaf, and even decide to throw the book away. In a centrally organized system, read, write, and modify rights can be controlled strictly.

Of course, the analogy isn't perfect, but I've used it with some success for several years.

Lesson 1: Active Directory Directory Services

This lesson does not describe the basic functions of Active Directory. As an experienced network professional, you should know how to add users and groups, assign rights and permissions, and use the AD Find function. If not, these topics are described adequately in the Help files, in white papers, and in many excellent publications. The object of this lesson is to describe the new and enhanced features of Windows Server 2008 and Windows Server 2008 R2 AD DS and to discuss the planning aspects of AD DS implementation. For example, it is easy enough to raise the domain functional level, but knowing when and whether you should do so is another matter, especially because you cannot reverse the process except by restoring from backup or reinstalling the operating system.

The lesson does not ask you to implement multiple domains or create multiple forests on your test network. Nevertheless, planning forest functional levels and forest trusts are tasks that you might be asked to perform when administering a large corporate network. You therefore need to consider the planning processes involved in interforest operations.

After this lesson, you will be able to:

- List and describe the new features and functions in Windows Server 2008 and Windows Server 2008 R2 AD DS.
- Plan and configure domain functional levels.
- Plan forest functional levels.
- Plan forest trusts.
- Use the Directory Server.

Estimated lesson time: 55 minutes

Planning the AD DS Server Role

You use a domain controller with the Windows Server 2008 or Windows Server 2008 R2 AD DS Server role (sometimes known as the Directory Server role) installed to manage users, computers, printers, or applications on a network. Windows Server 2008 AD DS introduced features that enable you to deploy AD DS more simply and securely and to administer it more efficiently. These features are retained in Windows Server 2008 R2, which also introduces further enhancements. The following features are common to both Windows Server 2008 and Windows Server 2008 R2:

- **Read-only domain controllers** Windows Server 2008 introduced read-only domain controllers (RODCs) that host read-only partitions of the Active Directory database. You can use RODCs where physical security cannot be guaranteed, such as at branch office locations, or where local storage of domain passwords is considered a primary threat (for example, in extranets or in an application-facing role). You can delegate RODC administration to a domain user or security group and can therefore use RODCs in locations where a local administrator is not a member of the Domain Admins group.

- **New and enhanced tools and wizards** Windows Server 2008 AD DS also introduced the AD DS Installation Wizard and enhances the Microsoft Management Console (MMC) snap-in GUI tools that manage users and resources. For example, the AD DS Installation Wizard lets you specify whether you are installing a writable domain controller or an RODC. If you are installing the former, you can specify the Password Replication Policy for that domain controller to determine whether it allows an RODC to pull user credential information.

- **Fine-grained security policies** Windows Server 2008 and Windows Server 2008 R2 AD DS let you apply different password and account lockout policies to users and global security groups in the same domain, thereby reducing the number of domains that you need to manage.

- **Restartable AD DS** You can stop and restart AD DS. This lets you perform offline operations such as the defragmentation of Active Directory objects without needing to restart a domain controller in Directory Services Restore Mode (DSRM).

- **AD DS data mining tool** You can use the AD DS data mining tool to view Active Directory data stored in snapshots online, compare data in snapshots that are taken at different times, and decide which data to restore without having to restart the domain controller.

NOTE **RESTORING DELETED OBJECTS AND CONTAINERS**

You cannot use the AD DS data mining tool to restore deleted objects and containers directly. You use it when you want to view snapshot data and need to perform data recovery as a subsequent step. However, you no longer need to restore from several backups to find the data you want.

- **Auditing enhancements** You can use the Directory Service Changes audit policy subcategory when auditing Windows Server 2008 and Windows Server 2008 R2 AD DS. This lets you log old and new values when changes are made to AD DS objects and their attributes. You can also use this feature when auditing Active Directory Lightweight Directory Services (AD LDS).

MORE INFO **AD LDS**

For more information about AD LDS, see *http://technet.microsoft.com/en-us/library/cc754361(WS.10).aspx.*

Windows Server 2008 R2 introduces the following enhancements to the AD DS Server role:

- **New domain and forest functional levels** Windows Server 2008 R2 introduces new Active Directory domain and forest functional levels. The Windows Server 2008 R2 domain functional level introduces authentication mechanism assurance (AMA) and automatic service principal name (SPN) management. The Windows Server 2008 R2 forest functional level introduces the Active Directory Recycle Bin. These features are discussed in more detail later in this lesson.

- **Enhanced command-line management**   You can now manage Active Directory server roles using Windows PowerShell.

- **Improved automated monitoring and notification**   The updated System Center Operations Manager 2007 R2 Management Pack improves the monitoring and management of Active Directory server roles.

- **Server Manager enhancement**   Server Manager allows you to pre-stage domain controllers. When the domain controller role is added from the Server Manager console, the files needed to perform the installation of the directory service are copied to the server. When you start the AD DS Installation Wizard (Dcpromo.exe), these files are cached and available.

- **Integrated Best Practices Analyzer**   Both Windows Server 2008 and Windows Server 2008 R2 fully comply with established standards and best practices. However, Windows Server 2008 R2 includes an integrated Best Practices Analyzer for each of the server roles. This tool creates a checklist within Server Manager for the role, which helps you perform all the configuration tasks.

- **Answer file creation**   If several domain controllers use the same settings when they are installed, the Summary page of the AD DS Installation Wizard allows you to export the settings from the current installation into an answer file. The password used for your DSRM administrator account is not exported with the answer file, and you can specify that the user who is installing the domain controller is always prompted for the administrator password. Passwords, therefore, are not accessible to users who have access to the location where the answer files are stored.

- **Simplified RODC installation**   You can define more easily who is allowed to install and manage an RODC. In the first phase of the installation, you specify the account that can install the RODC. Once defined, the user that you associate with the RODC has the rights to install the directory service.

The following Windows Server 2008 R2 enhancements to AD DS are of particular significance and are therefore described in more detail:

- **Active Directory Administrative Center**   This provides an improved additional method of managing directory service objects.

- **Active Directory module for Windows PowerShell**   This provides Windows PowerShell cmdlets that let you perform administrative, configuration, and diagnostic tasks.

- **Active Directory Recycle Bin**   This enhances your ability to preserve and recover accidentally deleted Active Directory objects.

The Active Directory Administrative Center

In previous editions of Windows Server operating systems, such as Windows Server 2003 and Windows Server 2008, you could manage and publish information in Active Directory by using the ADUC MMC console. In Windows Server 2008 R2, you can also manage directory service objects by using the Active Directory Administrative Center, available on the Administrative Tools menu.

You can use this tool to perform the following administrative tasks:

- Create new user accounts and manage existing user accounts.
- Create new groups and manage existing groups.
- Create new computer accounts and manage existing computer accounts.
- Create new OUs and containers and manage existing OUs.
- Connect to one or several domains or domain controllers and view and manage the directory information for those domains or domain controllers.
- Filter Active Directory data by using a query-building search.

You can use the Active Directory Administrative Center GUI, shown in Figure 3-1, to customize the Active Directory Administrative Center tool.

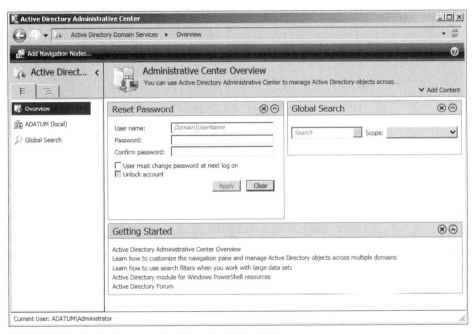

FIGURE 3-1 The Active Directory Administrative Center GUI

Active Directory Administrative Center installs automatically on any server running Windows Server 2008 R2 when you use Server Manager to install AD DS. It also installs automatically by default when you promote a server running Windows Server 2008 R2 to a domain controller by running Dcpromo.exe. You can also use Remote Server Administration Tools (RSAT) to install Active Directory Administrative Center on a server running Windows Server 2008 R2 or a client running Windows 7.

When you open the Active Directory Administrative Center on a server running Windows Server 2008 R2, your local domain appears in the Active Directory Administrative Center navigation pane. You can then view or manage the Active Directory objects in this domain.

When you open the Active Directory Administrative Center on a server running Windows
Server 2008 R2, your local domain appears in the Active Directory Administrative Center
navigation pane. You can then view or manage the Active Directory objects in this domain.

You can also use Active Directory Administrative Center and your current logon credentials
to view or manage Active Directory objects from other domains. You can view domains that
belong to the same forest as the local domain or have established a trust with your local
domain. Both one-way and two-way trusts are supported. You can also open the Active
Directory Administrative Center by using a set of logon credentials that is different from your
current set of credentials.

You can browse through the Active Directory Administrative Center navigation pane by
using either the tree view or the new list view. To see the tree view, move your cursor over the
left tab at the top of the navigation pane until the words "Tree View" appear, and then click
that tab. To see the list view, move your cursor over the right tab at the top of the navigation
pane until the words "List View" appear, and then click that tab.

In the list view, you can use the Column Explorer feature. Column Explorer simplifies
navigation by displaying all the child containers of the parent container in a single column.
The list view lets you take advantage of the Most Recently Used (MRU) list. This list
automatically appears under a navigation node when you visit at least one container in that
node. It lists the last three containers that you visited in a particular navigation node. You
can also view the current MRU list by expanding the Active Directory Administrative Center
breadcrumb bar (which will be described shortly).

You can customize your Active Directory Administrative Center navigation pane by adding
containers from the local domain or from any foreign domain to the navigation pane as
separate nodes. You can also rename or remove manually added navigation pane nodes,
move them up or down in the navigation pane, or create duplicates of existing nodes.

The breadcrumb bar is the box at the top of the Active Directory Administrative Center window. You can navigate directly to a specific container in a local domain or any trusted foreign domain by clicking the bar and specifying one of the following:

- A distinguished name (DN) for the desired container; for example, cn=Users,DC=adatum,DC=com
- A hierarchical path for the desired container; for example, Active Directory Domain Services/adatum (local)/Users
- A Lightweight Directory Access Protocol (LDAP) path for the desired container; for example, LDAP://cn=Users,DC=adatum,DC=com

You can use the breadcrumb bar to navigate directly to a specific container only if this container is stored in the domain directory partition of the local domain (or the trusted foreign domain) that you are managing in Active Directory Administrative Center. You cannot use the breadcrumb bar to navigate directly to containers that are stored in the configuration, schema, or application directory partitions of the local domain (or trusted foreign domains) that you are managing in Active Directory Administrative Center.

To navigate directly to a container by specifying its hierarchical path in the Active Directory Administrative Center breadcrumb bar, you must be managing the local domain (or a trusted foreign domain) that this container belongs to in the selected instance of Active Directory Administrative Center. However, this restriction does not apply to navigation to a specific container by specifying its LDAP path or a distinguished name in the breadcrumb bar.

For example, if adatum.com (the local domain) and fabrikam.com (a foreign domain) have an established trust relationship, you can specify the LDAP paths or distinguished names of the containers in the breadcrumb bar. You can navigate successfully to the desired containers in both adatum.com and fabrikam.com, regardless of whether adatum.com or fabrikam.com is currently added to the navigation pane. However, adatum.com and fabrikam.com must be added to the navigation pane for you to navigate successfully to the containers in these domains by specifying the hierarchical paths of these containers in the breadcrumb bar.

The object properties page in Active Directory Administrative Center consists of several property page sections and a preview feature. You can display, hide, or collapse any property page sections and the preview to customize this property page.

You can use the Active Directory Administrative Center query-building search and filtering mechanism to locate Active Directory objects quickly. You can save the queries that you build and use them again at a later time. Each saved query consists of the query criteria that you select, as well as the customized sorting and column information that you specify.

> **MORE INFO** **LOCATING ACTIVE DIRECTORY OBJECTS**
>
> For more information about locating Active Directory objects in Active Directory Administrative Center, see *http://technet.microsoft.com/en-us/library/dd560661(WS.10).aspx.*

Active Directory Module for Windows PowerShell

The Active Directory module for Windows PowerShell provides command-line scripting with a consistent vocabulary and syntax that lets you perform administrative, configuration, and diagnostic tasks. The module consolidates a group of cmdlets that you can use to manage Active Directory domains, AD LDS configuration sets, and Active Directory database mounting tool instances.

The Active Directory module installs on computers that are running Windows Server 2008 R2 (Standard, Enterprise, or Datacenter edition) when you install the AD DS or the AD LDS Server role. You can also install this module on workstation computers running Windows 7 as part of RSAT, provided that you have at least one domain controller running Windows Server 2008 R2 in your domain, or at least one instance of an AD LDS configuration set that is running on a server running Windows Server 2008 R2. To function correctly, the Active Directory module uses the ADWS service, which in turn requires TCP port 9389 to be open on the domain controller where the ADWS service is running.

The Active Directory module consists of the Active Directory module provider and the Active Directory module cmdlets. To connect to the module provider, click Active Directory Module For Windows PowerShell under Administrative Tools on the All Programs menu.

You can use the Active Directory module cmdlets to manage existing Active Directory user and computer accounts, groups, OUs, domains and forests, domain controllers, and password policies, or to create new ones.

Table 3-1 lists a selection of the cmdlets that are available in the release of the Active Directory module in Windows Server 2008 R2 current at this time of writing. You can access a full list by following the link given in the More Info reader aid, later in this section.

TABLE 3-1 Some Cmdlets in the Active Directory Module

CMDLET	DESCRIPTION
Enable-ADAccount	Enables an Active Directory account
Set-ADAccountControl	Modifies user account control (UAC) values for an Active Directory account
Set-ADAccountPassword	Modifies the password of an Active Directory account

CMDLET	DESCRIPTION
Set-ADComputer	Modifies an Active Directory computer
Get-ADComputerServiceAccount	Gets the service accounts that are hosted by an Active Directory computer
Set-ADDefaultDomainPasswordPolicy	Modifies the default password policy for an Active Directory domain
New-ADFineGrainedPasswordPolicy	Creates a new Active Directory fine-grained password policy
Set-ADGroup	Modifies an Active Directory group
Set-ADObject	Modifies an Active Directory object
Enable-ADOptionalFeature	Enables an Active Directory optional feature
New-ADServiceAccount	Creates a new Active Directory service account

> **MORE INFO** **THE ACTIVE DIRECTORY MODULE FOR WINDOWS POWERSHELL**
>
> For more information about the Active Directory module for Windows PowerShell, including a full list and description of the supported cmdlets, see *http://technet.microsoft .com/en-us/library/dd378783(WS.10).aspx*.

Active Directory Recycle Bin

The Active Directory Recycle Bin in Windows Server 2008 R2 builds on the existing tombstone reanimation infrastructure and enhances your ability to preserve and recover accidentally deleted Active Directory objects. It helps minimize directory service downtime by enhancing your ability to preserve and restore accidentally deleted Active Directory objects, such as OUs, without needing to restore Active Directory data from backups, restart AD DS, or reboot domain controllers.

> **MORE INFO** **TOMBSTONE REANIMATION**
>
> For more information about tombstone reanimation, see *http://technet.microsoft.com/ en-us/magazine/2007.09.tombstones.aspx*.

When you enable Active Directory Recycle Bin, all attributes of deleted Active Directory objects are preserved and the objects can be restored to the same consistent logical state that they were in immediately before deletion. For example, restored user accounts automatically regain all group memberships and corresponding access rights that they had immediately before deletion, within and across domains. Active Directory Recycle Bin works for both AD DS and AD LDS environments. As described later in this lesson, you can enable Active Directory Recycle Bin using the Active Directory Module for Windows PowerShell, provided your forest functional level is Windows Server 2008 R2. ADWS needs to be running on a server running Windows Server 2008 R2 in your domain if you want to use this module.

MORE INFO **RESTORING DELETED ACTIVE DIRECTORY OBJECTS**

For a step-by-step guide to restoring deleted Active Directory objects, see *http://technet .microsoft.com/en-us/library/dd392261(WS.10).aspx*.

MORE INFO **NEW AD DS FEATURES IN WINDOWS SERVER 2008 R2**

For more information about additional AD DS features introduced by Windows Server 2008 R2, access *http://technet.microsoft.com/en-us/library/dd378796(WS.10).aspx* and follow the links.

Planning and Using RODCs

In organizations that use Windows Server 2003 (or earlier) domains, users at remote branch locations typically authenticate with a domain controller at the central office through a wide area network (WAN) connection. This is far from ideal and can cause delays. If WAN connectivity is interrupted, users are unable to log on.

However, from a security point of view, logging on over a WAN is preferable to having a writable domain controller at a small location where physical security cannot be guaranteed. Also, it is a poor use of scarce administrative resource to locate a domain administrator at a small branch location, and administering a domain controller remotely over a WAN can be a time-consuming and frustrating task, particularly if the branch office is connected to a hub site over a low-bandwidth network.

Windows Server 2008 addressed this problem by introducing the RODC. RODCs offer improved security, faster logon times, and more efficient access to local resources. RODC administration can be delegated to users or groups that do not have administrative rights in the domain.

You might also choose to deploy an RODC if, for example, a line-of-business (LOB) application used at a branch office runs successfully only if it is installed on a domain controller. Alternatively, the domain controller might be the only server in the branch office and might host server applications. In both cases, the LOB application owner typically needs to log on to the domain controller interactively or use Terminal Services (called Remote Desktop Services in Windows Server 2008 R2) to configure and manage the application. This situation creates a security risk to the Active Directory forest. However, the risk is considerably reduced if the LOB application owner (typically not a domain administrator) is granted the right to log on to an RODC.

NOTE **PLANNING BRANCH OFFICES**

In a small branch office where the hardware budget is limited, you might need servers that perform a variety of roles, some of which conflict. An RODC can provide part of your solution to this problem, but you should also consider virtualization.

An RODC receives its configuration from a writable domain controller. Therefore, at least one writable domain controller in the domain must be running Windows Server 2008 or Windows Server 2008 R2. In addition, the functional level for the domain and forest must be Windows Server 2003 or later. Sensitive security information, such as user passwords, is not replicated to the RODC. The first time a user logs on at the branch office, his or her identity is validated across the WAN. However, the RODC can pull user credentials so that further logons by the same user are validated locally, although you need to permit this specifically in the domain Password Replication Policy with respect to that RODC. You can do this when you create a computer account for the RODC in Active Directory by using ADUC on a writable domain controller in the domain.

 Quick Check

- You plan to install RODCs in all your company's branch offices. What is the minimum forest functional level that allows you to do this?

Quick Check Answer

- Windows Server 2003

When an RODC requests credential information from the writable domain controller, that domain controller recognizes that the request is coming from an RODC and consults the Password Replication Policy in effect for that RODC. This addresses the security risk of having passwords for every user in a domain stored on a domain controller at a remote location.

> **MORE INFO** **RODC-FILTERED ATTRIBUTE SET**
>
> For more information about attributes that are filtered out and not replicated to an RODC, see *http://technet.microsoft.com/en-us/library/cc753223(WS.10).aspx?ppud=4*.

RODCs are particularly useful at remote locations that have relatively few users or users with little IT knowledge, inadequate physical security, low network bandwidth, or any combination of these features. They provide a read-only AD DS database, unidirectional replication (from the writable domain controller to the RODC only), credential caching (to streamline logon) and read-only Domain Name System (DNS) zones.

> **MORE INFO** **DEPLOYING AN RODC**
>
> For more information about the prerequisites for deploying an RODC, see *http://technet .microsoft.com/en-us/library/cc732801(WS.10).aspx* and *http://technet.microsoft.com/ en-us/library/cc772234(WS.10).aspx*. For more information about the adprep /rodcprep command, see *http://technet.microsoft.com/en-us/library/cc731728(WS.10).aspx*.

You can install the DNS Server service on an RODC, which can then replicate all application directory partitions that DNS uses, including ForestDNSZones and

DomainDNSZones. If a DNS server is installed on an RODC, clients can send name resolution queries as they would to any other DNS server.

However, the DNS server on an RODC does not support client updates directly and does not register name server (NS) resource records for any Active Directory–integrated zone that it hosts. When a client attempts to update its DNS records against an RODC, the server returns a referral to a writable DNS server. The RODC then requests the updated DNS record (only a single record) from the writable DNS server. The entire list of changed zone or domain data does not get replicated during this special replicate-single-object request.

> **NOTE THE** ADPREP **/RODCPREP COMMAND**
>
> This command updates permissions on application directory partitions so that these partitions can be replicated to RODCs. This operation contacts the infrastructure master in each domain to update the necessary permissions. You must be a member of the Enterprise Admins group to run this command, and you need to run this command only once in the forest (unless it fails to complete successfully because an infrastructure master is not available).

> **MORE INFO ADPREP**
>
> For more information about the adprep command, see *http://technet.microsoft.com/en-us/library/cc731728(WS.10).aspx*.

Planning RODC Implementation

You can plan to implement RODCs at remote locations either when you roll out a Windows Server 2008 or a Windows Server 2008 R2 upgrade or if you already have a Windows Server 2008 or Windows Server 2008 R2 AD DS domain. You can specify Password Replication Policy for a specific RODC when you create the computer account for the RODC in the domain as the first stage of a two-stage RODC installation, as described later in this lesson. Alternatively, you can open ADUC on an existing writable domain controller, right-click the account for an RODC in the Domain Controllers container, click Properties, and then click the Password Replication Policy tab to permit password caching for that RODC. Figure 3-2 shows the Password Replication Policy tab for an RODC named VAN-RODC1 in the adatum.com domain. Note that you will be unable to access this screen until you have precreated an RODC computer account for VAN-RODC1, as described later in this lesson.

For example, Margie's Travel has a number of very small branch offices located in remote rural areas where WAN links can sometimes be slow or unreliable. Because of the size and remote nature of these offices, the hardware budget is limited and servers need to perform several functions. No local domain administrators exist. Central administration from the head office requires that the branch office equipment is part of an Active Directory structure. One of

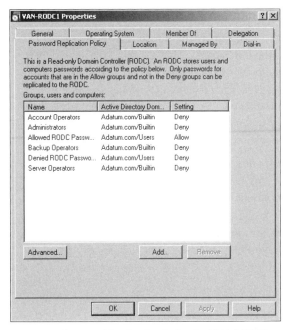

FIGURE 3-2 Password Replication Policy for VAN-RODC1

the current functions of the servers in the branch offices is to act as secondary DNS servers. The remote servers are also file and application servers, and some applications require interactive server logon. Offices at remote locations cannot offer the same level of physical security as can the head office, and logons at remote offices are validated by domain controllers at the head office. This can result in unacceptable logon delays.

In addition to upgrading the domain controllers at the main office, a planned Windows Server 2008 R2 upgrade could involve the installation of RODCs at branch offices. You can first create the accounts for these RODCs at the main office, and at that stage, you can set the Password Replication Policy for each RODC to allow the remote RODCs to pull account information and cache credentials for users who log on at the branch office. This would speed up logons. At the same time, users or a security group could be granted permission to install RODCs and to log on to these RODCs interactively at the branch office.

Installing DNS on RODCs (the default) implements a secondary DNS server that can replicate all application directory partitions that DNS uses, including ForestDNSZones and DomainDNSZones. In addition, if a local client record is amended or added, this DNS server can request the appropriate single updated DNS from the writable DNS server without needing to pull the entire list of changed zone or domain data.

You can permit interactive logon if the applications installed on the RODC require it without exposing writable Active Directory data to a user who is not a domain administrator. You should also consider virtualization. File and application servers are seldom virtualized, but RODCs and DNS servers can be.

Using AD DS Installation Wizard Enhancements

Windows Server 2008 enhanced the AD DS Installation Wizard to streamline and simplify AD DS and introduce new features such as the installation of RODCs. Windows Server 2008 also included changes to the MMC snap-in functions that manage AD DS. These features are retained in Windows Server 2008 R2, which offers further enhancements described earlier in this lesson. For example, AD DS Installation Wizard enhancements enable you to locate domain controllers in a large enterprise network easily, and to configure the Password Replication Policy for RODCs.

You start the AD DS Installation Wizard by clicking Add Roles in the Initial Configuration Tasks dialog box or in Server Manager, or by running Dcpromo from a command prompt or from the Run box. The wizard also starts when you precreate a computer account for an RODC. Some of the pages in the wizard appear only if you select Use Advanced Mode Installation on the Welcome page of the wizard. You can also enter **dcpromo /adv** to access advanced mode installation. Figure 3-3 shows the wizard page where you specify advanced mode installation.

FIGURE 3-3 Specifying advanced mode installation

 EXAM TIP

A domain administrator configures the Password Replication Policy for an RODC on a writable domain controller. You can discard any answer in the examination in which a designated user who is not a domain administrator opens ADUC on the RODC and configures Password Replication Policy.

Advanced mode installation gives you greater control over the installation process. If you do not specify this mode, the wizard uses default options that apply to most configurations. Additional installation options in advanced installation mode include the following:

- You can select the source domain controller for the installation. This domain controller is used to replicate domain data to the new domain controller initially.

- You can use backup media from an existing domain controller in the same domain to reduce network traffic that is associated with initial replication.

- You can create a new domain tree.

- You can change the default NetBIOS name.

- You can set forest and domain functional levels when you create a new forest or a new domain.

- You can configure the Password Replication Policy for an RODC.

You will discover other features as you go through the AD DS installation process. If you install an additional domain controller, for example, you can select the domain name rather than typing it into a dialog box. By default, the new AD DS Installation Wizard uses the credentials of the user who is currently logged on, provided that the user is logged on with a domain account. You can specify other credentials if you need to.

From the wizard's Summary page, you can export your settings to an answer file that you can use as a template for subsequent installations or uninstalls. Note that if you specify a value for the DSRM administrator password in the designated wizard page, and then export the settings to an answer file, the password does not appear in the answer file. If you want this information to be included, you need to modify the answer file manually.

However, the inclusion of clear-text passwords in answer files is not good security practice. For this reason, you can omit your administrator password from the answer file. If you type **password=*** in the answer file, the AD DS Installation Wizard prompts you for account credentials. Finally, the wizard lets you force the demotion of a domain controller that is started in Directory Services Restore Mode.

Delegating RODC Installation

When planning RODC installation, you can choose to implement two-stage installation. Working at the head office, you can delegate the appropriate permissions to a user or a group. At a branch office, a user with the delegated permissions can perform the installation, and subsequently can manage the RODC without needing domain administrator rights.

To delegate RODC installation, you first create an RODC account in ADUC by right-clicking the Domain Controllers container and selecting Pre-Create Read-Only Domain Controller Account. Figure 3-4 shows the computer name being specified.

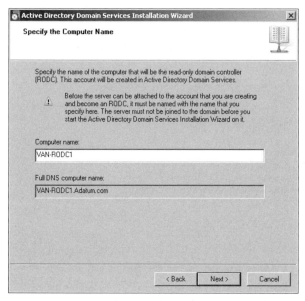

FIGURE 3-4 Specifying the computer name when precreating an RODC account

When you create the RODC account, you can delegate the installation and administration of the RODC to a user or a security group. Figure 3-5 shows installation and administration rights being delegated to Don Hall.

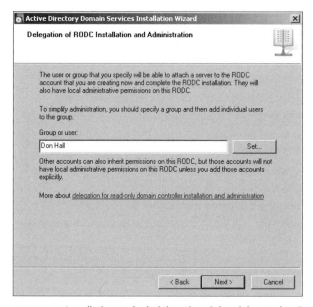

FIGURE 3-5 Installation and administration rights delegated to Don Hall

A user with delegated installation and administration rights can create an RODC on a designated server by running dcpromo /UseExistingAccount:Attach. This user (or all users in a designated security group) can log on to the RODC interactively and administer it without requiring administration rights in the rest of the domain or the forest.

> **NOTE DELETING AN RODC ACCOUNT**
>
> When you delete an RODC account, you are given the option of automatically forcing a password change on all accounts that were replicated to the RODC.

 Quick Check

- You are a domain administrator. You plan to use RODCs at your company's branch offices. Branch office staff who are not administrators will be promoting branch office servers to RODCs. What do you need to do as the first stage of a two-stage RODC installation?

Quick Check Answer

- You need to create the computer accounts for the RODCs in the domain. You need to give branch office staff (typically one member of staff in each branch office) the appropriate rights to install RODCs.

Utilizing MMC Snap-in Enhancements

Windows Server 2008 and Windows Server 2008 R2 enhance the functions of MMC snap-in tools such as ADUC. The next section of this lesson discusses enhancements to the schema and to ADUC that provide increased permission granularity and let you plan your permission structure and, in some circumstances, simplify your domain structure.

The Active Directory Sites And Services snap-in in Windows Server 2008 and Windows Server 2008 R2 includes a Find command on the toolbar and in the Action menu. This command lets you discover the site in which a domain controller is placed. This can help you to troubleshoot replication problems. In Microsoft Windows 2000 Server and Windows Server 2003, Active Directory Sites And Services did not provide you with this information easily.

When you install a computer account for an RODC, one of the advanced features of the AD DS Installation Wizard provides a Password Replication Policy page that lets you configure settings for that RODC. If you choose not to configure these settings at this stage, you can instead use the Password Replication Policy tab on the RODC's Properties dialog box. This was illustrated in Figure 3-2, earlier in this lesson.

If you click the Advanced button on this tab, you can determine what passwords have been sent to or are stored in the RODC and what accounts have authenticated to the RODC. This lets you discover who is using the RODC. You can use this information when planning your Password Replication Policy. You will not see entries in this dialog box until the RODC has been created physically and has validated logons for local users.

Planning Fine-Grained Password and Account Lockout Policies

In Active Directory implementations prior to Windows Server 2008, you could apply only one password and account lockout policy to all users in the domain. If you needed different password and account lockout settings for different sets of users, you needed to create a custom password filter or create multiple domains.

Windows Server 2008 and Windows Server 2008 R2 let you specify fine-grained password policies. You can specify multiple password policies and apply different password restrictions and account lockout policies to different sets of users within a single domain. For example, you might want to increase the minimum password length for administrative-level accounts. This facility also lets you apply a special password policy for accounts whose passwords are synchronized with other data sources.

Windows Server 2008 introduced the following two new object classes in the AD DS schema, and these are supported in Windows Server 2008 R2:

- Password Settings Container
- Password Settings

The Password Settings Container (PSC) object class is created by default under the System container in the domain. It stores the Password Settings Objects (PSOs) for that domain. You cannot rename, move, or delete this container. You can create a PSO by saving the parameters (such as password length) in a text file with an *.ldf* extension and using the ldifde command from the command prompt. Alternatively, you can use the ADSI Edit MMC snap-in, as described in the practice later in this lesson.

> **MORE INFO   CREATING PSOs**
>
> For more information about creating PSOs, see *http://technet.microsoft.com/en-us/library/cc754461(WS.10).aspx*.

EXAM TIP

The examination is unlikely to ask you to create a PSO under examination conditions, although you might be asked what tools you could use to do it. You are more likely to be asked about the planning considerations for using fine-grained passwords and what advantages they provide.

Before you plan a password policy, you need to know what the default settings are. Figure 3-6 shows the default settings for the adatum.com domain.

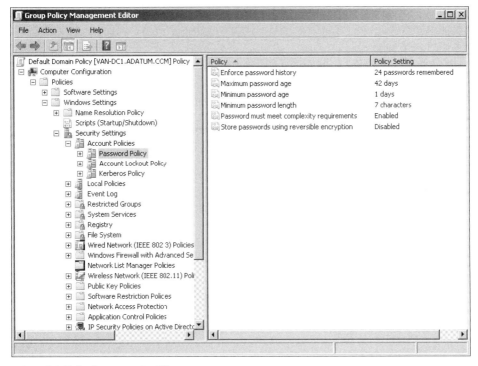

FIGURE 3-6 Default password settings

As a first step in planning fine-grained password and account lockout policies, you need to decide how many different password policies you need. Typically, your policy could include at least 3 but seldom more than 10 PSOs. At a minimum, you would probably want to configure the following:

- An administrative-level password policy with strict settings—for example, a minimum password length of 12, a maximum password age of 28 days, and password complexity requirements enabled.

- A user-level password policy with, for example, a minimum password length of 6, a maximum password age of 90 days, and password complexity requirements not enabled.

- A service account password policy with a minimum password length of 32 characters and complexity requirements enabled (service account passwords are seldom typed in). Because of their complexity, service account passwords typically can be set to have very long password ages or not to expire at all.

You also need to look at your existing group structure. If you have existing Administrators and Users groups, there is no point to creating new ones. Ultimately, you need to define a group and Active Directory structure that maps to your fine-grained password and account lockout policies.

You cannot apply PSOs to OUs directly. If your users are organized into OUs, consider creating shadow groups for these OUs and then applying the newly defined fine-grained password and account lockout policies to them. A shadow group is a global security group that is logically mapped to an OU to enforce a fine-grained password and account lockout policy. Add OU users as members to the newly created shadow group and then apply the fine-grained password and account lockout policy to this shadow group. If you move a user from one OU to another, you must update user memberships in the corresponding shadow groups.

> **NOTE SHADOW GROUPS**
>
> You will not find a control called Add Shadow Group in ADUC. A *shadow group* is simply an ordinary global security group that contains all the user accounts in one or more OUs. When you apply a PSO to a shadow group, you are effectively applying it to users in the corresponding OU.

Microsoft applies Group Policy objects (GPOs) to groups rather than OUs because groups offer better flexibility for managing various sets of users. Windows Server 2008 and Windows Server 2008 R2 AD DS create various groups for administrative accounts, including Domain Admins, Enterprise Admins, Schema Admins, Server Operators, and Backup Operators. You can apply PSOs to these groups or nest them in a single global security group and apply a PSO to that group. Because you use groups rather than OUs, you do not need to modify the OU hierarchy to apply fine-grained passwords. Modifying an OU hierarchy requires detailed planning and increases the risk of errors.

If you intend to use fine-grained passwords, you probably need to raise the functional level of your domain. To work properly, fine-grained password settings require a domain functional level of at least Windows Server 2008. Planning domain and forest functional levels is discussed later in this lesson. Changing functional levels involves irreversible changes. You need to be sure, for example, that you will never want to add a Windows Server 2003 domain controller to your domain.

By default, only members of the Domain Admins group can create PSOs and apply a PSO to a group or user. You do not, however, need to have permissions on the user object or group object to be able to apply a PSO to it. You can delegate Read Property permissions on the default security descriptor of a PSO object to any other group (such as Help desk personnel). This lets users that are not domain administrators discover the password and account lockout settings applied through a PSO to a security group.

You can apply fine-grained password policies only to user objects and global security groups (or inetOrgPerson objects, if they are used instead of user objects). If your plan identifies a group of computers that require different password settings, you need to look at techniques such as password filters. Fine-grained password policies cannot be applied to Computer objects.

If you use custom password filters in a domain, fine-grained password policies do not interfere with these filters. If you plan to upgrade Windows 2000 Server or Windows

Server 2003 domains that currently deploy custom password filters on domain controllers, you can continue to use those password filters to enforce additional password restrictions.

If you have assigned a PSO to a global security group, but one user in that group requires special settings, you can assign an exceptional PSO directly to that particular user. For example, the Chief Executive Officer of Northwind Traders is a member of the senior managers group, and company policy requires that senior managers use complex passwords. However, the CEO is not willing to do so. In this case, you can create an exceptional PSO and apply it directly to the CEO's user account. The exceptional PSO will override the security group PSO when the password settings (msDS-ResultantPSO) for the CEO's user account are determined.

 Quick Check

- By default, members of which group can create PSOs?

Quick Check Answer

- Domain Admins

Finally, you can plan to delegate management of fine-grained passwords. When you have created the necessary PSOs and the global security groups associated with these PSOs, you can delegate management of the security groups to responsible users or user groups. For example, a human resources (HR) group could add user accounts to or remove them from the managers group when staff changes occur. If a PSO specifying fine-grained password policy is associated with the managers group, the HR group is in effect determining to whom these policies are applied.

> **MORE INFO   FINE-GRAINED PASSWORD AND ACCOUNT LOCKOUT POLICY CONFIGURATION**
>
> For more information about fine-grained password and account lockout policies, see *http://technet.microsoft.com/en-us/library/cc770842(WS.10).aspx.*

> **NOTE   PSO PRECEDENCE**
>
> The PSO Precedence attribute is an integer value that is used to resolve conflicts if multiple PSOs are applied to a user or group object. A PSO with a lower Precedence priority number overrides a PSO with a higher Precedence priority number. You can edit PSO attributes using the Attribute tab of ADUC. This tab is visible when you specify Advanced View in the ADUC tool.

Planning the Use of the Data Mining Tool

The data mining tool (Dsamain.exe) makes it possible for deleted AD DS or AD LDS data to be preserved in the form of snapshots of AD DS taken by the Volume Shadow Copy Service (VSS). You can use an LDAP tool such as ldp.exe to view the read-only data in the snapshots. You can also use the ADUC tool to view this data. The data mining tool does not actually recover the deleted objects and containers—you need to perform data recovery as a subsequent step.

> **MORE INFO** **USING NTDSUTIL WITH THE DATA MINING TOOL**
>
> You can use the improved version of Ntdsutil introduced in Windows Server 2008 together with the data mining tool to create and view snapshots of data stored in AD DS or AD LDS. For more information, see *http://technet.microsoft.com/en-us/library/cc753609(WS.10).aspx.*

When you are planning a recovery strategy, you need to decide how best to preserve deleted data and recover that data if required. For example, you could schedule a task that regularly runs the Ntdsutil tool to take snapshots of the volume that contains the AD DS database. You can use the same tool to list the snapshots that are available, and mount the snapshot that you want to view.

The second stage of your strategy involves deciding what snapshot you should restore if data is lost or corrupted. Your plan can involve running Dsamain.exe to expose the snapshot volume as an LDAP server. As part of the `dsamain` command, you specify a port number for the LDAP port. If you want, you can also specify the LDAP-SSL, Global Catalog, and Global Catalog–SSL ports, but if you do not, the command derives these values from the LDAP port number. You can then run Ldp.exe and attach to the specified LDAP port. This lets you browse the snapshot just as you would any live domain controller.

If you know what objects or OUs you need to restore, you can identify them in the snapshots and record their attributes and back-links. You can then reanimate these objects by using the tombstone reanimation feature and manually repopulate them with the stripped attributes and back-links as identified in the snapshots. The data mining tool lets you do this without needing to restart the domain controller in Directory Services mode.

Your planning process should involve considerations other than when you take snapshots and how you use these snapshots in the data restoration. For example, you also need to take security into account. If an attacker obtains access to an AD DS snapshot, this is as serious as if an AD DS backup were compromised. A malicious user could copy AD DS snapshots from forest A to forest B and use domain or enterprise administrator credentials from forest B to examine the data. You should plan to encrypt AD DS snapshots to help reduce the chance of unauthorized access. As with any data encryption, you also need to draw up recovery plans to recover information if the encryption key is lost or corrupted.

Planning AD DS Auditing

In Windows Server 2008 and Windows Server 2008 R2, the Audit Directory Service Access global audit policy is enabled by default. This policy controls whether auditing for directory service events is enabled or disabled. If you configure this policy setting by modifying the Default Domain Controllers Policy, you can specify whether to audit successes, audit failures, or not audit at all. You can control what operations to audit by modifying the System Access Control List (SACL) on an object. You can set a SACL on an AD DS object on the Security tab in that object's Properties dialog box.

As an administrator, one of your tasks is to configure audit policy. Enabling success or failure auditing is a straightforward procedure. Deciding which objects to audit; whether to audit success, failure, or both; and whether to record new and old values if changes are made is much more difficult. Auditing everything is never an option—too much information is as bad as too little. You need to be selective.

In Windows 2000 Server and Windows Server 2003, you could specify only whether DS access was audited. Windows Server 2008 and Windows Server 2008 R2 give you more granular control. You can audit the following:

- DS access
- DS changes (old and new values)
- DS replication

Auditing DS replication is subdivided further so that you can choose between two levels of auditing—Normal and Detailed.

For example, you are a domain administrator at Litware, Inc. Previously, you found that the auditing that you configured had limitations. You could determine that the attributes of an object in Active Directory had been changed, but not what changes were made. If a change was erroneous, you relied on documentation maintained by the domain administration team to reverse or correct the alteration. Such documentation, if it existed at all, was seldom perfect.

Litware has recently upgraded its domain to Windows Server 2008 R2. You can now plan your auditing procedures so that if a change is performed on an object attribute, AD DS logs the previous and current values of the attribute. Only the values that change as a result of the modify operation are logged, so you do not need to search through a long list of attribute values to find the change.

 Quick Check

- You are setting up DS replication auditing. What are the two auditing levels from which you can choose?

Quick Check Answer

- Normal and Detailed

If a new object is created, AD DS logs values of the attributes that are configured or added at the time of creation. Attributes that take default values are not logged. If an object is moved within a domain, you can ensure that the previous and new locations are logged. When an object is moved to a different domain, you can access the Create event that is generated and logged on the domain controller in the target domain. If an object is undeleted, you can determine the location to which the object is moved. If attributes are added, modified, or deleted during an undelete operation, you can determine the values of those attributes from the Security event log.

If the Directory Service Changes setting is enabled, AD DS logs events in the Security event log when changes are made to objects that an administrator has set up for auditing. Table 3-2 lists these events.

TABLE 3-2 Security Events Related to AD DS Objects

EVENT ID	TYPE OF EVENT	EVENT DESCRIPTION
5136	Modify	A successful modification has been made to an attribute in the directory.
5137	Create	A new object has been created in the directory.
5138	Undelete	An object has been undeleted in the directory.
5139	Move	An object has been moved within the domain.

You need to decide whether to react to such events, and how to do so. By default, the events are logged in the Security event log and you can view them by opening Event Viewer. However, you can specify that an event written to the Security event log initiates a task, such as generating an alert or starting an executable program. To do this, select the event in Event Viewer and click Attach Task To This Event on the Action menu. Figure 3-7 shows this function.

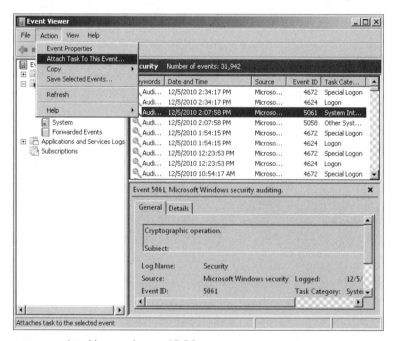

FIGURE 3-7 Attaching a task to an AD DS event

Planning Domain and Forest Functionality

When you upgrade your domains and forests to Windows Server 2008 or Windows Server 2008 R2, the temptation is always to raise the domain and forest functional levels. This is very easy to do, and your network will not achieve full functionality until the functional levels are raised. For example, for fine-grained password policy configuration to work properly, you need a domain functional level of at least Windows Server 2008.

Be careful. It is very easy to raise domain and forest functional levels, but it is almost impossible to lower them. (To do this, you need to go through uninstallations and reinstallations or restores from a backup taken before the functional level was changed.) If you are asked to add Windows Server 2003 domain controllers to your domain and you have raised the domain functional level to Windows Server 2008 or Windows Server 2008 R2, you have a problem. If you have raised your forest functional level to Windows Server 2008 and you find that you need to incorporate a Windows Server 2000 domain, you might regret your earlier decision. Planning functional levels is a delicate and difficult balancing act. You need to consider both the additional functionality that raising a functional level provides and the problems it could present.

> **NOTE ROLLING BACK THE WINDOWS SERVER 2008 R2 FOREST FUNCTIONAL LEVEL**
>
> Generally speaking, if you raise the forest functional level, you cannot roll back or lower it (except by restoring a backup that was taken before the functional level was raised). There is, however, one exception. If you raise the forest functional level to Windows Server 2008 R2 and if the Active Directory Recycle Bin is not enabled, you have the option of rolling the forest functional level back to Windows Server 2008.

To plan what functional level you need to set for your domains and forest and when you should raise functional levels, you need to know what domain controllers each functional level supports and what additional functionality raising the functional level provides. You also need to know the relationship between domain and forest functional levels. For example, if you raise the functional level of your forest to Windows Server 2008 R2, you ensure that the default functional level of all the domains in your forest is Windows Server 2008 R2.

> **IMPORTANT FUNCTIONAL LEVELS DO NOT AFFECT MEMBER SERVERS**
>
> Domain and forest functional levels support domain controllers. They do not affect member servers. For example, a file server in a Windows Server 2008 domain can have Windows 2000 Server or Windows Server 2003 installed.

Domain Functional Level Considerations

Domain functionality enables features that affect the domain. In Windows Server 2008 R2 AD DS, the following domain functional levels are available:

- Windows 2000 native
- Windows Server 2003

- Windows Server 2008
- Windows Server 2008 R2

A default installation of the Windows 2008 R2 AD DS Server role will create a domain with the Windows 2000 native functional level. You raise the functional level of a domain in the practice later in this lesson. To decide whether you should raise the domain functional level, you need to know what functional level supports all the domain controllers that currently exist in your domain, as well as any domain controllers that are likely to be added to the domain. Table 3-3 lists the domain functional levels and the domain controllers that each supports.

TABLE 3-3 Domain Functional Levels and Supported Domain Controllers

DOMAIN FUNCTIONAL LEVEL	SUPPORTED DOMAIN CONTROLLERS
Windows 2000 native	Windows 2000 Server
	Windows Server 2003
	Windows Server 2008
	Windows Server 2008 R2
Windows Server 2003	Windows Server 2003
	Windows Server 2008
	Windows Server 2008 R2
Windows Server 2008	Windows Server 2008
	Windows Server 2008 R2
Windows Server 2008 R2	Windows Server 2008 R2

If, for example, you have Windows Server 2003 domain controllers in your domain, you cannot raise the domain functional level to Windows Server 2008. If all your domain controllers are Windows Server 2008 R2 but you might need to add a Windows Server 2003 domain controller at a later date, you would be wise to postpone the decision to raise your domain functional level past Windows Server 2003.

You need to balance these restrictions against the advantages you gain through raising functional levels. For example, fine-grained password policies require a domain functional level of at least Windows Server 2008 to work properly. To help you make the decision and plan your domain functional levels, Table 3-4 lists the features that each functional level enables.

> **NOTE FIND OUT MORE ABOUT THE FEATURES**
>
> Table 3-4 lists the features, but it does not explain them—the table would be far too long. Most of these features are explained elsewhere in this book. If you see a feature that you do not recognize, consult this book's index, the Windows Server 2008 and Windows Server 2008 R2 Help files, or the Internet (for example, *http://technet.microsoft .com/en-us/library/cc787290(WS.10).aspx*).

TABLE 3-4 Features Enabled by Domain Functional Levels

DOMAIN FUNCTIONAL LEVEL	ENABLED FEATURES
Windows 2000 native	All default Active Directory features
	Universal distribution and security groups
	Group nesting
	Group conversion
	Security identifier (SID) history
Windows Server 2003	All default Active Directory features
	All Windows 2000 native domain functional level features
	The domain management tool (Netdom.exe)
	Logon time stamp update
	Setting the userPassword attribute as the effective password on the inetOrgPerson object and user objects
	Redirecting the Users And Computers containers
	Authorization Manager stores authorization policies in AD DS
	Constrained delegation
	Selective cross-forest authentication
Windows Server 2008	All default Active Directory features
	All Windows Server 2003 domain functional level features
	Distributed File System (DFS) replication support for SYSVOL
	Advanced Encryption Services (AES 128 and 256) support for the Kerberos authentication protocol
	Last Interactive Logon information
	Fine-grained password policies
Windows Server 2008 R2	All default Active Directory features
	All Windows Server 2008 domain functional level features
	Authentication mechanism assurance
	Automatic SPN management

Forest Function Level Considerations

Forest functionality enables features across all the domains in a forest. In Windows Server 2008 forests, the following forest functional levels are available:

- Windows 2000
- Windows Server 2003

- Windows Server 2008
- Windows Server 2008 R2

A default installation of the Windows 2008 R2 AD DS Server role that creates a new forest will set the forest functional level to Windows 2000. You can raise the forest functional level to Windows Server 2003, Windows Server 2008, or Windows Server 2008 R2. Forest functional levels are less restrictive than domain functional levels with regard to the domain controllers that can operate in the forest. However, you need to take account of both domain and forest functional levels if you want to determine what domain controllers can be supported or added. Table 3-5 lists forest functional levels and the domain controllers each supports. Note that Windows NT 4 backup domain controllers can operate in an Active Directory domain.

TABLE 3-5 Forest Functional Levels and Supported Domain Controllers

FOREST FUNCTIONAL LEVEL	SUPPORTED DOMAIN CONTROLLERS
Windows 2000	Windows NT 4
	Windows 2000 Server
	Windows Server 2003
	Windows Server 2008
	Windows Server 2008 R2
Windows Server 2003	Windows Server 2003
	Windows Server 2008
	Windows Server 2008 R2
Windows Server 2008	Windows Server 2008
	Windows Server 2008 R2
Windows Server 2008 R2	Windows Server 2008 R2

When you raise the forest functional level, domain controllers running earlier operating systems cannot be introduced into the forest. For example, if you raise the forest functional level to Windows Server 2003, domain controllers running Windows 2000 Server cannot be added to the forest. The domain functional level cannot be less than the forest functional level. For example, you cannot have a Windows 2000 native domain in a Windows Server 2003 forest, but you can have a Windows Server 2008 R2 domain in a Windows 2000 forest.

Raising the functional level of a forest is a decision that requires careful planning. You might be able to guarantee that you will not need to add a Windows Server 2003 domain controller to a Windows Server 2008 domain, but can you guarantee that you will never be called upon to add a Windows Server 2008 domain to a Windows Server 2008 R2 forest (possibly as part of a company acquisition)?

As with raising the domain functional level, you need to be aware of the advantages of higher functional levels before you can make your final decision. Table 3-6 lists the features enabled by each functional level.

TABLE 3-6 Features Enabled by Forest Functional Levels

FOREST FUNCTIONAL LEVEL	ENABLED FEATURES
Windows 2000	All default Active Directory features
Windows Server 2003	All default Active Directory features
	Forest trusts
	Domain renaming
	Linked-value replication
	RODC deployment
	Improved Knowledge Consistency Checker (KCC) algorithms and scalability—such as improved intersite topology generator (ISTG) algorithms
	The ability to create the dynamicObject class in a domain directory partition
	The ability to convert an inetOrgPerson object instance into a User object instance, and vice versa
	The ability to create application basic groups and LDAP query groups to support role-based authorization
	All domains in the forest operate at the Windows Server 2003 domain functional level
Windows Server 2008	All Windows Server 2003 features
	All domains in the forest operate at the Windows Server 2008 domain functional level
	No additional features
Windows Server 2008 R2	All Windows Server 2008 features
	All domains in the forest operate at the Windows Server 2008 R2 domain functional level
	Active Directory Recycle Bin

For example, the partner companies Coho Vineyard and Coho Vineyard and Winery plan to combine their Active Directory structures into a single forest. All of Coho Vineyard's servers have been upgraded recently to Windows Server 2008 R2. Coho Vineyard's managers foresee considerable benefits from fine-grained password policies that will enable the company's domain structure to be simplified to a single domain. As a long-term strategy, they want to enable the Active Directory Recycle Bin so that accidentally deleted AD DS objects can be recovered without the need to restore from backup. This is not an immediate requirement.

Most of Coho Vineyard and Winery's servers, including all current domain controllers, run Windows Server 2003. The company does not intend to promote any existing computers running Windows 2000 Server to domain controllers, and neither does it have any plans at present to upgrade its domain controllers to Windows Server 2008 R2. Coho Vineyard and Winery currently has a single domain structure and has no plans to install multiple domains. Both companies work very closely with Trey Research and plan to implement cross-forest trusts with that company's Windows Server 2003 forest.

In this situation, Coho Vineyard's redesigned domain can have a domain functional level of either Windows Server 2008 or Windows Server 2008 R2. This enables the company to use fine-grained password policy. At present, because the domain functional level of Coho Vineyard and Winery must support Windows Server 2003 domain controllers, the forest functional level cannot be raised beyond Windows Server 2003. Therefore, the Active Directory Recycle Bin (which requires a forest functional level of Windows Server 2008 R2) cannot be enabled. Coho Vineyard will probably choose a domain functional level of Windows Server 2008 R2 in anticipation of being able to raise the forest functional level in the future.

Coho Vineyard and Winery's domain level can be set to Windows Server 2003 because the company does not plan to add any Windows 2000 Server domain controllers. This in turn allows the forest functional level of the new forest to be raised to Windows Server 2003, enabling cross-forest trusts with Trey Research.

> **NOTE RAISING DOMAIN AND FOREST FUNCTIONAL LEVELS IN A PRODUCTION ENVIRONMENT**
>
> You should raise the domain functional level on a global catalog server in the domain. When all domains are at the required domain functional level, you should raise the forest functional level on a global catalog server on the root domain.

Enabling the Active Directory Recycle Bin

To enable the Active Directory Recycle Bin, you first need to raise the domain functional level of all the domains in your forest to Windows Server 2008 R2. You then raise your forest functional level to Windows Server 2008 R2. You can then run the Active Directory Module for Windows PowerShell as an administrator and enter a command based on the Enable-ADOptionalFeature cmdlet to enable this feature. You do this in the practice session later in this chapter. Note that ADWS needs to be running on a server running Windows Server 2008 R2 in your domain and that TCP port 9389 needs to be open on that server if you want to use the Active Directory Module for Windows PowerShell.

You can also use the Lpd.exe utility to enable the Active Directory Recycle Bin, but Microsoft recommends using the Enable-ADOptionalFeature cmdlet. Note also that if you enable the Active Directory Recycle Bin, every non-global catalog domain controller acts like an Infrastructure Master. As a result, the Infrastructure Master Flexible Single-Master (IM FSMO) placement no longer matters.

Planning Forest-Level Trusts

A forest trust (or forest-level trust) allows every domain in one forest to trust every domain in a second forest. Forest trusts were introduced in Windows Server 2003 and can be one-way incoming, one-way outgoing, or two-way. For example, you can configure all the domains in Forest A to trust all the domains in Forest B by creating a one-way trust in either Forest B or Forest A. If you also want all the domains in Forest B to trust all the domains in Forest A, you need to create a two-way trust.

You can use forest trusts with partner or closely associated organizations. For example, Coho Vineyard and Coho Vineyard and Winery might not choose to combine their Active Directory structures into a single forest but instead might decide to use a forest trust to give employees of one organization rights and permissions in the other.

Forest trusts can form part of an acquisition or takeover strategy. Northwind Traders has acquired Litware, Inc. The eventual plan is to reorganize the domain structures of both companies into a single forest, but until this process is complete, you might plan a forest trust between the organizations.

You can also use forest trusts for Active Directory isolation. You might, for example, want to run Exchange Server 2010 as part of a migration strategy to try out the new features and familiarize your technical staff with them. However, you do not want to install Microsoft Exchange Server 2010 into your production forest because this could affect your current Exchange Server 2007 deployment. You can create a separate forest in which you can run Exchange Server 2010, but access resources in your production forest while doing so, by setting up a forest trust.

Planning Trust Type and Direction

The most common type of trust that operates across forests is the forest trust, and this is the type of trust discussed in this lesson. You should, however, be aware of the other types of trusts that can be set up with entities outside your forest. These include the following:

- **Shortcut trust**   A forest trust will enable any domain in one forest to trust any domain in another forest. However, if forests are complex, with several layers of child domains, a client in a child domain might take some time to locate resources in a child domain in another forest, especially when the operation happens over a WAN link. If users in one child domain frequently need to access resources in another child domain in another forest, you might decide to create a shortcut trust between the two domains.

- **External trust** You set up a domain trust when a domain within your forest requires a trust relationship with a domain that does not belong to a forest. Typically, external trusts are used when migrating resources from Windows NT domains (many of which still exist). Windows NT does not use the concept of forests, and a Windows NT domain is a self-contained, autonomous unit. If you plan to migrate resources from a Windows NT domain into an existing Active Directory forest, you can establish an external trust between one of the Active Directory domains and the Windows NT domain.

- **Realm trust** If a UNIX realm uses Kerberos authentication, you can create a realm trust between a Windows domain and a UNIX realm. This is similar to an external trust, except that it is between a Windows domain and a UNIX realm.

When you have selected the type of trust you require—typically a forest trust because shortcut, external, and realm trusts are used in specific situations—you then need to decide whether the trust is one-way or two-way and, if the former, what the trust direction is. One-way trusts can be incoming or outgoing.

If users in Forest A require access to resources in Forest B and users in Forest B require access to resources in Forest A, you need to create a two-way trust. Because this is bidirectional, you do not need to specify a direction.

If, however, users in Forest A require access to resources in Forest B but users in Forest B do not require access to resources in Forest A, Forest A is the trusted forest and Forest B the trusting or resource forest. Forest B trusts the users in Forest A and allows them to access its resources. If you are creating a one-way forest trust in a resource forest, it is an incoming trust. If you are creating a one-way forest trust in a trusted forest, it is an outgoing trust.

Imagine the trust as an arrow. The resources are at the point of the arrow. The users that are trusted to use these resources are at the other end. Figure 3-8 shows this relationship. The arrow is incoming at the trusting (resource) forest and outgoing at the trusted forest.

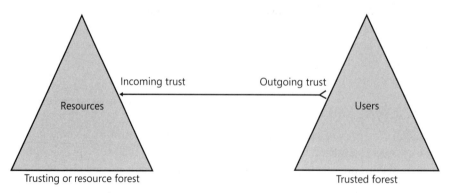

FIGURE 3-8 One-way forest trust relationship

Creating Forest Trusts

Before you can create a forest trust, you need to ensure that the forest functional level of both forests is Windows Server 2003 or later. (Forest functional levels were discussed earlier in this lesson.) Your next step is to ensure that each forest's root domain can access the root domain of the other forest. You need to create the required DNS records and use the nslookup tool to ensure that you can resolve domain names in the other forest. You also need to know the user name and password for an enterprise administrator account (an administrator account in the root domain) in each forest, unless you are setting up only one side of the trust and an administrator in the other forest is setting up the other end.

You create forest trusts by opening Active Directory Domains And Trusts from Administrative Tools. You need to connect the tool to a domain controller in the forest root domain. You then right-click the root domain in the tool's left pane and click Properties. On the Trust tab, click New Trust to start the New Trust Wizard.

The wizard prompts you to enter the domain, forest, or realm name of the trust. To create a forest trust, you enter the domain name of the root domain in the forest with which you want to establish the trust. The wizard asks if you are creating a realm trust or a trust with a Windows domain; select the Windows Domain option. You are then given the choice between creating a forest trust or an external trust. Choose the Forest Trust option and click Next.

At this point, the wizard asks you if you want to establish a one-way incoming, one-way outgoing, or two-way trust. If, for example, you are creating a one-way trust in a resource forest, the trust is incoming. (See Figure 3-8.) In practice, however, a two-way trust is typically the most appropriate choice.

The wizard now asks if you want to configure only your own side of the trust or both sides of the trust. An administrative password for both forest root domains is required to establish the trust. If you have only the administrative password for your own domain, choose the This Domain Only option, and the administrator of the other forest root domain repeats the procedure at the other end. If you know both passwords, you can configure both sides of the trust at the same time.

Next, you need to choose between Forest Wide Authentication and Selective Authentication. Selective Authentication allows you to specify the authentication process in more detail, but it involves a lot more effort. Typically, you will choose Forest Wide Authentication.

MORE INFO   **SELECTIVE AUTHENTICATION**

For more information about enabling Selective Authentication over a forest trust, see *http://technet.microsoft.com/en-us/library/cc794747(WS.10).aspx.*

The wizard displays a summary of the options you have chosen. Click Next to establish the trust. You can then confirm the link.

Active Directory Federation Services

You can create forest trusts between two or more Windows Server 2008 R2 forests (or any combination of Windows Server 2008 R2, Windows Server 2008, and Windows Server 2003 forests). This provides cross-forest access to resources that are located in disparate business units or organizations. However, forest trusts are sometimes not the best option, such as when access across organizations needs to be limited to a small subset of individuals. Active Directory Federation Services (AD FS) enables organizations to allow limited access to their infrastructure to trusted partners. AD FS acts like a cross-forest trust that operates over the Internet and extends the trust relationship to Web applications (a federated trust). It provides Web single sign-on (SSO) technologies that can authenticate a user over the life of a single online session. AD FS securely shares digital identity and entitlement rights (known as *claims*) across security and enterprise boundaries.

Windows Server 2003 R2 introduced AD FS and Windows Server 2008 expanded it. The AD FS features introduced in Windows Server 2008 and retained in Windows Server 2008 R2 include the following:

- **Improved application support**   Windows Server 2008 and Windows Server 2008 R2 integrate AD FS with Microsoft SharePoint Server 2007 and Active Directory Rights Management Services (AD RMS).

- **Improved installation**   AD FS is implemented in Windows Server 2008 and Windows Server 2008 R2 as a server role. The AD FS Installation Wizard includes new server validation checks.

- **Improved trust policy**   Improvements to the trust policy import and export functionality help to minimize configuration issues that are commonly associated with establishing federated trusts.

AD FS extends SSO functionality to Internet-facing applications. Partners experience the same streamlined SSO user experience when they access the organization's Web-based applications as they would when accessing resources through a forest trust. Federation servers can be deployed to facilitate business-to-business (B2B) federated transactions.

AD FS provides a federated identity management solution that interoperates with other security products by conforming to the Web Services Federation (WS-Federation) specification. This specification makes it possible for environments that do not use Windows to federate with Windows environments. It also provides an extensible architecture that supports the Security Assertion Markup Language (SAML) 1.1 token type and Kerberos authentication. AD FS can perform claim mapping—for example, modifying claims using business logic variables in an access request. Organizations can modify AD FS to coexist with their current security infrastructure and business policies.

Finally, AD FS supports distributed authentication and authorization over the Internet. You can integrate it into an organization's existing access management solution to translate the claims that are used in the organization into claims that are agreed on as part of a federation. AD FS can create, secure, and verify claims that move between organizations.

It can also audit and monitor the communication activity between organizations and departments to help ensure secure transactions.

> **MORE INFO** **AD FS**
>
> For more information about AD FS in Windows Server 2008 and Windows Server 2008 R2, access *http://technet.microsoft.com/en-us/library/cc733115.aspx* and follow the links.

Lesson Summary

- Windows Server 2008 introduced a number of new AD DS features, including RODCs, fine-grained security policies, and the data mining tool. These features continue to be implemented in Windows Server 2008 R2.

- RODCs can be installed in branch offices to improve logon and DNS resolution in situations where a writable domain controller would be a security risk.

- You can configure PSOs that hold password and account lockout policies different from the domain policies. You can associate users or security groups with a PSO.

- The data mining tool makes it possible for deleted AD DS or AD LDS data to be preserved in the form of snapshots of AD DS taken by the VSS.

- Windows Server 2008 introduced enhancements to MMC snap-in tools, including Active Directory Users And Computers and Active Directory Sites And Services. These features continue to be implemented in Windows Server 2008 R2.

- Enhancements to AD DS auditing let you determine what AD DS changes have been made and when these changes were made.

- Windows Server 2008 R2 introduces new domain and forest functional levels. If you raise a forest functional level to Windows Server 2008 R2, you can enable the Active Directory Recycle Bin in that forest.

- Forest-level trusts allow users in a domain in one forest to access resources in a domain in a second forest.

Lesson Review

You can use the following questions to test your knowledge of the information in Lesson 1, "Active Directory Directory Services." The questions are also available on the companion CD if you prefer to review them in electronic form.

> **NOTE** **ANSWERS**
>
> Answers to these questions and explanations of why each answer choice is correct or incorrect are located in the "Answers" section at the end of the book.

1. The root domain contoso.com has a domain functional level of Windows Server 2008. All domain controllers in this domain run either Windows Server 2008 or Windows Server 2008 R2. All of the other (non-domain controller) servers in the contoso.com domain run Windows Server 2003 or Windows Server 2008. The two child domains, denver.contoso.com and dallas.contoso.com, have domain functional levels of Windows Server 2008 and Windows Server 2003, respectively. All domain controllers in denver.contoso.com run Windows Server 2008. Some domain controllers in the dallas.contoso.com domain run Windows Server 2003 and the rest run Windows Server 2008. All non-domain controller servers in both child domains run Windows Server 2003. Contoso's technical director is convinced of the advantages offered by an Active Directory Recycle Bin. What do you need to do to activate this facility? (Each correct answer forms part of the solution. Choose four.)

   A. Upgrade all the Windows Server 2008 domain controllers on the contoso.com domain only to Windows Server 2008 R2.

   B. Ensure that every domain controller in all three domains is running Windows Server 2008 R2.

   C. Ensure that every domain controller in the contoso.com domain runs Windows Server 2008 R2 and every domain controller in the two child domains runs Windows Server 2008.

   D. Set the domain functional level to Windows Server 2008 R2 on the root domain only. Set the domain functional level to Windows Server 2008 on the two child domains.

   E. Set the domain functional level to Windows Server 2008 R2 on all three domains.

   F. Raise the forest functional level to Windows Server 2008 R2 on a global catalog server (domain controller) in the root domain.

   G. Raise the forest functional level to Windows Server 2008 R2 on a global catalog server (domain controller) in all three domains.

   H. Run a command based on the Enable-ADOptionalFeature cmdlet.

   I. Run a command based on the Enable-ADAccount cmdlet.

   J. Reconfigure IM FSMO placement.

2. You have created and configured a PSO that contains non-default account lockout policies. To which entities can you apply this PSO? (Each answer is a complete solution. Choose two.)

   A. A global security group

   B. A domain user account

   C. An OU

   D. A global distribution group

   E. A computer account

3. What tool can you use to view Active Directory data stored in snapshots?

   A. SACL

   B. PSC

   C. AS DS data mining tool

   D. AS DS Installation Wizard

4. You plan to migrate resources from a (past lifecycle) Windows NT 4 domain into an existing Active Directory forest. What type of trust do you set up?

   A. A forest trust

   B. An external trust

   C. A realm trust

   D. A shortcut trust

5. You are a domain administrator at Litware, Inc. In collaboration with colleagues at branch offices who are not domain administrators, you have set up RODCs in all of Litware's branch offices. The Password Replication Policy for one of the Litware RODCs needs to be changed. How should this be done?

   A. Ask your branch office colleague who has the right to log on to the RODC at the relevant branch to open Active Directory Users And Computers and ensure that the tool is connected to her branch RODC. She can then change the settings on the Password Replication Policy tab of the RODC's Properties dialog box.

   B. Add the branch office user who has the right to log on interactively to the relevant branch RODC to the Domain Admins group. Ask the user to log on to the RODC and open Server Manager. He can then expand Configuration and access the Password Replication Policy dialog box.

   C. Connect to the relevant RODC by using Remote Desktop. Open Server Manager and expand Configuration. Access the Password Replication Policy dialog box.

   D. Open Active Directory Users And Computers and ensure that the tool is connected to a writable domain controller at the head office. Locate the relevant RODC in the Domain Controllers container and open its Properties dialog box. Make the required change via the Password Replication Policy tab.

6. You are planning to create a two-way forest trust between your company forest and the forest of a recently acquired organization. What minimum forest functional level is required in both organizations?

   A. Windows 2000

   B. Windows 2000 native

   C. Windows Server 2003

   D. Windows Server 2008

   E. Windows Server 2008 R2

7. You plan to use the domain management tool (Netdom.exe) to rename a domain. All of your domain controllers currently run Windows Server 2003, Windows Server 2008, or Windows Server 2008 R2. You do not currently plan to upgrade the Windows Server 2003 domain controllers. What domain functional level supports this plan?

A. Windows Server 2008 R2

B. Windows Server 2008

C. Windows Server 2003

D. Windows 2000 native

E. Windows 2000 mixed

Lesson 2: Active Directory Certificate Services

Certificate Authorities (CAs) are as important to your organization's network infrastructure as domain controllers, DNS, and Dynamic Host Configuration Protocol (DHCP) servers. In this lesson, you learn how certificate templates affect the issuance of digital certificates, how to configure certificates to be assigned to users automatically, and how to configure supporting technologies such as Online Responders and credential roaming. A familiarity with these technologies helps you integrate the use of certificates in your organization's Windows Server 2008 or Windows Server 2008 R2 environment.

After this lesson, you will be able to:

- Install and manage AD CS.
- Configure autoenrollment for certificates.
- Configure credential roaming.
- Configure an Online Responder for Certificate Services.

Estimated lesson time: 45 minutes

Types of Certificate Authority

When planning the deployment of Certificate Services in your network environment, you must decide which type of CA best meets your organizational requirements. There are four types of CA:

- Enterprise Root
- Enterprise Subordinate
- Standalone Root
- Standalone Subordinate

The type of CA that you deploy depends on how certificates will be used in your environment and the state of the existing environment. You have to choose between an Enterprise or a Standalone CA during the installation of the Certificate Services role, as shown in Figure 3-9. You cannot switch between any of the CA types after the CA has been deployed.

Enterprise CAs require access to Active Directory. This type of CA uses Group Policy to propagate the certificate trust lists to users and computers throughout the domain and publish certificate revocation lists (CRLs) to Active Directory. Enterprise CAs issue certificates from certificate templates, which allow the following functionalities:

- Enterprise CAs enforce credential checks on users during the certificate enrollment process. Each certificate template has a set of security permissions that determines whether a particular user is authorized to receive certificates generated from that template.

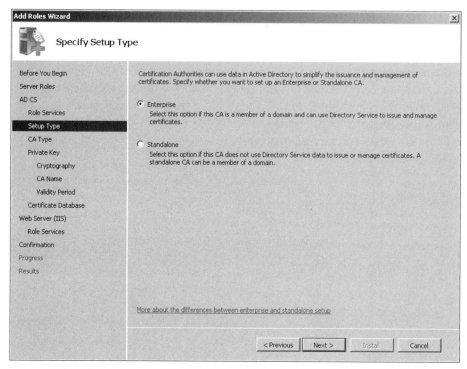

FIGURE 3-9 Selecting an Enterprise or Standalone CA

- Certificate names are generated automatically from information stored within Active Directory. The method by which this is done is determined by certificate template configuration.

- Autoenrollment can be used to issue certificates from Enterprise CAs, vastly simplifying the certificate distribution process. Autoenrollment is configured through applying certificate template permissions.

Enterprise CAs are fully integrated into a Windows Server 2008 or Windows Server 2008 R2 environment. This type of CA makes the issuing and management of certificates for Active Directory clients as simple as possible.

Standalone CAs do not require Active Directory. When certificate requests are submitted to Standalone CAs, the requestor must provide all relevant identifying information and manually specify the type of certificate needed. This process occurs automatically with an Enterprise CA. By default, Standalone CA requests require administrator approval. Administrator intervention is necessary because there is no automated method of verifying a requestor's credentials. Standalone CAs do not use certificate templates, which limits the ability for administrators to customize certificates for specific organizational needs.

You can deploy Standalone CAs on computers that are members of the domain. When installed by a user that is a member of the Domain Admins group, or one who has been delegated similar rights, the Standalone CA's information will be added to the Trusted Root

Certificate Authorities certificate store for all users and computers in the domain. The CA will also be able to publish its CRL to Active Directory.

Whether you install a Root or Subordinate CA depends on whether there is an existing certificate infrastructure. Root CAs are the most trusted type of CA in an organization's public key infrastructure (PKI) hierarchy. Root CAs sit at the top of the hierarchy as the ultimate point of trust and therefore must be as secure as possible. In many environments, a Root CA is used only to issue signing certificates to Subordinate CAs. When not used for this purpose, Root CAs are kept offline in secure environments to reduce the chance that they might be compromised.

If a Root CA is compromised, all certificates within an organization's PKI infrastructure should be considered compromised. Digital certificates are ultimately statements of trust. If you cannot trust the ultimate authority from which that trust is derived, it follows that you should not trust any of the certificates downstream from that authority.

Subordinate CAs are the network infrastructure servers that you deploy to issue the everyday certificates needed by computers, users, and services. An organization can have many Subordinate CAs, each of which is issued a signing certificate by the Root CA. In the event that one Subordinate CA is compromised, trust of that CA can be revoked from the Root CA. Only the certificates that were issued by that CA will be considered untrustworthy. You can replace the compromised Subordinate CA without having to replace the entire organization's certificate infrastructure. Subordinate CAs can be replaced, but a compromised Enterprise Root CA usually means you have to redeploy the Active Directory forest from scratch. If a Standalone Root CA is compromised, it also necessitates the replacement of an organization's PKI infrastructure.

> **MORE INFO** **CERTIFICATE SERVICES OVERVIEW**
>
> For more information about Active Directory Certificate Services in Windows Server 2008 R2, see *http://technet.microsoft.com/en-us/library/cc755071.aspx*.

Certificate Services Role-Based Administration

Because of the integral nature of Certificate Services to an organization's security infrastructure, many organizations use different staff members to manage different aspects of Certificate Services. One team is responsible for managing the CA itself, and a different team is responsible for managing the certificates that are issued by the CA. This separation is implemented through the assignment of Certificate Services roles.

The two critical roles are the CA Administrator and the Certificate Manager. Roles are designated by assigning permissions using the Security tab of the Properties dialog box of the certificate server (the server performing the CA role). You assign the CA Administrator role by granting the Manage CA permission to a user or group. You assign the Certificate Manager role by granting the Issue And Manage Certificates permission to a user or group. By default, the Domain Admins, Enterprise Admins, and local Administrators groups can assign these roles. Figure 3-10 shows that the Alpha global security group holds the Certificate Manager roles because the group is assigned the Issue And Manage Certificates permission.

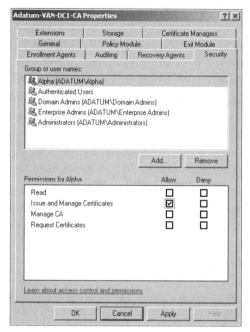

FIGURE 3-10 The Alpha group is assigned the Certificates Manager role

These roles have the following properties:

- **CA Administrator** This role should be assigned to staff who need to configure and maintain the CA itself. Users assigned this role can start and stop the certificate server, configure extensions, assign roles, renew CA keys, define key recovery agents, and configure certificate manager restrictions.

- **Certificate Manager** This role should be assigned to staff who are responsible for approving certificate enrollment and revocation requests. You can restrict certificate managers to specific groups or specific templates. Hence, you can configure one group with the permission to approve certificates issued from one template and configure another group with separate permission to approve certificates issued from a different template. You configure these restrictions on the Certificate Managers tab, shown in Figure 3-11.

MORE INFO **ROLE-BASED ADMINISTRATION**

For more information about implementing Certificate Services role-based administration, see *http://technet.microsoft.com/en-us/library/cc732590.aspx*.

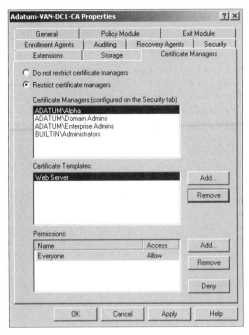

FIGURE 3-11 The Alpha user group can manage Web Server certificates

Installing a Root CA Certificate

Typically, a Root CA certificate is the first AD CS role service that you install in an organization. If your organization has a basic PKI, a Root CA may be the only CA that you need to deploy. The Root CA certificate establishes the basic rules that govern the issuing and use of certificates for your PKI. It defines standards for what is acceptable and unacceptable in the PKI hierarchy and AD CS applies those standards to any other CAs and AD CS role services.

A Root CA can be an Enterprise or Standalone CA. Many organizations minimize the exposure of their Root CA by keeping it offline except when it is needed to process a request for a Subordinate CA certificate.

To install a stand-alone Root CA on a server running Windows Server 2008 or Windows Server 2008 R2, you need (at a minimum) to be a member of the local Administrators group on that server. To install an Enterprise CA, you need (at a minimum) to be a member of the Domain Admins group for the domain. The high-level procedure to install a Root CA certificate is as follows:

1. Click Add Roles in Server Manager. Select the Active Directory Certificate Services role.

2. On the Select Role Services page, click Certification Authority.

3. On the Specify Setup Type page, select either Standalone or Enterprise as appropriate. Note that if you select Enterprise, you must have a network connection to a domain controller.

4. On the Specify CA Type page, click Root CA.

5. On the Set Up Private Key page, click Create A New Private Key.

6. On the Configure Cryptography page, select a cryptographic service provider, key length, and hash algorithm.

> **MORE INFO** **CRYPTOGRAPHIC OPTIONS**
>
> For more information about cryptographic service providers, key lengths, and hash algorithms, see *http://technet.microsoft.com/en-us/library/cc731828.aspx*.

7. On the Configure CA Name page, specify a unique name to identify the CA.

> **MORE INFO** **NAMING A CA**
>
> For more information about CA names, see *http://technet.microsoft.com/en-us/library/cc770402.aspx*.

8. On the Set Validity Period page, specify the number of years or months for which the Root CA certificate will remain valid.

9. On the Configure Certificate Database page, you typically accept the default locations. If you want, you can specify a custom location for the certificate database and the certificate database log.

> **MORE INFO** **THE CERTIFICATES DATABASE**
>
> For more information about the certificates database, see *http://technet.microsoft.com/en-us/library/cc770463.aspx*.

10. On the Confirm Installation Options page, review all your configuration settings. If these are satisfactory, click Install.

> **MORE INFO** **INSTALLING A ROOT CA CERTIFICATE**
>
> For a detailed, step-by step procedure, access *http://technet.microsoft.com/en-us/library/cc731183.aspx*. For more information, follow the links in this article.

Windows Server 2008 R2 Enhancements

Windows Server 2008 R2 retains all the enhancements to AD CS that were implemented by Windows Server 2008, and it introduces the following AD CS features and services that allow more flexible PKI deployments, reduce administration costs, and provide better support for Network Access Protection (NAP) deployments:

- **Certificate Enrollment Web Service and Certificate Enrollment Policy Web Service**   These services enable certificate enrollment over Hypertext Transport Protocol (HTTP).

- **Support for certificate enrollment across forests** This enables CA consolidation in multiple-forest deployments.
- **Improved support for high-volume CAs** This provides reduced CA database sizes for some NAP deployments and other high-volume CAs.

Certificate Enrollment Web Service and Certificate Enrollment Policy Web Service

These new AD CS role services enable policy-based certificate enrollment over HTTP by using methods such as autoenrollment (discussed later in this lesson). The Web services act as a proxy between a client and a CA. This makes direct communication between the client and CA unnecessary and allows certificate enrollment over the Internet and across forests. The certificate enrollment Web services are available in all editions of Windows Server 2008 R2.

For example, Northwind Traders is a large multinational organization whose network infrastructure uses multiple forests. The company has an existing PKI, but it can benefit from the expanded accessibility of certificate enrollment provided by the certificate enrollment Web services, which enable its clients running Windows 7 to use HTTP to enroll certificates from CAs in different forests with Windows Server 2008 R2 schemas. To take advantage of this feature, the organization's Enterprise CA needs to be running the Enterprise or Datacenter edition of Windows Server 2008 R2, Windows Server 2008, or Windows Server 2003.

Trey Research and Contoso, Ltd. are partner organizations whose network infrastructure forms an extranet. Contoso employs a number of mobile workers. The new Web services enable business partners and mobile workers to perform certificate enrollment over the Internet. As with the previous scenario, clients must be running Windows 7, both organizations' Active Directory forests must have Windows Server 2008 R2 schemas, and the Enterprise CAs in both organizations need to be running the Enterprise or Datacenter edition of Windows Server 2008 R2, Windows Server 2008, or Windows Server 2003.

> **CAUTION** **THE CERTIFICATE ENROLLMENT WEB SERVICE CAN MAKE AN EXTRANET MORE VULNERABLE**
>
> The certificate enrollment Web service submits requests on behalf of clients and must therefore be trusted for delegation. For this reason, deploying this Web service over an extranet makes the network infrastructure more vulnerable to attack. As a consequence, some organizations choose not to trust the service for delegation. In such cases, the certificate enrollment Web service and issuing CA can be configured to accept only renewal requests signed with existing certificates, so that delegation is not required.

Certificate Enrollment Across Forests That Have Two-Way Trust Relationships

Before the enhancements to AD CS introduced by Windows Sever 2008 R2, CAs could issue certificates only to members of the same forest, and each forest had its own PKI. Now, with added support for LDAP referrals, Windows Server 2008 R2 CAs can issue certificates across forests that have two-way trust relationships. This facility allows direct enrollment and does not use HTTP.

For instance, in the Northwind Traders example given earlier, if the organization's Enterprise CA is running Windows Server 2008 R2 Enterprise or Windows Server 2008 R2 Datacenter, if each forest had a PKI, and if two-way trust relationships were established between the forests, the CA could issue cross-forest certificates. There are fewer restrictions in this scenario. Provided that the Enterprise CA was running an appropriate edition of Windows Server 2008 R2, the forests would require only a forest functional level of Windows Server 2003 or greater, and clients could be running Window XP, Windows Server 2003, or Windows Vista. Clients do not have to be running Windows 7.

Support for High-Volume CAs

Windows Server organizations whose CAs process a high volume of requests can choose to bypass certain CA database operations to reduce CA database size. For example, a high volume of CA traffic is generated when an organization deploys NAP with Internet Protocol Security (IPsec) enforcement. NAP health certificates typically expire within hours after being issued, and the CA might issue multiple certificates for each computer every day. By default, records for each request and issued certificate are stored in the CA database. A high volume of requests increases the CA database growth rate and administration cost. You can specify that issued certificates are stored elsewhere, not in the CA database on Enterprise CAs running any edition of Windows Server 2008 R2.

If you specify this option, you need to bear in mind that because issued certificates are not stored in the CA database, certificate revocation is not possible. However, maintenance of a CRL for a high volume of short-lived certificates is often impractical or non-beneficial, and therefore you might choose to use this feature and accept the revocation limitation.

Configuring Credential Roaming

Credential roaming allows for the storage of certificates and private keys within Active Directory. For example, a user's Encrypting File System (EFS) certificate can be stored in Active Directory and provided to the user when she logs on to different computers within the domain. The same EFS certificate will always be used to encrypt files. This means that the user can encrypt files on an NTFS-formatted USB storage device on one computer and then decrypt them on another because the EFS certificate will be transferred to the second computer's certificate store during the logon process. Credential roaming also allows for all of a user's certificates and keys to be removed when she logs off the computer.

Credential roaming is enabled through the Certificate Services Client – Credential Roaming Policy, located through the Group Policy Management feature in Server Manager under User Configuration/Policies/Windows Settings/Security Settings/Public Key Policies, as shown in Figure 3-12.

FIGURE 3-12 Credential Roaming Policy

When a user logs on to a client in a domain where the Credential Roaming Policy has been enabled, the certificates in the user's store on the client are compared to certificates stored for the user within Active Directory.

- If the certificates in the user's certificate store are up to date, no further action is taken.
- If more recent certificates for the user are stored in Active Directory, these credentials are copied to the client.
- If more recent certificates are located in the user's store, the certificates stored in Active Directory are updated.

Credential roaming synchronizes and resolves any conflicts between certificates and private keys from any number of clients that a user logs on to, as well as certificates and private keys stored within Active Directory. Credential roaming is triggered whenever a private key or certificate in the local certificate store changes, whenever the user locks or unlocks a computer, and whenever Group Policy refreshes. Credential roaming is supported on Windows Server 2008 R2, Windows Server 2008, Windows Server 2003 SP1, Windows 7, Windows Vista, and Windows XP SP2.

> **MORE INFO** **CREDENTIAL ROAMING**
>
> For more information on credential roaming, see *http://technet.microsoft.com/en-us/library/cc770797.aspx.*

Configuring Autoenrollment

Autoenrollment allows certificates to be distributed to clients without direct client intervention. It also enables the automatic enrollment of subjects for specific certificates and allows for the retrieval of issued certificates and the automatic renewal of expiring certificates without the need for subject or administrator intervention. In most cases, autoenrollment occurs without the user being aware of it, although you can configure certificate templates in such a way that they do interact with the subjects.

Configuring a Template for Autoenrollment

Before a certificate can be enrolled automatically, it is necessary to configure several aspects of the certificate template. Certificate templates are modified using the Certificate Templates snap-in, which you will need to add to a custom MMC. Only users with the Certificate Manager role's permissions are able to create and modify certificate templates.

When using the Certificate Templates console, note that you cannot configure the autoenrollment permission for a Level 1 certificate template. Level 1 certificates have Windows 2000 as their minimum supported CA. Level 2 certificate templates have Windows Server 2003 as a minimum supported CA. Level 2 certificate templates are also the minimum level of certificate template that supports autoenrollment. Level 3 certificate templates are supported only by clients running Windows Server 2008, Windows Server 2008 R2, Windows Vista, or Windows 7. Level 3 certificate templates allow administrators to configure advanced Suite B cryptographic settings. These settings are not required to allow certificate autoenrollment, and most administrators find Level 2 certificate templates are adequate for their organizational needs.

If you do create a new certificate template based on an existing one, you should configure the template you copied as a superseded template. This allows certificates that are configured using previous settings to be updated to the new settings. You will also need to configure the CA to publish this new template through the Certification Authority console. To configure automatic certificate enrollment for a specific template, perform these steps:

1. Open the Certificate Templates snap-in.
2. Right-click the certificate template that you want to modify, and then click Properties.
3. Configure the General, Request Handling, and Issuance Requirements as necessary for the purposes of the certificate. (Note that not every certificate template has all three tabs in its Properties dialog box. For example, the Basic EFS certificate template does not have an Issuance Requirements tab. In addition, note that this step is not necessary for autoenrollment, but you should review these settings because they allow you to tune the automatic issuing of certificates better.)
4. On the Certificate Template's Security tab, select the group that you will allow to enroll certificates automatically and the select the Allow box next to the Autoenroll permission. Figure 3-13 shows autoenrollment configured for the Authenticated Users group for Kerberos authentication, which is a Level 2 certificate template.

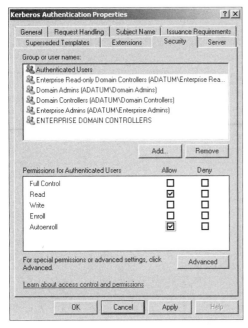

FIGURE 3-13 Enabling the autoenroll permission to allow automatic enrollment

Configuring Group Policy for Autoenrollment

After you have set up the permissions on certificate templates, your next step in deploying autoenrollment of certificates throughout your organization is to configure the default domain policy to support autoenrollment. To configure Group Policy for autoenrollment, perform the following steps:

1. Edit the Default Domain Policy GPO using the Group Policy Management Console feature located in Server Manager under Features.

2. Under User Configuration/Policies/Windows Settings/Security Settings/Public Key Policies, double-click Certificate Services Client – Auto-Enrollment. This will open the Certificate Services Client – Auto-Enrollment Properties policy dialog box.

3. Choose Enabled from the Configuration Model drop-down list and then configure the expiration and update settings as shown in Figure 3-14.

After you enable the Certificate Services autoenrollment policy, those certificates that have templates configured for autoenrollment will be deployed automatically. You can also enable the following policy options as a part of the autoenrollment policy:

■ **Renew Expired Certificates, Update Pending Certificates, And Remove Revoked Certificates** This policy primarily relates to certificate management. If you have enabled autoenrollment, you will probably want to ensure that expired certificates are renewed automatically, revoked certificates are removed, and pending certificates are updated. Enabling this option vastly reduces the workload of certificate administrators.

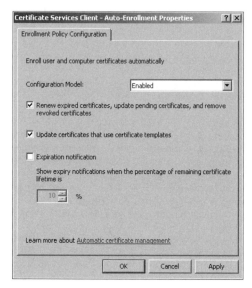

FIGURE 3-14 Configuring autoenrollment policies

- **Update Certificates That Use Certificate Templates** When this policy is enabled and the template that the certificate was issued from is revised or replaced, the issued certificate will be updated.
- **Expiration Notification** This policy is less necessary when you configure expired certificates to renew automatically, but it can be useful when certificate templates are configured so that automatic renewal (rather than automatic enrollment) does not occur.

MORE INFO **CONFIGURING AUTOENROLLMENT**

For more information about configuring autoenrollment, see *http://technet.microsoft.com/en-us/library/cc731522.aspx*.

 Quick Check

1. What sort of CA should you install as the first CA in your environment if you want to integrate certificates with Active Directory?

2. Which clients and CAs support Level 3 templates?

Quick Check Answers

1. Enterprise Root CA

2. Windows Vista, Windows 7, Windows Server 2008, and Windows Server 2008 R2 support Level 3 templates.

Configuring Web Enrollment Support

Web enrollment allows users of Windows Internet Explorer version 6 and later to submit certificate requests to a CA directly through a Web application. You can use Web enrollment to do any of the following:

- Request certificates and review existing certificate requests
- Access CRLs
- Perform smart card enrollment

Web enrollment is deployed primarily to provide an enrollment mechanism for organizations that need to issue and renew certificates for users and computers that are not joined to an Active Directory domain or who are using non-Microsoft operating systems. Users of browsers other than Internet Explorer version 6 and later are able to submit enrollment requests using the Web enrollment application, but they must first create a Public-Key Cryptography Standards (PKCS) #10 request before submitting it through the Web enrollment pages. Once the request is made successfully, users can reconnect to the Web enrollment application and are able to download and install their requested certificates.

> **MORE INFO   PKCS #10**
>
> For more information about PKCS #10, see *http://tools.ietf.org/html/rfc2986*. However, the examination is not likely to test your knowledge of detailed PKCS.

To configure a server to support Web enrollment, the Certification Authority Web Enrollment role service needs to be added to the server role. When the Certification Authority Web Enrollment role service is installed on a computer that is operating as a CA, no future configuration steps are required. If the Certification Authority Web Enrollment service is installed on a separate computer from the CA, the CA needs to be specified during the Certification Authority Web Enrollment role service installation process.

Web enrollment has the following limitations:

- Web enrollment cannot be used with version 3 certificate templates. Only version 1 and 2 certificate templates are supported by Web enrollment.
- Computer certificates cannot be requested using Web enrollment from a Windows Server 2008 or Windows Server 2008 R2 CA.
- If Microsoft Internet Information Services (IIS) is installed on a 64-bit version of Windows Server 2008 or on Windows Server 2008 R2, some 32-bit Web applications cannot be installed because this will force IIS to run in 32-bit mode. The Web enrollment role service will attempt to install as a 64-bit Web application, and the installation will fail. This does not apply to 32-bit versions of Windows Server 2008.

> **MORE INFO   SETTING UP WEB ENROLLMENT**
>
> For more information on setting up Web enrollment support, see *http://technet .microsoft.com/en-us/library/cc732895.aspx*.

Configuring CRLs

Certificate Services do more than issue certificates. Certificates are tokens of trust, and in certain cases those tokens of trust need to be revoked. This process is called *certificate revocation*. The most common method of publishing information about which certificates issued by a CA are no longer valid is the certificate revocation list (CRL). CRLs are lists of certificate serial numbers for certificates that have either been revoked or are placed on hold. CRLs are issued by the CA that issues the corresponding certificate, rather than an upstream or a downstream CA. When a certificate is to be used, a check against the issuing CA's CRL needs to be made. The location of the CRL is included with the certificate so that the client knows where on the network to look to verify that the certificate that it is about to accept is still actually valid.

Specifying a CRL Distribution Point

The Extensions tab on a Certificate Server's Properties dialog box, shown in Figure 3-15, allows you to add, remove, or modify CRL distribution points. When you make a modification to the list of distribution points, you should be aware that this will apply only to certificates issued from that point on; it does not apply retroactively. Your user account must have been assigned the Certificate Manager role to modify CRL distribution point configuration information. CRL Uniform Resource Locators (URLs) can use HTTP, FTP, LDAP, or FILE addresses.

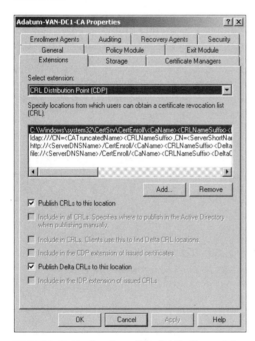

FIGURE 3-15 Configuring a CRL distribution point

Configuring CRL and Delta CRL Publication

Because CRLs can become very large, you can publish a smaller type of CRL called a delta CRL at a more frequent interval. A delta CRL contains only data about certificates that have been revoked since the publication of the last full CRL. This allows clients to retrieve the small delta CRL and add it to a cached copy of the full CRL to build a complete list of revoked certificates. Delta CRLs allow for revocation data to be published more frequently, which makes the deployment of Certificate Services more secure. An outdated CRL cannot be used to inform clients of the most recent revocations because these revocations will not be published until the next time the full CRL is published.

The CRL and delta CRL publication intervals are configured by modifying the properties of the Revoked Certificates node on a CA, as shown in Figure 3-16. You can access this dialog box by right-clicking Revoked Certificates under the CA in the Server Manager console and clicking Properties. The default CRL publication interval is once a week, and the default delta CRL publication interval is once a day.

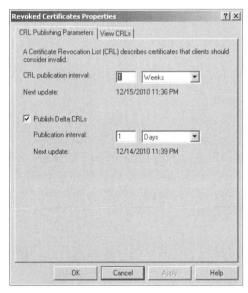

FIGURE 3-16 Configuring CRL publication interval

MORE INFO **REVOCATION**

For more information on configuring certificate revocation, see *http://technet.microsoft .com/en-us/library/cc771079.aspx.*

Configuring an Online Responder for Certificate Services

Significant delays in CRL publication can occur during periods of peak activity, such as when large numbers of users log on using smart cards, encrypt files, or use digital signatures. This is because the entire CRL has to be checked and, as mentioned earlier in the lesson, CRLs can become very large. CRL checks cannot be load-balanced to another CA if the issuing CA is experiencing a traffic spike. Attempts have been made to solve this problem using solutions such as partitioned CRLs, delta CRLs, and indirect CRLs. All these prior solutions ended up increasing the complexity of CA implementation without significantly reducing the problem of traffic spikes. This is where Online Certificate Status Protocol (OCSP) comes in.

An Online Responder receives and responds only to requests about the status of individual certificates. For example, rather than having to download the CA's entire CRL to see whether the signing certificate issued to Don Hall is valid, the client queries the Online Responder to see if Don Hall's signing certificate is valid and receives a response that provides only information about Don Hall's signing certificate. This significantly reduces the load on the issuing CA and also reduces network traffic. CRLs can get very large, and distributing a CRL to each of 100 clients can use a lot of bandwidth. Depending on the size of the CRL, providing revocation information about 100 different specific certificates may use less bandwidth than forwarding the current CRL to a single client.

Windows Server 2008 and Windows Server 2008 R2 OCSP includes the following features:

- **Web proxy caching**   The Online Responder Web proxy cache is the interface that clients connect with to access Online Responder data. It is implemented as an Internet Server Application Programming Interface (ISAPI) extension hosted by IIS.

- **Support for nonce and no-nonce requests**   You can set nonce and no-nonce request configuration options to prevent replay attacks on Online Responders. Replay attacks work by either repeating or delaying the transmission of legitimate data. A replay attack could be used to indicate that a revoked certificate is still valid.

> **MORE INFO   NONCE AND NO-NONCE REQUESTS**
>
> A *nonce* is a unique identifier included in an OCSP request. For more information about nonce and no-nonce requests, see *http://technet.microsoft.com/en-us/library/ee619783(WS.10).aspx*.

- **Advanced cryptography support**   You can configure OCSP to use elliptic curve and SHA-256 cryptography.

- **Kerberos protocol integration**   OCSP requests and responses can be processed with Kerberos password authentication, allowing for the validation of server certificates during the logon process.

- **Single point or responder array**   A single computer can function as an Online Responder, or multiple linked computers can host Online Responders, allowing for certificate validity checks to be balanced across multiple hosts.

You can install the Online Responder service on a CA, but Microsoft recommends deploying the Online Responder service on a separate computer. A single computer with the Online Responder service deployed can provide revocation status data for certificates issued by a single or multiple CAs. As mentioned earlier, a single CA's revocation data can be distributed across multiple Online Responders.

The Online Responder service is installed on computers running Windows Server 2008 and Windows Server 2008 R2 and is managed through the Online Responder MMC snap-in, shown in Figure 3-17. Note that you cannot access this console until you deploy an Online Responder, which you do in a practice later in this chapter.

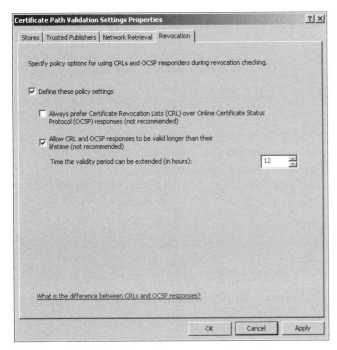

FIGURE 3-17 The Online Responder management console

You should deploy Online Responders after the deployment of CAs but prior to the issuance of client certificates. To deploy the Online Responder service to a computer running Windows Server 2008 or Windows Server 2008 R2, the following conditions must be met:

- IIS must already be installed on the computer that will host the Online Responder service.

- An OCSP Response Signing certificate template must be configured on the CA, and autoenrollment must be used to issue an OCSP Response Signing certificate to the computer that will host the Online Responder service. An Online Responder cannot provide status information for a certificate issued from a CA higher in the CA chain than the one that issued its signing certificate.

- The URL for the Online Responder must be included in the Authority Information Access (AIA) extension of certificates issued by the CA. This URL will be used by clients to locate the Online Responder so that certificate validation can occur.

After you have deployed the Online Responder, you create a revocation configuration for each CA and CA certificate that will be serviced by the Online Responder. Revocation configurations include all settings required to reply to client status requests with respect to certificates issued using a specific CA key. These settings include the CA certificate, signing certificate for the Online Responder, and the revocation provider that provides revocation data used by the revocation configuration. When configuring a single Online Responder for multiple CAs, ensure that the Online Responder has a key and signing certificate for each CA that it supports. In the practice at the end of this lesson, you will configure an Online Responder.

Configuring Responder Arrays

If the Online Responder that you have deployed in your network environment is unable to cope with projected traffic, you can deploy an array of computers functioning as Online Responders. As mentioned earlier in this lesson, an array of Online Responders can handle the revocation traffic of one or more issuing CAs. Online Responder Arrays are also often deployed for fault-tolerance purposes. Nodes in Online Responder Arrays can also be deployed at branch or satellite office locations that have only intermittent network connectivity to the site that hosts the issuing CA.

Online Responder Arrays have one member of the array configured as the Array controller and the rest as array members. Although each Online Responder in an array can be managed and configured separately when conflicts arise, the configuration settings for the Array controller override configuration settings for array members.

To create an Online Responder Array you need to perform the following general steps:

1. Configure the CAs in your organization that are used to issue certificates to support Online Responders.

2. Add the Online Responder service to all servers that will participate in the planned array.

3. Add the Online Responders to the array by opening the Online Responder console, selecting the Array Configuration Members node, and using the Add Array Members item in the Actions pane.

OCSP Group Policy Settings

Windows Server 2008 and Windows Server 2008 R2 include several Group Policy settings that enhance the management of OCSP and CRL data use. To access these settings, edit Default Domain Policy in the console tree of Server Manager and access the Revocation tab of the Properties dialog box located at Computer Configuration/Policies/Windows Settings/Security Settings/Public Key Policies/Certificate Path Validation Settings node. This is shown in Figure 3-18.

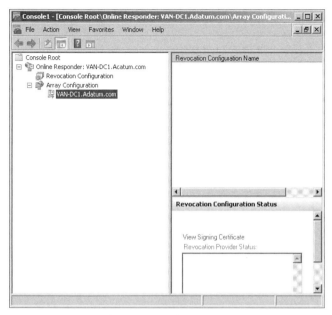

FIGURE 3-18 Group Policy options related to OCSP

One of the reasons for configuring these policies is that CRLs have expiration dates and if the expiration date passes prior to the update becoming available, the certificate chain validation might fail, even with an Online Responder deployed. Problems can occur when an Online Responder is forced to rely upon an expired CRL. By selecting Allow CRL And OCSP Responses To Be Valid Longer Than Their Lifetime, you can effectively issue an extension to CRLs in the event that they are not updated in a timely manner.

> **MORE INFO** **MANAGING ONLINE RESPONDERS**
>
> For more information about managing online responders, access *http://technet.microsoft .com/en-us/library/cc725644.aspx* and follow the links.

Network Device Enrollment Service

The Network Device Enrollment Service allows a Windows Server 2008 or Windows Server 2008 R2 CA to issue and manage certificates for routers and other network devices that do not have accounts within the Active Directory database. The Network Device Enrollment Service allows network devices to obtain certificates based on the Simple Certificate Enrollment Protocol (SCEP). The Network Device Enrollment Service provides the following functionalities to a network environment:

- Generates and provides one-time enrollment passwords to administrators of network devices
- Submits SCEP enrollment requests on behalf of network devices to a Windows Server 2008 CA
- Retrieves issued certificates from the CA and directs them to the network device

By default, the Network Device Enrollment Service can cache only five passwords at a time. This limits the number of network devices that can participate in the enrollment process to five. It is possible to flush stored passwords from the cache by restarting IIS, and it is also possible to configure the Network Device Enrollment Service to cache more than five passwords at a time.

> **MORE INFO** **ENROLLING NETWORK DEVICES**
>
> For more information about using the Network Device Enrollment Service to enroll devices, see *http://technet.microsoft.com/en-us/library/cc753784(WS.10).aspx*.

Using Enterprise PKI to Monitor CA Health

You can add the Enterprise PKI snap-in to a custom console (shown in Figure 3-19) to monitor the health of all CAs within a PKI. The Enterprise PKI tool allows you to view the status of your organization's PKI environment. In an organization that has multiple levels of issuing CAs, having an at-a-glance view of all certificate servers allows administrators to manage the CA hierarchy and troubleshoot CA errors easily and effectively. The Enterprise PKI snap-in provides data on the validity or accessibility of AIA locations and CRL distribution points.

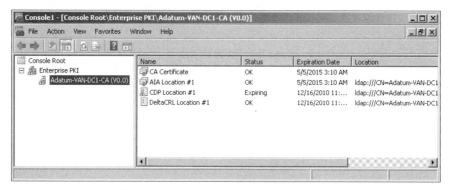

FIGURE 3-19 Enterprise PKI custom console

The Enterprise PKI snap-in works on both Windows Server 2008 and Windows Server 2003 Enterprise CAs. The Enterprise PKI tool provides the following status information about each CA in the PKI hierarchy:

- **Question Mark** Health status is being evaluated.
- **Green Indicator** CA is problem-free.
- **Yellow Indicator** CA has a non-critical problem.
- **Red Indicator** CA has a critical problem.
- **Red Cross Over CA Icon** CA is offline.

The most common configuration problems are likely to be the second AIA location, the second delta CRL location, and the CDP location. When confronted with CA configuration issues, you should use the following strategies in an attempt to resolve the issue:

■ If the issue is CA-related, such as problems connecting to a current CRL, use the Certification Authority console to manage the problem by connecting to the CA experiencing the problem.

■ If the issue relates to the Online Responder, use the Online Responder Management console to resolve the issue.

■ If the Enterprise PKI console reports that CA certificates are about to expire, you should use the Certificates snap-in of a custom console to renew these certificates.

■ It is possible to enable CryptoAPI 2.0 diagnostics to obtain detailed information about PKI-related issues. This is done by enabling the Operational log under Applications And Service Logs/Microsoft/Windows/CAPI2 log in Event Viewer, shown in Figure 3-20.

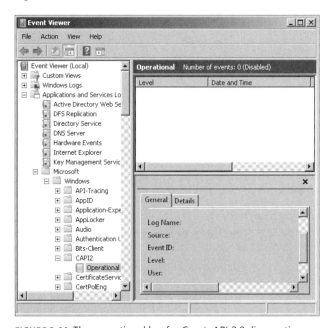

FIGURE 3-20 The operational log for CryptoAPI 2.0 diagnostics

---

MORE INFO **ENTERPRISE PKI**

For more information about the Enterprise PKI, access *http://technet.microsoft.com/ en-us/library/cc771400.aspx* and follow the links.

Lesson Summary

- Enterprise CAs are used to support Active Directory. Enterprise CAs are added automatically to the domain user's trusted certificate stores. Most certificate service deployments in Windows Server 2008 and Windows Server 2008 R2 network environments use Enterprise CAs.

- Standalone CAs do not require the deployment of Active Directory and cannot be configured to use certificate templates.

- Online Responders process requests for CRL data more efficiently than traditional CRL publishing methods.

- Credential caching ensures that a user's certificates are up to date by frequently comparing local certificates with certificates stored in Active Directory.

- Autoenrollment allows certificates to be deployed automatically, without user or administrator intervention, to eligible clients. Autoenrollment has to be enabled within a certificate template and within Group Policy.

- Windows Server 2008 R2 introduces AD CS features and services that allow more flexible PKI deployments, reduce administration costs, and provide better support for NAP deployments.

Lesson Review

You can use the following questions to test your knowledge of the information in Lesson 2, "Active Directory Certificate Services." The questions are also available on the companion CD if you prefer to review them in electronic form.

> **NOTE ANSWERS**
>
> Answers to these questions and explanations of why each answer choice is correct or incorrect are located in the "Answers" section at the end of the book.

1. Digital certificates distributed through autoenrollment are used widely at a company's head office location. Which of the following CA types would you deploy to a regional branch office to issue certificates in support of autoenrollment policies configured within the default domain GPO?

   A. Enterprise Root CA

   B. Enterprise Subordinate CA

   C. Standalone Root CA

   D. Standalone Subordinate CA

2. Which of the following steps must you take before deploying autoenrollment? (Each correct answer forms part of the solution. Choose two.)

   A. Configure Group Policy to support autoenrollment.

   B. Configure autoenrollment permissions on certificate templates.

C. Modify CRL publication settings.

   D. Configure an Online Responder.

   E. Configure Web Enrollment.

3. You want to configure the ocsp.adatum.com server as an Online Responder for ca1.
   adatum.com. The oscp.adatum.com server has IIS installed. Which of the following
   steps will you need to take as a part of this process? (Each correct answer forms part of
   the solution. Choose three.)

   A. Install an OCSP Response Signing certificate on ca1.adatum.com.

   B. Configure an OSCP Response Signing certificate template on ca1.adatum.com.

   C. Install an OCSP Response Signing certificate on ocsp.adatum.com.

   D. Configure the AIA extension with the URL ocsp.adatum.com.

   E. Configure the AIA extension with the URL ca1.adatum.com.

4. Your organization's Queensland branch office makes extensive use of digital
   certificates. Queensland satellite offices have similar usage patterns. The Queensland
   branch office has a single Enterprise Root CA, from which all certificates in Queensland
   are issued. Due to low-bandwidth WAN links, it sometimes takes a long time for clients
   in the satellite offices to validate the authenticity of certificates that have already been
   issued. Which of the following steps can you take to improve certificate validation
   times for clients in satellite offices?

   A. Deploy an Enterprise Subordinate CA at the branch office.

   B. Deploy an Enterprise Subordinate CA at each satellite office.

   C. Deploy a Standalone Subordinate CA at the branch office.

   D. Place an Online Responder at each satellite office. Configure an Online Responder
   Array.

5. Which of the following tools can you use to view the health of multiple CAs in your
   organization's PKI environment?

   A. The Certification Authority console

   B. The Online Responder Management console

   C. The Enterprise PKI

   D. The Certificates MMC snap-in

PRACTICE Raising Domain and Forest Functional Levels, Enabling
the Active Directory Recycle Bin, and Configuring
Fine-Grained Password Policy

In this practice, you create and configure a PSO that contains a password policy different than
the default policy in the contoso.internal domain. Before you do this, however, you need to
raise the functional levels of the domain and forest.

NOTE   **LOGGING ON TO THE DOMAIN CONTROLLER**

For the sake of brevity and convenience, this practice (and others in this book) asks you to log on interactively to the domain controller. You should be aware that in a production domain, you probably would not do so. You would instead log on at a workstation and create a Remote Desktop connection to the domain controller, or you would install RSAT on a workstation, open the relevant tool on the workstation, and connect it to the domain controller.

EXERCISE 1   Raise the Domain Functional Level

In this exercise, you raise the domain functional level. You do this first because the forest functional level cannot be higher than the functional level of any domain within the forest.

1. Log on to VAN-DC1 with the Kim Akers account.

2. On the Administrative Tools menu, open Active Directory Domains And Trusts.

3. In the console tree, right-click the adatum.com domain. Click Raise Domain Functional Level, as shown in Figure 3-21.

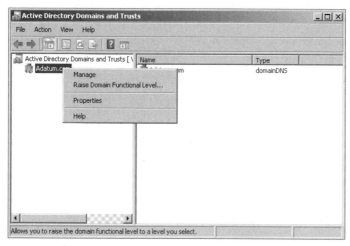

FIGURE 3-21 The Raise Domain Functional Level control

4. Check the functional level of the domain. If this is already Windows Server 2008 R2, you do not need to do the rest of this exercise. In this case, click Close, close Active Directory Domains And Trusts, and proceed to Exercise 2.

5. If the domain functional level is anything but Windows Server 2008 R2, select the highest available functional level from the Select An Available Domain Functional Level drop-down box, click Raise, click OK in the Raise Domain Functional Level dialog box, and then click OK again. Repeat this process until the domain functional level is Windows Server 2008 R2.

6. Click Close. Close Active Directory Domains And Trusts.

EXERCISE 2 Raise the Forest Functional Level

In this exercise, you raise the forest functional level. Do not attempt this exercise until you have completed Exercise 1 (if needed).

1. If necessary, log on to VAN-DC1 with the Kim Akers account and open Active Directory Domains And Trusts.

2. In the console tree, right-click Active Directory Domains And Trusts.

3. Right-click Raise Forest Functional Level.

4. Check the functional level of the forest. If this is already Windows Server 2008 R2, you do not need to do the rest of this exercise. In this case, click OK and then close Active Directory Domains And Trusts and go on to Exercise 3.

5. If the forest functional level is anything but Windows Server 2008 R2, select the highest available forest functional level from the Select An Available Forest Functional Level drop-down box. Figure 3-22 shows the selection of the Windows Server 2008 R2 forest functional level. Click Raise, click OK in the Raise Forest Functional Level dialog box, and then click OK again.

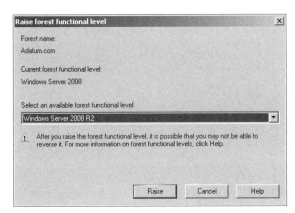

FIGURE 3-22 The Windows Server 2008 R2 forest functional level

6. Repeat this process until the forest functional level is Windows Server 2008 R2.

7. Click OK. Close Active Directory Domains And Trusts.

> **NOTE** **ALTERNATIVE METHODS OF RAISING THE DOMAIN AND FOREST FUNCTIONAL LEVELS**
>
> You can also use the Active Directory Administrative Center or the Active Directory Module for Windows PowerShell to raise domain and forest functional levels. As an extension to Exercises 1 and 2, find out how to do this.

EXERCISE 3   Enable the Active Directory Recycle Bin

When the forest functional level is Windows Server 2008 R2, you can enable the Active Directory Recycle Bin. Do not attempt this exercise until you have completed Exercises 1 and 2 (as needed).

1. If necessary, log off of VAN-DC1 with the Kim Akers account and log on again with the built-in domain Administrator account. (Note that this is one of the very few occasions when the Kim Akers account has insufficient privileges and the built-in Administrator account needs to be used.)

2. Click Start, click All Programs, and then open the Active Directory Module for Windows PowerShell from the Administrative Tools menu.

> *NOTE*   **OPENING THE ACTIVE DIRECTORY MODULE FOR WINDOWS POWERSHELL**
>
> If the VAN-DC1 domain controller is configured as described in Appendix A, this module should open without reporting an error. If, however, you get a message informing you that the module was unable to locate a default server running Active Directory Web Services (AD WS), then you might need to install a Root CA certificate and open TCP port 9389 on VAN-DC1. Refer to the server Help files if you are unsure how to carry out these tasks.

3. When the Active Directory Module for Windows PowerShell is running without reporting errors, enter the following command:

```
Enable-ADOptionalFeature -Identity 'CN=Recycle Bin Feature,CN=Optional
Features,CN=Directory Service,CN=Windows NT,CN=Services,CN=Configuration,
DC=adatum,DC=com' -Scope ForestOrConfigurationSet -Target 'adatum.com'
```

EXERCISE 4   Create a PSO

In this exercise, you create a PSO with password policies that are not the same as the default password policies for the adatum.com domain. You associate this with a global security group called special_password that contains the user Don Hall. Do not attempt this exercise until you have completed the previous three exercises.

1. If necessary, log on to VAN-DC1 with the Kim Akers account. If you are already logged on with the built-in domain Administrator account, you can complete the exercise. However, it is a good idea to use the built-in account as seldom as possible.

2. If you have not already done so, create a user account for Don Hall as described in the section entitled "Before You Begin," earlier in this chapter.

3. Create a global security group called special_password. Make Don Hall a member of special_password.

4. In the Run box, enter **adsiedit.msc**.

5. If this is the first time you have used the ADSI Edit console on your test network, right-click ADSI Edit, and then click Connect To. Type **adatum.com** in the Name box, and then click OK.

6. In the console tree, double-click adatum.com.

7. Double-click DC=adatum,DC=com.

8. Double-click CN=System.

9. Right-click CN=Password Settings Container. Click New. Click Object, as shown in Figure 3-23.

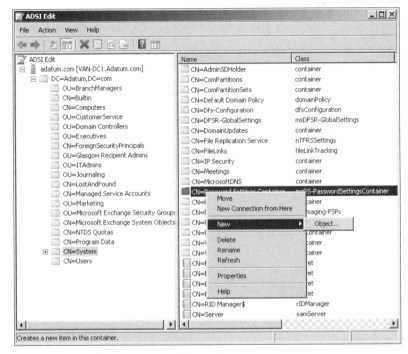

FIGURE 3-23 Creating a password settings object

10. In the Create Object dialog box, ensure that msDS-PasswordSettings is selected. Click Next.

11. In the CN box, type **PSO1**. Click Next.

12. In the msDS-PasswordSettingsPrecedence box, type **10**. Click Next.

13. In the msDS-PasswordReversibleEncryptionEnabled box, type **FALSE**. Click Next.

14. In the msDS-PasswordHistoryLength box, type **6**. Click Next.

15. In the msDS-PasswordComplexityEnabled box, type **FALSE**. Click Next.

16. In the msDS-MinimumPasswordLength box, type **6**. Click Next.

17. In the msDS-MinimumPasswordAge box, type **1:00:00:00**. Click Next.

18. In the msDS-MaximumPasswordAge box, type **20:00:00:00**. Click Next.

19. In the msDS-LockoutThreshold box, type **2**. Click Next.

20. In the msDS-LockoutObservationWindow box, type **0:00:15:00**. Click Next.

21. In the msDS-LockoutDuration box, type **0:00:15:00**. Click Next.

22. Click Finish.

23. Open Active Directory Users And Computers, click View, and then click Advanced Features.

24. Expand adatum.com, expand System, and then click Password Settings Container.

25. Right-click PSO1. Click Properties.

26. On the Attribute Editor tab, select msDS-PSOAppliesTo, as shown in Figure 3-24.

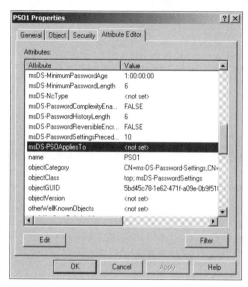

FIGURE 3-24 Selecting an attribute to edit

27. Click Edit.

28. Click Add Windows Account.

29. Type **special_password** in the Enter The Object Names To Select box. Click Check Names.

30. Click OK. The Multi-Valued Distinguished Name With Security Principal Editor dialog box should look similar to Figure 3-25.

31. Click OK, and then click OK again to close the PSO1 Properties dialog box.

32. Test your settings by changing the password for the Don Hall account to a non-complex, six-letter password, such as **simple**.

    It is interesting to note that when you access Active Directory Users And Computers when logged on as Kim Akers (or the domain Administrator) and change Don Hall's password to **simple**, you can then log off and test the setting by logging on as Don Hall. You cannot, however, log on as Don Hall using the original (complex) password and then use Ctrl-Alt-Del to change your password to **simple**. Experiment with the new settings and determine what you can and cannot do.

FIGURE 3-25 Adding the special_password global security group to PSO1

PRACTICE **Deploy Active Directory Certificate Services and an Online Responder**

In this practice, you install the Active Directory Certificate Services role on VAN-DC1, if this has not already been installed. You then deploy and configure an Online Responder. To complete this practice, perform the following steps:

EXERCISE 1   Deploying AD CS

1. Log on to VAN-DC1 using the Kim Akers user account. If you are already logged on with the built-in domain Administrator account, log off and log on as Kim Akers. When Server Manager opens, expand Roles in the console tree. (If the Server Manager console does not open automatically, open it from the Administrative Tools menu.) If the Active Directory Certificate Services role is already listed, you do not need to complete this exercise and should go on to Exercise 2.

2. Right-click Roles, and click Add Roles. On the Select Server Roles page, select Active Directory Certificate Services and click Next twice. On the Select Role Services page, verify that Certification Authority and Certification Authority Web Enrollment are selected. If you are prompted to install additional role services and features for the Web Server (IIS) and Windows Process Activation Service, click Add Required Role Services. Click Next.

3. On the Specify Setup Type page, ensure that Enterprise is selected, and then click Next.

4. On the Specify CA Type page, ensure that Root CA is selected, and then click Next.

5. On the Set Up Private Key page, ensure that Create A New Private Key is selected, and then click Next.

6. On the Configure Cryptography for CA page, verify that the RSA#Microsoft Software Key Storage Provider CSP is selected, that a Key Character Length of 2048 is selected, and that the hash algorithm is set to SHA1 and then click Next.

7. Verify that the Common Name For This CA: is set to Adatum-VAN-DC1-CA and then click Next.

8. Accept the default validity period of 5 years, and then click Next until you reach the Confirm Installation Selections page. Click Install. When the installation process completes, click Close.

EXERCISE 2 Deploying an Online Responder

In this exercise, you install the Online Responder service as a component of the Active Directory Certificate Services role.

1. If necessary, log on to VAN-DC1 with the Kim Akers account.

2. From the Administrative Tools menu, open the Certification Authority console. Verify that Adatum-VAN-DC1-CA has a green tick icon next to it.

3. Select the Certificate Templates node. Verify that the list of certificate templates matches the list in Figure 3-26.

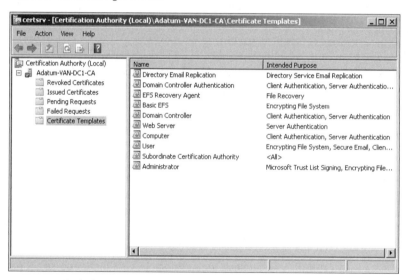

FIGURE 3-26 Default post-installation templates

4. Close the Certification Authority console.

5. If necessary, open Server Manager. Under the Roles node, right-click Active Directory Certificate Services, and then click Add Role Services.

6. On the Select Role Services page, select Online Responder. If prompted, click Add Required Role Services.

7. Click Next.

8. If the Web Server (IIS) page displays, click Next.

9. If the Select Role Services page displays, click Next.

10. Click Install on the Confirm Installation Selections page, shown in Figure 3-27, to install the Online Responder service. Click Close when the installation process completes.

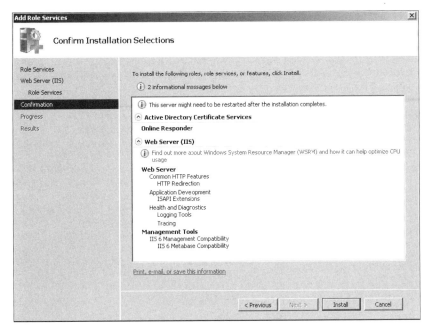

FIGURE 3-27 The Confirm Installation Selections page

11. Click Start, click Run, type **mmc**, and then click OK. Click Yes to close the User Account Control dialog box. On the File menu, click Add/Remove Snap-In. Add the Certificate Templates snap-in, as shown in Figure 3-28, and then click OK.

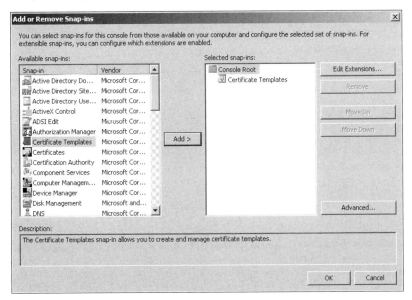

FIGURE 3-28 Adding the Certificate Template snap-in

12. Expand the Certificate Templates snap-in. Right-click the OCSP Response Signing template, and then click Properties.

13. On the Security tab, click Add. Click Object Types and ensure that the Computers object type is selected. Click OK to close the Object Types dialog box. Under the Enter The Object Names To Select, type **VAN-DC1** and then click OK.

14. When the VAN-DC1 object is selected, set the Read, Enroll, and Autoenroll permissions to Allow, as shown in Figure 3-29. Click OK.

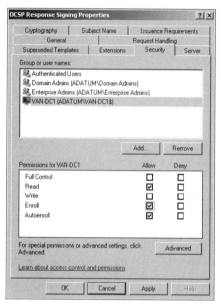

FIGURE 3-29 Configuring OCSP autoenrollment

15. Close the custom console without saving the console settings. Open the Certification Authority console from the Administrative Tools menu.

16. Right-click Adatum-VAN-DC1-CA and click Properties. On the Extensions tab, select Authority Information Access (AIA) from the Select Extension drop-down list.

17. Click Add to open the Add Location dialog box, type **http://van-dc1.adatum.com/ocsp,** and then click OK.

18. Check Include In the AIA Extension Of Issued Certificates and Include In The Online Certificate Status Protocol (OCSP) Extension, as shown in Figure 3-30, and then click OK.

19. You are informed that it is necessary to restart Active Directory Certificate Services for the changes to take effect. Click Yes to restart the service.

20. In the Certificate Authority console, right-click the Certificate Templates node, click New, and then click Certificate Template To Issue. Select the OCSP Response Signing template, and then click OK.

21. Review the list of Certificate Templates under the Certificate Template node, and verify that the OCSP Response Signing template is listed.

22. Minimize the Certification Authority console.

23. On the Administrative Tools menu, click Group Policy Management.

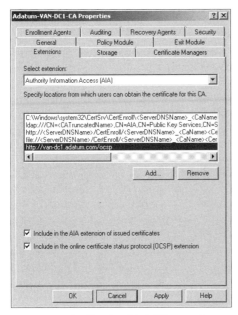

FIGURE 3-30 Configuring CA OCSP extensions

24. Edit the Default Domain Policy Group Policy Object (GPO). Enable the Certificate Services Client – Auto-Enrollment policy located under User Configuration/Policies/ Windows Settings/Security Settings/Public Key Policies, as shown in Figure 3-31. Do the same for the Certificate Services Client – Auto-Enrollment settings under the Computer Configuration section of the GPO.

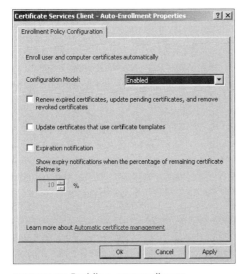

FIGURE 3-31 Enabling autoenrollment

25. Close the Group Policy Management Editor, close the Group Policy Management console, and reboot VAN-DC1.

Chapter Review

To further practice and reinforce the skills you learned in this chapter, you can perform the following tasks:

- Review the chapter summary.
- Review the list of key terms introduced in this chapter.
- Complete the case scenarios. These scenarios set up real-world situations involving the topics of this chapter and ask you to create a solution.
- Complete the suggested practices.
- Take a practice test.

Chapter Summary

- AD DS features give you more control over security policies, allow you to improve the user experience in branch offices, and help you to locate backed-up information that you need to restore.
- Improvements to GUI tools and auditing enhancements introduced in Windows Server 2008 are designed to make administrative tasks more straightforward and less time-consuming.
- Windows Server 2008 R2 introduces new domain and forest functional levels. If you raise the forest functional level to Windows Server 2008 R2, you can implement the Active Directory Recycle Bin.
- You can raise domain and forest functional levels to support new functionality, but apart from one specific exception, you cannot lower them (other than by restore or reinstallation). You can configure trusts between forests.
- Enterprise CAs are used to issue digital certificates to Active Directory user and computer accounts.
- The processes of autoenrollment and credential roaming can reduce the administrative burden of certificate deployment in Windows Server 2008 and Windows Server 2008 R2 environments.
- Online Responders and Online Responder Arrays reduce the bandwidth impact of CRL checks. A single Online Responder or Online Responder Array can provide CRL information for one or more CAs.

Key Terms

The following terms were introduced in this chapter. Do you know what they mean?

- Autoenrollment
- Certificate Authority (CA)
- Certificate Revocation List (CRL)
- Functional level
- Read-only domain controller (RODC)
- Shadow group
- Two-stage installation

Case Scenarios

In the following case scenarios, you will apply what you have learned about planning Directory Services and Certificate Services. You can find answers to these questions in the "Answers" section at the end of this book.

Case Scenario 1: Planning an Upgrade from Windows Server 2003 to Windows Server 2008 R2

You are a senior domain administrator at Northwind Traders. The company is planning to upgrade its domain controllers from Windows Server 2003 to Windows Server 2008 R2, although some senior managers are still unconvinced. You are currently attending a number of planning meetings. Answer the following questions:

1. Some members of the staff (for example, the CEO) want to use non-complex passwords, although the default policy for the northwindtraders.com domain enforces complex passwords. You are asked whether this facility will still be available when you upgrade to Windows Server 2008 R2. What is your reply?

2. The technical director is concerned that if you upgrade some of the domain controllers to Windows Server 2008 R2 and then raise the forest functional level to Windows Server 2008 R2 to take advantage of new features, domain controllers that still have Windows Server 2003 installed will become inoperable. She is also concerned that the domain currently contains member servers running Windows 2000 Server and Windows Server 2003 and the company has no immediate plans to upgrade these computers. What is your response?

3. Currently, users at remote branch offices are reporting that logon is sometimes unacceptably slow. A secondary DNS server is installed currently at each branch office, but domain controllers are not used at branch offices for security reasons and because the staff at branch offices are not domain administrators. You are asked if upgrading to Windows Server 2008 R2 will help address this problem. What is your reply?

Case Scenario 2: Deploying Certificate Services at Coho Vineyard

Coho Vineyard has recently installed a Windows Server 2008 R2 network in all its offices across the Yarra Valley wine-making region of Australia. Its managers have approached you for assistance with several network configuration issues that they hope you will be able to resolve. The first issue is that management feels that network communication across the Coho WAN and local area network (LAN) should be better protected. They want to implement IPsec and use certificate-based authentication for the process. The WAN links between the head office and the satellite offices are already choked with traffic. You have been asked to develop some method by which the impact of CRL checks on WAN bandwidth is minimized. Coho Vineyard deploys NAP with IPsec enforcement and as a result problems can occur due to large CA database sizes. With these facts in mind, answer the following questions:

1. What steps can be taken to ensure that IPSec certificates are deployed to all computers that are members of the domain?

2. What steps need to be taken to ensure that revocation checks occur with a minimum use of bandwidth?

3. Can the new functionality introduced by Windows Server R2 help reduce database sizes? If so, are there any disadvantages associated with this new functionality?

Suggested Practices

To help you master the examination objectives presented in this chapter, complete the following tasks.

Configure PSOs

- A PSO can contain a large number of settings, of which you configured only a small subset in the practice earlier in this chapter. Experiment with PSO settings and determine the effects each has on the security policies that affect the users associated with the GPO.

Find Out More About RODCs

- It is difficult to install and configure an RODC for real on your small test network, although you might consider using a virtual machine. Search the Internet for articles and online discussions that refer to RODCs. This is a new technology and more information should become available on a daily basis.

Configure Auditing

- Look at the new features available in Windows Server 2008 for AD DS auditing. Configure auditing to record AS DS changes, make changes, and then examine the Security event log.

Configure Web Enrollment

- Configure Web Enrollment on VAN-DC1.
- Use the VAN-SRV1 client to request a Web Server certificate using the Web Enrollment interface. Approve the request using the Certification Authority console and then download the Web Server certificate from the Web Enrollment pages.

Take a Practice Test

The practice tests on this book's companion CD offer many options. For example, you can test yourself on just one exam objective, or you can test yourself on all the 70-646 certification exam content. You can set up the test so that it closely simulates the experience of taking a certification exam, or you can set it up in study mode so that you can look at the correct answers and explanations after you answer each question.

> **MORE INFO** **PRACTICE TESTS**
>
> For details about all the practice test options available, see the "How to Use the Practice Tests" section in this book's Introduction.

CHAPTER 4

Group Policy Strategies

This chapter looks at how Group Policy is implemented in Active Directory Domain Services (AD DS). The focus of the chapter is planning and strategy rather than implementation. As an experienced administrator, you will have worked with Group Policy before and this chapter concentrates mainly on the enhancements introduced by Windows Server 2008 and Windows Server 2008 R2. You will use graphical user interface (GUI) and Command Line Interface (CLI) tools, but the most important consideration is not how you make configuration changes, but why and when. As you progress in your chosen career, you will spend more and more time planning rather than configuring.

Exam objectives in this chapter:

- Plan and implement group policy strategy.

Lessons in this chapter:

Before You Begin

To complete the exercises in the practice in this chapter, you need to have done the following:

- Installed a Windows Server 2008 R2 Enterprise server called VAN-DC1, configured as a domain controller in the adatum.com domain, as described in Appendix A, "Setup Instructions for Windows Server 2008 R2."

- If you configure VAN-DC1 as described in Appendix A, the Group Policy Management feature, and hence the Group Policy Management Console (GPMC), should be installed on that computer. However, if you have not performed this installation, the first exercise in the first practice in this chapter guides you through this process.

- Installed the Remote Desktop Services (RDS) Server role on VAN-DC1. This enables you to study features such as RemoteApp Manager. You will need the RDS Server role installed on VAN-DC1 in subsequent chapters.

- Installed a workstation client running Windows 7 Business, Enterprise, or Ultimate in the adatum.com domain. Unfortunately, the Enterprise server VAN-SRV1 running Windows Server 2008 R2 that you configured in previous chapters does not hold the Administrative Template files that you need to look at in this chapter. This workstation client can be a virtual machine, or you can use a physical computer if you have one available. If you do not have access to a computer running Windows 7, you can use a workstation client running Windows Vista Business, Enterprise, or Ultimate edition. As the practice exercises are written, this client is called VAN-CL1. If your client has a different computer name, amend the exercises accordingly.

- Created a user account in the adatum.com domain with the user name Kim Akers and password Pa$$w0rd, and added this account to the Domain Admins, Enterprise Admins, and Schema Admins groups. The procedure to do this is described in Appendix A.

- Created a user account in the adatum.com domain with the user name Don Hall and password Pa$$w0rd, and added this account to the Backup Operators group (to enable Don Hall to log on interactively to a domain controller).

- We recommend that you use an isolated network that is not part of your production network to do the practice exercises in this book. Internet access is not required for the exercises and you do not need to configure a default gateway. To minimize the time and expense of configuring physical computers, we recommend that you use virtual machines. For example, you can create virtual machines using the Hyper-V server role.

 REAL WORLD

Ian McLean

Books about a major new operating system or operating system revision tend to cover the new features that are introduced. Fortunately, most exams do the same. Unless they are writing about something completely new, authors tend to move quickly over what has come before. If they didn't, most technical books would be excessively long and very expensive.

However, although exams and books are mainly about what is new, real life does not reflect this situation. Every day, I call on skills and principles that I learned in the days of Microsoft Windows 2000 Server and even Microsoft Windows NT 4. Further, there is no guarantee that the exam will ask only about new features. If the objectives specify Group Policy, the examiner is entitled to include anything she likes about Group Policy, whether the feature was introduced in Windows 2000 Server or Windows Server 2008 R2.

I recall coming across a question in an exam a few years ago and thinking it was something I'd learned some time before and hadn't used much since. Fortunately, I knew the answer, but it wasn't one I found in any of the books I read as preparation. I've sometimes been accosted by colleagues who have read one of my books, and told about a topic on the exam that wasn't included. When that happens, I smile weakly and tell them it was in a book I wrote for a previous exam.

In particular, candidates for planning exams are expected to be experienced administrators and will be tested as such. I can't put a solid three years of experience, plus all the complex new features introduced by Windows Server 2008 and Windows Server 2008 R2, in a single book. I'd need an entire library. The solution is to make sure you have the experience. In the real world, you often do the same tasks repeatedly and let other members of your team take responsibility for other tasks. As part of your exam preparation, try to get at least some experience in everything. Books are valuable, but there's only one way to get qualifications and to advance your career. Hands on, hands on, and more hands on.

Lesson 1: Planning Group Policy Objects

This lesson considers a planning strategy for the configuration of Group Policy objects (GPOs) that you use to implement Group Policy in Windows Server 2008 and Windows Server 2008 R2. It specifically considers Administrative Templates and Administrative Template (ADM) files. The lesson discusses Starter GPOs, including the System Starter GPOs that are included with Windows Server 2008 R2.

In Windows Server 2008 and Windows Server 2008 R2, you can install the GPMC by using the Add Features Wizard in Server Manager. You do this in the practice later in this lesson. Using the GPMC, you can efficiently implement security settings, enforce IT policies, and consistently distribute software across sites, domains, or organizational units (OUs).

ADM files were introduced in Windows NT 4 and are used to describe registry-based Group Policy settings. In Windows Sever 2008 and Windows Server 2008 R2 (and in Windows Vista and Windows 7), ADM files are replaced by XML files known as ADMX files. These ADMX files make it easier to manage registry-based policy settings. Windows Server 2008 R2 introduces enhancements to the Properties dialog box for an Administrative Template policy setting and increases the number of registry types that Administrative Templates support. More than 300 Administrative Template policy settings are added in Windows Server 2008 R2 and Windows 7 with Remote Server Administration Tools (RSAT).

This lesson discusses Starter and System Starter GPOs and how you use these features when planning the implementation of your Group Policy design. It also discusses ADMX language-neutral and language-specific files.

After this lesson, you will be able to:

- Install the GPMC (if necessary) and use the console to administer Group Policy settings.
- Create, edit, back up, and restore Starter GPOs.
- Work with ADMX files.
- Configure a view filter for Administrative Template policy settings.

Estimated lesson time: 45 minutes

Using Starter GPOs

Windows Server 2008 Group Policy introduced Starter GPOs, and Windows Server 2008 R2 Group Policy introduces System Starter GPOs. Starter GPOs let you save baseline templates that you can use when you create new GPOs. You can also export Starter GPOs to domains other than those in which they were created.

System Starter GPOs are read-only Starter GPOs that provide a baseline of settings for a specific scenario. Like Starter GPOs, they store a collection of Administrative Template policy settings in a single object that you can import. You cannot, however, edit a System Starter GPO or create a custom System Starter GPO. You can determine whether a Starter GPO is a System Starter GPO by viewing the Starter GPO Type item on the Details tab of the Starter GPO. Figure 4-1 shows this tab for a custom (editable) Starter GPO.

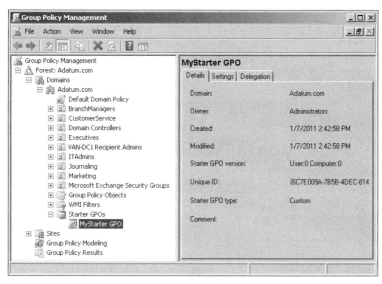

FIGURE 4-1 The Details tab for a Starter GPO

NOTE THE STARTER GPOS CONTAINER

Depending on your configuration, you may be prompted to create a Starter GPOs container. When you do, this is provisioned automatically with eight System Starter GPOs—four for clients running Windows XP, and four for clients running Windows Vista. You do not need to download these System Starter GPOs.

MORE INFO SYSTEM STARTER GPOS

For more information about System Starter GPOs, see *http://technet.microsoft.com/en-us/library/dd367854(WS.10).aspx*.

You create a Starter GPO by right-clicking the Starter GPOs container in the GPMC tree and clicking New. As shown in Figure 4-2, you are prompted to give a name to the Starter GPO, and you can also add a comment if you want. When you create a Starter GPO, you automatically create a new folder on the domain controller to which the GPMC is connected.

By default, this folder is placed in the C:\Windows\SYSVOL\domain\StarterGPOs path. This is replicated to other domain controllers as part of SYSVOL replication.

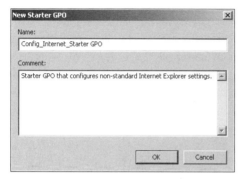

FIGURE 4-2 Creating a new Starter GPO

You can configure a Starter GPO as you would configure any GPO, except that only the Administrative Templates settings are available in both Computer Configuration and User Configuration. To do this, you right-click the Starter GPO and click Edit. Figure 4-3 shows the Config_Internet_Starter GPO with the Do Not Allow Users To Enable Or Disable Add-Ons setting in Windows Internet Explorer selected for editing. When you click Edit, you can enable or disable this policy setting or leave it unconfigured.

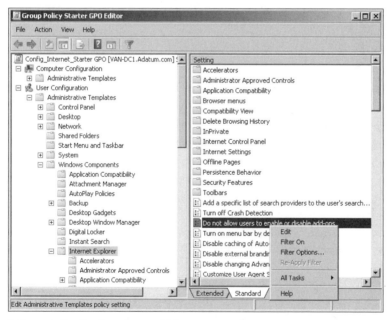

FIGURE 4-3 Configuring a Starter GPO

A Starter GPO lets you easily create multiple GPOs with the same baseline configuration. You then need to configure only the settings in these GPOs that are not contained in

Administrative Templates. You can create a new (normal) GPO using a Starter GPO as a template by right-clicking the Starter GPO and clicking New GPO From Starter GPO. Alternatively, you can right-click the Group Policy Objects container, click New, and then specify a Starter GPO from the Source Starter GPO drop-down list, as shown in Figure 4-4. You can access the same dialog box and specify a Starter GPO if you right-click an OU (or the domain) and click Create A GPO In This Domain, And Link It Here.

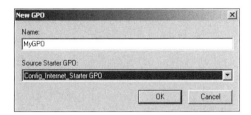

FIGURE 4-4 Specifying a Starter GPO when creating a new GPO

Backing Up and Restoring Starter GPOs

Unlike normal GPOs, Starter GPOs are not backed up when you right-click the Group Policy Objects container and click Back Up All, and they cannot be restored by clicking the Manage Backups function on the Domains or the Group Policy Objects container. Rather, you back up all Starter GPOs by right-clicking the Starter GPOs container and selecting Back Up All. You can also back up individual Starter GPOs by right-clicking the GPO and selecting Back Up. You can back up to a folder on a local disk, to an optical drive, or to a network share. Figure 4-5 shows the Backup Starter GPO dialog box.

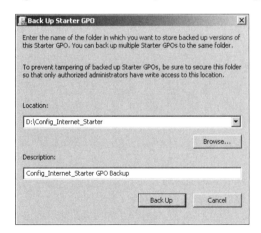

FIGURE 4-5 The Backup Starter GPO dialog box

You can restore a Starter GPO from backup by right-clicking the Starter GPOs container and clicking Manage Backups. The Restore Starter GPO Wizard prompts you for the backup location and then lets you select the Starter GPO to restore, as shown in Figure 4-6. You click Next, and then click Finish on the Summary page to restore the selected GPO.

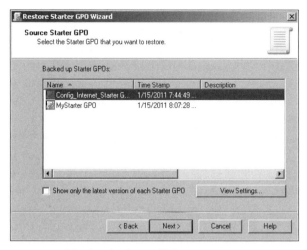

FIGURE 4-6 Selecting the Starter GPO to restore

Planning Administrative Templates

Administrative Templates, also known as registry-based policy settings, appear in the Group Policy Management Editor under the Administrative Templates node of both the Computer and User Configuration nodes for both normal and Starter GPOs. They are created from XML-based Administrative Template files. You can edit Administrative Template settings in any GPO (other than a System Starter GPO) easily by double-clicking any policy setting and changing it from its default state to Enabled or Disabled. You can then select any other available options that you want on the Setting tab.

However, it is bad practice and bad planning to change Administrative Templates policy settings at random to meet specific, isolated requirements. It is very easy to forget that a particular GPO has a nonstandard policy setting and, as a result, link it to an OU for which that policy setting is inappropriate. You also need to remember that when computer policy conflicts with user policy, computer policy generally takes precedence. However, this cannot be guaranteed for every application. If application authors disregard this convention, Group Policy cannot enforce it.

Therefore, you should plan to have a few groups of tried, tested, and well-documented Administrative Templates settings implemented in Starter GPOs. Where settings are the industry standard, they might be held in System Starter GPOs. The GPOs that you create should be based on Starter GPOs. You can edit Software Settings and Windows Settings for both user and computer configurations in an ordinary GPO, but you should not edit Administrative Templates, which are defined by the Starter GPO on which the ordinary GPO is based.

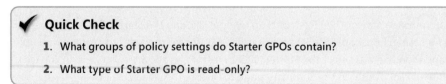

> ✔ **Quick Check**
> 1. What groups of policy settings do Starter GPOs contain?
> 2. What type of Starter GPO is read-only?

Filtering Administrative Templates Settings

If large numbers of Administrative Templates settings are available for a GPO in the Group Policy Management Editor and you want to view only those templates that meet specific criteria, you can filter the Administrative Template view based on those criteria. Filtering determines which settings are visible in the console—it does not affect the settings that are applied to the GPO. Even though you cannot see a template policy setting because it is filtered from a view, this policy setting is still present and is still applied. Also, filtering does not affect whether settings apply to users or computers. Filtering an Administrative Templates view is not the same as filtering the scope of Group Policy according to security group membership.

You can choose to display only configured policy settings or policy settings that can be fully managed. You can use Requirement Filters to include settings that match selected platforms. You can filter for text patterns within the policy setting title or associated help text. Windows Server 2008 introduced the ability to filter for text patterns within the comments that you can add to a policy configuration, and this functionality is supported in Windows Server 2008 R2. Figure 4-7 shows a configuration that views all policy settings that include the text pattern "Internet Explorer" in the Comments field.

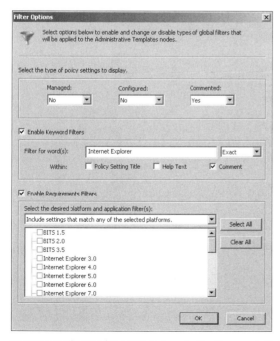

FIGURE 4-7 Filtering for a text pattern in the Comments field

Managing Group Policies by Using ADMX Files

ADMX files, based on XML, replace ADM files used in Windows Server 2003 and earlier. Unlike ADM files, ADMX files are not stored in individual GPOs. You can create a central store location for ADMX files that is accessible by anyone with permission to create or edit GPOs. Group Policy tools continue to recognize any ADM files that still exist in your existing environment, but they ignore any ADM file that has been superseded by an ADMX file. The Group Policy Management Editor automatically reads and displays Administrative Template policy settings from ADMX files that are stored either locally or in the ADMX central store. All Group Policy settings currently implemented by ADM files in legacy operating systems are available in Windows Server 2008 and Windows Server 2008 R2 as ADMX files.

Administrative Template files use an XML-based file format that describes registry-based Group Policy. ADMX files are divided into language-neutral resources (.admx files) and language-specific resources (.adml files). This enables Group Policy tools to adjust their user interfaces according to your chosen language. You can add a new language to a set of policy definitions so long as the language-specific resource file is available.

ADMX File Locations

ADMX files on domain controllers running Windows Server 2008 and Windows Server 2008 R2 can be held in a central store. This greatly reduces the amount of storage space required to maintain GPOs. In Windows Server 2008 and Windows Server 2008 R2, the Group Policy Management Editor does not copy ADMX files to each edited GPO. Instead, it provides the facility to read from a single domain-level location on the domain controller. If the central store is unavailable, the Group Policy Management Editor will read from the local administrative workstation running Windows Vista or Windows 7.

The central store is not available by default; you need to create it manually. You do this in the practice later in this lesson. In addition to storing standard Windows Server 2008 ADMX files in the central store, you can share a custom ADMX file by copying this file to the central store. This makes it automatically available to all Group Policy administrators in a domain. Table 4-1 shows locations for ADMX files on a domain controller (assuming a typical installation of Windows 2008 or Windows Server 2008 R2 and U.S. English ADMX language-specific files). Microsoft recommends that you manually create the central store on the primary domain controller on your domain—that is, the first domain controller running Windows 2008 or Windows Server 2008 R2 that you configure on your domain. This makes it quicker to replicate the files to all other domain controllers in your domain by using distributed file system replication (DFSR).

TABLE 4-1 Locations for ADMX Files on a Domain Controller

FILE TYPE	FILE LOCATION
ADMX language-neutral (.admx)	C:\Windows\SYSVOL\domain\policies\ PolicyDefinitions
ADMX language-specific (.adml)	C:\Windows\SYSVOL\domain\policies\ PolicyDefinitions\en-us

The central store for ADMX files allows all administrators that edit domain-based GPOs to access the same set of ADMX files. After you have created the central store, the Group Policy tools will use the ADMX files only in the central store, ignoring any locally stored versions. To edit GPOs using centrally stored ADMX files, you first create the central store and any subfolders that you need for language-specific files. You can then copy ADMX files from your administrative workstation to the central store. You do this in the practice later in this lesson.

Creating Custom ADMX Files

If the standard Group Policy settings that ship with Windows Server are insufficient for your needs, you might consider creating custom ADMX files. Take care if you choose to do this— ADMX files modify the registry. Be very wary of any registry modification, and make sure that you double- and triple-check your code. Do not install custom ADMX files on a production network before you have tested them on an isolated test network to make sure that you know how they will work.

Microsoft recommends downloading and installing sample files and modifying the elements that do not affect the registry until you are confident about using ADMX syntax. You can download the installation file from *http://www.microsoft.com/downloads/en/details. aspx?FamilyId=3D7975FF-1242-4C94-93D3-B3091067071A&displaylang=en*.

The ADMX schema defines the syntax for the ADMX files. If you want to view this schema, you can download it from *http://www.microsoft.com/downloads/details .aspx?FamilyId=B4CB0039-E091-4EE8-9EC0-2BBCE56C539E&displaylang=en*. Be aware, however, that the exam syllabus does not include schema management.

You can create and edit ADMX files by using an XML editor or a text editor such as Notepad. If you do not want to download sample files, you can use Notepad to open any of the ADMX files that you place in the central store in the practice later in this lesson. Be careful, however, to change the file name before saving any changes that you make.

ADMX files are created as one language-neutral file (.admx) and one or more language-specific files (.adml). Note that XML is case-sensitive. A language-neutral ADMX file contains the following elements:

- **XML declaration** This element is required for the file to validate as an XML-based file. It contains version and encoding information.

- **PolicyDefinitions element** This element contains all other elements for an .admx file.

- **PolicyNamespaces element** This element defines the unique namespace for the file. The element also provides a mapping to external file namespaces.

- **Resources element** This element specifies the requirements for the language-specific resources, such as the minimum required version of the associated .adml file.

- **SupportedOn element** This element specifies references to localized text strings defining the operating systems or applications affected by a specific policy setting.

- **Categories element** This element specifies categories under which the policy setting in the file will be displayed in the Group Policy Management Editor. Note that if you specify a category name that already exists in another ADMX file, you create a duplicate node.

- **Policies element** This element contains the individual policy setting definitions.

A language-specific (or language resource) ADMX file contains the following elements:

- **XML declaration** This element is required for the file to validate as an XML-based file. This element is the same in .admx and .adml files.

- **PolicyDefinitionResources element** This element contains all other elements for a language-specific ADMX file.

- **Resources element (.adml)** This element contains a StringTable element and a PresentationTable element for a specified language.

Lesson Summary

- The GPMC is integrated closely with Windows Server 2008 and Windows Server 2008 R2. You can install the tool by using Server Manager.

- ADMX language-neutral and language-specific files define configurable Group Policy settings in Windows 2008 Server domains. You can store these files in a central store on your domain controllers. You need to create the central store on one domain controller. DFSR replicates it to other domain controllers in the domain.

- Starter GPOs can contain Administrative Template settings for both user and computer configuration. You can create GPOs from Starter GPOs with known, tested Administrative Template settings, and you need only configure the non-Administrative Template settings.

- Windows Server 2008 R2 introduces read-only System Starter GPOs.

- You can back up all Starter GPOs or an individual System Starter GPO. You can use the Manage Backups function on the Starter GPOs container to restore an individual GPO from backup.

Lesson Review

You can use the following questions to test your knowledge of the information in Lesson 1, "Planning Group Policy Objects." The questions are also available on the companion CD if you prefer to review them in electronic form.

1. You want to restore the normal GPO called MyGPO from backup. What procedure do you follow? (Each answer is a complete solution. Choose three.)

   A. Right-click MyGPO under any OU to which it is linked. Click Restore From Backup. Follow the steps of the Restore Group Policy Object Wizard.

   B. Right-click MyGPO in the Group Policy Objects container. Click Restore From Backup. Follow the steps of the Restore Group Policy Object Wizard.

C. Right-click the Domains container. Click Manage Backups. Specify the backup location. Select MyGPO. Click Restore.

D. Right-click the Starter GPOs container. Click Manage Backups. Specify the backup location. Select MyGPO. Click Restore.

E. Right-click the Group Policy Objects container. Click Manage Backups. Specify the backup location. Select MyGPO. Click Restore.

2. You want to back up the Starter GPO MyStarterGPO. What procedure do you follow? (Each answer is a complete solution. Choose two.)

A. Right-click the Group Policy Objects container. Click Back Up All. Specify the backup location. Click Back Up.

B. Right-click the Starter GPOs container. Click Back Up All. Specify the backup location. Click Back Up.

C. Right-click the MyStarterGPO container. Click Back Up. Specify the backup location. Click Back Up.

D. Right-click the Starter GPOs container. Click Manage Backups. Specify the backup location. Click Back Up.

E. Right-click the Group Policy Objects container. Click Manage Backups. Specify the backup location. Click Back Up.

3. You want to display only the user configuration policy settings in the Starter GPO MyStarterGPO that have the term "Internet Settings" in the Comment field. You right-click the Starter GPO and click Edit. You right-click Administrative Templates under User Configuration and click Filter Options. What filter settings display the policy settings that you require? (Each answer forms part of the solution. Choose four.)

A. In the Select The Type Of Policy Settings To Display section, click Yes under Commented.

B. In the Select The Type Of Policy Settings To Display section, click No under Commented.

C. Select Enable Keyword Filters.

D. In the Filter For Word(s) section, Type **Internet Explorer** and select Exact.

E. In the Filter For Word(s) section, select only the Comment check box.

F. In the Filter For Word(s) section, select both the Policy Setting Title and Help Text check boxes. Do not select the Comment check box.

4. An element of an ADMX language-neutral file contains the following code:

```
<?xml version="1.0" encoding="utf-8"?>
```

What element is this?

A. The Policies element

B. The SupportedOn element

C. The PolicyNamespaces element

   D. The XML declaration

5. What element of an ADMX language-neutral file specifies references to localized text strings defining the operating systems or applications affected by a specific policy setting?

   A. The Categories element

   B. The SupportedOn element

   C. The PolicyNamespaces element

   D. The Resources element

Lesson 2: Group Policy Object Strategy

As an experienced administrator, you already know that Group Policy simplifies administration by automating many tasks related to managing users and computers. For example, you should be aware that you can use Group Policy to install permitted applications on clients on demand and to keep applications up to date.

You should already know that Group Policy settings contained in GPOs can be linked to OUs, and that OUs can either inherit settings from parent OUs or block inheritance and obtain their specific settings from their own linked GPOs. You also know that some policies—specifically security policies—can be set to enforced (formerly called no override in Windows Server 2003) so that they cannot be blocked or overwritten and force child OUs to inherit the settings from their parents.

Windows Server 2008 and Windows Server 2008 R2 change none of this, apart from the introduction of Password Setting Objects (PSOs), described in Chapter 3, "Planning Core Active Directory Infrastructure," that permit some security settings (such as password and account lockout settings) to be configured differently from the domain defaults and applied to security groups.

This lesson, therefore, does not cover the basic aspects of Group Policy in detail; rather, it discusses Group Policy strategy and the Group Policy enhancements that Windows Server 2008 and Windows Server 2008 R2 introduce. The lesson describes some of the more significant new Group Policy settings implemented in Windows Server 2008 and Windows Server 2008 R2 and discusses Group Policy troubleshooting.

After this lesson, you will be able to:

- List and apply the general principles that underlie a sound Group Policy design strategy.
- List the most significant new Group Policy settings introduced by Windows Server 2008 and Windows Server 2008 R2 and explain their functions.
- Discuss the various problems that can occur in Group Policy configuration and how you should troubleshoot them.

Estimated lesson time: 40 minutes

Planning Group Policy Strategy

Planning your Group Policy is partly about planning your organizational structure. If you have a large number of OUs—some inheriting policies, others blocking inheritance, several OUs linking to the same GPO, and several GPOs linking to the same OU—you have a recipe for disaster. While too few OUs and GPOs is also a mistake, most of us err on the side of having too many. Keep your structures simple. Do not link OUs and GPOs across site boundaries. Give your OUs and GPOs meaningful names.

Features such as block inheritance, enforced, security filtering, and loopback policies can be useful in the situations for which they were designed. However, they add complexity and make your Group Policy design more difficult to understand. You should use these features only where you can identify a real advantage in doing so.

If a GPO has no configured Computer Configuration policies, it is a good idea to disable Computer Configuration settings. Even if they are not configured, settings need to be processed, and disabling unconfigured settings saves processing time and resources. You can do this by right-clicking the GPO in Group Policy Management Editor and clicking Properties. Figure 4-8 shows this control. It is more unusual that no User Configuration policies are configured, but in this case, you have the option of disabling User Configuration settings.

FIGURE 4-8 Disabling Computer Configuration settings

> **NOTE PLANNING YOUR OU STRATEGY**
>
> When you plan your OU strategy, it is good practice to specify separate OUs for user and group objects and for computer objects. When a GPO is linked to an OU, you should then have the option to disable either Computer Configuration or User Configuration for the GPO. The exception is for GPOs linked to the domain container, which typically have both user and computer settings configured.

Use the Gpupdate command after Group Policy reconfiguration is complete. Even if changes to a GPO have been replicated across the domain, they do not take effect until the next time Group Policy is refreshed. The Gpupdate command forces a policy refresh. You can use the command on a domain controller or on any member server or client on the domain where you want Group Policy changes to take effect immediately.

Use standard combinations of Administrative Template settings predefined in Starter or System Starter GPOs and avoid the need to edit such settings in the normal GPOs that you create from Starter GPOs. Always store your ADMX files in a central store.

When you are planning Group Policy, you need to be aware of the new Group Policy settings that were introduced by Windows Server 2008 and are implemented in Windows Server 2008 R2. These are numerous, and it is not practical to memorize all of them, but you should know what the various categories are. Even if you do not edit any policies, exploring the Group Policy structure in the Group Policy Management Editor is worthwhile. You will develop a feel for what is available and whether you need to generate custom policies by creating ADMX files, as described in the previous lesson.

You also need a good understanding of how Group Policy is processed at the client. This happens in the following two phases:

- **Core processing** When a client begins to process Group Policy, it must determine whether it can reach a domain controller, whether any GPOs have been changed, and what policy settings must be processed. The core Group Policy engine performs the processing of this in the initial phase.

- **Client-side extension (CSE) processing** In this phase, Group Policy settings are placed in various categories, such as Administrative Templates, Security Settings, Folder Redirection, Disk Quota, and Software Installation. A specific CSE processes the settings in each category, and each CSE has its own rules for processing settings. The core Group Policy engine calls the CSEs that are required to process the settings that apply to the client.

CSEs cannot begin processing until core Group Policy processing is completed. Therefore, it is important to plan your Group Policy and your domain structure so that this happens as quickly and reliably as possible. The troubleshooting section later in this lesson discusses some of the problems that can delay or prevent core Group Policy processing.

New Group Policy Settings

Numerous new Group Policy settings were introduced in Windows Server 2008 and are retained in Windows Server 2008 R2. The following list describes those that are arguably the most significant, but is by no means exclusive:

- **Allow Remote Start Of Unlisted Programs** This computer-based policy setting allows you to specify whether remote users can start any program that is accessed remotely through Remote Desktop Services (RDS) on Windows Server 2008 R2 or Terminal Services (TS) on Windows Server 2008 when they start a remote session, or whether they can only start programs that are listed in the RemoteApp Programs list. You can use the RemoteApp Manager tool to create this list. By default, a user can start only programs in the RemoteApp Programs list during a remote session. Figure 4-9 shows the configuration dialog box for this setting.

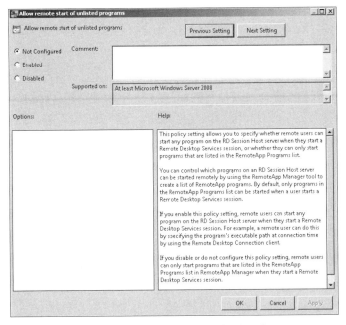

FIGURE 4-9 Configuring Allow Remote Start Of Unlisted Program

It is informative to compare the configuration dialog box shown in Figure 4-9 with the same dialog box for the same control on a Windows Server 2008 server, as shown in Figure 4-10. In Windows Server 2008 R2, you can configure the setting, add a comment, and see the explanation without needing to access different tabs.

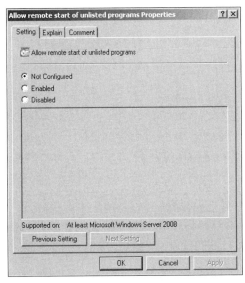

FIGURE 4-10 The same configuration dialog box on Windows Server 2008

■ **Allow Time Zone Redirection**   This user-based policy setting determines whether the
client redirects its time zone settings to the TS or RDS session. When you enable this
policy setting, clients that are capable of time zone redirection send their time zone
information to the server. Figure 4-11 shows the Group Policy Management Editor
accessing this policy.

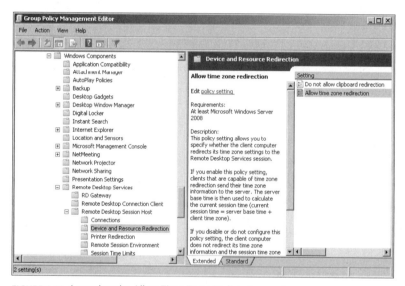

FIGURE 4-11 Accessing the Allow Time Zone Redirection policy

■ **Always Show Desktop On Connection**   This user-based policy setting determines
whether the desktop is always displayed when a client connects to a remote
computer, even if an initial program is already specified in the default user profile,
Remote Desktop Connection (RDC), TS client (for Windows Server 2008), RDS client
(for Windows Server 2008 R2), or through Group Policy. If an initial program is not
specified, the remote desktop is always displayed when the client connects.

- **Configure Custom Alert Text**   This computer-based policy setting requires that Desktop Experience is installed on a server running Windows Server 2008 or Windows Server 2008 R2. It substitutes custom alert text in the disk diagnostic message shown to users when a disk reports a Self-Monitoring, Analysis, and Reporting Technology (SMART) fault.

> **MORE INFO   SMART**
>
> Most hard disk manufacturers incorporate SMART logic into their drives. This acts as an early warning system for pending drive problems. For more information, see *http://www.pcguide.com/ref/hdd/perf/qual/featuresSMART-c.html*. This is not a Microsoft link, and the Uniform Resource Locator (URL) might change, in which case you can search the Internet for "Self-Monitoring, Analysis, and Reporting Technology." However, be aware that SMART is not a Microsoft technology and is unlikely to be featured in the exam.

- **Disk Diagnostic: Configure Execution Level**   This computer-based policy setting requires that Desktop Experience is installed on your server running Windows Server 2008 or Windows Server 2008 R2. It determines the execution level for SMART-based disk diagnostics. The Diagnostic Policy Service (DPS) will detect and log SMART faults to the event log when they occur. If you enable this policy setting, the DPS will also warn users and guide them through backup and recovery to minimize potential data loss.

- **Do Not Allow Clipboard Redirection**   This user-based policy setting specifies whether to prevent the sharing of Clipboard contents (Clipboard redirection) between a remote computer and a client during a TS or an RDS session. By default, TS and RDS allow Clipboard redirection. If the policy status is set to Not Configured, Clipboard redirection is not specified at the Group Policy level.

- **Do Not Display Initial Configuration Tasks Window Automatically At Logon**   This computer-based policy setting allows you to turn off the automatic display of the Initial Configuration Tasks window at logon. If you do not configure this policy setting, the Initial Configuration Tasks window opens when an administrator logs on to the server. However, if the administrator selects the Do Not Show This Window At Logon check box, the window does not open on subsequent logons.

- **Do Not Display Server Manager Automatically At Logon**   This computer-based policy setting allows you to turn off the automatic display of Server Manager at logon. If you enable this policy setting, Server Manager does not open automatically when an administrator logs on to the server. This setting is specific to the server rather than to a particular user account.

- **Enforce Removal Of Remote Desktop Wallpaper**   This computer-based policy setting specifies whether desktop wallpaper is displayed on remote clients connecting via TS or RDS. You can use this setting to enforce the removal of wallpaper during a remote session. If the policy status is set to Enabled, wallpaper never appears to a TS or an RDS client. If the status is set to Disabled, wallpaper might appear to a TS or an RDS client, depending on the client configuration.

- **Group Policy Management Editor**   This user-based policy setting permits or prohibits the use of the Group Policy Management Editor snap-in. If you enable this setting, the snap-in is permitted. If this setting is not configured, the Restrict Users To The Explicitly Permitted List Of Snap-Ins setting determines whether this snap-in is permitted or prohibited.

> **MORE INFO**   **RESTRICT USERS TO THE EXPLICITLY PERMITTED LIST OF SNAP-INS**
>
> The Restrict Users To The Explicitly Permitted List Of Snap-Ins policy setting is not new to Windows Server 2008 or Windows Server 2008 R2, and therefore it is not described in this lesson. If you have not come across this setting and need more information, see *http://technet.microsoft.com/en-gb/library/cc975962.aspx*.

- **Group Policy Starter GPO Editor**   This user-based policy setting permits or prohibits the use of the Group Policy Starter GPO Editor snap-in. If this setting is not configured, the Restrict Users To The Explicitly Permitted List Of Snap-Ins setting determines whether this snap-in is permitted or prohibited.

- **Redirect Only The Default Client Printer (User)**   This user-based policy setting allows you to specify whether the default client printer is the only printer redirected in TS or RDS sessions.

- **Redirect Only The Default Client Printer (Computer)**   This computer-based policy setting allows you to specify whether the default client printer is the only printer redirected in Terminal Services sessions. Because this is a computer-based setting, it is independent of the logged-on user.

- **Set The Number Of Synchronization Retries For Servers Running Password Synchronization**   This computer-based policy setting allows you to set the number of retries for synchronization on failure servers. If you enable this policy, all affected Password Sync servers use the number of retries specified by the policy setting. If you disable or do not configure this setting, the user preference will be used for individual Password Sync servers.

- **Set The Interval Between Synchronization Retries For Password Synchronization**   This computer-based policy setting allows you to set the interval in seconds between retries for synchronization failures. If you disable or do not configure this policy setting, the user preference will be used for individual Password Sync servers.

- **Set The Map Update Interval For NIS Subordinate Servers**   This computer-based policy setting allows you to set an update interval for pushing Network Information Service (NIS) maps to NIS subordinate servers. If you enable this policy, the specified update interval is used for all affected Server for NIS DCs. If you disable or do not configure the policy setting, the user preference will be used for individual Server for NIS DCs.

> **MORE INFO** **SERVER FOR NIS**
>
> For more information about NIS, access *http://technet.microsoft.com/en-us/library/ cc772394.aspx* and follow the links.

- **Use RD Connection Broker (or TS Session Broker) Load Balancing** This computer-based policy setting allows you to specify whether to use the RD Connection Broker or TS Session Broker load-balancing feature to balance the load between servers in a TS or RD farm. The RD Connection Broker role service is installed as part of the RDS Role on servers running Windows Server 2008 R2 and replaces the Windows Server 2008 TS Session Broker. If you enable this policy setting, RD Connection Broker or TS Session Broker will redirect users who do not have an existing session to the server in the farm with the fewest sessions.

> **MORE INFO** **RD CONNECTION BROKER**
>
> For more information about RD Connection Broker, see *http://technet.microsoft.com/ en-us/library/dd560675(WS.10).aspx?ppud=4*.

- **Turn On Extensive Logging For Password Synchronization** This computer-based policy setting allows you to manage the extensive logging feature for Password Sync servers. If you enable this policy, all the affected Password Sync servers log intermediate steps in synchronization attempts.
- **Turn On Extensive Logging For Active Directory Domain Services Domain Controllers Running Server For NIS** This computer-based policy setting allows you to manage the extensive logging feature for Server for NIS (SNIS) domain controllers.

Desktop Experience

The Desktop Experience feature on a server running Windows Server 2008 or Windows Server 2008 R2 lets you configure and thus install a variety of Windows 7 (or Windows Vista) features on your server. Desktop Experience includes the following components and features:

- Windows Media Player
- Desktop themes
- Video for Windows (AVI support)

- Windows SlideShow
- Windows Defender
- Disk Cleanup
- Sync Center
- Sound Recorder
- Character Map
- Snipping Tool

Installing Desktop Experience does not enable any of these features automatically. After installation, you must enable any features that require configuration changes manually. To use a desktop theme, for example, you need to open the Services MMC snap-in, enable and start the Themes service, and then select the theme.

To install Desktop Experience, open Server Manager and click Add Features in the Features Summary section. Select the Desktop Experience check box, and then click Next. If prompted, click Add Required Features and click Next again, and then click Install. You need to restart the server after installation.

Troubleshooting Group Policy

Group Policy very seldom "breaks." It is part of AS DS, and as such, it is sturdy and resilient. What is much more likely to happen is that policies will not be applied the way you or your users expect them to be. For example, a setting in a GPO will be configured incorrectly or, more commonly, policy inheritance and OU structure will not be designed correctly. As a result, users are unable to do things they need to do, or (more seriously and more difficult to debug) they can do things they should not be able to do. If you use loopback (machine-based) processing, the computers in the secure room may not be operating as securely as they should be.

Your first step in debugging Group Policy is typically to check that the domain infrastructure has been planned and implemented correctly. You need to ensure that required services and components are running and configured as expected. As with all system debugging, start at the lowest layer and ensure that you have full network connectivity. If a particular client is not working the way it should, verify that it is connected to the network, joined to the domain, and has the correct system time.

No administrator likes exceptions, but we are required to implement them. Typically you might have configured security filtering, Windows Management Instrumentation (WMI) filters, block inheritance settings, enforced settings, loopback processing, and slow-link settings. You need to check that these settings are not affecting normal GPO processing.

Using Group Policy Tools

Group Policy debugging tools are well known, and Windows Server 2008 and Windows Server 2008 R2 do not introduce any major changes (other than two new command-line switches that were added to the GPResult tool by Windows Server 2008 and retained in Windows Server 2008 R2). For example, GPResult.exe verifies all policy settings in effect for a specific user or computer. GPOTool.exe is a Windows Server 2003 Resource Kit Tools utility (available from *http://www.microsoft.com/downloads/en/details.aspx?familyid=9d467a69-57ff-4ae7-96ee-b18c4790cffd&displaylang=en*) that checks GPOs for consistency on each domain controller in your domain. The tool also determines whether the policies are valid and displays detailed information about replicated GPOs.

> **MORE INFO   GPRESULT COMMAND-LINE SWITCHES**
>
> For more information about the command-line switches /x and /h that are available in the GPResult tool, see *http://technet.microsoft.com/en-us/library/cc733160(WS.10).aspx*.

You can determine the Resultant Set of Policies (RSoP) for a specific user and a specific computer by using the Group Policy Results Wizard. This gives you information similar to that generated using GPResult.exe. To do this, double-click the forest at the top of the GPMC console tree, right-click Group Policy Results under Forest, and click Group Policy Results Wizard. The wizard asks you to specify a computer and a user (by default the current computer and the logged-on user), and then generates a report as shown in Figure 4-12.

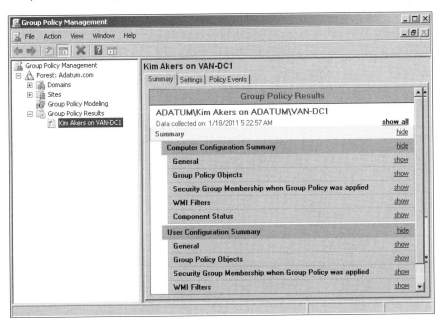

FIGURE 4-12 Generating an RSoP report

Arguably one of the most useful tools for isolating Group Policy problems is the reporting function in GPMC. You can select a GPO in the left pane of the tool and view the GPO report information on the Scope, Details, Settings, and Delegation tabs in the right pane, as shown in Figure 4-13. You can also right-click a GPO and select Save Report, as shown in Figure 4-14.

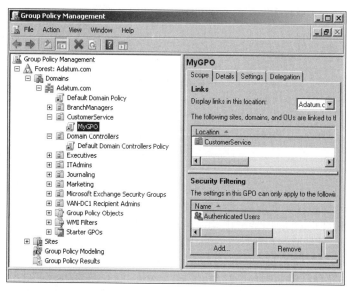

FIGURE 4-13 Viewing GPO information

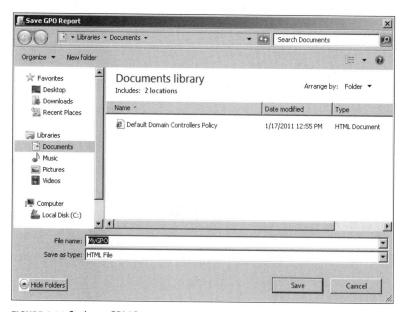

FIGURE 4-14 Saving a GPMC report

Figure 4-15 shows part of the output from a GPO report. By default, reports are saved in Hypertext Markup Language (HTML) format and opened in Internet Explorer.

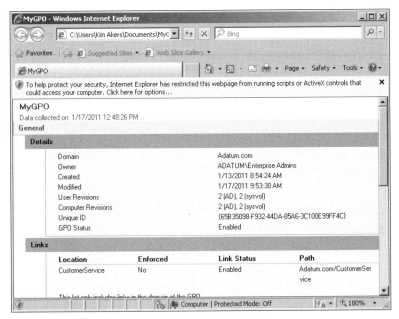

FIGURE 4-15 GPMC report output

You can examine GPMC reports and look for answers to the following questions:

- Does Group Policy Results list the GPO as applied?
- Is the setting listed in Group Policy Results Report?
- Is the GPO listed in the Denied List?

Addressing Core Processing Issues

If core processing does not happen quickly and efficiently, CSE processing might not begin and Group Policy will not be applied. A number of factors can affect core processing.

One of the most common causes of a GPO not being applied to a user or computer is that the GPO is not linked to the user or computer's site, domain, or OU. GPOs are delivered to clients based on the site and OU memberships of the computer and the logged-on user.

✔ **Quick Check**

- What command-line tool verifies all policy settings in effect for a specific user or computer?

Quick Check Answer

- GPResult.exe

Another issue that might cause core processing problems is that replication has not yet occurred. If GPOs are linked across sites (which is not recommended), this can be especially problematic. When you link a GPO to a site, domain, or OU in the hierarchy, the change must be replicated to the domain controller from which the client retrieved its GPO. If you add a user or computer to an OU, the GPOs that apply to that OU might not be applied to the client until the change in OU membership has been replicated.

After you make changes to a GPO, these changes need to reach the client. This occurs during Group Policy refresh. Sometimes Group Policy problems can be cured by using the Gpupdate command.

Network connectivity was mentioned at the start of this section. You need to ensure that the client can connect to the domain controller. Check that TCP/IP, DNS, and DHCP are configured and running. Make sure that a network cable has not fallen out.

Lesson Summary

- You can improve your Group Policy design by limiting the number of GPOs and OUs. However, you should avoid excessive use of block inheritance, enforced, security filtering, and loopback policies. Do not link GPOs to OUs across sites. You can disable User Configuration or Computer Configuration if either of them contains no configured policies.

- Windows Server 2008 introduced a number of new Group Policy settings, particularly settings related to the TS Server role. In Windows Server 2008 R2 the WDS Server role replaces the TS Server role, and the related Group Policy settings are retained.

- Various tools exist that help you troubleshoot Group Policy issues. One of the most useful is the ability to save a GPO report by using GPMC. You can also generate Group Policy Results and Group Policy Modeling reports.

Lesson Review

You can use the following questions to test your knowledge of the information in Lesson 2, "Group Policy Object Strategy." The questions are also available on the companion CD if you prefer to review them in electronic form.

> **NOTE   ANSWERS**
>
> **Answers to these questions and explanations of why each answer choice is correct or incorrect are located in the "Answers" section at the end of the book.**

1. Which Group Policy settings require that Desktop Experience be installed on a server running Windows Server 2008 or Windows Server 2008 R2? (Each is a complete answer. Choose two.)

    A. Disk Diagnostic: Configure Execution Level

    B. Do Not Allow Clipboard Redirection

C. Enforce Removal Of Remote Desktop Wallpaper

D. Set Update Interval To NIS Slaves

E. Disk Diagnostic: Configure Custom Alert Text

2. Which Group Policy settings are associated with Terminal Services in Windows Server 2008 and Remote Desktop Services in Windows Server 2008 R2? (Each is a complete answer. Choose three.)

A. Allow Time Zone Redirection

B. Disk Diagnostic: Configure Execution Level

C. Do Not Allow Clipboard Redirection

D. Enforce Removal Of Remote Desktop Wallpaper

E. Turn On Extensive Logging For Domain Controllers Running Server For NIS

3. You are planning your Group Policy strategy. Which of the following statements offer good advice? (Each is a complete answer. Choose three.)

A. Keep the number of GPOs to an absolute minimum by having a lot of configuration settings in any single GPO and by linking GPOs to OUs across site boundaries.

B. Store your ADMX files in a central store.

C. Give your OUs and GPOs meaningful names.

D. Make extensive use of features such as block inheritance, enforced, security filtering, and loopback policies.

E. Ensure that your policy for GPO updates and amendments mandates the use of the Gpupdate command when reconfiguration is complete.

4. Which resource kit utility checks GPOs for consistency on each domain controller in a domain, determines whether the policies are valid, and displays detailed information about replicated GPOs?

A. GPResult.exe

B. GPOTool.exe

C. The GPMC report function

D. Gpupdate.exe

5. You want to create an RSoP report for the logged-on user on the local domain controller. You open the GPMC. What procedure do you follow?

A. Expand the Forest container. Right-click the Group Policy Results container and click Group Policy Results Wizard. Follow the steps in the wizard using the default settings.

B. Expand the Forest container. Right-click the Group Policy Modeling container and click Group Policy Modeling Wizard. Follow the steps in the wizard using the default settings.

C. Expand the Forest container and expand the Domains container. Right-click the container identified by the domain name and click Group Policy Modeling Wizard. Follow the steps in the wizard using the default settings.

D. Expand the Forest container and expand the Domains container. Expand the container identified by the domain name and right-click the Default Domain Policy GPO. Click Save Report. Click Save to save the report in the Documents Library.

Installing the GPMC and Creating a Central Store for Group Policy Files

In this practice, you install the GPMC, unless it has already been installed when you installed AD DS. You also create and populate a central store for Group Policy (ADMX) definition files.

EXERCISE 1 Installing the GPMC

In this exercise, you check whether the GPMC is installed on VAN-DC1. This will depend on how you set up your computer (if VAN-DC1 is set up as described in Appendix A, the GPMC will already be installed). If the console is not installed, you install it.

1. Log on to VAN-DC1 with the Kim Akers account.

2. Look under Administrative Tools. If Group Policy Management already exists, as shown in Figure 4-16, you do not need to finish the remainder of this exercise, and you can proceed directly to Exercise 2. If not, go to step 3.

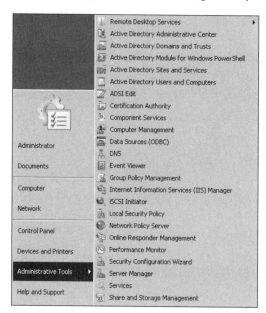

FIGURE 4-16 The GPMC installed on VAN-DC1

3. If necessary, open Server Manager under Administrative Tools.

4. Click Features in the console tree.

5. Click Add Features in the Features pane.

6. In the Add Features Wizard, select Group Policy Management from the list of available features.

7. Click Next.

8. Click Install.

EXERCISE 2 Creating a Central Store for ADMX Files

In this exercise, you create a folder that acts as a central store for language-neutral ADMX files. You then create a subfolder to hold language-specific ADMX files. You copy files from your client workstation (VAN-CL1) into these folders.

1. If necessary, log on to VAN-DC1 with the Kim Akers account.

2. Open Windows Explorer and browse to C:\Windows\SYSVOL\domain\policies. Create a subfolder called PolicyDefinitions.

3. Create a subfolder of the PolicyDefinitions folder called en-us. The file structure is shown in Figure 4-17.

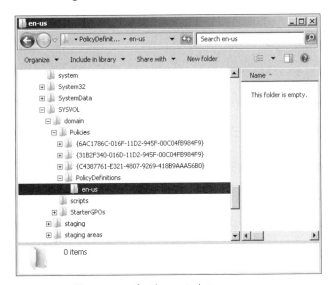

FIGURE 4-17 File structure for the central store

4. Share the PolicyDefinitions folder and give Kim Akers Full Control, as shown in Figure 4-18. Note that because this is a one-time operation, it is valid to set share permissions for a single user, although typically permissions are allocated to a security group.

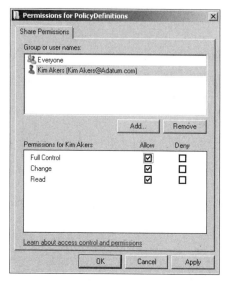

FIGURE 4-18 Setting permissions on the PolicyDefinitions shared folder

5. Log on to the VAN-CL1 client workstation as Kim Akers, or connect to it through Remote Desktop. Do not log off from VAN-DC1.

6. Locate any files with the file type .admx on the client workstation. Copy them to the shared PolicyDefinitions folder on VAN-DC1. Figure 4-19 shows the central store containing ADMX files.

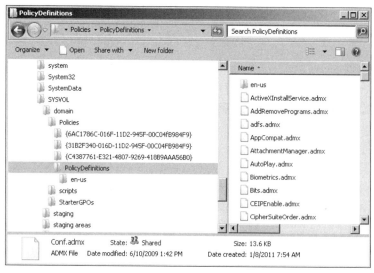

FIGURE 4-19 ADMX files in the central store

7. Locate any files with the file type .adml on the client workstation. Copy them to the shared PolicyDefinitions/en-us folder on VAN-DC1.

8. Open any ADMX file (.admx or .adml) on VAN-DC1 with Notepad and examine the contents. Figure 4-20 shows an ADMX file open in Notepad.

```
DCOM.admx - Notepad                                           _ □ X
File  Edit  Format  View  Help
<?xml version="1.0" encoding="utf-8"?>
<!-- (c) 2006 Microsoft Corporation  -->
<policyDefinitions xmlns:xsd="http://www.w3.org/2001/XMLSchema" xmlns:
  <policyNamespaces>
    <target prefix="dcom" namespace="Microsoft.Policies.DECOM" />
    <using prefix="windows" namespace="Microsoft.Policies.windows" />
  </policyNamespaces>
  <resources minRequiredRevision="1.0" />
  <categories>
    <category name="DCOM" displayName="$(string.DCOM)">
      <parentCategory ref="windows:System" />
    </category>
    <category name="DCOMAppCompatPolicies" displayName="$(string.DCOMA
      <parentCategory ref="DCOM" />
    </category>
  </categories>
  <policies>
    <policy name="DCOMActivationSecurityCheckAllowLocalList" class="Ma
      <parentCategory ref="DCOMAppCompatPolicies" />
      <supportedOn ref="windows:SUPPORTED_WindowsXPSP2" />
      <enabledValue>
        <decimal value="1" />
      </enabledValue>
      <disabledValue>
        <decimal value="0" />
```

FIGURE 4-20 ADMX file contents

PRACTICE   Creating and Configuring a GPO and Generating a Report

In this practice, you create and configure a GPO linked to one of the OUs in the adatum.com domain. You then use the GPMC reporting function to generate a report and the GPResult.exe tool to verify all policy settings that are in effect for the logged-in user Kim Akers.

EXERCISE 1   Creating and Configuring a GPO

In this exercise, you create and configure a GPO. The GPMC must be installed before you can carry out this exercise.

1. If necessary, log on to VAN-DC1 with the Kim Akers account.
2. Click Group Policy Management under Administrative Tools in the All Programs menu. This opens the GPMC.
3. In the GPMC, expand the Group Policy Management console tree and right-click an available OU (such as Marketing). Click Create A GPO In This Domain, And Link It Here.
4. Name the new GPO SampleGPO. If you want, specify a Source Starter GPO if one is available, as shown in Figure 4-21. Click OK.

FIGURE 4-21 Specifying a name and a Source Starter GPO

5. Right-click SampleGPO in the console tree and click Edit.

6. In the Group Policy Management Editor, expand User Configuration, expand Policies, expand Windows Settings, and expand Internet Explorer Maintenance.

7. In the Console pane, click Browser User Interface. In the Details pane, double-click Browser Title.

8. Customize the title displayed by the browser, as shown in Figure 4-22.

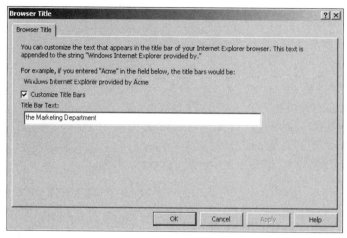

FIGURE 4-22 Specifying the browser title

9. Click OK. Close the Group Policy Management Editor.

EXERCISE 2   Generating a GPO Report

In this exercise, you generate and view a GPO report for the GPO that you created in Exercise 1.

1. If necessary, log on to VAN-DC1 with the Kim Akers account and open the GPMC.

2. In the GPMC, expand the Group Policy Management console tree and right-click SampleGPO. Click Save Report.

3. Click Save to save the report in the Documents Library in VAN-DC1, as shown in Figure 4-23. Note that on a production domain controller, you would probably create a folder specifically to store such reports.

4. Access the Documents Library on VAN-DC1. Double-click SampleGPO. The file opens in Internet Explorer.

5. Examine the SampleGPO report. In particular, note the changes to User Configuration generated by your reconfiguration and (if appropriate) in the Source Starter GPO. Figure 4-24 shows a typical User Configuration report.

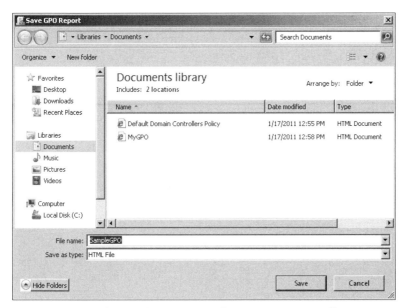

FIGURE 4-23 Saving the SampleGPO Group Policy report as an HTML file

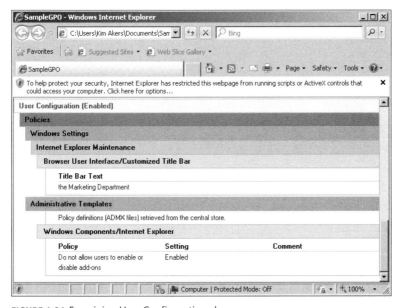

FIGURE 4-24 Examining User Configuration changes

EXERCISE 3 Verifying Policy Settings

In this exercise, you use the GPResult.exe tool to verify all policy settings that are in effect for the logged-in user Kim Akers.

1. If necessary, log on to VAN-DC1 with the Kim Akers account.

2. Open the command prompt from the Accessories menu under All Programs.

3. Enter the following command:

   `gpresult /R`

4. Read the output of this command for the user Kim Akers. Figure 4-25 shows part of this output.

FIGURE 4-25 Policy settings for Kim Akers

Chapter Review

To further practice and reinforce the skills you learned in this chapter, you can perform the following tasks:

- Review the chapter summary.
- Review the list of key terms introduced in this chapter.
- Complete the case scenarios. These scenarios set up real-world situations involving the topics of this chapter and ask you to create a solution.
- Complete the suggested practices.
- Take a practice test.

Chapter Summary

- Starter GPOs and System Starter GPOs contain Administrative Template policy settings for user and computer configuration. You can create GPOs from Starter GPOs without the need to configure such settings.
- Group Policy definition files can be held in a central AS DS store that is replicated between domain controllers. You can create custom files if required.
- Policy settings introduced in Windows Server 2008 and retained in Windows Server 2008 R2 give you additional Group Policy functionality. Troubleshooting tools are available, but as always, troubleshooting policy and planning is mainly common sense.

Key Terms

The following terms were introduced in this chapter. Do you know what they mean?

- Administrative Template setting
- GPMC reporting
- Group Policy setting
- Resultant Set of Policies (RSoP)
- Starter GPO
- System Starter GPO

Case Scenarios

In the following case scenarios, you will apply what you have learned about planning GPOs and GPO strategy. You can find answers to these questions in the "Answers" section at the end of this book.

Case Scenario 1: Using Starter GPOs

Don Hall wants to generate a number of GPOs, all of which have the same User Configuration Administrative Template settings but different User Configuration Windows settings. The GPOs do not contain any configured Computer Configuration policies. You advise Don to create a Starter GPO with the User Configuration Administrative Template settings defined and use this to create normal GPOs. He would then need only to configure the User Configuration Windows Settings on his normal GPOs. Don comes back to you with the following questions:

1. Should he disable Computer Configuration on his GPOs, and what is the advantage in doing so?

2. Don has attempted to back up his Starter GPO by right-clicking the Group Policy Objects container and clicking Back Up All. However, he cannot find the GPO in his list of GPO backups. What should he have done?

Case Scenario 2: Planning and Documenting Troubleshooting Procedures

You worked on the help desk at Litware, Inc for a number of years. One of your tasks was resolving issues related to Group Policy. You were promoted recently, and one of your new responsibilities is to create a Procedures and Planning document that will help less experienced administrators to carry out troubleshooting tasks efficiently. Answer the following questions:

1. What should the procedure be if a user reports that she does not have access to the same facilities as her colleagues?

2. What should the procedure be if changes in policy settings are not being applied to a particular client, but they are working on similar computers?

3. Administrators at Litware frequently use the Save Report feature of GPMC to generate GPO reports. What questions should they ask when studying these reports?

Suggested Practices

To help you master the exam objectives presented in this chapter, complete the following tasks.

Use GPMC and Group Policy Management Editor

- An administrator typically needs to configure only a few policy settings in the course of her work. A senior administrator, responsible for planning rather than implementation, needs a broader knowledge of what settings are available. Look at GPMC, and especially Group Policy Management Editor. Expand the lists of policy settings. Use the Explain function to find out what each one does.

Examine ADMX Files

- The ability to understand and create code is invaluable if you want to develop your career. Administrators are not software designers, but the ability to generate simple files in XML (for example) is a valuable asset. Examine the standard ADMX files. Install and experiment with the sample ADMX files that Microsoft provides. (The link is given in Lesson 1.)

Examine GPO Reports

- Use the Save Report function in the GPMC to generate and save GPO reports. Examine these reports until you feel comfortable with their structure and know what information they provide. Also, generate and examine RSoP reports as described in Lesson 2.

Examine RemoteApp Programs

- RemoteApp programs run on a Remote Desktop Services Host or Terminal Server and are accessed from a client through Remote Desktop. They then appear as if they are running locally on the client. Find out more about RemoteApp programs and the RemoteApp Manager, and then use your client running Windows 7 to test this feature. Note that the RDS Server role needs to be installed on the VAN-DC1 computer for you to do this practice.

Take a Practice Test

The practice tests on this book's companion CD offer many options. For example, you can test yourself on just one exam objective, or you can test yourself on all the 70-646 certification exam content. You can set up the test so that it closely simulates the experience of taking a certification exam, or you can set it up in study mode so that you can look at the correct answers and explanations after you answer each question.

MORE INFO **PRACTICE TESTS**

For details about all the practice test options available, see the "How to Use the Practice Tests" section in this book's Introduction.

CHAPTER 5

Planning Server Administration

Planning how servers will be managed is as important as planning their deployment. If you, as the system administrator, do not put enough care into determining the method by which servers will be managed, your job becomes much more difficult. As a system administrator, your time is important. In a large organization, you do not have enough time to deal with every small problem that comes across your desk. You should consider delegating minor administrative tasks to trusted users so that you can focus your attention on more complicated matters. In this chapter, you will learn how to plan which remote administration technology to use in your organization. You will also learn how to delegate trivial administrative tasks to subordinates so that you can spend more time on complex tasks.

Exam objectives in this chapter:

- Plan server management strategies.
- Plan for delegated administration.

Lessons in this chapter:

Before You Begin

To complete the exercises in the practice in this chapter, you need to have done the following:

- Complete the setup tasks outlined in Appendix A, "Setup Instructions for Windows Server 2008 R2."

No additional configuration is required for this chapter.

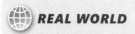

REAL WORLD

Orin Thomas

I used to have one of the world's longest telecommutes. For a couple of years, I used remote desktop technology to perform daily management tasks on a server hosted in a data center in Minneapolis, Minnesota, from where I live in Melbourne, Australia. Rather a long drive to work if I had ever needed to change a backup tape manually! Today, in the age of offshoring and outsourcing, such an arrangement is less unusual. Remote management technology is a boon and a bane to system administrators: a boon because it lets you manage a server from anywhere in the world; but a bane because you are expected to be able to manage a server from anywhere in the world. When you have a laptop with a built-in cellular modem, you can find yourself in a pub in Wagga Wagga restoring data on a server hosted in a London data center.

Lesson 1: Server Management Technologies

In this lesson, you will learn several methods of remotely administering Windows Server 2008 and Windows Server 2008 R2. When you understand these technologies, you can apply this knowledge to planning how to manage and monitor servers on an organization-wide basis. The key to applying this knowledge is understanding the difference between the functionality of a particular technology when you use it directly in the server room and applying that technology to managing servers in another state, or even on another continent.

After this lesson, you will be able to:
- Plan the local and remote administration of Windows Server 2008.
- Determine which server management technology to deploy in a given situation.

Estimated lesson time: 60 minutes

Tools for the Administration of Windows Server 2008 and Windows Server 2008 R2

In many cases, the tools that you decide to use to manage the servers on your organization's network will be more a matter of personal preference than technical necessity. You have a great deal of flexibility in how you can manage servers, but as a system administrator, you will be called upon to advise people in your organization on the best way to manage servers in a given set of circumstances. Throughout this lesson, you will learn about different management technologies with Windows Server 2008 and Windows Server 2008 R2 and situations in which you might choose to use one technology over another to achieve the most efficient server management outcome.

Server Manager Console

The Server Manager console, shown in Figure 5-1, is an expanded Microsoft Management Console (MMC) that allows you to manage all aspects of a computer running Windows Server 2008 or Windows Server 2008 R2. The Server Manager console contains the most commonly used tools that an administrator will need. As you add or remove roles and features, the relevant components are added or removed from the Server Manager console. The Server Manager console is not available on Server Core installations.

MORE INFO **SERVER MANAGER**

To learn more about the Server Manager console, consult the following TechNet article: *http://technet.microsoft.com/en-us/library/cc732131(WS.10).aspx.*

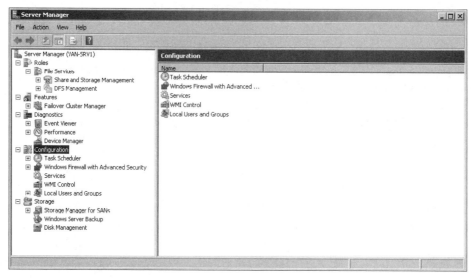

FIGURE 5-1 The Server Manager console

Servermanagercmd.exe is a command-line utility that can be run from an elevated command prompt on both the Full Core and Server Core installation options of Windows Server 2008 to add and remove server roles and features. Executing the command `servermanagercmd.exe –query` will display a list of all roles, role services, and features available to a computer running Windows Server 2008 and information about whether they are installed on the computer. You are most likely to use Servermanagercmd.exe on Server Core installations to install roles and features and then use tools such as the Remote Server Administration Tools (RSAT) to manage those roles and features remotely from a management computer. You can also use Oclist.exe and Ocsetup.exe on a computer running with the Server Core installation option to achieve the same goals. Although Servermanagercmd.exe is available on Windows Server 2008 and Windows Server 2008 R2, the command is being deprecated in favor of the Add-WindowsFeature cmdlet in Windows PowerShell. This cmdlet is available with the ServerManager module in PowerShell. You will learn more about PowerShell later in this lesson.

> **MORE INFO** **SERVERMANAGERCMD.EXE**
>
> To learn more about ServerManagerCmd.exe, consult the following TechNet article:
> *http://technet.microsoft.com/en-us/library/cc748918(WS.10).aspx.*

Microsoft Management Consoles

Although a default set of MMC consoles is available in the Administrative Tools menu, the snap-ins that you can use to create a custom console allow for greater functionality and customization. A custom console allows you to access a common toolset quickly. You also can copy the console to other computers, such as a management workstation, so that you have the same toolkit available regardless of where you are logged on. With some snap-ins, you can specify a set of credentials when running the snap-in against a remote computer. Creating a custom console is straightforward. To do this, perform the following steps:

1. From the Start menu, type **mmc** in the Run dialog box. This will open a blank MMC console.

2. From the File menu, click Add/Remove Snap-in. This will open the Add Or Remote Snap-ins dialog box, shown in Figure 5-2. Add the snap-ins that you want to use with the console, and then click OK.

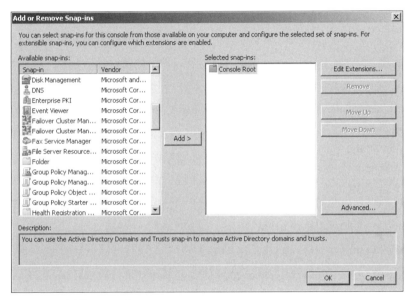

FIGURE 5-2 Adding snap-ins

3. If you are asked which computer to focus the MMC on, select that computer and then click OK.

4. From the File menu, save the console.

Snap-ins are available for all roles and features that are present on the server. Snap-ins for services and features that are not installed will not be available unless you install the appropriate RSAT features, which are covered in the section entitled "Remote Server Administration Tools (RSAT)," later in this lesson.

PowerShell

PowerShell is a scripting and command-line shell language specifically designed for system administration tasks. Although PowerShell can look daunting to system administrators who are not used to performing a significant number of their duties from the command prompt, after a few hours spent using PowerShell to accomplish day-to-day server management tasks, you might be reluctant to go back to GUI-based system administration utilities.

Windows Server 2008 R2 includes PowerShell 2.0, which is enabled by default. You can add PowerShell 2.0 to Windows Server 2008 by downloading it from Microsoft's website. You can add the modules automatically to PowerShell by right-clicking the PowerShell item on the Taskbar and clicking Import System Modules. When you do this, modules that are relevant to the features and roles that you have installed on the server will become active. If you install all the RSAT tools, you will have access to the following system modules:

- ActiveDirectory
- AD RMS
- ADRMSAdmin
- AppLocker
- BestPractices
- BitsTransfer
- FailoverClusters
- NetworkLoadBalancingClusters
- PSDiagnostics
- ServerManager
- TroubleshootingPack
- WebAdministration

You can also add these modules individually. For example, to load the ServerManager module, issue the following command:

```
Import-Module ServerManager
```

From the perspective of planning server 2008 management strategies, you can use PowerShell scripts to automate almost all complex system administration tasks. You can call PowerShell scripts from the Task Scheduler, allowing you to automate many daily system administration tasks. Because PowerShell is also a scripting language, you can build conditional logic into your scripts, allowing automated tasks to execute in a certain manner depending on the conditions that exist when the script is run. PowerShell scripts work best for planned tasks where you know exactly what needs to be done. PowerShell scripts do not work as well when you are performing tasks that require you to make a significant number of on-the-spot decisions about which way to proceed.

PowerShell 2.0 also has powerful remote administration capabilities. You will learn more about configuring Windows Server 2008 R2 to support remote PowerShell functionality later in this lesson.

> **MORE INFO** **POWERSHELL AND WINDOWS SERVER 2008 AND WINDOWS SERVER 2008 R2**
>
> PowerShell is a complex topic that cannot be done justice in a few pages. Several good books are available from Microsoft Press that will teach you about how to best use PowerShell in your environment. To get started, consult the PowerShell and Windows Server 2008 page on the Microsoft website at *http://technet.microsoft.com/en-us/library/ bb978526.aspx.*

Scripting and Command-Line Tools

Command-line tools and scripts are available for all the server roles and features that you can install on Windows Server 2008 and Windows Server 2008 R2. Although the command-line tools are not as straightforward to use as the GUI-based utilities, with a little effort, you can use them to perform all the tasks that you can complete with the GUI tools. An advantage of the command-line tools is that you can use them in scripts that you create. If you can create a script that automates a complicated administrative task that works on one server, you can then copy that script to use on other servers.

Traditional scripting using Windows Scripting Host as an administrative tool has been deprecated in favor of PowerShell. That does not mean that you cannot use existing management scripts with Windows Server 2008 and Windows Server 2008 R2; it simply means that Microsoft recommends that you use PowerShell, which was designed specifically as a scripting and command-line shell for system administration in a way that Windows Scripting Host scripts are not. In some circumstances—especially in terms of the script-based management of computers running in the Server Core configuration—you will not have any choice but to use traditional scripts because PowerShell is not fully compatible with Windows Server Core on Windows Server 2008. This is not the case with Windows Server 2008 R2, where PowerShell is much better supported in the Server Core configuration.

Emergency Management Services (EMS)

Emergency Management Services (EMS) allows a server to be controlled when it is in a minimally functional state, such as the network card and display adapter being nonfunctional. EMS allows an out-of-band connection, generally through a serial or USB port using an application such as Telnet or another terminal emulator. With the appropriate hardware, you can also perform many server management tasks through EMS, although you must complete all these tasks from the command line.

An advantage to EMS is that it is accessible when other methods of administration are not. You can access EMS when the computer is in the process of starting up or shutting down. For example, EMS allows access to a server if it has frozen during shutdown or in some cases even when a STOP error has occurred. You can also use EMS when a server is not responsive to traditional input methods because of a runaway process. As a example: In your experience as a system administrator, you might have encountered a server that appears to have frozen and you are unable to log on. In this situation, you might be able to use EMS to manage the server and even shut down the errant process. This will not always be the case—sometimes you cannot do much with a frozen server other than manually turn it off, but EMS provides you with a final fallback position for working with a server before that last resort.

EMS must be enabled on a server. How you enable it depends on the type of hardware configuration that a computer has. For example, the method of enabling and configuring EMS on a computer with Extensible Firmware Interface (EFI) firmware is different from the method of enbling and configuring EMS on a computer that has an Advance Configuration and Power Interface (ACPI) Serial Port Console Redirection (SPCR) table. Enabling requires you to use the `bcdedit` command to edit the boot settings of Windows Server 2008 and Windows Server 2008 R2, but the exact syntax is dependent on a server's hardware configuration. From a planning perspective, you should enable EMS on servers prior to deployment. That way, if you do encounter a situation in which the tools might be useful, they will be available to you.

> **MORE INFO**   **ENABLE EMS**
>
> To learn how to enable EMS on a computer running Windows Server 2008 or Windows Server 2008 R2, consult the following page on TechNet: *http://technet.microsoft.com/ en-us/library/cc731245(WS.10).aspx*.

Although you can use EMS to perform almost all management tasks on a server through a command-prompt interface, most organizations primarily use EMS to manage a server that is not responding to normal management technologies. The Special Administration Console (SAC) is an EMS-specific tool, but it is available only if Windows is functioning normally. The !SAC console, which provides a subset of SAC commands, is available when the operating system is not operating normally and the SAC console has failed to load and has ceased to operate. Typing **help** or **?** at either the SAC or !SAC prompt brings up a list of commands that you can use with EMS at its current level of functionality.

Remote Administration Technologies

You are not limited to one option when considering which remote administration technology to deploy to manage the servers in your organization's environment. Each technology has its benefits and drawbacks. It will make sense to perform some management tasks using a remote desktop connection (RDC) in some situations, while in others you might be better served by connecting to a server using a Telnet application when you need to execute a script. The next part of this lesson covers remote administration using Remote Desktop, RSAT, PowerShell remoting, and Telnet.

Remote Desktop

Remote Desktop is likely to be the most commonly used remote administration technology deployed in your Windows Server 2008 environment because it most closely simulates the experience of being directly in front of a server. Administrators connect to servers using the Remote Desktop Client software that is included with Windows operating systems.

After you enable Remote Desktop, members of the local Administrators group and Remote Desktop Users group are able to connect automatically. It is important to note that on domain controllers, just being a member of the Remote Desktop Users group does not confer the right to log on using Remote Desktop. You can change this by editing the Log On Through Remote Desktop policy, located in the Computer Configuration/Policies/Windows Settings/Security Settings/Local Policies/User Rights Assignment/ node of a Group Policy object (GPO).

Remote Desktop allows two administrators to make simultaneous remote connections to a computer running Windows Server 2008 or Windows Server 2008 R2. To ensure that you make an administrator connection, use the /admin switch after the server address in Remote Desktop Connection. If two administrators are already connected, you can force one of those administrators to log off, as shown in Figure 5-3.

FIGURE 5-3 Forcing disconnection

As shown in Figure 5-4, the Remote Desktop firewall exception is enabled automatically when you enable Remote Desktop for administration. Although Windows Firewall is configured automatically to allow remote desktop traffic, other firewalls might exist between the client and the server you want to manage. If you encounter this situation, you must ensure that you configure the firewalls to allow traffic on TCP port 3389.

FIGURE 5-4 Firewall exception for Remote Desktop

In certain situations, you will need to perform administrative tasks on servers located on private networks at organizations that you can connect to only using the Internet. These servers are likely to be protected by firewalls and also will not be directly addressable by Internet hosts. For example, you cannot make a direct connection to a computer running Windows Server 2008 or Windows Server 2008 R2 that is using IP address 192.168.15.100 on a remote organization's network, if the only way that you can connect to that network is through the Internet.

If you do need to perform regular administrative duties on servers on private networks that you do not have a direct connection to, you have two options:

- You can configure a VPN server on the remote screened subnet. After a VPN connection is established from your workstation to the remote private network, you can make an administrative connection to the server that you want to manage.

- You can install a Remote Desktop Gateway (RD Gateway) on the remote screened subnet. You can then make a Remote Desktop Protocol (RDP) connection through this gateway to any server located on the remote organization's private network.

Although configuring a VPN server on the remote organization's screened subnet is an option in many circumstances, setting up a VPN server involves a significant amount of effort. If you need to make RDP connections only to remote servers, installing a RD Gateway server is a simpler process.

RD Gateways allow users on the Internet to connect to Remote Desktop servers on a protected network through an RD Gateway server hosted behind a firewall on a screened subnet. RD Gateway works by using RDP over HTTPS, which means that external firewalls only need to have port 443 open, rather than opening up the Remote Desktop port. A direct connection is made from the Internet host through the firewall to the RD Gateway server, and that gateway server then forwards authorized traffic to servers located on a protected private network. Although primarily used to allow normal users to access Remote Desktop Services applications when connecting from clients on the Internet, RD Gateway also can be used to assist in the remote administration of servers on a protected network.

> **MORE INFO** **RD GATEWAY**
>
> To learn more about RD Gateway, consult the following TechNet article:
> *http://technet.microsoft.com/en-us/library/dd560672(WS.10).aspx.*

Remote Server Administration Tools (RSAT)

By default, only the administration tools for the services and features installed on a computer running Windows Server 2008 or Windows Server 2008 R2 are available on that computer. Therefore, if you wanted to manage a remote server running Active Directory Rights Management Server (AD RMS), you would not be able to add that snap-in or access the tool from the Administrative Tools menu unless you had installed the RSAT tools or the specific AD RMS component of the RSAT tools. If you add the RSAT tools feature to a server, you will have access to all administrative tools even if the relevant roles and features are not installed locally. You can also choose to add only specific RSAT components depending on your need. RSAT tools are added using the Add Feature functionality. You can add all the RSAT tools by using the following PowerShell cmdlet when the ServerManager module is installed:

```
Add-WindowsFeature RSAT
```

The RSAT tools are available as features in Windows Server 2008 and Windows Server 2008 R2 and available as a download for computers running the following operating systems:

- Windows Vista SP1 Business, Enterprise, or Ultimate edition
- Windows 7 Professional, Enterprise, or Ultimate edition

The RSAT tools cannot be installed on computers running Windows XP Professional or Windows Server 2003.

PowerShell Remoting

PowerShell remoting allows you to execute PowerShell commands against remote computers. Remoting is supported on computers running Windows 7, Windows Vista SP 1 or later, Windows Server 2008, and Windows Server 2008 R2. PowerShell remoting must be enabled on the computer that you intend to manage remotely. To enable PowerShell remoting, perform the following steps:

1. Start an elevated PowerShell session.

2. Configure the WinRM service to start automatically, and then start the service by running the following commands:

   ```
   Set-Service Winrm -startuptype automatic

   Start-service winrm
   ```

3. Enable PowerShell remoting with the following command:

   ```
   Enable-PSRemoting -force
   ```

Once PowerShell remoting is enabled, you can use remote commands through the Invoke-Command cmdlet with the -computername parameter. For example, to list all features installed on a remote computer when the ServerManager module is installed, issue the following command:

```
Invoke-Command -script {Import-Module ServerManager; Get-WindowsFeature} -computername
VAN-SRV1
```

You will configure PowerShell remoting in the practice at the end of this chapter.

> **MORE INFO POWERSHELL REMOTING**
>
> To learn more about PowerShell remoting, consult the following TechNet article: *http://technet.microsoft.com/en-us/library/dd347744.aspx*.

Remote Administration Tools for Non-Administrators

In Lesson 2, "Delegating Authority," you will learn techniques for delegating administrative privileges to non-administrators. Before non-administrators can perform the tasks that they have been delegated, they need to have access to the tools that allow them to perform those tasks.

One method that you can use to provide them with those tools is to create and distribute custom MMCs. You simply add the console that is related to the delegated task to the custom console, save that console, and deploy it to the user. Although you could install the RSAT tools on the workstation of a staff member with non-administrative privileges, having 30 consoles available when the staff member needs only 1 to perform her job function may prove confusing.

Although you might be tempted to, you should not give normal users access to a server through Remote Desktop. In general, when planning for remote administration, you should limit the number of people who are able to access a server directly. Users that have been delegated limited administrative responsibilities almost always can complete their tasks by using tools that have been installed on their workstations.

Using Telnet for Remote Administration

A final method of performing Remote Administration on computers running Windows Server 2008 or Windows Server 2008 R2 is by connecting through Telnet. Telnet allows you to make a text-based connection over the network to a command console. You can run any text-based commands remotely that you normally would be able to run locally on a command prompt. The advantage of Telnet as a remote administration technology is that you can use it over extremely low bandwidth connections, such as those that are below-normal 56-kilobit dialup speeds and might not be able to support Remote Desktop.

After the Telnet Server feature is installed, you can configure options by running the tlntadmn.exe command from an elevated command prompt. Options that you can configure include the idle session timeout, the maximum number of supported Telnet connections, the port that Telnet operates on, and the maximum number of failed login attempts. The default authentication mechanism for the Telnet server is NTLM. Because Telnet is not an encrypted protocol, you should secure connections to a Telnet Server using IPSec and ensure that Telnet-related firewall rules require an authenticated connection.

With PowerShell remoting now supported in Windows Server 2008 and Windows Server 2008 R2 with the release of PowerShell 2.0, Telnet is less likely to be used as a remote administration tool.

 Quick Check

- Which PowerShell 2.0 module must you add to your PowerShell session before you can use the Add-WindowsFeature cmdlet?

Quick Check Answer

- You must add the ServerManager module to your PowerShell session before you can use the Add-WindowsFeature cmdlet.

Managing Event Logs

A significant component of planning for the managing servers involves determining how to deal with event logs. The core problem with event logging is ensuring that you are aware that something important has happened by ensuring that you not only have logged the relevant event, but that you also can actually find it. You face two problems when doing this:

- If you log everything, how do you ensure that you do not miss that one important event in the tens of thousands that are recorded?

- If you restrict the amount of data that you log, how can you be sure that you are not missing something vitally important because you have chosen to record only a select number of events?

When you have to manage tens (or even hundreds) of servers, you can be flooded with data quickly. In the following section, you will learn how to use the Event Viewer that ships with Windows Server 2008 and Windows Server 2008 R2 to make event log data more manageable.

By default, Windows Server 2008 and Windows Server 2008 R2 have the following logs available under the Windows Logs node in the Event Viewer:

- **Application** The Application log stores data generated by applications that are installed on the server. This includes applications such as the Certificate Services client, Desktop Windows Manager, and other applications such as Notepad. With the Application log, you must remember that there is also a node in the Event Viewer called Applications And Service Logs, which also stores application and server role log data. In general, you should check under the Applications And Service Logs node for application-related information before you check the Application log itself. Alternatively, you can set up a filter. You will learn how to set up filters later in this lesson.

- **Security** The Security log contains audited security events, such as logons or the accessing of audited objects such as files. What is important to remember about this log is that you must configure auditing to ensure that the events you want logged actually are. You will not be able to determine who has attempted to access a specific file unless you have configured auditing for that file. If you have configured auditing, the related events are written to the security log file.

- **Setup** The Setup log contains events related to the setup of applications on the server.

- **System** The System log stores events logged by system components, including events such as the failure of a device driver or the failure of a service.

- **Forwarded Events** The Forwarded Events log stores events collected from other computers. This log is very useful for administrators who want to view important log data in a single location rather than by checking the individual logs of each server that they manage. You can collect events from other computers only by using subscriptions, which is covered in the section entitled "Configuring Log Subscriptions," later in this lesson.

Another important planning decision related to event logs is deciding how large the logs can be and what to do when the log file reaches the maximum specified log size. This is often described as setting a log retention policy. As you can see in Figure 5-5, the options are Overwrite Events As Needed, Archive The Log When Full, and Do Not Overwrite Events (Clear Log Manually). If you set this final policy security log, remember that depending on how you configure Group Policy, a server could become unavailable until the appropriate log file is cleared manually. It is often good policy to ensure that security event logs are never overwritten.

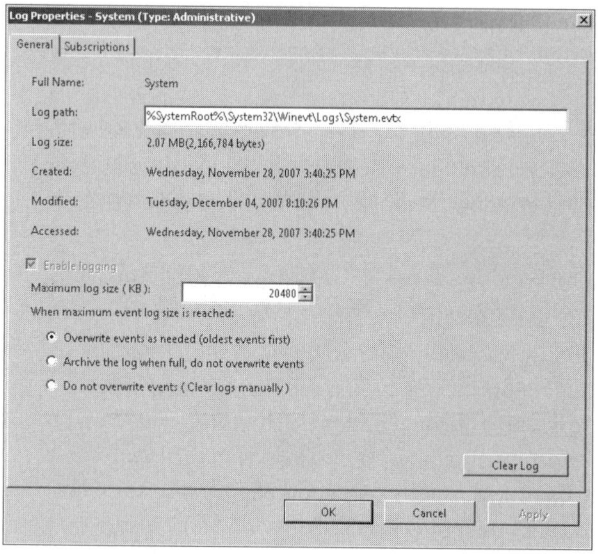

FIGURE 5-5 Log file properties

Filters

Filters are a way of restricting the number of events displayed in a log to those that are pertinent to your interests. For example, the filter shown in Figure 5-6 will display only Critical, Warning, and Error events in the System log that were recorded between 10:49 P.M. on January 3, 2011, and 10:49 P.M. on January 17, 2011. To use a filter, you need to know something about the type of event you are looking for. The higher the number of conditions that you place on the filter, the fewer events will be displayed. Unlike custom views, you cannot save filters—they must be generated each time you want to use them.

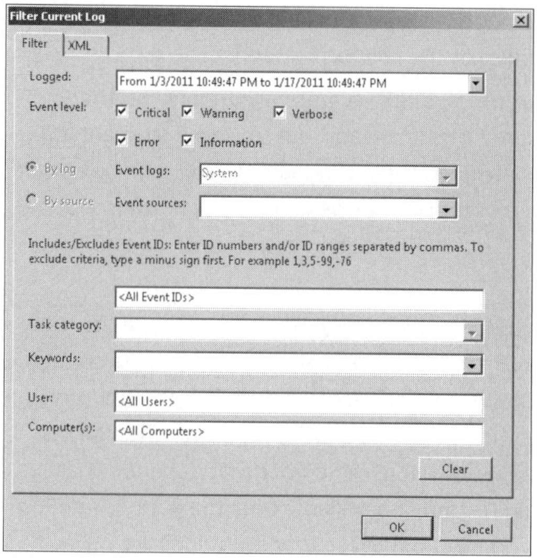

FIGURE 5-6 Log filter

Custom Views

You can think of a custom view, such as the one shown in Figure 5-7, as a special filter that can be saved. You can also apply a custom filter to multiple logs rather than to a single log. Rather than having to create the filter, you can create a custom view and select that view each time you enter the Event Viewer console. You can also import and export custom views if you want to use them on other computers running Windows Server 2008 and Windows Server 2008 R2.

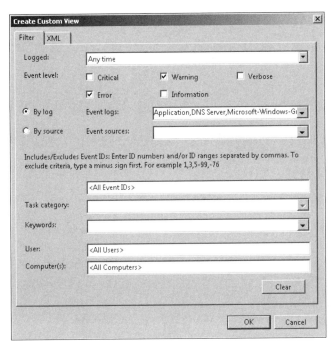

FIGURE 5-7 A custom view

Attaching Tasks to Events

As shown in Figure 5-8, attaching a task to an event allows you to start a program, send an email, or display a message each time a specific event is written to a particular event log. Attaching tasks to events allows you to be more proactive about the management of important events. Rather than finding out about the event only when you examine the log files after the event occurs, you can be informed immediately that the event has occurred, which allows you to take direct action. As with any direct notification, you should avoid setting up too many of them. If you do, you may start to feel flooded by tasks that might not require your immediate attention. You should arrange to receive a direct notification only for the kind of event to which you would need to respond urgently. Tasks that are attached to event logs are stored in Task Scheduler. If you want to remove an attached task, you must do this from Task Scheduler rather than from Event Viewer.

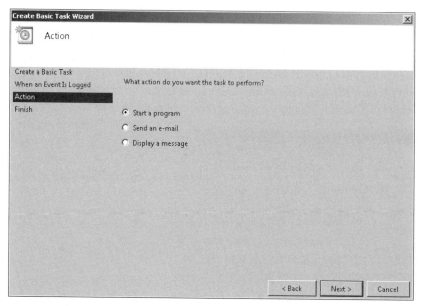

FIGURE 5-8 Creating a basic task

The limitations of attaching tasks to events are that the event must exist already within the log file; you cannot attach tasks to events in analytic or debug logs; and you cannot assign a task to an event stored in a saved log file. You cannot use this functionality to run a task to an event if the event has not occurred, although you can mimic such functionality by creating a PowerShell script that runs on a scheduled basis. Using PowerShell with log files is covered in more detail later in this lesson. You will attach a task to an event in the practice at the end of this chapter.

Configuring Log Subscriptions

Log subscriptions are a form of centralized log management. Rather than having to check the logs of each server that you are responsible for, you can use log subscriptions to centralize all important events that occur across the organization in a single place. Then, by applying custom views, you can single out specific events of interest quickly.

You can configure two types of subscriptions. In a collector-initiated subscription, the computer that will store the collected events (the collector) retrieves them from the computer that generates the event (the source computer). In a source computer–initiated subscription, the computers that generate the events forward the events to the collector computer.

To set up a collector-initiated subscription, perform the following steps:

1. On each source computer, open an elevated command prompt and issue the command `winrm quickconfig`. You also will need to accept the request to create a firewall exception.

2. On each source computer, add the computer account of the collector computer to the local Administrators group.

3. On the computer that will function as the collector, open an elevated command prompt and issue the command `wecutil qc`. This will start the Windows Event Collector service and configure it to start automatically, with a delayed start.

4. Open Event Viewer on the collector computer and click the Subscriptions item. In the Actions pane, click Create Subscription, which will open the Subscription Properties dialog box shown in Figure 5-9.

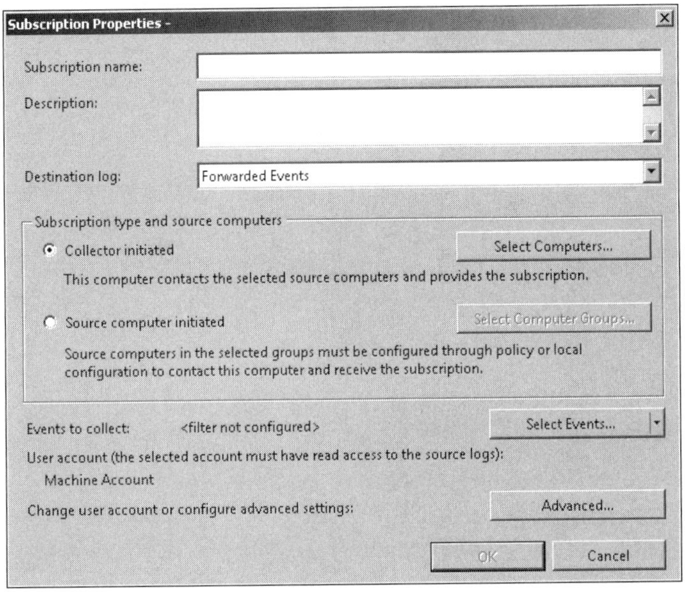

FIGURE 5-9 Configuring a subscription

5. Click Select Computers to select the source computers.

6. When all source computers are selected, click Select Events to configure a filter for the type of events that you want the collector computer to gather.

7. When you have completed the creation of the filter, click OK twice to activate the subscription.

The configuration of a subscription filter is more like the configuration of a custom view in that you are able to specify multiple event log sources, rather than just a single event log source. In addition, the subscription will be saved, whereas you need to re-create a filter each time you use one. By default, all collected event log data will be written to the Forwarded Event log. You can forward data to other logs by configuring the properties of the subscription. Even though you use a filter to retrieve only specific events from source computers and place them in the destination log, you can still create and apply a custom view to data that is located in the destination log. You could create a custom view for each source computer, which would allow you to limit events to that computer rather than viewing data from all source computers at the same time.

You configure collector-initiated subscriptions through the application of Group Policy. To do this, you must configure the collector computer in the same manner as you did in the previous steps. When configuring the subscription type, select Source Computer Initiated rather than Collector Initiated. To set up the source computers, apply a GPO where you have configured the Computer Configuration/Policies/Administrative Templates/Windows Components/Event Forwarding node and configure the Server Address, Refresh Interval, And Issuer Certificate policy with the details of the collector computer, as shown in Figure 5-10.

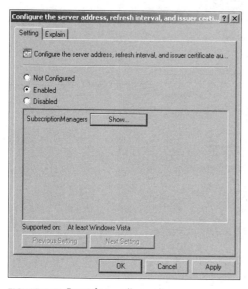

FIGURE 5-10 Event forwarding policy

MORE INFO   EVENT LOG SUBSCRIPTIONS

For more information on event log subscriptions, consult the following TechNet Web page: *http://technet.microsoft.com/en-us/library/cc749183.aspx.*

Applications and Service Logs

When you install an application or role on a computer running Windows Server 2008 or Windows Server 2008 R2, it will most likely add a new log under the Applications And Services log node of the Event Viewer. Application And Service Logs is a new category of event logs introduced with Windows Server 2008. Because this category of event log is new, applications produced prior to the release of Windows Server 2008 might still write events to the traditional application log, covered earlier in this lesson. As Figure 5-11 shows, you can also view the analytic and debug logs of a server under this node. These logs are viewable only if you select the Show Analytic And Debug logs option under the View menu in the Event Viewer console.

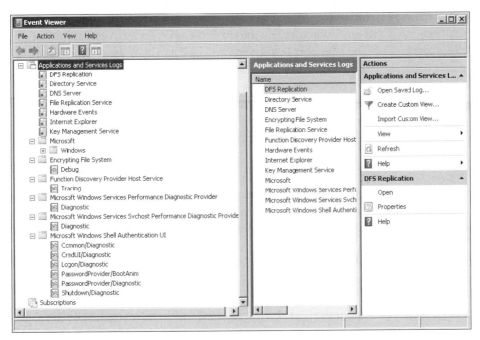

FIGURE 5-11 Viewing the analytic and debug logs

Application and service logs can be defined by four broad categories:

- **Admin** Admin logs describe a problem and suggest a solution that an administrator can implement. Messages in admin logs almost always tell an administrator how to rectify a problem.

- **Operational** Operational events provide information to assist in the analysis and diagnosis of problems. Although these events will not provide information on how to resolve the problem that generated the event, you can use these events as a task trigger to alert an administrator that this event has just occurred.

- **Analytic** Only viewable when enabled, analytic events are written in high volume and indicate problems that generally cannot be resolved easily.

- **Debug** Debug logs are used by developers who are troubleshooting applications that they have created.

Using Event Viewer on a Remote Computer

Just as you can with other management consoles, you can use the Event Viewer console to connect to remote computers running Windows Server 2008 or Windows Server 2008 R2. To do this, select the Connect To Another Computer option on the Action menu of the console. To view event logs remotely on a computer that has Windows Firewall enabled, you must enable the Remote Event Log Management exception.

When you connect to another computer remotely using the Event Viewer, the custom views that you can access are those stored on the local computer. Custom views stored on the remote computer will be unavailable. When you run a local custom view when connected to a remote computer, the custom view will be run against the remote event logs rather than the local ones. For example, if you have a custom view that shows only Error events from the System log, when connected to a remote computer, your custom view will show only Error events from the remote computer's system log.

Because you are likely to use subscriptions to forward event data to a centralized location for analysis, from a planning perspective, you are likely to make remote connections with Event Viewer only when you have found an event worthy of your attention and you want to dig deeper by looking at other events on that original computer. Forwarding everything that is interesting to a centralized location and allowing a local follow-up provides a good balance between storing details and displaying what is probably important.

Archiving Event Logs

When planning the management of event log data in an organization, be sure to consider your event log storage policies. You will need to create a policy that specifies how long event log data has to be retained. For example, if an employee is caught accessing confidential data, evidence of this activity might exist in security logs that were taken over the last several months. If logs are overwritten automatically once they reach a particular size, or simply deleted after a cursory examination, information pertinent to an investigation might be lost. The simplest way to manage the archiving of an organization's server event logs is to implement Event Log forwarding and then to export the collected event log data to files that can be backed up separately and stored securely for the required period. You can save log files by clicking Save Log File As on the Action menu. You can select from the following formats:

- Event Files (*.evtx)
- XML (*.xml)
- Text (Tab delimited) (*.txt)
- CSV (Comma Separated) (*.csv)

When you save log files using the Event Viewer Save Log File function, you are prompted about whether you want to save display information. If you do not include this information with the saved log file, the log file may not display properly when imported to other computers. You can also save log files when you apply filters or custom views. This can reduce the size of saved log files, though you might fail to save an event that later turns out to be important when you are performing an investigation. Although the other file types can be useful in specific circumstances, only files stored in Event Viewer format can be reopened in the Event Viewer on another computer.

Managing Event Logs with Wevtutil and PowerShell

Wevtutil has much of the same functionality as the Event Viewer GUI. It allows administrators to view, filter, and manage event log data directly from a command line. For example, to use Wevtutil to export a log to a file, use the following command:

```
wevtutil epl Logname Filename.evtx
```

Given this information, it is a relatively simple exercise for most administrators to create a script based on Wevtutil to perform a daily export of all log files to a shared directory. The Event Viewer console does not allow for this type of automation. Automating the backup of log file data is useful when you are considering the management of event logs on an organization-wide basis.

> **MORE INFO** **WEVTUTIL**
>
> To learn more about Wevtutil, consult the following TechNet page:
> *http://technet.microsoft.com/en-us/library/cc732848(WS.10).aspx.*

Although Wevtutil does provide the ability to analyze event log data, it provides only simple event management functionality. A more extensible option is PowerShell, which provides another method of monitoring and managing event logs through the Get-Eventlog cmdlet. The advantage of using PowerShell is that you can create more complicated scripts than you can with Wevtutil. All data analysis and manipulation occurs within the PowerShell script, whereas with Wevtutil, your script will call an outside application and then attempt to deal with that outside application's output. Put another way, PowerShell components are designed to interact with one another, and this makes writing and managing PowerShell scripts a simpler task for you as a system administrator.

You can use a PowerShell command to list all instances of an event in a specified log. For example, to find all events with event ID 1000 in the System log, you would enter the following PowerShell command:

```
Get-Eventlog System | where {$_.EventID -eq 1000}
```

> **MORE INFO** **GET-EVENTLOG**
>
> To learn more about the Get-EventLog cmdlet, consult the following TechNet page:
> *http://technet.microsoft.com/en-us/library/dd315250.aspx.*

As a programming and scripting language, PowerShell allows you to build complicated commands quickly for analyzing Windows event log data. From a planning perspective, you should consider PowerShell scripts for the management of event logs when built-in tools such as custom views, filters, and attaching tasks to specific events are not providing you with enough control to meet your needs. The functionality built into the Event Viewer is likely to meet the majority of your needs, but if you need to go further, using PowerShell will help you achieve your goals.

Microsoft System Center Operations Manager 2007 R2

When planning the centralized monitoring and management of large numbers of computers running Windows Server 2008 or Windows Server 2008 R2, you should consider implementing Microsoft System Center Operations Manager 2007 R2. System Center Operations Manager 2007 R2 allows you to manage and monitor thousands of servers and applications centrally and provides a complete overview of the health of your network environment. System Center Operations Manager 2007 R2 is the most recent version of Microsoft Operations Manager. System Center Operations Manager 2007 R2 provides the following features:

- Proactive alerts that recognize conditions that are likely to lead to failure of critical services, applications, and servers in the future

- The ability to configure tasks to execute automatically to resolve problems when given events occur

- The collection of long-term trend data from all servers and applications across the organization with the ability to generate comparison reports against current performance

- Correlation of auditing data generated across the organization, allowing the detection of trends that might not be apparent when examining server auditing data in isolation

In addition to the monitoring components that are part of a default Operations Manager 2007 R2 installation, you can use management packs, which are add-on components that extend Operations Manager 2007 R2 monitoring capability. Microsoft provides more than 60 different management packs that you can use with Operations Manager 2007 R2, covering everything from Microsoft Exchange Server 2010 to Microsoft SQL Server 2008 R2. You can use a management pack to determine whether a particular technology is configured according to best practices. You can also use management packs to analyze the performance of a technology and make recommendations on what configuration changes should be made to best suit the way that the technology is being used. This is similar to using the Best Practices Analyzer (BPA), but instead of being limited to analyzing one computer at a time, you can examine a specific technology's deployment across the organization.

Like other enterprise-wide monitoring and management solutions, such as Microsoft System Center Virtual Machine Manager 2008 R2, System Center Operations Manager 2007 R2 requires access to a database running SQL Server 2005 SP1 or later to store data. Because SQL Server instances are able to host multiple databases, a single server running SQL Server can host configuration databases for System Center Virtual Machine Manager 2008 R2 and System Center Operations Manager 2007 R2. Even if an organization does not require a database server as an application server, in enterprise environments, SQL Server increasingly finds a place as a core component of network infrastructure.

> **MORE INFO**   **SYSTEM CENTER OPERATIONS MANAGER 2007 R2**
>
> You can find out more about System Center Operations Manager 2007 R2 and download a 180-day evaluation version of the software from the following Microsoft website: *http://www.microsoft.com/systemcenter/en/us/operations-manager.aspx.*

Lesson Summary

- You must enable Remote Desktop on Windows Server 2008 or Windows Server 2008 R2 before you can make connections to the server. By default, members of the local Administrators and Remote Desktop Users groups can log on to a server using Remote Desktop. This does not apply to domain controllers, where only members of the Administrators group can log on.

- EMS allows you to manage a computer that has become nonfunctional.

- The RSAT tools include consoles for administering all the roles and features that ship with Windows Server 2008 or Windows Server 2008 R2. The RSAT tools are included as an installable feature on Windows Server 2008 or Windows Server 2008 R2 and can be downloaded and installed onto computers running Windows Vista SP1 or Windows 7.

- Filters allow you to limit the display of a single event log to a specific set of events. You cannot save filters, although custom views allow you to apply a saved filter to multiple event logs.

- You can attach tasks to specific logs or events. When the event occurs, the task is triggered. You can edit or delete existing event log–based tasks in Task Scheduler.

Lesson Review

You can use the following questions to test your knowledge of the information in Lesson 1, "Server Management Technologies." The questions are also available on the companion CD if you prefer to review them in electronic form.

> **NOTE ANSWERS**
>
> Answers to these questions and explanations of why each answer choice is correct or incorrect are located in the "Answers" section at the end of the book.

1. Which of the following operating systems support the RSAT? (Each answer is a complete solution. Choose all that apply.)

   A. Windows Vista Enterprise edition with SP1

   B. Windows XP Professional edition with SP3

   C. Windows 7 Home Premium edition

   D. Windows 7 Enterprise edition

   E. Windows Server 2008 Standard edition

2. By default, members of which of the following groups are able to connect via Remote Desktop to a stand-alone computer running Windows Server 2008 or Windows Server 2008 R2? (Each answer is a complete solution. Choose all that apply.)

   A. Administrators

   B. Remote Desktop Users

C. Power Users

D. Print Operators

E. Backup Operators

3. Which of the following technologies can you use to cleanly turn off a computer running Windows Server 2008 R2 that continues to function after an electrical surge has burned out its graphics and network adapters?

A. Remote Desktop

B. Telnet

C. EMS

D. PowerShell

4. It will be necessary in the coming months for you to perform regular administrative tasks on several computers at a subsidiary company's office that are running Windows Server 2008 R2. Because this is a subsidiary of your company, there is no direct WAN link to their office from your company's head office. However, both the subsidiary company and yours have a direct connection to the Internet and the third-party firewall is configured to allow port 443 traffic through if the source address is within your company's head office public IP address range. Which of the following solutions should you implement to allow for the remote administration of these computers from your head office location?

A. Configure an RD Gateway server and place it at the subsidiary office.

B. Configure an RD Gateway server and place it at your company's head office.

C. Configure the subsidiary office's firewall to allow port 25 traffic if the source IP address is within your company's head office's public IP address range.

D. Configure the subsidiary office's firewall to allow port 25 traffic if the source IP address is within your company's head office's private IP address range.

5. You have configured a collector computer to collect event log data from 50 different computers running Windows Server 2008 R2 that are scattered across your organization. When you open the Forwarded Events log in the Event Viewer, you are overwhelmed with data. Each time you open the Event Viewer, you want to be able to ascertain quickly whether any critical events have occurred within the last 24 hours. Which of the following solutions should you implement?

A. Create a custom filter.

B. Create a custom view.

C. Create a subscription.

D. Configure a Windows System Resource Manager (WSRM) policy.

Lesson 2: Delegating Authority

As a system administrator, you often have the privileges to do everything. As a valuable asset to your organization, however, you should minimize time spent attending to trivial tasks so that you can focus on accomplishing the more complex ones. Delegation of authority is a technology that allows nonprivileged users to perform a limited and highly specific set of simple administrative tasks. In this lesson, you will learn how you can plan the delegation of authority to make the management of your organization's network more efficient.

> **After this lesson, you will be able to:**
> - Plan delegation policies and procedures.
> - Delegate authority.
> - Delegate the management of applications.
>
> **Estimated lesson time: 60 minutes**

Delegation Policies

Human resources staff is rarely knowledgeable about the capabilities of AD DS. Delegation of authority is an area that combines both the technical aspects of what can be accomplished through the application of a system administrator's knowledge and the legal and policy framework that must be interpreted and implemented by the human resources department. System administrators are trusted with critical information by the organizations that they work for. If a system administrator is the only one who can perform a particular task, such as user account creation, permissions modification, or resetting a CEO's password, the system administrator is clearly to blame if something goes wrong. As you will learn in this lesson, system administrators have the ability to delegate their powers. Delegation of privilege should be done only in situations covered by existing policy, not only because it is the ethical thing to do, but also because there needs to be a clear chain of responsibility.

Delegation Procedures

You can delegate authority by configuring the security settings of objects within AD DS. Figure 5-12 shows the advanced security settings for an OU where the Kim Akers user account has been delegated permissions. The drawback of performing a manual edit is that it requires far more precision than using the Delegation Of Control Wizard, which performs the configuration automatically. You can also perform delegations by using the dsacls.exe command. Similar to using the GUI, the dsacls.exe command requires that you use precise syntax to set permissions on AD DS objects. You can learn more about the syntax of the dsacls.exe command by issuing the dsacls.exe /? command from an elevated command prompt on a computer running Windows Server 2008 or Windows Server 2008 R2. You can also create PowerShell scripts to modify the permissions assigned to an OU as a method of delegation. Because the dsacls.exe command-line utility is designed specifically for the task of modifying the permissions of directory objects, it offers a more direct route for this task than a PowerShell script that achieves the same results for simple delegation tasks.

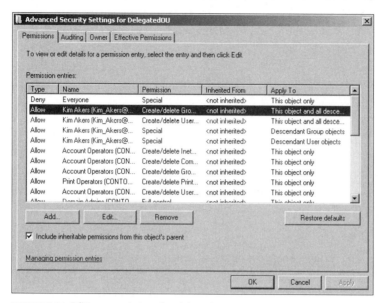

FIGURE 5-12 Editing permissions for delegation

When planning delegations for your environment, the Delegation Of Control Wizard is the best tool to use for a small number of delegations because it reduces the likelihood of errors and is relatively straightforward to use. When you need to perform a large number of complex delegations, getting a script that uses dsacls.exe or PowerShell functioning is worth the time investment. When you are deciding between using dsacls.exe and PowerShell, you need to assess the complexity of the delegation. You can perform a large number of relatively simple delegations using dsacls.exe. A large number of complex delegations might be better performed using a PowerShell script, because then you can add other components more easily, such as having the script extract data from a database or spreadsheet that describes which delegations need to be performed. In summary, use the following criteria to make your decision:

- If you have a small number of delegations, use the Delegation Of Control Wizard.
- If you have a large number of simple delegations, use the dsacls.exe command-line utility.
- If you have a large number of complex delegations involving components such as CSV files, use a PowerShell script.

Delegation of Administrative Privileges

As mentioned earlier in the lesson, the primary tool for performing delegations is the Delegation Of Control Wizard, shown in Figure 5-13. You can use the wizard at the domain level, although in most organizations, delegations will occur at the OU level. Using this wizard, you can delegate the following tasks:

- Create, Delete, And Manage User Accounts
- Reset User Passwords And Force Password Change At Next Logon
- Read All User Information
- Create, Delete, And Manage Groups
- Modify The Membership Of A Group
- Manage Group Policy Links
- Generate Resultant Set Of Policy (Planning)
- Generate Resultant Set Of Policy (Logging)
- Create, Delete, And Manage InetOrgPerson Accounts
- Reset InetOrgPerson Passwords And Force Password Change At Next Logon
- Read All InetOrgPerson Information

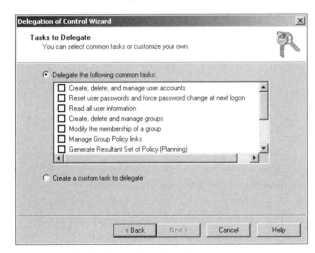

FIGURE 5-13 Tasks that can be delegated

You can use the Delegation Of Control Wizard to delegate one, some, or all these tasks to users or groups. You can also, when using the Delegation Of Control Wizard, create a custom task to delegate. When creating a custom task to delegate, you can delegate control of the folder, existing objects of the container, and the creation of new objects in the container, or specific objects. You can delegate control over more than 100 different objects. Figure 5-14 shows some of these objects in the Delegation Of Control Wizard.

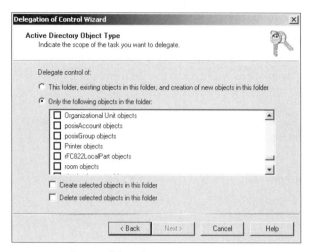

FIGURE 5-14 Custom delegation

The main reason to plan the delegation of control is that you want to give limited administrator rights to users. This is very important in environments where IT support is centralized and many branch offices are without a member of the IT support staff. It is important because security risks are involved in having some important administrative tasks, such as password resets, performed by someone in a remote headquarters office. For example, an attacker could phone the help desk pretending to be a particular user to get that user's user account password changed. If your organization has robust policies, you need something more than a declaration of "I am Rooslan" before Rooslan's password is changed. In many organizations, this involves a personal visit to the help desk and presentation of some form of identification, such as a driver's license. Identity verification becomes more difficult when someone at a branch office forgets her password and no local IT person is available to verify her identity or reset her password.

Using the Delegation Of Control Wizard, you can plan policies that allow a trusted person at a branch office site the ability to reset passwords. Because only that particular right is delegated, the trusted person does not have any other administrative rights. When someone at the branch office needs a password changed, he can verify his identity directly with the trusted delegate. The trusted delegate then performs the password reset.

Removing Existing Delegations

Although it is possible, by viewing the Advanced Security Settings for Delegation Properties, to figure out which user accounts have been delegated administrative permissions, it can sometimes be difficult to work out exactly which rights have been delegated, especially if the custom delegation options are used. In a situation in which you are unsure of what has happened previously in terms of delegation and no written records exist, you would be prudent to reset settings to their default configuration. The next time that a delegation is requested, you can make sure that a paper trail exists to explain why (and for whom) the delegation was performed.

The Restore Defaults button in the Advanced Security Settings for Delegation dialog box—which you can locate by clicking Advanced on the Security tab of the OU Properties dialog box—allows you to reset the OU to a default, nondelegated state. You can also reset existing delegations using the dsacls.exe command-line utility. For example, to reset the OU named Delegation in the adatum.com domain, you would issue the following command:

```
Dsacls "OU=Delegation,DC=adatum,DC=com" /resetDefaultDACL
```

Delegating the Management of a Group

You can delegate control over the membership of a group through specifying a manager with the Managed By tab of a user account's Properties dialog box. The user account specified as the manager can edit the membership of the group, adding and removing users as necessary. Figure 5-15 shows that Kim Akers's user account has been given the ability to update the membership list of the group named ExampleGroup. The manager can either be a user account or a group that exists within AD DS.

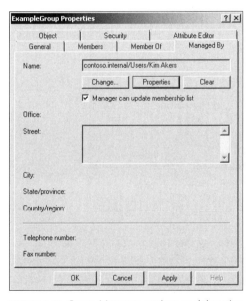

FIGURE 5-15 Group Manager settings as delegation

Credential Delegation

Credential delegation is an automatic process that is different from delegation of control. Delegation of control allows someone with a large set of rights to grant a subset of those rights to another user. Credential delegation, also known as *delegated authentication*, allows a computer to impersonate a user for the purposes of gaining access to resources that the user would normally be able to access.

When the domain and forest functional level are set to Windows Server 2008 or Windows Server 2008 R2, the Delegation tab, shown in Figure 5-16, becomes available on the computer account's Properties dialog box in Active Directory Users And Computers.

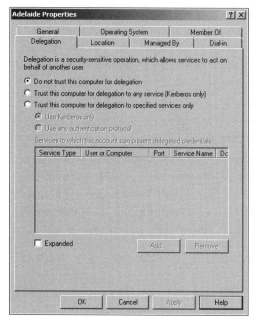

FIGURE 5-16 Computer account delegation settings

You can configure the following delegation settings by editing the properties of a computer account:

- Do Not Trust This Computer For Delegation
- Trust This Computer For Delegation To Any Service (Kerberos Only)
- Trust This Computer For Delegation To Specified Services Only

In terms of planning, you should deny the ability to participate in delegated authentication to any computers that are not physically secure. If this is not practical, you can plan to use constrained delegation. Constrained delegation allows you to select specific services that can be requested through delegation by a computer that you trust for delegation. For example, in Figure 5-17, the computer account for the computer named Adelaide is configured so that it can only be used to present delegated credentials to the DNS service on computer GLASGOW.contoso.internal.

You can block important user accounts from participating in delegation. In Active Directory User And Computers, on the Account tab of a user account's Properties dialog box, under Account Options, you will find the option to set an account as sensitive and not to be delegated, as shown in Figure 5-18. Delegated authentication allows a network service to assume a user's identity when connecting to a second network service. For example, if Encrypting File System (EFS) is used in an organization, delegated authentication allows for the storage of encrypted files on file servers because the file server needs to assume the user's identity to obtain the necessary certificates to encrypt the file. Although this is acceptable for normal user accounts, Microsoft recommends that all domain-level

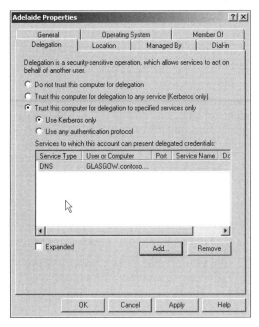

FIGURE 5-17 Limiting delegation

administrator accounts be marked as sensitive and prohibited from delegation. That way, there is no chance that administrative rights will be hijacked by a sophisticated attack that uses delegation and impersonation.

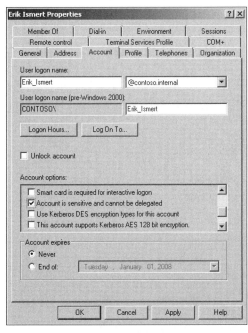

FIGURE 5-18 Stopping the delegation of a sensitive user account

Quick Check
- Which types of user accounts should be marked as sensitive and prohibited from participating in credential delegation?

Quick Check Answer
- Administrator accounts, specifically domain- and enterprise-level administrator accounts, should be marked as sensitive and be prohibited from participating in credential delegation.

Delegating the Management of Applications

In many large organizations, different people are responsible for different administrative tasks. The person who installs the application often is not the person who is responsible for maintaining that application. An example of this might be Exchange Server 2010, where the person who is responsible for the network overall and who has administrative privileges over all computers running Windows Server 2008 R2 is not actually responsible for managing the Exchange Server 2010 infrastructure.

Role-Based Delegation

Almost all Microsoft server products, such as Exchange Server 2010, SQL Server 2008 R2, and System Center Operations Manager 2007 R2, use a method of role-based delegation, where users are assigned particular administrative roles. In almost all cases, users that are delegated administrative roles for a particular application require no separate administrative rights on the server that hosts that application.

Role Based Access Control (RBAC), a technology available in Exchange Server 2010, allows you to delegate specific administrative privileges over a specific scope. For example, you might give a particular group the ability to manage all mailboxes on all servers at the Sydney site, but not grant them any mailbox administration privileges on any other mailbox servers in the organization.

> *MORE INFO* **RBAC IN EXCHANGE SERVER 2010**
>
> To learn more about RBAC in Exchange Server 2010, consult the following TechNet article: *http://technet.microsoft.com/en-us/library/dd298183.aspx*.

IIS Configuration Delegation

Microsoft Internet Information Services (IIS) 7.0 configuration delegation, a feature new to IIS 7.0 and available in IIS 7.5, allows administrators of computers hosting the Web Server role to delegate website configuration tasks. This means that rather than requiring the administrator of the computer running Windows Server 2008 or Windows Server 2008 R2 to configure settings such as a website's default document or SSL settings, these configuration tasks can be delegated to website owners or users without server-level administrative rights on a per-website basis. To perform feature delegation, it is necessary to be logged on or invoke the built-in Administrator account. You cannot perform feature delegation with an account that is a member of the local Administrators group on the computer hosting IIS 7 or IIS 7.5 because of the security architecture of Windows Server 2008 and Windows Server 2008 R2.

> **MORE INFO** **CONFIGURING IIS DELEGATION**
>
> To learn more about delegated management in IIS, consult the following page on IIS.NET: *http://learn.iis.net/page.aspx/159/configuring-remote-administration-and-feature-delegation-in-iis-7/.*

Authorization Manager

Authorization Manager provides an authorization model framework for applications on the Windows Server platform. By using Authorization Manager, application developers can create roles and scopes that allow them to implement the principles of RBAC in their applications. You can use Authorization Manager only on applications that have been created specifically to use Authorization Manager. You can start Authorization Manager using the azman.msc command on a computer running Windows Server 2008 or Windows Server 2008 R2. The Authorization Manager console is displayed in Figure 5-19.

FIGURE 5-19 Authorization Manager

Authorization Manager stores information in authorization stores. In Windows Server 2008 R2, Authorization Manager supports authorization stores in the following locations: SQL Server databases, AD DS, Active Directory Lightweight Directory Services (AD LDS), or in XML files. The domain must be at the Windows Server 2003 or higher functional level to support an Authorization Manager store. SQL Server must be running SQL Server 2005 SP1 or later to support Authorization Manager stores.

Authorization Manager has two modes: Administrator mode and Developer mode. Developer mode allows you to create, deploy, and maintain applications, access all Authorization Manager features, and create new authorization stores. Administrator mode allows you to deploy or maintain existing applications, but it does not allow you to create new applications or define operations.

MORE INFO AUTHORIZATION MANAGER

To learn more about Authorization Manager, consult the following TechNet Web page: *http://technet.microsoft.com/en-us/library/cc726036(WS.10).aspx.*

Lesson Summary

- You should consult with the human resources department and develop written delegation policies before proceeding with an actual delegation.

- Delegation is usually performed using the Delegation Of Control Wizard. You can also perform delegation using the dsacls.exe command. It is also possible to reset delegation settings back to their defaults using the dsacls.exe command.

- Domain Administrator accounts should be marked as sensitive and be prohibited from participating in delegation.

- Application delegation usually involves adding users to special groups that are added to the domain by an application's installation routine.

- Authorization Manager allows you to implement RBAC in custom applications.

Lesson Review

You can use the following questions to test your knowledge of the information in Lesson 2, "Delegating Authority." The questions are also available on the companion CD if you prefer to review them in electronic form.

NOTE ANSWERS

Answers to these questions and explanations of why each answer choice is correct or incorrect are located in the "Answers" section at the end of the book.

1. You have just logged on to a computer running Windows Server 2008 R2 that hosts the Web Server role using Remote Desktop. The server is a member of your organization's domain. You are in the process of configuring the server to host websites for several different departments in your company. You want to delegate authority in such a way that each department can manage its own website. When you attempt this, you are unable to perform the feature delegation. Which of the following strategies should you pursue to accomplish this goal?

    A. Log on using the built-in Administrator account.

    B. Add your domain account to the local Administrators group.

    C. Add your domain account to the Domain Admins group.

    D. Add your local account to the local Administrators group.

2. You are planning a Windows Server 2008 R2 network for your organization. Your organization has a head office and five branch offices scattered around the country. IT personnel will be located only in the head office. You want to avoid having branch office users contact the head office when they need a password changed, but you do not want to grant non-IT staff unnecessary privileges. Which of the following plans would meet these goals?

   A. Delegate the Create, Delete, And Manage Groups task to a trusted user at each branch office using the Delegation Of Control Wizard.

   B. Delegate the Create, Delete, And Manage User Accounts task to a trusted user at each branch office using the Delegation Of Control Wizard.

   C. Delegate the Read All User Information task to a trusted user at each branch office using the Delegation Of Control Wizard.

   D. Delegate the Reset User Passwords And Force Password Change At Next Logon task to a trusted user at each branch office using the Delegation Of Control Wizard.

3. You want give Hazem Abolrous the ability to change the membership of the Interns universal security group. The group is located in the Contractors OU, which hosts the user accounts and security groups related to temporary workers at your organization. Which of the following steps should you take to accomplish this goal?

   A. Use the Delegation Of Control Wizard to grant Hazem's user account the Modify The Membership Of A Group right on the Contractors OU.

   B. Use the Delegation Of Control Wizard on the Interns security group. Grant the Modify The Membership Of A Group right to Hazem's user account

   C. Use the Delegation Of Control Wizard on the Interns security group. Grant the Create, Delete, And Manage Groups right to Hazem's user account.

   D. Set the Interns security group to be managed by Hazem's user account. Ensure that Hazem has the ability to update the membership list.

4. The Students OU contains 300 user accounts and 40 groups. Your assistant reports that she made an error when using the Delegation Of Control Wizard, and she is not sure which rights she may have delegated away. Which of the following actions could you take to return the Students OU to the state it existed in prior to delegation occurring? (Each answer is a complete solution. Choose two.)

   A. Use the dsacls command with the /resetDefaultDACL option.

   B. Use the Restore Defaults button in the Advanced Security Settings for Delegation dialog box for the OU.

   C. Use the Clear button on the Managed By tab of the OU Properties dialog box.

   D. Use the Change button on the Managed By tab of the OU Properties dialog box.

   E. Use the dsquery command.

PRACTICE Remote Management and Delegation

In this set of practices, you will perform several common Windows Server 2008 R2 remote management and delegation tasks, including installing a feature remotely through PowerShell and delegating administrative privileges over an OU.

EXERCISE 1 Remote Management with PowerShell 2.0

In this exercise, you will configure two servers so that you can perform remote management tasks using PowerShell 2.0. To complete this exercise, perform the following steps:

1. Power on server VAN-DC1, VAN-SRV1, and VAN-SRV2. Log on to server VAN-SRV1 with the Kim_Akers user account.

2. Open an elevated PowerShell prompt and issue the following commands:

   ```
   Import-Module ServerManager

   Set-Service Winrm -startuptype automatic

   Start-Service winrm

   Enable-PSRemoting -force
   ```

3. Log on to server VAN-SRV2 with the Kim_Akers user account.

4. Open an elevated PowerShell session and run the following commands:

   ```
   Import-Module ServerManager

   Invoke-Command -script {Import-Module ServerManager; Get-WindowsFeature}
   -computername VAN-SRV1
   ```

5. Verify that the XPS Viewer feature is not installed on server VAN-SRV1.

6. Install the XPS Viewer feature remotely on server VAN-SRV1 using the command:

   ```
   Invoke-Command -script {Import-Module ServerManager; Add-WindowsFeature
   XPS-Viewer} -computername VAN-SRV1
   ```

7. Verify that the XPS Viewer feature is now installed on server VAN-SRV1 by running the command:

   ```
   Invoke-Command -script {Import-Module ServerManager; Get-WindowsFeature}
   -computername VAN-SRV1
   ```

EXERCISE 2 Delegating the Management of User Passwords for All User Accounts in an OU

In this exercise, you will delegate the ability to manage user passwords for a specific OU to a specified user account. You are likely to perform this procedure when you want to allow a designated person at a branch office location to reset passwords, but you do not want to give that person the ability to perform tasks such as creating user accounts or managing groups. To complete this exercise, perform the following steps:

1. Log on to VAN-DC1 with the Kim_Akers user account.

2. From the Administrative Tools menu, click Active Directory Users And Computers.

3. In Active Directory Users And Computers, create an account for Andy_Jacobs in the Users container. Assign the password P@ssword.

4. In Active Directory Users And Computers, create a new OU called Delegation under the adatum.com domain.

5. Right-click the Delegation OU and then click Delegate Control. This will start the Delegation Of Control Wizard. Click Next.

6. On the Selected Users And Groups page, click Add, then add andy_jacobs@adatum.com and click OK. Click OK again, and then click Next.

7. On the Tasks To Delegate page, ensure that the Delegate The Following Common Tasks option is selected and then select the Reset User Passwords And Force Password Change At Next Logon option. Click Next.

8. Click Finish to close the Delegation Of Control Wizard.

EXERCISE 3   Resetting a Delegation Using the dsacls **Command**

In this exercise, you will undo the delegation that you performed in Exercise 2. You can achieve this goal by several methods. You will examine the first method and then perform the second. To complete this exercise, perform the following steps:

1. Log on to VAN-DC1 with the Kim_Akers user account.

2. On the Administrative Tools menu, click Active Directory Users And Computers.

3. Click View, and then click Advanced Features. This will display extended properties for AD DS objects.

4. Right-click the Delegation OU, click Properties, and then click the Security tab. Click Advanced. You should be able to see that the Andy Jacobs user account has been assigned permissions. Note the Restore Defaults button on this dialog box. You can also use this button to reset a delegated OU to its initial configuration.

5. Click Cancel twice to close the Permissions and OU Properties dialog boxes.

6. Open an Administrative command prompt by right-clicking Command Prompt on the Start menu and then clicking Run As Administrator.

7. When the command prompt opens, issue the following command:

   ```
   dsacls "OU=Delegation,DC=adatum,DC=com" /resetDefaultDACL
   ```

8. When you receive the message The Command Completed Successfully, close the command prompt.

9. View the Advanced Security Settings dialog box for the Delegation OU using the procedure outlined in step 4. Verify that the Andy Jacobs user account no longer has any permissions to the Delegation OU.

Chapter Review

To further practice and reinforce the skills you learned in this chapter, you can perform the following tasks:

- Review the chapter summary.
- Review the list of key terms introduced in this chapter.
- Complete the case scenarios. These scenarios set up real-world situations involving the topics of this chapter and ask you to create a solution.
- Complete the suggested practices.
- Take a practice test.

Chapter Summary

- Remote Desktop is commonly used for the remote administration of computers running Windows Server 2008. The RSAT tools allow the roles and features of a computer running Windows Server 2008 to be managed from a client workstation. PowerShell is a powerful administrative scripting language that allows administrators to automate repetitive and complex system administration tasks.
- Event log subscriptions allow all an organization's events to be forwarded to a single collector computer for analysis. Custom views are persistent filters that allow an administrator to locate important event log data quickly.
- The Delegation Of Control Wizard can be used to delegate the ability to perform administrative duties to non-administrative users.

Key Terms

The following terms were introduced in this chapter. Do you know what they mean?

- Collector computer
- Data collector set
- Delegation
- Privilege
- Reliability

Case Scenarios

In the following case scenarios, you will apply what you have learned about planning server installs and upgrades. You can find answers to these questions in the "Answers" section at the end of this book.

Case Scenario 1: Fabrikam Event Management

One of the members of the System Administration team at Fabrikam is retiring early in the new year and, rather than replace that member of the staff, management has offered you a deal in which they will increase your salary if you can implement more-efficient server management technologies. One of the most time-consuming tasks has been the management of event log data on the company's many servers. You have decided to implement some of the new log management functionality that ships with Windows Server 2008 as a way of becoming more efficient. To do this, you need to answer the following questions:

1. What steps need to be taken to configure a single computer running Windows Server 2008 as a log collector?

2. There are 30 servers, all located within an OU named AppServers. How can you ensure that the events written to the event logs from these 30 servers are forwarded to the log collector?

3. You want to be notified by a text message sent to your cellular phone when a particular error event occurs. You have written a PowerShell script that generates the text message based on the event data, but you need some way to trigger this script when the event occurs. What steps do you need to take to implement this?

Case Scenario 2: Delegating Rights to Trusted Users at Wingtip Toys

You are helping to plan administrative procedures and policy for a new Windows Server 2008 environment that is to be implemented in Wingtip Toys, a medium-sized business. Wingtip Toys has approximately 500 staff members who work in one office and two factory locations. Wingtip Toys wants to minimize the number of staff members who have a direct IT responsibility and wants to delegate specific IT-related tasks to trusted users throughout the organization. For example, departmental administrative assistants should be able to reset the passwords of members of their departments, and team leaders should be able to add and remove user accounts from security groups that correspond to their teams. Team leaders should not be able to modify the membership of other team leaders' security groups. All user accounts currently are stored in the Users container and each department is represented by a security group. Given this information, answer the following questions:

1. What steps must you take to allow departmental administrative assistants to reset passwords of the user accounts of staff within their respective departments?

2. What steps must you take to allow team leaders to add and remove user accounts from security groups that correspond to their teams?

Suggested Practices

To help you successfully master the exam objectives presented in this chapter, complete the following tasks.

Plan Server Management Strategies

Do all the practices in this section.

- Practice 1: Create a comma-delimited file with the details of five users. Create a PowerShell script to import these users into AD DS.

- Practice 2: Create a second comma-delimited file with the details of five more users. Do not use the user names that you configured for the first part of this practice. Use the traditional `csvde.exe` command-line utility to import the second set of five users into AD DS.

Plan for Delegated Administration

Do all the practices in this section.

- Practice 1: Create a new OU called CompanyContacts. Create a new security group named ContactAdmins. Delegate the ability to create and delete Contact objects in the CompanyContacts OU to members of the ContactAdmins security group.

- Practice 2: In IIS, create a new virtual host called cohovineyard.com. Create a new security group named CohoAdmins. Delegate control of the newly created website to the Cohoadmins group.

Take a Practice Test

The practice tests on this book's companion CD offer many options. For example, you can test yourself on just one exam objective, or you can test yourself on all the 70-646 certification exam content. You can set up the test so that it closely simulates the experience of taking a certification exam, or you can set it up in study mode so that you can look at the correct answers and explanations after you answer each question.

> **MORE INFO** **PRACTICE TESTS**
>
> For details about all the practice test options available, see the section "How to Use the Practice Tests" in this book's Introduction.

CHAPTER 6

Presentation and Application Virtualization

Presentation virtualization is a method through which an application runs on one computer, but the graphical output of that application displays on another. Presentation virtualization includes technologies such as Remote Desktop Services (RDS), which had the name "Terminal Services" in Windows Server 2008 and Windows Server 2003. Microsoft Application Virtualization (App-V) allows administrators to deliver applications to computers without installing them directly. The application runs locally, but it is not installed locally. When App-V is configured properly, only those parts of the application that are required for successful execution are transmitted across the network. In this chapter, you will learn about presentation virtualization and App-V, including how to deploy applications so that clients will open virtualized applications automatically when a user double-clicks the appropriate document type.

Exam objectives in this chapter

- Plan application servers and services.
- Provision applications.

Lessons in this chapter:

Before You Begin

To complete the exercises in the practice in this chapter, you need to have done the following:

- Complete the setup tasks outlined in Appendix A, "Setup Instructions for Windows Server 2008 R2."

No additional configuration is required for this chapter.

REAL WORLD

Orin Thomas

The first Terminal Server (now called RD Session Host server) that I deployed was put in place as an experimental solution to help out some of the accountants at the company I worked for. The accountants had been running a custom application on a single server running Microsoft Windows NT 4.0 that interfaced with Microsoft SQL Server 7. The setup was such that only one person could work on the application at a time, which caused a bottleneck because time with the server would have to be scheduled in advance. The application itself wasn't network-aware and had to be installed and used on the same server that hosted the database. Eventually, a new server was purchased because the original server performed poorly as a result of inadequate hardware.

Although the easiest course of action would have been just to install Windows NT 4.0 on the new hardware and to continue as before, Microsoft Windows 2000 had just been released, and I was itching to see whether I could use Terminal Services as a solution. After we ascertained that the application ran without problems on Windows 2000, we uninstalled it, reconfigured the server to run Terminal Services, reinstalled the application, and began a trial with multiple users. It worked like a charm, which left us with one last problem: licensing. We contacted the local company who had written the custom application. They had never heard of anyone trying to get their application working with Terminal Services, so they came out to have a look at the server. They didn't have any rules about licensing this sort of setup, but they were quite impressed with how multiple users were able to interact with their non-network-aware application at once. Because they were going to start recommending the configuration to other customers, they decided that we were still in compliance, and everyone ended up happy.

Lesson 1: Presentation Virtualization

This lesson will teach you about the factors that you should consider in planning the deployment of the Windows Server 2008 R2 RDS role in your organization's environment. You will learn what to take into consideration when planning a licensing strategy for RD Session Host server clients, and what impact new technologies such as the RD Connection Broker service will have on the deployment of the RD Session Host server at headquarters and branch office sites.

> **After this lesson, you will be able to:**
> - Deploy RDS.
> - Ensure the reliability and redundancy of presentation virtualization.
>
> **Estimated lesson time: 60 minutes**

Planning Remote Desktop Infrastructure

An RD Session Host server provides a remotely accessible desktop to clients. A computer only needs to have a compatible Remote Desktop Protocol (RDP) client, and it will be able to connect to an RD Session Host server that hosts everything else. Many organizations save money by providing cheap client hardware and having their users connect to an RD Session Host server session to run more powerful applications, such as word processors, Internet browsers, and email clients. The benefits to implementing this configuration include the following:

- User workstations run a minimal amount of software and need little direct attention. If a problem occurs with a user workstation, the user's desktop environment exists on the RD Session Host server, so the failed workstation can be swapped out without requiring any data to be migrated to the replacement.
- User data is always stored in a central location rather than on user workstations, simplifying the data backup and recovery process.
- Anti-spyware and antivirus software is installed and updated on the RD Session Host server, ensuring that all definition files are up to date.
- Rather than updating each application installed on a user's workstation, applications are updated centrally.

When used in a sustained manner, remote desktop connections to an RD Session Host server require high bandwidth and low latency. This is because users expect a certain level of responsiveness from the applications that they use on a daily basis. Although it is possible to optimize the remote desktop experience for low-bandwidth connections, the better the bandwidth between your clients and the RD Session Host server, the happier those users are going to be. This means that you need to consider deploying an RD Session Host server to each branch office site. You also need to consider the necessity of balancing the number of clients that will connect to the RD Session Host server with the cost of deploying the RD Session Host server to that location. For example, if you have only three users at your organization's Yarragon branch office that need access to the same applications you deploy using an RD Session Host server farm to your Melbourne head office, it might be easier to install the applications on each user's computer directly or optimize the RDP connection to use the WAN link from Melbourne to Yarragon. Unless a really good business case can be made, most organizations are going to be reluctant to deploy server-class hardware to meet the occasional needs of only three users!

Planning RD Session Host Server Software

Software that is going to be used by clients connecting to an RD Session Host server must be installed after the RD Session Host server role is deployed. Many applications perform a check during installation to determine whether the target of the installation is an RD Session Host server. In some cases, different executable files will be installed when the installation target is an RD Session Host server as opposed to a normal, stand-alone computer. Alternatively, some applications will generate a pop-up dialog box informing you that installing the application on an RD Session Host server is not recommended and that the vendor does not support this deployment configuration.

Applications that are deployed on an RD Session Host server might conflict with one another. Prior to deploying a new RD Session Host server configuration in a production environment, you should plan a testing period. During this testing period, you should organize a small group of users and get them to use the RD Session Host server as a part of their day-to-day activities. If you follow this procedure, you will become aware of any possible problems and conflicts prior to deploying the RD Session Host server more widely in your organization's production environment. The section entitled "App-V," in Lesson 2, "Application Deployment and Virtualization," has more information on how to deploy applications that conflict or are incompatible with a default RDS deployment.

RDS Licensing

All clients that connect to an RD Session Host server require a special license called a Remote Desktop Services client access license (RDS CAL). This license is not included with Windows 7 or Windows Vista and is not a part of the standard CALs that you use when licensing a server. RDS CALs are managed by an RD license server, which uses the RD Licensing role service of the RDS server.

You need to make several decisions when planning an RD license server deployment. The most important of these decisions revolve around the following questions:

- What is the scope of the license server?
- How will the license server be activated?
- How many license servers are required?
- What type of licenses will be deployed?

License Server Scope

The license server's discovery scope determines which RD Session Host servers and clients can detect the license server automatically. The license server scope is configured during the installation of the RD License Server role service, as shown in Figure 6-1. You can change the scope once it is set. The three possible discovery scopes are as follows:

- **This Workgroup**   This scope is not available if the computer is joined to an Active Directory Directory Services (AD DS) domain. This discovery scope is most often installed on the same computer as the RD Session Host role. RD Session Host servers and clients in the same workgroup can discover this license server automatically.

- **This Domain**   The domain discovery scope allows RD Session Host servers and clients that are members of the same domain to acquire RDS CALs automatically. This scope is most useful if RDS CALs are going to be purchased on a per-domain basis.

- **This Forest**   The forest discovery scope allows RD Session Host servers and clients located anywhere in the same AD DS forest to acquire RDS CALs automatically. A drawback to this scope is that in large forests with many domains, RDS CALs can be acquired rapidly. Microsoft recommends that you configure this scope because most organizations manage licenses centrally.

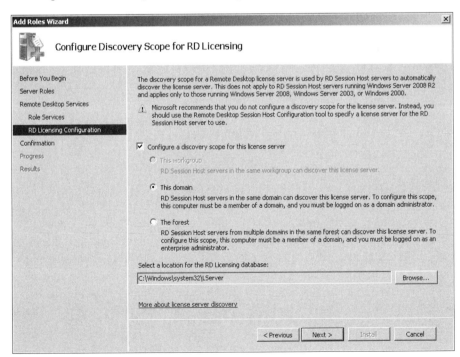

FIGURE 6-1 License server discovery scope

License Server Activation

Before an RD license server can issue CALs, it must be activated with Microsoft in a procedure similar to Windows Product Activation. During the activation process, a Microsoft-issued digital certificate (used to validate both server ownership and identity) is installed on the RD license server. This certificate will be used in transactions with Microsoft for the acquisition and installation of further licenses. As shown in Figure 6-2, a license server can be activated through three methods.

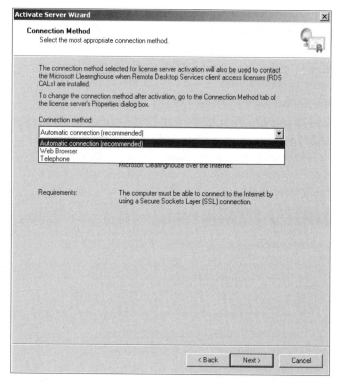

FIGURE 6-2 Three methods of activating an RD license server

The first method occurs transparently through a wizard, like Windows Product Activation. This method requires that the server be able to connect directly to the Internet using an SSL connection, which means that it will not work with certain firewall configurations. The second method involves navigating to a Web page. This method can be used on a computer other than the license server and is appropriate in environments where the network infrastructure does not support a direct SSL connection from the internal network to an Internet host.

The third method involves placing a telephone call to a Microsoft Clearinghouse operator (which is a toll-free call from most locations). The method used for activation will also be used to validate RDS CALs that are purchased later, although you can change this method by editing the RD license server's properties. If a license server is not activated, it can issue only temporary CALs. These CALs are valid for 90 days.

If the certificate acquired during the activation process expires or becomes corrupted, you might need to deactivate the license server. A deactivated license server cannot issue permanent RDS Per Device CALs, although it can still issue RDS Per User CALs and temporary RDS Per Device CALs. You can deactivate RD license servers using the automatic method or over the telephone, but you cannot deactivate them using a web browser on another computer.

RDS Client Access Licenses

An RD license server running Windows Server 2008 R2 can issue two types of CAL: the Per Device CAL and the Per User CAL. The differences between these licenses are as follows:

- **RDS Per Device CAL**   The RDS Per Device CAL gives a specific computer or device the ability to connect to an RD Session Host server. RDS Per Device CALs are reclaimed automatically by the RD license server after a random period between 52 and 89 days. This will not affect clients that regularly use these CALs because any available CAL will simply be reissued the next time the device reconnects. If you run out of available CALs, 20 percent of issued RDS Per Device CALs for a specific operating system can be revoked using the RD Licensing Manager console on the license server. For example, 20 percent of issued Windows 7 RDS Per Device CALs can be revoked, or 20 percent of issued Windows Vista Per Device CALs can be revoked, at any one time. Revocation is not a substitute for ensuring that your organization has purchased the requisite number of RDS Per Device CALs for your environment.

- **RDS Per User CAL**   An RDS Per User CAL give a specific user account the ability to access any RD Session Host server in an organization from any computer or device. RDS Per User CALs are not enforced by RD Licensing, and it is possible to have more client connections occurring in an organization than there are actual RDS Per User CALs installed on the license server. Failure to have the appropriate number of RDS Per User CALs is a violation of license terms. You can determine the number of RDS Per User CALs by using the RD Licensing Manager console on the license server. You can either examine the Reports node or use the console to create a Per User CAL Usage report.

You can purchase RDS CALs automatically if the RD Session Host server is capable of making a direct SSL connection to the Internet. Alternatively, just as when you activate the RD Session Host server, you can use a separate computer that is connected to the Internet to purchase RDS CALs by navigating to a website or calling the Microsoft Clearinghouse directly.

MORE INFO   **RDS CALS**

For more information about RDS CALs, consult the following TechNet Web page: *http://technet.microsoft.com/en-us/library/cc753650.aspx.*

Backing Up and Restoring a License Server

To back up an RD license server, you need to back up the System State data and the folder where the RD Licensing database is installed. You can use the Review Configuration page of the Add Roles Wizard to determine the location of the RD Licensing database. To restore the license server, rebuild the server and reinstall the RD Licensing Server role, restore the System State data, and then restore the RD Licensing database. When restored to a different computer, unissued licenses will not be restored, and you will need to contact the Microsoft Clearinghouse to get the licenses reissued.

License Server Deployment

When planning the deployment of RD Session Host servers running Windows Server 2008 R2 in an environment where Terminal Services are running, consider the fact that Windows Server 2003 TS license servers and Windows 2000 Server TS license servers cannot issue licenses to Windows Server 2008 R2 RD Session Host servers or Windows Server 2008 Terminal Services servers. Windows Server 2008 R2 RD Session Host servers, however, support earlier versions of RDS. If your organization is going to have a period where servers running Terminal Services will coexist with RD Session Host servers running Windows Server 2008 R2, you should first upgrade your organization's license servers to Windows Server 2008 R2 so that they can support both the new and existing servers.

 Quick Check

- Which type of RDS CAL can be revoked?
- At what point should you install the applications that are going to be used by RDS clients on the RD Session Host server?

Quick Check Answer

- Per Device CALs can be revoked.
- This can occur after the RD Session Host server role has been installed on the server.

Configuring RD Session Host Servers

When planning the deployment of RD Session Host servers, you should be aware of what configuration settings can be applied at the RD Session Host server and the protocol level. You will be interested primarily in configuration settings at the protocol level. You can edit settings at the protocol level by opening the Remote Desktop Session Host Configuration console located in the Remote Desktop Services folder of Administrative Tools on the Start menu, right-clicking the RDP-Tcp item in the Connections area, and clicking Properties. This will bring up the RDP-Tcp Properties dialog box.

The General tab of this dialog box, shown in Figure 6-3, allows the administrator to configure the Security Layer, Encryption Level, and other connection security settings. The default setting for the Security layer security level is Negotiated; the default setting for the Encryption level is Client Compatible. By default, an attempt will be made to negotiate the strongest security layer and encryption, but administrators can set a specific level. Clients that cannot meet this level will be unable to establish a connection to an RD Session Host server. Clients running Windows 7, Windows Vista, and Windows XP SP2+ can make traditional RDS connections when the security settings are set to their strongest level, although this rule does not apply to RemoteApp connections made through RD Web Access, which are covered in more detail in Lesson 2.

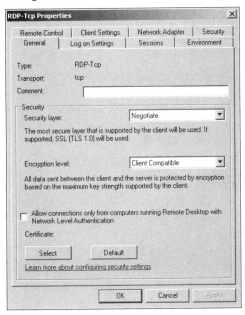

FIGURE 6-3 The General tab of the RDP-Tcp Properties dialog box

The Security Layer settings are used to configure server authentication, which is how the server verifies its identity to the client. This allows an SSL certificate issued by a trusted certificate authority to be installed as a method of verifying the RD Session Host server's identity to a connecting client. Use this setting when clients are connecting to an RD Session Host server from untrusted networks, such as the Internet. Verification of an RD Session Host server's identity reduces the risk that a user in your organization will provide authentication credentials to a rogue RD Session Host server through a phishing attack. Although it is possible to use a self-signed certificate generated by the RD Session Host server, this can lead to problems if clients are not configured properly to trust the server's SSL certificate.

The Encryption level is used to protect the contents of the RD Session Host server from interception by third parties. The four settings have the following properties:

- **High** This level of encryption uses a 128-bit key and is supported by RDP 5.2 clients (Windows XP SP2+, Windows Server 2003 SP1+, Windows Vista, Windows Server 2008, Windows 7, and Windows Server 2008 R2).

- **FIPS** Traffic is encrypted using Federal Information Process Standard (FIPS) 140-1 validated encryption methods. This is used primarily by government organizations.

- **Client Compatible** This method negotiates a maximum key length based on what the client supports.

- **Low** Data sent from the client to the server is encrypted using a 56-bit key. Data sent from the server to the client remains unencrypted.

The Security tab of the RDP-Tcp Properties dialog box allows you to specify which groups of users can access the RD Session Host server and what level of control they have. With the Sessions tab, shown in Figure 6-4, you can specify how long an RD Session Host server allows active connections to last and how to treat idle and disconnected sessions. In environments where every extra session places pressure on an RD Session Host server's resources, ensuring that idle and disconnected sessions are disconnected can be an excellent way of managing an RD Session Host server.

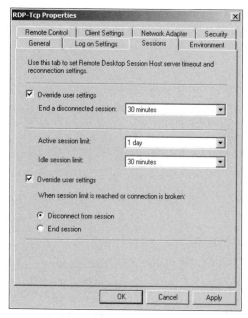

FIGURE 6-4 The Sessions tab of the RDP-Tcp Properties dialog box

The Remote Control tab of the RDP-Tcp Properties dialog box allows you to specify what level of control an administrator has over connected sessions. You can ensure that remote control sessions—which are used primarily by support staff—can be enacted only if the connected user provides permission for support personnel to connect in a similar manner to the remote assistance functionality that ships with Windows Vista and Windows 7. The Network Adapter tab, shown in Figure 6-5, allows administrators to limit the number of active connections to the RD Session Host server and to specify which network adapter clients will use to connect. This setting is important on RD Session Host servers when the number of clients connecting can exhaust hardware resources and a limit needs to be put in place to ensure that server functionality does not diminish to the point of user frustration.

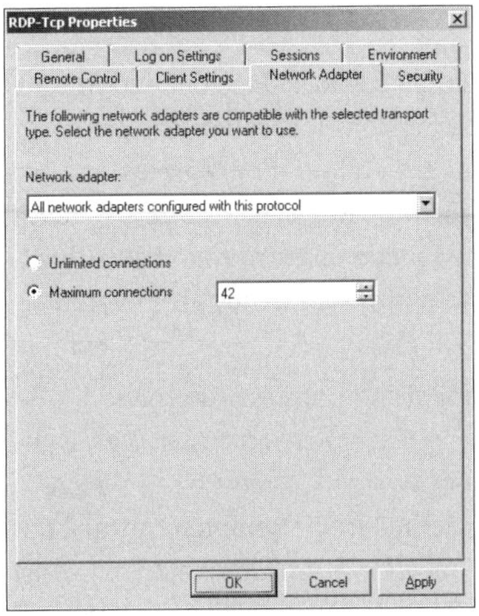

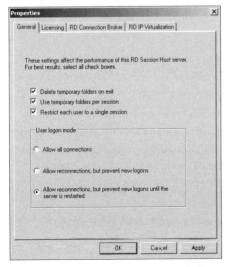

FIGURE 6-5 Network Adapter settings

Server Properties

In addition to the RDP connection properties covered earlier, the properties of each RD Session Host server affect the client experience. As shown in Figure 6-6, you can configure each RD Session Host server to use temporary folders for each session and have those folders deleted when the session completes. You can also restrict a user to a single session on an RD Session Host server. This setting is important because if the RDP connection settings are not set to disconnect idle sessions, a user could be responsible for multiple idle sessions on a server. You should use the User Logon Mode settings when you need to take an RD Session Host server offline for maintenance. For example, if you set the User Logon Mode to Allow Reconnections, But Prevent New Logons Until The Server Is Restarted, you can monitor the number of active connections and then shut down the server and perform maintenance tasks without interrupting the user's work.

FIGURE 6-6 The RD Session Host server's Properties dialog box

Configuring RDS with Group Policy

In large RD Session Host server deployments, you will not configure RDP-Tcp connection settings and RD Session Host server properties on a per–RD Session Host server basis. You would apply these settings through AD DS. The Computer Configuration/Policies/ Administrative Templates/Windows Components/Remote Desktop Services/RD Session Host server node of Group Policy contains several policies whose functionality mirrors the settings that can be applied on the server. Because of the vast number of policies, they are covered only briefly here.

- **Connections** The Connections node contains the following policies: Automatic Reconnection, Allow Users To Connect Remotely Using Remote Desktop Services, Deny Logoff Of An Administrator Logged In To The Console Session, Configure Keep-Alive Connection Interval, Limit Number Of Connections, Set Rules For Remote Control Of Remote Desktop Services User Sessions, Allow Reconnection From Original Client Only, Restrict Remote Desktop Services Users To A Single Remote Session, Allow Remote Start Of Unlisted Programs, and Turn of Fair Share CPU Scheduling.

- **Device and Resource Redirection** The Device And Resource Redirection node contains the following policies: Allow Audio Redirection, Do Not Allow Clipboard Redirection, Do Not Allow COM Port Redirection, Do Not Allow Drive Redirection, Do Not Allow LPT Port Redirection, Do Not Allow Supported Plug And Play Device Redirection, Do Not Allow Smart Card Device Redirection, and Allow Time Zone Redirection.

- **Licensing** The Licensing node contains the following policies: Use The Specified Remote Desktop License Servers, Hide Notifications About RD Licensing Problems That Affect The RD Session Host Server, and Set The Remote Desktop Services Licensing Mode.

- **Printer Redirection** The Printer Redirection node contains the following policies: Do Not Set Default Client Printer To Be Default Printer In A Session, Do Not Allow Client Printer Redirection, Specify RD Session Host Server Fallback Printer Driver Behavior, Use Remote Desktop Services Easy Print Printer Driver First, and Redirect Only The Default Client Printer.

- **Profiles** The Profiles node contains the following policies: Set Remote Desktop Services User Home Directory, Use Mandatory Profiles On The RD Session Host Server, and Set Path For Remote Desktop Services Roaming User Profile.

- **Remote Session Environment** The Remote Session Environment node contains the following policies: Limit Maximum Color Depth, Enforce Removal Of Remote Desktop Wallpaper, Remove Disconnect Option From Shut Down Dialog Box, Remove Windows Security Item From Start Menu, Set Compression Algorithm For RDP Data, Start A Program On Connection, and Always Show Desktop On Connection.

- **Security** The Security node contains the following policies: Server Authentication Certificate Template, Set Client Connection Encryption Level, Always Prompt For Password Upon Connection, Require Secure RPC Communication, Require Use

Of Specific Security Layer For Remote (RDP) Connections, Do Not Allow Local Administrators To Customize Permissions, and Require User Authentication For Remote Connections By Using Network Level Authentication.

- **Session Time Limits**   The Session Time Limits node contains the following policies: Set Time Limit For Disconnected Sessions, Set Time Limit For Active But Idle Remote Desktop Services Sessions, Set Time Limit for Active Remote Desktop Services Sessions, Terminate Session When Time Limits Are Reached, and Set Time Limit For Logoff Of RemoteApp Sessions.

- **Temporary Folders**   The Temporary Folders node contains the following policies: Do Not Delete Temp Folder Upon Exit, and Do Not Use Temporary Folders Per Session.

- **RD Connection Broker**   The policies in this folder are covered in detail in the section entitled "Remote Desktop Services Session Broker," later in this lesson.

Although this list may seem daunting at first, it is reproduced here to give you an idea of how you can configure RDS to best meet the requirements of your organization, not because you will be expected to recite it by rote on the exam. You should read through the list and consider how each policy might affect the number of clients that can be serviced, as well as how each policy might influence the number of RD Session Host servers that need to be deployed. Some policies will be irrelevant to your pursuit of these objectives; other policies will be critical.

From the perspective of an administrator who needs to plan the deployment of RDS, the most important policy groups are located in the Connections and Session Time Limits nodes. With these nodes, you control how many clients are connected to each RD Session Host server and how long they remain connected, both of which directly affect the RD Session Host server's capacity. If you allow lots of idle sessions to take up memory in the RDS environment, you will need to plan the deployment of more RD Session Host servers because the existing ones will reach their natural capacity quickly. If you limit idle sessions to a specified period of time, you will ensure that capacity is not wasted, but you might also disrupt the way that people in your organization actually work. As with everything else related to deployment and planning, getting the settings right is a matter of finding your organization's unique balance point.

RD Web Access

RD Web Access allows clients to connect to an RD Session Host server through a Web page link rather than by entering the RD Session Host server address in the Remote Desktop Connection client software. Unlike the similar functionality that was available in Windows Server 2003, RD Web Access in Windows Server 2008 R2 does not rely on an ActiveX control to provide the Remote Desktop Connection (RDC), but instead uses the RDC client software that is installed on clients. This means that to use RD Web Access, clients need to be running Windows XP SP2, Windows Vista, Windows 7, Windows Server 2003 SP1, Windows Server 2008, or Windows Server 2008 R2. To deploy RD Web Access, you must not only install the RD Web Access server role, but also the Web Server (IIS) role and a feature called Windows Process Activation Service.

RD Connection Broker

A single RD Session Host server can support only a limited number of clients before it begins to run out of resources and the client experience deteriorates. The precise number will depend on what applications and tasks the clients are performing, as well as the specific hardware configuration of the RD Session Host server itself. Eventually, as the number of clients grows, you will need to add a second RD Session Host server to your environment to take some load off the first. From a planning perspective, this is fairly obvious, but it gives rise to the question, "How do I ensure that clients are distributed equally between the new and the old RD Session Host server?" If everyone jumps on the new server, it will soon have the same resource pressure problem that the old server had. The RD Connection Broker role service simplifies the process of adding capacity, allowing the load balancing of RD Session Host servers in a group and the reconnection of clients to existing sessions within that group. In RD Connection Broker terminology, a group of RD Session Host servers is called a *farm*.

The RD Connection Broker service consists of a database that keeps track of RD Session Host server sessions. RD Connection Broker can work with DNS Round Robin or with Network Load Balancing (NLB) to distribute clients to RD Session Host servers. When configured with load balancing, the RD Connection Broker service monitors all RD Session Host servers in the group and allocates new clients to the RD Session Host servers that have the largest amount of free resources. When used with DNS Round Robin, clients are still distributed; the main benefit is that the RD Connection Broker remembers where a client is connected. Thus, a disconnected session is reconnected appropriately rather than a new session being created on a different RD Session Host server. The limitation of the RD Connection Broker service is that it can be used only with RD Session Host servers running Windows Server 2008 R2 or Terminal Services servers running Windows Server 2008. Terminal Services servers running Windows Server 2003 cannot participate in an RD Connection Broker farm.

To deploy RD Connection Broker load balancing in your organization, you must ensure that the clients support RDP 5.2 or later. RD Connection Broker also supports the User Logon Mode settings, discussed in the section entitled "Configuring and Monitoring RD Session Host Server," earlier in this lesson. These settings allow you to prevent new connections from being made to an individual server in the farm until you have completed pending maintenance tasks.

You can join an RD Session Host server to a farm using the RDS configuration MMC, available from the Remote Desktop Services folder of the Administrative Tools menu. Joining a farm is a matter of specifying the address of an RD Connection Broker Server, a farm name, the condition that the server should participate in session broker load balancing, and the relative weight of the server—based on its capacity—in the farm. You should configure more powerful servers with higher-weight values than those that you configure for less powerful servers. You should clear the IP Address Redirection option only if your load-balancing solution uses RD Connection Broker Routing Tokens, which are used by hardware load-balancing solutions and which means that the load balancing is not handled by the RD Connection Broker server. As discussed earlier, you can also apply these configuration settings through Group Policy, with the relevant policies located under the Computer Configuration/Policies/Administrative Templates/Windows Components/Remote Desktop Services/RD Session Host server/RD Connection Broker node of a Group Policy object (GPO) on Windows Server 2008 R2.

In conjunction with these configuration settings, you must add the RD Session Host server's Active Directory computer account to the Session Directory Computers local group on the computer hosting the RD Connection Broker service. After you complete these tasks, you then need to configure the load-balancing feature on each of the computers in the farm.

> **MORE INFO**   **REMOTE DESKTOP CONNECTION BROKER**
>
> For more information on Remote Desktop Connection Broker, consult the following TechNet article: *http://technet.microsoft.com/en-us/library/dd560675(WS.10).aspx.*

RD Gateway Server

RD Gateway servers allow you to provide access to RD Session Host servers to clients that are not on your organization's internal network without having to provision virtual private networks (VPNs) or DirectAccess. Although you'll learn more about RD Gateway servers in Chapter 9, "Remote Access and Network Access Protection," an important aspect of RD Gateway Server functionality is that you can integrate it with Network Access Protection (NAP). This allows you to ensure that clients that connect to your organization's RD Session Host servers have met a minimum health benchmark. This can be useful when you need to provide access to clients that you do not manage but that require access to RD Session Host servers.

> **MORE INFO**   **RD GATEWAY SERVER**
>
> To learn more about RD Gateway servers, consult the following TechNet article: *http://technet.microsoft.com/en-us/library/cc725706.aspx.*

Remote Desktop Virtualization Host

Remote Desktop Virtualization Host (RD Virtualization Host) is a role that first became available with Windows Server 2008 R2. RD Virtualization Host allows clients to connect using Remote Desktop to personal virtual machines running on Hyper-V hosts on Windows Server 2008 R2. This type of virtualization allows each user to be assigned an individual virtual machine that is accessed through the Remote Desktop Client. The 70-646 exam objectives do not address desktop or server virtualization directly.

> **MORE INFO**   **RD VIRTUALIZATION HOST**
>
> To learn more about RD Virtualization Host, consult the following TechNet article: *http://technet.microsoft.com/en-us/library/dd759193.aspx.*

Monitoring RDS

You need to monitor RD Session Host servers regularly to ensure that the user experience remains acceptable and that the RD Session Host server still has adequate hardware resources with which to perform its role. Hardware bottlenecks on RD Session Host servers primarily occur around the processor and memory resources. These are the resources that you need to be most careful in monitoring because although you can make estimates about a server's capacity, until clients are actually performing day-to-day tasks, you will not really know how much load the server can take before the user experience begins to deteriorate. You will use two specific tools to manage and monitor RD Session Host server resources: System Monitor and the Windows System Resource Manager.

Using Performance Monitor to Monitor RDS

In addition to the typical Windows Server 2008 R2 monitoring tools that you will be familiar with, System Monitor contains RD Session Host server–specific performance counters that help you determine what level of use the current client sessions are having on the server that hosts them. The two broad categories of counters are those located under the Remote Desktop Services category and those located under the Remote Desktop Services Sessions category. The Remote Desktop Services category tracks the number of active, inactive, and total sessions. The Remote Desktop Services Sessions category gives details about resource usage. You can use this category to track memory and processor usage, as well as receive detailed troubleshooting information such as the number of frame errors and protocol cache hits.

Windows System Resource Manager

Windows System Resource Manager (WSRM) is a feature that you can install on a computer running Windows Server 2008 R2 that controls how resources are allocated. The WSRM console, shown in Figure 6-7, allows an administrator to apply WSRM policies. WSRM includes four default policies and also allows administrators to create their own. The policies that will most interest you as someone responsible for planning and deploying Remote Desktop Services infrastructure are Equal_Per_User, Weighted_Remote_Session, and Equal_Per_Session.

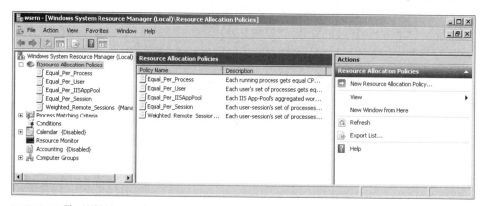

FIGURE 6-7 The WSRM console

The Equal_Per_User WSRM policy ensures that each user is allocated resources equally, even when one user has more sessions connected to the RD Session Host server than other users. Apply this policy when you allow users to have multiple sessions with the RD Session Host server—it stops any one user from monopolizing hardware resources by opening multiple sessions. The Weighted_Remote_Sessions policy allows processes to be grouped according to the priority assigned to the user account. The Equal_Per_Session policy ensures that each session is allocated resources equally. If applied on an RD Session Host server where users are allowed to connect with multiple sessions, this policy can allow those users to gain access to a disproportionate amount of system resources compared to users with single sessions.

> **MORE INFO** **WINDOWS SYSTEM RESOURCE MANAGER AND RD SESSION HOST**
>
> To learn more about using WSRM with RD Session Host, consult the following TechNet article: *http://technet.microsoft.com/en-us/library/cc742814.aspx*.

Lesson Summary

- RD license servers must be activated before you can install RDS CALs. The discovery scope of a license server determines which clients and RD Session Host servers can detect the server automatically.
- RD Connection Broker allows you to create RD Session Host farms. RD Connection Broker can be paired with DNS Round Robin or NLB and ensures that disconnected clients are always reconnected to the correct session on the appropriate server.
- RD Web Access allows clients to connect to an RD Session Host server using a browser shortcut, but it still requires that the latest RDC software be installed.
- RD Gateway Servers can allow clients from the Internet to connect to RD Session Host servers behind the firewall without having to implement a VPN solution.

Lesson Review

You can use the following questions to test your knowledge of the information in Lesson 1, "Presentation Virtualization." The questions are also available on the companion CD if you prefer to review them in electronic form.

> **NOTE** **ANSWERS**
>
> Answers to these questions and explanations of why each answer choice is correct or incorrect are located in the "Answers" section at the end of the book.

1. Your organization has a single RD Session Host server. Users are allowed to connect to the RD Session Host server with up to two concurrent sessions. You want to ensure that users who are connected to two sessions do not use more resources on the RD Session Host server than a user connected with a single session. Which of the following strategies should you pursue?

   A. Apply the Equal_Per_User WSRM policy.

   B. Apply the Equal_Per_Session WSRM policy.

   C. Configure the server's properties in the RD Session Host server's Management console.

   D. Configure RDP-tcp properties.

2. Your organization has two offices, one located in Sydney and one located in Melbourne. A data center in Canberra hosts infrastructure servers. Both the Melbourne and Sydney offices have their own RD Session Host server farms. The offices are connected by a high-speed WAN link. Each office has its own AD DS domain, which are both a part of the same forest. The forest root domain is located in the Canberra data center and does not contain standard user or computer accounts. For operational reasons, you want to ensure that CALs purchased and installed at each location are allocated only to devices at that location. Which of the following license server deployment plans should you implement?

   A. Deploy a license server to each location and set the discovery scope of each license server to Domain.

   B. Deploy a license server to each location and set the discovery scope of each license server to Forest.

   C. Deploy a license server to the Canberra data center and set the discovery scope of the license server to Forest.

   D. Deploy a license server to the Canberra data center and set the discovery scope of the license server to Domain.

3. Which of the following steps do you need to take prior to installing CALs on an RD license server? (Each answer forms part of the solution. Choose all that apply.)

   A. Select the license server scope.

   B. Set the domain level to the Windows Server 2008 R2 functional level.

   C. Activate the license server.

   D. Select the license type.

4. The organization that you work for is going through a period of growth. Users access business applications from client terminals. You are concerned that the growth in users will outstrip the processing capacity of the host RD Session Host server. Which of the following solutions allows you to increase the client capacity without requiring client reconfiguration?

   A. Use WSRM to ensure that all users are able to access resources equally.

   B. Install Hyper-V on a computer running Windows Server 2008 R2 Enterprise edition and add virtualized servers as required.

   C. Add RD Session Host servers as required and reconfigure clients to use specific RD Session Host servers.

   D. Create an RD Session Host server farm and add RD Session Host servers as required.

5. You need to ensure that clients connecting to your RD Session Host servers have passed a health check. Which of the following deployments should you implement?

   A. Install Forefront Endpoint Protection on the RD Session Host servers.

   B. Implement RD Connection Broker.

   C. Mediate access using a TS Gateway server.

   D. Mediate access using Microsoft ISA Server 2006.

Lesson 2: Application Deployment and Virtualization

This lesson looks at application deployment and virtualization. There are several methods through which you can deploy applications, the most common of which is Group Policy. This lesson will also look at the steps you need to take to deploy web applications to servers running Microsoft Internet Information Services (IIS) 7.0 or IIS 7.5. Application Virtualization (App-V) is a process where applications are run locally in their own separate environments, but where the application is not actually installed on the local machine. Running an application in its own environment ensures that no conflicts occur as each operating system or application is located in the equivalent of its own sealed environment. This lesson also will teach you about RemoteApp, a special type of presentation virtualization technology that allows you to run RDS applications without having to run them in a normal RDS window.

> **After this lesson, you will be able to:**
> - Plan App-V deployment.
> - Plan virtual application deployment.
> - Plan web application deployment.
>
> **Estimated lesson time: 60 minutes**

Traditional Application Deployment

Traditional application deployment involves installing the program files for the application locally on a person's workstation. This can occur directly by having someone manually execute the program installer. In large environments, this generally occurs automatically where you use a network process to have the installation occur without direct human intervention. In many organizations, applications are built into the operating system image.

When locally installed applications need updates, it is necessary to have those updates deployed to every client in the organization that has a local copy of that application. Traditional applications are most often deployed as a part of operating system image deployment. An image is built that includes the applications, and that image is applied directly to users' computers.

In general, applications come as executable files or Windows Installer packages. Windows Installer Packages, which have the *.msi* file extension, are easier to manage because they include information that the computer can use not only to install the package, but also to repair the package and to uninstall the package. It can be tricky to remove or repair an application that was installed through a traditional executable such as Setup.exe, especially when you are dealing with a deployment across hundreds, if not thousands, of computers.

> *MORE INFO*   **WINDOWS INSTALLER**
>
> To learn more about Windows Installer, consult the following TechNet article:
> *http://technet.microsoft.com/en-us/library/dd316071(WS.10).aspx.*

You can use AD DS as a method of pushing out applications to clients, but this works only if the application has already been packaged in Windows Installer format. Application deployment through Group Policy has the following conditions:

- When you publish an application, users can use Add Or Remove Programs to install an application manually. You can also associate the application with a particular type of document so that the application will be installed automatically if the user attempts to open a document of that type.

- When you assign an application, the application is installed to the computer the next time the computer boots. When you assign an application to a user, the application is installed the next time the user logs on.

- If you want to deploy applications that are not already packaged and in another format, such as *.exe,* you'll need to use a product such as System Center Essentials 2010 or System Center Configuration Manager 2007 R3.

> **MORE INFO   GROUP POLICY SOFTWARE DEPLOYMENT**
>
> To learn more about deploying software through Group Policy, consult the following article on Microsoft's website: *http://support.microsoft.com/kb/816102.*

Deploying Web Applications

A website is a container for web applications. Web applications are a collection of content, scripts, and executable files that provide some functionality to the user. Web applications are stored on the file server running Windows Server 2008 R2 in their own directories that host these files, scripts, and executables. Most organizations create and update their web applications in a development environment before they deploy those applications to production web servers. From a planning standpoint, this means that you need to have a strategy to deploy web applications to the production web servers from the development environment.

In general, web application deployment means moving a set of files and directories from a set of folders on one server running IIS to a location set up exactly the same way on a second server running IIS. While a simple use of Robocopy.exe to move files from one server to another is generally straightforward, organizations have to take into account the following:

- Production servers are usually located on perimeter networks, whereas development servers are almost always located on internal networks.

- Production servers are generally stand-alone systems and not members of domains. Development servers may or may not be members of domains, but they will have separate account databases from production servers.

- Production servers are protected by firewalls. Most administrators are reluctant to place a file share where users have write access on a server that is hosted on a perimeter network.

There are two general methods through which web applications are published to servers running IIS:

- Publication using WebDAV
- Publication using FTP

WebDAV in Windows Server 2008 R2

Web Distributed Authoring And Versioning (WebDAV) allows you to publish content through a firewall using HTTP or HTTPS protocols. This makes it an excellent protocol to use when deploying web applications from a development server on the internal network to a production server on a perimeter network. Sites that support WebDAV can be stored as network places in Windows Explorer or opened as web folders in Windows Internet Explorer on computers running Windows XP, Windows 7, Windows Vista, Windows Server 2003, Windows Server 2008, and Windows Server 2008 R2.

WebDAV supports the same authentication protocols that are supported with IIS, so you can ensure that credentials are not passed to the server in unencrypted format. WebDAV also supports SSL connections as a further security measure. WebDAV was not included in the RTM version of Windows Server 2008, but it is included as a role service in Windows Server 2008 R2. WebDAV settings are configured on a per-site basis through the IIS Manager and are shown in Figure 6-8.

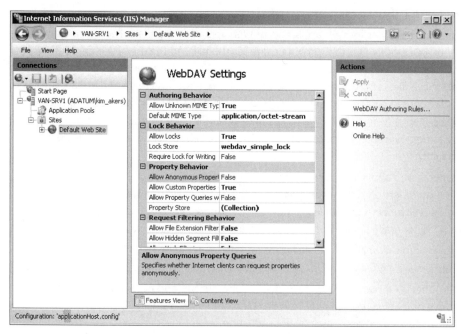

FIGURE 6-8 WebDAV settings

FTP 7.5 in Windows Server 2008 R2

File Transfer Protocol (FTP) is a protocol traditionally used to publish content to websites. Windows Server 2008 R2 includes FTP 7.5. This version was available as an add-on for IIS 7.0 in Windows Server 2008, but it has several important differences from FTP 7.0, the default version that shipped with Windows Server 2008. One of the main ones is that FTP 7.5 now supports SSL. FTP allows you to upload files and folders from one server to another, and numerous FTP clients, including a command-line client available in all versions of Windows, which means that you can almost always publish content to a web server if it is configured with FTP. The key is to map the FTP site to the website so that content can be deployed to the folders that host the site. You manage FTP 7.5 through the IIS Manager. The FTP management tools are shown in Figure 6-9.

FIGURE 6-9 FTP management tools

As added security, you can use the IP address and domain name restrictions to limit which hosts are able to connect to the server. For example, you might create a restriction so that content can be uploaded through FTP only if the connecting host is on the development server, rather than just any host on the internal network. It is also possible to configure a firewall rule that allows FTP traffic to require authentication from the connecting host, although this is beyond what most administrators do when securing an FTP server to allow traffic only from hosts on the internal network.

> **MORE INFO**   **FTP 7.5**
>
> To learn more about FTP 7.5, consult the following TechNet page: *http://technet.microsoft.com/en-us/library/dd722686(WS.10).aspx.*

> **MORE INFO**   **DEPLOY WEBSITES ON IIS 7.5**
>
> To learn more about deploying websites, consult the following page on Microsoft's official IIS website: *http://learn.iis.net/page.aspx/37/deploying-web-sites-on-iis-7/.*

RDS RemoteApp

RemoteApp differs from a normal RD Session Host server session in that instead of connecting to a window that displays a remote computer's desktop, an application executed on the RD Session Host server appears as if it is being executed on the local computer.

A benefit of this technology is that all the memory, disk, and processor resources required by the application are provided by the RD Session Host server hosting the application rather than the client. This allows applications that require significant amounts of RAM and CPU resources to run quickly on computers that do not have sufficient resources for a traditional installation and application execution.

When multiple applications are invoked from the same host server, the applications are transmitted to the client using the same session. This means that if you have configured an RD Session Host server to allow a maximum of 20 simultaneous sessions, a user having three separate RemoteApp applications open will account for only one open session instead of three.

RemoteApp includes the following benefits:

- It is easier to deploy application updates. Updates need to be applied only on the RD Session Host server rather than having to be deployed to clients.
- The application upgrade path is simpler. As with the application of updates, it is only necessary to upgrade the application on the RD Session Host server to a newer version. The client does not need to be upgraded.
- Any application that can be run on the RD Session Host server can be run as a RemoteApp application.
- RemoteApp applications can be associated with local file extensions, meaning that the RemoteApp application starts when the user attempts to open an associated document.
- Users are often unaware that an application is running remotely.

Through RemoteApp Manager, you can configure RD Gateway settings. This allows users to access RemoteApp applications when their computers are located on the Internet by connecting indirectly through an RD Gateway server. As shown in Figure 6-10, you can use three methods to deploy RemoteApp applications to the clients in your organization. These methods are as follows:

- Create an RDP shortcut file and distribute this file to clients. You can do this by placing the RDP shortcut on a shared folder or emailing the shortcut to the user.

- Create and distribute a Windows Installer package. The benefit of this is that you can associate the RemoteApp with a particular file extension. When a user attempts to open the file, the RemoteApp application executes automatically.

- Get clients to connect to the RD Web Access website and start the RemoteApp application from a link on the page. You can use RemoteApp Manager to specify whether an application is published to the RD Web Access site or not.

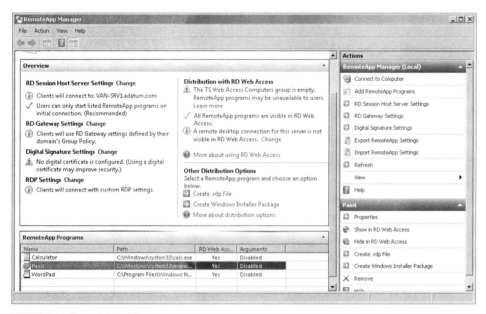

FIGURE 6-10 RemoteApp Manager

RemoteApp users still need to be members of the Remote Desktop Users group on the RD Session Host server. If you are in the situation in which RemoteApp applications are being deployed from a computer that is also functioning as a domain controller, you will need to modify the Allow Log On Through RDS policy to enable RemoteApp access.

MORE INFO **REMOTEAPP**

To learn more about RemoteApp, consult the following TechNet link:
http://technet.microsoft.com/en-us/library/cc755055.aspx.

App-V

App-V allows applications to run locally on computers without being installed locally on those computers. App-V creates a separate partitioned space, called a *silo,* for a specific application, and the application executes within this silo. The advantage of this approach is that applications that might not be able to execute on the computer because of compatibility problems with the host operating system will be able to execute when run within the silo through App-V. App-V ships as part of the Microsoft Desktop Optimization Pack (MDOP).

> **MORE INFO** MDOP
>
> For more information on MDOP, consult the following page on Microsoft's website: *http://www.microsoft.com/windows/enterprise/products/mdop/default.aspx.*

App-V uses streaming technology to transmit only the parts of the application that are actually being used by the client over the network. As different parts of the application are required by the client, those parts will be streamed across the network.

Because the application is virtualized in a silo, App-V allows you to do the following:

■ Deploy multiple versions of the same application from the same server. It is even possible to run multiple versions of the same application on a local client as the silos, ensuring that the two applications will not conflict. This is especially useful in application development environments where different versions of the same application need to be tested simultaneously.

■ Deploy applications that normally would conflict with each other from the same server. When deploying applications using RemoteApp, you can only install applications that do not conflict with one another on the same RD Session Host server.

■ Deploy applications that are not compatible with RD Session Host server. Because of conflicts with the RD Session Host server architecture, not all applications work with RD Session Host server. App-V allows these applications to be deployed to clients in a manner similar to that of the RD Session Host server.

■ Deploy App-V applications as Windows Installer packages.

Lesson Summary

- You can use AD DS to deploy applications to clients so long as those applications are in Windows Installer packages.
- Windows Installer packages use the *.msi* file extension.
- Deploying web applications involves copying files to a server running IIS. You can use FTP 7.5 or WebDAV to deploy web applications securely.
- RemoteApp applications are a form of presentation virtualization where only the application display is transmitted across the network.
- You should deploy RemoteApp applications in Windows Installer format when you want to ensure that certain file types are associated with the RemoteApp application.
- App-V allows applications that might conflict with one another to run in silos on the same client.
- App-V allows applications to be streamed across the network as needed.
- App-V applications can be deployed using Windows Installer packages.

Lesson Review

You can use the following questions to test your knowledge of the information in Lesson 2, "Application Deployment and Virtualization." The questions are also available on the companion CD if you prefer to review them in electronic form.

1. Which of the following methods can you use to deploy an RD RemoteApp application to users in your organization? (Each answer is a complete solution. Choose all that apply.)

   A. Deploy a bookmark to RD Web Access through Group Policy.

   B. Use a Windows Installer package deployed through Group Policy.

   C. Place an RDP shortcut on an accessible shared folder.

   D. Install the application on an accessible shared folder.

2. You work as a systems administrator for a software development company. During the application development phase, it is necessary to deploy several versions of the same software from the same RD Session Host server. When you attempt to install the applications side by side, it causes a conflict. Which of the following solutions should you plan to use?

   A. Deploy the applications using TS RemoteApp.

   B. Deploy an RD Gateway server.

   C. Deploy App-V.

   D. Deploy the applications using RD Web Access.

3. Clients running Windows XP in your organization are unable to connect to RemoteApp applications using the RD Web Access Web page. Clients running Windows Vista are able to connect without any problems. Which of the following steps should you take to resolve this issue?

   A. Install Internet Explorer 6.0 on the clients running Windows XP.

   B. Disable the Windows XP firewall.

   C. Upgrade the clients running Windows XP to SP3.

   D. Install Windows Defender on the clients running Windows XP.

4. Your organization has a server running Windows Server 2008 R2 that is hosted on the perimeter network and that has IIS 7.5 installed through the Web Server role. You want to ensure that when developers deploy web applications to your organization's IIS server, they do not pass their credentials across the network in an insecure way. The server is not a member of the domain, and you do not want to open ports related to the Server Message Block (SMB) protocol on the firewall between the internal and perimeter network. Which of the following steps should you take to allow web applications to be deployed to the server on the perimeter network? (Each answer is a complete solution. Choose all that apply.)

   A. Install DFS on the server on the perimeter network.

   B. Install the FTP role service.

   C. Configure a file share on the server on the perimeter network.

   D. Install WebDAV publishing.

PRACTICE **Installing and Configuring RDS and RemoteApp**

In this set of exercises, you will install and configure RDS and deploy applications using RD Web Access and RemoteApp.

EXERCISE 1   Prepare Server and Install RDS

In this exercise, you will install and configure RDS on server VAN-SRV1. To complete this practice, perform the following steps:

1. Ensure that servers VAN-DC1 and VAN-SRV1 are turned on.

2. Log on to server VAN-SRV1 with the Kim_Akers user account. To ensure that no existing Remote Desktop or Web Server role components are installed on the server, run the following commands from an elevated Windows PowerShell prompt:

```
Import-Module ServerManager

Remove-WindowsFeature Web-Server

Remove-WindowsFeature Remote-Desktop-Services
```

3. If necessary, restart the server and log on using the Kim_Akers user account.

4. Open Windows Explorer and create and share a folder from volume C: named RemoteApp.

5. Open the Server Manager console, and click the Roles node. In the Details pane, click Add Roles. This opens the Add Roles Wizard. Click Next.

6. On the Server Roles page, select Remote Desktop Services and then click Next twice.

7. On the Role Services page, select Remote Desktop Session Host and Remote Desktop Web Access. When prompted to add extra role features, click Add Required Role Services. Click Next twice.

8. On the Specify Authentication Method for Remote Desktop Session Host page, click Require Network Level Authentication, and then click Next.

9. On the Licensing Mode and User Groups page, click Next.

10. On the Configure Client Experience page, select all options, and then click Next three times. Click Install.

11. Click Close. When prompted to restart the server, click Yes.

EXERCISE 2   Configure RD Web Access

In this exercise, you will configure RD Web Access. To complete this practice, perform the following steps:

1. Log on to server VAN-SRV1 with the Kim_Akers user account. Click Close on the Resume Configuration Wizard.

2. On the Administrative Tools menu, in the Remote Desktop Services folder, click Remote Desktop Web Access Configuration.

3. On the page that provides a warning about a problem with the website's security certificate, click Continue To This Website (Not Recommended).

4. On the Remote Desktop Services Default Connection page, enter the credentials **adatum\Kim_Akers** and the password **Pa$$w0rd**. Select This Is A Private Computer, and then click Sign In.

5. Click RemoteApp Programs, and verify that no programs are displayed. Leave Internet Explorer open.

6. On the Administrative Tools menu, in the Remote Desktop Services folder, click RemoteApp Manager. This opens the RemoteApp Manager console.

7. In the Actions pane, click Add RemoteApp Programs. This opens the RemoteApp Wizard. Click Next. On the Choose Programs To Add To The RemoteApp Programs List page, select Calculator, and then click Next. Click Finish.

8. Return to Internet Explorer and refresh the RemoteApp Programs page. Verify that Calculator is now displayed. On the RemoteApp Programs page, click Calculator. In the RemoteApp warning box, click Connect. On the Enter Your Credentials page, enter the password **Pa$$w0rd** and then click OK. Verify that the calculator displays.

9. Open Task Manager. On the Applications tab, verify that the Calculator program includes the fully qualified domain name (FQDN) of the RD Session Host server. Close Calculator.

EXERCISE 3   Configure RemoteApp and Windows Installer

In this exercise, you will configure a RemoteApp installer for WordPad. To complete this practice, perform the following steps:

1. While logged on to computer VAN-SRV1 as Kim_Akers, in the Remote Desktop Services folder of the Administrative Tools menu, click RemoteApp Manager.

2. In the Actions pane, click Add RemoteApp Programs. This opens the RemoteApp Wizard. Click Next. On the Choose Programs To Add To The RemoteApp Programs List page, select WordPad, and then click Next. Click Finish.

3. In RemoteApp Manager, in the RemoteApp Programs list, select WordPad. In the Actions pane, click Create Windows Installer Package. This opens the RemoteApp Wizard. Click Next.

4. On the Specify Package Settings page, enter the directory **C:\RemoteApp** that you created in step 4 of Exercise 1, and then click Next.

5. On the Configure Distribution Package page, ensure that the Desktop and Start Menu Folder items are selected. Click Next, and then click Finish.

6. Log on to server VAN-DC1 using the Kim_Akers user account. Navigate to the network folder \\VAN-SRV1\RemoteApp. Double-click the file WordPad.msi. In the Open File - Security Warning dialog box, click Run.

7. In the User Account Control dialog box, click Yes. When the RemoteApp application has installed, view the desktop. Double-click the WordPad shortcut on the desktop. In the warning message box, click Connect. Enter the password **Pa$$w0rd** and then click OK. Verify that WordPad opens.

8. Open Task Manager. On the Applications tab, verify that the program is listed as Document - WordPad (Remote). Close the RemoteApp application.

Chapter Review

To further practice and reinforce the skills you learned in this chapter, you can perform the following tasks:

- Review the chapter summary.
- Complete the case scenarios. These scenarios set up real-world situations involving the topics of this chapter and ask you to create a solution.
- Complete the suggested practices.
- Take a practice test.

Chapter Summary

- Presentation virtualization involves running an application on one computer and displaying it on another. The benefit of presentation virtualization is that it allows an application to be updated once on the host server rather than repeatedly across all clients in the organization.
- App-V involves streaming an application from a host server so that it executes, but does not install, on the client. App-V allows conflicting applications to be run on the same computer. App-V requires the MDOP.
- You can publish web applications to web servers on perimeter networks securely using FTP 7.5 or WebDAV.

Case Scenarios

In the following case scenarios, you will apply what you have learned about planning server installs and upgrades. You can find answers to these questions in the "Answers" section at the end of this book.

Case Scenario 1: Planning an RDS Strategy for Wingtip Toys

You are planning the deployment of RDS for the Wingtip Toys company. Wingtip Toys has an office in each state of Australia. Because of the decentralized nature of the Wingtip Toys organization, each state office has its own domain in the Wingtiptoys.internal forest. All clients in the organization are running Windows XP SP2 and Windows Vista without any service packs applied. Taking this into consideration, how will you resolve the following design challenges?

1. Each state office should be responsible for the purchase and management of RDS CALs. What plans should be made for RD license server deployment?

2. The RD Session Host server in the Queensland office is reaching capacity and cannot be upgraded further. How can you continue to service clients in the Queensland office and ensure that interrupted sessions are reconnected?

3. What steps need to be taken to ensure that clients can access RemoteApp applications through RD Web Access?

Case Scenario 2: App-V at Contoso

Contoso develops custom applications for computers running Windows 7. A new version of a certain application is released every year, and while customers upgrade, you need to give support staff at Contoso the ability to run the current and previous versions of the application. The technical problem is that both the current and the previous version of the application cannot be installed on the same computer running Windows 7. You have also deployed RDS at Contoso to support several important applications. You want to ensure that the application hosted on the RD Session Host server is started when users click file attachments sent to them through email. You have deployed an RD Gateway server on the Contoso perimeter network. With these facts in mind, answer the following questions:

1. Which technology should you provision to allow users in the testing department to be able to run different versions of the same application?

2. How should you deploy RemoteApp applications to ensure that the application will open when a user double-clicks an associated file type?

3. How can you ensure that users who are using their computers on the Internet are able to access RemoteApp applications?

Suggested Practices

To help you successfully master the exam objectives presented in this chapter, complete the following tasks.

Provision Applications

Perform all the practices in this section.

- Practice 1: Using the RD RemoteApp Manager, create a Windows Installer package for Notepad.

- Practice 2: Install the RD Licensing role service. Activate the computer using the Web page method using another computer that is connected to the Internet.

Plan Application Server and Services

Perform all the practices in this section.

- Practice 1: Install the Web Server and FTP 7.5 role services. Use FTP to upload content to a site hosted on the web server.

- Practice 2: Install and configure the WebDAV role service and use it to upload content to a site hosted on the web server.

Take a Practice Test

The practice tests on this book's companion CD offer many options. For example, you can test yourself on just one exam objective, or you can test yourself on all the 70-646 certification exam content. You can set up the test so that it closely simulates the experience of taking a certification exam, or you can set it up in study mode so that you can look at the correct answers and explanations after you answer each question.

> **MORE INFO** **PRACTICE TESTS**
>
> For details about all the practice test options available, see the section "How to Use the Practice Tests" in this book's Introduction.

CHAPTER 7

Provisioning File and Print Servers

This chapter looks at the Print and Document Services and File Services server roles and describes how you can plan to meet your organization's printing, file storage, and access security needs. It discusses printer publishing and availability and looks at access permissions for both printers and files. The chapter covers file quotas and availability and describes how you can plan the deployment of the BranchCache For Network Files feature in both Distributed and Hosted Cache mode.

Exam objectives in this chapter:

- Plan file and print server roles.

Lessons in this chapter:

Before You Begin

To complete the exercises in the practice session in this chapter, you need to have done the following:

- Installed a server called VAN-DC1 running Windows Server 2008 R2 Enterprise that is configured as a domain controller in the Adatum.com domain, as described in Exercise 1 of the Appendix, "Setup Instructions for Windows Server 2008 R2."

- Optionally installed a server called VAN-SRV1 running Windows Server 2008 R2 Enterprise that is configured as a member server in the Adatum.com domain, as specified in Exercise 2 of the Appendix. This server is not required to carry out the practices in this chapter, but you may want to use it if you are trying out the new BranchCache For Network Files feature.

- Created a user account in the Adatum.com domain with the user name Kim Akers and password Pa$$w0rd, and added this account to the Domain Admins, Enterprise

Admins, and Schema Admins groups. This procedure is described in Exercise 1 of the Appendix.

- We recommend that you use an isolated network that is not part of your production network to do the practice exercises in this book. Internet access is not required for the exercises, and you do not need to configure a default gateway. To minimize the time and expense of configuring physical computers, we recommend that you use virtual machines. For example, you can create virtual machines using the Hyper-V server role.

 REAL WORLD

Ian McLean

In July 1993, Microsoft introduced the new technology file system (NTFS). This was a remarkable development in its time. With its advent, folders and files could be protected from interactive as well as network users, and protection could be implemented at file level rather than folder level. I won't go into the many other developments that NTFS enabled—this isn't a history book—but I know that I have lost data on NTFS disks far less often than on FAT disks.

However, NTFS was not unalloyed good news, particularly for a network engineer (me) who was studying for his first MCSE at the time. NTFS introduced a level of complexity in calculating user permissions that almost guaranteed examination failure to those who couldn't quite understand how permissions interacted, particularly when the old No-Access permission was replaced by the more granular Deny.

Software was developed for determining resultant user permissions, but you can't take that into the examination room. My solution was much simpler. I drew three rectangular boxes next to each other. I marked the right box "File," the middle box "Folder," and the left box "Share."

Then I wrote in the NTFS permissions a user had on a file, and the permissions that the same user had on the folder that contained the file. File overrides folder, so I had my resultant NTFS permissions. If I were logged on locally, those were my permissions on the folder. I wrote the shared folder permission into the Share box. If I were accessing remotely, my permissions would be more restrictive between share and resultant NTFS. I had worked out my user permission.

I used this technique in exams and in my profession. When I became an MCT, I taught it to my students, and rectangular boxes appeared on whiteboards throughout the land. It's a simple technique. Some have even called it dumb.

It works. Try it.

Lesson 1: Planning Print Services Management

As far as the users in your organization are concerned, one of the major functions they require from a computer network is the ability to print files easily and without fuss. You need to publish printers so that your users can print to them, while at the same time controlling the use of expensive printing assets. You need to plan your print infrastructure so that urgent print jobs are completed quickly while large, non-urgent print jobs are done outside normal working hours. This lesson looks at the Print and Document Services server role and how you manage availability and access permissions and publish printers.

> **After this lesson, you will be able to:**
> - Install the Print and Document Services server role and install and manage printers and print drivers.
> - Manage printer access permissions and printer availability.
>
> **Estimated lesson time: 35 minutes**

Planning the Print and Document Services Server Role

As an experienced administrator, you will almost certainly be familiar with administering printers and print devices. What is new in Windows Server 2008 R2 is that the Print Services server role, introduced in Windows Server 2008, is now the Print and Document Services server role. You need to install this server role on a server to create a print server. You will install this role in the practice later in this lesson. The Print Management console has been enhanced in Windows Server 2008 R2 and is described in this lesson.

The Print and Document Services server role lets you manage print servers and printers. If you configure a server running Windows Server 2008 R2 as a print server, you reduce administrative and management workload by centralizing printer management tasks through the Print Management console.

By default, installing the Print and Document Services server role installs the Print Server role service, which lets you share printers on a network and publish them to Active Directory Directory Services (AD DS). If you want, you can install the Line Printer Daemon (LPD), which lets you print to printers connected to a UNIX server; the Distributed Scan Server role service (new to Windows Server 2008 R2), which you use to communicate with scanners that support Web Services on Devices (WSD), run scan processes, route scanned documents, and log scan-related events; and Internet Print, which lets you use a web interface to connect to and manage printers.

Planning the Print and Document Services server role involves analyzing current and required printing needs within an organization and configuring printer scheduling and access permissions. Do you have a department that sends very large but non-urgent jobs to a print device? In this case, you need to configure a printer that sends such jobs to a print device outside of office hours.

Does everyone in your organization need to print in color? If you give people the opportunity to print in color, they are likely to do so whether they need to or not. You cannot prevent users from habitually clicking Print several times whenever they want to print a document, or from printing out all their email messages. You can, however, set up auditing to detect high printer usage and identify those users with bad printing habits. As this book states in several places, an administrator needs to be able to solve people problems as well as technical problems.

Some of your planning decisions will be practical and pragmatic. It might be a good idea to have a print device with multiple input trays for special paper types, but it is probably a bad idea to use this device for general-purpose printing. A print device that stops and flashes an error message, thus blocking other jobs in the print queue, whenever a user specifies the wrong size of paper (which could happen easily and frequently) is also a bad choice for general printing needs. Also, you should consider using a printer pool—where a single printer controls several print devices—if you need to provide high availability of print devices.

Managing Printer Entities

If the Print and Document Services server role is installed on your server, you can manage the following entities:

- **Print queue**   A print queue is a representation of a print device. Opening a print queue displays the active print jobs and their status. If a print job at the head of the queue is not being processed (possibly because an incorrect paper size is specified), you can delete this job and allow the remainder of jobs in the queue to be processed.

- **Print spooler service**   A print server has a single print spooler service. This manages all the print jobs and print queues on that server. Typically, the print spooler service starts automatically. If, however, the service has stopped for any reason, you need to restart it. A symptom of this is a print job at the head of a queue that is not being processed but cannot be deleted.

- **Printer driver**   A print queue requires a printer driver to print to a print device. You need to ensure that the print driver exists on your print server, is working correctly, and is up to date.

- **Network printer port**   A printer driver uses a network printer port to communicate with a physical device across a network. These ports may, for example, be TCP/IP printer ports, Line Printer Remote (LPR) ports, or standard COM and LPT ports.

- **Print server cluster**   Printing is typically a mission-critical operation and you might choose to cluster your print servers to ensure high availability and failover support. Chapter 11, "Clustering and High Availability," discusses cluster administration.

Publishing Printers

If you share a printer on a network but do not publish it in Active Directory, users then need to know its network path to use it. If you do publish the printer in Active Directory, it is easier to locate. If you decide to move a printer to another print server, you do not need to change the settings on clients—you only need to change its record in Active Directory.

If a printer is shared but not published, you can publish it by selecting the List In The Directory check box on the Sharing tab of the printer's Properties dialog box, shown in Figure 7-1.

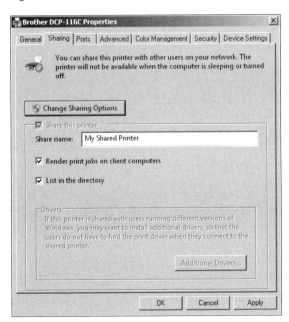

FIGURE 7-1 Publishing a printer

If you add a printer on a print server running Windows Server 2008 R2 and share it, the printer is published automatically, provided that the Group Policy settings called Automatically Publish New Printers In Active Directory and Allow Printers To Be Published are enabled. Figure 7-2 shows the Allow Printers To Be Published setting. A published printer needs to be shared. If you stop sharing the printer, it is no longer published.

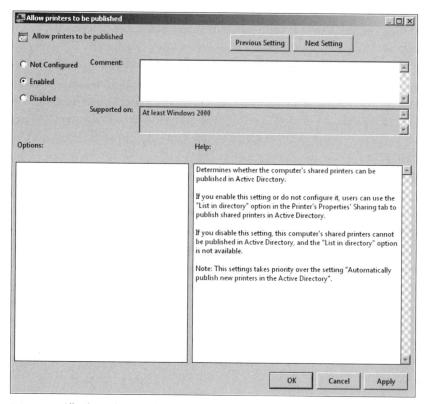

FIGURE 7-2 Allowing printers to be published

Using Windows Server 2008 R2 Print Enhancements

Windows Server 2008 R2 provides users with enhanced printer and Print and Documents Services server role performance through the use of XML Paper Specification (XPS) documents, print paths, and printer drivers. It provides improved Print Management tools and, in particular, enhances the Print Management console. It also provides built-in support for WSD. It enhances efficiency and reduces the processing load on the Print Server and Documents server by performing print rendering on clients.

XPS Documents

Windows Server 2008 R2 integrates XPS throughout the print subsystem. This provides an enhanced level of efficiency, compatibility, and document quality. The XPS Document format is based on a fixed-layout document technology. The Microsoft XPS and Open Packaging Conventions (OPC) define the format, and these specifications are built on industry standards, such as XML and ZIP.

The XPS Document format provides broad platform support and is standard with Windows Vista. It is also supported by Microsoft .NET Framework 3.0 in Windows XP, Windows Vista, Windows 7, and Windows Server 2003. Cross-platform solutions are made possible by the open specifications. Many vendors of print and scan products are already developing solutions around XPS technologies to take advantage of the performance available and quality improvements to both .NET Framework 3.0 and Win32 applications.

XPSDrv printer drivers use a modular architecture that allows them to process documents in the print queue more efficiently. Windows Server 2008 R2 XPSDrv printer drivers use an architecture that extends the existing driver infrastructure with new features and capabilities while retaining compatibility with existing printers and applications. The XPSDrv printer driver architecture provides the following features:

- It supports Windows Presentation Foundation (WPF) and is also compatible with Win32-based applications.

MORE INFO WPF

For more information about WPF, access *http://msdn.microsoft.com/en-us/library/ ms754130.aspx* and follow the links. Be aware, however, that the examination is unlikely to ask in-depth questions on this topic.

- It allows you to include custom filters that perform such functions as adding a corporate watermark or implementing quota management and print job accounting.
- It enables independent hardware vendors to share common functionalities between similar driver models. This can improve the reliability of driver components and enhance print server driver post-processing by supporting the reuse of common printer driver components.

The print architecture gives existing applications the ability to use features that can be found only in the XPSDrv printer drivers. New applications that are written to use the .NET Framework 3.0 and .NET Framework 3.5 can take advantage of all the features that are offered throughout the print path.

MORE INFO .NET FRAMEWORK 3.0 AND .NET FRAMEWORK 3.5

For more information about .NET Framework 3.0 and .NET Framework 3.5, including download links, see *http://www.microsoft.com/downloads/en/details. aspx?FamilyID=10CC340B-F857-4A14-83F5-25634C3BF043&displaylang=en* and *http:// www.microsoft.com/downloads/en/details.aspx?FamilyID=333325FD-AE52-4E35-B531- 508D977D32A6&displaylang=en*, respectively.

XPSDrv printer drivers provide your users with better print quality. The drivers are not limited to using only the graphics device interface (GDI) processing functions. This enables them to process graphics in alternate color spaces and to use higher-performance graphics libraries that were not available to the older, GDI based printer drivers.

Print Paths

Windows Server 2008 R2 supports the XPS print paths that use the XPS Document format throughout the print path from the application to the printer. This makes it possible to achieve true WYSIWYG print output. Print paths in Windows Server 2008 R2 provide the following advantages:

- They eliminate the file format conversions that are common with GDI-based printer drivers. This improves print performance and printed output quality, and helps reduce the overall size of spool files.

- They provide support for advanced color spaces and technologies in the printer driver components.

- They use 32-bit-per-channel color and CMYK color space. CMYK refers to the four inks used in some color printing: cyan, magenta, yellow, and key black.

- They provide direct support for transparencies and gradients.

- They implement conversion print paths to support existing applications and printer drivers.

The Print Management Console

Print and Document Services in Windows Server 2008 R2 enables you to share printers on a network and centralize print server and network printer management tasks by using the Print Management MMC snap-in. This console, shown in Figure 7-3, helps you monitor print queues and receive notifications when print queues stop processing print jobs. It also enables you to migrate print servers and deploy printer connections using Group Policy. You access the Print Management console by clicking Print Management on the Administrative Tools menu. Note that this tool is not available unless you have installed the Remote Server Administration Tools (RSAT) or have installed the Print and Document Services server role. You install this server role in a practice later in this chapter.

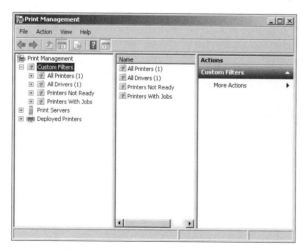

FIGURE 7-3 The Print Management console

The enhanced Windows Server 2008 R2 Print Management console includes support for print server migration from Windows 2000 Server and Windows Server 2003 to Windows Server 2008 R2. It also features an improved Network Printer Installation Wizard, which reduces the number of steps that you need to perform when adding network printers. The wizard automatically locates printers and installs the appropriate printer driver if this is available.

 Quick Check

- What three features does the XPSDrv printer driver architecture provide in Windows Server 2008 R2?

Quick Check Answer

- It supports WPF.
- It allows you to include custom filters that perform such functions as adding a corporate watermark or implementing quota management and print job accounting.
- It enables independent hardware vendors to share common functionality between similar driver models.

Web Services on Devices (WSD)

Windows Server 2008 R2 provides built-in support for WSD, which is a set of protocols for accessing and controlling services on network-connected devices. WSD makes it easier to connect, install, and use printers. Microsoft is working in collaboration with several printer manufacturers to support this protocol in its devices.

Improving Scalability

To reduce the processing load on the computer running the Print and Document Services server role, print rendering is performed on the client (in particular, on clients running Windows Vista). In some cases, performing print rendering on the client considerably reduces network bandwidth. The size of this reduction in bandwidth depends on the print job content and the Page Description Language (PDL).

The print spooler in Windows Server 2008 R2 uses remote procedure calls (RPCs) to communicate between the client and the server. Windows Server 2008 R2 significantly reduces the number of separate processing threads required for RPCs. This can greatly enhance performance in medium- to large-scale print environments.

> **MORE INFO** **PRINT MANAGEMENT**
>
> For more information about Print Management on computers running Windows Server 2008 R2, and also on computers running Windows Vista and Windows 7, access *http://technet.microsoft.com/en-gb/library/cc766474.aspx* and follow the links.

Managing Printers with the Print Management Console

The Print Management console is installed as part of the Print and Document Services server role in Windows Server 2008 R2. You can also install it by opening Server Manager, clicking Features in the console tree, and then clicking Add Features. You then expand Remote Server Administration Tools, expand Role Administration Tools, and select the Print And Document Services Tools check box. Click Next, and then click Install. Click Close when the tool is installed.

The Print Management console lets you implement single-seat administration in a large organization that has a number of print servers (typically a large number). When you have installed the Print Management console as part of RSAT (it is also installed by default when you add the Print and Document Services role), you can open it from the Administration Tools menu or from within Server Manager. When you have installed the Print Management console, you need to configure it to identify the printers and print servers that you want to manage. You can add printers manually, or you can scan the network to identify printers automatically by clicking Printers on the Print Management console tree, as shown in Figure 7-4.

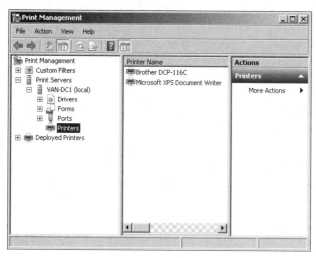

FIGURE 7-4 Scanning for printers automatically in the Print Management console

You can add a print server to the Print Management console by right-clicking Print Servers and selecting Add/Remove Servers. You can add new printers to a Windows Server 2008 R2 network by using the Add Printer wizard that was available in previous Windows versions. In Windows Server 2008 R2, this has been renamed the Network Printer Installation Wizard. The Print Management console gives you the option of running this wizard on a remote print server in both Windows Server 2008 and Windows Server 2008 R2; previously, you needed to run it locally.

To start the Network Printer Installation Wizard within the Print Management console, expand Print Servers and right-click the print server that you want to host the printer. Then click Add Printer, as shown in Figure 7-5, and follow the steps of the wizard. The Network Printer Installation Wizard lets you install a printer that is on a remote print server.

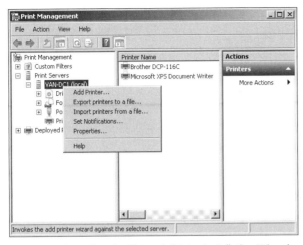

FIGURE 7-5 Accessing the Network Printer Installation Wizard

If you have added remote print servers to the Print Management console and configured printers on these servers, you can view, manage, and administer these printers and print servers centrally. Some of the tasks that you now can perform from the Print Management console, such as changing printer ports, adding or modifying forms, and viewing the status of printers, you previously had to carry out locally on a print server. Other tasks on the Print Management console are new, including creating custom printer filters that allow you and other administrators to view and manage selected printers based on their site, rights, and roles. The procedure to create a printer filter is described in the next section.

Creating a Printer Filter and a Print Driver Filter

Printer filters are used to display only those printers that meet specified criteria. You can create custom printer filters that filter by manufacturer or by printer type (such as laser, color laser, and plotter). This lets you view assets by make, model, location, or configuration. For example, you could set a filter to display all the printers in a single building, regardless of the print server they use.

The Print Management console provides two default filters named Printers Not Ready and Printers With Jobs. When you create a new custom filter, you have the option to set up an email notification or to run a script when the conditions of the filter are met. The procedure to create a custom printer filter is as follows:

1. Open the Print Management console.
2. Right-click Custom Filters. Click Add New Printer Filter. This starts the New Printer Filter Wizard.
3. On the Printer Filter Name And Description page, specify a name for the printer filter. This name will appear in the Custom Printer Filters folder in the Print Management console tree.
4. If you want, type a description.

5. If you want to display the number of printers that satisfies the conditions of a filter, select the Display The Total Number Of Items Next To The Name Of The Filter check box.

6. The Filter Name And Description page should look similar to Figure 7-6. Click Next.

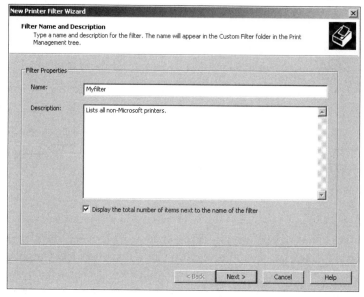

FIGURE 7-6 The Filter Name And Description page

7. On the Define A Printer Filter page, specify a printer status characteristic or print queue on the Field list. Specify a Condition and a Value for that condition, as shown in Figure 7-7. Click Next.

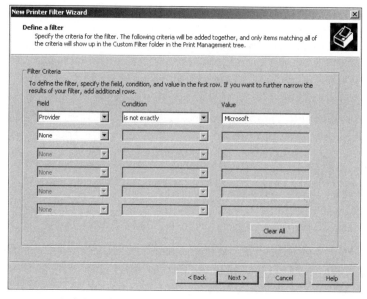

FIGURE 7-7 Defining a filter

8. If you want, on the Set Notifications (Optional) page, set an email notification, set a script to run, or specify both. Click Finish.

9. Click the name of the filter that you created in the Custom Filters container, as shown in Figure 7-8. View the list of printers in the middle pane.

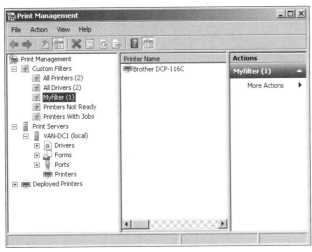

FIGURE 7-8 Viewing the printers specified by a printer filter

Similarly, you can use the Print Management console to create custom print driver filters that display only those print drivers that meet a certain set of criteria. The procedure for creating a custom print driver filter is almost identical to that for creating a custom printer filter, except that in step 2 you right-click Custom Filters and click Add New Driver Filter. You specify a name and (if you want) a description, and then select whether to display the number of items next to the filter.

As with a printer filter, you configure the print driver filter by specifying Field, Condition, and Value, and you have the option of configuring an email notification, running a script, or both.

EXAM TIP

Custom filters are new to the Print Management console and can be configured only on print servers running Windows Server 2008 or Windows Server 2008 R2.

 Quick Check
■ What are the two default filters provided by the Print Management console in Windows Server 2008 R2?

Quick Check Answer
■ Printers Not Ready and Printers With Jobs

Managing Drivers, Ports, Forms, and Printers

You can expand any of the print servers listed in the Print Management console tree and manage drivers, ports, forms, or printers. You can also add a driver, a port, or a printer.

When you right-click Drivers and click Manage Drivers, this opens the Properties dialog box for the print server with the Drivers tab selected, as shown in Figure 7-9. You can add a new driver, remove a driver, or view the properties of any driver in the list.

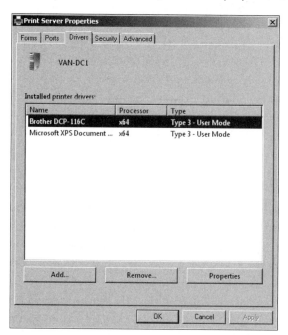

FIGURE 7-9 The Drivers tab of the Print Server Properties dialog box

When you right-click Ports and click Manage Ports, this opens the Properties dialog box for the print server with the Ports tab selected, as shown in Figure 7-10. You can delete an existing port, add a new port, or configure a selected port. To configure a port, click Configure Port, enter a value (in seconds) for the transmission timeout retry interval, and then click OK.

When you right-click Forms and click Manage Forms, this opens the Properties dialog box for the print server with the Forms tab selected. When you select the Create A New Form check box, you can give the form a name and specify paper size and print area margins, as shown in Figure 7-11. When you are satisfied with your configuration, you click Save Form to create the form. Note that the Delete button becomes active only if you have already saved one or more custom forms and select a custom form on the Forms tab. You cannot delete standard forms from this tab.

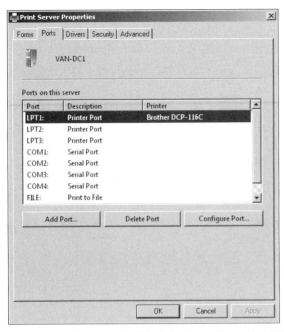

FIGURE 7-10 The Ports tab of the Print Server Properties dialog box

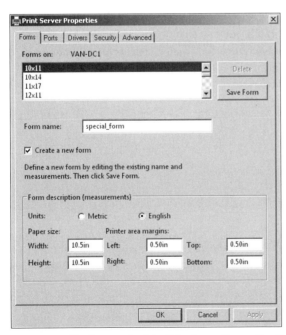

FIGURE 7-11 The Forms tab of the Print Server Properties dialog box

When you right-click Printers under a print server, you can add a printer or show or hide Extended view. If you choose to show Extended view, then more details are given for any printer that you select in the Print Management console. You can view the print jobs currently running on the printer and access the printer Web page (if one exists). Figure 7-12 shows Extended view details for a selected printer.

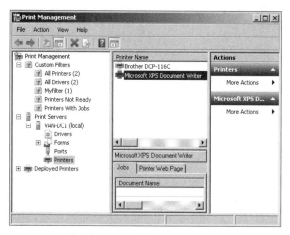

FIGURE 7-12 Showing Extended view

You can also access the Properties dialog box for a print server by right-clicking the server in the Print Management console tree and clicking Properties. By default, this accesses the Advanced tab, shown in Figure 7-13. On this tab, you can change the location of the print spool folder and select whether an audible warning will be generated if an error is detected on a remote document and whether to show informational notifications for local printers, remote printers, or both.

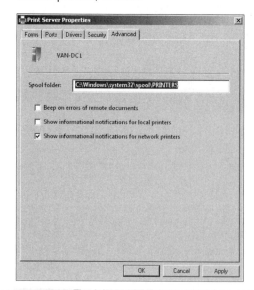

FIGURE 7-13 The Advanced tab of the Print Server Properties dialog box

Planning and Managing Security and Access Permissions

To secure a print server and control access to specific printers, you must consider what rights users and groups should have. As an experienced administrator, you have probably configured permissions for both files and printers. You should be aware that you should grant permissions to groups rather than individual users, and you should use explicit Deny permissions as sparingly as possible.

You have probably dealt with the situation where a user who should have access to a printer does not and (more difficult to diagnose) where a user who should not have access to a printer does. Setting permissions and debugging permission configuration are common administrative tasks.

Planning permissions is a much more difficult task. Should you configure two print drivers for an expensive print device, so that the Managers security group has full-time access while the Everyone security group has access only at off-peak times? How should you plan access to color printers or A3 printers? What type of auditing and monitoring should you set up so you can identify users with bad printing habits (such as sending a job to a printer several times if it does not immediately appear on the print device)? Should you use printer pools to handle heavy print traffic?

EXAM TIP

Remember that you can have several printers controlling a single print device and giving different groups different levels and times of access. You can also have several print devices controlled by a single print driver so that they form a printer pool.

The Security tab of the Print Server Properties dialog box lets you configure access settings for all printers on the print server, as well as to the print server itself. You are probably aware of the print permissions available, but they are listed here to remind you:

- **Print**   This permission is assigned to the Everyone group by default. The user can connect to a printer and send documents. Members of the Administrators, Print Operators, and Server Operators groups also have explicit Print permission.

- **Manage Documents**   This permission is assigned explicitly to members of the Creator Owner group and is the only permission assigned to that group. Members of the Administrators, Print Operators, and Server Operators groups are granted the Manage Documents permission but are also granted the Manage Printers permission. The user can pause, resume, restart, cancel, and rearrange the order of documents submitted by all other users. A user who has only the Manage Documents permission, however, cannot send documents to the printer or control the status of the printer.

- **Manage Printers**   This permission is assigned to members of the Administrators, Print Operators, and Server Operators groups. The user can perform the tasks associated with the Print permission and has complete administrative control of the printer. The user can pause and restart the printer, change spooler settings, share a printer, adjust printer permissions, and change printer properties.

The Security tab of the Print Server Properties dialog box also lets you assign permissions to the server itself. The View Server permission allows a user to view the print server. Without the View Server permission, a user cannot see printers that are managed by the server, and for this reason, this permission is given to members of the Everyone group.

The Manage Server permission lets users create and delete print queues (with already installed drivers), add or delete ports, and add or delete forms. By default, the Administrators, Server Operators, and Print Operators groups are granted this permission. A standard user who is granted this permission is called a delegated print administrator.

> **MORE INFO**   **ASSIGNING DELEGATED PRINT ADMINISTRATOR AND PRINTER PERMISSION SETTINGS**
>
> For more information about delegating print server management,
> see *http://msdn.microsoft.com/en-us/library/ee524015(WS.10).aspx.*

Figure 7-14 shows the Security tab of the Print Server Properties dialog box and the permission settings for the Everyone group. A group or an individual user can be specifically allowed permission, although as a best practice individual users should inherit permissions through group membership.

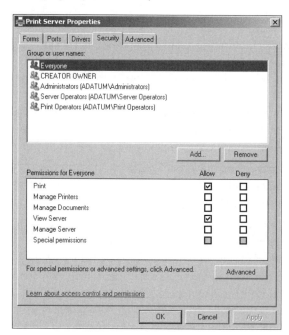

FIGURE 7-14 The Security tab of the Print Server Properties dialog box

A user or group can also be specifically denied permission. A user who has been specifically denied a permission, or who is a member of a group that has been specifically denied a permission, cannot be granted the permission through being a member of other groups. For this reason, the explicit Deny permission should be used as seldom as possible, and any instance should be documented carefully.

If appropriate, you can grant special permissions to a user or a group by allocating a non-standard combination of the available permissions. To confer special permissions to a user or security group, select the user or group in the Security tab and then click Advanced. The Advanced Security Settings dialog box, shown in Figure 7-15, allows you to configure permissions for a listed group or user by selecting the group or user and clicking Edit. You can also add a group or user and edit its permissions.

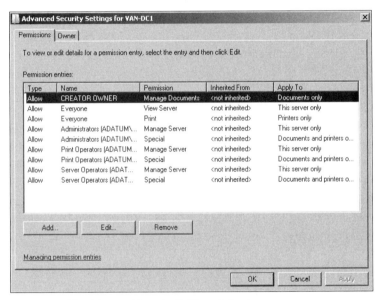

FIGURE 7-15 The Advanced Security Settings dialog box

In addition to granting permissions on a print server, you can configure permissions on an individual printer. Permissions specifically configured at the printer level override permissions inherited from the print server configuration. You can assign Print, Manage Documents, and Manage Printers permissions to groups or users, and you can configure and assign special permissions. As with all permission configurations, it is good practice to confer permissions to groups rather than individual users and to be very sparing in the use of explicit Deny and special permissions. The Security tab of a printer's Properties dialog box is shown in Figure 7-16.

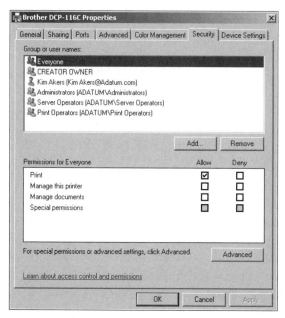

FIGURE 7-16 The Security tab of a printer's Properties dialog box

Lesson Summary

- When you install the Print and Document Services server role, you can install and manage printers and print drivers, add and manage ports, and configure forms.
- The Print Management console provides single-seat management of printers on remote print servers on your network.
- You can configure printer and server permissions on the Print Server Properties dialog box. You can configure permissions to an individual printer on the printer's Properties dialog box.

Lesson Review

You can use the following questions to test your knowledge of the information in Lesson 1, "Planning Print Services Management." The questions are also available on the companion CD if you prefer to review them in electronic form.

> **NOTE ANSWERS**
>
> Answers to these questions and explanations of why each answer choice is correct or incorrect are located in the "Answers" section at the end of the book.

1. When you install the Print and Document Services server role, you can use the Print Management console to carry out a number of jobs remotely that previously you needed to do locally on the print server that held the printer. The console also introduces features that were not available in Windows versions earlier than Windows Server 2008. Which of the following tasks is new to the Print Management console?

   A. Changing printer ports

   B. Viewing the printer status

   C. Adding or modifying forms

   D. Creating custom printer filters

2. Which permission, assigned by default to the Creator Owner security group, allows a user to pause, resume, restart, cancel, and rearrange the order of documents submitted by all other users, but does not permit the user to send documents to the printer or control the status of the printer?

   A. Print

   B. Manage Documents

   C. Manage Printers

   D. Manage Server

3. Jeff Hay is a standard user. You want him to be a delegated print administrator on the print server DEN-PRS1. What permission do you grant him?

   A. Manage Server

   B. View Server

   C. Manage Documents

   D. Manage Printers

4. If you add and share a printer on a print server running Windows Server 2008 R2, the printer is published automatically, provided that two Group Policy settings are enabled. What are these settings? (Each answer forms part of the solution. Choose two.)

   A. Disallow Installation Of Printers Using Kernel Mode Drivers

   B. Always Render Print Jobs On The Server

   C. Automatically Publish New Printers In Active Directory

   D. Pre-Populate Printer Search Location Text

   E. Allow Printers To Be Published

Lesson 2: Planning File Servers

Your users need to be able to create files and save these files where they can be retrieved easily. You, on the other hand, need to ensure that users cannot read confidential files unless they are allowed to. You need to control usage so that users cannot clog the network with high numbers of large files. This lesson discusses file server configuration, file access permissions, quotas, storage availability, and the new BranchCache For Network Files feature introduced by Windows Server 2008 R2.

After this lesson, you will be able to:

- Plan your file and folder infrastructure and install the role services that you require to implement this plan.
- Manage file access permissions and storage availability.
- Plan and implement file quotas.
- Use the new BranchCache For Network Files feature.

Estimated lesson time: 45 minutes

Configuring a File Server

A file server provides a central network location where users can store files and share them with other users on the network. If a user requires a file that typically is accessed by many users, such as a company policy document, she should be able to access the file remotely. For the purposes of centralized administration, backup and restore, and the implementation of shadow copies, you need to store user files on a file server rather than on individual computers, although users typically also need to have the facility of working with their files offline.

You configure a server running Windows Server 2008 R2 as a file server by adding the File Services role, which consists of a number of role services. The File Server role service is installed automatically if you share a folder on the server. Figure 7-17 shows the role services that you can install as part of the File Services role.

As part of your planning process, you need to decide what role services you require and how these should be configured. The temptation is to install everything just in case you need it. Resist this temptation. The more services you install on a server, the more pressure you put on limited resources and the larger the footprint for attack.

The Role Services server role provides the following role services:

- Share And Storage Management (provided by File Server), which includes Disk Management, which in turn enables you to configure shadow copies
- Distributed File System (DFS), which includes DFS Namespaces (DFSN) and DFS Replication (DFSR)
- File Server Resource Manager (FSRM)

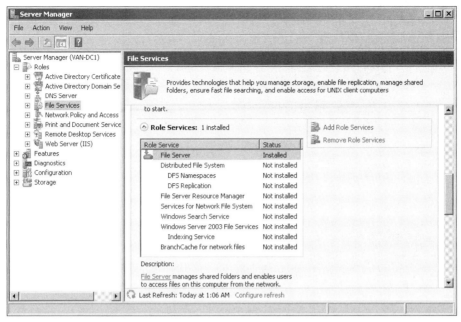

FIGURE 7-17 Role services provided by the File Services server role

- Services For Network File System
- Windows Search Service
- Windows Server 2003 File Services, which includes the legacy Indexing Service
- BranchCache For Network Files, which is new in Windows Server 2008 R2

> *NOTE* **OPTIONAL FEATURES**
>
> Often the Windows Server Backup, Storage Manager for SANs, Failover Clustering, and
> Multipath I/O (MPIO) features are installed at the same time as the role services provided
> by the File Services server role. Chapter 13, "Backup and Recovery," and Chapter 10,
> "Provision Data and Plan Storage," discuss these features.

Share and Storage Management

Share And Storage Management is installed by default with the File Server role service. You can access the Share And Storage Management console through Server Manager or directly from Administrative Tools. It uses the Microsoft Server Message Block (SMB) 2.0 protocol to share the content of folders and to manage shared folders.

Figure 7-18 shows the Share And Storage Management console (accessed from Administrative Tools rather than from Server Manager) and lists the shared folders on the VAN-DC1 domain controller. Your domain controller might have additional shares if you created them when you were experimenting with your network.

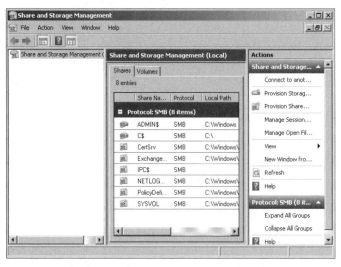

FIGURE 7-18 The Share And Storage Management console

> **MORE INFO** **THE SMB PROTOCOL**
>
> If you want to learn more about the SMB protocol, as well as the Common Internet File System (CIFS) protocol that is a dialect of the SMB protocol, see *http://msdn2.microsoft.com/en-us/ library/aa365233.aspx*. However, the examination is unlikely to ask you detailed questions about this protocol.

You can manage volumes and disks by using the Share And Storage Management console, as shown in Figure 7-19. Again, the volumes on your VAN-DC1 domain controller might differ from those seen here.

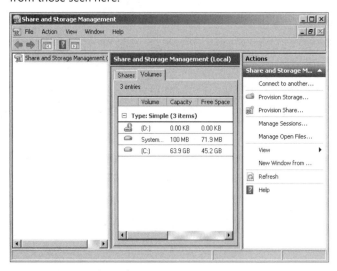

FIGURE 7-19 Managing volumes

If you access Share And Storage Management from Server Manager, you can access the Disk Management console, shown in Figure 7-20. Again, the disks in your VAN-DC1 domain controller might differ from those seen here.

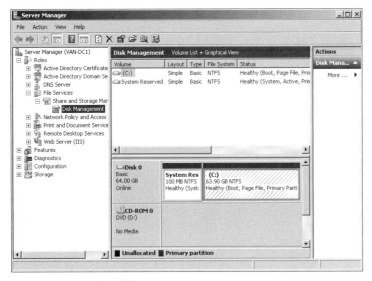

FIGURE 7-20 Managing disks

You can share the content of folders and volumes on a server running Windows Server 2008 or Windows Server 2008 R2 over the network by using the Provision A Shared Folder Wizard, which you can access by selecting Provision Share from the Actions pane in the Share And Storage Management console. Figure 7-21 shows this wizard, which guides you through the steps required to share a folder or volume and configure its properties.

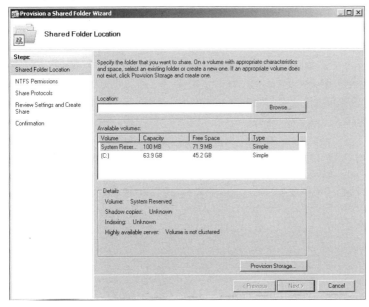

FIGURE 7-21 The Provision A Shared Folder Wizard

You can use the Provision A Shared Folder Wizard to do the following:

- Specify a folder or volume to share, or create a new folder to share.
- Specify the network sharing protocol used to access the shared resource.
- Change the local NTFS permissions for the folder or volume you are sharing.
- Configure the share access permissions, user limits, and offline access to files in the shared resource.
- Publish the shared resource to a DFS namespace.

If you have installed the Services For Network File System role service, you can specify Network File System (NFS)–based access permissions for the shared resource. If you have installed the File Server Resource Manager role service, you can apply storage quotas to the new shared resource and limit the type of files that can be stored in it.

You can use Share And Storage Management to stop sharing a resource by selecting the resource on the Shares tab (shown previously in Figure 7-18) and clicking Stop Sharing in the Actions pane. If a folder or volume is shared for access by both the SMB and the NFS protocols, you need to stop sharing for each protocol individually. Before you stop sharing a folder or volume, you need to ensure that it is not in use by using the Manage Sessions and Manage Open Files features of Share And Storage Management. These features are described later in this section.

You can also use Share And Storage Management to view and modify the properties of a shared folder or volume, including the local NTFS permissions and the network access permissions for that shared resource. To do this, you again select the shared resource on the Shares tab and select Properties in the Actions pane (or right-click the shared resource and then click Properties). Figure 7-22 shows the Properties dialog box for a Public folder that has been shared. Clicking Advanced on the Sharing tab lets you configure user limits and caching and disable or enable access-based enumeration (ABE). ABE is enabled by default and lets you hide files and folders from users who do not have access to them. The Permissions tab lets you specify share and NTFS permissions.

> **NOTE ADMINISTRATIVE SHARES**
>
> You cannot modify the access permissions of folders or volumes shared for administrative purposes, such as C$ and ADMIN$.

If you want to view and close open sessions and open files—for example, if you intend to stop sharing a resource—you can click Manage Sessions or Manage Open Files as appropriate in the Share And Storage Management Actions pane. Figure 7-23 shows the Manage Sessions dialog box.

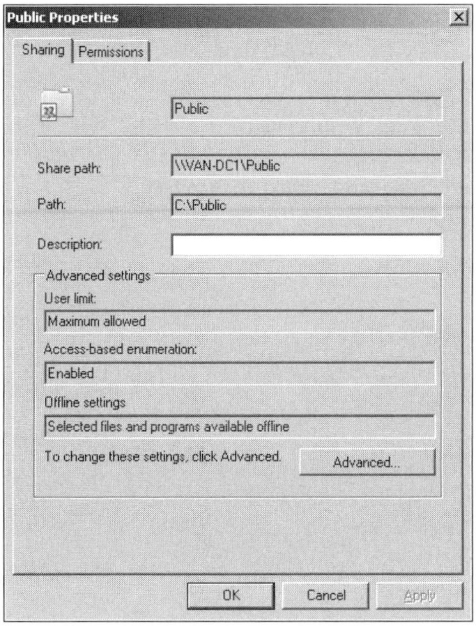

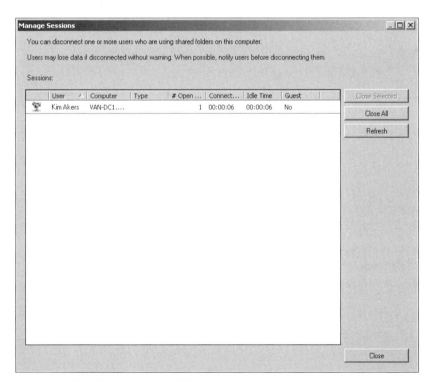

FIGURE 7-22 The Properties dialog box for a shared resource

FIGURE 7-23 The Manage Sessions dialog box

Share And Storage Management enables you to provision storage on disks on your server running Windows Server 2008 or Windows Server 2008 R2, or on storage subsystems that support Virtual Disk Service (VDS). The Provision Storage Wizard, shown in Figure 7-24, guides you through the process of creating a volume on an existing disk or on a storage subsystem, such as a storage area network (SAN), attached to your server. You access this wizard from Share And Storage Management by clicking Provision Storage on the Actions pane.

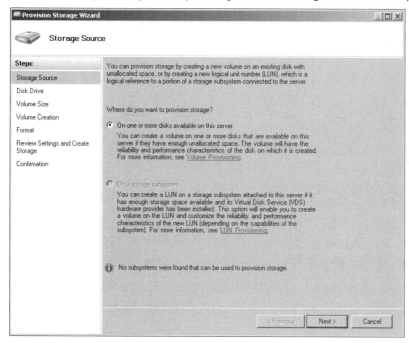

FIGURE 7-24 The Provision Storage Wizard

If you create a volume on a storage subsystem, the wizard enables you to create a Logical Unit Number (LUN) to host that volume. You can also use the wizard to create a LUN, and use the Disk Management console (shown previously in Figure 7-20) to create the volume later.

> **NOTE RUNNING THE PROVISION STORAGE WIZARD**
>
> You can run the Provision Storage Wizard only if your server can access disks with unallocated space or storage subsystems with available storage for which a VDS hardware provider is installed. Also, you can create a volume only on a disk that is online. Chapter 10 discusses storage provisioning in more detail.

Provided that you have the available disk or storage subsystem resources, the Provision Storage Wizard can perform the following functions:

- Choose the disk on which the volume is created.
- Specify the volume size.

- Assign a drive letter or a mount point.
- Format the volume. (You can also do this from the Disk Management console.)

You can use Share And Storage Management to monitor and manage volumes on your server. The tool enables you to perform the following operations:

- Extend the size of a volume.
- Format a volume.
- Delete a volume.
- Change volume properties, including compression, security, offline availability, and indexing.
- Access disk tools for error checking, defragmentation, and backup.

LUNs

A LUN refers to a portion of a storage subsystem. It can include a disk, a section of a disk, a whole disk array, or a section of a disk array. LUNs simplify storage management by providing logical identifiers through which you can assign access and control privileges.

You can use the Provision Storage Wizard in Share And Storage Management to create LUNs on Fibre Channel and iSCSI disk drive subsystems connected to your server. You can then assign the LUN to your server or to other servers on the network. While creating the LUN, you can also create a volume on that LUN and format it. Alternatively, you can create the LUN first and the volume later.

If you want to create a LUN on a disk storage subsystem, you need to ensure that all the following requirements are met:

- The storage subsystem supports VDS.
- The VDS hardware provider for the storage subsystem is installed on the server.
- Storage space is available on the subsystem.
- The storage subsystem is attached directly to the server or is accessible over the network.

If you need to assign a LUN to a server or cluster other than the server on which you run the Provision Storage Wizard, you need to configure the server connections by using Storage Manager for SANs. (See Chapter 10 for more information about this.) If you want to assign the LUN to a cluster, ensure that each server in the cluster is a member of only one cluster and has been configured by installing Failover Clustering. Also, if you enable multiple Fibre Channel ports or iSCSI Initiator adapters for LUN access, make sure that that the server supports MPIO.

Distributed File System

DFS is considerably enhanced in Windows Server 2008 and Windows Server 2008 R2 and is installed as a role service under File Services. This topic is discussed in detail in Chapter 10 and is introduced only briefly here. DFS consists of two technologies, DFSN and DFSR, that you can use (together or independently) to provide fault-tolerant and flexible file sharing and replication services.

DFSN lets you group shared folders on different servers (and in multiple sites) into one or more logically structured namespaces. Users view each namespace as a single shared folder with a series of subfolders. The underlying shared folders structure is hidden from users, and this structure provides fault tolerance and the ability to connect users automatically to local shared folders, when available, instead of routing them over wide area network (WAN) connections.

DFSR provides a multimaster replication engine that lets you synchronize folders on multiple servers across local or WAN connections. It uses the Remote Differential Compression (RDC) protocol to update only those files that have changed since the last replication. You can use DFS Replication in conjunction with DFS Namespaces or by itself.

File Server Resource Manager

FSRM is a role service that you can install as part of File Services in Windows Server 2008 R2. When you install the role service you can access tools that enable you to understand, control, and manage the quantity and type of data stored on your servers. You can use FSRM to place quotas on folders and volumes, actively screen files, and generate storage reports. Details of the facilities available from FSRM are given later in this lesson. You install the FSRM server role in a practice later in this chapter.

Services For Network File System

You can install Services For Network File System as a role service under File Services. NFS provides a file sharing solution for organizations with a mixed Windows and UNIX environment. Services For Network File System lets you transfer files between computers running Windows Server 2008 or Windows Server 2008 R2 and the UNIX operating system by using the NFS protocol. The Windows Server 2008 and Windows Server 2008 R2 versions of Services For NFS support the following enhancements:

- **Active Directory lookup**   Identity management for the UNIX extension of the Active Directory schema includes the UNIX user identifier (UID) and group identifier (GID) fields. This enables Server For NFS and Client For NFS to refer to Windows-to-UNIX user account mappings directly from Active Directory Domain Services (AD DS). Identity management for UNIX simplifies mapping user accounts from Windows to UNIX in AD DS.

- **64-bit support**   You can install Services For NFS on all editions of Windows Server 2008, including 64-bit editions, and on all editions of Windows Server 2008 R2.

- **Enhanced server performance**   Services For NFS includes a file filter driver, which significantly reduces server file access latencies.

- **UNIX special device support**   Services For NFS provides support for UNIX special devices based on the *mknod* (make a directory, a special file, or a regular file) function.

> **MORE INFO**   **MKNOD**
>
> For more information on the *mknod* function, see *http://www.opengroup.org/ onlinepubs/009695399/functions/mknod.html*. However, the exam is unlikely to ask about UNIX functions.

- **Enhanced UNIX support**   Services For NFS supports the following UNIX versions: Sun Microsystems Solaris version 9, Red Hat Linux version 9, IBM AIX version 5L 5.2, and Hewlett Packard HP-UX version 11i.

> **NOTE**   **WINDOWS SERVER 2008 R2 ENHANCEMENTS**
>
> The Services For NFS role service is enhanced in Windows Server 2008 R2 and supports netgroups, which you can use to support network-wide named groups of hosts. The role service is also enhanced to support the Remote Procedure Call Security_Generic Security Services (RPCSEC_GSS) protocol, which enables applications to take advantage of the Generic Security Services_Application Programming Interface (GSS_API) to verify authentication and integrity. It lets you use Windows Management Instrumentation (WMI) for remote NFS management and makes an unmapped UNIX user option available for NFS shares.

Quick Check

■ What are the three main tasks that FSRM enables you to perform?

Quick Check Answer

■ FSRM enables you to place quotas on folders and volumes, actively screen files, and generate storage reports.

Windows Search Service

The Windows Search Service role service enables you to perform fast file searches on a server from clients that are compatible with Windows Search. It creates an index of the most common file and non-file data types on your server, such as email, contacts, calendar appointments, documents, photographs, and multimedia. Indexing files and data types enables you to perform fast file searches on your server running Windows Server 2008 or Windows Server 2008 R2 from clients running Windows Vista or Windows 7, or from clients running Windows XP with Windows Desktop Search installed.

Windows Search Service replaces the Indexing Service feature that was provided in Windows Server 2003. Although you have the option of installing the Windows Server 2003 File Services role service—including the Indexing Service—as part of the File Services server role on a server running Windows Server 2008 or Windows Server 2008 R2, you cannot install Indexing Services if you choose to install Windows Search Service.

When you install Windows Search Service, you are given the option to select the volumes or folders that you want to index. Microsoft recommends that you select a volume rather than a folder only if that volume is used exclusively for hosting shared folders.

Windows Server 2003 File Services

The File Services role in Windows Server 2008 or Windows Server 2008 R2 includes the role services that are compatible with Windows Server 2003. If you want, you can include the legacy Indexing Service that catalogs contents and properties of files on local and remote computers. Note that if you install the Windows Search Service, you cannot install the legacy Indexing Service.

In Windows Server 2008, you also have the option of installing the File Replication Service (FRS), which enables you to synchronize folders with file servers that use FRS. However, Microsoft recommends that where possible, you should use the DFSR service. In Windows Server 2008 R2, FRS has been replaced by DFSR for replicating DFS folders and for replicating the SYSVOL folder. The option to install the FRS role service is not available in Windows Server 2008 R2.

BranchCache For Network Files

The BranchCache For Network Files role service helps you reduce WAN utilization and enhance the responsiveness of network applications when users in branch office locations access content held in a central office. This role service is new to Windows Server 2008 R2 and is therefore discussed in detail later in this lesson.

Optional Features

If you want, you can install the following additional features to complement the role services in the File Services role:

- **Windows Server Backup**   Windows Server Backup provides a reliable method of backing up and recovering the operating system, certain applications, and files and folders stored on your server.

> **MORE INFO   WINDOWS SERVER BACKUP**
>
> For more information, open the command prompt and enter **hh backup.chm**.

- **Storage Manager for SANs**   Storage Manager for SANs lets you provision storage on one or more Fibre Channel or iSCSI storage subsystems on a SAN.

> **MORE INFO   STORAGE MANAGER FOR SANS**
>
> For more information about SANs, open the command prompt and enter **hh sanmgr.chm**.

- **Failover Clustering**   The Failover Clustering feature enables multiple servers to work together to increase the availability of services and applications. If one of the clustered servers (or nodes) fails, another node provides the required service through failover.

> **MORE INFO   FAILOVER CLUSTERS IN WINDOWS SERVER 2008 R2**
>
> For more information about failover clusters and the enhancements introduced in Windows Server 2008 R2, access *http://technet.microsoft.com/en-us/library/ff182338(WS.10).aspx* and follow the links.

- **MPIO**   MPIO, introduced earlier in this lesson, provides support for multiple data paths between a file server and a storage device (known as multipathing). You can use MPIO to increase data availability by providing redundant connections to storage subsystems. Multipathing can also load-balance I/O traffic and improve system and application performance.

Using Windows Server 2008 R2 File Services Enhancements

Windows Server 2008 R2 helps you manage data more effectively, as well as more efficiently. It provides features that help you gain insight into organizational data and reduce the cost of data storage, maintenance, and management. It assists you to enforce company policies and mitigate the risks of leaking data.

File Classification Infrastructure

File Classification Infrastructure (FCI) in Windows Server 2008 R2 helps you manage your data more effectively, reduce costs, and mitigate risks. It provides a built-in solution for file classification that allows you to automate manual processes with predefined policies based on the business value of the data.

File systems on servers running previous operating systems stored files and allowed access based on user permissions. They did not, however, classify files according to their business value. When you have no indication about the business value of data in a file, it is difficult to make decisions about when stale files should expire or which files require a higher level of protection. By being able to both automatically and manually classify files according to predefined rules, you can manage organizational data more effectively and decide what should be retained and where it should be stored.

You can access Classification Properties and Classification Rules under Classification Management in the FSRM MMC snap-in and use the functionality built into Windows Server 2008 R2 to classify files based on content and location so that the files can be protected and managed more effectively based upon business value. An organization's files can be classified to enable you to perform the following tasks:

- Identify sensitive data on public servers.
- Configure automated expiration of stale data.
- Use custom IT scripts. For example, you can use a script to move low-business-value files to cheaper storage hardware.
- Integrate with third-party storage software solutions.

Figure 7-25 shows the Create Classification Property Definition dialog box. If you click Classification Rules, you can create a new classification rule or configure a classification schedule. Figure 7-26 shows a classification schedule configured on the Automatic Classification tab of the File Server Resource Manager Options dialog box, which you access by clicking Classification Rules under Classification Properties in the FSRM MMC snap-in and then clicking Configure Classifications Schedule in the Actions pane.

> **MORE INFO** **FCI**
>
> For more information about FCI, see *http://www.microsoft.com/windowsserver2008/en/us/FCI.aspx.*

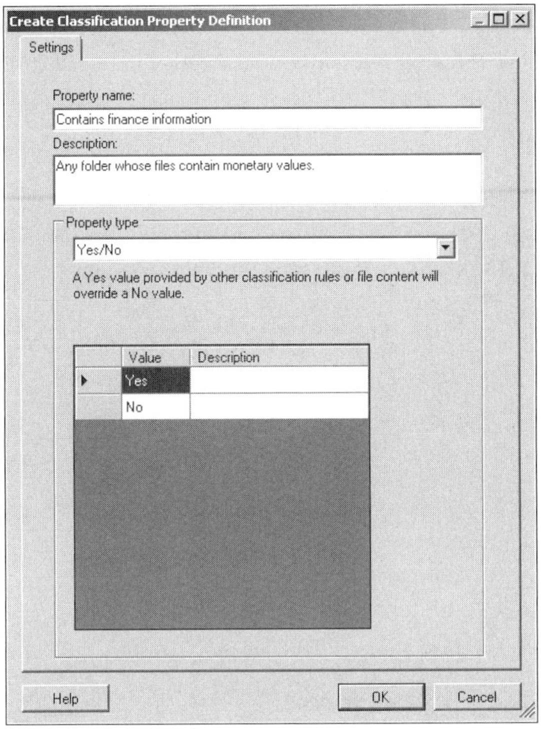

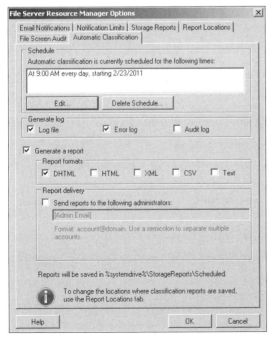

FIGURE 7-25 The Create Classification Property Definition dialog box

FIGURE 7-26 Configuring a classification schedule

Distributed File Management

Windows Server 2008 R2 file services include DFSR and DFSN, introduced earlier in this lesson, to provide customers with better access to data and simplified access to files and shares across a network-wide infrastructure. DFSR efficiently and bidirectionally replicates partial file changes to keep multiple file copies in synchronization. DFSN makes file shares easier to locate and more resilient by enabling users to access their data without regard to the physical file server(s) on which the files reside. Replicated copies and transparent redirection enable your users to be more productive because their data is closer to them and highly available.

DFS is discussed in more detail in Chapter 10. Briefly, DFS technologies offer WAN-friendly replication as well as simplified, highly available access to geographically dispersed files. DFS is enhanced and operates more efficiently in Windows Server 2008 R2. It provides the following benefits:

- Better access to data
- Simplified access to files
- Increased productivity and data availability
- Support for failover clusters
- Read-only replicated folders

> **MORE INFO** **DFS MANAGEMENT IN WINDOWS SERVER 2008 R2**
>
> For more information about the DFS management facilities provided by Windows Server 2008 R2, see *http://technet.microsoft.com/en-gb/library/cc732006.aspx*.

Disk Management

You use the Disk Management console, described earlier in this lesson, to manage hard disks and the volumes or partitions that they contain. You can initialize disks, create volumes, and format volumes with the FAT, FAT32, or NTFS file system. Disk Management enables you to perform most disk-related tasks without restarting the system or interrupting users, and most configuration changes take effect immediately.

The following Disk Management features are provided by Windows Server 2008 R2:

- **More efficient disk partition creation**   When you right-click a volume, you can choose directly from a shortcut menu whether to create a basic, spanned, or striped partition.
- **Disk conversion options**   If you add more than four partitions to a basic disk, you are prompted to convert the disk to dynamic or to the GUID partition table (GPT) partition style.
- **The ability to extend and shrink partitions**   You can extend and shrink partitions directly from the Disk Management console.

FSRM

As mentioned earlier in this lesson, the FSRM role service installs the Classification Management console. In Windows Server 2008 R2, FSRM delivers better-managed file services across Common Internet File System/Server Message Block (CIFS/SMB) and NFS. By centralizing several different file service utilities available in previous Windows Server operating systems, FSRM provides a single management interface that lets you manage all the file allocation, quota, and sharing options in one place. Windows Server 2008 R2 FSRM provides built-in reporting, which lets you determine how your file-serving resources can be used for management, audit, and planning purposes, and offers the following advantages:

- Better-managed file services
- Improved control and compliance over files
- Insight into how your file servers are being used

Using the FSRM MMC snap-in to configure quotas and file screen policy is discussed later in this lesson.

Removable Storage

You can use the Removable Storage component to track removable storage media easily and to manage the libraries that contain them. Removable Storage labels, catalogs, and tracks media; controls library drives, slots, and doors; and provides drive-cleaning operations. It works with data-management programs, such as Backup, which manage the data stored on the media. Removable Storage makes it possible for multiple programs to share the same storage media resources and organizes all the media in your libraries into different media pools. It also moves media between media pools to provide the amount of data storage that your applications require.

Microsoft has removed Removable Storage Manager (RSM) from Windows Server 2008 R2 in favor of new archiving technology. The Ntbackup utility is not available in Windows Server 2008 R2, and it is currently impossible to restore files or folders or entire volumes from old archives created with Ntbackup on Windows Server 2008 and previous versions of Windows unless you download and install the Windows NT Backup Restore Utility for Windows 7 and for Windows Server 2008 R2. This is available at *http://support.microsoft.com/kb/974674.*

MORE INFO   REMOVABLE STORAGE IN WINDOWS SERVER 2008 R2

For more information about Removable Storage in Windows Server 2008 R2, access
http://technet.microsoft.com/en-gb/library/cc772263(WS.10).aspx and follow the links.

Services For NFS

As stated earlier in this lesson, Services For NFS is a role service that you can install as part
of the File Services server role. It includes Server For NFS and Client For NFS and provides
a file-sharing solution for organizations that have a mixed Windows and UNIX environment.
Services For NFS enables you to transfer files between servers running Windows Server 2008
R2 and UNIX operating systems using the NFS protocol. The Windows Server 2008 R2 version
of Services For NFS offers the following improvements:

- **Simplified administration**   The configuration for supporting NFS clients has been
  simplified by the introduction of the Unmapped UNIX User Access feature.
- **Active Directory lookup**   The Identity Management for UNIX Active Directory schema
  extension includes UNIX UID and GID fields. This enables Server For NFS and Client For
  NFS to look up Windows-to-UNIX user account mappings directly from AD DS.
- **Enhanced server performance**   Services For NFS includes a file filter driver. This
  significantly reduces access latencies when accessing common server files.
- **UNIX special device support**   Services For NFS supports UNIX special devices.
- **Enhanced UNIX support**   Services For NFS supports Sun Microsystems Solaris version
  9, Red Hat Linux version 9, IBM AIX version 5L 5.2, and Hewlett Packard HP-UX version
  11i. NFS security is enhanced with the Kerberos protocol.

MORE INFO   SERVICES FOR NFS IN WINDOWS SERVER 2008 R2

For more information about Services For NFS in Windows Server 2008 R2, see
http://technet.microsoft.com/en-gb/library/cc753495.aspx.

Shadow Copies of Shared Folders

Shadow Copies of Shared Folders provides point-in-time copies of files that are located on
shared resources. It enables users to access shared files and folders as they existed at points
of time in the past. Accessing previous versions of files, or shadow copies, lets users recover
files that were accidentally deleted (or recent versions of such files), recover from accidentally
overwriting a file, and compare versions of a file while working.

The following is a list of the aspects that are part of the Shadow Copies of Shared Folders
managed entity in Windows Server 2008 R2:

- **Volume Snapshot driver integrity** Shadow Copies of Shared Folders uses the Volume Snapshot driver (Volsnap.sys) to create shadow copies in Windows Server 2008 R2. This driver uses storage space allocated on a volume to maintain a snapshot of the contents of the shared folders. This storage space is called the Diff Area.

- **Diff Area integrity** A snapshot is a block-level set of information that represents the differences between the current content and content from a previous point in time. Shadow Copies of Shared Folders allocates the Diff Area storage space on a volume to maintain snapshots of the contents of shared folders. The integrity of existing and new snapshots depends on the integrity of the Diff Area.

- **Volume Revert operations** Shadow Copies of Shared Folders enables you to return a volume to the state that it was in when a shadow copy was created.

NOTE **REVERTING A VOLUME**

When you revert a volume, all changes made to files and folders on the volume since the shadow copy was created are lost.

MORE INFO **SHADOW COPIES IN WINDOWS SERVER 2008 R2**

For more information about shadow copies of shared folders in Windows Server 2008 R2, see *http://technet.microsoft.com/en-us/library/dd364797(WS.10).aspx*.

Share and Storage Management

Share and Storage Management, discussed earlier in this lesson, provides a centralized location where you can manage folders and volumes that are shared on the network and volumes in disks and storage subsystems. You can use the Provision A Shared Folder Wizard to share the content of folders and volumes on your server over your network. Share and Storage Management enables you to provision storage on disks that are available on your server, or on storage subsystems that support VDS.

The wizard guides you through the process of creating a volume on an existing disk, or on a storage subsystem attached to your server. If the volume is created on a storage subsystem, the wizard also guides you through the process of creating a LUN to host that volume. You also have the option of creating the LUN and then using Disk Management to create the volume. Share and Storage Management also helps you monitor and manage the volumes that you have created, along with any other volumes that are available on your server.

MORE INFO **SHARE AND STORAGE MANAGEMENT IN WINDOWS SERVER 2008 R2**

For more information about Share and Storage Management in Windows Server 2008 R2, access *http://technet.microsoft.com/en-gb/library/cc731574.aspx* and follow the links.

Shared Folders

In Windows Server 2008 R2, you can use the Shared Folders MMC snap-in, shown in Figure 7-27, to manage file shares centrally on a computer. This enables you to create file shares, set permissions, and view and manage open files and users connected to file shares on the computer.

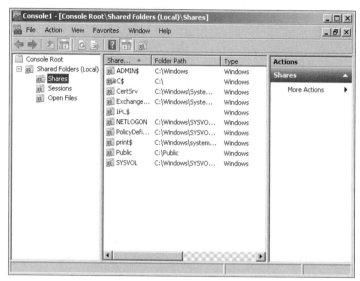

FIGURE 7-27 The Shared Folders MMC snap-in

MORE INFO **SHARED FOLDERS IN WINDOWS SERVER 2008 R2**

For more information about the Shared Folders MMC snap-in in Windows Server 2008 R2, access *http://technet.microsoft.com/en-gb/library/cc770406.aspx* and follow the links.

Storage Explorer

A fabric is a network topology in which devices are connected to each other through one or more high-efficiency data paths. In the case of a Fibre Channel fabric, the network includes one or more Fibre Channel switches that allow servers and storage devices to connect to each other through virtual point-to-point connections. For iSCSI fabrics, the network includes one or more Internet Storage Name Service (iSNS) servers that provide discoverability and partitioning of resources. Storage Explorer enables you to view and manage the Fibre Channel and iSCSI fabrics that are available in your SAN.

The Storage Explorer console, shown in Figure 7-28, can display detailed information about servers connected to the SAN, as well as components in the fabrics such as host bus adapters (HBAs), Fibre Channel switches, and iSCSI Initiators and targets. You can also perform administrative tasks on an iSCSI fabric—for example, you can log on to iSCSI targets, configure iSCSI security, add iSCSI target portals, add iSNS servers, and manage discovery domains and discovery domain sets.

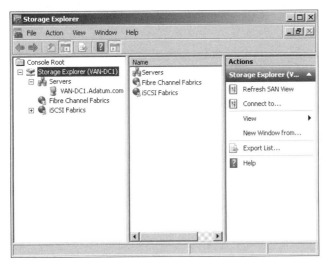

FIGURE 7-28 The Storage Explorer console

> **MORE INFO** **DISCOVERY DOMAINS AND DISCOVERY DOMAIN SETS**
>
> For more information about discovery domains and discovery domain sets, see
> *http://technet.microsoft.com/en-us/library/cc753442.aspx*.

> **MORE INFO** **STORAGE EXPLORER IN WINDOWS SERVER 2008 R2**
>
> For more information about the Storage Explorer console in Windows Server 2008 R2, see
> *http://technet.microsoft.com/library/cc731884.aspx*.

Storage Manager for SANs

The Storage Manager for SANs console lets you create and manage LUNs on Fibre Channel and iSCSI disk drive subsystems that support VDS in your SAN. Using LUNs simplifies the management of storage resources in your SAN because LUNs serve as logical identifiers through which you can assign access and control privileges.

As described previously in this lesson, a LUN is a logical reference to a portion of a storage subsystem. A LUN can comprise a disk, a section of a disk, a whole disk array, or a section of a disk array in the subsystem.

> **MORE INFO** **STORAGE MANAGER FOR SANS IN WINDOWS SERVER 2008 R2**
>
> For more information about the Storage Manager for SANs console in Windows Server
> 2008 R2, access *http://technet.microsoft.com/en-gb/library/cc771378.aspx* and follow
> the links.

Folder Redirection

Folder Redirection lets you redirect the path of a folder to a new location, such as a directory on a network file share. Users can then work with files on a file server as if these files were stored on a local drive on their clients. The documents in the folder are available to a user from any client on the network. Folder Redirection is a Group Policy setting and can be configured for any Group Policy object (GPO) that has User Configuration enabled. You can right-click any of the folders, click Properties, and configure the redirection options. Figure 7-29 shows the redirection options available for the Start Menu folder.

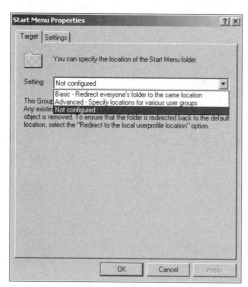

FIGURE 7-29 Redirection options for the Start Menu folder

Folder Redirection is not a new feature, but Windows Server 2008 R2 includes the following enhancements:

- The ability to redirect more folders in the user profile folders than in earlier Windows operating systems. These include the Contacts, Downloads, Favorites, Links, Music, Saved Games, Searches, and Videos folders.

- The ability to apply settings for redirected folders to clients running earlier versions of Windows.

- The option to have the Music, Pictures, and Videos folders follow the Documents folder.
- The ability to redirect the Start Menu folder to a specific path for all users.

> **MORE INFO** **FOLDER REDIRECTION IN WINDOWS SERVER 2008 R2**
>
> For more information about Folder Redirection, especially the enhancements introduced by Windows Server 2008 R2, see *http://technet.microsoft.com/en-us/library/cc732275.aspx*.

The Offline Files Feature

Offline files enable users such as mobile workers and branch office employees to access files that are available on a shared network resource and continue to work with network files when the computer is not connected to the network.

The Offline Files feature maintains a local cache of remote files and folders on your computer, so that they are available to users when they are working offline. Users can access these files in the same way that they accessed them online because the shared network resource paths and namespaces are preserved. The cache also speeds up the access to these files and folders over a slow connection.

When a network connection is restored, any changes that a user made while working offline are updated to the network by default. Any changes a user makes while working on a slow link are synchronized automatically with the version on the server at regular intervals as a background task.

The major enhancement to the Offline Files feature in Windows Server 2008 R2 is significantly improved file access over WANs, resulting in an improved network file experience for remote users. Other enhancements include the following:

- Fast First Logon
- Usually Offline Support With Background Sync
- Exclusion List
- Transparent Caching

> **MORE INFO** **THE OFFLINE FILES FEATURE IN WINDOWS SERVER 2008 R2**
>
> For more information about enhancements to the Offline Files feature in Windows Server 2008 R2, see *http://technet.microsoft.com/en-us/library/ff183315(WS.10).aspx*.

BranchCache For Network Files

As mentioned previously in this lesson, BranchCache For Network Files is a role service that can be installed as part of the File Services server role in Windows Server 2008 R2. This role service was not available in previous versions of Windows Server. BranchCache For Network Files helps reduce WAN utilization and enhances the responsiveness of network applications when users in branch office locations access content held in a central office.

The role service caches, within a branch office, a copy of the content that is retrieved from a web server or file server at a central location such as a head office. If another client in the branch requests the same content, that client can download it directly from the local branch network without needing to retrieve the content over the WAN. You install the BranchCache For Network Files role service in a practice later in this chapter.

Users at branch offices can experience poor performance when they use network applications that connect to servers over a WAN connection. It might take a significant amount of time for a branch office user to open a large file on a shared folder located on a server at the central office—and remember that user expectations are now such that even a few seconds can seem like a long time. For instance, a user viewing a video through a web browser might have to wait an appreciable period of time before the video loads.

If BranchCache For Network Files is used, a branch office user should experience the same level of service as a user at the central office. The first branch office client to download data from a web server or file server (known as the *content server*) caches a copy on the local branch network. Subsequent clients download the locally cached copy of the content from within the branch after it is authenticated and authorized by the content server.

BranchCache For Network Files is designed to work with existing network and security infrastructures and supports IPv4, IPv6, and end-to-end encryption methods such as SSL and IPSec. It ensures that the most up-to-date content version is served and that clients are authorized by the content server before they can retrieve content from within the branch. BranchCache For Network Files requires that clients are running Windows 7 with the BranchCache feature enabled, and that web servers and file servers are running Windows Server 2008 R2 with the BranchCache For Network Files role service installed. You can enable BranchCache For Network Files for a shared folder by accessing the Properties dialog box for that folder and clicking Offline Settings on the General tab. Figure 7-30 shows the Offline Settings dialog box with Enable BranchCache selected.

FIGURE 7-30 Enabling BranchCache For Network Files

Depending on the cache location, BranchCache For Network Files can operate in one of the following modes:

■ **Hosted Cache**   This mode deploys a computer running Windows Server 2008 R2 as a host in the branch office. Clients are configured with the fully qualified domain name (FQDN) of the host computer so that they can retrieve content from the hosted cache. If the content is not available in the hosted cache, it is retrieved from the content server over the WAN and then stored in the hosted cache for access by subsequent clients.

■ **Distributed Cache**   This mode typically is used in branch offices with fewer than 50 users. In Distributed Cache mode, a local client running Windows 7 keeps a copy of the content and makes it available to other authorized clients. This eliminates the need for a server in the branch office. However, Distributed Cache mode works across only a single subnet (unlike Hosted Cache mode). This means that the content needs to be retrieved over the WAN for each subnet in the branch office. Also, clients that disconnect from the network (for example, clients that hibernate) cannot, while disconnected, provide content when requested.

To reduce bandwidth, BranchCache For Network Files sends content metadata to clients, which in turn retrieve the content from within the branch. The content metadata is significantly smaller than the actual content. Prior to sending content metadata, the server authorizes the client. The content server needs to send the content metadata to each client to ensure that the client always receives hashes for the most up-to-date content.

The content is broken into blocks. A block hash is computed for each block. A segment hash is also computed on a collection of blocks. Content metadata is primarily composed of block hashes and segment hashes. The hash algorithm that is used is SHA 256. The compression ratio achieved is approximately 2,000 to 1; that is, the size of the metadata is approximately 2,000 times smaller than the size of the original data itself.

> **MORE INFO   SHA 256**
>
> If you have a professional interest in secure hash algorithms and want to learn more about SHA 256, see *http://csrc.nist.gov/publications/fips/fips180-2/fips180-2withchangenotice.pdf*. Be aware, however, that the exam will not test hash algorithms in the depth described in this document.

Segment hashes help reduce the total number of lookups performed for given content (compared to looking up every block). When a client needs to retrieve data from the hosted cache or from another client, it downloads the content in units defined by block hashes.

> **NOTE   MINIMUM SIZE OF CONTENT CACHED**
>
> The minimum size of content that BranchCache For Network Files caches is 64 KB. When content is less than 64 KB, data is directly retrieved from the content server through the WAN.

Windows Storage Server 2008 R2

Windows Storage Server 2008 R2 offers the same file services that are included in Windows Storage Server 2008, along with additional file services and enhancements. It is built upon Windows Server 2008 R2 and provides a platform for network-attached storage (NAS) appliances. The Windows Storage Server 2008 R2 family—Windows Storage Server 2008 R2 Enterprise edition, Windows Storage Server 2008 R2 Standard edition, and Windows Storage Server 2008 R2 Workgroup edition—offers advanced storage solutions to all sizes of organizations and includes storage technologies such as file deduplication (the removal of duplicate files and data) and an iSCSI software target for unified file services and block I/O storage.

> **MORE INFO**   **MICROSOFT ISCSI INITIATOR IN WINDOWS SERVER 2008 R2**
>
> For more information about the Microsoft iSCSI Initiator in Windows Server 2008 R2, see *http://technet.microsoft.com/en-us/library/dd878522(WS.10).aspx*.

Windows Storage Server 2008 R2 provides simplified deployment and management of individual appliances and dual-node, highly available storage clusters. Windows Storage Server 2008 R2 Enterprise edition includes wizards that enable automated two-node failover cluster setup.

Single Instance Storage (SIS) reduces the amount of storage used by data by replacing multiple identical copies with logical links to a single source copy, hence performing file deduplication. SIS now supports 128 volumes on a single server. Windows Storage Server 2008 R2 includes a set of Windows PowerShell cmdlets to manage SIS, such as Install-SisVolume, Enable-SisVolume, and Get-SisVolume.

> **MORE INFO**   **POWERSHELL CMDLETS TO MANAGE SIS**
>
> For more information about the PowerShell cmdlets that manage SIS in Windows Storage Server 2008 R2, see *http://technet.microsoft.com/en-us/library/gg278036.aspx*.

Windows Storage Server 2008 R2 enables file access over a network using the SMB and NFS protocols. It uses DFS and DFSR to implement a unified namespace and file-replication for data publishing to satellite offices. You can administer Windows Storage Server 2008 R2 remotely from Windows Internet Explorer using an ActiveX control, and from non-Microsoft browsers using a Java Remote Desktop Protocol (RDP) control. Windows Storage Server 2008 R2 provides a cost-effective, reliable, and scalable solution to challenges about how file data is accessed, moved, and managed. It offers the following file service features:

- **Distributed access to file services**   Windows Storage Server 2008 R2 file services enable you to provide better access to files, which typically are distributed widely across an organizational network. Distributed access increases storage management efficiency. Regardless of platform or location, data is more quickly accessible and easier to manage.

- **Centralized management of file services** Centralized file services management provides controls that exclude unwanted data and management tools that improve the management of wanted data. These tools centralize management and reduce administrative overhead while simultaneously providing information about file infrastructures. This information helps you to meet requirements for file service availability and compliance more efficiently.

- **Cost-effective scalability and increased productivity** Windows Storage Server 2008 R2 file services enable you to expand IT services and support a growing base of users affordably and efficiently.

These improved file service features are implemented by means of the following file service components that are introduced by Windows Storage Server 2008 R2 (and Windows 7):

- **SMB version 2.1** The SMB 2.1 protocol is faster and more efficient than previous versions of SMB. SMB 2.1 is also optimized for low-bandwidth connectivity and improved for better flexibility, compatibility, and resiliency for clients running Windows 7.

- **NFS** The NFS protocol enables organizations with heterogeneous environments to consolidate their file-sharing resources on Windows Storage Server 2008 R2. It enables computers running both Windows and non-Windows operating systems to share data easily.

- **DFS** DFSR and DFSN provide organizations with better access to data and simplified access to files and shares across a network-wide infrastructure. DFS also extends traditional file serving by making file shares easier to locate and more resilient.

- **FSRM** This server role provides a single management interface that delivers better-managed file services across CIFS/SMB and NFS and improves control and compliance over files. FSRM also provides built-in reporting that lets you determine how your file-serving resources are used for auditing and planning purposes.

- **FCI** This feature automates classification processes to help you manage your data more effectively. Your organization can save money and reduce risk by storing and retaining files based on their business value or impact, and FCI provides expiration, custom tasks, and reporting.

The File Server Migration Toolkit

When you migrate from a previous version of Windows Server to Windows Server 2008 R2, you need to ensure that permissions are set properly, and that the way users access files and the file naming conventions are preserved. The Microsoft File Server Migration Toolkit (FSMT) is a downloadable toolkit that contains two step-by-step wizards to help you migrate existing file servers to Windows Server 2008 R2. You can download the FSMT at *http://www.microsoft.com/downloads/en/details.aspx?FamilyID=d00e3eae-930a-42b0-b595-66f462f5d87b&displaylang=en.*

Managing Access Control

Access control is the process of permitting users, groups, and computers to access objects on the network or on a computer. It involves permissions, permission inheritance, object ownership, user rights, and auditing.

Permissions define the type of access granted to a user or group for an object. When a folder or volume is shared over a network and users access its contents remotely (as is the case with files on a file server), share or shared folder permissions apply to these users. A folder or file on an NTFS volume also has NTFS permissions, which apply whether it is accessed locally or across the network. Access permissions to files on a file server are typically a combination of NTFS permissions and the shared folder permissions set on the folder or folder hierarchy that contains the files. Printer objects have associated print permissions.

Every container and object on a network has associated (or attached) access control information defined within a security descriptor. This controls the type of access allowed to users and security groups. Permissions defined within an object's security descriptor are associated with, or assigned to, specific users and security groups. Each assignment of permissions to a user or group is represented in the system as an access control entry (ACE). The entire set of permission entries in a security descriptor is known as a permission set, or access control list (ACL).

You can set NTFS permissions for objects such as files, Active Directory objects, registry objects, or system objects such as processes. You set NTFS permissions on the Security tab of the object's Properties dialog box, sometimes known as the Access Control User Interface. Permissions can be granted to individual users, security groups, computers, and other objects with security identifiers in the domain. It is a good practice to assign permissions to security groups rather than to individual users.

The permissions attached to an object depend on the type of object. For example, the permissions that can be attached to a file are different from those that can be attached to a printer or to a registry key. When you set permissions, you specify the level of access for groups and users. For example, you can let one user read the contents of a file, let another user make changes to the file, and prevent all other users from accessing the file.

Microsoft states that permission inheritance allows administrators to assign and manage permissions easily and ensures consistency of permissions among all objects within a given container. Inheritance automatically causes objects within a container to inherit all the inheritable permissions of that container. For example, child folders by default inherit the permissions of their parent, and files within a folder have their permissions set automatically depending upon folder permissions.

Undoubtedly, inheritance is convenient when configuring permissions. You can block folder inheritance and assign explicit rather than inherited permissions to child objects. You can change file permissions so that some files in a folder can have different access permissions than others. This gives you a lot of flexibility, but it also can lead to complexity, so inheritance can make permissions more difficult to manage rather than easier. As with all administrator tasks, the key is to plan carefully to avoid exceptions. You should also limit the use of explicit Deny permissions. If a user is a member of a group that has a Deny permission, or if the user has been explicitly denied a permission, she will be denied that permission no matter what other groups she is a member of.

An owner is assigned to an object when that object is created—typically, an object is owned by the user that creates it, so files saved in a Documents folder in a user profile are owned by that user. The owner of the object can always change the permissions on an object.

> **MORE INFO** **OBJECT OWNERSHIP**
>
> For more information on object ownership, see *http://technet.microsoft.com/en-us/ library/cc732983(WS.10).aspx.*

User rights grant specific privileges and logon rights to users and security groups. You can assign specific rights to group accounts or to individual user accounts. These rights authorize users to perform specific actions, such as logging on to a system interactively or backing up files and directories.

User rights are different from permissions because user rights apply to user accounts and permissions are attached to objects. Although you can apply user rights to individual user accounts, it is good practice to apply them to security groups rather than to individual users. You can administer user rights through the Local Security Settings MMC snap-in.

You can audit successful or failed access to objects on a per-user basis. You select which object's access to audit by using the Access Control User Interface, but first, you must enable the Audit Policy by selecting Audit Object Access under Local Policies in the Local Security Settings snap-in. You can then view these security-related events in the Security log in Event Viewer.

> **MORE INFO** **SECURITY AUDITING**
>
> For more information on security auditing, see *http://technet.microsoft.com/en-us/library/ cc771475(WS.10).aspx.*

Configuring Access Permissions

By default, File Sharing is enabled and Public Folder Sharing is disabled on a computer running Windows Server 2008 or Windows Server 2008 R2. You can enable and disable these features by clicking Change Advanced Sharing Settings in the Network And Sharing Center, which you can access through the Control Panel. Figure 7-31 shows the Advanced Sharing Settings dialog box.

You can also open the MMC and add the Shared Folders snap-in. If you then right-click Shares and select New Share, the Create A Shared Folder Wizard starts. This wizard lets you specify the path to a folder you want to share, the name of the share, and the shared folder access permissions.

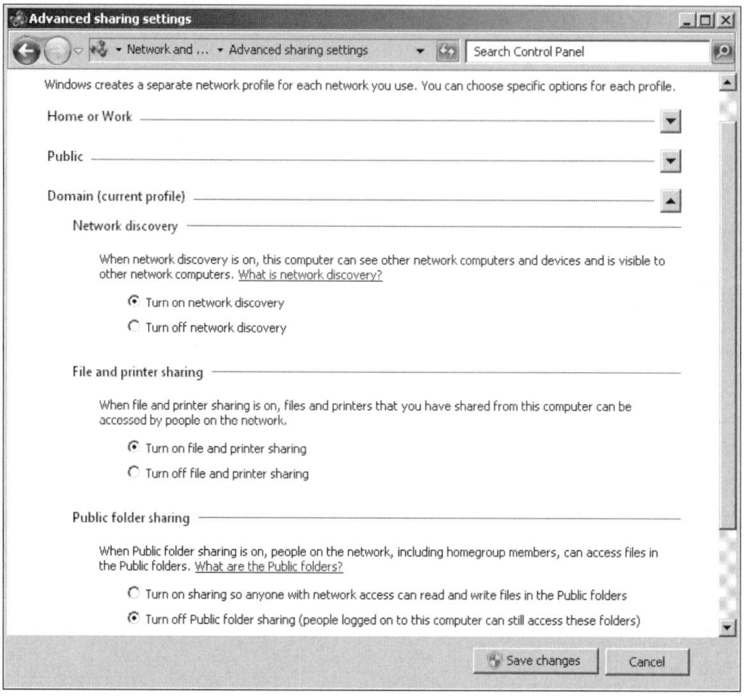

FIGURE 7-31 The Advanced Sharing Settings dialog box

On the Shared Folder Permissions page of the wizard, shown in Figure 7-32, you can specify standard shared folder permissions—for example, All Users Have Read-Only Access (the default) or Administrators Have Full Access; Other Users Have Read-Only Access. You can also select Customize Permissions and click Custom to set custom permissions. Figure 7-33 shows the Customize Permissions dialog box. The wizard also lets you configure offline settings. You can share a folder or a volume.

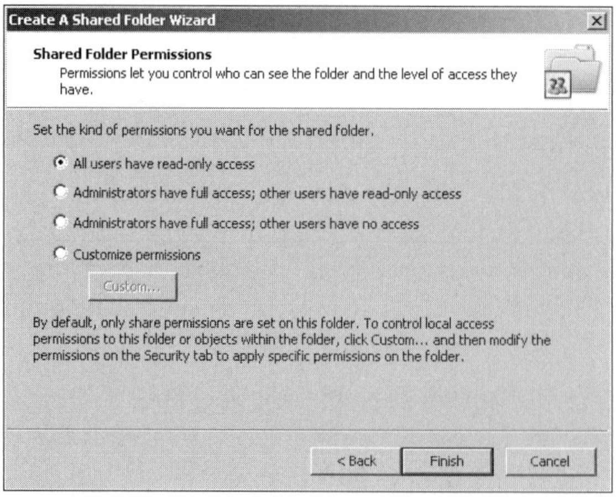

FIGURE 7-32 The Shared Folder Permissions page

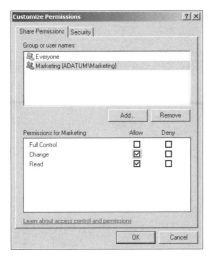

FIGURE 7-33 The Customize Permissions dialog box

If you choose to customize permissions, you can also access a Security tab that lets you set NTFS permissions by selecting a user or group and clicking Edit. For users who access folders on a server over a network (the vast majority of users), access permissions are a combination of shared folder and NTFS permissions. Figure 7-34 shows the Security tab on which you can configure NTFS permissions.

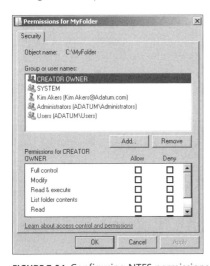

FIGURE 7-34 Configuring NTFS permissions by clicking Edit on the Security tab

You can also create and provision a shared folder by using the Share And Storage Management MMC snap-in. You click Provision Share in the Actions pane and specify the path to the folder that you want to share and provision. This starts the Provision A Shared Folder Wizard. The wizard lets you modify the default NTFS permissions if you want. You can then select the protocol over which users can access the shared folder—SMB, NFS, or both. Note that you can specify NFS only if you have installed the Services For NFS role service.

You then have the option of clicking Advanced, which lets you set a user limit, disable user-based enumeration, and reconfigure offline settings. Figure 7-35 shows the caching options available for offline settings.

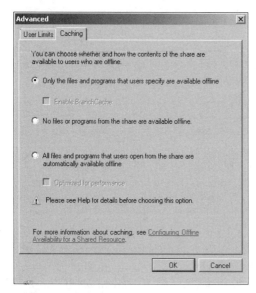

FIGURE 7-35 Caching options

If you are configuring SMB permissions (which is typically the case), you can either choose one of three standard shared folder permission configurations or to customize these permissions. The SMB Permissions page is shown in Figure 7-36. If you choose to customize shared folder permissions, the wizard presents you with a dialog box very similar to the Customize Permissions dialog box in the Create A Shared Folder Wizard, which was shown earlier in Figure 7-33.

> **NOTE SMB AND NTFS PERMISSIONS**
> If your SMB permissions differ from your NTFS permissions for the same shared folder, then the more restrictive set of permissions applies.

The wizard then prompts you to publish the share in a DFS namespace. Note that you cannot do this unless you have installed the appropriate role services. Finally, the wizard summarizes your settings, and you click Create to create the share.

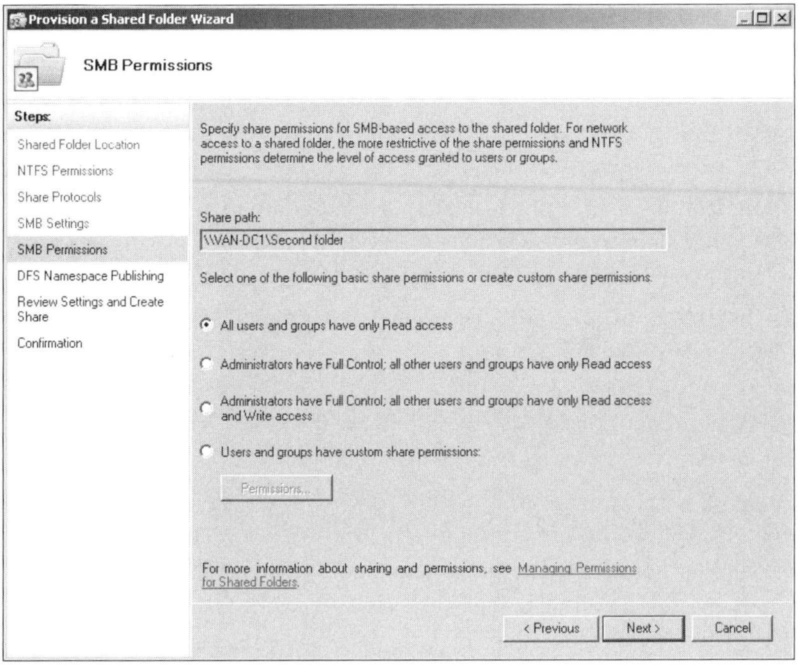

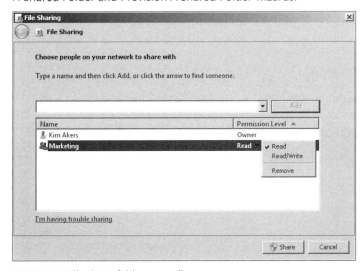

FIGURE 7-36 The SMB Permissions page

You can also share a folder manually and set shared folder and NTFS permissions
by right-clicking a folder or volume in Windows Explorer or My Computer and clicking
Properties. If you choose to share a folder by this method, you will see a dialog box similar to
that shown in Figure 7-37. If you click the Security tab on the folder's Properties dialog box,
you can configure NTFS permissions using a dialog box similar to that provided by the Create
A Shared Folder and Provision A Shared Folder wizards.

FIGURE 7-37 Sharing a folder manually

Combining Share and NTFS Permissions

Files, folders, and other objects typically are accessed across a network, such as when they are held on a file server. ACEs, however, are applied at both the share level (share permissions) and at the file system level (NTFS permissions). This means that you need to remember to change permissions in two different places.

For example, if you want members of the Managers security group to be able to add, edit, and delete files in a folder called Reports, when previously they could only view them, you would change the NTFS permission for the security group to Modify. However, if the share permission of the folder is Read and you forget to change this, group members will still only be able to view the contents of the files.

One solution to this problem is to grant everyone full access at the share level and to assign restrictive NTFS permissions. The NTFS permissions are then the effective permissions because they are more restrictive. However, many administrators are not happy about assigning nonrestrictive share permissions. The security best practice in this situation is to use (at most) the Change share permission.

To figure out what permissions a security group has on a file, you first figure out the effective NTFS permissions, remembering that any explicit permissions that are set at the file level override the folder permissions. You then compare share and NTFS permissions; the effective permissions are the more restrictive of the two. This process becomes even more complex when you want to figure out access permissions for a user that might be a member of several security groups.

You can figure out a user's effective permissions manually. This is a tedious process, but it gets easier with practice. Currently, no Windows Server 2008 or Windows Server 2008 R2 tool exists to automate the process, but you should consider downloading Server Share Check from the Windows Server 2003 Resource Kit. This tool can be used on servers running Windows Server 2008 or Windows Server 2008 R2. You can download this resource kit at *http://www.microsoft.com/downloads/details.aspx?familyid=9d467a69-57ff-4ae7-96ee-b18c4790cffd&displaylang=en.*

> **MORE INFO** **SERVER SHARE CHECK**
>
> For more information on Server Share Check, see *http://searchwindowsserver.techtarget.com/tip/Checking-access-permissions-with-Server-Share-Check.* Also, you need to become a member of SearchWindowsServer.com, but membership is free. If you cannot access this URL or do not want to register with this site, search the Internet for "Server Share Check."

Using FSRM to Configure Quotas, File Screen Policy, and Storage Reports

Windows Server 2008 and Windows Server 2008 R2 offer enhanced quota management. You can apply quotas to folders as well as volumes, and you have a set of quota templates that you can use to create quotas quickly and easily. You can create a custom quota or derive a quota from an existing template.

Microsoft recommends deriving quotas from templates. This simplifies the management of quotas because you can update automatically all quotas that are based on a specific template by editing that template. You then have the option of updating the settings of any quotas that you created by using the template. You can also exclude specified quotas from this update. For example, if you created a quota from a template and then manually changed some of its settings, you might not want to update that quota when you change the template because you could lose these settings.

You can create an auto-apply quota and assign a quota template to a parent volume or folder. Quotas based on that template are then automatically generated and applied to each of the existing subfolders and to any subfolders that you create in the future.

Creating Quotas

If the FSRM File Services server role is installed, you can use the FSRM MMC snap-in to create quotas. The Create Quota dialog box is shown in Figure 7-38. Note that you will be unable to access this box if you have not installed the appropriate server role, which you will do in the practice later in this chapter. You can also choose to create a quota from a template, which you also will do in the practice.

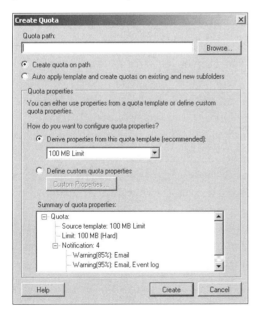

FIGURE 7-38 The Create Quota dialog box

You specify a path to the volume or folder for which you want to create the quota and then specify whether you want to create a quota only on that path or whether a template-based quota will be generated and applied to existing and new subfolders on the path of the parent volume or folder automatically. To specify the latter action, select Auto Apply Template And Create Quotas On Existing And New Subfolders.

Typically, you would select Derive Properties From This Quota Template (Recommended) and select a template. You can define custom quota properties if you want, but this is not recommended. You can select templates that specify the quota size that is allocated to each user and whether the quota is hard or soft. A hard quota cannot be exceeded. A user can exceed a soft quota, but exceeding the quota limit typically generates a report, in addition to sending an email notification and logging the event. Soft quotas are used for monitoring. Quota templates include the following:

- **100 MB Limit**   This is a hard quota. It emails the user and specified administrators if the 100 percent quota limit has been reached and writes an event to the event log.

- **200 MB Limit Reports To User**   This is a hard quota. It generates a report, sends emails, and writes an event to the event log if the 100 percent quota limit has been reached.

- **200 MB Limit With 50 MB Extension**   Technically, this is a hard quota because it performs an action when the user attempts to exceed the limit rather than merely monitoring the exceeded limit. The action is to run a program that applies the 250 MB Extended Limit template and effectively gives the user an additional 50 MB. Emails are sent and the event is logged when the limit is extended.

- **250 MB Extended Limit**   The 250-MB limit cannot be exceeded. Emails are sent and the event is logged when the limit is reached.

- **Monitor 200 GB Volume Usage**   This is a soft quota that can be applied only to volumes. It is used for monitoring.

- **Monitor 50 MB Share**   This is a soft quota that can be applied only to shares. It is used for monitoring.

You can also configure templates to send emails and write to the event log if a defined percentage of the quota is reached. Figure 7-39 shows the properties of the 200 MB Limit Reports To User template.

When you have created a quota or an auto-apply quota, you can edit it. Figure 7-40 shows a Quota Properties box. You can change the Quota Template, Space Limit, and Notifications Thresholds and add a label. You can add new Notification Thresholds and specify what action should be taken if a threshold is reached. For example, you can specify whether an email is sent to the user and to one or more specified administrators. You can also specify a command, generate a report, and specify whether the event is to be logged. If you edit quota settings or create a custom quota, you can use the quota to create a new template.

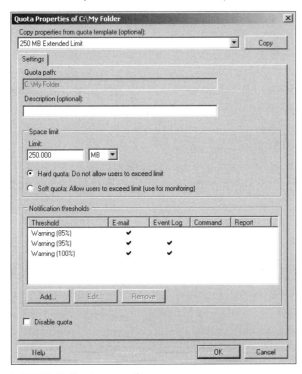

FIGURE 7-39 Properties of the 200 MB Limit Reports To User template

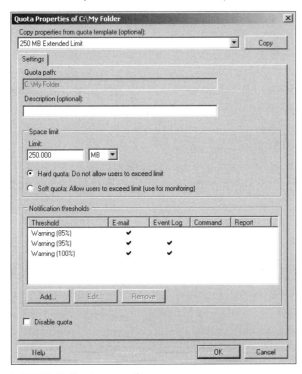

FIGURE 7-40 Quota properties

Creating Templates

If none of the supplied templates is suitable for your purposes, you can create a new template. If you like, you can copy settings from an existing template and edit them, or you can specify new settings. Figure 7-41 shows the Create Quota Template dialog box. Many of the settings are similar to those that you can configure when editing a quota.

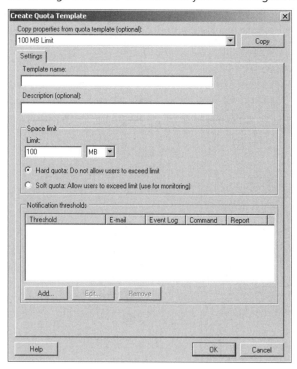

FIGURE 7-41 Creating a quota template

Managing File Screens

You can use FSRM to create and manage file screens that control the types of files that users can save and generate notifications when users attempt to save unauthorized files. You can also define file screening templates that you can apply to new volumes or folders and use across your organization.

FSRM also enables you to create file screening exceptions that extend the flexibility of the file screening rules. You could, for example, ensure that users do not store music files in personal folders, but you could allow storage of specific types of media files, such as training files that comply with company policy. You could also create an exception that allows members of the senior management group to save any type of file they want (provided that they comply with legal restrictions).

You can also configure your screening process to notify you by email when an executable file is stored on a shared folder. This notification can include information about the user who stored the file and the file's exact location.

Managing Storage Reports

FSRM provides a Storage Reports Management node. This enables you to generate storage-related reports, such as reports about duplicate files, the largest files, which files are accessed most frequently, and which files are seldom accessed. It also lets you schedule periodic storage reports, which help you identify trends in disk usage, and monitor attempts to save unauthorized files.

For example, you could schedule a report to run at midnight every Sunday and provide you with information about the most recently accessed files from the previous two days. This lets you monitor weekend storage activity and plan server downtime so that it has a minimum impact on users who connect from home over the weekend.

You could use the information in a report that identifies duplicate files so that you can reclaim disk space without losing data, and you could create other reports that enable you to analyze how individual users are using shared storage resources.

MORE INFO   FSRM

For more information about FSRM, open the command prompt and enter **hh fsrm.chm.**

Lesson Summary

- The File Server role service in the File Services server role is installed by default and allows access to the Share And Storage Management MMC snap-in. This in turn provides access to the Provision A Stored Folder Wizard and lets you configure access control and manage shared folders, volumes, open sessions, and open files. The Shared Folders MMC snap-in also enables you to share a folder and set permissions.

- If you want, you can install the DFS, FSRM, Services For NFS, Windows Search Service, and BranchCache For Network Files role services. DFS includes DFSN and DFSR. You can also install the Windows Server 2003 File Services server role to create compatibility with earlier versions of Windows.

- The FSRM console lets you configure quotas and file screens and generate storage reports. You can set quotas on shared folders as well as volumes.

- BranchCache For Network Files caches files downloaded from a central location on a computer in a branch office. Other computers in the branch that need to access these files can then do so locally.

Lesson Review

You can use the following questions to test your knowledge of the information in Lesson 2, "Planning File Servers." The questions are also available on the companion CD if you prefer to review them in electronic form.

> **NOTE   ANSWERS**
>
> Answers to these questions and explanations of why each answer choice is correct or incorrect are located in the "Answers" section at the end of the book.

1. Which of the following wizards can you access from the Share And Storage Management console?

   A. Provision A Shared Folder Wizard

   B. New Namespace Wizard

   C. Create Quota Wizard

   D. Create File Screen Wizard

2. You have not installed any additional role services for the File Services server role; only the default File Server role service is installed. You start the Provision A Shared Folder Wizard. All your volumes are formatted with NTFS. Which of the following tasks can you carry out by using the wizard? (Each answer is a complete solution. Choose three.)

   A. Specify a folder to share.

   B. Create a new folder to share.

   C. Specify the network sharing protocol that is used to access the shared resource.

   D. Change the local NTFS permissions for the folder or volume that you are sharing.

   E. Publish the shared resource to a DFS namespace.

3. Which of the following quota templates, available by default, creates a soft quota that can be applied only to volumes?

   A. 100 MB Limit

   B. 200 MB Limit Reports To User

   C. Monitor 200 GB Volume Usage

   D. Monitor 50 MB Share Usage

4. Which mode of which server role deploys a computer running Windows Server 2008 R2 as a host in a branch office? The host stores files downloaded from a central location across a WAN so that other clients in the branch can access these files locally.

   A. FSRM in Hosted Cache mode

   B. FSRM in Distributed Cache mode

C. BranchCache For Network Files in Distributed Cache mode

D. BranchCache For Network Files in Hosted Cache mode

PRACTICE **Adding the Print and Document Services Server Role**

In this practice, you add the Print and Document Services server role and the Internet Printing role service. Here, you log on to the domain controller interactively. In a production network, you typically would access the domain controller remotely from your administrator workstation.

EXERCISE **Installing the Print and Document Services Server Role**

In this exercise, you install the Print and Document Services server role. This lets you share (or publish) printers on a network. To complete the exercise, follow these steps:

1. Log on to VAN-DC1 with the Kim Akers account and, if necessary, open Server Manager.

2. In the console tree, expand Server Manager. Locate the Roles Summary in the right pane, as shown in Figure 7-42. Check that the Print and Document Services role is not listed. If this role is listed, it is installed, and you do not need to complete the rest of this exercise.

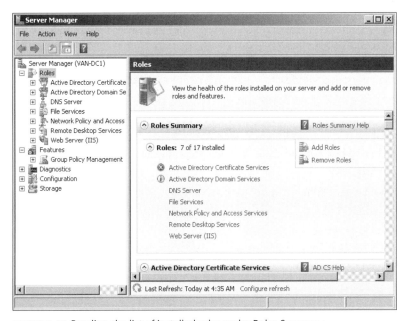

FIGURE 7-42 Reading the list of installed roles under Roles Summary

3. Click Add Roles. The Add Roles Wizard starts. If the Before You Begin page appears, click Next.

4. On the Select Server Roles page, select Print And Document Services, as shown in Figure 7-43. Click Next.

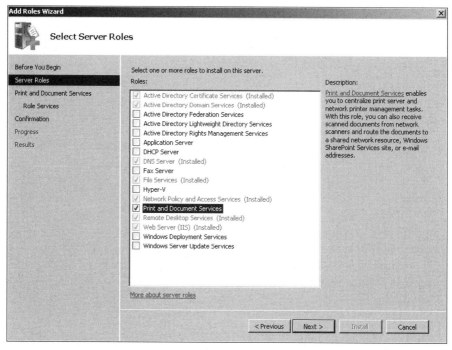

FIGURE 7-43 Selecting Print and Document Services

5. Read the information under Introduction To Print And Document Services and under Things To Note. If you want, you can also click the links to the Help files. Click Next.

6. On the Select Role Services page, shown in Figure 7-44, Print Server should be selected by default. Select Internet Printing. If the Add Role Services Required For Internet Printing dialog box appears, click Add Required Role Services. Click Next on the Select Role Services page.

7. If the Web Server (IIS) page appears, read the information presented and then click Next.

8. The Select Role Services page should now look similar to Figure 7-45, and it should show that the Web Server role service is already installed. If this server role is not installed, select Web Server. Click Next.

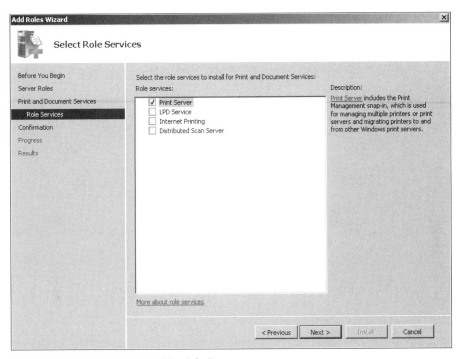

FIGURE 7-44 Print Server, selected by default

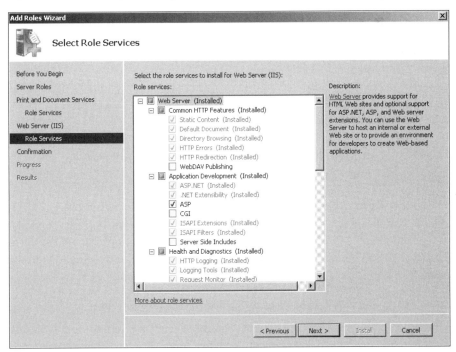

FIGURE 7-45 The Web Server role service, already installed

9. Read the information on the Confirm Installation Selections page, which should look similar to Figure 7-46. Note that you might need to reboot your server when installation is complete. Click Install.

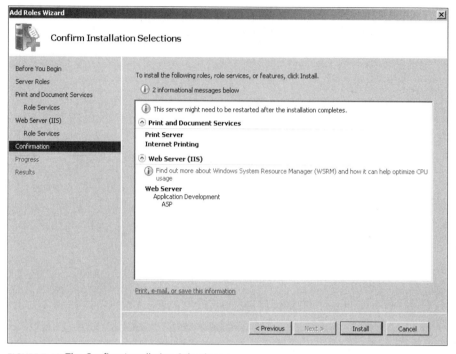

FIGURE 7-46 The Confirm Installation Selections page

10. Click Close when installation completes. Check that Print And Document Services is now listed under Roles Summary in Server Manager.

11. Save any unsaved files and close all open windows. Reboot VAN-DC1 if prompted to do so.

PRACTICE **Adding Role Services to the File Services Server Role and Configuring a Quota**

In this practice, you add selected role services to the File Services server role on your domain controller, VAN-DC1. You then create a shared folder on that domain controller and configure a quota for that folder. As with the previous practice, you will log on to VAN-DC1 interactively. In a production network, you typically would access the domain controller remotely.

EXERCISE 1 Adding Role Services to the File Services Server Role

In this exercise, you open Server Manager and add selected role services to the File Services server role. You do not add any of the optional features associated with this server role. The folder C:\Public should exist on your domain controller by default—if it is not, create it before you start this exercise. To complete the exercise, follow these steps:

1. If necessary, log on to VAN-DC1 with the Kim Akers account, share the C:\Public folder with default permissions, and open Server Manager.

2. Expand Roles and click File Services. In the right pane, locate the list of Role Services, as shown in Figure 7-47.

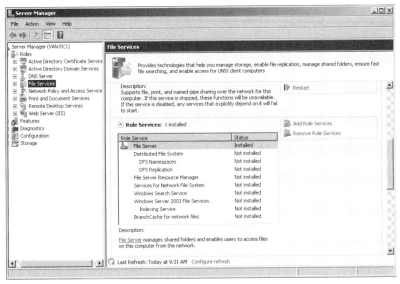

FIGURE 7-47 Role services that can be added to the File Services role

3. Click Add Role Services.

4. In the Select Role Services dialog box, select all uninstalled role services except the Windows Server 2003 File Services and its associated Indexing Service, as shown in Figure 7-48.

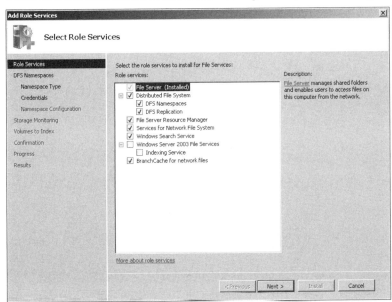

FIGURE 7-48 Selecting role services

5. Click Next.

6. Call the DFS namespace **MyNameSpace**, as shown in Figure 7-49. Click Next.

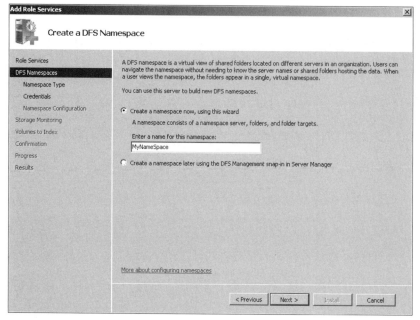

FIGURE 7-49 Specifying a DNS namespace

7. Specify a domain-based namespace (the default), as shown in Figure 7-50. Click Next.

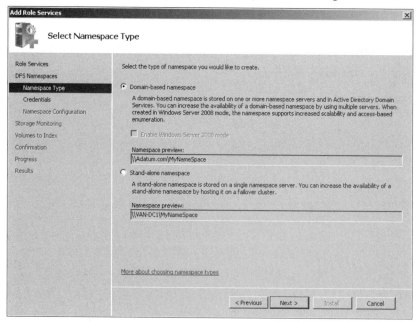

FIGURE 7-50 Specifying a DNS namespace type

NOTE **DOMAIN-BASED AND STAND-ALONE NAMESPACES**

Chapter 10 discusses domain-based and stand-alone namespaces.

8. On the Provide Credentials To Create A Namespace page, click Select. Specify the user name and password for the Kim Akers account, and then click OK. Click Next.

9. In the Configure Namespace dialog box, click Add. Click Browse in the Add Folder To Namespace dialog box.

10. In the Browse For Shared Folders dialog box, click Show Shared Folders. Ensure that Public is selected, as shown in Figure 7-51. Click OK.

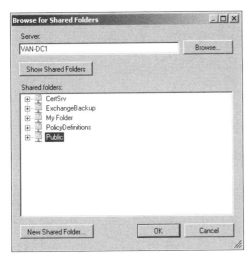

FIGURE 7-51 Selecting a shared folder

11. By default, the corresponding folder in your namespace takes the same name as the shared folder you selected. Click OK to accept this default.

12. Your Configure Namespace wizard page should look similar to Figure 7-52. Click Next.

13. In the Configure Storage Usage Monitoring page, select your C: volume, as shown in Figure 7-53. Your volume size and usage probably will differ from what is shown here. Do not change the default options. Click Next.

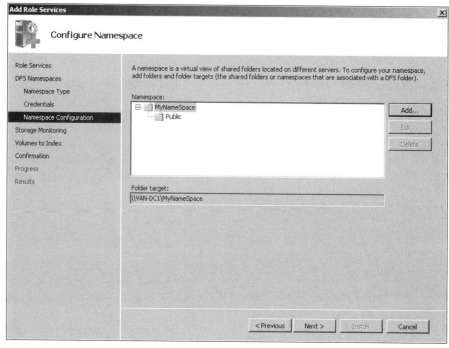

FIGURE 7-52 Configuring a namespace

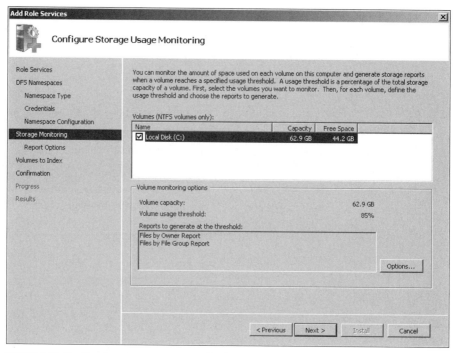

FIGURE 7-53 Configuring storage usage monitoring

14. The Set Report Options page should look similar to Figure 7-54. Click Next to accept the default settings.

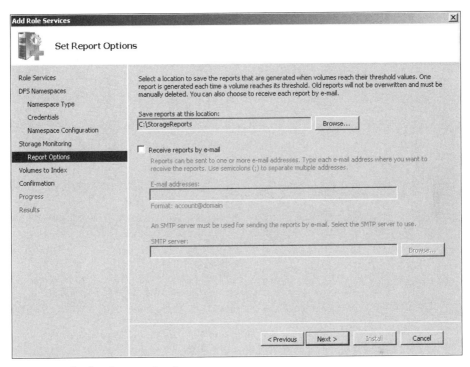

FIGURE 7-54 Configuring report options

15. Choose to index a volume that does not contain your operating system. If the only volume on your server is C:, do not index any volumes. Click Next.

16. Check your installation selections. If you are satisfied with them, click Install.

17. When installation completes, click Close.

EXERCISE 2 Configure a Quota

In this exercise, you create a shared folder on domain controller VAN-DC1 and configure a quota for that folder. If you prefer, you can access the File Server Resource Manager tool from the Administrative Tools menu rather than adding the snap-in to the MMC.

1. If necessary, log on to VAN-DC1 with the Kim Akers account.

2. Create a folder named My Folder in the root of your C: drive and share it, giving the Everyone group Read Access. If you are unsure how to do this, refer to Lesson 2.

3. On the Start menu, click Run. Enter **mmc**.

4. If necessary, click Yes to close the User Account Control (UAC) dialog box.

5. In the MMC, click File. Click Add/Remove Snap-In.

6. Click File Server Resource Manager, as shown in Figure 7-55. Click Add, and then click OK.

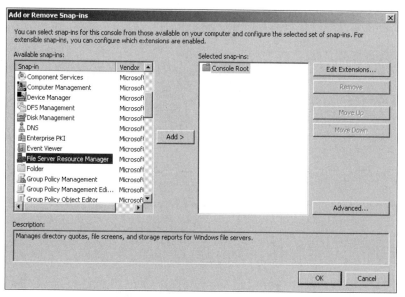

FIGURE 7-55 Adding the File Server Resource Manager snap-in

7. Expand File Server Resource Manager (Local), expand Quota Management, and then click Quota Templates, as shown in Figure 7-56.

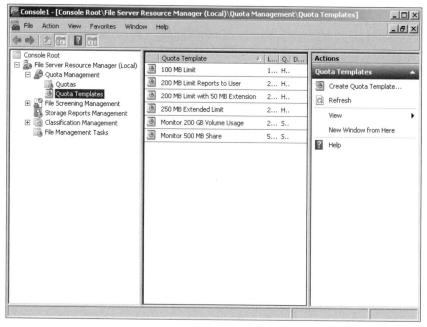

FIGURE 7-56 Accessing the quota templates

8. Click 250 MB Extended Limit, and then, in the Actions pane, click Create Quota From Template.

9. In the Create Quota dialog box, click Browse and browse to C:\My Folder. Click OK. The dialog box should look similar to Figure 7-57.

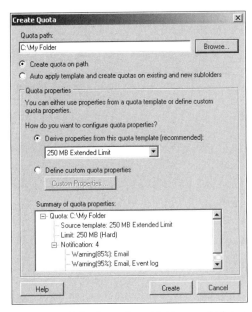

FIGURE 7-57 Selecting a shared folder on which to apply the quota

10. Click Create.

Chapter Review

To further practice and reinforce the skills you learned in this chapter, you can perform the following tasks:

- Review the chaptter summary.
- Review the list of key terms introduced in this chapter.
- Complete the case scenario. These scenarios set up real-world situations involving the topics of this chapter and ask you to create a solution.
- Complete the suggested practices.
- Take a practice test.

Chapter Summary

- The Print and Document Services server role lets you manage printers, print drivers, print queues, and printer permissions, both on locally installed printers and on printers installed on other print servers on your network.
- The role services in the File Services server role let you configure access control; manage shared folders, volumes, open sessions, and open files; manage DFS, DFSN, and DFSR; configure quotas and file screens; generate storage reports; configure offline file settings; configure indexing; and implement the caching of files in branch offices.

Key Terms

The following terms were introduced in this chapter. Do you know what they mean?

- Access control entry (ACE)
- Access control list (ACL)
- Access control
- Caching
- DFS Namespace (DFSN)
- DFS Replication (DFSR)
- Distributed File System (DFS)
- Offline file
- Quota

Case Scenario

In the following case scenario, you will apply what you have learned about provisioning file and print servers. You can find answers to these questions in the "Answers" section at the end of this book.

Planning a Windows Server 2008 R2 Upgrade

You are a senior administrator at Blue Yonder Airlines. All the company's servers run Windows Server 2008, and all its clients run Windows 7. The company's network infrastructure consists of a central office and a number of branch offices in distant locations that currently access files on a central office server through WAN links. Sometimes it can take an unacceptable length of time for a large file to download. All the branch offices are small (typically using between 10 and 15 clients), and all the computers in each branch office are on a single subnet. The company plans to upgrade all its domain controllers and some of its member servers at its central office to Windows Server 2008 R2. Answer the following questions:

1. The technical director is concerned with the slow transfer of files to branch offices. She wants to know if installing Windows Server 2008 R2 will improve the situation. What do you tell her?

2. There is no budget for upgrading servers at branch offices. How will this affect branch office caching?

3. The financial director is concerned that files currently can be classified by criteria such as size, what folders they are stored in, and when they were last updated. He asks you if the planned expenditure will assist in classifying files by other criteria, such as the business value of the information they contain. What do you tell him?

4. The technical director is also concerned about the time it takes and the number of steps that are required to install network printers. She wants to know if it is worthwhile to install Windows Server 2008 R2 on a computer running the Print Services server role. What do you tell her?

Suggested Practices

To help you master the examination objectives presented in this chapter, complete the following tasks.

Use the Enhanced Print Management Console

- You can become familiar with a tool only through practice. Use the enhanced Print Management console provided in Windows Server 2008 R2 and become familiar with the various wizards that it provides. If you also have access to a computer running Windows Server 2008, compare the printer management facilities provided by both operating systems and note the differences if you want.

Use the FSRM Console

- You may be familiar with the facilities provided through the FSRM role service in Windows Server 2008, and these continue to be implemented in Windows Server 2008 R2. This role service is not significantly changed, but it remains important, and the exam is likely to ask about quotas, file screening, and report generation. Ensure that you are familiar with the FSRM console.

- Arguably, the most significant feature implemented by the FSRM role service is the facility to implement quotas. Make sure that you are familiar with the process of configuring quotas, that you are familiar with the various standard quota templates available, and that you can distinguish between hard and soft quotas.

Learn More About Windows Storage Server 2008 R2

- Windows Storage Server 2008 R2 is based on Windows Server 2008 R2, and you should know about it. It is described only briefly in this chapter. Look for articles in online technical magazines and on TechNet.

Learn More About BranchCache For Network Files

- BranchCache For Network Files is new to Windows Server 2008 R2. Read any online articles and discussions you can discover, including TechNet articles.

Take a Practice Test

The practice tests on this book's companion CD offer many options. For example, you can test yourself on just one exam objective, or you can test yourself on all the certification exam content. You can set up the test so that it closely simulates the experience of taking a certification exam, or you can set it up in study mode so that you can look at the correct answers and explanations after you answer each question.

> *MORE INFO* **PRACTICE TESTS**
>
> For details about all the practice test options available, see the "How to Use the Practice Tests" section in this book's Introduction.

CHAPTER 8

Planning Security Policies

This chapter examines how you configure, manage, and monitor server security, and the planning that is required to ensure the protection that you configure is adequate but not excessive and is maintained and kept up to date. To plan your security, you need to know how different auditing policies can be used to track sensitive items and data within your organization; and you need to know about authentication and authorization, how to secure your data, and how to audit your security policies.

Keeping your operating system and applications up to date is an essential part of server security because many updates are issued to address security issues. As part of your security planning, you need to examine the centralized deployment of updates through Windows Server Update Services (WSUS). You need to manage operating system and application updates and to plan an appropriate update schedule. You need to ensure that centralized patch deployment is working as expected.

Exam objectives in this chapter:

- Monitor and maintain security and policies.
- Implement update management strategy.

Lessons in this chapter:

Before You Begin

To complete the exercises in the practice in this chapter, you need to have done the following:

- Installed a server called VAN-DC1 running Windows Server 2008 R2 Enterprise edition and configured as a domain controller in the adatum.com domain, as described in Exercise 1 of Appendix A, "Setup Instructions for Windows Server 2008 R2."

- Created a user account in the adatum.com domain with the user name Kim Akers and password Pa$$w0rd, and added this account to the Domain Admins, Enterprise Admins, and Schema Admins groups. This procedure is described in Exercise 1 of the Appendix, "Setup Instructions for End-of-Chapter Labs."

- Created a user account in the adatum.com domain with the user name Don Hall and password Pa$$w0rd. In previous chapters, you added this account to the Backup Operators security group. This is not essential in this chapter, but it does not affect the exercises and there is no need to remove the account from that group. However, it is sufficient for this chapter that Don Hall is in the default Domain Users security group.

- Ensured that a user account with the user name Jim Hance and a global security group with the name DonGroup do not exist in the adatum.com domain. If either or both entities exist, delete them.

- We recommend that you use an isolated network that is not part of your production network to do the practice exercises in this book. Internet access is not generally required for the exercises. However, the second practice in this chapter requires Internet access, and for this reason, it is optional. More detail is given in the practice. To minimize the time and expense of configuring physical computers, we recommend that you use virtual machines. For example, you can create virtual machines using the Hyper-V server role.

 REAL WORLD

Ian Mclean

As an experienced administrator, your aim should be to implement a carefully planned and appropriate security policy and carry out regular security checks carefully and rigorously. The key words here are "planned" and "appropriate." There is no such thing as perfect security, and if you try too hard to make everything as secure as possible, you are likely to defeat your own aims. A rigorous password policy is useless if it is so onerous that users scribble their passwords on bits of notepaper and paste them to their monitors.

You cannot always allow for the careless user, no matter how hard you try. An inexperienced or overconfident administrator can cause all sorts of problems on your network. A malicious internal user typically poses more of a danger than any external attack. You can do your best to counter threats from users and administrative users, but you will always be fighting a losing battle unless the vast majority of your users appreciate and agree with what you are trying to do.

Your users want to get on with their jobs. If they see security procedures as restrictions that give them problems and slow them down, they will find ways of circumventing the most elegant and well-designed security policies. You need to inform the people who use the servers that you manage on a day-to-day basis why certain security policies have been enforced. You need to advise them about the steps that they can take to resolve any problems that your security policies might cause them. You need to get your users on your side.

Always remember that securing your servers is more than the technical process of planning and configuring server security policies. It also involves educating and informing the people who use those servers how they can continue to do their jobs with those security settings in place. Security administration, as with any other type of administration, is as much about people skills as it is about technical competence.

Lesson 1: Developing Security Policies

Security is an ongoing process. You first need to plan your security and decide how you should set up your permissions model and the security events that you need to monitor, and how to configure Windows Firewall (as described in Chapter 9, "Remote Access and Network Access Protection"). You then need to plan a strategy that ensures that the protective shield that you have placed around a server is effective in keeping the server secured. Not only must you plan, design, and configure server security, you need to monitor security events to ensure that the shield that you have implemented is working in the intended manner. In this lesson, you learn about security planning, security policies, data security, and auditing.

> **After this lesson, you will be able to:**
> - Plan server security policies.
> - Deploy and manage security policies.
> - Monitor server security.
> - Monitor authentication and authorization.
> - Monitor data security.
> - Configure auditing.
>
> **Estimated lesson time: 50 minutes**

Planning Server Security

Before you implement security policy and deploy software such as malware scanners on your servers running Windows Server 2008 R2, you need to plan your security strategy. It is impossible to monitor everything, and you need to decide what servers are most likely to be targets for external attacks or unauthorized logon attempts and what you should do to prevent administrator errors that incorrectly set permissions and allow user accounts to use resources to which these accounts should not have permission to access. It is not possible to monitor and audit all the large amount of security information generated by even a single server—much less a server farm—and you need to plan your monitoring and auditing to make the best use of scarce and valuable administrator time.

Identifying Security Requirements

Your organization faces several challenges when attempting to implement effective security on a production network. You need to consider the following:

- **The need to protect information**   You need to decide what information needs to be protected, how sensitive and business-critical this information is, and how high a protection level is required.

- **Authorization levels** You need to define authorization and permission levels for both administrators and users.
- **Security monitoring** You need to implement a workable monitoring policy that is nevertheless as comprehensive as possible and correlate this policy with detected security events.

You need to correlate the scope of security deployment, monitoring, and auditing with the known range of potential threats and attacks to your production network. You can define a policy violation as any deviation from organizational policies. Thus, if an administrator changes a policy setting that is specified by written company policy, this is a policy violation. If a user discovers that she can access confidential business information that should be available only to senior management, this is also a policy violation. Policy violations are discussed in more detail in the section entitled "Planning to Detect and Deal with Policy Violations," later in this lesson.

Servers are seldom used to browse the Internet and some types of external attack (such as phishing attacks) are rare. Nevertheless, a server typically requires an Internet connection so that packages (for example, Process Explorer, described in Chapter 12, "Performance Evaluation and Optimization") can be downloaded. Also, an external attacker will put considerable effort into attempting to install a trojan horse (known as "trojans" for short) into your file servers or domain controllers. Web servers are typically on peripheral networks and are the target for Denial of Service (DoS) attacks. Therefore, you must identify the types of external attack that are likely to occur and what servers are the most likely to be targets.

If an external attack or a policy violation occurs, you need to plan forensic analysis techniques that tell you the likely reasons for the violation, or whether and why the attack succeeded or failed. You need to have auditing in place so that you can fulfill regulatory requirements.

Planning Security Monitoring

The Event Viewer tool is described in detail in Chapter 12. In this chapter, we are concerned only with the security event log, which this tool can monitor. You can attach a task to an event or create a custom view that shows only events that meet specified criteria. You also can configure different security audit levels for different users. You can use all these features when you are planning security event logging.

The security event log, shown in Figure 8-1, records two types of events—success audits and failure audits. A success audit event indicates that an operation performed by a user, service, or program completed successfully. A failure audit indicates that a similar operation did not complete successfully. For example, if you enable logon audits for failure events, the security event log records unsuccessful logon attempts.

In Group Policy Management Editor, you can expand Computer Configuration, expand Policies, expand Windows Settings, expand Advanced Audit Policy Configuration, and click Audit Policies to view security event auditing categories. Table 8-1 lists these categories and the events that each category logs in Windows Server 2008 R2.

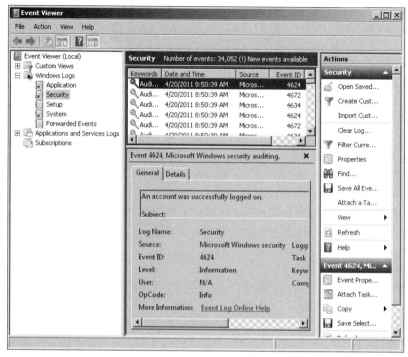

FIGURE 8-1 Monitoring the security event log

TABLE 8-1 Security Event Auditing Categories

CATEGORY	EFFECT
Account Logon	Records logon attempts by a local account on a computer. If the user account is a domain account, this event also appears on the domain controller.
Account Management	Records the creation, modification, and deletion of user and group accounts, in conjunction with password changes and resets.
Detailed Tracking	Records events generated when encryption or decryption requests are made to the Data Protection Application Interface (DPAI) events generated when a process is created or starts, or when it ends; and events generated by inbound Remote Procedure Call (RPC) connections.
Directory Service (DS) Access	Records access to objects in Active Directory Domain Services (AD DS).
Logon/Logoff	Records attempts to log on to workstations and member servers. Also records logoff events, account lockout, and Internet Protocol Security (IPsec) events.

CATEGORY	EFFECT
Object Access	Records attempts to access an object such as a file, folder, registry key, or printer that has defined audit settings within that object's System Access Control List (SACL).
Policy Change	Records any change to user rights assignment, audit, account, or trust policies.
Privilege Use	Records each instance that a user exercises a user right, such as changing the system time.
Process Tracking	Records application behavior such as program starts or terminations.
System	Records computer system events, such as startup and shutdowns, and events that affect system security or the security log.
Global Object Access Auditing	Allows you to configure a global SACL on the file system and on the registry of an entire computer.

The Audit Policy Group Policy container, which controls which events create entries in the security logs, is shown in Figure 8-2. You can configure the Audit Policy settings through the Local Security Settings console, or at the site, domain, or organizational unit (OU) level through Group Policy in conjunction with AD DS.

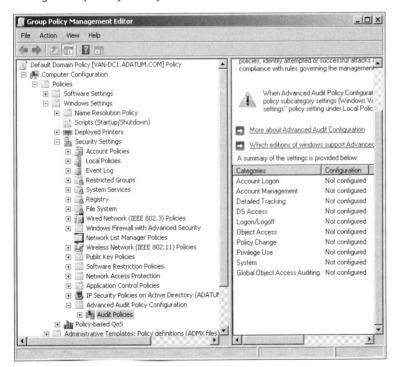

FIGURE 8-2 The Audit Policy Group Policy container

Security logs provide a good basis around which you can plan a comprehensive security monitoring policy. Group Policy settings provide centralized configuration of security log audit levels and the default security settings allow only administrators to access the security logs. However, monitoring distributed attacks and implementing forensic analysis requires a monitoring system that can correlate audit events centrally. Event forwarding (also described in Chapter 12) enables you to collect events on your servers—and also on clients if you want to monitor your entire network—on a single collector computer. However, for a full analysis of collected events you might plan to use a software package such as Microsoft System Center Operations Manager 2007 R2.

> **MORE INFO** **SYSTEM CENTER OPERATIONS MANAGER 2007 R2**
>
> For more information about System Center Operations Manager 2007 R2, see *http://www.microsoft.com/systemcenter/en/us/operations-manager.aspx*. You can download an evaluation version at *http://technet.microsoft.com/en-us/evalcenter/bb738014.aspx*.

> **NOTE** **COMPUTERS ON A PERIMETER NETWORK**
>
> Because computers in a perimeter network (such as web servers) are typically members of a workgroup rather than a domain, you cannot configure these computers with AD DS Group Policy settings. Instead, you should use local policies and template files.

Planning to Detect and Deal with Policy Violations

Policy violations typically form the largest category of security issues with which an organization needs to cope. They can include the following:

- The creation of user accounts outside the proper process
- The use of administrator privileges without proper authorization
- The use of service accounts for interactive logons
- The deletion of files that users have permission to access
- The execution of unapproved programs
- Attempts to access files to which a user does not have permission

The most common type of policy violation is unintentional user access attempts, such as when an ordinary user tries to open a directory that is available only to members of a security group to which that user does not belong. However, access restrictions and limited rights usually prevent users from doing any significant damage. Policy violations by administrators, whether deliberate or accidental, are a much greater concern.

Mistakes by network administrators pose a significant threat to an organization. Administrators need high levels of access rights and privileges to carry out their jobs. They can create user accounts, reset passwords, and change ownership of files and folders. However, just because an administrator can carry out a procedure does not mean that he or she is authorized to do so. Administrator rights also may enable administrators to view network resources that they should not see, such as financial records or human resource department reports.

The probability of policy violations occurring is high, as is their potential for causing damage. You should make the detection of policy violations a priority when you are planning your security policy. As a senior administrator, you may have a say in the hiring of staff for your administrative team. Make sure that the background checks carried out on potential new administrators are strict, and ensure that follow-up checks are carried out at regular intervals. However, this book is about technical rather than human resource issues. From a technical viewpoint, carry out the following tasks:

- Maintain independent security checks on administrator actions.
- Perform regular checks of the security monitoring system so that you can identify security breaches quickly.
- Confirm the extent of any security breach so that you can limit the damage that security breaches cause.

You need to ensure that internal users (who are not always company employees) sign explicit terms and conditions that alert them to your network security monitoring requirements. They must understand that if they try to open a file or access a share to which they do not have permission, the security logs will record that failed attempt. Internal users who work with high-value files should know that the security logs will track each time that they access those files. As an administrator (however senior you might be), you might not have the direct authority to enforce such a policy. Lobby your human resources and IT departments to ensure that this is done.

Your organization should implement strict separation of duties so that different individuals or groups are responsible for the inspection of the actions of administrators. Members of such inspection groups probably would not have permission to perform administrator actions themselves.

Your plan should include carrying out regular tests of monitoring functions. For example, you need to ensure that alerts function correctly. Perform such tests on an irregular schedule each week to prevent a potential internal attacker from using the test as a strike opportunity.

Your plan needs to identify security breaches quickly. You need to identify comprehensive processes that define how to perform particular network operations. For example, although administrators can create user accounts directly, organizational policy might specify that they should not do so. Hence, if the security monitoring system detects the appropriate event (Event ID 624—creation of a user account) you should ensure that the event is not linked to an individual administrator's account.

To limit the damage that security breaches cause, your plan must define suitable responses to anticipated incidents. The speed and effectiveness of incident responses can provide significant enhancement to your organization's security profile—if users or administrators know that a vigorous investigation will follow any security incident, they are less likely to attempt to breach a security policy.

Typically, the probability of data loss or compromise from external attackers is significantly lower than the probability of data loss from incorrect configuration by network administrators. You should not become complacent about external threats, but remember that it is easy to buy solutions that keep external intruders out of your network. It is much more difficult to keep your administrators from making mistakes.

Planning to Identify and Counter External Attacks

External attacks can be perpetrated directly by the attacker or can be carried out by malicious applications that the attacker installs, such as a trojan. Each type of attack has different characteristics and threat profiles. Human attackers can learn about the target network and modify their attacks accordingly; malicious applications can affect multiple computers and leave back doors for attackers to exploit.

Malicious applications include (for example) viruses, worms, and trojans. Although these applications can be troublesome and cause significant disruption, these attacks are easier to prevent than those perpetrated by people.

You need to identify malicious applications, particularly if your organization operates in the financial sector or in another environment that is constrained by regulations. You always need to be concerned about spyware applications that can reside on a server or workstation and communicate confidential information to external third parties, but blocking such applications is especially important in such environments.

It is not always easy to tell whether malicious applications exist on a network. If, for example, the malicious software component is a toolkit, it could take complete control of a computer and then mask the fact that an attacker now controls that computer. It is difficult to be sure that a server does not have such a malicious application running.

You should plan to identify malicious applications by tracking processes. Then you can identify each program that starts or stops on a workstation or server. The downside of this approach is that it generates a large number of events, the majority of which are not of interest.

The following areas can present difficulties when you are analyzing tracked processes:

- Web servers that use Common Gateway Interface (CGI), where each page hit creates a new process
- Application builds on development workstations that create a large number of processes within a short period

Where your planned monitoring activity can cause very high numbers of events in a short time or can create numerous events continually, you need effective filters to separate the attack events from legitimate events.

Attackers have great flexibility when it comes to choosing their intrusion methods. External attackers can penetrate networks through the following mechanisms:

- Password cracking
- Attempts to change or reset passwords
- Tricking a user into running a malicious application

- Exploiting vulnerabilities
- Using privilege escalation to compromise additional computers (this is called *island hopping*)
- Installing what appears to be a toolkit
- Installing a trojan
- Using a phishing attack, in which a fraudulent email points to a malicious website (this occurs less often with servers)

The best way to detect attackers and malicious applications is (arguably) to track processes. You need to apply process tracking carefully and integrate it with software restriction policies in Group Policy. In particular, you need to define very strict policies that dictate what programs can run on computers within perimeter networks.

Your plan to identify external attackers will likely overlap with your plan to identify internal threats. It should include the following:

- Effective security audit logs
- Automated analysis of the security logs to identify attack signatures
- Centralized collection of security logs, such as by using Event Forwarding

To detect malicious applications, your planned solution requirements should include the following:

- Effective procedures that audit any unauthorized software on the network
- Security audit logs that have been configured properly
- Reliable centralized collection and filtering of security logs
- Automated analysis of the security logs to identify suspicious behavior

Planning Forensic Analysis

You can use forensic analysis to track the timing, severity, and consequences of a security breach and to identify the systems that attackers have compromised. Forensic analysis records the following:

- The time of the attack
- The duration of the attack
- The computers that were affected
- The changes that the attacker made to the network

Forensic analysis investigates incidents after they have occurred instead of at the time. Therefore, it must provide a detailed list of all events of interest from one or more computers. You need to plan an analysis system that is able to handle and archive large amounts of data in a suitable database.

You need to decide how long you should preserve forensic data. You need to identify the maximum age for forensic data, after which the information becomes obsolete. Table 8-2 shows typical retention times for forensic data.

TABLE 8-2 Storage Limits for Forensic Analysis

STORAGE FACTORS	STORAGE LIMIT	COMMENTS
Online storage (database)	21 days	This provides rapid access to recent events.
Offline storage (backup)	180 days	This is a reasonable limit for most organizations.
Regulatory environment	7 years	Typically, regulatory agencies require data to be retained for this amount of time.
Intelligence agencies	Permanent	If your data affects national security, you must not delete it.

You can use online databases to retain the last three weeks of events and then archive older events into a compressible format for offline storage. If necessary, you can import these files back into the database for analysis.

Whatever system you use, you need to ensure that it matches your requirements for rapid investigation of recent events, with the ability to recover older events if necessary. Your experience of security events within your own environment should guide you as to the best combination of data retention times for online and offline storage. Implementation of security monitoring for forensic analysis requires reliable collection and storage of very large numbers of events. You need to plan to implement the following:

- Reliable and secure storage for online data
- Reliable backup of old events to archive media, and automatically moving older backups to a suitable archive store
- The ability to restore information from old backups
- The provision of large amounts of high-performance disk space for online storage

Typically, the data gathered for forensic analysis grows continuously. One specified person, such as an enterprise security administrator (and nobody else), might very occasionally need to access this information. Security must be comprehensive, so that only one or (at the most) two highly trusted individuals can access the security data.

Deploying Security Policies to Implement a Solution

When you have devised a plan for a security monitoring and attack detection system, your next step is to configure the solution design that addresses the solution requirements. This solution design must target the issues that affect the three previously defined scenarios:

- Detect policy violations.
- Identify external attacks.
- Implement forensic analysis.

The precise implementation of this solution will vary, based on your organization's network topology, but your solution should use the same basic components for all three scenarios, although the forensic analysis implementation may require additional online, offline, and archive storage resources. Before you start your implementation, you need to carry out the following tasks:

- **Review current security settings** You need to review your organization's current security audit and security event log file settings to provide a baseline for the planned changes. You need to know the current effective security audit settings, the level to which these settings apply (local computer, site, domain, or OU), and the current log file settings (such as the maximum log size and the behavior when the maximum log size is reached). You need to know about any additional security audit settings—for example, your production network—that might be configured currently so that the use of backup and restore privileges is audited.

- **Identify vulnerable computers** You need to identify the servers that an external attacker is most likely to attempt to access first. These computers typically are part of the perimeter network (such as web servers). You should perform a comprehensive review of all vulnerable computers to ensure that all service packs and security updates have been applied, that you have disabled unnecessary services and user accounts, configured services to run under Local Service or Network Service accounts rather than user accounts wherever possible, and applied high-security computer policy templates. Note that you should take certain precautions with any server, but they are particularly important on vulnerable computers.

- **Identify high-value assets** It is likely that you have already identified your organization's high-value assets and protected them using access control lists (ACLs) and encryption. However, you need to identify these protected files and amend written company policy formally to state that unauthorized users or administrators should not attempt to access them. Administrators and users should be made aware of this restriction. You then can investigate any changes to the ACL on these protected files. Changes in ownership are particularly important because ownership changes can indicate that an attacker (or an inexperienced administrator) attempted to access a file without proper authorization.

- **Assess administrator roles and user tasks** You need to ensure that you know what roles and responsibilities each member of your administrator team holds. For example, domain administrators can create new domain user accounts. However, your organizational policies might specify that only the provisioning system can create new accounts. In this situation, if an administrator creates a user account, this action should be logged and generate an alert. Users have significantly less access to network resources than administrators. For example, users do not usually have access to the file systems of servers in the perimeter network, and it is unlikely that you need to monitor such servers for user activity.

- **Review organizational policies and procedures**   You need to correlate your review of organizational policies and procedures with your assessment of administrator roles and responsibilities. For example, you need to define who can and cannot add users to security groups. Departments in your organization should establish procedures for change requests and define methods for implementation of these requests. If, for example, a user is added to a group outside the approved process, this requires investigation.

- **Identify sensitive or suspicious accounts**   You need to review all sensitive accounts and identify the accounts that need higher audit levels. Such accounts include the default Administrator account; any members of the Enterprise, Schema, and Domain Admins groups; and any accounts that services use to log on. When you notice suspicious activity by an individual, your security policy requirements should require higher audit levels for that person.

- **Identify authorized programs**   Attackers run programs to discover information about a network. Restricting the programs that can run significantly reduces the threat of external attacks. You should perform an audit of all authorized programs and treat any unrecognized programs as suspicious.

- **Check your firewall and anti-malware protection**   Both Microsoft and third-party products are available that scan for and delete or quarantine viruses and other malware. Sometimes such programs can alter your firewall settings, and you need to check these settings, as discussed in Chapter 9. Your malware definitions need to be up to date. If a server is connected to the Internet continuously to receive updates, malware definition updates should download automatically. However, the use of WSUS (described in Lesson 2, "Managing Server Security") enables you to run some servers without an Internet connection most of the time, making them much less vulnerable to external attacks. When you do connect such a server to the Internet, however, your first task is to update your malware definitions.

The tasks listed here, implemented on servers running Windows Server 2008 R2, should make these servers as secure as possible given your current security settings. The various checks and reviews that you perform should help identify any security improvements that are required and confirm that your security planning is sound. From the baseline created by your review, you can implement the additional configuration that your plan calls for.

Deploying Audit Policies

Part of your security plan typically will involve enabling Audit Policies under Advanced Audit Policy Configuration in the Security settings of either the Default Group Policy Object (GPO) or a GPO that you have created for this purpose. If you want different audit policies on different servers, you can group your servers in OUs and apply a GPO to each OU.

A list of audit policy categories appears in the Result pane of the Group Policy Management Editor when you click Audit Policies, as shown previously in Figure 8-2. You can expand Audit Policies so that these categories appear in the tree pane, and then select a category to view the available settings. The categories are listed and summarized in Table 8-1 previously, but they are listed here again for convenience and then described in more detail:

- Account Logon
- Account Management
- Detailed Tracking
- DS Access
- Logon/Logoff
- Object Access
- Policy Change
- Privilege Use
- System
- Global Object Access Auditing

Figure 8-3 shows the subcategories under Account Logon. You can audit Success, Failure, or both for each subcategory.

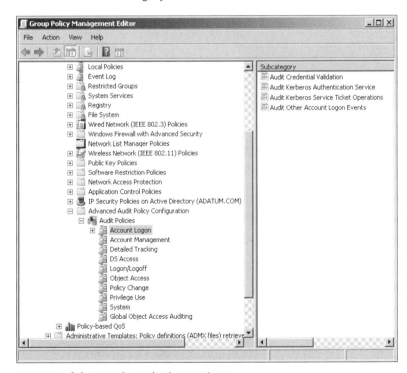

FIGURE 8-3 Subcategories under Account Logon

When you double-click a subcategory, you can configure it on the Policy tab of its Properties dialog box. Before you do this, however, you should ensure that you know exactly what you are auditing by clicking the Explain tab. Figure 8-4 shows the explanation of the Audit Credentials subcategory. Some settings are more useful than others; for example, Audit Other Account Logon Events does not contain any events. Space does not permit a description of every subcategory setting; only the more relevant are discussed here. However, one of the Suggested Practices (seen at the end of this chapter) is to look at the explanations of all of these settings.

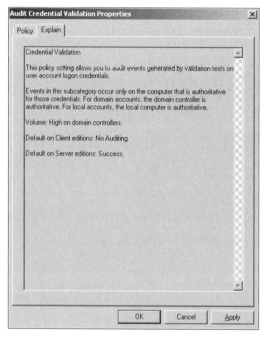

FIGURE 8-4 Explanation of the Audit Credentials subcategory

The Account Management category lets you audit the creation, deletion, or alteration of application, distribution, and security groups, and computer and user accounts. The Audit Other Account Management Events subcategory lets you configure auditing for less common events, such as when the password hash for a user account is accessed during account migration. Figure 8-5 shows the subcategories of the Account Management category. You audit the creation of user accounts and adding users to security groups in a practice later in this chapter.

The Detailed Tracking category allows you to audit events generated when encryption or decryption requests are made to the DPAPI, when a process is created, starts, or ends, and when inbound RPC connections are made.

The DS Access category allows you to audit events related to DS access, DS replication, and modifications to AD DS objects.

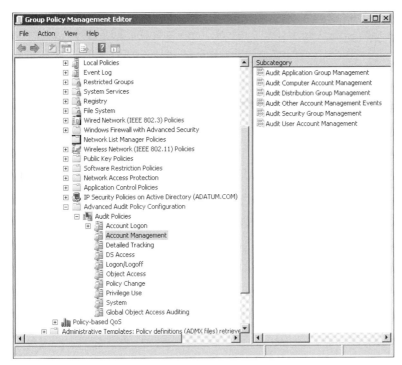

FIGURE 8-5 Subcategories of the Account Management category

The Logon/Logoff category lets you audit events related to successful logons, failed logon attempts, and logons using explicit credentials (such as when the Runas command is used). You can also audit events related to the termination of a logon session and account lockout. You can configure the auditing of events related to Terminal Service (TS) sessions, privilege elevation, Network Access Protection (NAP), and IPsec.

The Object Access category lets you audit a wide range of access events and events related to operations. Access events include access to the registry, to a network share and the files and folders it contains, to file system objects, to COM+ objects, to Security Accounts Manager (SAM) objects, and to kernel objects. This category also lets you audit Active Directory Certificate Services (AD CS) operations, connections that are allowed or blocked by the Windows Filtering Platform (WFP), and events generated when the handle to an object is opened or closed.

The Audit Policy category lets you audit changes to audit policy settings, to authentication settings, and to authorization settings. You can configure this category to audit changes to the WPF and to enable auditing of events generated by changes to policy rules applied to the Microsoft Protection Service (MPSSVC), which is used by Windows Firewall.

You can audit the Privilege Use category to determine whether other members of your administrative team are making proper use of their administrator privileges. For example, are they adding workstations to a domain, adjusting memory quotas, or allowing or denying Log On Locally rights to another user? You also can audit the use of more sensitive privileges.

Is an administrative user attempting to use privileges that should be confined to operating system operations? Is such a user attempting to reconfigure auditing and the security log? Figure 8-6 shows the subcategories available for the Privilege Use category. Note that there are currently no settings available under Audit Other Privilege Use Events.

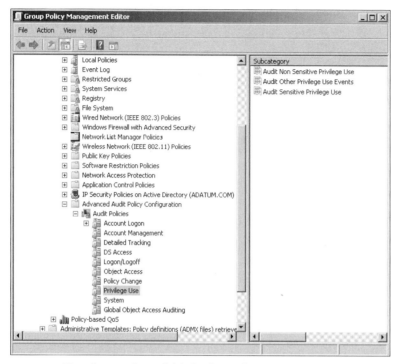

FIGURE 8-6 The subcategories available for the Privilege Use category

The System category allows you to audit events related to the IPsec driver and the security system. The Global System Access Auditing category allows you to configure global SACLs for the file system and the registry for an entire computer.

Protecting Vulnerable Computers

Typically, web servers in the peripheral zone are the most likely class of server to be attacked. These servers are not part of your domain and cannot be protected through domain Group Policy settings. You need to set up monitoring on such servers so that usage that would indicate a DoS attack, for example, is identified and countered quickly. You need to implement IP filtering so that traffic from addresses in the private address ranges or from other suspicious IP addresses is not permitted.

Your domain controllers typically access the Internet much less frequently than your web servers, if at all, and therefore are less vulnerable to external attacks. However, attacks from a malicious insider or careless configuration by an inexperienced administrator can pose a serious threat. For example, you need to monitor failed and successful logon attempts. Multiple failed logons could indicate a brute-force attack to crack the administrator password.

A successful logon by a user who should not have that right might indicate that an administrator has abused his or her administrative privileges and granted that user Log On Locally rights.

Monitoring Server Security

Auditing is the primary method through which you monitor the security of a computer running Windows Server 2008 R2. In the first part of this lesson, you learned about how you would plan to use the different auditing categories that can be applied to computers running Windows Server 2008 R2. In this section, you consider in more detail the types of situation that you would use each auditing policy to monitor.

Monitoring Security Log

Auditing events are written to the security log in Event Viewer. In Chapter 12, you will learn how to use Event Viewer to perform actions such as attaching tasks to specific events. Using the attached task functionality allows you to be alerted if a particular security event occurs. You also can configure attached tasks to start more detailed logging by triggering data collector sets. With appropriate configuration, data collector sets can allow you to collect detailed data about events on a computer running Windows Server 2008 R2, such as the particular applications that have been opened, processes that are executing, and other diagnostic information.

Another technique that you will learn in Chapter 12 is using event forwarding and subscriptions. When you are tracking user logon information, especially when users might authenticate against any one of multiple domain controllers at a site, there is a considerable advantage in configuring event log subscriptions so that event data flows to a centralized location at which you can view it. You need to make sure that the server that is configured as the collector has enough disk space to store the large log files that will be generated when you forward security events from all your organization's servers running Windows Server 2008 R2 to a centralized location.

Finally, Chapter 12 covers custom views. When you implement auditing in a Windows Server 2008 R2 environment, you are likely to be flooded with data. Creating a set of custom views allows you to focus on a set of events that you already have defined as interesting. Going through the security event log line by line can lead quickly to boredom and distraction. If you are distracted (or bored, for that matter), you might miss something. When you discover an interesting event, consider creating a custom view so that you can find similar events easily the next time you examine the Security event log.

Auditing Account Logon and Logon Events

There are two types of logon event auditing, and even experienced systems administrators can get confused and need to check documentation to be sure that they are using the correct auditing category. These two logon-related auditing policies are the following:

- Audit Account Logon Events
- Audit Logon Events

Account Logon Events are generated when a domain user account authenticates against a domain controller. Events are written to the logs on the domain controller, and you should configure event forwarding on the domain controller if you want to centralize auditing of domain logons and logoffs. If you do not use event forwarding, you must check the logs of each domain controller at a site because any domain controller in a site can authenticate account logon events.

Audit Logon Events records local logons. If both Audit Account Logon Events and Audit Logon Events are enabled for successful events, a user logging on to a member server in a domain will generate a Logon Event in the member server's event log and an Account Logon Event in the domain controller's event log.

Auditing Account Management

When the Auditing Account Management policy is enabled, events related to account management on a domain controller or a local computer are written to the event log. Account management events include:

- Creation, deletion, or modification of user accounts
- Creation, deletion, or modification of security or distribution groups
- Changing of user password

This auditing policy is used most often to keep an independent record of the activities of help-desk and human resource department staff when they perform the management of user accounts. Rigorous auditing of account management events allows you to answer questions about whether a user account has been modified without permission, such as a member of the help-desk staff changing the CEO's password after hours to gain access to sensitive data on a file server.

Auditing DS Access

DS Access auditing allows you to record access to objects within AD DS that have been configured with SACLs. This auditing policy is useful in situations where you need to track whether changes have been made to critical objects in Active Directory, such as OUs.

Auditing Object Access

Object Access policy is used for auditing access to all objects except those stored within AD DS. You can use this policy to record access to specific files, folders, registry keys, and printers. When securing sensitive data, you should configure this policy so that it is possible to audit access attempts to that data. Not only should you record which user account successfully accessed the data, but you also should record which user accounts have attempted to access the data unsuccessfully. This way, you can determine if someone who should not be able to access the data actually is and you will also be able to determine if someone is trying to access the data when they should not be.

Auditing Policy

The Auditing Policy policy is used to audit changes to users' rights, audit policies, or trust policies. This policy often is used to track modifications to accounts used by IT staff. In environments with rigorous security policies, it is necessary to keep track of which user accounts have been delegated specific rights. It sometimes can be difficult to keep track of the rights that have been delegated to a specific account or group. Auditing this type of activity allows you to ensure that accounts are not delegated undue rights. You do not want to go on leave for a week and come back to find that one of your help-desk staff has managed to delegate himself the privileges of an Enterprise Administrator without adding his user account to that group.

Auditing Privilege Use

When enabled, the Auditing Privilege Use policy allows you to track the use of user rights. In high-security environments, it is useful for recording how administrator-level accounts are used and to ensure that administrators do not exceed their authority by making changes that they can do because their account has administrative-level privileges, but which they are not officially authorized to perform.

Auditing System Events and Process Tracking

The Audit System Events and Audit Process Tracking policies monitor computer-related events rather than user-related events. Audit Process Tracking policy can be used to audit the activation of programs, how programs access objects, and when applications terminate. The Auditing System Events policy records information about the startup or shutdown of a computer. It also can be used to record data when an event occurs that changes the security log.

> **MORE INFO   AD DS AUDITING**
>
> For more information about auditing AD DS in Windows Server 2008 and Windows Server 2008 R2, see *http://technet.microsoft.com/en-us/library/cc731607(WS.10).aspx*.

Using the Encrypting File System

The Encrypting File System (EFS) enables you to ensure the integrity of data. EFS allows for the encryption of individual files and folders using a public encryption key tied to a specific user account. The encrypted file can be decrypted only using a private encryption key that is accessible to the user alone. It is also possible to encrypt documents to another user's public EFS certificates. A document encrypted to another user's public EFS certificate can be decrypted only by that user's private certificate.

Security groups cannot hold encryption certificates, so the number of users that can access an encrypted document is always limited to the individual EFS certificates that have been assigned to the document. Only a user who originally encrypts the file or a user whose certificate is already assigned to the file can add another user's certificate to that file.

With EFS, there is no chance that an encrypted file on a departmental shared folder might be accessed and read by someone who should not have access because of incorrectly configured NTFS or Shared Folder permissions. As many administrators know, teaching regular staff to configure NTFS permissions can be challenging. The situation gets even more complicated when you take into account shared folder permissions. Teaching staff to use EFS to limit access to documents is significantly easier than explaining NTFS ACLs to them.

If you are considering deployment of EFS throughout your organization, you should remember that the default configuration of EFS uses self-signed certificates. These are certificates generated by the user's computer rather than a Certificate Authority (CA), and they can cause problems in sharing documents because they are not necessarily accessible from other computers where the user has not encrypted documents. A more robust solution is to modify the default EFS Certificate Template, which is provided with a Windows Server 2008 R2 Enterprise CA so that autoenrollment is enabled. EFS certificates automatically issued by an Enterprise CA can be stored in AD DS and applied to files that need to be shared between multiple users. Another EFS deployment option involves smart cards. In organizations where users authenticate using smart cards, their private EFS certificates can be stored on a smart card and their public certificate stored within AD DS.

MORE INFO **EFS**

For more information about EFS, see
http://technet.microsoft.com/en-us/library/cc749610(WS.10).aspx.

Microsoft BitLocker Drive Encryption

BitLocker provides an alternative method of protecting files stored on a Windows Server 2008 R2 drive and on fixed data drives, such as internal hard drives. BitLocker To Go is used to protect files stored on removable data drives, such as external hard drives or USB flash drives. BitLocker encrypts entire drives; EFS enables you to encrypt individual files.

If your files are encrypted using BitLocker, you can log on and work with them normally, but hackers cannot access system files and discover your password. BitLocker prevents an attacker from accessing your drive by removing it from your computer and installing it in a different computer.

When you add new files to a drive that is encrypted with BitLocker, these files are encrypted automatically. Files on an encrypted drive are decrypted if you copy them to another drive or computer. If you share files with other users, these files are encrypted while stored on the encrypted drive, but they can be accessed normally by authorized users.

If you encrypt a Windows Server 2008 R2 drive, BitLocker checks the server during startup for any condition that could represent a security risk (for example, a change to any of the startup files). If a potential security risk is detected, BitLocker locks the operating system drive and you require a BitLocker recovery key to unlock it. You create this recovery key when you turn on BitLocker for the first time.

BitLocker is most effective when used with a Trusted Platform Module (TPM) version 1.2. TPM is a hardware component installed by the computer manufacturer. If your computer has the TPM chip, BitLocker uses it to seal the keys that are used to unlock the encrypted operating system drive. When you start your computer, BitLocker asks the TPM for the keys to the drive and unlocks it.

You still can use BitLocker to encrypt the Windows Server 2008 R2 drive on computers that do not have a TPM chip. However, you need to insert a USB startup key to start the computer, and this does not provide the pre-startup system integrity verification offered by BitLocker with a TPM.

If you need to use a BitLocker USB startup key, be careful to store it in a secure location. If you lose it and your operating system drive is locked, you could lose access to all the files stored on that drive permanently.

If you encrypt fixed or removable data drives, you can unlock an encrypted drive with a password or a smart card. You also can set the drive to unlock automatically when you log on to the computer. You can turn off BitLocker at any time, either temporarily, by suspending it, or permanently, by decrypting the drive.

For more information about BitLocker on computers running Windows Server 2008 R2, see *http://technet.microsoft.com/en-us/library/cc732774.aspx*.

EXAM TIP

BitLocker is not explicitly mentioned in the exam objectives and is unlikely to be tested in depth. However, you should be aware that BitLocker works on a per-volume basis and (unlike EFS) cannot be used to restrict access on a per–user account basis.

 Quick Check

- What type of auditing policy should you implement to track access to sensitive files?

Quick Check Answer

- Auditing Object Access

Lesson Summary

- As part of your security planning process, you need to review your current security settings, identify vulnerable computers and high-value assets, review organizational policies and procedures, and assess administrator roles and user tasks. You need to identify sensitive or suspicious accounts and authorized programs and check and review firewall and anti-malware protection.

- Part of your security review plan likely will involve configuring security audit policies, which enable you to identify security risks posed by malicious or careless insiders and incorrect settings configured by less experienced administrators.

- EFS allows for the encryption of individual files and folders using a public encryption key tied to a specific user account.

Lesson Review

You can use the following questions to test your knowledge of the information in Lesson 1, "Developing Security Policies." The questions are also available on the companion CD if you prefer to review them in electronic form.

> **NOTE ANSWERS**
>
> Answers to these questions and explanations of why each answer choice is correct or incorrect are located in the "Answers" section at the end of the book.

1. There are three domain controllers at your organization's headquarters. You want to configure a member server named SRV-Records so that it has a record of all domain logon and logoff activity that occurs at the headquarters. Which of the following actions should you take?

   A. Configure event forwarding on the domain controllers. Forward events generated by the Audit Account Logon Events policy to the server SRV-Records.

   B. Configure event forwarding on the domain controllers. Forward events generated by the Audit Account Management policy to the server SRV-Records.

   C. Configure event forwarding on the domain controllers. Forward events generated by the Audit Logon Events policy to the server SRV-Records.

   D. Configure event forwarding on the domain controllers. Forward events generated by the Audit Directory Service Access policy to the server SRV-Records.

2. Five accountants want to use the Accounting shared folder to share confidential client information with each other temporarily. Thirty accountants have access to this folder and past experience has shown that file and folder permissions are almost always incorrectly applied by non-technical users. Which of the following methods could

these five accountants use to secure this confidential data while it is being hosted on the Accounting shared folder?

A. Use BitLocker to encrypt the confidential data.

B. Use EFS to encrypt the confidential data using a special group account.

C. Use EFS to encrypt the confidential data to each accountant's EFS certificate.

D. Use BitLocker to encrypt the confidential data to each accountant's encryption certificate.

3. You are planning to use forensic analysis to track security breaches that occur on your network. You hope to use this information provided by this analysis when you are designing a plan that identifies threats and leads to better security. Which of the following should your forensic analysis record? (Choose four; each answer forms part of the solution.)

A. The identity of the attacker

B. The time of the attack

C. The duration of the attack

D. The identity of the computer from which the attack was made

E. The computers that were affected

F. The changes that the attacker made to the network

4. During a routine investigation of the configuration of AD DS in a domain that you are responsible for administering, you notice that a number of security groups have been added that were not required by the domain's security configuration plan, and other security groups that should be there have been deleted. You suspect that a newly appointed administrator has exceeded her authority. Which Audit Policy category should you configure settings for so that you can track the creation and deletion of security groups?

A. DS Access

B. Detailed Tracking

C. Object Access

D. Account Management

5. You are planning forensic analysis of security data for a regulatory agency. You need to decide how long you should preserve forensic data. Typically, how long should data be retained in a regulatory environment?

A. 21 days

B. 180 days

C. 7 years

D. Permanently

Lesson 2: Managing Server Security

Windows Server Update Services (WSUS) is an add-on component for Windows Server 2008 R2 that functions as a local Microsoft Update server. Rather than having every computer in your organization download megabytes of updates over the Internet, you can configure a WSUS server to be the only computer that downloads updates and then configure every other computer in your organization to use the WSUS server as the source of update files. In this lesson, you learn how to configure WSUS as the primary method of managing updates in your Windows Server 2008 R2 environment. You also will learn about advanced software solutions, such as System Center Essentials 2010 and System Center Configuration Manager 2007 R3, which you can use to ensure that the computers in your environment are fully updated and compliant with relevant rules and regulations.

> **After this lesson, you will be able to:**
> - Manage operating system patch level maintenance.
> - Manage Application patch level maintenance.
> - Manage WSUS.
>
> **Estimated lesson time: 40 minutes**

Deploying Updates with WSUS

WSUS 3.0 Service Pack 2 (SP2) is a freely available component that you can install on a computer running Windows Server 2008 R2. WSUS 3.0 SP2 allows for the centralized deployment of software updates and service packs for Microsoft software on your organization's network. Provided that installation requirements are satisfied, you can deploy WSUS 3.0 SP2 on a computer running Windows Server 2008 R2 in your organization by downloading the WSUS 3.0 SP2 software from Microsoft's website. WSUS 3.0 SP2 can be installed as a role in Windows Server 2008 R2. WSUS 3.0 SP2 cannot be installed on computers running Windows Server Core, although this functionality may be available in later versions of the update server software.

Software Installation Requirements

Installation of WSUS 3.0 SP2 requires that the following software is installed:

- Internet Information Services (IIS) 6.0 or later
- The Microsoft .NET Framework 2.0 or later
- Microsoft Management Console (MMC) 3.0
- Microsoft Report Viewer Redistributable 2008 or later

All the software listed above should be installed by default on a server running Windows Server 2008 R2, with the exception of Microsoft Report Viewer, Redistributable 2008 or later (the latest version is Report Viewer, Redistributable 2010). It is not available as an add-on role or feature and must be downloaded from Microsoft's Download website. The WSUS 3.0 SP2 installation file works with Report Viewer, Redistributable 2008, but not with Report Viewer, Redistributable 2008 SP1 or Report Viewer, Redistributable 2010. This may have changed by the time you read this book, but the relevant practice in this chapter has been written accordingly.

Database software is required for WSUS reporting. WSUS 3.0 SP2 can operate with any one of the following:

- Microsoft SQL Server 2008 Standard or Enterprise edition
- Microsoft SQL Server 2005 SP3 or later

If one of the supported versions of SQL Server is not installed, however, the WSUS 3.0 SP2 Setup Wizard will install Windows Internal Database.

WSUS 3.0 SP2 can be installed only if the following Windows Server 2008 R2 components are enabled:

- Windows Authentication
- Static Content
- ASP.NET
- IIS 6.0 (or later) Management Compatibility
- IIS 6.0 (or later) Metabase Compatibility

When the components listed here are enabled and Report Viewer is installed, you can install WSUS 3.0 SP2.

The installation of WSUS 3.0 SP2 on a computer running Windows Server 2008 R2 generates two local groups. These groups function as WSUS administrative roles, and you can assign roles to users by adding their user account to the relevant groups. These groups are as follows:

- **WSUS Administrators**   Users who have accounts that are members of this local group are able to administer the WSUS server. This includes WSUS administration tasks, from approving updates and configuring computer groups through to configuring automatic approvals and the WSUS server's update source. A user that is a member of this group can use the Update Services console to connect remotely to manage WSUS.
- **WSUS Reporters**   Users who have accounts that are members of this local group are able to create reports on the WSUS server. A user that is a member of this group can connect remotely to the WSUS server using the Update Services console to run these reports.

As stated previously in this section, you use a database running SQL Server 2005 SP3 or later to store WSUS configuration and reporting information. (SQL Server 2008 R2 is the latest version, and SQL Server 2008 R2 SP1 is available for testing.) Organizations that want to generate customized reports use this option, writing their own applications to interact with the SQL Server database rather than relying on the default reporting options available from the Update Services console. For example, developers in your organization could write a database application that extracts data from the database and forwards it to administrators on a daily basis through email. Organizations considering this type of deployment might also consider using System Center Essentials 2010 as an update management solution as it includes more detailed reporting functionality. System Center Essentials 2010 is discussed later in this lesson.

Deployment Scenarios

How WSUS is deployed in your organization depends on your organization's network architecture. The following section details four common WSUS deployment configurations and the network environments that they suit best.

SINGLE WSUS SERVER DEPLOYMENT

In a single WSUS server deployment, one WSUS server is deployed in a protected environment and synchronizes content directly with Microsoft Update. Updates are distributed to clients, as shown in Figure 8-7.

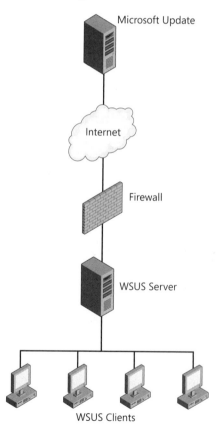

FIGURE 8-7 Single WSUS server deployment

MULTIPLE INDEPENDENT WSUS SERVERS

The multiple independent WSUS deployment is common in organizations that have branch offices in disparate locations. Each WSUS server functions as an upstream server. Configuration and approval data is managed on a per–WSUS server basis, usually by administrators that are onsite. Figure 8-8 shows a multiple independent WSUS server deployment.

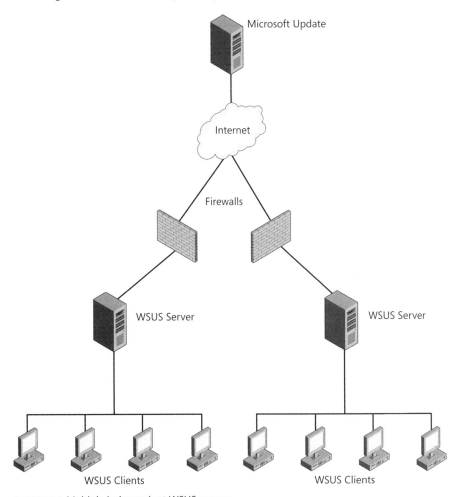

FIGURE 8-8 Multiple independent WSUS servers

MULTIPLE INTERNALLY SYNCHRONIZED WSUS SERVER

In this deployment model, the WSUS server that receives updates from the Microsoft Update server is designated as the upstream server. A WSUS server that retrieves updates from another WSUS server is designated a downstream server. This type of deployment is becoming less common because WSUS 3.0 SP2 supports up to 25,000 clients and Background Intelligent Transfer Service (BITS) peer caching allows updates to be shared in a peer-to-peer manner among clients on the LAN. BITS peer-caching allows one computer on a local subnet to download an update from a WSUS server and then share it with other compatible clients on the same subnet.

> **MORE INFO   BITS**
>
> For more information about BITS and BITS peer caching, access
> *http://msdn.microsoft.com/en-us/library/aa362708(VS.85).aspx* and follow the links. Be
> aware, however, that BITS is unlikely to be tested in depth on the exam.

When studied on Microsoft's network, BITS peer caching reduced the load on the WSUS servers so much that it was determined that 70 percent of updates were retrieved from other computers on the same LAN rather than being downloaded directly from the WSUS server. This means that except for the purpose of redundancy, a single WSUS server can provide updates to all but the largest sites. The multiple internally synchronized deployment model is shown in Figure 8-9.

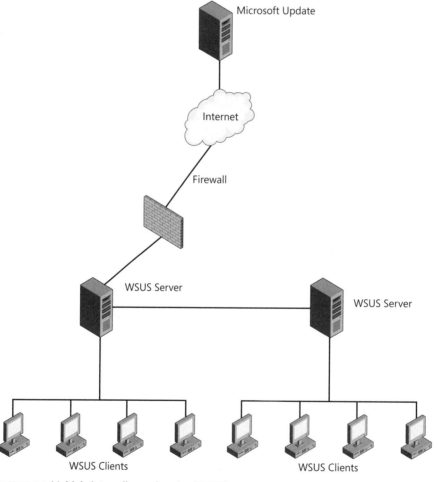

FIGURE 8-9 Multiple internally synchronized WSUS servers

DISCONNECTED WSUS SERVERS

In the disconnected model, one server retrieves updates from the Internet, those updates are then transferred using other media, either writable DVD-ROM or removable USB hard disk drive, and installed on other servers, which deploy them to clients. Many administrators use a variant of this model when dealing with remote branch offices. Rather than transfer gigabytes of existing updates across slow WAN links to the new WSUS server at the remote office, the data is physically transported and added to the new WSUS server. Figure 8-10 shows the disconnected WSUS server deployment model.

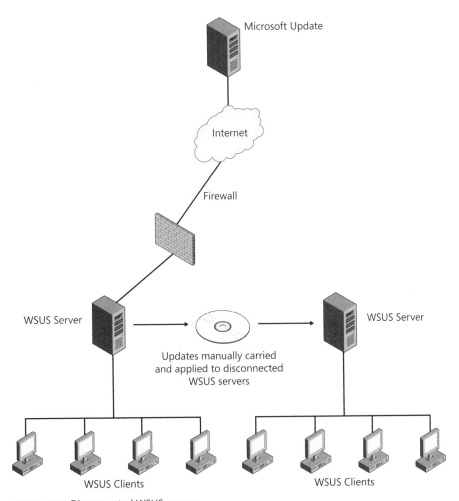

FIGURE 8-10 Disconnected WSUS servers

New Features in WSUS 3.0 SP2

WSUS 3.0 SP2 is an update of WSUS 3.0 SP1 rather than a new edition. Nevertheless, it offers significant new features and enhancements with which you need to be familiar. A WSUS server running Windows Server 2008 R2 requires WSUS 3.0 SP2 (although WSUS Server 3.0 SP2 will run on other server operating systems, such as Windows Server 2008 SP1). If your server is running Windows Server 2008 R2, then you should install WSUS 3.0 SP2. Microsoft's release notes specifically state that you should not install WSUS 3.0 SP1 on a server running Windows Server 2008 R2.

> **NOTE   UPGRADE IN THE CORRECT ORDER**
>
> If you install WSUS 3.0 SP2 on a computer running Windows Server 2008 and then attempt to upgrade the operating system to Windows Server 2008 R2, the upgrade will fail.

WSUS 3.0 SP2 can be installed as a server role on a computer running Windows Server 2008 SP2. Arguably the most significant new features in WSUS 3.0 SP2 are support for clients running Windows 7 and support for the BranchCache feature. Chapter 7, "Provisioning File and Print Servers," describes BranchCache. WSUS 3.0 SP2 also offers considerable improvements to the Windows Update Agent (WUA) client. Client scan times are shorter, and WSUS clients can run scoped scans against a WSUS server, instead of performing a full scan. This results in considerably faster scans for applications that use Microsoft Update application programming interfaces (APIs), such as Windows Defender.

WSUS 3.0 SP2 auto-approval rules let you specify the approval deadline date and time for all computers or specific computer groups. Language selection for downstream servers now includes a new warning dialog box that appears when you decide to download updates only for specified languages. You can run Update and Computer Status reports from the WSUS console or use APIs to incorporate this information into your own reports. Update reports let you filter updates that are approved for installation.

Changes have been made to the software requirements for the installation of WSUS 3.0 SP2. They are described in the section entitled "Software Installation Requirements," earlier in this lesson. Possibly the most significant of these is that the installation of WSUS 3.0 SP2 requires that Report Viewer Redistributable 2008 or later is installed. WSUS 3.0 SP1 required the installation of Report Viewer 2005 or later.

> **MORE INFO   WSUS 3.0 SP2 RELEASE NOTES**
>
> To access the WSUS 3.0 SP2 release notes, which contain more information about new features and software requirements, see
> *http://technet.microsoft.com/en-us/library/dd939886(WS.10).aspx.*

Autonomous and Replica Mode

You have several options when configuring your organization's downstream WSUS servers. The first option, shown in Figure 8-11, is to configure the downstream WSUS server as a replica of the upstream server. You can access this dialog box by clicking Updates on the Updates Services console and then clicking Update Source and Proxy Server. You will not be able to do this until you have installed WSUS 3.0 SP2, as described in a practice later in this lesson.

When you configure a WSUS server in this way, all approvals, settings, computers, and groups from the upstream server are used on the downstream server. The downstream server cannot be used to approve updates when configured in replica mode, although it is possible to change a replica server to autonomous mode should an update need to be urgently deployed. The second option is called *autonomous mode*. Autonomous mode allows for a local WSUS administrator to configure separate update approval settings but still retrieves updates from the upstream WSUS server.

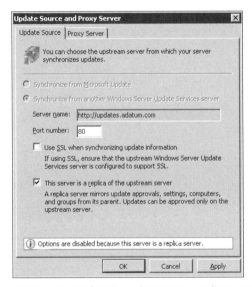

FIGURE 8-11 Configuring a downstream replica server

Using Computer Groups

In the most basic form of WSUS deployment, every computer that is a client of the WSUS server receives approved updates at the same time. Although this method works well for many organizations, other organizations prefer to perform staggered rollouts of updates. Groups allow the staggered and targeted deployment of updates. Microsoft does everything possible to ensure that the updates that it releases do not cause problems with other software. However, if your organization deploys custom applications, it is possible that a conflict may arise between a newly released update and your organization's important custom business application. By creating a test group, you can deploy newly released updates to a subset of the computers in your organization. This gives you a chance to verify that new updates do not conflict with existing deployed configurations before rolling out the update to everyone in your organization.

WSUS computer groups have the following properties:

- The two default computer groups are All Computers and Unassigned Computers. When a client contacts the WSUS server for the first time, it is added to the Unassigned Computers group unless it is already assigned to a group.

- Groups can be organized in a hierarchy. An update added to a group at the top of the hierarchy also will be deployed to computers that are in groups lower in the hierarchy. The Unassigned Computers group is a part of the All Computers hierarchy.

- Computers can be assigned to multiple groups.

Administrators can use two methods to assign computer accounts to WSUS groups. The first method is known as *server-side targeting*. This method is selected by choosing the Use The Update Services Console option under the Computers item in the Options section of the Update Services console, as shown in Figure 8-12. When a computer contacts the WSUS server for the first time, it is placed in the Unassigned Computers group. A user with WSUS Administrator privileges then manually assigns the computer to a Computers group using the WSUS console.

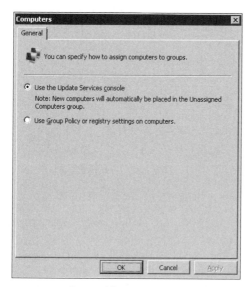

FIGURE 8-12 Server-side targeting

The second method of assigning computers to groups is to use Group Policy or registry settings on clients of the WSUS server. This method is less onerous in large environments and simplifies the group assignment process. Regardless of which method you use to assign computers to groups, you must first create the groups using the WSUS console. To configure a GPO to support client-side targeting, perform the following steps:

1. Edit the GPO that you will use to assign the computer group.

2. In Computer Configuration\Policies\Administrative Templates\Windows Components\ Windows Update, double-click the Enable Client-Side Targeting policy item.

3. Select the Enabled option and then specify the Target Group Name For This Computer, as shown in Figure 8-13.

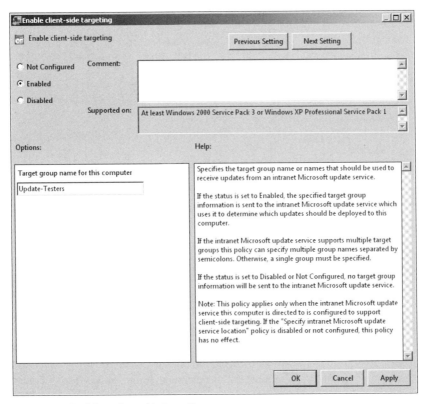

FIGURE 8-13 Enabling client-side targeting

WSUS Client Configuration

Although WSUS clients can be configured manually, in most enterprise environments WSUS clients will be configured using Group Policy. The policies related to WSUS are located in the Computer Configuration\Policies\Administrative Templates\Windows Components\Windows Update node of the Group Policy Management Editor and are shown in Figure 8-14. If you want a computer running Windows Server 2008 R2 that is hosting WSUS to receive updates, it is necessary to configure it like you would any other client.

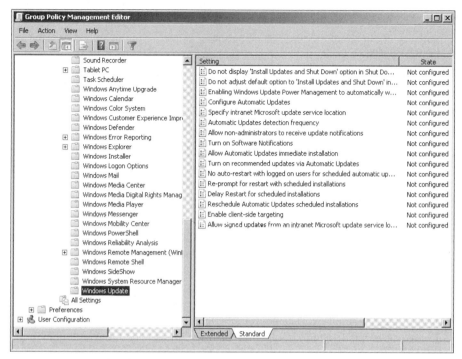

FIGURE 8-14 WSUS-related policies

Update Installation Behavior

Other than the policies that determine the assignment of computers to WSUS groups and the location of the local WSUS server, the most important WSUS-related policies relate to how and when WSUS updates are downloaded and installed. As an administrator, you want to avoid the situation of having updates never being installed, either because a user intervenes to cancel update installation or the updates are always scheduled to be installed when the computer turns off. Stopping user intervention must be balanced with interrupting a user's work. No one will be particularly happy to lose several hours of work on an important spreadsheet because you have configured the update settings to install and reboot the computer without giving the user a chance to do anything about it.

When planning the scheduling of update deployments, you should take the following policy items into account:

- **Enabling Windows Update Power Management To Automatically Wake Up The System To Install Scheduled Updates** This policy works only with clients running Windows Vista or Windows 7 that have compatible hardware and an appropriately configured BIOS. Rather than worrying about whether users will be interrupted by reboots during the update deployment process, this policy allows computers to be woken in the middle of the night (or another specified period of low usage), have the relevant updates deployed, and then be returned to a sleep state.

- **Configure Automatic Updates**   This policy allows you to specify whether updates are downloaded and scheduled for installation automatically or if the user is notified that updates (either already downloaded or on the WSUS server) are available.

- **Automatic Updates Detection Frequency**   If this policy is not enabled, the default detection frequency is 22 hours. If you want to configure a more frequent interval, you can do so with this policy.

- **Allow Automatic Updates Immediate Installation**   When enabled, this policy automatically installs all updates that do not require a service interruption or for Windows to restart.

- **No Auto-Restart With Logged On Users For Scheduled Automatic Updates Installations**   When this policy is enabled, the computer does not restart automatically but will wait for the logged-on user to initiate a restart. The user is notified that the computer needs to be restarted before the installation of updates is completed. If this policy is not enabled, the computer automatically restarts 5 minutes after the updates are installed to complete update installation.

- **Delay Restart For Scheduled Installations**   This policy enables you to vary the automatic restart period. As mentioned previously, the default period is 5 minutes. This policy allows you to set a delay period of up to 30 minutes.

- **Reschedule Automatic Updates Scheduled Installations**   This policy ensures that a scheduled installation that did not occur (perhaps because the computer was switched off or disconnected from the network) will occur a specified number of minutes after the computer is next started. If this policy is disabled, a missed scheduled installation will occur with the next scheduled installation.

WSUS Support for Roaming Clients

Many organizations have employees who regularly move between locations. These employees typically are assigned laptop computers. In terms of the deployment of updates, this means that unless a technology like NAP is installed, these computers might not receive updates until the staff member who uses them logs back on at their home office. NAP is discussed in Chapter 9.

You can ensure that roaming clients can access updates on any WSUS server in your organization by configuring all update clients to point to the same WSUS server name through group policy and then configure DNS so that the fully qualified domain name (FQDN) resolves to the local IP address in each subnet. To do this, open DNS Manager and configure DNS Round Robin with netmask ordering in the computer's Properties dialog box, as shown in Figure 8-15. When DNS Round Robin is configured with Netmask Ordering, the DNS server will return the host record that is located on the querying computer's subnet. Note that for this solution to work, you need to ensure that each WSUS server in your organization is configured to use the same FQDN.

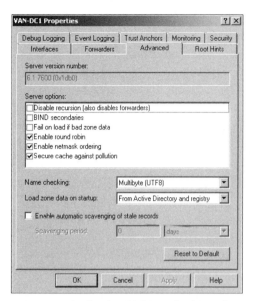

FIGURE 8-15 Configuring DNS Round Robin with netmask ordering

Updates and Synchronization Strategies

When updates are downloaded to a WSUS server, either from Microsoft Update or an upstream server, the metadata and the update files are stored in separate locations. The update metadata is stored in the WSUS database. Depending on the configuration of WSUS, the actual update files themselves are stored on the WSUS server or on the Microsoft Update servers. This configuration setting is determined during the installation of WSUS. When updates are stored on the Microsoft Update servers, approved updates are downloaded by clients directly from Microsoft's servers rather than from the WSUS server.

Automatic approval rules allow you to approve specific categories of updates automatically. In WSUS 3.0 SP2, automatic approval rules now enable you to specify the approval deadline date and time for all computers or specific computer groups. Updates can be configured for a specific classification and for specific products, and applied to specific WSUS computer groups. The available classifications are Critical Updates, Definition Updates, Drivers, Feature Packs, Security Updates, Service Packs, Tools, Update Rollups, and Updates. The product category includes almost all current Microsoft products, which are too numerous to list here. You can have multiple automatic approval rules and can enable and disable them as necessary. Automatic approval rules are configured through the Automatic Approvals dialog box, shown in Figure 8-16, and available under Options in the Update Services console. By default, no updates are approved automatically for distribution by WSUS 3.0 SP2.

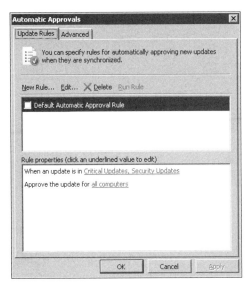

FIGURE 8-16 Configuring automatic approvals

To approve an update, you need to perform the following steps:

1. Open the Update Services console, and under the Updates node, click All Updates.

2. Set the Approval drop down list to Unapproved and the Status drop-down list to Any.

3. Right-click an update and then click Approve. This will open the Approve Updates dialog box.

4. Click Connect To All Computers and then click Approved For Install.

5. Right-click the newly approved update in the All Computers Group, click Deadline, and then click 2 Weeks. The approved update now will be deployed with the set deadline.

NOTE **FORCING UPDATES**

If you want an update to be deployed immediately, set the Update Deadline to a date in the past.

✔ **Quick Check**

1. What mode should you deploy a downstream WSUS 3.0 SP2 server in if you want it to use the approvals and computer group configuration of the designated upstream server?

2. Aside from WSUS 3.0 SP2, what other software must be downloaded from Microsoft's website prior to the installation of WSUS?

Update Management and Compliance

Compliance means ensuring that a computer is configured in a mandated way. This involves not only having a specific set of updates installed, but ensuring that other configuration settings, such as a strong password policy, strong firewall configuration, and anti-spyware software are set up correctly.

WSUS Reporting

WSUS 3.0 SP2 offers basic reporting functionality. The reports are based on information communicated with WSUS. WSUS does not scan computers to determine whether updates are missing, but instead records whether updates have been downloaded to target computers and whether the target computers have reported back to the WSUS server that the update has been successfully installed. You can access WSUS reporting by clicking the Reports node on the Update Services console, as shown in Figure 8-17.

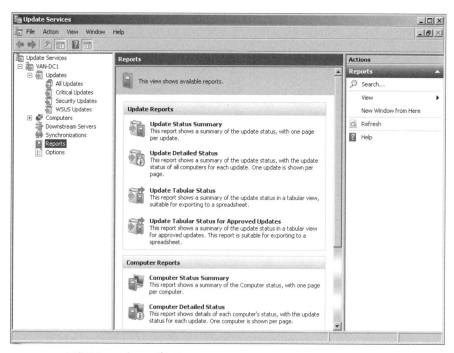

FIGURE 8-17 WSUS Reporting options

WSUS reports can be printed or exported to Microsoft Excel or PDF format. If WSUS data is written to a SQL Server database, you have the ability to perform your own separate analyses using your own set of database queries. You can generate the following reports using WSUS 3.0 SP2 if your user account is a member of the WSUS Reporters or WSUS Administrators groups:

- **Update Status Summary Report**   This report provides basic information about update deployment, including the number of computers the update is installed on, needed on, or failed to install on, and for which WSUS has no data. One page per update is available.

- **Update Detailed Status**   This report provides significantly more information about the deployment of updates. It returns a list of computers and their update status on an update-per-page basis. When you run a detailed update, you can view the report in summary or tabular format.

- **Update Tabular Status**   This report format provides data in a table on a per-update basis. Once this report is generated you can switch the report to summary or update detailed status. This form of report is the best to export to Excel because it is already in tabular format.

- **Update Tabular Status For Approved Updates**   This report shows a summary of the update status in a tabular view for approved updates. You can export it to a spreadsheet.

- **Computer Status Summary**   This is similar to the update detailed status report. It provides update information on a per-computer rather than a per-update basis. Data is in summary form.

- **Computer Detailed Status**   This report format provides details about the status of specific updates for a particular computer. Once this report is generated, you can switch the report to summary or tabular form.

- **Computer Tabular Status**   This report provides a table of update status information, with individual computers as rows. Once this report is generated, you can switch the report to summary or tabular form. Note that Computer Tabular Status is not the same as Update Tabular Status.

- **Synchronization Results**   This report shows the result of the WSUS server's last synchronization.

Enabling the Reporting Rollup For Downstream WSUS Servers option allows update, computer, and synchronization data for replica downstream servers to be included in reports generated on the upstream WSUS server.

Other Patch Management Tools

Although WSUS is the primary patch management tool covered by the exam, there are other patch management tools of which you should be aware. These include, but are not limited to, the Microsoft Baseline Security Analyzer, System Center Essentials 2010, and System Center Configuration Manager 2007 R3.

Microsoft Baseline Security Analyzer

The Microsoft Baseline Security Analyzer (MBSA) tool is not used for deploying updates, but it allows systems administrators to scan the network to determine which computers are missing updates or are configured incorrectly. The MBSA tool can integrate with WSUS, so rather than scanning target systems to see whether any updates are missing from the entire catalog of updates, it will check whether approved updates are missing from a target computer.

System Center Essentials 2010

System Center Essentials 2010 is the next step up from WSUS 3.0 SP2 in terms of patch management in a Windows Server 2008 R2 environment. It can manage up to 50 servers and provides significantly more detailed patch deployment reporting functionality than WSUS. System Center Essentials 2010 also can be used to deploy software updates to non-Microsoft products and provides advanced update distribution control and scheduling flexibility. It provides basic compliance checking functionality and inventory management. Virtual Machine Manager 2008 R2 technology is built into the product, so that System Essentials 2010 provides a single console and management solution for managing both physical and virtual servers. This includes support for converting physical servers to virtual machines and support for live migration. System Center Essentials 2010 requires access to SQL Server 2008 (Standard or Enterprise edition) with SP1.

> **MORE INFO**   **SYSTEM CENTER ESSENTIALS 2010**
>
> For more information about System Center Essentials 2010, access the product home page on Microsoft's website at *http://www.microsoft.com/systemcenter/essentials/default.mspx*. For more information about upgrading to System Center Essentials 2010, see *http://technet.microsoft.com/en-us/library/cc339466.aspx*.

System Center Configuration Manager 2007 R3

System Center Configuration Manager 2007 R3 is the latest iteration of the Systems Management Server product line. This product provides more detailed functionality than System Center Essentials and can be used to monitor almost all aspects of a network environment. System Center Configuration Manager 2007 R3 provides advanced compliance reporting and is designed for very large environments, such as those that would exceed the 50-server capacity of System Center Essentials 2010.

> **MORE INFO**   **SYSTEM CENTER CONFIGURATION MANAGER 2007 R3**
>
> For more information about System Center Configuration Manager 2007 R3, access *http://www.microsoft.com/systemcenter/en/us/configuration-manager/cm-overview.aspx* and follow the links.

Lesson Summary

- WSUS enables a single server to obtain updates online from Microsoft Update and to deliver these updates to clients on a network. This means that WSUS clients on the network do not all need to access Microsoft Update through an Internet connection to obtain updates.

- WSUS replicas are downstream servers that inherit the configuration of their upstream server. Autonomous mode WSUS servers are downstream servers that retrieve updates from an upstream server, but on which approvals are configured by a local administrator.

- Server-side targeting assigns computers to WSUS groups using the WSUS administration console. Client-side targeting assigns computers to WSUS groups using Group Policy or by editing the client's registry. Deploying updates in a staggered manner allows you to test whether a particular update has an adverse impact on clients.

- System Center Essentials 2010 provides greater functionality than WSUS. It requires access to a database running under SQL Server 2008 (Standard or Enterprise edition) with SP1 or later.

- System Center Configuration Manager 2007 R3 has advanced reporting functionality that can be used to verify that computers meet compliance requirements.

Lesson Review

You can use the following questions to test your knowledge of the information in Lesson 2, "Managing Server Security." The questions are also available on the companion CD if you prefer to review them in electronic form.

> **NOTE ANSWERS**
>
> Answers to these questions and explanations of why each answer choice is correct or incorrect are located in the "Answers" section at the end of the book.

1. A total of 30 percent of your organization's workforce uses laptop computers running Windows 7. Most of these employees visit different branch offices each week. Your organization has 30 branch offices spread out across Europe. After doing some compliance reporting, you have determined that these laptop computers are being updated only when they connect to the branch office from which they were originally deployed. How can you ensure that these laptop computers always receive updates from the local branch office WSUS server, no matter which branch office they are connecting to? (Choose two; each answer forms a part of the solution.)

    A. Configure Network Load Balancing (NLB) on each site's WSUS server.

    B. Configure DNS Round Robin and netmask ordering on each DNS server in your organization.

    C. Configure each WSUS server in your organization to use the same FQDN.

    D. Configure Berkley Internet Name Daemon (BIND) secondaries on each DNS server in your organization.

    E. Configure the host file on each client with the host name and IP address of all WSUS servers in the organization.

2. You are in the process of planning the deployment of WSUS at a university. The university is made up of five faculties, each of which has its own IT staff. You want to minimize the amount of data downloaded from the Microsoft Update servers, but each faculty's IT staff should have responsibility to approve updates. Which of the following WSUS deployments should you implement?

    A. Configure one upstream server. Configure five downstream servers as replicas of the upstream server.

    B. Configure five replica servers.

    C. Configure one upstream server. Configure five downstream servers as autonomous servers.

    D. Configure five autonomous servers.

3. You want to stagger the rollout of updates from your organization's WSUS 3.0 SP2 server on a departmental basis. The accounts for the computers in each department are located in departmental OUs. Which of the following should you do? (Choose two; each answer forms a part of the solution.)

    A. Create WSUS computer groups for each department.

    B. Create GPOs and link them to the domain. In each GPO, specify the name of a departmental WSUS computer group.

    C. Create GPOs and link them to each OU. In each GPO, specify the name of a departmental WSUS computer group.

    D. Create separate security groups for all the computer accounts in each departmental OU.

    E. Create separate security groups for all the user accounts in each departmental OU.

4. What method should you use to ensure that all Security and Critical updates are deployed to computers in the PatchTest computer group?

    A. Create a scheduled task.

    B. Create an Automatic Approval rule that uses the All Computers group as a target.

    C. Create an Automatic Approval rule that uses the PatchTest WSUS computer group as a target.

    D. Create an Automatic Approval rule that uses the PatchTest security group as a target.

5. You need a list of computers that a recent update did not install on so that you can send a technician to investigate. Which of the following reports should you generate so that you can locate this information quickly?

    A. Update Status Summary

    B. Computer Status Summary

    C. Update Detailed Status

    D. Computer Detailed Status

PRACTICE **Monitoring Account Creation by an Inexperienced Administrator**

Kim Akers is the senior administrator at the Adatum Corporation. Don Hall has been promoted to domain administrator, and Kim needs to give him the appropriate rights. However, Kim wants to check what users and security groups Don creates. In this practice, you configure auditing to record user and security group creation, promote Don to domain administrator, and determine how he uses his new rights.

EXERCISE 1 **Configure Auditing of User and Security Group Creation and Promote Don Hall to Domain Administrator**

In this exercise, you configure auditing of user and group creation before you add Don Hall to the Domain Admins group. It is good practice to configure security auditing before making any changes that might affect your organization's security.

1. Log on to the VAN-DC1 domain controller using the Kim Akers user account.

2. On the Start menu, under Administrative Tools, open Group Policy Management.

3. If necessary, expand Forest: Adatum.com, expand Domains, and then expand Adatum.com.

4. Expand Domain Controllers.

5. Right-click Default Domain Controller Policy and then click Edit. This opens the Group Policy Management Editor.

6. Under Computer Configuration, expand Policies, expand Windows Settings, expand Security Settings, expand Advanced Audit Policy Configuration, expand Audit Policies, and then click Account Management, as shown in Figure 8-18.

7. In the Result pane, double-click Audit User Account Management.

8. In the Audit User Account Management Properties dialog box, select Configure The Following Audit Events, select Success, as shown in Figure 8-19, and then click OK.

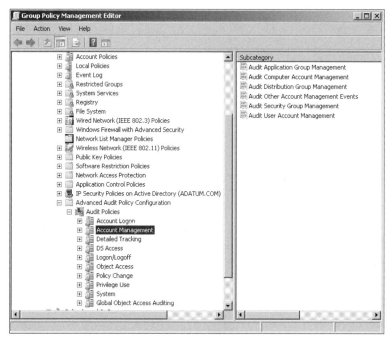

FIGURE 8-18 Account Management configuration

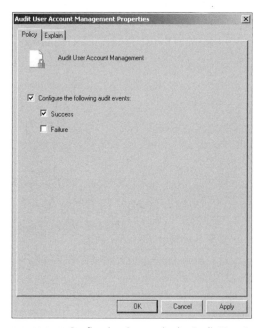

FIGURE 8-19 Configuring Success in the Audit User Account Management Properties dialog box

9. In the Result pane of Group Policy Management Editor, double-click Audit Security Group Management.

10. In the Audit Security Group Management Properties dialog box, select Configure The Following Audit Events, select Success, and then click OK.

11. Close the Group Policy Management Editor. In Administrative Tools, open Active Directory Users And Computers.

12. Expand Adatum.com. Double-click Users. In the Result pane, double-click Domain Admins. Click Add.

13. In the Select Users, Contacts, Service Accounts, Or Groups dialog box, type **Don Hall** in the Enter Object Names To Select box, as shown in Figure 8-20. Click OK. Click OK again to close the Domain Admins Properties dialog box. Close Active Directory Users And Computers.

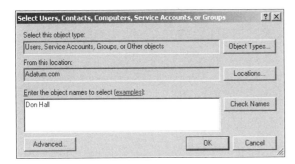

FIGURE 8-20 Adding Don Hall to Domain Admins

14. Open an elevated command prompt. Type **gpupdate /force** and press Enter. Close the elevated command prompt.

15. Log off of VAN-DC1.

EXERCISE 2 Log On as Don Hall and Create a User and a Security Group

In this exercise, you log on as the new domain administrator Don Hall, create a new security group, create a user, and place the user in the security group.

1. Log on to the VAN-DC1 domain controller using the Don Hall user account.

2. In Administrative Tools, open Active Directory Users And Computers.

3. Expand Adatum.com. Right-click Users. Click New and then click Group.

4. In the New Object – Group dialog box, specify the Group Name as **DonGroup**. Accept the default settings of Global and Security, as shown in Figure 8-21, and click OK.

5. In Active Directory Users And Computers, right-click Users, click New, and then click User.

6. Specify the user as **Jim Hance**, as shown in Figure 8-22. If this user already exists, create a user with another name instead. Click Next.

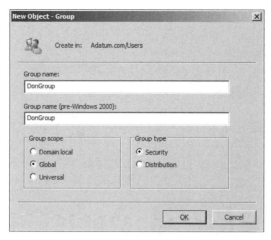

FIGURE 8-21 Creating the DonGroup global security group

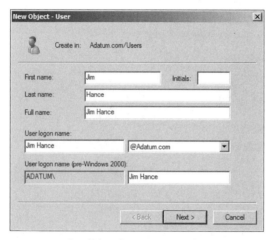

FIGURE 8-22 Specifying the new user as Jim Hance

7. Clear User Must Change Password At Next Logon. Select Password Never Expires. Specify the password as **Pa$$w0rd** in the Password and Confirm Password boxes. Click Next.

8. Click Finish.

9. In Active Directory Users And Computers, double-click Users. In the Result pane, double-click Jim Hance.

10. Click the Member Of tab. Click Add.

11. In the Select Groups dialog box, type **DonGroup** in the Enter Object Names To select box, as shown in Figure 8-23. Click OK.

12. Click OK to close the Jim Hance Properties dialog box. Close Active Directory Users And Computers.

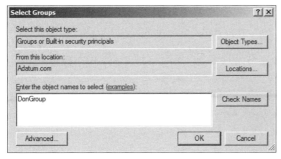

FIGURE 8-23 Adding Jim Hance to the DonGroup security group

13. Open an elevated command prompt. Type **gpupdate /force** and press Enter. Close the elevated command prompt.

15. Log off of VAN-DC1.

EXERCISE 3 Checking User and Security Group Creation

In this exercise, you log in as Kim Akers and audit Don Hall, creating a user and adding that user to a security group.

1. Log on to the VAN-DC1 domain controller using the Kim Akers user account.

2. In Administrative Tools, open Event Viewer.

3. Expand Windows Logs and then double-click Security.

4. Double-click the most recent event on the event list with the Event ID 4720.

5. Check that Event Viewer has recorded that Don Hall created the user account Jim Hance, as shown in Figure 8-24.

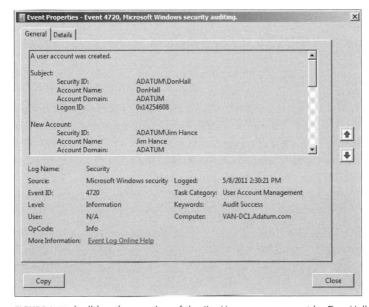

FIGURE 8-24 Auditing the creation of the Jim Hance user account by Don Hall

6. Double-click the most recent event on the event list with the Event ID 4728.

7. Check that Event Viewer has recorded that Don Hall added the user account Jim Hance to the DonGroup security group, as shown in Figure 8-25.

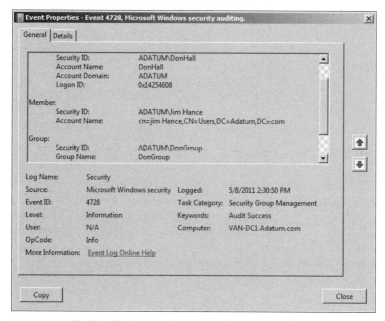

FIGURE 8-25 Checking that Don Hall has added Jim Hance to the DonGroup security group

8. Open Active Directory Users And Computers and remove Don Hall from the Domain Admins security group.

PRACTICE Installing WSUS 3.0 SP2 on Windows Server 2008 R2 (Optional)

In this practice, you install WSUS 3.0 SP2 on a computer running Windows Server 2008 R2. This installation will be configured so that updates are stored on the Microsoft Update servers. This practice is optional because it requires Internet access. You can configure the domain controller VAN-DC1 to access the Internet by adding a second network card, using a wireless connection (if available), or (if you are using virtual machines) adding a virtual network card and configuring Virtual Machine network settings appropriately. This practice also assumes that you have not installed IIS on server VAN-DC1. If IIS has been installed, use the Add Role Services functionality to add additional required components listed in step 7 instead of performing steps 5 and 6.

If you do not want to expose your test network to the Internet, you can download the Report Viewer and WSUS 3.0 SP2 installation files to another computer that can access the Internet and then transfer these files (by using a USB flash memory device or a CD-ROM, for example) to VAN-DC1. You then can install Report Viewer, the IIS server role, and WSUS on

VAN-DC1. However, in this scenario, you cannot run the Windows Software Update Services Configuration Wizard and will need to cancel the exercise at step 15. Because installing WSUS 3.0 SP2 as a role service requires an Internet connection throughout, this practice does not use this method; instead, it installs WSUS from a downloaded installation file.

> **NOTE DOWNLOAD LOCATIONS**
>
> For this practice, you should install Report Viewer 2008 Redistributable rather than Report Viewer 2010 Redistributable. The Report Viewer 2008 Redistributable installation file can be downloaded from *http://www.microsoft.com/downloads/en/ details.aspx?FamilyID=cc96c246-61e5-4d9e-bb5f-416d75a1b9ef*. The WSUS 3.0 SP2 installation file can be downloaded from *http://www.microsoft.com/downloads/en/details .aspx?FamilyId=a206ae20-2695-436c-9578-3403a7d46e40&displaylang=en*. Rather than type in these URLs, it is probably easier to access the Microsoft Download Center at *http://www.microsoft.com/downloads/en/default.aspx* and search for these products.

EXERCISE   Installing WSUS 3.0 SP2

In this exercise, you install Report Viewer, add the IIS role (if necessary), add additional required components to IIS, and install WSUS. To complete the exercise, perform the following steps:

1. Log on to the VAN-DC1 domain controller using the Kim Akers user account.

2. Download the Report Viewer 2008 installer and the WSUS 3.0 SP2 installer (64-bit version) to the C:\Temp folder. (This folder should already exist; if not, create it.)

3. Double-click the Report Viewer installer (ReportViewer.exe) and click Run to start the installation of Report Viewer on server VAN-DC1. Click Yes if prompted by the User Account Control dialog box.

4. Click Next. Accept the terms of the license agreement and then click Install. Click Finish when the installation process completes.

5. If necessary, open Server Manager from the Administrative Tools menu. If prompted, click Yes to close the User Account Control dialog box. In Server Manager, expand Roles. If the Web Server (IIS) role has already been added, click Add Role Services and go to step 7. Otherwise, right-click Roles and click Add Roles.

6. Select the Web Server (IIS) role, as shown in Figure 8-26. Click Next. Read the information presented and then click Next again to access the Select Role Services page.

7. On the Select Role Services page, select ASP.NET. This brings up the dialog box shown in Figure 8-27, asking you to add further role services. Click Add Required Role Services.

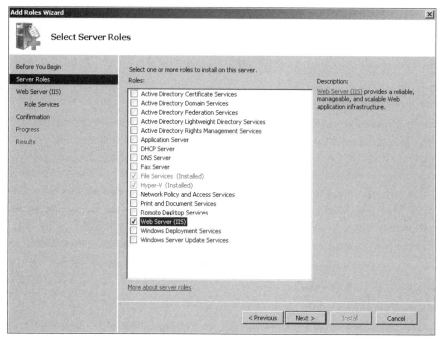

FIGURE 8-26 Selecting the Web Server (IIS) role

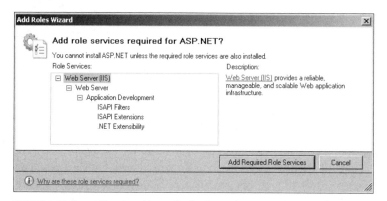

FIGURE 8-27 Prompting to add required role services

8. On the Select Role Services page, under Security, select Windows Authentication. Under Management Tools, select IIS 6 Metabase Compatibility, as shown in Figure 8-28. Click Next.

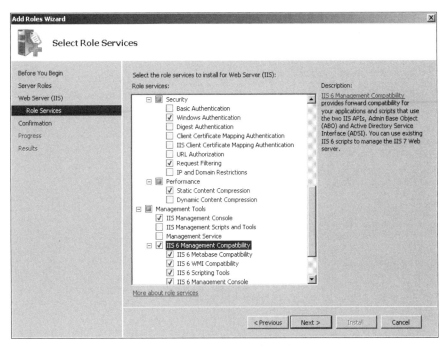

FIGURE 8-28 Specifying Security and Management Tools settings

9. Verify that the features listed in the Confirm Installation Selections dialog box match those shown in Figure 8-29, and then click Install.

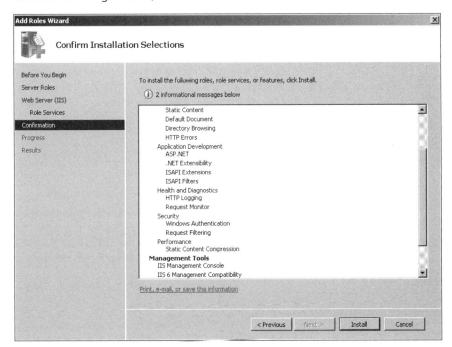

FIGURE 8-29 Preparing IIS for the installation of WSUS

10. When the installation process completes, click Close.

11. In the C:\Temp folder, double-click the WSUS installation file (currently WSUS30-KB972455-x64.exe). If necessary, click Yes to close the User Account Control box and then click Run.

12. The Windows Server Update Services 3.0 SP2 Setup Wizard starts, as shown in Figure 8-30. Click Next.

FIGURE 8-30 The Windows Server Update Services 3.0 SP2 Setup Wizard

13. Select Full Server Installation Including Administration Console. Click Next.

14. Select I Accept The Terms Of The License Agreement. Click Next. If prompted during the installation, click Yes to close the User Account Control dialog box. Click Finish when installation completes.

15. The Windows Software Update Services Configuration wizard automatically starts when the installation of WSUS 3.0 SP2 is complete.

    If you are not connected to the Internet, click Cancel at this point to end the exercise. Otherwise, click Next twice.

16. On the Choose Upstream Server page, select Synchronize From Microsoft Update, as shown in Figure 8-31, and then click Next.

17. On the Specify Proxy Server page, click Next.

18. On the Connect To Upstream Server page, click Start Connecting. The server will contact Microsoft Update to determine the type of updates available, the products that can be updated, and the available languages. When the connection routine completes, click Next.

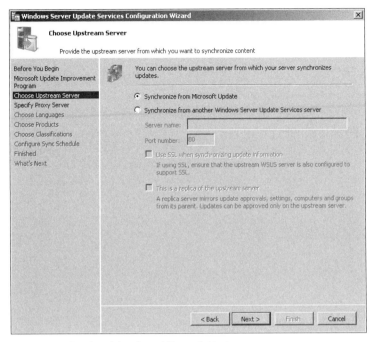

FIGURE 8-31 Synchronizing from Microsoft Update

19. On the Choose Products page, shown in Figure 8-32, select All Products and then click Next.

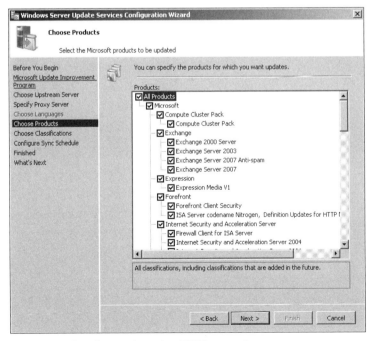

FIGURE 8-32 Choosing products that WSUS can update

20. On the Choose Classifications page, select All Classifications and then click Next.

21. On the Set Sync Schedule page, select Synchronize Manually and then click Next.

22. Ensure that the Launch The Windows Server Update Services Administration Console and Begin Initial Synchronization check boxes are not selected, and then click Finish.

23. Because all the other practice exercises in this book run on an isolated network, it is strongly recommended that you disable the Internet connection on VAN-DC1 when you have finished experimenting with WSUS.

Chapter Review

To further practice and reinforce the skills you learned in this chapter, you can perform the following tasks:

- Review the chapter summary.
- Review the list of key terms introduced in this chapter.
- Complete the case scenarios. These scenarios set up real-world situations involving the topics of this chapter and ask you to create a solution.
- Complete the suggested practices.
- Take a practice test.

Chapter Summary

- Security audit policies enable you to identify security risks posed by malicious or careless insiders and incorrect settings configured by less experienced administrators.
- WSUS Server can be used to centralize the deployment of updates in a Windows Server 2008 R2 environment.
- System Center Configuration Manager 2007 R3 has advanced reporting functionality that can be used to verify that computers meet compliance requirements.

Key Terms

The following terms were introduced in this chapter. Do you know what they mean?

- Autonomous Mode
- Downstream Server
- Encrypting File System (EFS)
- Replica Mode

Case Scenarios

In the following case scenarios, you will apply what you've learned about planning security policies. You can find answers to these questions in the "Answers" section at the end of this book.

Case Scenario 1: Implementing a Security Plan for the Adatum Corporation

You are a senior administrator working for the Adatum Corporation. Adatum hosts websites, specifically sites controlled by government organizations. You are given the task of assessing network and server security at Adatum and are drawing up a plan to improve the security settings that the company currently implements. Answer the following questions.

1. Your plan involves detecting and dealing with policy violations, such as the creation of user accounts outside the proper process, attempts to access files to which a user does not have permission, and the execution of unapproved programs. What do you need to monitor, and what tools do you use to do this?

2. You are planning to use forensic analysis to discover more about attempts to access the Adatum network and discover information to which the attacker should not have access. Some of the data held securely by the Adatum Corporation affects national security. For how long do you need to retain forensic data related to attacks that attempt to access this information?

3. All the servers in the Adatum Corporation's network run Windows Server 2008 R2. The internal network consists of a single domain that contains domain controllers, file and print servers, and database servers. The peripheral network contains Microsoft Exchange Server 2010 servers and web servers. You are implementing protection against DoS attacks. Which servers are the most likely to be attacked in this way and thus most need to be protected?

Case Scenario 2: Deploying WSUS 3.0 SP2 at Fabrikam

After using an ad-hoc approach to patch management over the last few years, the CIO at Fabrikam has decided to upgrade all existing servers running Microsoft Windows 2000 to Windows Server 2008 R2. WSUS 3.0 SP2 also should be deployed. Fabrikam is located in the state of Victoria, Australia. The head office is located in Melbourne, and there are suburban satellite offices in Moonee Ponds, Cheltenham, Endeavour Hills, and Glen Waverley.

The current plan is for a WSUS 3.0 SP2 server to be installed on a host running Windows Server 2008 R2 at the head office and then for a phased rollout of WSUS servers at the suburban satellite offices. Because all the IT staff work in the Melbourne office, the servers at the satellite offices should use the computer group configuration and the update approvals that are configured on the head office server.

One reason for the ad-hoc approach in the past has been that Fabrikam uses custom software that sometimes conflicts with updates, causing the installation of those updates to fail. The CIO wants to be able to run reports on updates from her desktop computer to determine when these events occur. The CIO does not require administrative access to the server and never performs hands-on administrative tasks, always delegating them to the systems administrators on her team.

With this information in mind, answer the following questions.

1. To which local group on the computer running Windows Server 2008 R2 that hosts WSUS should you add the CIO's user account?

2. How should you configure the update source of downstream WSUS servers at the Fabrikam satellite offices?

3. Which type of report should you instruct the CIO to generate to gain detailed information about the specific computers where a particular update's installation has failed?

Suggested Practices

To help you successfully master the exam objectives presented in this chapter, carry out the following practices.

Monitor Server Security

Do all the practices in this section.

- Configure success and failure auditing of privilege use.
- Configure auditing of Account Logon Events and verify that these events are being logged on server VAN-DC1.

Implement a Patch Management Strategy

Complete the following practice exercises:

- Install WSUS 3.0 SP2 on a second computer running Windows Server 2008 R2. (If you configured the VAN-SRV1 member server in previous chapters, you can use that server for this purpose.)
- Configure the second computer running Windows Server 2008 R2 as a downstream replica of the WSUS 3.0 SP2 server (VAN-DC1) that you configured in the practice at the end of the second lesson.
- Synchronize the downstream WSUS server with the upstream server.

Take a Practice Test

The practice tests on this book's companion CD offer many options. For example, you can test yourself on just one exam objective, or you can test yourself on all the 70-646 certification exam content. You can set up the test so that it closely simulates the experience of taking a certification exam, or you can set it up in study mode so that you can look at the correct answers and explanations after you answer each question.

> **MORE INFO**   **PRACTICE TESTS**
>
> For details about all the practice test options available, see the "How to Use the Practice Tests" section in this book's Introduction.

CHAPTER 9

Remote Access and Network Access Protection

You can use VPNs to allow remote users to connect to your organization's internal network resources, whether they are using a hotel wireless hotspot in Gundagai or are connecting through an ADSL connection in Canberra. When you plan how to provision VPN access, you need to take into account a host of factors. You need to know how your organization's external firewall will be configured, the operating system used by the client, and the types of resources that remote clients will need to access.

Network Access Protection (NAP) allows you to restrict network access on the basis of client health. Put simply, NAP allows you to enforce a rule that if the client is not up to date with patches and antivirus definitions, you can block it from getting full access to the network. In this chapter, you will learn how to configure and deploy NAP and the various methods that are available to deal with noncompliant computers. You will also learn how to plan and deploy Windows Server 2008 R2 remote access services to ensure that your organization's clients can connect to your internal resources no matter where in the world they are.

Exam objectives in this chapter:

- Plan infrastructure services server roles.
- Monitor and maintain security and policies.

Lessons in this chapter:

Before You Begin

To complete the exercises in the practice in this chapter, you need to have done the following:

- Complete the setup tasks outlined in Appendix A, "Setup Instructions for Windows Server 2008 R2."

No additional configuration is required for this chapter.

 REAL WORLD

Orin Thomas

Traditional models of networks and firewalls had all the bad stuff "out there" and all the safe stuff "in here." Today, however, the internal network can be as hostile an environment as the Internet. In the past, every computer that connected to the network was stationary, and very few people took their workstations home with them. But today, most computers sold are laptops, and increasing numbers of people take their primary computer with them when they leave the office for the day. Unfortunately, once people take their computers out of the protected glasshouse that is your internal network, all sorts of bad things can happen to them. Malware, which might have been blocked by the external firewall, will be inadvertently downloaded on the home ADSL connection. Computers that you were able to keep completely healthy when they were under your control are now exposed on a daily basis to all manner of Internet nasties. The biggest problem is that after those computers go out of your safe environment, they are brought back into work the next day and are plugged into your organizational network. Technologies such as Windows Firewall with Advanced Security and NAP go some distance toward protecting hosts on your internal network from whatever "the cat drags in" on a regular basis when the people you work with bring their computers back from home. When you plan your organizational security strategy, don't assume that hosts that have a local IP address are any safer than hosts with an Internet IP address unless they've gone through some process, such as NAP, to provide evidence that they are secure.

Lesson 1: Managing Remote Access

If your organization is going to allow workers to telecommute, you need to provide those workers with some way to access resources on your organization's internal network. In this lesson, you will learn how to plan the deployment of VPN servers to allow remote access to your internal network from locations that are external to your organization's network. You will also learn about DirectAccess, a technology available with Windows 7 and Windows Server 2008 R2 that dramatically simplifies the remote access process from the user perspective. The lesson will also cover traditional remote access protocols, including Point to Point Tunneling Protocol (PPTP), Layer 2 Tunneling Protocol/Internet Protocol Security (L2TP/IPsec), Secure Socket Tunneling Protocol (SSTP), and another technology new to Windows Server 2008 R2 called IKEv2.

After this lesson, you will be able to:

- Plan remote access infrastructure server roles.
- Monitor and maintain remote access security policies.
- Implement remote access technologies, including IKEv2 VPNs and DirectAccess.

Estimated lesson time: 60 minutes

The Routing and Remote Access Service (RRAS) role service is available as part of the Network Policy And Access Services server role. You should deploy the Remote Access Service (RAS) component of the RRAS role service when you want to provide either of the following resources to your network environment:

- VPN remote access server
- Dial-up remote access server

In this lesson, you will learn how to configure and monitor a VPN remote access server running Windows Server 2008 and Windows Server 2008 R2. To install the RRAS role service, use the Add Roles Wizard and then select Network Policy And Access Services. RRAS is a role service within this role. As an alternative, open an elevated Windows PowerShell prompt on a computer running Windows Server 2008 R2 and issue the following commands:

```
Import-Module ServerManager
Add-WindowsFeature NPAS-RRAS-Services
```

To remove RRAS completely from a server running Windows Server 2008 R2, issue the command:

```
Remove-WindowsFeature NPAS
```

Once installed, you must configure RAS manually. Only members of the local Administrators group are able to configure the RAS. In domain environments, you should perform this action using a user account that is a member of the Domain Admins group. If your user account is not a member of the Domain Admins security group, organize a domain admin to add the RAS server account manually to the RAS And IAS Servers domain security group. It is not necessary to add the RAS server to this group if the RAS server will be using local authentication or authenticating against a Remote Authentication Dial-In User Service (RADIUS) server.

To enable Remote Access, open the Routing and Remote Access console from the Administrative Tools menu, right-click the computer running Windows Server 2008 R2 that you want to host this role, and then click Configure And Enable Routing And Remote Access. Performing this action starts the Routing And Remote Access Server Setup Wizard. The configuration page of this wizard, shown in Figure 9-1, allows you to select the combination of services that this particular server will provide. The Remote Access (Dial-Up Or VPN) option is selected when you want to provide either remote access option or both options to clients outside your organization.

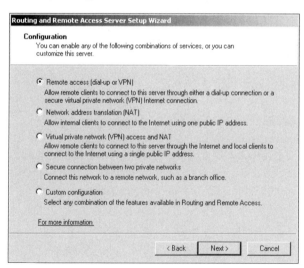

FIGURE 9-1 The Routing And Remote Access Server Setup Wizard

If you have chosen to install a VPN server, you will need to specify which network interface connects to the Internet on the VPN Connection page shown in Figure 9-2. This will be the interface that has the public IP address, rather than the interface that has the private IP address. If additional network adapters are installed on the server that hosts the RAS role after the RAS server is deployed, they can be configured for use with RAS using the RRAS console. If the computer running Windows Server 2008 R2 has fewer than two network adapters, you will not be able to perform a standard VPN server setup and will need to perform a custom configuration instead.

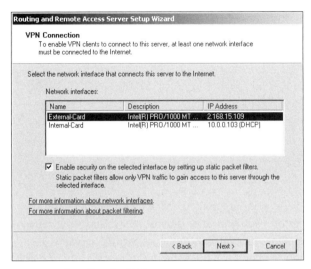

FIGURE 9-2 Installing the RAS

When you configure a remote access server, the process applies packet filters that allow only VPN protocols to the Internet interface. This means that the server is limited to providing VPN access. If you have deployed other services on the server that will host the RAS role, you will need to configure new packet filters to allow this traffic to the server. As a deployment strategy, you should seriously consider keeping the RAS server separate from other services.

After you identify the external interface, the next step in configuring the RAS role is specifying how to assign IP addresses to clients. You can do this in several ways:

- Client addresses can be leased from a DHCP server within the organization.

- The RAS server can generate the addresses itself.

- You can specify a range of addresses to assign to connecting clients.

When using your organization's DHCP infrastructure, the RAS server will lease blocks of 10 addresses, requesting new blocks if previously requested blocks are all currently in use.

DHCP servers running Windows Server 2008 and Windows Server 2008 R2 have a predefined user class, known as the Default Routing And Remote Access Class. This class allows administrators to assign specific options only to Routing And Remote Access clients. This class is configured through the Advanced tab of DHCP Server Options, as shown in Figure 9-3.

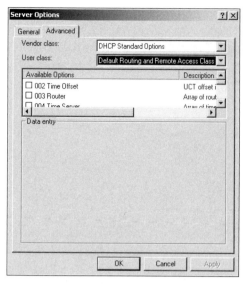

FIGURE 9-3 The RRAS DHCP class

The next step in configuring an RAS server is determining how authentication will occur. You can configure the RAS server to perform authentication against Active Directory Domain Services (AD DS) or the local account database, or you can configure the RAS server as a RADIUS client and allow the RADIUS server to perform the authentication and authorization of client connection requests. You will learn more about RADIUS options later in this lesson. After you have performed these steps, the RAS server will be functional.

VPN Authentication

A VPN is an extension of a private network that encompasses encapsulated, encrypted, and authenticated links across shared or public networks. A client connects to a public network, such as the Internet, and initiates a VPN connection to a remote server. This remote server is usually located on the perimeter network of the organization that the client wants to connect to. After the connection is made, an encrypted tunnel forms between the client and the VPN server. This encrypted tunnel carries local area network (LAN) traffic between the client and the remote network that the client is connected to. Clients are connected to the network in the same way that they would be if they were in the office. Instead of a network cable connecting them to a switch somewhere in the office, a virtual cable in the form of a VPN tunnel connects them to their organization's network infrastructure.

The following authentication protocols can be used by a computer running Windows Server 2008 or Windows Server 2008 R2 to authenticate incoming VPN connections. These protocols are listed in order from most secure to least secure:

- **Extensible Authentication Protocol-Transport Level Security (EAP-TLS)** This is the protocol that you deploy when your VPN clients are able to authenticate using smart cards or digital certificates. EAP-TLS is not supported on stand-alone servers and can be implemented only when the server hosting the RAS role service is a member of an AD DS domain.

- **Microsoft Challenge Handshake Authentication Protocol (MS-CHAPv2)**   This protocol provides mutual authentication and allows for the encryption of both authentication data and connection data. MS-CHAPv2 is enabled by default in Windows Server 2008 and Windows Server 2008 R2.

- **Challenge Handshake Authentication Protocol (CHAP)**   An older authentication method that encrypts authentication data using MD5 hashing. CHAP does not support the encryption of data and is used most often to provide compatibility with older, non-Microsoft clients.

- **Extensible Authentication Protocol-Message Digest 5 Challenge Handshake Authentication Protocol (EAP-MD5 CHAP)**   A version of CHAP that has been ported to the EAP framework. This authentication protocol supports encryption of authentication data through MD5 hashing and is generally used to provide compatibility with non-Microsoft clients.

- **Shiva Password Authentication Protocol (SPAP)**   A weakly encrypted authentication protocol that does not support the encryption of connection data.

- **Password Authentication Protocol (PAP)**   When this protocol is used, authentication data is not encrypted, but is passed across the network in plain text. Does not support the encryption of protection data.

The authentication process always attempts to negotiate the use of the most secure authentication protocol. The default authentication protocol used for VPN clients connecting to a Windows Server 2008 and Windows Server 2008 R2 VPN is MS-CHAPv2.

VPN Protocols

Windows Server 2008 R2 supports four different VPN protocols: Point to Point Tunneling Protocol (PPTP), Layer 2 Tunneling Protocol over IPsec (L2TP/IPsec), Secure Socket Tunneling Protocol (SSTP), and IKEv2. The factors that will influence the protocol you choose to deploy in your own network environment include client operating system, certificate infrastructure, and how your organization's firewall is deployed.

PPTP

PPTP connections can only be authenticated using MS-CHAP, MS-CHAPv2, EAP, and PEAP. PPTP connections use MPPE to encrypt PPTP data. PPTP connections provide data confidentiality but do not provide data integrity or data origin authentication. It is possible to use PPTP with certificates if EAP-TLS is selected as the authentication protocol, although the advantage of PPTP over the other VPN protocols supported by Windows Server 2008 and Windows Server 2008 R2 is that it does not require certificates be installed on the client making the connection. With PPTP, you do not need to be concerned about shared secrets or computer certificates or ensuring that the appropriate Certificate Authority (CA) is trusted. PPTP is often used with non-Microsoft operating systems.

MORE INFO   **PPTP**

For more information on configuring PPTP-based remote access, consult the following TechNet article: *http://technet.microsoft.com/en-us/library/ff687676(WS.10).aspx.*

L2TP/IPsec

L2TP connections use encryption provided by IPsec. L2TP/IPsec is the protocol that you need to deploy if you are supporting remote access clients running Microsoft Windows XP because such clients cannot use SSTP. L2TP/IPsec provides per-packet data origin authentication, data integrity, replay protection, and data confidentiality.

L2TP/IPsec connections use two levels of authentication. Computer-level authentication occurs either using digital certificates issued by a CA trusted by the client and VPN server or through the deployment of preshared keys. PPP authentication protocols are then used for user-level authentication. L2TP/IPsec supports all the VPN authentication protocols available on Windows Server 2008 and Windows Server 2008 R2.

MORE INFO   **L2TP/IPSEC**

To learn more about L2TP/IPsec, consult the following TechNet article: *http://technet.microsoft.com/en-us/library/ff687761(WS.10).aspx.*

SSTP

SSTP is a VPN technology that made its debut with Windows Server 2008 and is available in Windows Server 2008 R2. SSTP VPN tunnels allow traffic to pass across firewalls that block traditional PPTP or L2TP/IPsec VPN traffic. SSTP works by encapsulating PPP traffic over the Secure Sockets Layer (SSL) channel of the Secure Hypertext Transfer Protocol (HTTPS). Expressed more directly, SSTP piggybacks PPP over HTTPS. This means that SSTP traffic passes across TCP port 443, which is almost certain to be open on any firewall between the Internet and a public-facing web server on an organization's perimeter network.

The PPP of SSTP allows for the deployment of advanced authentication methods such as EAP-TLS, which is used most commonly with smart cards. The SSL component of SSTP provides the VPN tunnel with encryption, enhanced key negotiation, and integrity checking. This means data transferred using this method is encoded and that it is possible to detect whether someone has attempted to intercept the contents of the tunnel between the source and destination points.

When planning for the deployment of SSTP, you need to take into account the following considerations:

- SSTP is supported only with Windows Server 2008, Windows Server 2008 R2, Windows 7, and Windows Vista with SP1.
- SSTP requires that the client trust the CA that issues the VPN server's SSL certificate.

- The SSL certificate must be installed on the server that will function as the VPN server prior to the installation of RRAS; otherwise, SSTP will not be available.

- The SSL certificate subject name and the host name that external clients use to connect to the VPN server must match, and the client running Windows 7 or Windows Vista SP1 must trust the issuing CA.

- SSTP does not support tunneling through web proxies that require authentication.

- SSTP does not support site-to-site tunnels. (PPTP and L2TP, however, do.)

> **MORE INFO** **SSTP**
>
> For more information on SSTP, consult the following TechNet article:
> *http://technet.microsoft.com/en-us/library/ff687819(WS.10).aspx.*

IKEv2

IKEv2 is a VPN protocol that is new to Windows 7 and Windows Server 2008 R2. This protocol is not present in previous versions of Windows, and clients running Windows 7 will be able to use this protocol only if the remote access server is running Windows Server 2008 R2. IKEv2 has the following properties:

- Supports IPv6.

- Has a VPN Reconnect feature.

- Supports EAP and computer certificates for client-side authentication. This includes the Microsoft: Protected EAP (PEAP), Microsoft: Secured Password (EAP-MSCHAP v2), and Microsoft Smart Card Or Other Certificate options in the user interface.

- IKEv2 does not support PAP, CHAP, or MS-CHAPv2 (without EAP) as authentication protocols. IKEv2 supports data origin authentication, data integrity, replay protection, and data confidentiality.

- IKEv2 uses UDP port 500.

- When you configure a new Windows 7 VPN connection with the default settings, the client will attempt to make an IKEv2 connection first.

- IKEv2 requires a client running Windows 7 and an RRAS server running Windows Server 2008 R2.

The benefit of using IKEv2 over other protocols is that it supports VPN Reconnect. When you connect to a VPN server using the PPTP, L2TP/IPsec, or SSTP protocol and you suffer a network disruption, you can lose your VPN connection and need to restart it. This often involves reentering your authentication credentials. If you are transferring a file, downloading email, or sending a print job, and something interrupts your connection, you need to start over from the beginning. VPN Reconnect allows clients running Windows 7 to reconnect automatically to a disrupted VPN session even if the disruption has lasted for up to 8 hours.

VPN Reconnect uses the IKEv2 tunneling protocol with the *.mobike* extension. The *.mobike* extension allows VPN clients to change their Internet addresses without having to renegotiate authentication with the VPN server. For example, a user might be using a VPN connection to his corporate network while connected to a wireless network at an airport coffee shop. As the time of his flight's departure approaches, he moves from the coffee shop to the airport lounge, which has its own Wi-Fi network. With VPN Reconnect, the user's VPN connection is reestablished automatically when he achieves Internet connectivity with the new network. With a traditional VPN solution, this user would have to reconnect manually once he connected to the new wireless network in the airport lounge, and any existing operations occurring across the VPN would be lost. Unlike DirectAccess, which only some editions of Windows 7 support, all editions of Windows 7 support IKEv2 with VPN Reconnect.

> **MORE INFO IKEV2**
>
> For more information on setting up IKEv2 VPNs, consult the following TechNet article: *http://technet.microsoft.com/en-us/library/ff687731(WS.10).aspx.*

 Quick Check

- Which clients support SSTP?

Quick Check Answer

- Clients running Windows Vista SP1 and Windows 7 support SSTP.

DirectAccess

DirectAccess is an always-on, IPv6, IPsec VPN connection. If a properly configured computer is able to connect to the Internet, DirectAccess automatically connects that computer to a properly configured corporate network. DirectAccess differs from the VPN solutions outlined earlier in the following ways:

- The connection process is automatic and does not require user intervention or logon. The DirectAccess connection process starts from the moment the computer connects to an active network. From the user's perspective, the computer always has access to the corporate intranet, whether she is sitting at her desk or when she has just connected to a Wi-Fi hotspot at a beachside cafe. Traditionally, users must initiate VPN connections to the corporate intranet manually.

- DirectAccess is bidirectional, with servers on the intranet being able to interact with the client running Windows 7 in the same way that they would if the client was connected to the LAN. In many traditional VPN solutions, the client can access the intranet, but servers on the intranet cannot initiate communication with the client.

- DirectAccess provides administrators with greater flexibility in controlling which intranet resources are available to remote users and computers. Administrators can integrate DirectAccess with NAP to ensure that remote clients remain up to date with virus definitions and software updates. Administrators can also apply connection security policies to isolate servers and hosts.

The DirectAccess process is automatic. It requires no intervention on the part of the person who is logging on to the computer running Windows 7. A portable computer that is taken home and connected to a home Internet network can still receive software and Group Policy updates from servers on the corporate network even if the user has not logged on. Clients running Windows 7 use the following process to establish a DirectAccess connection:

1. The client running Windows 7 configured with DirectAccess connects a network. This occurs prior to user logon when the client running Windows 7 first connects to the network.

2. During the network identification phase, whenever a computer running Windows 7 detects that it is connecting to a new network or resuming a connection to an existing network, the client attempts to connect to a specially configured intranet website. An administrator specifies this website address when configuring DirectAccess on the DirectAccess server. If the client can contact the website, Windows 7 concludes that it has connected to the corporate network and no further action is necessary.

3. If the client running Windows 7 is unable to contact the specially configured intranet website, the client attempts to determine whether a native IPv6 network is present. If a native IPv6 network is present and the client has been assigned a public IPv6 address, DirectAccess makes a direct connection to the DirectAccess server across the Internet.

4. If a native IPv6 network is not present, Windows 7 attempts to establish an IPv6 over IPv4 tunnel using first the 6to4 and then the Teredo transition technologies.

5. If the client running Windows 7 cannot establish a Teredo or 6to4 connection due to an intervening firewall or proxy server, the client running Windows 7 attempts to connect using IP-HTTPS. IP-HTTPS encapsulates IPv6 traffic over an HTTPS connection. IP-HTTPS is likely to work because few firewalls that allow connections to the Internet block traffic on TCP port 443.

6. The DirectAccess IPsec session is established when the client running Windows 7 and the DirectAccess server authenticate with each other using computer certificates. DirectAccess supports only certificate-based authentication.

7. The DirectAccess server checks the appropriate AD DS group to verify that the computer and user have authorization to connect using DirectAccess.

8. The DirectAccess client now has access to appropriately configured resources on the corporate network.

Table 9-1 summarizes DirectAccess client configurations and the corresponding method of communicating using IPv6 with the DirectAccess server. When you configure the DirectAccess server, you configure it to support all these different connection methods. You do this because you cannot be certain of what conditions exist on the remote network from which the DirectAccess client is attempting to connect. IP-HTTPS is tried last because it provides a poorer performance compared to the other connection methods.

TABLE 9-1 DirectAccess Connection Methods

CLIENT NETWORK CONNECTION	DIRECTACCESS CONNECTION METHOD
Public IPv6 Address	Public IPv6 Address
Public IPv4 Address	6to4
Private (NAT) IPv4 Address	Teredo
Client unable to connect through firewall, but is connected to the Internet	IP-HTTPS

Only domain-joined clients running Windows 7 Enterprise and Ultimate editions support DirectAccess. You cannot use DirectAccess with other editions of Windows 7 or earlier versions of Windows, such as Windows Vista or Windows XP. When configuring a client for DirectAccess, you must add the client's domain computer account to a special security group. You specify this security group when running the DirectAccess wizard on the DirectAccess server.

Clients receive their DirectAccess configuration through Group Policy. This differs from traditional VPN configuration, where connections are configured manually or distributed through the Connection Manager Administration Kit (CMAK). Once you have added the computer's client account to the designated security group, you need to install a computer certificate on the client for the purpose of DirectAccess authentication. An organization needs to deploy Active Directory Certificate Services (AD CS) so that clients can enroll automatically with the appropriate certificates.

You configure DirectAccess primarily by configuring the DirectAccess server. When you configure the DirectAccess server, you also end up configuring the necessary Group Policy objects (GPOs) that support DirectAccess. Prior to installing DirectAccess, you should ensure that the DirectAccess server meets the following requirements:

- The computer needs to have Windows Server 2008 R2 installed and be a member of a domain.
- This server must have two network adapters.
- One of these network adapters needs to have a direct connection to the Internet. You must assign this adapter two consecutive public IPv4 addresses.
- The second network adapter needs a direct connection to the corporate intranet.
- The computer needs digital certificates to support server authentication. This includes having a computer certificate that matches the fully qualified domain name (FQDN) that is assigned to the IP addresses on the DirectAccess server's external network interface.

You should also create at least one global security group in AD DS that you use with DirectAccess. You can give this group any name that you like, although it is easier to keep track of it if you give it a DirectAccess-related name. It is possible to create and specify multiple DirectAccess-related security groups if necessary. You create multiple groups when you need to differentiate access to segments of the corporate intranet.

To install DirectAccess on a server running Windows Server 2008 R2, add the DirectAccess Management Console feature using the Add Features Wizard or the following PowerShell command:

```
Add-WindowsFeature DAMC
```

Installing the DirectAccess Management console allows you to configure and manage DirectAccess features. Installing the DirectAccess Management console also requires that you add the Group Policy Management feature. The Group Policy Management feature is necessary because the DirectAccess setup wizard creates DirectAccess-related GPOs that configure DirectAccess clients. You need to run the DirectAccess Setup wizard with a user account that has permission to create and apply GPOs in the domain.

After you have installed the DirectAccess Management console, you can configure the DirectAccess server. To do this, perform the following steps:

1. Open the DirectAccess Management console from the Administrative Tools menu on the computer running Windows Server 2008 R2. This console is shown in Figure 9-4.

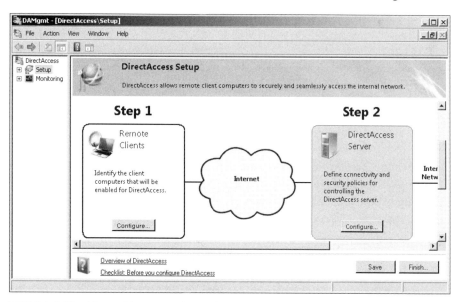

FIGURE 9-4 DirectAccess Management console

2. Select the Setup node. In the details pane, in the Remote Clients area, click Configure. This opens the DirectAccess Client Setup dialog box. Click Add and then specify the name of the security groups to which you add computer accounts when you want to

grant access to DirectAccess to specific clients running Windows 7. These groups can have any names.

3. Use the DirectAccess Server Setup item to specify which interface is connected to the Internet and which interface is connected to the internal network. Performing this step will enable IPv6 transition technologies on the DirectAccess server, as shown in Figure 9-5. You use this item to specify the CA that client certificates must ultimately come from, either directly or through a subordinate CA. You also must specify the server certificate used to secure IP-HTTPS traffic.

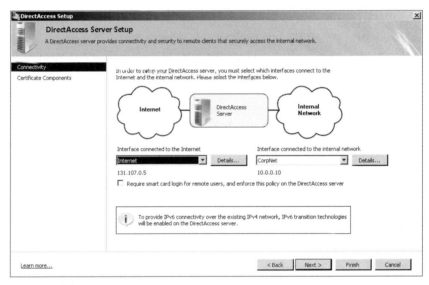

FIGURE 9-5 DirectAccess Server Setup

4. On the Infrastructure Server Setup page, you specify the location of the internal website (known as the Network Location Server) that DirectAccess clients attempt to contact to determine whether they are connected to the corporate intranet or a remote location. You must ensure that you secure this website with a web server certificate. You also use this dialog box to specify which DNS servers and domain controllers the DirectAccess clients are able to contact for authentication purposes.

5. The final step involves specifying which resources on the corporate intranet are accessible to DirectAccess clients. The default setting is to allow access to all resources. In more secure environments, it is possible to use isolation policies to limit the contact to the membership of specific security groups. For example, you might create a security group and add the computer accounts of some file servers and mail servers, but not others.

6. When you click Finish, DirectAccess interfaces with a domain controller and creates two new GPOs in the domain. The first of these is targeted at the security groups that contain the computer accounts of DirectAccess clients. The second GPO is targeted at the DirectAccess server itself.

DirectAccess relies upon several other components in a Windows Server 2008 R2 network infrastructure. The domain in which you install the DirectAccess server must also have the following:

- At least one domain controller running Windows Server 2008 R2 and a DNS server on the internal network
- A server running Windows Server 2008 or later with AD CS installed, either as an Enterprise Root CA or an Enterprise Subordinate CA

To make internal network resources available to remote DirectAccess clients, you need to do one of the following:

- Ensure that all internal resources that will be accessed by DirectAccess support IPv6.
- Deploy ISATAP on the intranet, which allows intranet servers and applications to be reached by tunneling IPv6 traffic over an IPv4 intranet.
- Deploy a NAT-PT device, which allows hosts that support only IPv4 addresses to be accessible to DirectAccess clients using IPv6.

All application servers that DirectAccess clients access need to allow ICMPv6 traffic in Windows Firewall with Advanced Security (WFAS). You can accomplish this by enabling the following firewall rules using Group Policy:

- Echo Request – ICMPv6-in
- Echo Request – ICMPv6-out

The following ports on an organization's external firewall must be open to support DirectAccess:

- **UDP port 3544**   Enables Teredo traffic
- **IPv4 protocol 41**   Enables 6to4 traffic
- **TCP port 443**   Allows IP-HTTPS traffic
- **ICMPv6 and IPv4 protocol 50**   Required when remote clients have IPv6 addresses

> *MORE INFO*   **DIRECTACCESS**
>
> To learn more about DirectAccess, consult the following TechNet article:
> *http://technet.microsoft.com/en-us/network/dd420463.aspx.*

NPS RADIUS Servers

In addition to its ability to provide RRAS gateways, Network Policy Server (NPS) can function as a RADIUS server and as a RADIUS client, which also is known as a RADIUS proxy. When an organization has more than one remote access server, an administrator can configure a server that has NPS installed as a RADIUS server and then configure all remote access servers as RADIUS clients. The benefit of doing this is that network policy management is centralized rather than requiring management on a per-remote-access-server basis.

When RADIUS is used as an authentication provider for RAS servers, the connection request is sent in a RADIUS request message format to a RADIUS server. The RADIUS server performs the authentication and authorization and then passes this information back to the RAS server. The RADIUS server must be a member of an AD DS domain, but the RAS VPN server passing authentication requests to the RADIUS server can be a stand-alone computer.

NPS and RADIUS clients

RADIUS clients are network access servers such as VPN servers, wireless access points, and 802.1x authenticating switches. Although the computers that access these network access servers are called *remote access clients*, they are not considered RADIUS clients. RADIUS clients provide network access to other hosts.

To configure a RADIUS client using NPS, open the Network Policy Server console from the Administrative Tools menu. Right-click RADIUS Clients and then click New RADIUS Client. This will open the dialog box shown in Figure 9-6.

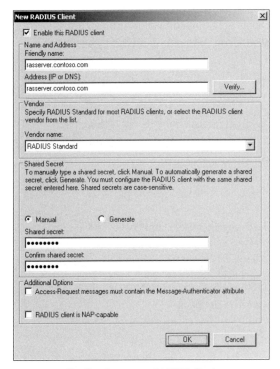

FIGURE 9-6 Configuring a new RADIUS client

Configuration involves providing the following information:

- Friendly Name
- Address (IP or DNS)
- Vendor Name (with more than 20 separate vendors available in this drop-down menu)
- Shared Secret (configured using the NPS snap-in on the RADIUS client)

NPS as a RADIUS Proxy

RADIUS proxies route RADIUS messages between remote access servers configured as RADIUS clients and the RADIUS servers that perform authentication, authorization, and accounting. When configured as a RADIUS proxy, an NPS will record information in the accounting log about the messages that it passes on from RAS clients to the RADIUS servers. NPS functions as a RADIUS client when it is configured as a RADIUS proxy.

You should deploy NPS as a RADIUS proxy when you need to provide authentication and authorization for accounts from other AD DS forests. The NPS RADIUS proxy uses the realm name (which identifies the location of the user account) portion of a user name to forward the request to a RADIUS server in the target forest. This allows connection attempts for user accounts in one forest to be authenticated for the network access server in another forest. Using a RADIUS proxy for inter-forest authentication is not necessary when both forests are running at the Windows Server 2003 functional level or higher and a forest trust exists.

You should also deploy NPS as a RADIUS proxy when you need authentication and authorization to occur against a database other than the Windows account database. Connection requests that match a specific realm name are forwarded to a RADIUS server, often running on a platform other than Windows, that accesses a separate database of user accounts and authorization data. Hence, you would deploy NPS as a RADIUS proxy when authentication and authorization have to occur against a RADIUS server that uses Novell Directory Services or one that runs on UNIX.

A final reason to consider the deployment of NPS as a RADIUS proxy server is when you need to process a large number of connection requests between RAS RADIUS clients and RADIUS servers. An NPS RADIUS proxy can load balance traffic across multiple RADIUS servers—something that is difficult to configure when dealing with just RADIUS clients and RADIUS servers.

Remote Access Accounting

You can configure NPS to perform RADIUS accounting. RADIUS accounting allows you to keep track of who is connecting and who has failed to connect to your RADIUS infrastructure. You can use NPS accounting to monitor the following information:

- User authentication requests
- Access-Accept messages

- Access-Reject messages
- Accounting requests and responses
- Periodic status updates

As Figure 9-7 shows, you have two separate ways of recording log data. Logs can be stored locally or written to a database in Microsoft SQL Server 2005 SP1, SQL Server 2008, or SQL Server 2008 R2. Locally written logs are suitable if you have a small number of remote access clients. If you have a significant number of remote access clients, writing data to a SQL Server database will provide you with a much better way of managing what is likely to be a mountain of information.

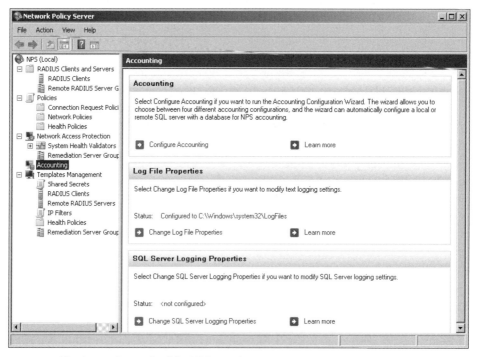

FIGURE 9-7 The Accounting node of the NPS console

Local File Logging

NPS log files can be written in two formats: IAS and database-compatible. The default format is database-compatible. The frequency at which new log files are created should be adjusted to suit your organization's needs. The benefit of having a single file of unlimited size is that locating a specific event is simpler, because you have to search for only one log file. The drawback of larger log files is that on systems where a log of NPS accounting data is logged, the log files can become huge, making the process of opening them and searching them difficult.

Although logs are written by default to the %Systemroot%/System32/LogFiles folder, Microsoft recommends that you keep log files on a partition separate from the operating system and application or file share data. Log files, unless strictly monitored, have a way of filling all available disk space. If this happens on a critical partition, the server could become unavailable. It is very important to note that NPS accounting data logs are not deleted automatically. You can configure the log retention policy to ensure that older log files are deleted automatically when the disk is full. This works best when log files are written to an isolated partition, so that the only impact of a disk that is full of NPS log files is on the storage of existing NPS log files. If NPS log files must be stored on a partition with other data or on the same volume as the operating system, you should consider writing a script that automatically removes logs when they reach a certain age.

Log files can be written to remote shares. This is done by specifying the UNC path of the share. If you configure this option, it will be necessary to ensure that the share permissions are configured to allow the account that writes the logs to write data to the shared folder. The Log File tab of the Local File Logging properties dialog box is shown in Figure 9-8.

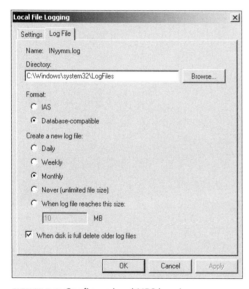

FIGURE 9-8 Configure local NPS logging

Configure SQL Server Logging

The alternative to logging NPS accounting data locally is to have it written to a computer running SQL Server that is installed either locally or on the local network. NPS sends data to the *report_event* stored procedure on the target computer running SQL Server. This stored procedure is available on SQL Server 2000, SQL Server 2005, SQL Server 2008, and SQL Server 2008 R2.

You can configure which NPS accounting data is sent to the computer running SQL Server by selecting options in the SQL Server Logging properties dialog box shown in Figure 9-9. Clicking Configure in this dialog box allows you to specify the properties of the data link to the computer running SQL Server. When configuring the data link properties for the SQL Server connection, you must provide the server name, the method of authentication that will be used with the computer running SQL Server, and the database on the computer running SQL Server that you will use to store the accounting data. Just as it is a good idea to have a separate partition on a computer to store NPS accounting data, it is a good idea to have a separate database that stores NPS accounting data.

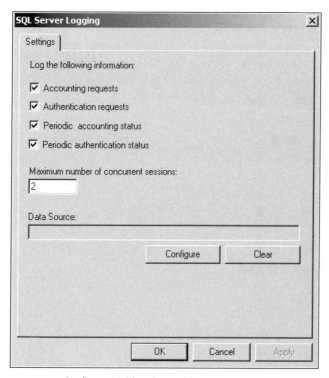

FIGURE 9-9 Configure NPS logging to SQL Server

> **MORE INFO   NPS CHANGES IN WINDOWS SERVER 2008 R2**
>
> For more information about the changes to NPS in Windows Server 2008 R2, consult the following TechNet article: *http://technet.microsoft.com/en-us/library/ dd365355(WS.10).aspx.*

Remote Desktop Gateway Servers

Remote Desktop Gateway (RD Gateway) servers allow Remote Desktop Protocol (RDP) over HTTPS connections to RDP servers located on protected internal networks to clients on the Internet. This functionality allows clients on the Internet to access RemoteApp applications, standard Remote Desktop Server sessions, and remote desktop sessions to appropriately configured clients.

An advantage of RD Gateway is that you do not need to set up RAS VPNs to grant access to resources. Instead of having to deploy client connection kits to everyone in the organization that needs to be able to access resources from the Internet side of the firewall, you can email them an RDP shortcut file and allow them to connect with their clients running Windows XP SP2, Windows Vista, or Windows 7. RD Gateway is essentially an SSL VPN that is restricted to RDP. With a regular VPN connection, you can access all resources directly once connected (in theory, anyway). For example, a VPN can be used to connect to internal file shares and shared printers. With RD Gateway, you can access an RDS server or remote desktop session and, through that, access resources such as shared drives and printers.

Follow these steps to configure an RD Gateway server:

1. Install the RD Gateway Role Service on a computer running Windows Server 2008 R2 that is located on a screened subnet. The perimeter firewall should be configured so that the RD Gateway server is accessible on port 443.

2. Obtain an SSL certificate. The certificate name must match the name that clients use to connect to the server. Install the certificate on the server and then use the RD Gateway Manager console to map the server certificate. It is important that you only use RD Gateway Manager to map the SSL certificate. If you use another method, the RD Gateway server will not function properly.

3. Configure Remote Desktop Connection Authorization Policies (RD-CAPs) and Remote Desktop Resource Authorization Policies (RD-RAPs). (These are covered in the next section.)

Connection Authorization Policies

Remote Desktop Connection Authorization Policies (RD-CAPs) specify which users are allowed to connect through the RD Gateway server to resources located on your organization's internal network. This is usually done by specifying a local group on the RD Gateway server or a group within AD DS. Groups can include user or computer accounts. You can also use RD-CAPs to specify whether remote clients use password or smart-card authentication to access internal network resources through the RD Gateway server. You can use RD-CAPs in conjunction with NAP; this scenario is covered in more detail in Lesson 2, "Firewalls and Network Access Protection."

Resource Authorization Policies

Remote Desktop Resource Authorization Policies (RD-RAPs) are used to determine the specific resources on an organization's network that an incoming RD Gateway client can connect to. When you create an RD-RAP, you specify a group of computers that you want to grant access to and the group of users that you will allow this access to. For example, you could create a group of computers called AccountsComputers that will be accessible to members of the Accountants user group. To be granted access to internal resources, a remote user must meet the conditions of at least one RD-CAP and at least one RD-RAP.

Lesson Summary

- SSTP piggybacks PPP over HTTPS. The SSL certificate installed on the RAS server must match the host name that the SSTP client is connecting to. SSTP can be used only by clients running Windows 7 and Windows Vista SP1. SSTP cannot be used for site-to-site tunnels.
- IKEv2 VPNs can be used only by clients running Windows 7 that are connected to VPN servers running Windows Server 2008 R2. IKEv2 VPNs support the VPN Reconnect feature.
- DirectAccess is an always-on IPv6 remote access technology. DirectAccess is supported only on Windows 7 Enterprise and Ultimate editions and requires a DirectAccess server running Windows Server 2008 R2.
- NPS servers can be configured to write accounting data to local log files or to computers running SQL Server that have the *report_event* stored procedure available.
- RADIUS proxies are a useful way of load balancing requests from RAS servers to RADIUS servers.
- RD Gateway servers provide another method of remote access, allowing clients running Windows Vista to connect to RDP servers using port 443.

Lesson Review

You can use the following questions to test your knowledge of the information in Lesson 1, "Managing Remote Access." The questions are also available on the companion CD if you prefer to review them in electronic form.

> **NOTE** **ANSWERS**
>
> Answers to these questions and explanations of why each answer choice is correct or incorrect are located in the "Answers" section at the end of the book.

1. Which of the following VPN protocols would you deploy if your firewall blocked all traffic from the Internet except traffic on TCP ports 25, 80, and 443?
   - **A.** L2TP/IPsec
   - **B.** SSTP

C. PPTP

D. IKEv2

2. Users at your organization have all been issued laptops running Windows 7 Enterprise edition. These users often need to place their computers into hibernation and do not want to have to reauthenticate to access their VPN connection when they resume using them. Which of the following VPN protocols allows users to reconnect to a VPN session that they initiated in the last few hours when they resume from hibernation?

A. L2TP/IPsec

B. SSTP

C. PPTP

D. IKEv2

3. Which of the following clients can connect to your organization's VPN server running Windows Server 2008 R2 if the only ports that are available for VPN connections are ports 25, 80, and 443? (Each answer is a complete solution. Choose all that apply.)

A. Windows Vista with SP1

B. Windows 7

C. Windows XP Professional with SP3

D. Microsoft Windows 2000 Professional with SP2

4. Servers VPN1, VPN2, and VPN3 host the RAS server role and accept incoming VPN connections from clients on the Internet. Server NPS1 is configured as a RADIUS server using the NPS server role. Servers VPN1, VPN2, and VPN3 use NPS1 to authenticate incoming connections. Server SQL1 is a computer running Windows Server 2008 R2 that has SQL Server 2008 R2 installed. You want to improve your ability to search through RADIUS accounting data. Which of the following strategies should you pursue?

A. Configure VPN1, VPN2, and VPN3 so that NPS accounting data is forwarded to SQL1.

B. Configure VPN1, VPN2, and VPN3 so that NPS accounting data is forwarded to NPS1.

C. Configure SQL1 so that NPS accounting data is forwarded to server NPS1.

D. Configure NPS1 so that NPS accounting data is forwarded to server SQL1.

5. Computers running which of the following operating systems are able to use DirectAccess to access your organization's internal network from locations on the Internet?

A. Windows XP Professional with SP3

B. Windows Vista Enterprise edition

C. Windows 7 Enterprise edition

D. Windows 7 Home Premium edition

Lesson 2: Firewalls and Network Access Protection

You deploy NAP on your network as a method of ensuring that computers accessing important resources meet certain client health benchmarks. These benchmarks include (but are not limited to) having the most recent updates applied, having antivirus and anti-spyware software up to date, and having important security technologies such as Windows Firewall configured and functional. In this lesson, you will learn how to plan and deploy an appropriate NAP infrastructure and enforcement method for your organization.

After this lesson, you will be able to:

- Plan NAP server roles.
- Monitor and maintain NAP policies.

Estimated lesson time: 60 minutes

Windows Firewall with Advanced Security

The simplest method of enforcing a standardized firewall configuration across an organization is to use Group Policy. You can configure inbound and outbound rules, as well as enable and disable Windows Firewall with Advanced Security for specific profiles, through the Computer Configuration/Policies/Windows Settings/Windows Firewall With Advance Security node of Group Policy.

You can configure new rules based on a specific program, port, or predefined rule. Rules can be applied to inbound and outbound traffic. In many domain environments, administrators use outbound rules as a way of blocking the use of specific programs such as file sharing or instant messaging programs. Although the best way to block this sort of traffic is to stop the software from being installed in the first place or restricting its use with AppLocker policies, many domain environments have users with laptops that are taken on and off the network. In some cases, laptop users are given local administrative control over their computers. Applying firewall rules to each computer through Group Policy allows administrators to block programs that may use SSL tunnels to get around perimeter firewall configuration.

> **MORE INFO CONFIGURE WINDOWS FIREWALL THROUGH GROUP POLICY**
>
> To learn more about configuring Windows Firewall with Advanced Security through Group Policy, consult the following TechNet article: *http://technet.microsoft.com/en-us/library/ff602918(WS.10).aspx.*

Domain Isolation

Windows Firewall with Advanced Security can be used to create connection security rules that secure traffic by using IPsec. Domain isolation uses an AD DS domain, domain membership, and Windows Firewall with Advanced Security Group Policy settings to enforce a policy that forces domain member computers to accept incoming communication requests only from other computers that are members of the same domain. When enforced, computers that are members of the domain are isolated from computers that are not members of the domain. It is important to remember that in domain isolation scenarios, isolated computers can initiate communication with hosts outside the domain, such as web servers on the Internet. However, they will not respond when network communication is initiated from a host outside the domain.

Domain isolation policies are applied through the Computer Configuration/Policies/ Windows Settings/Security Settings/Windows Firewall with Advanced Security node of a GPO by accessing the Connection Security Rules item.

> **MORE INFO** **DOMAIN ISOLATION**
>
> To learn more about domain isolation, consult the following TechNet article:
> *http://technet.microsoft.com/en-us/library/cc730709(WS.10).aspx.*

Server Isolation

Server isolation works in a similar way to domain isolation except that instead of applying to all computers within a domain, a server isolation policy applies only to a specific set of servers in a domain. You do this by placing the computer accounts of the servers that will be isolated in a specific OU and then applying a GPO that has an appropriately configured connection security rule to that OU. When enforced, only computers that are members of the domain are able to communicate with the isolated servers. This can be an effective way of protecting servers when you must grant network access to third-party computers. The third-party computers are able to access some network resources, such as intranet web and DNS servers, but you can isolate specific network resources, such as file servers and databases, by configuring server isolation policies.

> **MORE INFO** **SERVER ISOLATION**
>
> To learn more about domain isolation, consult the following TechNet article:
> *http://technet.microsoft.com/en-ca/library/cc770626(WS.10).aspx.*

Forefront Threat Management Gateway

While Windows Firewall with Advanced Security is an appropriate solution to protect individual servers, you should look toward a more fully featured firewall, such as Microsoft Forefront Threat Management Gateway (TMG) 2010, as a solution between your organization's perimeter network and the Internet. Perimeter networks are networks that exist between the Internet and an organization's internal network. Organizations host resources that need to be available to the Internet on perimeter networks. This allows them to provide an external firewall to protect the resource and then also to provide a firewall between the perimeter network and the internal network as a second layer of protection. In most configurations, traffic can pass from the Internet to the perimeter network and back, or from the internal network to the perimeter network and back, but never directly from the internal network to the Internet without passing in some way across the perimeter network.

Forefront TMG 2010 includes the following advanced features:

- Packet inspection and application filtering

- Intrusion Prevention System (IPS)

- Secure proxy

- Web filtering based on URL or URL category (for example, filtering sports or entertainment websites)

- Web traffic monitoring

- HTTPS inspection

- Publish reverse proxy services to the Internet, such as websites, Microsoft Outlook Web Access, and Microsoft SharePoint sites including SSL bridge functionality

- Create site-to-site VPNs

- The ability to publish VPN servers to the Internet

You can install Forefront TMG 2010 on computers running Windows Server 2008 with SP2 or Windows Server 2008 R2. When you install Forefront TMG 2010, the installation routine automatically installs the Network Policy Server, RRAS, and Active Directory Lightweight Directory Services (AD LDS) roles and role services.

Usually, you would install Forefront TMG on a computer that has two network cards, with one computer connected to the Internet and the other network adapter connected to your perimeter or internal network. It is possible to deploy Forefront TMG on a computer with a single network adapter, but in general, you would do this only when you have deployed an additional perimeter firewall solution. ForeFront TMG is the latest version of the product once known as Microsoft Internet Security and Acceleration (ISA) Server. You manage Forefront TMG using the Forefront TMG console, shown in Figure 9-10.

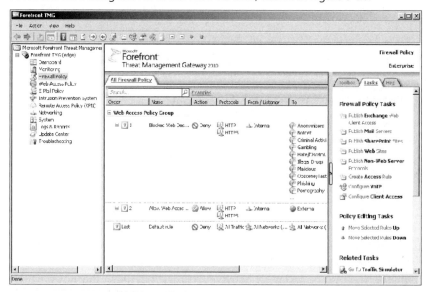

FIGURE 9-10 The Forefront TMG console

MORE INFO **FOREFRONT TMG 2010**

To learn more about Forefront TMG 2010, consult the following TechNet website:
http://technet.microsoft.com/en-us/library/ff355324.aspx.

Network Access Protection

Network Access Protection (NAP) is a technology that allows you to restrict network access
on the basis of a client's health. System Health Agents (SHAs) and System Health Validators
(SHVs) are the components that validate a computer's health against a configured set of
benchmarks. The SHV specifies which benchmarks the client must meet. The SHA is the
component against which those benchmarks are tested. The SHVs in Windows 7, Windows
Vista, and Windows XP can be configured through the System Health Validators node
under NAP in the NPS. Figure 9-11 shows the settings that you can configure for the SHV in
Windows 7 and Windows Vista.

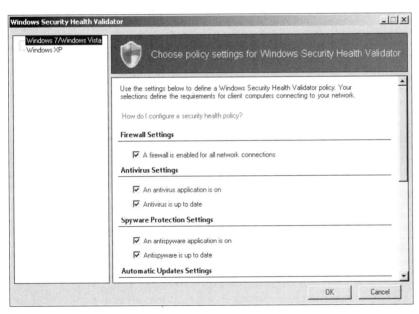

FIGURE 9-11 An SHV in Windows 7 and Windows Vista

Third-party organizations can provide SHAs and SHVs that you can use with their
own products and NAP. Deploying third-party SHAs and SHVs involves installing the SHA
components on all clients and the SHV on the computer running Windows Server 2008 or
Windows Server 2008 R2 that hosts the Network Policy Server server role. Once installed,
you create a new health policy that uses the new SHV as a compliance benchmark. A health
policy can call on multiple SHVs. For example, you might create a health policy that requires
all conditions on the SHV on Windows 7 or Windows Vista and the Fabrikam SHV to be met
before a client is granted access to all network resources.

NAP Enforcement Methods

When a computer is found to be noncompliant with the enforced health policy, NAP enforces limited network access. This is done through an Enforcement Client (EC). Windows 7, Windows Vista, Windows XP SP3, Windows Server 2008, and Windows Server 2008 R2 include NAP EC support for IPsec, IEEE 802.1X, Remote Access VPN, and DHCP enforcement methods. Windows 7, Windows Vista, Windows Server 2008, and Windows Server 2008 R2 also support NAP enforcement for RD Gateway connections.

NAP enforcement methods can be used either individually or in conjunction with each other to limit the network access of computers that are found not to be in compliance with configured health policies. Hence, you can apply the remote access VPN and IPsec enforcement methods to ensure that internal clients and clients coming in from the Internet are granted access to resources only if they meet the appropriate client health benchmarks.

IPsec NAP Enforcement

IPsec enforcement works by applying IPsec rules. Only computers that meet health compliance requirements are able to communicate with each other. IPsec enforcement can be applied on a per-IP address, per-TCP port number, or per-UDP port number basis. For example: You can use IPsec enforcement to block RDP access to a web server so that only computers that are healthy can connect to manage that server but allow clients that do not meet health requirements to connect to view Web pages hosted by the same web server.

IPsec enforcement applies after computers have received a valid IP address, either from DHCP or through static configuration. IPsec is the strongest method of limiting network access communication through NAP. Where it might be possible to subvert other methods by applying static addresses or switching ports, the IPsec certificate used for encryption can be obtained by a host only when it passes the health check. No IPsec certificate means that communication with other hosts that encrypt their communications using a certificate issued from the same CA is impossible.

To deploy IPsec enforcement, a network environment must have a Windows Server 2008 or 2008 R2 Health Registration Authority (HRA) and a Windows Server 2008 or Windows Server 2008 R2 CA. Clients must be running Windows 7, Windows Vista, Windows Server 2008, Windows Server 2008 R2, or Windows XP SP3, all of which include the IPsec EC.

802.1X NAP Enforcement

802.1X enforcement uses authenticating Ethernet switches or IEEE 802.11 Wireless Access Points. These compliant switches and access points grant unlimited network access only to computers that meet the compliance requirement. Computers that do not meet the compliance requirement are limited in their communication by a restricted access profile. Restricted access profiles work by applying IP packet filters or virtual local area network (VLAN) identifiers. This means that hosts that have the restricted access profile are allowed only limited network communication. This limited network communication generally allows access to remediation servers. You will learn more about remediation servers later in this lesson.

An advantage of 802.1X enforcement is that the health status of clients is assessed constantly. Connected clients that become noncompliant will be placed under the restricted access profile automatically. Clients under the restricted access profile that become compliant will have that profile removed and will be able to communicate with other hosts on the network in an unrestricted manner. For example, suppose that a new antivirus update comes out. Clients that have not checked the update server recently are put under a restricted access profile until they check the server and retrieve the update. Once the check has been performed successfully, the clients are returned to full network access.

A computer running Windows Server 2008 or Windows Server 2008 R2 with the Network Policy Server role is necessary to support 802.1X NAP enforcement. It is also necessary to have switch or Wireless Access Point hardware that is 801.1X-compliant. Clients must be running Windows 7, Windows Vista, Windows Server 2008 R2, Windows Server 2008, or Windows XP SP3 because only these operating systems include the EAPHost EC.

> **MORE INFO 802.1X ENFORCEMENT**
>
> To learn more about 802.1X enforcement, consult the following TechNet page: *http://technet.microsoft.com/en-us/library/cc770861.aspx.*

VPN NAP Enforcement

VPN enforcement is used on connecting VPN clients as a method of ensuring that clients granted access to the internal network meet system health compliance requirements. VPN enforcement works by restricting network access to noncompliant clients through the use of packet filters. Rather than being able to access the entire network, incoming VPN clients that are noncompliant have access only to the remediation server group.

As is the case with 802.1X enforcement, the health status of a connected client is monitored continuously. If a client becomes noncompliant, packet filters restricting network access will be applied. If a noncompliant client becomes compliant, packet filters restricting network access will be removed. VPN enforcement requires an existing remote access infrastructure and an NPS server. The enforcement method uses the VPN EC, which is included with Windows 7, Windows Vista, Windows Server 2008, Windows Server 2008 R2, and Windows XP SP3.

MORE INFO   VPN ENFORCEMENT

To learn more about VPN enforcement, consult the following TechNet page:
http://technet.microsoft.com/en-us/library/cc753622.aspx.

DHCP NAP Enforcement

DHCP NAP enforcement works by providing unlimited-access IPv4 address information to compliant computers and limited-access IPv4 address information to noncompliant computers. Unlike VPN and 802.1X enforcement methods, DHCP NAP enforcement is applied only when a client lease is obtained or renewed. Organizations using this method of NAP enforcement should avoid configuring long DHCP leases because this will reduce the frequency at which compliance checks are made.

To deploy DHCP NAP enforcement, you must use a DHCP server running Windows Server 2008 or Windows Server 2008 R2 because this includes the DHCP Enforcement Service (ES). The DHCP EC is included in the DHCP Client service on Windows 7, Windows Vista, Windows Server 2008, Windows Server 2008 R2, and Windows XP SP3.

The drawback of DHCP NAP enforcement is that you can get around it by configuring a client's IP address statically. Only users with local administrator access can configure a manual IP, but if your organization gives users local administrator access, DHCP NAP enforcement may not be the most effective method of keeping these computers off the network until they are compliant.

MORE INFO   DHCP ENFORCEMENT

To learn more about DHCP enforcement, consult the following TechNet page:
http://technet.microsoft.com/en-us/library/cc733020.aspx.

 Quick Check

1. Which NAP enforcement method uses VLANs?
2. Which NAP enforcement methods can you get around by configuring a static IP address?

Quick Check Answer

1. The 802.1X NAP enforcement method uses VLANs.
2. You can get around the DHCP NAP enforcement method by configuring a static IP address.

RD Gateway NAP Enforcement

RD Gateway NAP enforcement ensures that clients running Windows 7, Windows Vista, Windows Server 2008, and Windows Server 2008 R2 located on the Internet that are connecting to an RD Gateway meet health compliance requirements before the RD Gateway allows connections to RDP servers on the internal network. To configure RD Gateway for NAP, you must perform the following basic steps:

1. Enable NAP health policy checking on the RD Gateway server by configuring the RD Gateway server to request that clients send a statement of health.

2. Remove any existing RD-CAPs. It is not necessary to remove existing RD-RAPs.

3. Configure a Windows SHV on the RD Gateway server by editing the properties of the Windows SHV in the Network Policy Server console on the RD Gateway server.

4. Create NAP Policies on the RD Gateway server using the Configure NAP Wizard. You will need to create two health policies (one for compliant and one for noncompliant computers), a connection request policy, and three network policies (compliant, noncompliant, and non-NAP-capable).

> **MORE INFO** **RD GATEWAY ENFORCEMENT**
>
> For more information on using NAP with RD Gateway enforcement, consult the following TechNet page: *http://technet.microsoft.com/en-us/library/cc771213.aspx*.

DirectAccess NAP Enforcement

You can incorporate NAP into your DirectAccess infrastructure as a way of ensuring that clients that are attempting to connect using DirectAccess from remote networks will be successful only if they meet network health requirements. Using NAP with DirectAccess requires similar infrastructure to the NAP IPsec enforcement method. It is necessary to ensure that your organization has at least one HRA as well as CAs that are configured to support NAP, NAP health policy servers, and necessary remediation servers. If your remediation and HRA servers are on the Intranet, you'll need to perform the following steps:

- Add the IPv6 addresses of the HRA and remediation servers to the list of management servers when running the DirectAccess Setup Wizard.

- Configure the intranet tunnel rule in the DirectAccess server GPO to require health certificates.

> **MORE INFO** **DIRECTACCESS WITH NAP**
>
> For more information on DirectAccess with NAP enforcement, consult the following TechNet article: *http://technet.microsoft.com/en-us/library/ff528477(WS.10).aspx*.

Remediation Servers

Remediation servers generally host software updates and antivirus and anti-spyware definition files and are used to bring a client that has not passed a health check up to date. Remediation servers are accessible from the restricted networks that noncompliant clients are relegated to when they do not pass system health checks. Remediation servers allow these clients to be brought into compliance so that they can have unrestricted access to the network. Remediation server groups are added through the Remediation Server Group node of the Network Policy Server console, as shown in Figure 9-12.

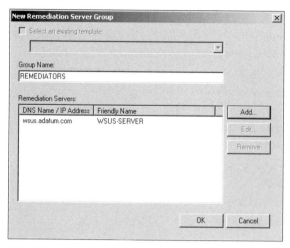

FIGURE 9-12 Remediation Server Group node

Monitoring-Only Mode

While you usually use NAP to restrict access to noncompliant clients, when you deploy NAP for the first time, you should use NAP in monitoring-only mode. This is because when you start out, you are likely to have a large number of noncompliant clients and if you enforce NAP policies right at the start, a large number of the computers that you are responsible for managing will be unable to access the network. By using monitoring-only mode, you can get a good idea about how many clients in your organization do not comply with current health policies. You can then take steps to correct these problems on the clients so that when you do enforce NAP, only a small number of clients will be forced into remediation.

> *MORE INFO* **NO ENFORCEMENT**
>
> To learn more about configuring NAP for monitoring rather than enforcement, consult the following TechNet article: *http://technet.microsoft.com/en-us/library/dd314142(WS.10).aspx.*

> *MORE INFO* **HOST CREDENTIAL AUTHORIZATION PROTOCOL**
>
> Host Credential Authorization Protocol (HCAP) allows the integration of NAP with Cisco's Network Admission Control technology. HCAP allows the NPS server running on Windows Server 2008 and Windows Server 2008 R2 to perform authorization for Cisco 802.1X access clients. To learn more about HCAP, consult the following TechNet page: *http://technet.microsoft.com/en-us/library/cc732681.aspx.*

Lesson Summary

- An SHV is a set of conditions that a computer must meet to be considered healthy. An SHA is what the NPS server checks with to determine whether a connecting client meets all the conditions of the SHV.

- The four methods of NAP enforcement that can be applied to Windows Server 2008 R2, Windows Server 2008, Windows 7, Windows Vista, and Windows XP SP3 clients are IPsec, DHCP, VPN, and 802.1X enforcement. You can use RD Gateway NAP only with Windows 7, Windows Vista, Windows Server 2008, and Windows Server 2008 R2.

- NPS servers are installed as a part of the Network Policy And Access Services role. These servers are where you configure health policies and SHVs that dictate the health compliance benchmark.

- Domain isolation allows you to use IPsec to limit network communication to computers that are members of a specific domain.

- Forefront TMG 2010 is an advanced firewall application that can be installed on servers running Windows Server 2008 and Windows Server 2008 R2. It is often installed between a perimeter network and the Internet.

Lesson Review

You can use the following questions to test your knowledge of the information in Lesson 2, "Firewalls and Network Access Protection." The questions are also available on the companion CD if you prefer to review them in electronic form.

> **NOTE ANSWERS**
>
> Answers to these questions and explanations of why each answer choice is correct or incorrect are located in the "Answers" section at the end of the book.

1. You want only healthy computers on your network to be able to connect to a computer running Windows Server 2008 used as an intranet web server role for management tasks, but you want to allow all clients, healthy or unhealthy, to be able to access Web pages on the same servers. Which of the following NAP enforcement methods should you implement without having to configure the firewall or IP address restrictions on the intranet server running Windows Server 2008?

   A. IPsec

   B. 802.1X

   C. DHCP

   D. VPN

2. Your network contains a mixture of Windows Vista SP1 and Windows XP SP3 clients. You want to enable NAP enforcements for the clients running Windows Vista SP1. Clients running Windows XP SP3 should not be subjected to NAP enforcement. Which of

the following strategies should you pursue? (Each answer forms a part of the solution. Choose two.)

A. Create a network policy that specifies the operating system as a condition.

B. Create a VLAN for all clients running Windows XP.

C. Configure the network policy to allow computers running Windows Vista to bypass the health check.

D. Configure the network policy to allow computers running Windows XP to bypass the health check.

3. Your organization has one domain controller running Windows Server 2003, named 2K3DC, and one domain controller running Windows Server 2008, named 2K8DC. The domain functional level is Windows Server 2003. DNS is installed on a stand-alone computer named DNS1 running Windows Server 2003 R2. DHCP is installed on a stand-alone computer named DHCP1 running Windows Server 2003 R2. NPS is installed on a computer named NPS1 running Windows Server 2008. Which of the following computers must you upgrade if you want to use DHCP NAP enforcement?

A. 2K3DC

B. DNS1

C. DHCP1

D. NPS1

4. Which of the following server roles must be available on your network if you plan to configure IPsec rules so that only healthy computers can connect to each other? (Each answer forms a part of the solution. Choose two.)

A. HRA

B. Windows Server 2008 CA

C. Windows Server 2008 DHCP server

D. HCAP server

5. Other than 802.1X-compatible switches, which of the following components must be deployed in your network environment to support 802.1X NAP enforcement? (Choose two; each solution forms a complete answer.)

A. The NPS server role on a computer running Windows Server 2008

B. A RADIUS proxy server

C. EAPHost EC on clients

D. The HCAP server role on a computer running Windows Server 2008

PRACTICE **Installing and Configuring NAP with DHCP Enforcement**

In this set of practices, you will configure Windows Server 2008 R2 with the Network Policy Server role to support NAP with the DHCP.

EXERCISE 1   Network Policy Server Installation and DHCP Configuration

In this exercise, you will install the NPS server role on server VAN-DC1. To complete this practice, perform the following steps:

1. Log on to server VAN-DC1 with the Kim_Akers user account.

2. Open an elevated PowerShell session and issue the following commands to ensure that the DHCP and NPS role services, if installed, are removed from the server. If these roles are present, it will be necessary to reboot the server, log in, restart PowerShell, and import the ServerManager module again.

    ```
    Import-Module ServerManager
    Remove-WindowsFeature DHCP, NPAS
    ```

3. From the elevated PowerShell session, issue the following commands to install DHCP and the NPS server roles:

    ```
    Add-WindowsFeature DHCP, NPAS
    ```

4. From the Administrative Tools menu, click DHCP. The DHCP console will open. Right-click the DHCP node and then click Manage Authorized Servers. Click Authorize. In the Authorize DHCP Server dialog box, enter the name **VAN-DC1** and then click OK. Verify that the IP address of the DHCP server matches 10.10.0.10, and then click OK. Highlight VAN-DC and then click OK.

5. Open the Services console. Set the properties of the DHCP Server service to start automatically. Start the service.

6. In the DHCP console, expand the IPv4 node under van-dc.adatum.com and then delete the scope Alpha Scope.

7. Select and right-click the IPv4 node under van-dc.adatum.com, and then click New Scope. This will start the New Scope Wizard. Click Next.

8. On the Scope Name page, enter the scope name **NAP_Scope**. Click Next.

9. Set the start IP address as **10.100.0.1** and the end IP address as **10.100.0.254**. Set the Subnet Mask Length at **24**. Click Next three times.

10. On the Configure DHCP Options page, select the No, I Will Configure These Options Later option, and then click Next. Click Finish.

EXERCISE 2   Configure NPS

In this exercise, you will configure NPS. To complete this practice, perform the following steps:

1. From the Administrative Tools menu, click Network Policy Server. The Network Policy Server console will open.

2. On the Getting Started page, shown in Figure 9-13, click Configure NAP.

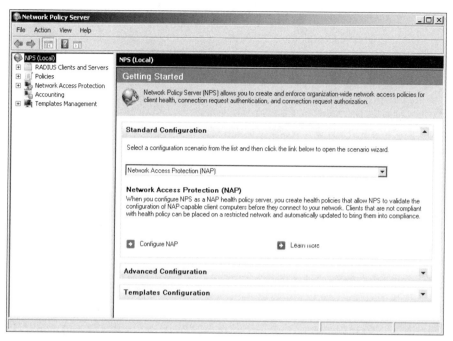

FIGURE 9-13 NPS NAP Getting Started page

3. On the Select Network Connection Method For Use With NAP page, use the drop-down menu to select Dynamic Host Configuration Protocol (DHCP), and then click Next.

4. On the RADIUS Clients page, click Next.

5. On the DHCP Scopes page, click Add. In the Specify The Profile Name That Identifies Your DHCP Scope box, type **NAP_Scope** and click OK. Click Next.

6. On the Configure Machine Groups page, click Next.

7. On the Specify A NAP Remediation Server Group And URL page, click Next.

8. On the Define NAP Health Policy page, clear the Enable Auto-Remediation Of Client Computers option and select Allow Full Network Access To NAP-Ineligible Client Computers, as shown in Figure 9-14. Click Next, and then click Finish.

EXERCISE 3 Configure SHV

In this exercise, you will configure an SHV to support your NAP DHCP deployment. To complete this practice, perform the following steps:

1. In the Network Policy Server console, navigate to the Network Access Protection/ System Health Validators/Windows Security Health Validator/Settings node. In the details pane, right-click Default Configuration and then click Properties. This will open the Windows Security Health Validator dialog box.

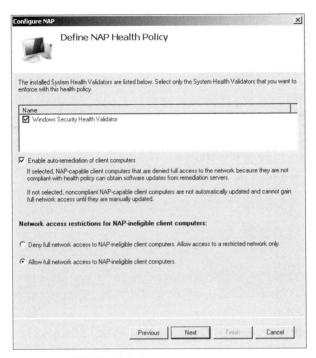

FIGURE 9-14 NAP Health Policy

2. In the details pane of the Windows Security Health Validator dialog box, scroll down to the Security Updates Settings section. Enable the Restrict Access For Clients That Do Not Have All Available Security Updates Installed option and change the severity level to Moderate And Above, as shown in Figure 9-15.

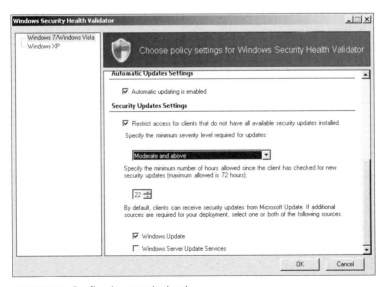

FIGURE 9-15 Configuring severity level

Chapter Review

To further practice and reinforce the skills you learned in this chapter, you can perform the following tasks:

- Review the chapter summary.
- Review the list of key terms introduced in this chapter.
- Complete the case scenarios. These scenarios set up real-world situations involving the topics of this chapter and ask you to create a solution.
- Complete the suggested practices.
- Take a practice test.

Chapter Summary

- VPN servers running Windows Server 2008 and Windows Server 2008 R2 support the PPTP, L2TP/IPsec, and SSTP protocols. SSTP can be used only by computers running Windows Vista or Windows 7.
- VPN servers running Windows Server 2008 R2 support IKEv2 VPNs. VPNs using IKEv2 support automatic reconnection, but they can be used only by computers running Windows 7.
- DirectAccess is an always-on IPv6 remote access solution. It requires a computer running Windows Server 2008 R2 and supports only clients running Windows 7 Enterprise and Ultimate editions.
- You can configure a computer running Windows Server 2008 or Windows Server 2008 R2 to function as a RADIUS server, RADIUS proxy, or RADIUS client.
- The four methods of local NAP enforcement are IPsec, DHCP, VPN, and 802.1X enforcement. You can also configure NAP enforcement for RD Gateway and DirectAccess.

Key Terms

The following terms were introduced in this chapter. Do you know what they mean?

- DirectAccess
- EAP-TLS
- IKEv2
- L2TP/IPsec
- PPP
- PPTP
- SSTP
- RADIUS
- VPN

Case Scenarios

In the following case scenarios, you will apply what you have learned about planning server installs and upgrades. You can find answers to these questions in the "Answers" section at the end of this book.

Case Scenario 1: Remote Access at Wingtip Toys

Wingtip Toys has branch office locations in Sydney and Melbourne, Australia. The branch office firewalls are configured to let traffic from the Internet through only to hosts on the screened subnet on TCP ports 25, 80, and 443. An RD Gateway server has been installed on the screened subnet at the Sydney location. A multihomed computer running Windows Server 2008 R2 with the Remote Access role installed will be deployed on the Melbourne screened subnet next week. Given this information, provide answers to the following questions:

1. What type of policy should you configure to limit access at the Sydney location to a list of authorized users?

2. When the Melbourne server is deployed, what VPN protocol would you use to provide access if you are not able to modify the existing firewall rules?

3. What sort of NAP enforcement should you use in the Melbourne location?

Case Scenario 2: Coho Vineyard NAP

You are in the process of improving network security at Coho Vineyard's head office. Coho Vineyard has 20 servers running Windows Server 2008 R2 and 400 clients running Windows 7 Enterprise edition. As a part of this process, you intend to deploy NAP, but must deal with the following design constraints:

- Management at Coho want to do a six-month trial before they commit to purchasing any new hardware. The pilot program should allow NAP to be tested and ensure that noncompliant clients are remediated.

- If the pilot program proves to be successful, NAP should be implemented in such a way that unhealthy clients are blocked from accessing the network at the switch level.

- Coho Vineyard does not have the necessary hardware infrastructure at this time to implement switch-level network access demarcation, but the hardware will be purchased at the conclusion of a successful pilot program.

- Several of Coho Vineyard's legacy third-party systems do not support the IPsec protocol.

With this information in mind, answer the following questions:

1. Which NAP method should be used at Coho Vineyard during the pilot program?

2. Which NAP method should be used at Coho Vineyard once the pilot program is deemed successful?

3. What steps should you take to allow for remediation?

Suggested Practices

To help you successfully master the exam objectives presented in this chapter, complete the following tasks.

Monitor and Maintain Security Policies

Do all the practices in this section.

- Practice 1: Configure an RD Gateway server on a stand-alone computer running Windows Server 2008 R2 that has two network cards, one connected to a public network such as the Internet, and the other connected to the internal network.

- Practice 2: Configure and test an RD-RAP and RD-CAP.

Plan Infrastructure Services Server Roles

Do all the practices in this section.

- Practice 1: Create a server isolation policy using Windows Firewall with Advanced Security.

- Practice 2: Configure IPsec enforcements so that only healthy clients on the network are able to communicate with each other.

Take a Practice Test

The practice tests on this book's companion CD offer many options. For example, you can test yourself on just one exam objective, or you can test yourself on all the exam content. You can set up the test so that it closely simulates the experience of taking a certification exam, or you can set it up in study mode so that you can look at the correct answers and explanations after you answer each question.

> **MORE INFO** **PRACTICE TESTS**
>
> For details about all the practice test options available, see the section "How to Use the Practice Tests" in this book's Introduction.

CHAPTER 10

Provision Data and Plan Storage

Data is organizational memory. People create word processing documents, spreadsheets, and add rows to database tables so that at some stage in the future, they or someone else can retrieve that stored information. Having a great data provisioning and storage strategy is about making sure that data is available to those who need to access it under all conditions, whether that be the failure of the wide area network (WAN) or failure of a hard disk drive. In this lesson, you will learn how to provision data so that it is available through Distributed File System (DFS) or Microsoft SharePoint Foundation 2010. You will learn how to connect Windows Server 2008 R2 to an iSCSI for Fibre Channel storage area networks (SANs) and learn what steps you need to take to provision a Logical Unit Number (LUN) so that you can provision storage centrally to your organization's critical servers.

Exam objectives in this chapter:

- Provision data.
- Plan storage.

Lessons in this chapter:

Before You Begin

To complete the exercises in the practice in this chapter, you need to have done the following:

- Complete the setup tasks outlined in Appendix A, "Setup Instructions for Windows Server 2008 R2."

No additional configuration is required for this chapter.

REAL WORLD

Orin Thomas

Hardware redundancy is important and can save you a lot of time. I was in my first few weeks in a new systems administrator position when a server that a colleague was responsible for managing lost a hard disk drive. The server that went down happened to be the one that hosted the management team's mailboxes. The colleague was new to the position as well, and had been at the company only a few more weeks than I had. There was an agreement with the hardware vendor that any failed components had to be replaced in a couple of hours, and as soon as my colleague notified the vendor, it had a tech come straight out to our site in a taxi. The server itself had three hard disk drive bays and had a BIOS that supported hardware RAID. When the tech arrived, we learned that the person who had actually built the server 18 months before had, for some unknown reason, decided not to configure RAID at all and had, instead, set the server up with three separate volumes. Because the volume that had failed hosted the operating system, my colleague had to spend quite a few hours rebuilding the server so that it was functional again. If the person who had built the server 18 months before had turned on the built-in hardware RAID 5 functionality, the complexity involved in recovering the server would have been reduced and the server would have been functional much sooner.

Lesson 1: Provisioning Data

Data is useless unless it is available to those who need it. A volume that can't be accessed because a hardware component has failed is about as accessible as it would be if you put it in an ice cream container and hid it at the back of your refrigerator. In this lesson, you will learn all about how to make data available, from the basics of ensuring that your organization's important servers use redundant storage to more complex schemes involving data replication and offline availability. You will also learn what steps you can take to index information, to make the task of finding a specific document more efficient. Finally, you will learn how you can integrate SharePoint Foundation 2010 into your organization so that you can go beyond the simple sharing of files and deploy a more rigorous document management solution.

> **After this lesson, you will be able to:**
> - Plan data availability.
> - Configure DFS.
> - Configure indexing.
> - Provide offline data access.
> - Configure collaboration.
>
> **Estimated lesson time: 60 minutes**

Planning Data Availability

The accessibility of data is of pivotal importance to the functioning of your organization. Ensuring that data remains available requires taking action at several levels. You must ensure that data is available at the server level, but you also have to make sure that data is available at the organizational level. You can pursue three basic strategies to ensure that data is available to the users of your organization. These strategies include:

- **Ensuring availability through hardware redundancy** You ensure that data remains available if a hardware component fails by providing component-level redundancy. This could mean installing multiple power supplies in the server and, more commonly, configuring disks in redundant arrays. You will learn more about redundant arrays of disks later in this lesson.

- **Ensuring availability through server redundancy**   You ensure that data remains available in the event of server failure by making critical servers redundant. This could be as simple as configuring intrasite replication using DFS. You could also look at configuring failover clustering. You will learn more about configuring storage used by clusters in Lesson 2, "Planning Windows Server 2008 R2 Storage." You will learn more about the process of clustering in Chapter 11, "Clustering and High Availability."

- **Ensuring availability through site redundancy**   Failover clusters do insure you against the failure of a single server, but do not ensure that colleagues in other sites have access to data should the WAN link fail. A holistic data availability strategy includes provisions for ensuring that data remains available even when a headquarters or branch office site is inaccessible to the network.

Hardware Redundancy

The more important a server is to your organization, the more you will need to spend on it to ensure that it remains available. If accountants balk at the thought of spending a couple of extra thousand dollars when provisioning server components, ask them to calculate how much it costs to have people in your organization sitting around, unable to complete their work because the server that they "nickel and dimed" will not be available until the replacement hardware arrives. Although you will learn about disk redundancy later in the lesson, there are a few general rules that you should consider when provisioning server hardware to ensure that it remains available. These include, but are not limited to:

- **Have a plan to deal with hardware failure.**   If possible, have replacement components on-site so if something does fail, you can replace it quickly and then wait, at your leisure, for the vendor to replace the spare.

- **Ensure that the server has multiple power supplies.**   Because they contain moving parts, power supplies and hard disk drives are amongst the most likely components to fail. Redundant power supplies ensure that when this happens, your servers keep working.

- **Ensure that you have your multiple power supplies plugged into separate UPS units.**   The worst time to find out that a UPS does not work is just after the power has gone out. When the power goes out is when most administrators make this realization.

- **Ensure that the server has multiple network cards.**   Unless you have a hot-swappable network cards, a network card failure will take a server off the network as effectively as a blown motherboard.

- **Ensure that you have redundant switches.**   Redundant network cards are great, but you do not want every server in the data center to become inaccessible because a single switch fails.

- **Try to figure out where your single points of failure are and work around them.** Systems administration is often an exercise in pessimism. Try to think of what type of hardware failure will inconvenience you the most, and then develop a plan to deal with it.

Redundant Array of Inexpensive Disks

Redundant array of inexpensive disks (RAID) allows you to use multiple disks to provide redundancy. Windows Server 2008 and Windows Server 2008 R2 support several different versions of software RAID, specifically disk mirroring and disk striping with parity. Although support for software RAID is built into the operating system, most real-world deployments rely upon hardware RAID rather than software RAID. You implement hardware RAID either in BIOS or through a dedicated RAID controller. The most common forms of RAID are as follows:

- **RAID 0. Disk striping** Offers improved performance, but if you lose a disk in a RAID 0 set, you'll lose all the data hosted on the volume. You can configure this using the operating system software in Windows Server 2008 R2. Requires a minimum of two disks.

- **RAID 1. Disk mirroring** A second disk keeps a copy of all the data stored on the first. Offers no performance benefit over a normal volume, but if the disk fails, the mirror can assume its role. You can configure this in software in Windows Server 2008 R2, but disk failure will require a reboot. Requires a minimum of two disks.

- **RAID 5. Disk striping with parity** Offers part of the performance boost of disk striping, with a special parity calculation that allows the contents of a disk to be regenerated in the event that one disk in the set fails. Requires a minimum of three disks and the equivalent of one disk across the set is consumed by parity data. You can configure this in software in Windows Server 2008 R2.

- **RAID 1+0. A stripe of mirrors** Sometimes called "RAID 10." For example, you create three mirrored sets and then stripe data across them. You can implement this only at the hardware level when using Windows Server 2008 R2.

- **RAID 0+1. A mirror of stripes** You create a stripe set across multiple disks, and then use the same amount of disks to mirror that content. You can implement this only at the hardware level when using Windows Server 2008 R2.

To create a RAID 5 volume using the software RAID capabilities of Windows Server 2008 R2, you need to have at least three disks available and to perform the following steps:

1. Open the Server Manager console and then click the Storage/Disk Management node.

2. Ensure that the disks that you want to add to the RAID 5 volume are in an online state and initialized.

3. Right-click one of the disks and then click New RAID 5 Volume. This will start the New RAID 5 Volume Wizard.

4. Add disks to the RAID volume, as shown in Figure 10-1, and then click Next.

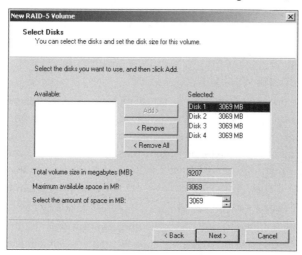

FIGURE 10-1 Creating the RAID volume

5. Assign a drive letter or a mount point, and then click Next. Format the disk and select a volume label, and then click Finish.

Distributed File System (DFS)

DFS is a method of both simplifying your organization's shared folder structure and providing data redundancy through replication. DFS lets you collect shared folders located on different servers into one or more logically structured namespaces. Rather than having to remember which server hosts a specific shared folder, they can access the DFS namespace and find all shared folders.

You can replicate a DFS namespace and folders within a site and across WAN links. A user connecting to files within the shared folder structures contained in the DFS namespace will connect automatically to shared folders in the same Active Directory Directory Services (AD DS) site (when available) rather than across a WAN. You can have several DFS Namespace servers in a site and spread over several sites, so if one server goes down a user can still access files within the shared folder structure. The architecture of DFS ensures that a change to a file on a DFS share is replicated quickly and efficiently to all other replicas of that DFS share.

Creating a DFS Namespace

You can create a namespace when you install the DFS Management role service, as shown in Figure 10-2, or create it later. You can add additional namespaces by right-clicking DFS Namespaces in the DFS Management console and selecting New Namespace. You can create namespaces on a member server or domain controller running Windows Server 2008. However, you cannot create more than one namespace on a server running Windows Server 2008 Standard edition. You can create multiple namespaces on servers running Windows Server 2008 Enterprise and Datacenter editions.

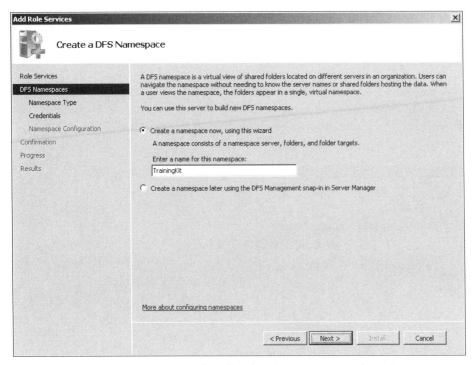

FIGURE 10-2 Creating a namespace when installing the DFS Management role service

A namespace is a virtual view of shared folders in an organization, and it has a path to a namespace similar to a Universal Naming Convention (UNC) path to a shared folder. You can create two types of namespaces:

- A domain namespace uses a domain as its namespace root, such as \\adatum.com\ MyNameSpace. A domain-based namespace can be hosted on multiple namespace servers to increase its availability, and its metadata is stored in AD DS. Domain-based namespaces can be created on one or more member servers or domain controllers in the same domain, and metadata for a domain-based namespace is stored by AD DS. Each server must contain an NTFS volume to host the namespace. Multiple namespace servers increase the availability of the namespace. A domain-based namespace cannot be a clustered resource in a failover cluster. However, you can locate the namespace on a server that is also a node in a failover cluster provided that you configure the namespace to use only local resources on that server.

- A stand-alone namespace uses a namespace server as its namespace root, such as \\ServerA\MyNameSpace. A stand-alone namespace is hosted on only one server. You would choose a stand-alone namespace if your organization does not use AD DS, if you needed to create a single namespace with more than 5,000 DFS folders but your organization did not support Windows Server 2008 mode, or if you wanted to use a failover cluster to increase availability.

Windows Server 2008 Namespace Mode

If you choose a domain-based namespace, you can use the Windows 2000 Server mode or the Windows Server 2008 mode. The Windows Server 2008 mode includes support for access-based enumeration and provides increased scalability (more than 5,000 DFS folders). Whenever possible, Microsoft recommends that you choose the Windows Server 2008 mode. To use this mode, the domain needs to be at the Windows Server 2008 domain functional level or later, and all namespace servers must be running Windows Server 2008 or later. Figure 10-3 shows the creation of a domain-based namespace using the Windows Server 2008 mode.

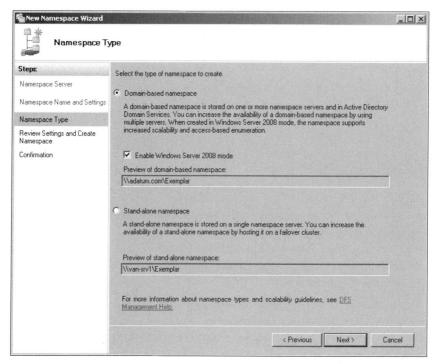

FIGURE 10-3 Choosing a namespace mode

> **MORE INFO** **CHOOSE A DFS NAMESPACE**
>
> For more information on choosing a DFS namespace, consult the following TechNet article:
> *http://technet.microsoft.com/en-us/library/cc770287(WS.10).aspx.*

Setting Target Priority to Override Referral Ordering

A referral is an ordered list of targets that a client receives from a domain controller or namespace server when a user accesses a namespace root or a folder that has folder targets in the namespace. Each folder target in a referral is ordered according to the method defined for the namespace root or folder, such as Random Order or Lowest Cost. You can refine how targets are ordered by setting a priority on individual targets. For example, you can specify that the target is first among all targets, last among all targets, or first (or last) among all targets of equal cost.

To set target priority on a root target for a domain-based namespace, you expand the namespace in the DFS Management console, click the relevant folder, right-click the folder target, and click Properties. On the Advanced tab, shown in Figure 10-4, you can select the Override Referral Ordering check box and specify one of the following options:

- **First Among All Targets**   Users are always referred to this target if it is available.
- **Last Among All Targets**   Users are never be referred to this target unless all other targets are unavailable.
- **First Among Targets Of Equal Cost**   Users are referred to this target before other targets of equal cost (typically in the same site).
- **Last Among Targets Of Equal Cost**   Users are never referred to this target if there are other targets of equal cost available (typically in the same site).

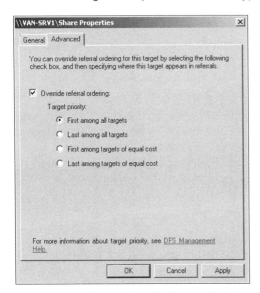

FIGURE 10-4 Setting the Override Referral Ordering option

Access-Based Enumeration

Access-based enumeration allows users to see only files and folders on a file server that they have permission to access. Access-based enumeration is supported in a DFS namespace only when the namespace is a stand-alone namespace hosted on a computer running Windows Server 2008, or a domain-based namespace in Windows Server 2008 mode. To enable access-based enumeration in a namespace, edit the properties of the namespace as shown in Figure 10-5.

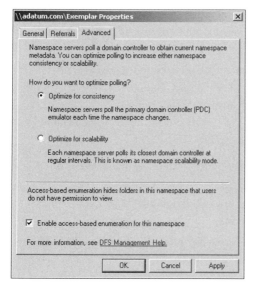

FIGURE 10-5 Enabling access-based enumeration

Configuring Replication

DFS Replication (DFSR) ensures that the changes made to a file on one shared folder replicate to other replicas in the organization. You can use the New Replication Group Wizard in the DFS Management console to create a replication group, and the New Member Wizard adds a member. The New Replicated Folders Wizard in the same tool adds a replicated folder to a replication group. Note that when you add a new replicated folder, it is not replicated immediately. DFSR settings must first be replicated to all domain controllers, and each member in the replication group needs to poll its closest domain controller to obtain the new settings. The amount of time this takes depends on AD DS replication latency and the long polling interval (typically 60 minutes) on each member.

When you are configuring replication groups, you must choose between the following two types:

- **Multipurpose Replication Group**   This most commonly used replication group type allows you to configure replication between two or more servers.
- **Replication Group For Data Collection**   This group type is used to transfer data from a hub site to a branch office site.

To create a replication group, perform the following steps:

1. Ensure that the DFSR feature is installed on all servers that you want to add to the replication group.
2. Open the DFS Management console and select the Replication node. In the Actions pane, click New Replication Group. This will start the New Replication Group Wizard.
3. On the Replication Type page, select Multipurpose Replication Group.

4. On the Name And Domain page, enter a name for the replication group and then specify the domain that the replication group is associated with.

5. On the Replication Group Members page, click Add, and then add the computers that will be members of the replication group. These computers must have the DFSR feature installed. Click Next.

6. On the Topology Selection page, select Full Mesh Topology. You will learn more about topologies later in this lesson.

7. On the Replication Group Schedule And Bandwidth page, select the Replicate Continuously Using The Specified Bandwidth option and then ensure that the Full option is selected. Click Next.

8. On the Primary Member page, select the server that has the seed content that you want to replicate to other servers, and then click Next.

9. On the Folders To Replicate page, click Add. In the Add Folder To Replicate dialog box, shown in Figure 10-6, enter the local path on the seed server that hosts the content that you want to replicate, click OK, and then click Next.

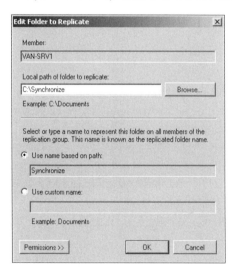

FIGURE 10-6 Selecting the folder to replicate

10. On the Local Path Of <foldername> On Other Members page, edit the properties of the other members of the replication group to specify the local path to which the folder will replicate. Click Next, and then click Create to create the replication group.

Managing DFS

You can configure replication filters so that certain file types are exempt from replication. To edit the replication filters for a replicated folder, perform the following steps:

1. In the DFS Management console, select the replication group that hosts the replicated folder for which you want to configure the filter.

2. In the details pane, on the Replicated Folders tab, select the folder that you want to modify, and then, on the Actions pane, click Properties.

3. On the General tab, modify the filter settings as shown in Figure 10-7.

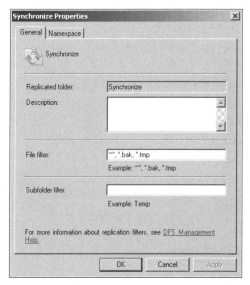

FIGURE 10-7   Replication filter

When a member detects a new or modified filter, it scans its database and removes the records of files that match the filter. Because the files are no longer listed in the database, future changes to the files are ignored. When a member detects that a filter has been removed, it scans the file system, adds records for all files that match the removed filter, and replicates the files.

You can enable file sharing on a replicated folder and specify whether to add (publish) the folder to a DFS namespace by performing the following steps:

1. In the DFS Management console, click the replication group that contains the replicated folder that you want to share.

2. In the details pane, on the Replicated Folders tab, right-click the replicated folder that you want to share, and then click Share And Publish In Namespace.

3. In the Share And Publish Replicated Folder Wizard, click Share The Replicated Folder and follow the steps in the Share And Publish Replicated Folder Wizard, specifying whether to publish the folder when you are prompted for that setting. If you do not have an existing namespace, you can create one in the Namespace Path page in the wizard. To do so, click Browse in the Namespace Path page, and then click New Namespace.

Specifying the Replication Topology

The replication topology defines the logical connections that DFS uses to replicate files among servers. When choosing or changing a topology, remember that two one-way connections are created between the members you choose, thus allowing data to flow in both directions. To create or change a replication topology in the DFS Management console, right-click the replication group for which you want to define a new topology, and then click New Topology. The New Topology Wizard lets you choose one of the following options:

- **Hub and spoke**   This topology requires three or more members. For each spoke member, you should choose a required hub member and an optional second hub member for redundancy. This optional hub ensures that a spoke member can still replicate if one of the hub members is unavailable. If you specify more than one hub member, the hub members will have a full-mesh topology between them.

- **Full mesh**   In this topology, every member replicates with all the other members of the replication group. This topology works well when there are 10 or fewer members in the replication group.

> *MORE INFO*   **DFS IN WINDOWS SERVER 2008 R2**
>
> To learn about the Windows Server 2008 R2–specific features for DFS, consult the following TechNet page: *http://technet.microsoft.com/en-us/library/ee307957(WS.10).aspx*.

 Quick Check

- What must you ensure is installed on servers before you add them to a replication group?

Quick Check Answer

- The DFS Replication role service

Configuring Offline Data Access

Offline files allow users to access files that are hosted on shared folders when they are not connected to the network. Offline file functionality works by creating a copy of the file in a local encrypted cache and then synchronizing that copy back to the file share when network connectivity is reestablished. In the rare event that a file is modified on the file share when it is also modified on the client when offline, the user is notified and asked to resolve the situation by making a copy, discarding his or her changes, or overwriting the modified file stored on the file server. You can use the Share and Storage Management console to configure offline file settings. You can configure whether users are able to access offline file functionality through Group Policy.

In the Share and Storage Management console, you can access a shared folder on the Shares tab and click Properties. You then click Advanced on the Sharing tab of the share's Properties dialog box. This enables you to access the settings on the Caching tab of the Advanced dialog box, as shown in Figure 10-8.

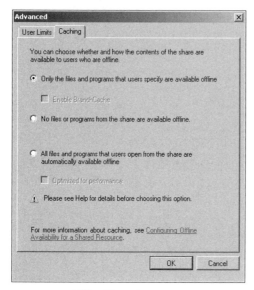

FIGURE 10-8 Offline file settings

You can choose an offline availability option for the shared resource. If you want, you can configure each shared resource on your server with the offline setting that you choose. The available settings are as follows:

- **Only The Files And Programs That Users Specify Are Available Offline** This is the default option. With this option, no user or program files are available offline unless the user specifies that they should be. The user chooses the files that are synchronized and available offline. You would use this option if your users are relatively sophisticated and can sensibly choose the files they want to work with. If you have enabled BranchCache on a server, you can enable BranchCache with this option.

- **All Files And Programs That Users Open From The Share Are Automatically Available Offline** Whenever a user accesses the shared folder or volume and opens a user or program file, that file or program is made available offline to that user automatically. This has the advantage that users do not need to choose the files that are synchronized.

- **No Files Or Programs From The Share Are Available Offline** This option blocks the Offline Files feature on the client from making copies of the files and programs on the shared resource. Typically, you would select this option to prevent secure shared resources from being stored offline on nonsecure computers.

MORE INFO **OFFLINE FILES**

To learn more about configuring offline file functionality, consult the following TechNet link: *http://technet.microsoft.com/en-us/library/cc732663.aspx*.

Configuring Indexing in the Windows Search Service

The Windows Search Service provides an indexing solution that creates an index of the most common file and nonfile data types on the server. When you index files and data types, this enables you to perform fast file searches on your server from clients running Windows 7, Vista, or Windows XP or Windows Server 2003 with Windows Desktop Search installed.

You can instead install the legacy Indexing Service that was used in previous versions of Windows as part of the Windows Server 2003 role service. However, you should do this only if you have a customized or non-Microsoft application that requires you to run this service on your server. You cannot install the Windows Search Service and the Indexing Service on the same computer, and Microsoft recommends that you upgrade any applications that require the Indexing Service to be compatible with Windows Search Service, which offers several enhancements, especially in the areas of extensibility, usability, and performance.

Selecting Volumes and Folders to Index

You are given the option to select volumes to index when you add the Windows Search Service role service. You should always index shared resources only. The Windows Search Service enables you to search for files on your server from a client, and there is little point in indexing folders that cannot be accessed over the network.

Microsoft recommends that you select a volume that is used exclusively for hosting shared folders. You are not required to specify a volume to install the role service, and you can add individual shared folders after the service is installed. When you install Windows Search Service, default indexing locations are selected, even if you do not select a volume to index. You can review the default locations by opening Indexing Options in the Control Panel.

When you add a new location, indexing will begin. You can click Pause if you need to pause indexing to do something else. As before, you need to clear a UAC dialog box to get to this dialog box. You can also click Advanced in the Indexing Options dialog box. This lets you access the Advanced Options dialog box. The Index Settings tab of this dialog box is shown in Figure 10-9.

On the Index Settings tab, you can choose to index encrypted files and to treat similar words with diacritics as different words. Diacritics are marks above, through, or below letters (for example, accents). You can also choose to rebuild your index or re-index selected locations and to change the location of your index. If you change the index location, you need to stop and restart the service.

On the File Types tab of the same dialog box, you can add or remove file types that you want to index and specify whether to index by properties only or by properties and content. You can also specify a file extension that is not on the list and click Add New Extension.

> **MORE INFO** **WINDOWS SEARCH SERVICE**
>
> To learn more about the Windows Search Service, consult the following TechNet link:
> *http://technet.microsoft.com/en-us/library/dd364879(WS.10).aspx.*

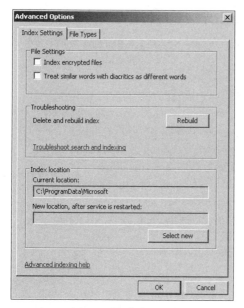

FIGURE 10-9 Advanced indexing options

Collaboration with SharePoint Foundation 2010

SharePoint Foundation 2010 is the successor product to Windows SharePoint Services that allows organizations to perform more advanced file collaboration tasks than is possible using DFS and traditional file shares. SharePoint Foundation 2010 has many of the features of the more comprehensive SharePoint Server 2010 product, but has the advantage of being free to customers that have a Windows Server 2008 or Windows Server 2008 R2 license. SharePoint Foundation 2010 supports features such as Access Services, Business Connectivity Services, Central Administration, Health Monitoring, Sandboxed Solutions, and PowerShell while not including advanced features such as Digital Asset Management, Enterprise Search, Excel Services, Managed Metadata, PerformancePoint Services, Records Management, Social Computing, and Visio Services.

SharePoint Foundation 2010 allows organizations to apply workflow and collaboration functionality when provisioning data. This means that you can allow users to create their own document libraries and can control who can check files in and out. SharePoint Foundation 2010 also provides versioning functionality, allowing changes that have been made to one document to be rolled back easily by another author. Accomplishing this using DFS or standard shared folders is difficult because the standard shared folder infrastructure is not designed to keep track of document versions, just to keep a most recent copy of an updated document.

SharePoint Foundation 2010 works using web applications, site collections, sites, and document libraries. A web application is a collection of settings and functionality related to a URL. When you install SharePoint Foundation 2010, the default web application is available at the default URL of the server hosting SharePoint. It is important to note that Microsoft Office applications can connect to SharePoint in the same way that they would connect to an ordinary shared folder. This means that rather than connecting to a website, downloading a document, and then editing that document, this entire process can happen in a way that is transparent to the user, just as it would if the user was accessing the document from a DFS share.

To create a new site in a SharePoint Foundation 2010 web application, perform the following steps:

1. Open SharePoint Central Administration. On the Central Administration site, shown in Figure 10-10, click Manage Web Applications.

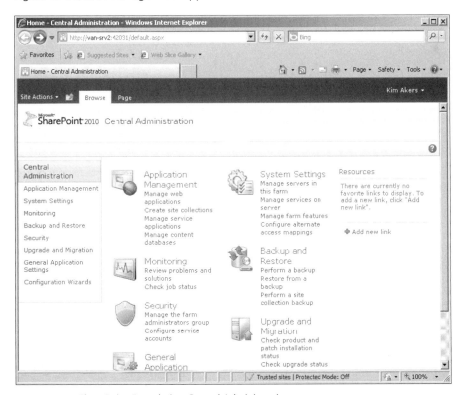

FIGURE 10-10 SharePoint Foundation Central Administration

2. On the toolbar, click New to create a new web application.

3. On the Create New Web Application page, review the settings, such as the public URL of the site and the port number and security account used by the web application, and then click OK.

SharePoint libraries are collections of documents. When you use SharePoint to store documents, the shared documents are stored within SharePoint libraries. To manage shared documents within a SharePoint Foundation web application library, connect to the application using Windows Internet Explorer and then perform the following steps:

1. Open Internet Explorer and navigate to the SharePoint web application. On the Welcome To Your Site page, click Shared Documents.

2. In the Library Tools section, click Documents to get access to the Documents menu.

3. Click New Folder to create a document folder. In the New Folder dialog box, shown in Figure 10-11, enter a folder name and then click Save.

FIGURE 10-11 New SharePoint folder

4. On the server, click Start, All Programs, Accessories, and then open WordPad.

5. Create a document called Example and save it in Office Open XML format on the desktop.

6. In Internet Explorer, enter the Example folder and then, on the Ribbon, click Upload Document.

7. Browse to the Example document on the desktop and then click OK.

8. Place your mouse over the document until you can see the menu shown in Figure 10-12, and then click Check Out. Once you have checked out the document successfully, click View Properties.

MORE INFO **SHAREPOINT FOUNDATION 2010**

To learn more about SharePoint Foundation 2010, consult the following TechNet article: *http://technet.microsoft.com/en-us/library/cc288070.aspx.*

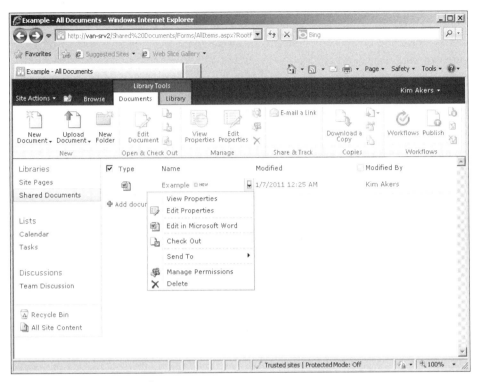

FIGURE 10-12 Checking out a document

Lesson Summary

- Windows Server 2008 and Windows Server 2008 R2 support software implementations of RAID 0, RAID 1, and RAID 5, also known as striping, mirroring, and striping with parity.

- The DFS Namespaces tool in the DFS Management console lets you group shared folders at different locations into logically structured namespaces so that users can view each namespace as a single shared folder with a series of subfolders. This structure provides fault tolerance and the ability to connect users to local shared folders automatically when available.

- The DFS Replication tool in the DFS Management console lets you manage DFSR, which provides a multimaster replication engine that lets you synchronize folders on servers across local or WAN connections. It updates only those files that have changed since the last replication. You can use DFSR in conjunction with DFS Namespaces, or by itself.

- You can use the Share and Storage Management console to configure how files and programs in a shared folder or volume on your Windows Server 2008 server are made available offline.

- The Windows Search Service role service indexes files, folders, and volumes to enable fast searches of server files to be implemented from a client. You can configure indexing settings from the Indexing Options tool in the Control Panel.

Lesson Review

You can use the following questions to test your knowledge of the information in Lesson 1, "Provisioning Data." The questions are also available on the companion CD if you prefer to review them in electronic form.

> **NOTE ANSWERS**
>
> Answers to these questions and explanations of why each answer choice is correct or incorrect are located in the "Answers" section at the end of the book.

1. Which type of volume would you create using Windows Server 2008 R2 if you had two disks and you wanted to prioritize fault tolerance over performance?
   - **A.** RAID 0
   - **B.** RAID 1
   - **C.** RAID 5
   - **D.** RAID 1+0

2. You are planning the deployment of a domain-based DFS namespace at wingtiptoys.com. The name of the namespace will be Accounting, and the namespace server hosting the namespace will be Actuary-Alpha. Which of the following names will users in the domain use to access the folders under this namespace?
   - **A.** \\Accounting\Wingtiptoys.com
   - **B.** \\wingtiptoys.com\Accounting
   - **C.** \\Accounting\Actuary-Alpha
   - **D.** \\Actuary-Alpha\Accounting

3. You want to provide versioning and collaboration functionality to a group of users in the research department at your organization. Which of the following technologies should you deploy to accomplish this goal with a minimum of administrative effort?
   - **A.** File Server Resource Manager
   - **B.** Stand-alone DFS
   - **C.** Domain-based DFS
   - **D.** SharePoint Foundation 2010

4. You want to ensure that users are able to see files and folders only in the DFS namespace to which they have access. Which of the following features must you enable to accomplish this goal?
   - **A.** Override referral ordering
   - **B.** Offline Files
   - **C.** BranchCache
   - **D.** Access-based enumeration

5. You are configuring offline access on a file server running Windows Server 2008 R2. Users in your organization's domain use clients running Windows 7 Enterprise edition, all of which are configured through Group Policy to use the Offline Files feature. You want to ensure that executable files that a client runs from the shared resource are cached automatically on that client, and that the next time the client needs to run one of those executable files, it will access its local cache instead of the shared resource on the server. In the Share and Storage Management console, you access the Offline tab of the Advanced dialog box for the shared folder that stores the files to be synchronized and used offline. What settings do you configure? (Each answer forms part of a complete solution. Choose two.)

   A. Select Only The Files And Programs That Users Specify Are Available Offline.

   B. Select No Files Or Programs From The Share Are Available Offline.

   C. Select All Files And Programs That Users Open From The Share Are Automatically Available Offline.

   D. Select the Optimize For Performance check box.

Lesson 2: Planning Windows Server 2008 R2 Storage

This lesson covers LUNs, SANs, iSCSI, Multipath I/O (MPIO), Virtual Disk Service (VDS), and Fibre Channel. As intimidating as these acronyms can be, by the end of this lesson, you will understand how the concepts that they represent fit together so that you can plan the deployment of SANs in your Windows Server 2008 environment.

> **After this lesson, you will be able to:**
> - Plan the assignment of LUNs.
> - Plan the deployment of iSCSI SANs.
> - Plan the deployment of Fibre Channel SANs.
> - Plan MPIO.
> - Plan the deployment of VDS.
>
> **Estimated lesson time: 60 minutes**

Logical Unit Numbers

A LUN is a logical reference to a portion of a storage subsystem. A LUN can represent a disk, a section of a disk, an entire disk array, or a section of a disk array in the storage subsystem. Conceptually, there are similarities to the concept of a volume, which can also consume part of a disk, the whole disk, or span multiple disks. When you assign a LUN to a server, it acts as a physical disk drive on which the server is able to perform read and write operations. LUNs are used to simplify storage resource management on SANs.

You can use any LUN type that is supported by the storage subsystem that you are deploying. The different LUN types are the following:

- **Simple** A simple LUN uses either an entire physical drive or a portion of that drive. The failure of a disk in a simple LUN means that all data stored on the LUN is lost.

- **Spanned** A spanned LUN is a simple LUN that spans multiple physical drives. The failure of any one disk in a spanned LUN means that all data stored on the LUN is lost.

- **Striped** Data is written across multiple physical disks. This type of LUN, also known as RAID 0, has improved I/O performance because data can be read and written to multiple disks simultaneously. However, like a spanned LUN, all data will be lost if one disk in the array fails.

- **Mirrored** This LUN type, also known as RAID 1, is fault-tolerant. Identical copies of the LUN are created on two physical drives. All read and write operations occur concurrently on both drives. If one disk fails, the LUN continues to be available on the unaffected disk.

- **Striped with Parity**   This LUN type, also known as RAID 5, offers fault tolerance and improved read performance, although write performance is hampered by parity calculation. This type requires a minimum of three disks, and the equivalent of one disk's worth of storage is lost to the storage of parity information across the disk set. This LUN type will retain data if one disk is lost, but all data will be lost if two disks in the array fail at the same time. If one disk fails, you should replace it as quickly as possible.

The Provision Storage Wizard, which is accessible from the Storage Manager For SANs console, allows you to create a LUN on a Fibre Channel or iSCSI disk storage subsystem. Prior to attempting to create a LUN, you should verify that the following requirements have been met:

- The storage subsystem supports VDS.
- You have installed the VDS hardware provider for the storage subsystem.
- Storage space is available on the storage subsystem.
- If you are assigning the LUN to a server, ensure that you have configured server connections. You will learn more about how to configure server connections to iSCSI and Fibre Channel SANs later in this lesson.

After you have assigned a LUN to a server or cluster, you will be able to create a volume on the disk. The LUN type determines the disk performance and reliability characteristics.

Managing LUNs

You can extend a LUN if storage space is available in the subsystem where you created the LUN. Extending a LUN will not extend its file system partition. You must use the Disk Management console or a similar tool to extend the file system partition from the server that has access to the LUN after the LUN has been extended using Storage Manager for SANS.

Deleting a LUN will remove all data on all volumes on the LUN. This operation is irreversible. You can delete a LUN only if all applications that access the LUN have been shut down. An alternative to deleting a LUN is to unassign it. When you unassign a LUN, you make the LUN invisible to the server or cluster but retain the data stored in the LUN. The LUN can be reassigned later. LUNs are deleted using Storage Manager For SANs. Select the target LUN under the LUN Management node and, from the Actions pane, click Delete LUN. To unassign a LUN, perform the same actions, except click Unassign LUN instead of Delete LUN.

Virtual Disk Service (VDS)

VDS provides a standard set of application programming interfaces (APIs) that provide a single interface through which disks can be managed. VDS provides a complete solution for managing storage hardware and disks and enables you to create volumes on those disks. This means that you can use a single tool to manage devices in a mixed storage environment rather than tools provided by different hardware vendors. Before you can manage a LUN using Storage Manager For SANs, you must install its VDS hardware provider. This will usually be provided by the hardware vendor. Prior to purchasing a storage device to be used on your organization's SAN, you should verify that a compatible VDS hardware provider exists.

VDS defines a software and a hardware provider interface. Each of these providers implements a different portion of the VDS API. The software provider is a program that runs on the host and is supported by a kernel-mode driver. Software providers operate on volumes, disks, and partitions. The hardware provider manages the actual storage subsystem. Hardware providers are usually disk array or adapter cards that enable the creation of logical disks for each LUN type. The LUN type that can be configured will depend on the options allowed by the VDS hardware provider. For example, some VDS hardware providers will allow the RAID striped with parity LUN type to be implemented, while others might be limited to providing the mirrored or spanned LUN type.

> **MORE INFO** **INSTALLING VDS PROVIDERS**
>
> For more information about installing VDS providers, consult the following TechNet page: *http://technet.microsoft.com/en-us/library/gg232643(WS.10).aspx.*

 Quick Check

1. Your storage subsystem consists of five 1-terabyte drives. Which LUN type will allow you to create a volume of approximately 5 terabytes?
2. You have just extended a LUN using Storage Manager For SANs. Which tool should you use to extend the file system partition on this LUN?

Quick Check Answer

1. Spanned LUN type
2. The Disk Management console or an equivalent tool. You cannot use Storage Manager For SANS to increase the size of the file system, only the size of the LUN.

Storage Manager For SANs

You can use the Storage Manager For SANs console to create LUNs on Fibre Channel and iSCSI storage arrays. You install Storage Manager For SANs as a feature of Windows Server 2008 or Windows Server 2008 R2. To use Storage Manager for SANs to manage LUNs, the following criteria must be met:

- The storage subsystems that you are going to manage must support VDS.
- The VDS hardware provider for each subsystem must already be installed on the computer running Windows Server 2008.

When you open Storage Manager For SANs from the Administrative Tools menu, you are presented with three main nodes, which have the following functionalities:

- **LUN Management** This node lists all the LUNs created with Storage Manager For SANs. From this node, you can create new LUNs, extend the size of existing LUNs, assign and unassign LUNs, and delete LUNs. You can also use this node to configure the Fibre Channel and iSCSI connections that servers use to access LUNs.

- **Subsystems** This node lists all of the storage subsystems currently discovered within the SAN environment. You can rename subsystems using this node.

- **Drives** This node lists all the drives in the storage subsystems discovered in the SAN. You can use this node to identify drives that you are working with by making the drive light blink.

Managing Fibre Channel LUNs

In a Fibre Channel environment, LUNs created on a Fibre Channel disk storage subsystem are assigned directly to a server or cluster. Servers access the LUN through one or more Fibre Channel host bus adapter (HBA) ports. Using Storage Manager For SANs, you can identify the server that will access the LUN and then specify which HBA ports will be used for LUN traffic. You can add ports manually by specifying their World Wide Name. You can also view detailed information about Fibre Channel HBAs for servers in your SAN by using the Storage Explorer console. Storage Explorer is covered in more detail later in this lesson.

Managing iSCSI LUNs

iSCSI is a SAN protocol that uses traditional network technologies—rather than the special cabling used by Fibre Channel—to send SCSI commands from initiators installed on servers to SCSI-based storage devices located on the network. Unlike Fibre Channel, iSCSI LUNs are not assigned directly to a server or cluster, but are assigned to logical entities called targets. These targets manage the connections between the iSCSI hardware and the servers that access it. A target includes the IP address, or portal, of the iSCSI device as well as the device's security settings—usually whatever credentials the server needs to provide to authenticate with the device. The specifics of the credentials vary from vendor to vendor.

To connect to a target, a server uses an iSCSI Initiator. An iSCSI Initiator is a logical entity that allows communication with the target from the server. The Windows Server 2008 R2 iSCSI Initiator is located in Control Panel. The iSCSI Initiator logs on to the target and, when granted access, allows the server to read and write to all LUNs assigned to that target. Each iSCSI Initiator can communicate through one or more network adapters. The Windows Server 2008 R2 iSCSI Initiator is shown in Figure 10-13.

> **MORE INFO** **ISCSI INITIATOR**
>
> For more information on the iSCSI Initiator, see the following TechNet page:
> *http://technet.microsoft.com/en-us/library/ee338477(WS.10).aspx.*

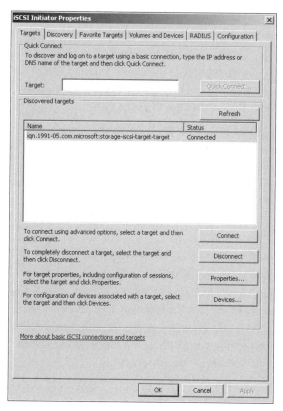

FIGURE 10-13 Windows Server 2008 R2 iSCSI Initiator

Multipath I/O

MPIO is a feature of Windows Server 2008 that allows a server to use multiple data paths to a storage device. This increases the availability of storage resources because it provides alternate paths from a server or cluster to a storage subsystem in the event of path failure. MPIO uses redundant physical path components (such as adapters, switches, and cabling) to create separate paths between the server or cluster and the storage device. If one of the devices in these separate paths fails, an alternate path to the SAN device will be used, ensuring that the server is still able to access critical data. You configure failover times through the Microsoft iSCSI Software Initiator driver or by modifying the Fibre Channel HBA driver parameter settings, depending on the SAN technology deployed in your environment.

If the server will access a LUN through multiple Fibre Channel ports or multiple iSCSI Initiator adapters, you must install MPIO on servers. You should verify that a server supports MPIO prior to enabling multiple iSCSI Initiator adapters or multiple Fibre Channel ports for LUN access. If you do not do this, data loss is likely to occur. In the event that you are unsure whether a server supports MPIO, enable only a single iSCSI Initiator adapter or Fibre Channel port on the server.

Windows Server 2008 R2 MPIO supports iSCSI, Fibre Channel, and Serially Attached Storage (SAS) SAN connectivity by establishing multiple connections or sessions to the storage device. The Windows Server 2008 R2 MPIO implementation includes a Device Specific Module (DSM) that works with storage devices that support the asymmetric logical unit access (ALUA) controller model as well as storage devices that use the Active/Active controller model. MPIO also supports the following load-balancing policies:

- **Failover** When this policy is implemented, no load balancing is performed. The application specifies a primary path and a group of standby paths. The primary path is used for all device requests. The standby paths are used only if the primary path fails. Standby paths are listed from most preferred path to least preferred path.

- **Failback** When this policy is configured, I/O is limited to a preferred path while that path is functioning. If the preferred path fails, I/O is directed to an alternate path. I/O will switch back to the preferred path automatically when that path returns to full functionality.

- **Round-robin** All available paths are used for I/O in a balanced fashion. If a path fails, I/O is redistributed among the remaining paths.

- **Round-robin with a subset of paths** When this policy is configured, a set of preferred paths is specified for I/O and a set of standby paths is specified for failover. The set of preferred paths will be used until all paths fail, at which point failover will occur to the standby path set. The preferred paths are used in a round-robin fashion.

- **Dynamic Least Queue Depth** I/O is directed to the path with the least number of outstanding requests.

- **Weighted path** Each path is assigned a weight. The path with the least weight is chosen for I/O.

Load-balancing policies are dependent on the controller model (ALUA or true Active/Active) of the storage array attached to the computer running Windows Server 2008. MPIO is added to a computer running Windows Server 2008 R2 by using the Add Features item in the Features area of Server Manager.

> **MORE INFO** **UNDERSTANDING MPIO**
>
> To learn more about MPIO, see the following TechNet page: *http://technet.microsoft.com/ en-us/library/ee619734(WS.10).aspx*.

Storage Explorer

Storage Explorer, shown in Figure 10-14 and available from the Administrative Tools menu, is used to manage Fibre Channel and iSCSI fabrics on the SAN. A *fabric* is a network topology where storage devices are interconnected through one or more data paths. In a Fibre Channel fabric, this network will include multiple Fibre Channel switches that are used to connect servers and storage devices to each other through virtual point-to-point connections. In iSCSI fabrics, the network will include multiple Internet Storage Name Service (iSNS) servers that allow for the discovery and partitioning of resources.

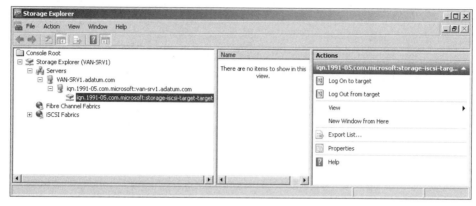

FIGURE 10-14 Storage Explorer

The Storage Explorer console can display detailed information about servers that are connected to the SAN, as well as data about fabric components such as host bus adapters, Fibre Channel switches, iSCSI Initiators, and iSCSI targets. Storage Explorer can be used to configure iSCSI security, configure iSCSI target portals, add iSNS servers, and manage Discovery Domains and Discovery Domain Sets. To view and manage an iSCSI fabric, you must enable the WMI exception in Windows Firewall on each server running Windows Server 2008 that is a part of the fabric. Many of the iSCSI-related management tasks that you can perform using Storage Explorer can also be performed using the Microsoft iSCSI Initiator (located in Control Panel) or from the Microsoft iSNS Server.

> **MORE INFO** **STORAGE EXPLORER**
>
> To learn more about Storage Explorer, consult the following TechNet page:
> *http://technet.microsoft.com/en-us/library/cc731884.aspx.*

Lesson Summary

- A LUN is a logical reference to a portion of a storage subsystem. A LUN can represent a disk, a section of a disk, an entire disk array, or a section of a disk array in the storage subsystem.
- MPIO supports multiple data paths to storage devices. MPIO must be installed on a server if a LUN will be accessed through multiple Fibre Channel HBA ports or multiple iSCSI Initiators.
- Servers and clusters connect to Fibre Channel arrays using HBA ports. Servers and clusters use iSCSI Initiators to connect to iSCSI targets, which manage iSCSI arrays.
- Storage Manager For SANS is used to create and manage LUNs on iSCSI and Fibre Channel devices. Storage Explorer is used to manage iSCSI and Fibre Channel fabrics.

Lesson Review

You can use the following questions to test your knowledge of the information in Lesson 2, "Planning Windows Server 2008 R2 Storage." The questions are also available on the companion CD if you prefer to review them in electronic form.

> **NOTE ANSWERS**
>
> Answers to these questions and explanations of why each answer choice is correct or incorrect are located in the "Answers" section at the end of the book.

1. Which of the following features of Windows Server 2008 R2 should you install prior to enabling access to a LUN through multiple Fibre Channel ports?

   A. Remote Differential Compression

   B. Universal Description, Discovery, and Integration (UDDI)

   C. MPIO

   D. RPC over HTTP Proxy

2. Assuming that your iSCSI storage device supports all LUN types, which LUN type would you select when you want to maximize I/O performance but retain fault tolerance?

   A. Spanned

   B. Striped

   C. Simple

   D. Striped with parity

3. Which of the following MPIO policies should you choose to ensure that a server that is configured with four paths between the server and the SAN array directs traffic equally to all paths during normal operation?

   A. Failback

   B. Round-robin

   C. Weighted Path

   D. Dynamic Least Queue Depth

4. Which of the following tools in Windows Server 2008 R2 would you use to create LUNs on a Fibre Channel storage array?

   A. Storage Manager For SANs

   B. Storage Explorer

   C. Device Manager

   D. Disk Management

PRACTICE **Install and Configure DFS**

In this practice, you will install and configure DFS. You will also configure offline settings for DFS shares.

EXERCISE 1   Install DFS

In this exercise, you will install the DFS role on servers VAN-SRV1 and VAN-SRV2. To complete this practice, perform the following steps:

1. Turn on computer VAN-DC1. When computer VAN-DC1 has booted completely, turn on servers VAN-SRV1 and VAN-SRV2.

2. Log on to server VAN-SRV1 with the Kim_Akers user account. Open an administrative Windows PowerShell prompt and run the following commands:

   ```
   Import-Module ServerManager
   ```

   ```
   Add-WindowsFeature FS-DFS
   ```

3. Log on to server VAN-SRV2 with the Kim_Akers user account. Open an administrative PowerShell prompt and run the following commands:

   ```
   Import-Module ServerManager
   ```

   ```
   Add-WindowsFeature FS-DFS
   ```

EXERCISE 2   Configure DFS Namespace and Add a Namespace Server

In this exercise, you will use the DFS Management console to create a DFS namespace. You will then ensure that this domain-based namespace is highly available by adding a second namespace server. To complete this practice, perform the following steps:

1. While logged on to server VAN-SRV1 with the Kim_Akers user account, open the DFS Management console from the Administrative Tools menu.

2. Select the Namespaces node. In the Actions pane, click New Namespace. This will open the New Namespace Wizard.

3. On the Namespace Server page, enter the name **VAN-SRV1** and then click Next.

4. On the Namespace Name and Settings page, enter the name **TrainingKit** and then click Next.

5. On the Namespace Type page, ensure that Domain-Based Namespace and Enable Windows Server 2008 Mode are selected, and then click Next. Click Create, and then click Close.

6. Click the \\adatum.com\TrainingKit node under the Namespaces node. In the Actions pane, click Add Namespace Server.

7. In the Add Namespace Server dialog box, type **VAN-SRV2,** as shown in Figure 10-15, and then click OK.

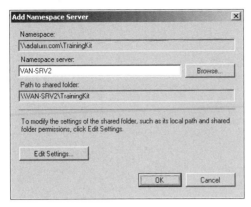

FIGURE 10-15 The Add Namespace Server dialog box

EXERCISE 3   Create a New DFS Folder and Replication Group

In this exercise, you will create a new shared folder that will use DFS to replicate between VAN-SRV1 and VAN-SRV2. To complete this practice, perform the following steps:

1. Under the Namespaces node, click the \\adatum.com\TrainingKit node. In the Actions pane, click New Folder.

2. In the New Folder dialog box, enter the name **Synchronize** and then click Add. In the Add Folder Target dialog box, click Browse.

3. In the Browse For Shared Folders dialog box, click New Shared Folder. In the Create Share dialog box, enter the name **Synchronize.** Next to the Local Path Of Shared Folder text box, click Browse. In the Browse For Folder dialog box, click c$, and then click Make New Folder. Enter the name **Synchronize** and then click OK. Verify that the Create Share dialog box matches Figure 10-16, and then click OK three times to return to the New Folder dialog box.

4. Click Add again. On the Add Folder Target page, click Browse. Click Browse again and select server VAN-SRV2. Click New Shared Folder. In the Create Share dialog box, enter the name **Synchronize.** Next to the Local Path Of Shared Folder text box, click Browse. In the Browse For Folder dialog box, click c$, and then click Make New Folder. Enter the name **Synchronize** and then click OK four times until the Replication dialog box is displayed.

5. In the Replication dialog box, click Yes. This will start the Replication Folder Wizard. On the Replication Group And Replicated Folder Name page, verify that the name is set to adatum.com\trainingkit\synchronize and the Replicated Folder Name is set to Synchronize, and then click Next.

6. On the Replication Eligibility page, click Next.

7. On the Primary Member page, use the drop-down menu to select VAN-SRV1, and then click Next.

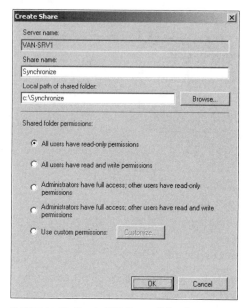

FIGURE 10-16 Create DFS Share dialog box

8. On the Topology Selection page, select the Full Mesh option, and then click Next.

9. On the Replication Group Schedule And Bandwidth page, verify that the Replicate Continuously Using The Specified Bandwidth option is selected and the Bandwidth setting is configured as Full, and then click Next. Click Create and then click Close. Click OK to close the dialog box.

EXERCISE 4 Configure Offline File Settings for Shares

In this exercise, you will configure the offline file settings for the Synchronize share and enable access-based enumeration for the share rather than for the entire DFS namespace. To complete this practice, perform the following steps:

1. Ensure that you are logged on to server VAN-SRV1 with the Kim_Akers user account.

2. From the Administrative Tools menu, open the Share And Storage Management console.

3. In the details pane of the Share And Storage Management console, click the Synchronize folder. On the Actions menu, click Properties.

4. On the Sharing tab of the Synchronize Properties dialog box, click the Advanced button. Select the Enable Access-Based Enumeration check box.

5. On the Caching tab, select the All Files And Programs That Users Open From The Share Are Automatically Available Offline item, and then select the Optimized For Performance option. Click OK twice.

Chapter Review

To further practice and reinforce the skills you learned in this chapter, you can perform the following tasks:

- Review the chapter summary.
- Review the list of key terms introduced in this chapter.
- Complete the case scenarios. These scenarios set up real-world situations involving the topics of this chapter and ask you to create a solution.
- Complete the suggested practices.
- Take a practice test.

Chapter Summary

- You can configure storage redundancy using software RAID 1 and RAID 5 in Windows Server 2008 and Windows Server 2008 R2 if you have an appropriate number of disks.
- DFS allows you to provision data across sites in your organization through replication.
- SharePoint Foundation 2010 allows you to provide your organization with a file collaboration and versioning infrastructure beyond what is offered by file-sharing services and DFS.
- A LUN is a logical reference point to a portion of a storage subsystem, ranging from a partition on a disk to an entire storage array.
- MPIO is used to provide fault-tolerant paths from servers to SAN arrays.

Key Terms

The following terms were introduced in this chapter. Do you know what they mean?

- DFS
- LUN
- Versioning

Case Scenarios

In the following case scenarios, you will apply what you have learned about planning server installs and upgrades. You can find answers to these questions in the "Answers" section at the end of this book.

Case Scenario 1: DFS at Wingtip Toys

Wingtip Toys has several sites across Australia. You want to ensure that important documents are replicated to each site, so you are planning to install DFS. All sites have VPN links to every other site, and every site will have a computer running Windows Server 2008 R2 that is dedicated to hosting local replicas of each DFS shared folder. You want to ensure that the namespace is still accessible in the event that a site's Internet connection fails for several hours. With this information in mind, answer the following questions:

1. What service should you add to the computer running Windows Server 2008 R2 at each site prior to configuring it as a replica?

2. How can you ensure that the namespace is accessible if the site's VPN connections fail?

3. How can you ensure that any replica is able to update any other replica?

Case Scenario 2: Provision Data at Contoso

You are in the process of developing a data provisioning strategy for Contoso. You want to be able to ensure that users from the Accounting group can track who has made modifications to files. You want to be able to ensure that users in the Management group are able to access files that are stored on shared folders even when they are travelling, and you want to ensure that the Management Group file servers are able to survive the failure of a hard disk drive. With this information in mind, answer the following questions:

1. Which technology should you deploy so that you can meet your file workflow objectives for the Accounting group?

2. What feature should you enable to ensure that Management users are able to access shared files when they take their portable computers home?

3. Which software version of RAID could you implement on the servers hosting the shared files for the Management group to meet your objectives?

Suggested Practices

To help you successfully master the exam objectives presented in this chapter, complete the following tasks.

Provision Data

Do all the practices in this section if you have access to the appropriate hardware:

- Practice 1: Create an additional DFS namespace and populate it with replicated folders.

- Practice 2: Download and install SharePoint Foundation 2010. Create, upload, and check out documents.

Configure Storage

Do all the practices in this section if you have access to the appropriate SAN array hardware:

- Configure the iSCSI Initiator to connect to an iSCSI target.

- Configure a LUN of the RAID 5 type on a SAN.

- Assign the LUN to a computer running Windows Server 2008 R2.

Take a Practice Test

The practice tests on this book's companion CD offer many options. For example, you can test yourself on just one exam objective, or you can test yourself on all the exam content. You can set up the test so that it closely simulates the experience of taking a certification exam, or you can set it up in study mode so that you can look at the correct answers and explanations after you answer each question.

> **MORE INFO   PRACTICE TESTS**
>
> For details about all the practice test options available, see the section "How to Use the Practice Tests" in this book's Introduction.

CHAPTER 11

Clustering and High Availability

High availability is about ensuring that important services and applications remain available to clients on the network if a server suffers a catastrophic failure. You can take several different approaches to implementing high availability. The one that you choose depends on the resources you have available at your disposal. The cheapest way of ensuring high availability is using DNS Round Robin. DNS Round Robin has the advantage of being a cross-platform solution, but it has the disadvantage of not being aware when one of the DNS Round Robin target servers fails. Network Load Balancing (NLB) allows you to balance traffic across multiple servers and is failure-aware, but it doesn't work well directly with server applications, such as file servers. Failover clustering ensures that you still will have access to the network service or application in the event of catastrophic server failure, but it has the disadvantage of requiring access to a storage area network (SAN). In this chapter, you will learn about each of these high-availability solutions and how you can decide which one of them is appropriate to deploy to support your organization's specific needs.

Exam objectives in this chapter:
- Plan high availability.

Lessons in this chapter:

Before You Begin

To complete the exercises in the practice in this chapter, you need to have done the following:
- Complete the setup tasks outlined in Exercises 1 through 4 in Appendix A, "Setup Instructions for Windows Server 2008 R2."

No additional configuration is required for this chapter.

REAL WORLD

Orin Thomas

The big disadvantage of failover clustering is that not only do you need to perform all the mucking about to get the storage on the SAN running properly, you also need to allocate an expensive server to sit in place doing nothing until the server that is actually doing something fails. This is why many applications are moving toward a continuous replication method of providing high availability rather than the traditional "one node is active, one node does nothing" approach of the traditional failover cluster. A great example of this new approach to high availability is the Database Availability Groups in Microsoft Exchange Server 2010. Database Availability Groups provide the essential functionality of a failover cluster without all the mucking about required to set up a SAN. If one Exchange Server 2010 mailbox server fails, another server, hosting a passive copy of the first server's mailbox databases, automatically takes over. So although Microsoft made configuring failover clusters a lot easier with the release of Windows Server 2008 and Windows Server 2008 R2, technologies such as Database Availability Groups mean that in the future, you are less likely to actually need to configure a failover cluster.

Lesson 1: DNS Round Robin and Network Load Balancing

This lesson covers DNS Round Robin and NLB, two technologies that you can use as part of a basic high-availability strategy. Both DNS Round Robin and NLB are supported on all editions of Windows Server 2008 and Windows Server 2008 R2.

> **After this lesson, you will be able to:**
> - Plan and deploy DNS Round Robin as an appropriate availability solution.
> - Plan and deploy NLB as an appropriate availability solution.
>
> **Estimated lesson time: 60 minutes**

Simple Availability Strategies

DNS Round Robin and NLB are two relatively simple technologies that you can use to provide application availability. These technologies allow you to add capacity to an overloaded service by adding more servers. For example, if you were using one of these technologies to support a website and you found your website overloaded with traffic, you could deal with this problem by adding more web servers. Either DNS Round Robin or NLB would distribute the traffic across those servers, reducing the load and increasing your capacity.

These technologies require that the content hosted on each node is the same—for example, if used with Remote Desktop, that each Remote Desktop server hosts the same applications, or if used with websites, that each website connects to the same back-end SQL Server database. You can't use DNS Round Robin or NLB with services such as file shares because the content of the file share needs to be in one place, not spread across multiple servers.

DNS Round Robin

DNS Round Robin works by providing different IP responses from a DNS server to requests for the same host name. For example, with DNS Round Robin, you can associate the DNS record for the fully qualified domain name (FQDN) *www.contoso.internal* with two different IP addresses, 10.10.111.111 and 10.10.222.222. When one client queries the DNS server for the *www.contoso.internal* host address, the DNS server returns 10.10.111.111. The next client to query the same DNS server will receive the address 10.10.122.222.

If more than two IP addresses are associated with the same host name, the DNS server provides each address to requesting clients in a round-robin fashion. Providing the next IP address in the list associated with the host name allows the DNS Round Robin technology to provide a crude form of traffic aggregation. While there is no hard limit to the number of IP addresses that can be associated with a specific host name, the capacity of the DNS server that hosts the zone determines the functional limit to the number of records that can exist within a DNS zone. With DNS Round Robin, you can associate 200 or 2,000 different IP addresses with a single host name. If you did associate 2,000 different IP addresses with one name, the DNS server would work through the list of all the IP addresses in response to queries for the host name before returning to the top of the list and starting again.

Netmask Ordering

Netmask ordering is an extension to DNS Round Robin that allows the DNS server to take into account the IP address of the querying client when providing a response. When you enable netmask ordering, the DNS server will attempt to return a host IP address that is on the same subnet as the querying client. For example, if you had associated the IP addresses 10.10.111.111 and 10.10.222.222 with the host name *www.contoso.internal* and enabled netmask ordering, and a client that had the IP address 10.10.222.100 queried the DNS server for that host name, the DNS server would always respond with IP address 10.10.222.222. This is because netmask ordering always attempts to provide the client with the host address that is on the same network. If the querying client is not on the same subnet as any of the DNS Round Robin records, the round-robin process functions as normal.

The DNS role on Windows Server 2008 and Windows Server 2008 R2 has DNS Round Robin and netmask ordering enabled by default. To verify the status of DNS Round Robin and netmask ordering on a DNS server, perform the following steps:

1. From the Administrative Tools menu, open the DNS Manager console.

2. Open the DNS server properties and click the Advanced tab.

3. Verify that the Enable Round Robin and Enable Netmask Ordering options are selected, as shown in Figure 11-1.

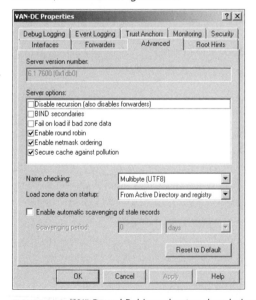

FIGURE 11-1 DNS Round Robin and netmask ordering status

Creating DNS Round Robin Entries

As DNS servers running Windows Server 2008 and Windows Server 2008 R2 support DNS Round Robin by default, all you need to do to use it is create multiple A or AAAA records associated with the same host name. For example, to add multiple records for the host name *www.contoso.internal* on the DNS server that hosts the Contoso.internal primary zone, you could use the dnscmd command in the following fashion:

```
Dnscmd /recordadd Contoso.internal www A 10.10.111.111
Dnscmd /recordadd Contoso.internal www A 10.10.111.222
Dnscmd /recordadd Contoso.internal www A 10.10.222.222
Dnscmd /recordadd Contoso.internal www A 10.10.222.111
```

Figure 11-2 shows the result of adding these records to the Contoso.internal zone.

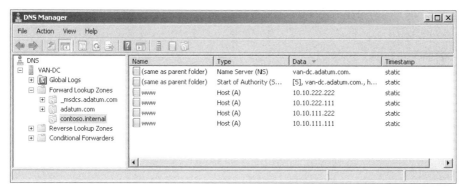

FIGURE 11-2 DNS Round Robin records

To remove a DNS Round Robin record, simply delete it from the zone that hosts the record.

Remember that the DNS server is unaware whether the host that it is directing the client to actually exists or is available. When you create a DNS record, no check is performed to verify that the host you are pointing to is available. If a host fails, the DNS server will continue to direct clients to that host until such time as the DNS record for that host is removed.

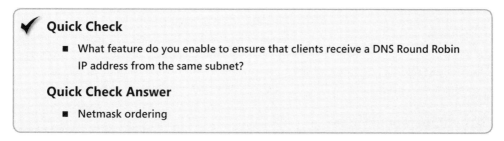

✔ **Quick Check**

- What feature do you enable to ensure that clients receive a DNS Round Robin IP address from the same subnet?

Quick Check Answer

- Netmask ordering

Network Load Balancing

When you create an NLB cluster, it creates a virtual network address and adapter, with traffic to this address distributed across a number of hosts. The virtual network adapter has an IP address and a media access control (MAC) address.

A Windows Server 2008 R2 NLB cluster supports up to 32 nodes, although Microsoft's testing has found that using more than 8 nodes in a single cluster decreases cluster efficiency. Microsoft recommends that if you need clusters larger than 8 nodes, you should build multiple clusters with no more than 8 nodes per cluster and then use DNS Round Robin to spread traffic across these clusters.

A big advantage of NLB over DNS Round Robin is that NLB automatically reconfigures as nodes join or fail out of the cluster. An administrator can add and remove nodes through the NLB Manager interface or on the command line. For example, suppose that an administrator needs to apply an operating system update that requires a server reboot. The administrator can apply the update to each node of the cluster in turn, blocking new incoming connections to that node until the node is servicing no active clients, applying the update, rebooting the node, and then allowing the node to resume servicing cluster traffic. The administrator can continue this process for each node of the cluster while ensuring continuity of service to hosts accessing the cluster over the network.

Although all members of an NLB cluster should be running the same operating system, it is possible to run a mixed-mode NLB cluster containing nodes that are running Windows Server 2003, Windows Server 2008, and Windows Server 2008 R2. If you are in a situation where different nodes within a cluster are running different versions of Windows Server, you should upgrade nodes with older operating systems so that they are all running the newest operating system present in the cluster operating system. You will create an NLB cluster in the practice at the end of the chapter.

> **MORE INFO** **NETWORK LOAD BALANCING DEPLOYMENT GUIDE**
>
> For more information on deploying NLB, consult the Network Load Balancing Deployment Guide at *http://technet.microsoft.com/en-us/library/cc754833(WS.10).aspx*.

Heartbeat and Convergence

Servers within NLB clusters constantly communicate with each other, verifying which nodes are available using a process known as heartbeat and convergence. The heartbeat is a message sent every second by each node participating in an NLB cluster to all other nodes. If a cluster node fails to transmit five consecutive heartbeats, the convergence process begins and the cluster reconfigures itself. Convergence can be triggered by the unexpected loss of a host, a host returning to functionality, or an administrator manually adding or removing nodes from the cluster. Convergence also occurs when you modify port rules.

Cluster Operation Mode

When you create a new NLB cluster, you have to determine which cluster operation mode to use. Cluster operation mode is primarily dependent on the number of network adapters installed on each cluster node. NLB has two modes of operation: unicast and multicast. All servers within a cluster must operate in one mode or the other. You cannot mix the two operation modes. These operational modes function as described in the following sections.

NLB UNICAST MODE

The MAC address created for the virtual network adapter is shared among the participants within the cluster. If the cluster nodes have only one network card, the cluster's virtual MAC address logically replaces the physical MAC address for that network card and the server will respond to network traffic targeted at the virtual MAC address. While the server still retains its original IP address, that original IP address will resolve to the virtual MAC address rather than the physical MAC address.

When you use NLB unicast mode on servers that have a single network adapter, only computers within the same subnet as that server will be able to communicate with that server using its original IP address. This means that if you need to perform management tasks on that server, you need to connect from the same subnet as the NLB cluster. For example, suppose that one of the servers in a unicast-mode NLB cluster has an original IP address of 192.168.15.10 and the cluster IP address is 192.168.15.100. You have configured NLB to support a web server, and a port rule is set up for port 80. If you wanted to connect to this server using Remote Desktop, you would be able to make a connection to IP address 192.168.15.10 only from a host on the same subnet. You would not be able to make a successful Remote Desktop connection to IP address 192.168.15.10 from a remote subnet because the unicast configuration replaces the physical MAC address with the cluster virtual MAC address.

NLB unicast mode is most appropriate when there are two network cards installed on a host. The first network card participates in the cluster, while you use the other for management and inter-server communication. When you configure a server to have two network cards as a member of a unicast-mode NLB cluster, you can make management connections to the server from remote subnets.

NLB MULTICAST MODE

NLB multicast mode is more suitable than NLB unicast mode for computers that have single network adapters. This is because when using NLB multicast mode, the server retains its original MAC address and IP address in addition to being able to use the virtual MAC address and IP address created for the cluster. This means that you can perform remote administration from separate subnets as in the scenario described earlier, even though the server only has a single network card. The only drawback of NLB multicast mode is that network devices, such as the switches and routers, must support multicast MAC addressing. This is less of a problem today than it was in the past.

IGMP MULTICAST MODE

IGMP multicast mode is a special version of NLB multicast mode that enhances network performance by limiting switch flooding. Enabling IGMP support means that multicast traffic passes through only switch ports that service the NLB cluster rather than all switch ports, which is the case with standard NLB multicast mode. It is possible to use IGMP multicast mode only if your switch hardware supports this technology.

Managing NLB Clusters

You manage NLB clusters using the Network Load Balancing Manager console, accessible from the Administrative Tools menu and shown in Figure 11-3. Using this tool, you can perform tasks such as altering the port rules and parameters under which the cluster operates. To manage NLB clusters, you must be a member of the local Administrators group on each node of the cluster.

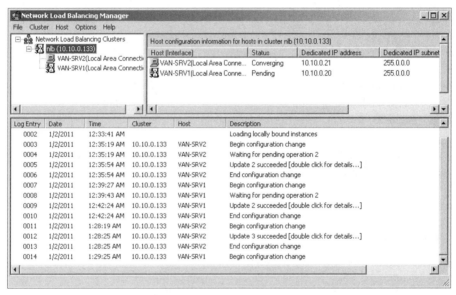

FIGURE 11-3 The Network Load Balancing Manager console

To remove hosts from NLB clusters through the Network Load Balancing Manager, simply right-click the host that you want to remove and select Delete Host. You can remove the entire cluster by right-clicking the cluster and selecting Delete Cluster.

If you want to perform maintenance on a cluster node, you have the option of blocking incoming connections while retaining existing connections. You can then wait for the existing connections to terminate before performing your maintenance task. You have the following options for controlling NLB cluster nodes:

- **Start**   Starts a cluster that has been stopped.
- **Stop**   Stops a cluster. This will terminate any active connections.

- **Drainstop** This stops a cluster node from receiving any new connections but does not terminate existing connections. You would use Drainstop prior to shutting down a cluster node gracefully.

- **Suspend** This pauses the cluster node until the Resume command is issued. This differs from the Stop option in that Stop shuts down the cluster service on the targeted node.

- **Resume** Resume the cluster node after it has been suspended.

> **MORE INFO STOPPING AND STARTING TRAFFIC ON AN NLB NODE**
>
> For more information about stopping, starting, and using Drainstop on NLB cluster nodes, consult the following TechNet article: *http://technet.microsoft.com/en-us/library/cc770345(WS.10).aspx*.

NLB Port Rules

NLB port rules allow you to control how NLB clusters deal with traffic to a specific port, such as port 80 for web traffic. Port rules are set on the Port Rules tab of the Cluster Properties dialog box, as shown in Figure 11-4. Port rules must match for each host within the NLB cluster. When you configure port rules on the cluster level, the port rules for all nodes in the cluster are configured automatically. A node will be unable to join the cluster if it has a different set of port rules. The default port rule for an NLB cluster redirects all traffic in a balanced way to all nodes in the cluster. You should delete this default rule if you want to create specific rules.

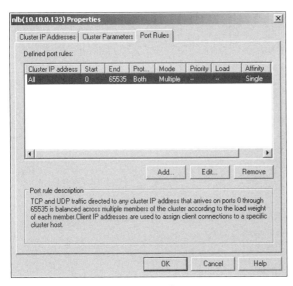

FIGURE 11-4 Setting cluster port rules

When creating an NLB cluster port rule, you choose a filtering mode. Filtering modes allow you to specify whether only a single node, some nodes, or all nodes in the cluster respond to requests from a single client during the session. This is important for some applications, such as e-commerce websites, because they require all session traffic to occur only between a single host and the client. The following three filtering modes are used:

- **Single Host** A single node handles all traffic sent to the cluster matching the port rule. For example, all traffic to the cluster IP address on port 25 goes to server ALPHA.

- **Disable Port Range** Use this mode to configure the cluster not to respond to traffic on specific ports. NLB discards traffic sent to the cluster IP on these ports.

- **Multiple Host Filtering** This mode allows traffic to be directed to all nodes in the cluster. When you configure multiple host settings, you also configure an affinity setting. Affinity settings work as follows:

  - **None.** All requests are distributed equally across the cluster, even if a client has an established session.

  - **Network.** This is similar to netmask ordering and directs clients to the closest node on the basis of the subnet.

  - **Single.** After a client establishes a session, all subsequent requests in the session will be directed to the same node in the cluster. This allows sessions that require stateful data, such as ecommerce transactions, to be completed. This is the default filtering mode on port rules.

To create an NLB cluster port rule, perform the following steps:

1. From the Administrative Tools menu, open the NLB console.

2. Right-click the cluster and then click Cluster Properties.

3. On the Port Rules tab of the Properties dialog box, click Add.

4. In the Add/Edit Port Rule dialog box, specify the port range the rule applies to, the protocols the rule applies to, and the filtering mode, as shown in Figure 11-5.

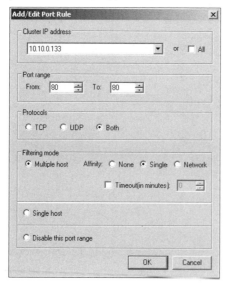

FIGURE 11-5 Setting a new NLB port rule

Comparing DNS Round Robin to Network Load Balancing

As you learned earlier in this lesson, DNS Round Robin can work in conjunction with NLB in situations where you create multiple NLB clusters and then use DNS Round Robin to spread traffic across those clusters. One of the advantages of DNS Round Robin is that it is not tied to a specific operating system, so you can configure it to forward client requests not only to web servers running on Microsoft operating systems but also to web servers running on third-party operating systems.

DNS Round Robin suffers from the following drawbacks when compared to NLB:

- **DNS has no control over the distribution of the load**   DNS Round Robin offers no way to allocate load evenly across hosts. This can result in an unbalanced load, with more clients using one server and fewer using another.

- **DNS Round Robin is not fault-tolerant**   There is no way for DNS Round Robin to compensate for the failure of a host. The DNS server will still redirect clients to the failed host until you manually update the DNS zone. You should also be careful to configure a short Time to Live (TTL) on DNS host records to ensure that records related to failed hosts do not persist in DNS client caches after you have removed them from the DNS zone. If the DNS server fails, then DNS Round Robin ceases to work.

- **DNS Round Robin is not session-friendly**   If you set a DNS TTL too short, the TTL may expire while a client is actively using an application. When this occurs, the client will query for the server's address. With DNS Round Robin, you have no way to control which address the client will receive, meaning that the client's next request could be sent to a different server that does not have session information for that client.

Lesson Summary

- DNS Round Robin works by providing DNS clients with different IP addresses for the same host name.

- DNS Round Robin can be configured to use netmask ordering. When netmask ordering is enabled, the DNS server will attempt to provide the client with the address of a host on the same subnet.

- DNS Round Robin and netmask ordering are enabled by default when you install the DNS Server role on computers running Windows Server 2008 or Windows Server 2008 R2.

- NLB is a feature that you can install on computers running all editions of Windows Server 2008 and Windows Server 2008 R2.

- NLB unicast mode is recommended for computers with two or more network cards. It is possible to use NLB unicast mode if a server has one network card, but you will be able to perform network management tasks against that server only from its local subnet.

- NLB multicast mode uses multicast addresses for cluster traffic. IGMP multicast mode uses special switch functionality to reduce the impact of multicast mode on network devices.

- NLB port rules allow you to determine how NLB clusters manage traffic. Affinity settings determine whether traffic is sent to one specific node or whether traffic is sent to any available node. Affinity settings can be configured to ensure that disconnected sessions always reconnect to the same node.

- You can use the Drainstop functionality to block new sessions for a specific node without terminating existing sessions to that node.

Lesson Review

You can use the following questions to test your knowledge of the information in Lesson 1, "DNS Round Robin and Network Load Balancing." The questions are also available on the companion CD if you prefer to review them in electronic form.

> *NOTE* **ANSWERS**
>
> Answers to these questions and explanations of why each answer choice is correct or incorrect are located in the "Answers" section at the end of the book.

1. You have configured DNS Round Robin for the host name www.contoso.com. You want to ensure that the DNS server returns the IP address of the server on the same subnet as the requesting client if the situation arises. Which of the following steps should you take to accomplish this goal?

   A. Enable netmask ordering.

   B. Configure a secondary DNS zone.

   C. Configure a DNS stub zone.

   D. Enable affinity.

2. You need to place an SMTP server on one node of a four-node NLB cluster. Which of the following port rules should you configure to accomplish this goal?

   A. Single Host

   B. Disable Port Range

   C. Multiple Host Filtering, single affinity

   D. Multiple Host Filtering, no affinity

3. You are configuring a port rule for an NLB cluster in your organization. You want to ensure that clients are redirected to the NLB node on their subnet. Which of the following filtering modes and affinities should you use when creating your port rule?

   A. Single Host, no affinity

   B. Multiple Host Filtering, no affinity

   C. Multiple Host Filtering, network affinity

   D. Multiple Host Filtering, single affinity

4. You are preparing to perform an operating system update that will require a reboot on the four nodes in your organization's NLB cluster. You want to stop new sessions being created on each node that you will service without disrupting existing sessions. Which of the following options should you use to accomplish this goal?

   A. Stop

   B. Start

   C. Drainstop

   D. Suspend

Lesson 2: Windows Server 2008 Cluster Tools

Failover clustering in Windows Server 2008 and Windows Server 2008 R2 allows you to provide an availability solution for network services that rely on a single data source, such as a Hyper-V virtual machine, that can be hosted in only one place at a time. You manage failover clusters using the Failover Cluster Manager console interface in Windows Server 2008 and Windows Server 2008 R2. Failover clustering is available only to computers running the Enterprise and Datacenter editions of Windows Server 2008 and Windows Server 2008 R2.

After this lesson, you will be able to:

- Understand failover clustering.
- Configure failover clusters.
- Perform a cluster migration.

Estimated lesson time: 60 minutes

Failover clusters support two types of application: single-instance and multiple-instance. The difference between these two applications is as follows:

- **Single-instance application**   A single-instance application can run on only one server at a time. An example of this is an authentication server. If an authentication server service is running on multiple servers simultaneously, the client might receive multiple answers to a request for authentication, and some of those answers might conflict, with one answer sending successful authentication and another server sending an answer of a failed authentication attempt. When running in a cluster, single-instance applications must operate on one node, with the other nodes operating in standby mode.

- **Multiple-instance application**   Multiple-instance applications can either share data or partition data in such a way that one node in the cluster can provide an answer for a particular part of the data. Advanced database servers and some email servers can operate in this fashion. Multiple-instance applications are less common than single-instance applications.

To run on a cluster, an application must meet the following criteria:

- The cluster application must use an IP-based protocol.

- Applications that require access to local databases must allow you to configure where data can be stored—for example, configuring a virtual machine to be hosted on shared storage rather than a local hard disk drive.

- If an application needs to have access to data regardless of the cluster node on which it is running, the data needs to be stored on a shared disk resource that will fail over with the Services And Applications group. This shared disk can be running on iSCSI, Serial Attached SCSI, or Fibre Channel.

- If an application can run and store data only on the local system or boot drive, you should choose the Node Majority or the Node and File Share Majority quorum model.

You will also need a separate file replication mechanism for the application data. You will learn about quorum models later in this lesson.

- If an application encounters a network disruption or fails over to an alternate cluster node, client sessions must be able to reestablish connectivity. No client connectivity exists during the failover process until an application is brought back online. If the client software does not try to reconnect and instead times out when a network connection is broken, the application is not suited for failover (or NLB) clusters.

> **MORE INFO**   **REQUIREMENTS FOR WINDOWS SERVER 2008 R2 FAILOVER CLUSTERS**
>
> To learn more about the requirements for a Windows Server 2008 R2 failover cluster, consult the following TechNet article: *http://technet.microsoft.com/en-us/library/ ff182359(WS.10).aspx*.

Understanding Cluster Concepts

Setting up a cluster in Windows Server 2008 and Windows Server 2008 R2 has few requirements. Like Windows Server 2003, Windows Server 2008 requires the same processor architecture—32-bit or 64-bit—and you cannot mix processor architectures within a cluster. Unlike Windows Server 2003, Windows Server 2008 and Windows Server 2008 R2 clustering no longer support direct SCSI connections to shared storage. You can use Fibre Channel, Serially Attached SCSI (SAS), and iSCSI for network shared storage. All servers within a cluster must be within the same Active Directory Domain Services (AD DS) domain and should be running the same operating system.

Understanding Cluster Quorum Models

Clusters stop running after a certain number of failures to protect data integrity and prevent problems that could occur because of failed or failing communication between nodes. Quorum determines the number of failures that a cluster tolerates before it stops running. Quorum exists as a database in the registry and is maintained on the witness disk or witness share. The witness disk or share keeps a copy of this configuration data so that servers can join the cluster at any time, obtaining a copy of this data to become part of the cluster. One server manages the quorum resource data at any given time, but all participating servers also have a copy. Windows Server 2008 and Windows Server 2008 R2 use four quorum models:

- **Node Majority**   This quorum model suits failover cluster deployments that contain an odd number of cluster nodes. A Node Majority cluster retains quorum if the number of available nodes exceeds the number of failed nodes. For example, for a seven-node cluster to remain online, four nodes must be available. If four nodes fail in a seven-node Node Majority cluster, the entire cluster shuts down. You should use Node Majority clusters in geographically or network-dispersed cluster nodes. To operate successfully, this model requires an extremely reliable network, high-quality hardware, and a third-party mechanism to replicate back-end data.

- **Node and Disk Majority** This quorum model suits clusters that contain even numbers of cluster nodes. So long as the witness disk remains available, a Node and Disk Majority cluster keeps running when half or more of its nodes are available. For instance, a six-node cluster will retain quorum if three or more nodes plus its witness disk are available. In this model, the cluster quorum is stored on a cluster disk that is accessible to all cluster nodes through a shared storage device using Serial Attached SCSI (SAS), Fibre Channel, or iSCSI connections. You should use the Node and Disk Majority Quorum model in failover clusters with shared storage, all connected on the same network and with an even number of nodes. In the case of a witness disk failure, a majority of the nodes needs to keep running. For example, a six-node cluster will run if three nodes and the witness disk are available. If the witness disk is offline, the same six-node cluster requires that four nodes are available.

- **Node and File Share Majority** This configuration is similar to the Node and Disk Majority model, but the quorum is stored on a network share rather than on a witness disk. You can deploy a Node and File Share Majority cluster in a similar fashion to a Node Majority cluster.

- **No Majority: Disk Only** This model can be used with clusters that have an odd number of nodes, but Microsoft recommends that you do not use this model in a production environment because the disk containing the quorum is a single point of failure. No Majority: Disk Only clusters are best suited for testing the deployment of built-in or custom services and applications on a Windows Server 2008 R2 failover cluster. In this model, provided that the disk containing the quorum remains available, the cluster can sustain the failover of all nodes except one. Should the disk hosting the quorum fail, the cluster fails even if other nodes remain online.

EXAM TIP

Even though the cluster quorum model is selected automatically during cluster creation, you should be familiar with the requirements of each model and how many nodes each model requires to remain available.

Before you deploy a failover cluster, you need to determine whether to use shared storage. If you are going to use shared storage, ensure that each node can communicate with each Logical Unit Number (LUN) the shared storage device presents. You can verify that shared storage is available to each node by using the storage-based tests in the Validate A Configuration Wizard, as shown in Figure 11-6.

When you configure the cluster, the Create Cluster Wizard will suggest the most appropriate quorum model for that cluster. For example, when you create a single-node cluster, the wizard will suggest the Node Majority quorum model. However, if you do not agree with the model chosen, you can change this from within the Failover Cluster Manager interface. If the chosen model uses shared storage and a witness disk, the smallest available LUN will be selected for this disk. If needed, you can change this after the cluster is created.

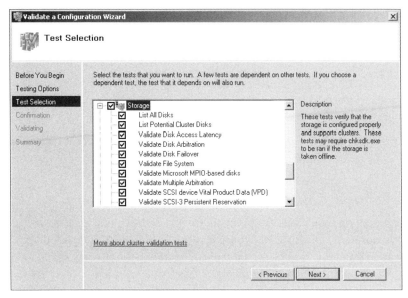

FIGURE 11-6 Validating cluster shared storage

To view the currently used cluster quorum model, perform the following steps:

1. Open the Failover Cluster Manager. In the Actions pane, click More Actions, and then click Configure Cluster Quorum Settings. This will open the Configure Cluster Quorum Wizard.

2. On the Select Quorum Configuration page, select the quorum model. The page will display the recommended quorum model, as shown in Figure 11-7.

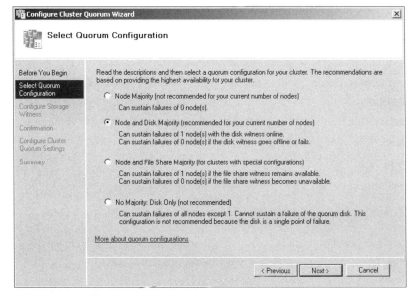

FIGURE 11-7 Configuring a quorum

Installing Failover Clustering

You can install the Failover Clustering feature using Server Manager in Windows Server 2008 and Windows Server 2008 R2. As an alternative, you can also use the following Windows PowerShell command on Windows Server 2008 R2 if the Server Manager PowerShell Module is installed:

```
Add-WindowsFeature Failover-Clustering
```

The Failover Clustering feature is supported only on the Enterprise and Datacenter editions of Windows Server 2008 and Windows Server 2008 R2.

Validating a Failover Cluster Configuration

Prior to creating a cluster, you should validate the configuration of the computers that will become nodes in the cluster. Windows Server 2008 and Windows Server 2008 R2 include several cluster validation tests. You validate component configuration like storage, network, and the server itself using the Validate A Configuration Wizard. Validating the servers that will be part of the cluster will perform tests against those servers to ensure compatibility and functionality with the proposed cluster configuration.

It is recommended that you deploy similar components, including matching computers, as part of a cluster. Other considerations for failover clustering include the following:

- Remove single points of failure, such as nodes with one network connection or more than one network connection where all connections connect to the same switch. Failure to do so may result in a warning during validation, although the tests will pass.

- Parallel SCSI cannot be used for storage and NTFS is recommended for cluster partitions. NTFS is required for the witness disk.

- Any storage using multipath I/O must be verified with the vendor to ensure that it is appropriate for Windows Server 2008 or Windows Server 2008 R2 failover clusters.

As Figure 11-8 shows, the Validate A Configuration Wizard contains five test categories:

- **Cluster Configuration**   Checks that the cluster-level components are compatible with the proposed configuration.

- **Inventory Test**   Creates an inventory of components and settings in the node.

- **Network Test**   Ensures that network settings are appropriate for clustering.

- **Storage Test**   Examines storage for compatibility with clustering.

- **System Configuration Test**   Validates system settings across servers.

MORE INFO   **CLUSTER VALIDATION TESTS**

To learn more about cluster validation tests, consult the following TechNet page: *http://technet.microsoft.com/en-us/library/cc726064.aspx*.

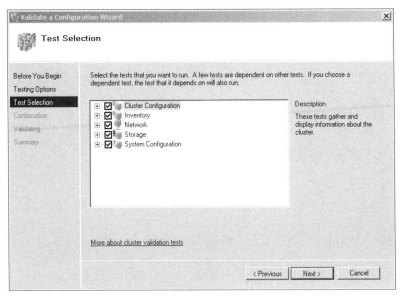

FIGURE 11-8 Cluster validation tests

Creating a Failover Cluster

Prior to creating a failover cluster, ensure that all potential cluster nodes have the Failover Cluster feature installed. To create a failover cluster, perform the following steps:

1. Open the Failover Cluster Manager from the Administrative Tools menu of one of the nodes that you want to be a member of the failover cluster.

2. In the Actions pane, click Create A Cluster. This will start the Create Cluster Wizard. Click Next.

3. On the Select Servers page, enter each of the names of the servers that will function as cluster nodes and click Add. Click Next.

4. On the Validation Warning page, choose whether to run validation tests and then click Next. If you choose to run the validation tests, the Validate A Configuration Wizard will run. If you run this wizard, choose which tests you want to run and then have the tests execute. This process will take several minutes. When the process finishes, the wizard will inform you whether the configuration is suitable for clustering, as shown in Figure 11-9. Click Finish to close this wizard.

5. In the Access Point For Administering The Cluster dialog box, enter a cluster name and an IP address and then click Next. On the Confirmation page, click Next. The cluster will now be created. Click Finish to close the wizard.

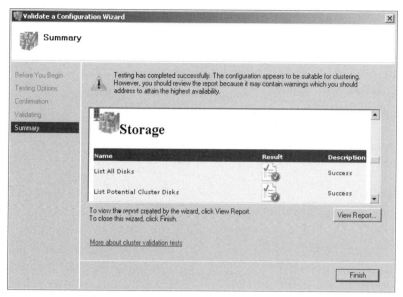

FIGURE 11-9 A configuration suitable for clustering

MORE INFO **CREATING CLUSTERS**

For more information about creating failover clusters or adding nodes to existing failover clusters, consult the following TechNet article: *http://technet.microsoft.com/en-us/library/cc730647.aspx.*

Configuring Services for High Availability

You can configure several services and applications for use in a failover cluster. Use the High Availability Wizard to configure these services and applications. Several applications and services have specific settings and are available for selection from within the High Availability Wizard. Services and applications not listed within the wizard should use the Generic Service, Generic Application, or Generic Script option. Services and applications specifically listed include the following:

- **DFS Namespace Server**   Provides a virtual view of an organization's shared folders.
- **DHCP Server**   Provides IP address information to clients.
- **Distributed Transaction Coordinator (DTC)**   Provides support for distributed applications that are used to perform transactions. A *transaction* is a set of tasks that must either succeed or fail together.
- **File Server**   Provides the ability to store files on the network.
- **Internet Storage Name Service (iSNS)**   Provides a directory of iSCSI targets.

- **Message Queuing** Used by distributed applications for communication.
- **Other Server** Provides both a client access point and storage for an application that you configure after creating the cluster.
- **Print Server** Manages the printer queue for a shared printer.
- **Remote Desktop Connection Broker** Allows sessions to be load-balanced across a Remote Desktop Server farm.
- **Virtual Machine** Allows a virtual machine to be highly available on a Hyper-V cluster.
- **WINS Server** Allows the Windows Internet Naming Service (WINS) server to remain available.

To configure a service for high availability, perform the following steps:

1. Open the Failover Cluster Manager. In the Actions pane, click Configure A Service Or Application. This will start the High Availability Wizard. Click Next.

2. On the Select Service Or Application page, shown in Figure 11-10, select the service that you want to make highly available, and then click Next. This service must be installed on the cluster nodes already.

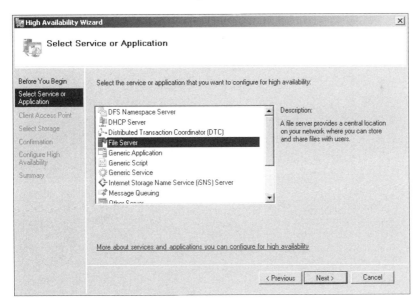

FIGURE 11-10 Add service to cluster

3. On the Client Access Point page, specify the address that clients will use to access the highly available service, and then click Next.

4. On the Select Storage page, select the storage volumes that you want to assign to the highly available application and then click Next. On the Confirmation page, click Next. The application will be made highly available. Click Finish to close the wizard.

Managing a Failover Cluster

Cluster management is performed within the Failover Cluster Manager console. Expanding a cluster reveals available options for that cluster, including nodes, networks, cluster events, and storage, as shown in Figure 11-11.

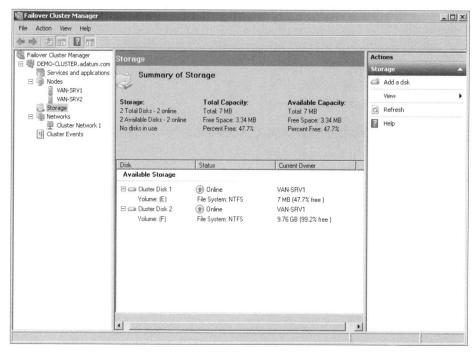

FIGURE 11-11 The Failover Cluster Manager console

To pause a node, select the node and then, from the Actions menu, click Pause. To resume the node, click the node and then select Resume. You can also use the Cluster.exe command-line tool to pause and resume nodes. To pause the VAN-SRV1 node of the DEMO-CLUSTER using the command line, open the Command Prompt window by clicking Start and selecting Command Prompt. Type the following at the command prompt:

```
cluster DEMO-CLUSTER node VAN-SRV1 /pause
```

Type the following to resume the node:

```
cluster DEMO-CLUSTER node VAN-SRV1 /resume
```

You perform maintenance on cluster services and applications from the Services And Applications node of the Failover Cluster Manager, as shown in Figure 11-12. The three main service- and application-related management tasks that you can perform are as follows:

- **Take the service or application offline** You might want to perform maintenance on the application, so take it offline. Doing this disconnects all active connections to the application.

- **Bring the service or application online** Bring the application back online after it has been taken offline.

- **Move the service or application to another cluster node** This is done most often when you want to perform maintenance on a node rather than an application. You should perform maintenance on the passive node first, and then transfer the application across to the passive node before performing maintenance on the node that was originally the active node.

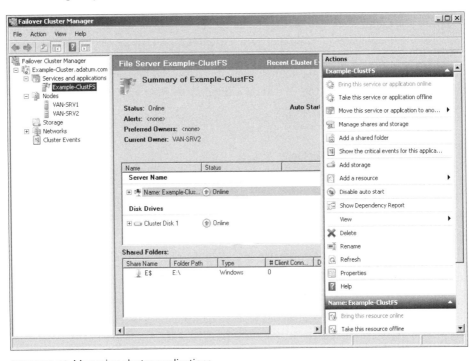

FIGURE 11-12 Managing cluster applications

Lesson Summary

- Failover clustering is used for session-aware applications that have the need for shared data storage and are capable of using shared data storage.

- The four quorum models in Windows Server 2008 are Node Majority, Node and Disk Majority, Node and File Share Majority, and No Majority: Disk Only.

- Failover clustering is managed through the Failover Cluster Manager snap-in or with the Cluster.exe command-line tool.

- Shared storage must be available to all nodes in the cluster. The most common forms of shared storage are iSCSI and Fibre Channel.

- You use wizards for validation of clusters, nodes, network, and storage and for configuration of clusters.

Lesson Review

You can use the following questions to test your knowledge of the information in Lesson 2, "Windows Server 2008 Cluster Tools." The questions are also available on the companion CD if you prefer to review them in electronic form.

NOTE ANSWERS

Answers to these questions and explanations of why each answer choice is correct or incorrect are located in the "Answers" section at the end of the book.

1. Which of the following quorum models can be used for failover clusters with an odd number of nodes? (Each answer is a stand-alone solution. Choose two.)

   A. Node and File Share Majority

   B. Node Majority

   C. No Majority: Disk Only

   D. Node and Disk Majority

2. You have a two-node cluster operating with a file share that is located on a different server and running in Node and File Share Majority mode. What happens to the application and cluster when one of the servers in the cluster has a hardware failure?

   A. The application still will run because the quorum model allows it to continue.

   B. The application will fail because the witness disk is no longer available.

   C. The answer depends on which server housed the cluster resource at the time.

   D. The application will fail because the quorum model used requires that it stop servicing requests if half of the nodes become unavailable.

3. Which of the following operating systems support failover clustering? (Each answer is a stand-alone solution. Choose two.)

   A. Windows Server 2008 R2 Foundation edition

   B. Windows Server 2008 R2 Standard edition

   C. Windows Server 2008 R2 Enterprise edition

   D. Windows Server 2008 R2 Datacenter edition

4. Your cluster uses the Node and Disk Majority quorum model and has eight nodes. Assuming that the shared disk remains online, what is the minimum number of servers that must fail before the cluster fails?

    A. One

    B. Three

    C. Four

    D. Five

<table>
<tr><td>PRACTICE</td><td>

Installing and Configuring a Windows Server 2008 R2 NLB Cluster
</td></tr>
</table>

In this set of exercises, you will create and test an NLB cluster.

EXERCISE 1   Prepare DNS and Member Servers for the NLB Cluster

In this exercise, you prepare VAN-DC1, VAN-SRV1, and VAN-SVR2 for the deployment of an NLB cluster. To complete this exercise, perform the following steps:

1. Log on to server VAN-DC1 with the Kim Akers user account. Open an elevated command prompt and issue the following command:

```
Dnscmd /recordadd adatum.com nlb-cluster A 10.10.0.131
```

2. Log on to server VAN-SRV1 with the Kim Akers user account and open an elevated PowerShell session. Run the following commands:

```
Import-Module ServerManager
Add-WindowsFeature NLB,Web-Server
```

3. Log on to server VAN-SRV2 with the Kim Akers user account and open an elevated PowerShell session. Run the following commands:

```
Import-Module ServerManager
Add-WindowsFeature NLB,Web-Server
Mspaint.exe \inetpub\wwwroot\welcome.png
```

4. In MSPaint, draw over the Welcome.png image with the paintbrush and save the result. You will use this modified image to differentiate between VAN-SRV1 and VAN-SRV2.

5. On VAN-DC1, open Windows Internet Explorer and then navigate to the pages *http://van-SRV1* and *http://van-SRV2*. Verify that they have different Welcome pages.

EXERCISE 2   Configure and Test an NLB Cluster

In this exercise, you will configure an NLB cluster. You will then create a port rule and verify that the cluster works. To complete this practice, perform the following steps:

1. Ensure that you are logged on to server VAN-SRV1 with the Kim Akers user account.

2. From the Administrative Tools menu, open the Network Load Balancing Manager console. Click Yes when prompted by User Account Control.

3. From the Cluster menu, select New. This will open the New Cluster: Connect wizard. In the Host text box, type **VAN-SRV1** and then click Connect. Click Next.

4. On the New Cluster: Host Parameters page, verify that 1 is selected for Priority (Unique Host Identifier) and then click Next.

5. On the New Cluster: Cluster IP Addresses page, click Add. In the Add IP Address box, enter the IP address **10.10.0.131** and subnet mask **255.0.0.0,** and then click OK. On the New Cluster: Cluster IP Address page, click Next.

6. On the New Cluster: Cluster Parameters page, enter the full Internet name as **nlb-cluster.adatum.com,** and then select Multicast, as shown in Figure 11-13. Click Next.

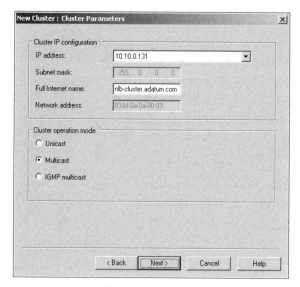

FIGURE 11-13 Configuring multicast

7. On the New Cluster: Port Rules page, click Finish.

8. Right-click nlb-cluster.adatum.com, and then click Add Host To Cluster. In the Add Host To Cluster: Connect dialog box, enter the name **VAN-SRV2,** and then click Connect. Verify that the Local Area Connection with IP address 10.10.0.21 interface appears in the list of available interfaces. Click Next twice and then click Finish.

9. When both nodes of the NLB cluster have reached a status where they are listed as Converged, right-click nlb-cluster.adatum.com and then click Cluster Properties. On the Port Rules tab, select the existing rule, and then click Remove.

10. Click Add. In the Port Range section, enter **80** in both the From and the To box. Set the Filtering Mode to Multiple Host and the Affinity to None, and then click OK. Click OK again to close the Cluster Properties dialog box. Wait until both nodes are listed as Converged. You may need to click Refresh.

11. On VAN-DC1, open Internet Explorer to *http://nlb-cluster.adatum.com*. Close Internet Explorer. Open Internet Explorer again to *http://nlb-cluster.adatum.com*. Repeat this process until you have seen both the modified and unmodified Microsoft Internet Information Services (IIS) 7 Welcome pages.

12. Shut down server VAN-SVR2. On VAN-DC1, verify that you can still connect to *http://nlb-cluster.adatum.com*.

EXERCISE 3 Remove NLB from the NLB Cluster

In this exercise, you will remove the NLB cluster and then remove both the NLB feature and IIS from servers VAN-SRV2 and VAN-SRV1. To complete this practice, perform the following steps:

1. Turn on server VAN-SRV2 and log on with the Kim Akers user account.

2. From the Administrative Tools menu, open the Network Load Balancing Manager. Click Yes when prompted by User Account Control. Click OK when presented with a warning.

3. Right-click nlb-cluster.adatum.com and then click Delete Cluster. Click Yes when prompted by the warning.

4. When the cluster has been removed, open an elevated PowerShell session and run the following commands:

```
Import-Module ServerManager
Remove-WindowsFeature NLB,Web-Server -Restart
```

5. Log on to server VAN-SRV1, open an elevated PowerShell session, and run the following commands:

```
Import-Module ServerManager
Remove-WindowsFeature NLB,Web-Server -Restart
```

6. Shut down all servers to complete the practice.

Chapter Review

To further practice and reinforce the skills you learned in this chapter, you can perform the following tasks:

- Review the chapter summary.
- Review the list of key terms introduced in this chapter.
- Complete the case scenario. These scenarios set up real-world situations involving the topics of this chapter and ask you to create a solution.
- Complete the suggested practices.
- Take a practice test.

Chapter Summary

- Windows Server 2008 and 2008 R2 use three key methods for providing high availability and redundancy: DNS Round Robin, NLB, and failover clustering.
- You can use DNS Round Robin and NLB for applications that can use their own data store, such as websites. You use failover clustering for applications that have a shared data store, such as virtual machines or Microsoft SQL Server databases.
- If you intend to use a shared data store with a Windows Server 2008 failover cluster, the shared volume must be accessible to all nodes in the cluster.
- NLB creates a virtual network adapter and has two modes of operation: unicast and multicast. NLB unicast is suitable for network adapters with two or more network adapters. It can be used with NLB clusters where nodes have one adapter, but this makes remote management difficult. NLB multicast mode can be used when nodes have one adapter. You can use IGMP multicast mode to prevent switches being flooded with multicast traffic.

Key Terms

The following terms were introduced in this chapter. Do you know what they mean?

- DNS Round Robin
- Failover clustering
- Network Load Balancing (NLB)
- Quorum model

Case Scenario

In the following case scenario, you will apply what you have learned about planning high availability. You can find answers to these questions in the "Answers" section at the end of this book.

Choose the Appropriate Availability Strategy

You are the administrator for a company running a network in which 98 percent of the servers run Windows Server 2008 servers and 2 percent of the servers run Linux. The business has just deemed three applications business-critical, meaning that the applications need to be available in the event of server failure without losing any data. These applications have the following properties:

- The first is a customer relationship database running on SQL Server 2008 R2. SQL Server 2008 R2 is installed on a computer running Windows Server 2008 R2.

- The company's main website that contains just static, informational pages running on IIS on Windows Server 2008 R2.

- An internal customer service application that uses web servers running on Linux. You have access to additional computers running Windows Server 2008 R2.

You also have access to a SAN to meet your availability requirements. With these facts in mind, answer the following questions:

1. What could be done to improve the application availability?

2. What steps do you need to take to implement failover clustering?

3. If you choose failover clustering for any of the applications, which quorum model should be used, and why?

Suggested Practices

To help you successfully master the exam objectives presented in this chapter, complete the following tasks.

Plan for High Availability

- Practice 1: Create a failover cluster that does not have access to shared storage.

- Practice 2: Configure the DHCP service as a highly available service.

- Practice 3: Add two additional nodes to the NLB cluster that you created in the practice exercise.

- Practice 4: Create two new NLB port rules. Create a port rule for port 25 that assigns all traffic to that port to one node in the failover cluster. Configure a second port rule that causes all traffic from ports 1025 to ports 2024 to be dropped by the cluster.

Take a Practice Test

The practice tests on this book's companion CD offer many options. For example, you can test yourself on just one exam objective, or you can test yourself on all the exam content. You can set up the test so that it closely simulates the experience of taking a certification exam, or you can set it up in study mode so that you can look at the correct answers and explanations after you answer each question.

> **MORE INFO** **PRACTICE TESTS**
>
> For details about all the practice test options available, see the section "How to Use the Practice Tests" in this book's Introduction.

CHAPTER 12

Performance Evaluation and Optimization

This chapter looks at how you would plan to monitor resources and performance on a computer running Windows Server 2008 R2. It considers the various tools that tell you what resources are available on a computer and that report problems encountered when using a resource, and it discusses monitoring servers and services for performance and optimization, establishing baselines and logs to identify and interpret trends, and determining where bottlenecks might occur before they happen.

It also looks at checking the potential of the computer to perform resource-intensive tasks and how to capture both local events and events on other computers. This chapter is about forward planning, identifying trends, and solving issues before they become apparent to the user. However, planning requires that you know exactly what each tool can offer, and the chapter describes the facilities you have available to you to do this. Sometimes, services, processes, and applications encounter problems, and the chapter considers how you can deal with them.

Exam objectives in this chapter:

- Monitor servers for performance evaluation and optimization.

Lessons in this chapter:

Before You Begin

To complete the exercises in the practice in this chapter, you need to have done the following:

- Installed a server called VAN-DC1 running Windows Server 2008 R2 Enterprise edition and configured as a domain controller in the Adatum.com domain, as described in Exercise 1 of Appendix A, "Setup Instructions for Windows Server 2008 R2."

- Created a user account in the Adatum.com domain with the user name Kim Akers and password Pa$$w0rd, and added this account to the Domain Admins, Enterprise Admins, and Schema Admins groups. This procedure is described in Exercise 1 of the appendix, "Setup Instructions for End-of-Chapter Labs."

- Installed a server called VAN-SRV1 running Windows Server 2008 R2 Enterprise edition and configured as a member server in the Adatum.com domain, as described in Exercise 2 of the appendix. This computer is not used in the practice but is required if you want to configure both a source and collector computer for event subscriptions, as described in the chapter text and included as a suggested practice.

- We recommend that you use an isolated network that is not part of your production network to do the practice exercises in this book. Internet access is not required for the exercises, and you do not need to configure a default gateway. To minimize the time and expense of configuring physical computers, we recommend that you use virtual machines. For example, you can create virtual machines using the Hyper-V server role.

- The practice in this chapter requires that you have access to an additional storage device that you attach to domain controller VAN-DC1. In this chapter, you need only very limited storage capacity, and if you are using real computers, a USB flash memory device with 500 MB free space is sufficient. However, Chapter 13, "Backup and Recovery," requires an extra disk that is able to store 40 GB of data. This disk can be an extra virtual disk if you are using virtual machines, or a physical disk or an attached USB 2.0 or IEEE 1394 disk if you are using real hardware. If you decide to install and use this extra disk in this chapter, you will have it available for Chapter 13.

 REAL WORLD

Ian McLean

I made a rather dumb statement in a previous book. I said that it was typically less difficult to get funding for upgrading servers than for upgrading clients. My reasoning was that there aren't many servers, and that with virtualization, there are fewer than ever before. I argued that you can justify the amount of extra cash needed to upgrade half a dozen servers a lot more easily than the expense of upgrading 500 workstations.

The book was published, and the worldwide recession started around the same time. (I hope the two events weren't connected.) Under today's stringent financial conditions, it is very difficult to get a budget to upgrade anything. Also, to most senior managers, servers are mysterious black boxes that do incomprehensible things. They need to be convinced that they are important before they will agree to spend money on them.

Senior managers typically may not be technically aware, but they are emphatically not fools. They know that their organization's servers are important, even if they don't fully understand why. So when their network administrator says the servers need an upgrade, they are prepared to listen, but only if that administrator can present a convincing case, backed up by hard statistics.

So, gathering statistics about the performance of your servers is more important now than it has ever been. Inevitably, you will need to upgrade your hardware— if not right now, then in a year or two. Start preparing your case. Ensure that you have defined sensible baselines. Keep track of the small but cumulative performance drops as your equipment ages and user expectations increase. Start preparing a good case right now for the upgrades you need in the future. Don't wait for tomorrow, because if you do, somebody else might end up doing your job tomorrow.

Lesson 1: Monitoring Data

As an experienced administrator, you will already have come across most of the tools and utilities described in this lesson. Windows Server 2008 R2 offers tools to measure performance, set baselines, identify bottlenecks, display resources, measure system stability and reliability, and other functions. You probably are very aware of the importance of generating baselines for busy, quiet, and normal periods and of comparing the results of your current monitoring activities against these baselines to identify trends. It is important to remember that result comparisons and trend analysis are not activities carried out at random. They need to be planned.

It is sometimes not easy to select the right tool for the job, and this is where planning becomes important. Often, you can use several tools to obtain the same information or carry out the same configuration, but one of them does it more efficiently than the others or gives more information that helps you to identify trends and generate reports that justify needed upgrades. It is relatively straightforward to use one or more tools to gather information about a computer system. Interpreting that information may be more difficult. This lesson attempts to split the various tools into different functional groups and describe how the tools in each group can complement each other in an overall plan.

> **After this lesson, you will be able to:**
> - Use performance tools to view real-time performance data.
> - Collect data in Data Collector Sets (DCSs).
> - Generate reports that identify actual or potential resource bottlenecks.
> - Examine failures and potential problems related to software installations and other significant system changes.
> - Monitor what services are running and use the Services administrative tool.
> - Gather event subscriptions from source computers and forward them to a destination computer.
>
> **Estimated lesson time: 50 minutes**

Performance Monitoring and Reporting

Monitoring performance data and comparing it to established baselines is crucial to determining the health of your server, as is examining events in the event logs. Many events are informational, but you should not ignore them because of that. Your skill and experience as an administrator must determine what you should address and what you can safely ignore. You should never ignore warning and error events that indicate real and immediate problems.

You probably have experience with Windows performance tools such as Performance Monitor and the Reports tool. You might not be familiar with DCSs that use performance counters to generate performance logs and can in turn be read by Performance Monitor and the Reports tool. DCSs provide a replacement for Performance Logs And Alerts in earlier server operating systems.

Your aim is to plan how best to monitor and improve performance, identify potential bottlenecks, and upgrade the appropriate resources. You especially want to identify sources of critical performance problems that could make a computer unacceptably slow or completely unusable.

Performance Monitor

In Windows Server 2008 R2, you can open the Performance Monitor console from the Administrative Tools menu or by entering **perfmon** in the Search box of the Start menu or in the command prompt. The Performance Monitor console, shown in Figure 12-1, lets you access Performance Monitor, Data Collector Sets, and the Reports tool. You can then click Performance Monitor in the tree pane to access the Performance Monitor tool.

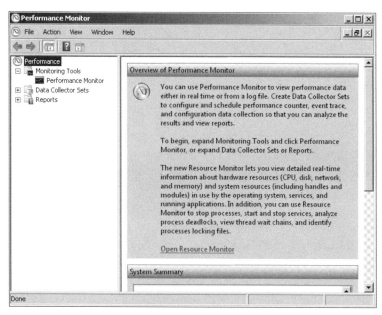

FIGURE 12-1 The Performance Monitor console

You can add counters by clicking the green + button on the Performance Monitor toolbar, expanding the object (such as Memory), selecting the counter, and clicking Add. You can specify whether you want to display a single instance of a counter or a total of all instances. For example, if a server has more than one CPU, you could select a counter that monitors the usage of a single CPU or a counter that monitors total CPU usage. Figure 12-2 shows the Performance Monitor tool displaying real-time data.

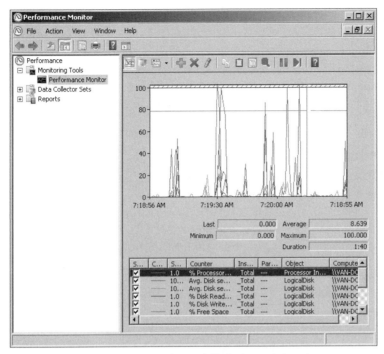

FIGURE 12-2 The Performance Monitor tool displaying real-time data

Each line on the graph appears in a different color. To make it easier to view a specific graph, select its counter and press Ctrl+H. The selected counter appears bold and in black on the graph. To change the appearance and refresh rate of the chart, right-click Performance Monitor and then select Properties. The five tabs of the Performance Monitor Properties dialog box provide access to different configuration options, as follows:

- **General**   In the Graph Elements group, you can type a value into the Sample Every box to change how frequently the graph updates and into the Duration box to determine the period of the scan. You can also specify whether the Legend, Value Bar, and Toolbar are displayed and whether the Report and Histogram views show Default, Maximum, Minimum, Average, or Current values. Figure 12-3 shows the General tab.

- **Source**   On this tab, you can choose whether to display current activity in real time or show log files that you have saved using a DCS. If you have a server running Microsoft SQL Server on your network and are using Open Database Connectivity (ODBC), you can specify a database by its System Data Source Name (System DSN) and select from the log sets that it contains.

FIGURE 12-3 The General tab of Performance Monitor Properties

- **Data** On this tab, in the Counters list, select the counter that you want to configure and adjust Color, Scale, Width, and Style.

- **Graph** By default, Performance Monitor begins overwriting graphed counter values on the left portion of the chart after the specified duration is reached. If you want to record counter values over a long period of time, you likely want to see the chart scroll from right to left. To do this, select the Scroll style. You can also select one of the following chart types by clicking the Change Graph Type button on the toolbar or by pressing Ctrl+G:

  - **Line** This is the default setting and shows values as lines on the chart.

  - **Histogram Bar** This shows a bar graph with the current, maximum, minimum, or average counter values displayed. If you have a large number of counters, a histogram is easier to read than a line chart.

  - **Report** This lists the current, maximum, minimum, or average counter values in a textual report.

- **Appearance** If you keep multiple Performance Monitor windows open simultaneously, you can use this tab to change the color of the background or other elements.

Data Collector Sets

DCSs gather system information, including configuration settings and performance data, and store it in a data file. You can use Performance Monitor to examine the data file and analyze detailed performance data, or you can generate a report that summarizes this information.

Windows Server 2008 R2 includes the following built-in DCSs:

- **System Performance**   You can use this DCS when troubleshooting a slow computer or intermittent performance problems. It logs processor, disk, memory, and network performance (IPv4 and IPv6) counters and kernel trace data.

- **System Diagnostics**   You can use this DCS when troubleshooting reliability problems such as problematic hardware, driver failures, or STOP errors. It logs all the information included in the System Performance DCS, plus detailed system information.
  Figure 12-4 shows some of the counters included in the System Diagnostics data set.

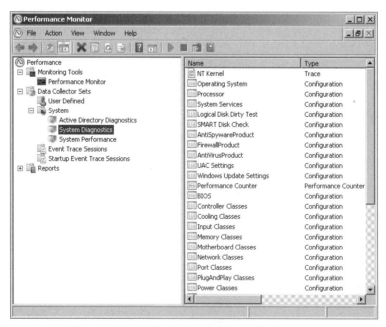

FIGURE 12-4 Counters included in the System Diagnostics data set

- **Active Directory Diagnostics** If your server running Windows Server 2008 R2 is a domain controller, the Active Directory Diagnostics DCS is also included. This enables you to collect performance data (for example in the ADDS Performance Counter) and generate diagnostic reports that help you analyze Active Directory Domain Services (AD DS) performance issues.

To use a DCS, right-click it and then select Start. The System Performance DCS has a default overall duration of 10 minutes; the System Diagnostics DCS has a default overall duration of 1 minute; and the Active Directory DCS has a default overall duration of 5 minutes. To stop a DCS manually, right-click it and then click Stop.

After running a DCS, you can view a summary of the data that it has gathered in the Performance Monitor Reports node. To view the most recent report for a DCS, right-click the DCS and then click Latest Report. You can then view the report by accessing it in the Reports node. Figure 12-5 shows a report generated by running the Active Directory DCS on VAN-DC1. You need to expand the headings in the right pane to access detailed information.

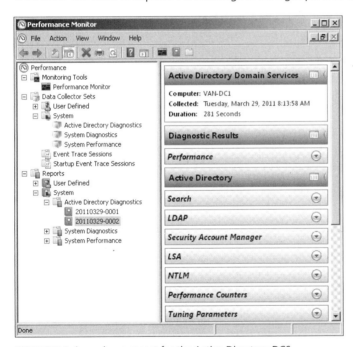

FIGURE 12-5 Accessing a report for the Active Directory DCS

You can also add performance counter alerts to DCSs. This enables you to monitor a counter and detect an alert, which you can then use to start a batch file, send you an email, or call you on a pager. For example, if you configured an alert to trigger when free space on a logical volume falls below 30 percent, you could add this to a DCS and use it to trigger a batch file that archives the data on the volume.

Data logging uses a large amount of system resources, and performance log files can become very large. To minimize the performance impact of performance data logging, log the minimum amount of information that you require. For example, use System Performance instead of System Diagnostics whenever possible because System Performance includes fewer counters.

Creating a Data Collector Set

If you have a performance problem or want to analyze and possibly improve the performance of a server, you can use DCSs to gather performance data and compare it against your baselines. The following procedure creates a custom DCS:

1. In the Performance Monitor console (or the Performance Monitor tool), expand Data Collector Sets, right-click User Defined, select New, and then select Data Collector Set. This starts the Create New Data Collector Set Wizard.

2. On the Create New Data Collector Set page, specify a name for the set. Ensure that Create From A Template (Recommended) is selected. Click Next.

3. On the Which Template Would You Like To Use? page, choose one of the standard templates (Basic, System Diagnostics, or System Performance). On a domain controller, you can also select Active Directory. Click Next.

4. On the Where Would You Like The Data To Be Saved? page, click Next to accept the default location for the data.

5. On the Create The Data Collector Set page, leave Run As set to the default to create and run the DCS using the logged-on user's credentials. Alternatively, click Change and specify alternative administrative credentials.

6. Select one of the following three options, and then click Finish:
   - Open Properties For This Data Collector Set
   - Start This Data Collector Set Now
   - Save And Close

Custom DCSs are located under the User Defined node within DCSs. You can schedule when a DCS runs and configure its stop conditions. You can also start a DCS manually by right-clicking it and selecting Start.

> **MORE INFO**   **CREATING DCSs**
>
> For more information about the various methods of creating DCSs, see *http://technet.microsoft.com/en-us/library/cc749337.aspx*.

Customizing Data Collector Sets

A newly created custom DCS logs only the performance data defined in the template that you choose. To add your own data sources to a DCS, you must update it after you create it.

To add a performance data source (such as a performance counter) to a DCS, right-click the DCS, select New, and then select Data Collector. The Create New Data Collector Wizard opens. On the What Type Of Data Collector Would You Like To Create? page, specify the data collector name, select the type, and then click Next. You can choose from the following types of data collectors:

- **Performance Counter Data Collector**   This type of data collector enables you to collect performance statistics over long periods of time for later analysis. You can use it to set baselines and analyze trends.

- **Event Trace Data Collector**   This type of data collector enables you to collect information about system events and activities.

- **Configuration Data Collector**   This type of data collector stores information about registry keys, Windows Management Instrumentation (WMI) management paths, and the system state.

- **Performance Counter Alert**   This type of data collector (sometimes termed an *Alert data connector*) enables you to configure an alert that is generated when a particular performance counter exceeds or drops below a specific threshold value.

You can add as many data collectors to a DCS as you need. For example, if you selected Performance Counter Data Collector on the What Type Of Data Collector Would You Like To Create? page, you can click Add on the Which Performance Counters Would You Like To Log? page and add a performance counter in the same way that you would add a counter to Performance Monitor. You can then click Add again on the Which Performance Counters Would You Like To Log? page and add another counter. You can repeat this process until you have added all the counters you need. You can then click Finish. Figure 12-6 shows the Which Performance Counters Would You Like To Log? page.

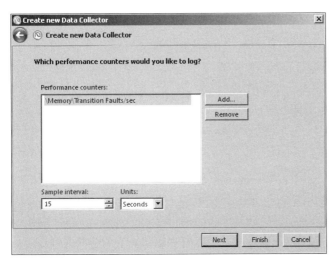

FIGURE 12-6 The Which Performance Counters Would You Like To Log? page

To edit a data collector in a custom DCS, select the DCS in the Data Collector Sets\User Defined node. In the Details pane, right-click the data collector that you want to edit and click Properties.

MORE INFO **DCS PROPERTIES**

For more information about configuring DCS properties, see *http://technet.microsoft.com/ en-us/library/cc749267.aspx*.

If a DCS includes performance counters, you can view the counter values in Performance Monitor by selecting the report generated by running the DCS, right-clicking the selected report, clicking View, and then clicking Performance Monitor. Performance Monitor then displays the data logged by the DCS rather than real-time data. The performance Monitor output is likely to look very complex in Graph or even Histogram Bar view, and you will likely need to look at it in Report view.

Creating Data Collectors from the Command Prompt

You can create data collectors from an elevated command prompt by using the Logman utility. For example, you can use the following commands to create the various types of data collector listed in the previous section:

- **logman create counter**   This command creates a Performance Counter data collector. For example, the `following` command creates a counter called my_perf_log that records values for the % Processor Time counter in the Processor(_Total) counter instance:

```
logman create counter my_perf_log -c "\Processor(_Total)\% Processor Time"
```

- **logman create trace**   This command creates an Event Trace data collector. For example, the following command creates an event trace data collector called my_trace_log and outputs the results to the C:\trace_log_file location:

```
 logman create trace my_trace_log -o c:\trace_log_file
```

- **logman create config**   This command creates a Configuration data collector. For example, the following command creates a configuration data collector called my_cfg_log using the HKEY_LOCAL_MACHINE\SOFTWARE\Microsoft\Windows\ CurrentVersion\\ registry key:

```
logman create cfg my_cfg_log -reg
HKEY_LOCAL_MACHINE\SOFTWARE\Microsoft\Windows\CurrentVersion\\
```

- **logman create alert**   This command creates an Alert data collector. For example, the following command creates an alert called my_alert that fires when the % Processor Time performance counter in the Processor(_Total) counter instance exceeds a value of 90:

```
logman create alert my_alert -th "\Processor(_Total)\% Processor Time>90"
```

You can also use the Logman utility to query data collector output; for example, the following command lists the data collectors contained in the my_perf_log DCS:

```
logman query "my_perf_log"
```

Figure 12-7 shows the output of this command.

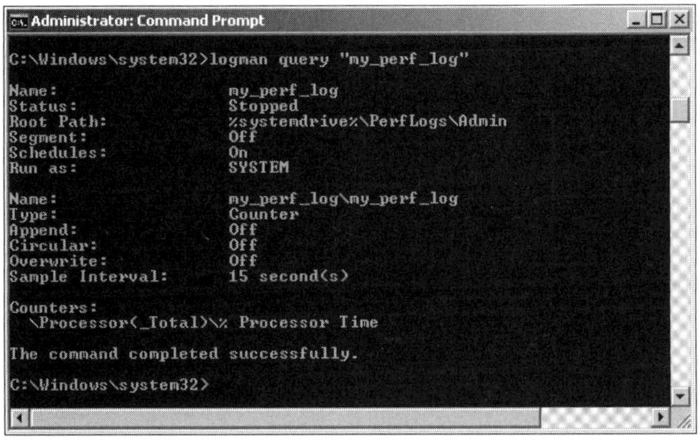

FIGURE 12-7 Listing the data collectors contained in the my_perf_log DCS

You can start and stop DCSs by using the commands `logman start` and `logman stop`; for example, `logman start my_perf_log` and `logman stop my_perf_log`. You can use the command `logman delete` to delete a DCS, for example, the command `logman delete my_perf_log`; and you can use `logman update` to update a performance counter, a trace counter, an alert, or a configuration. Logman enables you to export the information in DCSs to and import information from an XML file.

> **MORE INFO** **LOGMAN**
>
> For more information about the Logman utility, see *http://technet.microsoft.com/en-us/library/cc753820(WS.10).aspx*.

Generating a System Diagnostics Report

When you create and use a DCS, you generate a report that is placed in User Defined Reports under Reports in the Performance Monitor console. However, the Reports tool can also display a system diagnostic report, sometimes known as a *computer health check*.

A system diagnostics report gives you details about the status of hardware resources, system response times, and processes on the local computer, along with system information and configuration data. You would generate a system diagnostics report if you were looking for ways to maximize performance and streamline system operation. You need to be a member of the local Administrators group or equivalent to generate a system diagnostics report.

If you use the Performance Tools console to look at the system diagnostics report, you see a copy of that report the last time it was compiled (if it has never been compiled, you will not see it). To generate and display a system diagnostic report that is completely up to date, enter the following into the Search box on the Start menu:

`perfmon /report`

If you prefer, you can enter **perfmon.exe /report** in an elevated command prompt instead. Whatever method you choose, the command generates a diagnostics report (this typically takes 60 seconds) and automatically displays it in the Resource And Performance Monitor, as shown in Figure 12-8. You can scroll down the report and expand any of its sections.

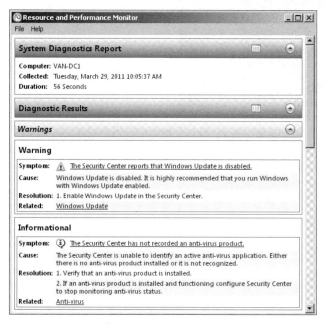

FIGURE 12-8 System diagnostics report in the Resource And Performance Monitor

For example, expanding Security Center Information in the Resource And Performance Monitor results in the screen shown in Figure 12-9, which indicates there is a problem with antivirus protection on VAN-DC1. Because VAN-DC1 is on an isolated test network not connected to the Internet, no antivirus software is installed.

You can expand Performance, Software Configuration, Hardware Configuration, CPU, Network, Disk, Memory, and Report Statistics. For example, expanding Report Statistics lets you access Computer Information, Files, and Processed Events and discover Payload GUIDs, as shown in Figure 12-10.

FIGURE 12-9 Displaying the basic system check for Security Center Information

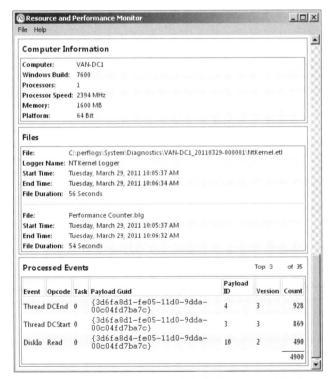

FIGURE 12-10 Expanding Report Statistics in Resource and Performance Monitor

Tracking System Reliability, Stability, and Overall Performance

Windows Server 2008 R2 offers tools that enable you to assess system reliability and stability. Reliability Monitor keeps a record of software changes and updates and lets you correlate system changes with crashes and reboots. It generates a Stability Index that measures the reliability and stability of a computer over a rolling 28-day period. The Action Center monitors a computer and reports problems with security, maintenance, and related services.

Reliability Monitor

Reliability Monitor tracks a computer's stability. Computers that have no reboots or failures are considered stable and can (eventually) achieve the maximum system stability index of 10. The more reboots and failures that occur on a computer, the lower the system stability becomes. The minimum index value is zero. The system stability index is not an exact measure of reliability because installing a new service pack or update sometimes requires a reboot, which initially lowers the index value but ultimately makes a system more reliable than before. However, Reliability Monitor provides valuable information about what system changes were made before a problem occurred.

Reliability Monitor uses data provided by the RACTask scheduled task. In Windows Server 2008 R2, this task is enabled the first time you open Reliability Monitor. If, however, data collection has been disabled, RACTask must be enabled manually from the Task Scheduler MMC snap-in. Your account needs to be a member of the local Administrators group, or equivalent, to carry out this procedure. If you need to enable the RACTask scheduled task, perform the following steps:

1. Click Start, click in the Search box, type **taskschd.msc**, and then press ENTER.
2. In the navigation pane, expand Task Scheduler Library, expand Microsoft, expand Windows, and click RAC.
3. In the Actions pane, click View, and then click Show Hidden Tasks.
4. Click RACTask in the Results pane.
5. On the Action menu, click Enable. Figure 12-11 shows the RACTask enabled.

The easiest way to open Reliability Monitor is to type **perfmon /rel** in the Search box on the Start menu and click View Reliability History. Reliability Monitor will start displaying a Stability Index rating and specific event information 24 hours after it first starts.

You can use Reliability Monitor to diagnose intermittent problems. For example, if you install an application that causes the operating system to fail intermittently, it is difficult to correlate the failures with the application installation. Figure 12-12 shows how Reliability Monitor can be used to indicate that Windows and application failures and a video hardware error occurred on VAN-DC1 on June 22, following an update of a video driver on June 21. If you obtained this result on a test network, you might consider obtaining more information before updating the driver on your production network.

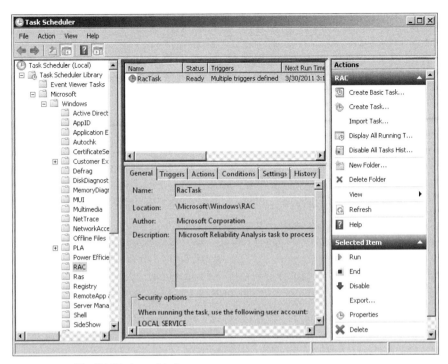

FIGURE 12-11 The RACTask, enabled

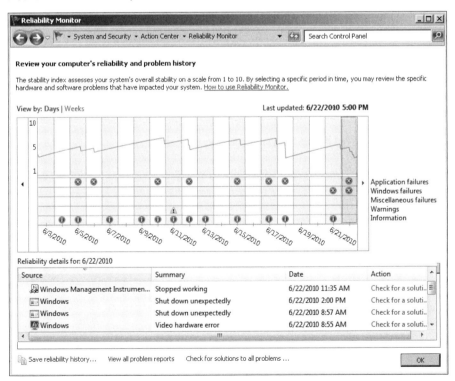

FIGURE 12-12 Reliability Monitor

The Stability Index

The stability index is based on data collected over the lifetime of a system. Each day in the stability chart is associated with a graph point showing its stability index rating. The stability index is a weighted measurement calculated from the number of failures seen over a rolling historical period. The index value is calculated over the preceding 28 days, although the results for considerably more days can be displayed.

Recent failures are weighted more heavily than past failures, so improvement over time is reflected in an ascending stability index when a reliability issue has been resolved. (Days when the computer is turned off are not included when calculating the stability index. If you are interpreting the stability index on a client rather than a server, you need to remember that days when the computer is in a sleep or hibernate state are also not included.)

If there is not enough data to calculate a steady stability index, the line on the graph is dotted. For example, until Reliability Monitor has 28 days of data, the stability index is displayed as a dotted line, indicating that it has not yet established a valid baseline. When enough data has been recorded to generate a steady stability index, the line is solid. If there are any significant changes to the system time, an Information icon appears on the graph for each day on which the system time was adjusted.

Reliability Monitor maintains up to a year of history for stability and reliability events. The Stability Chart displays a rolling graph organized by date.

 Quick Check

- What would a stability index of 10 indicate?

Quick Check Answer

- The maximum value of the stability index is 10. This value indicates that the computer has been stable over the previous 28 days with no failures or reboots. It also indicates that no software updates and service packs that require a reboot have been applied during that time.

The Stability Chart

The Stability Chart in Reliability Monitor displays a graph of the stability index on a day-to-day basis. Rows in the lower half of the chart track reliability events that either contribute to the stability measurement for the system or provide related information about software installation and removal. When one or more reliability events of each type are detected, an icon appears in the column for that date.

For software installs and uninstalls, an information icon indicates a successful event and a warning icon indicates a failure. For all other reliability event types, an error icon indicates a failure. If more than 30 days of data are available, you can use the left and right arrow keys on the keyboard to find dates outside the visible range.

Using the Action Center

The Action Center, available under System And Security in Control Panel, monitors your computer and reports problems with security, maintenance, and related settings that help indicate your computer's overall performance. It notifies users if there is a problem with the network firewall, antivirus, anti-spyware, or Windows Update on a server running Windows Server 2008 R2. When the status of a monitored item changes (for example, antivirus software becomes out of date), Action Center notifies you with a message in the notification area on the taskbar. The status of the item in Action Center changes color to reflect the severity of the message, and Action Center recommends an action. The Action Center is shown in Figure 12-13.

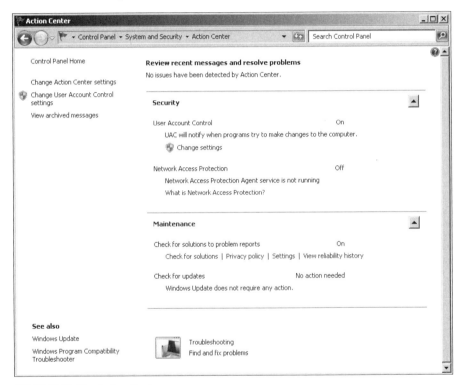

FIGURE 12-13 The Action Center

Changing Action Center Settings

If you prefer to keep track of an item yourself and you do not want to see notifications about its status, you can turn off notifications for the item in the Change Action Center Settings dialog box, shown in Figure 12-14.

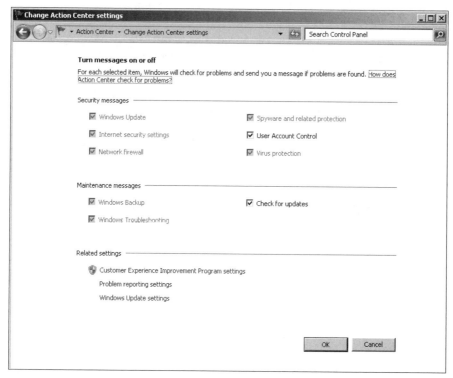

FIGURE 12-14 The Change Action Center Settings dialog box

When you clear the check box for an item on the Change Action Center Settings dialog box, you no longer receive any messages and do not see the item's status in Action Center. Microsoft recommends checking the status of all items listed because that can help warn you about security issues.

From Action Center, you can archive messages and view the messages you have archived. You can also access Action Center Settings and disable User Account Control (UAC) messages.

Using System Tools to Investigate Processes and Services

As an experienced administrator, you probably have used Task Manager and accessed Resource Manager from that tool, although you may not be aware of the Resource Manager enhancements that Windows Server 2008 R2 provides. Process Explorer is a downloadable advanced system tool that offers many of the features of Task Manager and Resource Manager and you can use this tool to investigate resource usage, handles, and dynamic-link library (DLL) files.

As part of the planning process, you need to decide what system tools you should use for routine checks or when problems are detected, and how often you should run regular system checks. Sometimes a task can be performed by more than one tool; for example, much of what you can do with Task Manager and Resource Manager can also be done using Process

Explorer. To plan your system checks and choose the best tool for the job, you need to be aware of how each tool works and the functionality it provides.

Task Manager

If an application stops responding, Windows Server 2008 R2 tries to find the problem and fix it automatically. Alternatively, if the application seems to have crashed completely and Windows Server 2008 R2 has not resolved the problem, you can end the application by opening Task Manager and accessing the Applications tab.

The Performance tab in Task Manager provides details about how a computer is using system resources—for example, RAM and CPU. As shown in Figure 12-15, the Performance tab has four graphs. The first two show the percentage of CPU resources that the system is using, both at the moment and for the past few minutes. A high percentage usage over a significant period indicates that programs or processes require a lot of CPU resources. This can affect computer performance. If the percentage appears frozen at or near 100 percent, a program might not be responding.

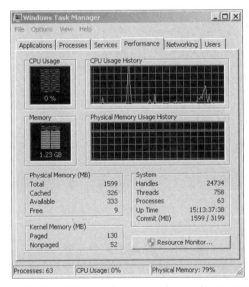

FIGURE 12-15 The Performance tab in Task Manager

> **NOTE SPLIT CPU USAGE HISTORY GRAPH**
>
> If the CPU Usage History graph is split, the computer either has multiple CPUs, a single dual-core CPU, or both.

If processor usage is consistently high—say 80 percent or higher for a significant period—you should consider installing a second processor or replacing the current processor. However, before you do so, it is worth capturing processor usage data by using Performance Monitor rather than relying on snapshots obtained by using Task Manager.

The next two graphs display how much RAM is being used, both at the moment and for the past few minutes. The percentage of memory being used is listed at the bottom of the Task Manager window. If memory use appears consistently high or slows your computer's performance noticeably, try reducing the number of programs that are open at one time. If the problem persists, you might need to install more RAM.

Three tables below the graphs list various details about memory and resource usage. In the Physical Memory (MB) table, Total is the amount of RAM installed on your computer, Cached refers to the amount of physical memory used recently for system resources, Available is the amount of memory currently available, and Free is the amount of memory that is unused.

The Kernel Memory (MB) table shows how memory is being used by the core part of Windows, called the kernel; Paged refers to the amount of virtual memory the kernel is using; Nonpaged is the amount of RAM memory used by the kernel.

The System table has five fields: Handles, Threads, Processes, Up Time, and Commit (MB) Handles are unique object identifiers, or pointers, in use by processes that refer to system elements. They include (but are not limited to) files, registry keys, events, or directories.

Threads are objects or processes running within larger processes or programs. Processes refers to the number of individual processes running on the computer (you can view more detailed information about processes on the Processes tab). Up Time is the amount of time that has passed since the computer was last restarted. The Commit (MB) value describes virtual memory use (also known as *paging file use*). The paging file is space on your hard disk that Windows uses in addition to RAM. The first value is the amount of RAM and virtual memory currently in use, and the second value is the amount of RAM and virtual memory available on your computer.

If you need more information about how memory and CPU resources are being used, click Resource Monitor on the Task Manager Performance tab. This displays the Resource Monitor, which is discussed in the section entitled "Resource Monitor," later in this lesson. You require elevated privileges to access Resource Monitor.

You can determine how much memory an individual process uses by selecting the Task Manager Processes tab, shown in Figure 12-16. The values in the Memory (Private Working Set) column (which is displayed by default) indicate the amount of memory a process is using that other processes cannot share. This information can be useful in identifying a "leaky" application—that is an application which, if left open, uses more and more memory resources and does not release memory resources that it is no longer using.

You can click View, click Select Columns, and then select other memory usage values to view (for example) Memory – Paged Pool or Memory – Commit Size on the Processes tab. You can use the Task Manager Processes tab to end a process, to end a process tree (which stops the process and all processes on which it depends), and to set process priority. To change the priority of a process, right-click the process and click Set Priority. You can choose Realtime, High, Above Normal, Normal, Below Normal, or Low.

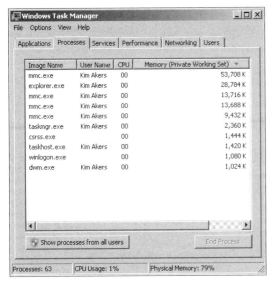

FIGURE 12-16 The Processes tab in Task Manager

The Task Manager Services tab shows which services are running and which are stopped. You can stop or start a service or go to a process that depends on that service. If you want more details about or more control over the services available on a computer, you can click Services to access the Services administrative tool. You require elevated privileges to use the Services tool. This tool is discussed in the section entitled "The Services Console," later in this lesson.

The Task Manager Networking tab lets you view network usage. The Users tab tells you what users are connected to the computer and lets you disconnect a user. The Applications tab shows you the running applications and (as previously stated) enables you to close a crashed application.

✔ Quick Check

- You want to change the priority of a process on a computer. How do you do this?

Quick Check Answer

- Open Task Manager. On the Processes tab, right-click the process and click Set Priority. You can choose Realtime, High, Above Normal, Normal, Below Normal, or Low.

Resource Monitor

Windows Server 2008 R2 offers an enhanced version of the Resource Monitor tool. This tool allows you to view information about hardware and software resource use in real time. You can filter the results according to the processes or services that you want to monitor.

You can also use Resource Monitor to start, stop, suspend, and resume processes and services and to troubleshoot unresponsive applications. You can start Resource Monitor from the Performance tab of Task Manager or by entering **resmon** in the Search box on the Start menu.

Resource Monitor always starts in the same location and with the same display options as the previous session. You can save your display state at any time and then open the configuration file to use the saved settings. However, filtering selections are not saved as part of the configuration settings.

Resource Monitor includes five tabs: Overview, CPU, Memory, Disk, and Network. The Overview tab, shown in Figure 12-17, displays basic system resource usage information. The other tabs display information about each specific resource. If you have filtered results by selecting one or more processes or services on one tab, these processes or services are selected on the other tabs on which they appear.

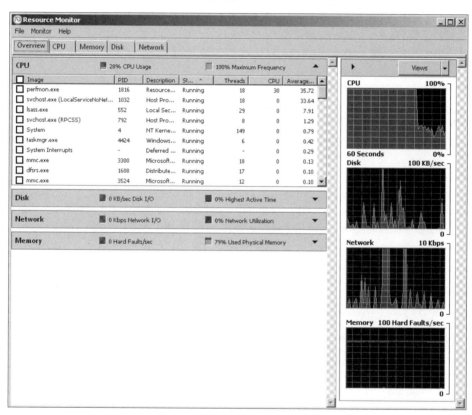

FIGURE 12-17 The Resource Monitor Overview tab

Each tab in Resource Monitor includes multiple tables that provide detailed information about the resource featured on that tab. The first table displayed is always the key table, and it always contains a complete list of processes that are using the resource included on that tab. For example, the key table on the Overview tab contains a complete list of processes running on the system.

You can filter the detailed data in tables other than the key table by one or more processes or services. To filter, select the check box in the key table next to each process or service that you want to highlight. To stop filtering for a single process or service, clear its check box. To stop filtering altogether, clear the check box in the Image column header bar. If you have filtered results, the resources used by the selected processes or services are shown in the graphs as an orange line.

You can change the size of the graphs by clicking Views and selecting a different graph size. You can hide the chart pane by clicking the arrow at the top of the pane. To view the definitions of data displayed in the tables, move the mouse pointer over the column title about which you want more information.

For example, to identify the network address that a process is connected to, click the Network tab and then click TCP Connections to expand the table. Locate the process whose network connection you want to identify. You can then view the Remote Address and Remote Port columns to see which network address and port the process is connected to. Figure 12-18 shows the System process is currently connected to IPv6 address fe80::ada5:5657:9e68:c03b on local port 445 and remote port 58946.

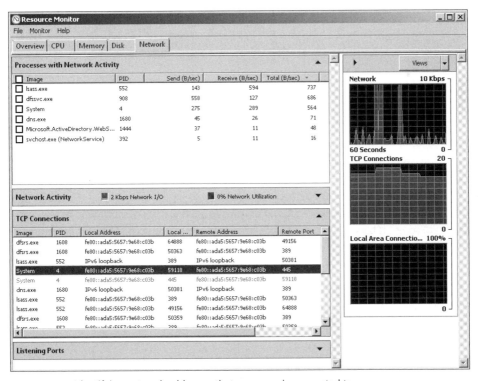

FIGURE 12-18 Identifying network addresses that a process is connected to

On the Memory tab, shown in Figure 12-19, you can review the memory that is available to programs. Available memory is the combined total of standby memory and free memory. Free memory includes zero page memory.

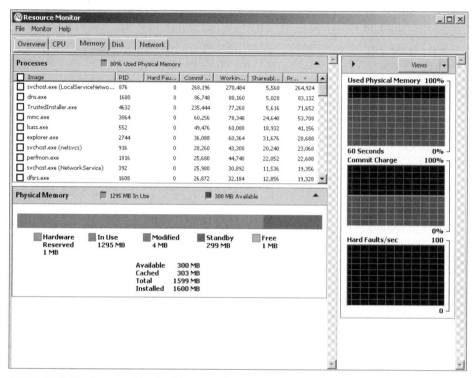

FIGURE 12-19 The Resource Monitor Memory tab

Resource Monitor displays real-time information about all the processes running on your system. If you want to view only the data related to selected processes, you can filter the detailed results by selecting the check boxes next to the names of the processes that you want to monitor in any of the tabs. Selected processes are moved to the top of the Image column. After you have selected at least one process for filtering, the Associated Handles and Associated Modules tables on the CPU tab contain data related to your selection. Tables that contain only filtered results include an orange information bar below the title bar of the table.

Resource Monitor allows you to end or suspend processes and start, stop, or restart services. You should use Resource Monitor to end a process only if you are unable to close the program by normal means. If an open program is associated with the process, it closes immediately and you lose any unsaved data. If you end a system process, it might result in system instability and data loss.

To end a process, right-click the executable name of the process that you want to end in the Image column of the key table of any Resource Monitor tab and click End Process. To end all processes dependent on the selected process, click End Process Tree. To resume a process, right-click the executable name of the program that you want to resume, and then click Resume Process.

To stop, start, or restart a service using Resource Monitor, access the CPU tab and click the Services title bar to expand the table. Under Name, right-click the service that you want to change, and then click Stop Service, Start Service, or Restart Service.

Applications that are not responding might be waiting for other processes to finish or for system resources to become available. Resource Monitor allows you to view a process wait chain and to end processes that are preventing a program from working properly. A process that is not responding appears as a red entry in the CPU table of the Overview tab and in the Processes table of the CPU tab. To view the process wait chain, right-click the executable name of the process that you want to analyze in the Image column on the key table of any Resource Monitor tab and click Analyze Wait Chain.

If the process is running normally and is not waiting for any other processes, no wait chain information is displayed. On the other hand, if the process is waiting for another process, a tree organized by dependency on other processes is displayed. If a wait chain tree is displayed, you can end one or more of the processes in the tree by selecting the check boxes next to the process names and clicking End Process.

As stated previously in this section, handles are pointers that refer to system elements. They include—but are not limited to—files, registry keys, events, and directories. Modules are helper files or programs. They include but are not limited to DLL files.

To use Resource Monitor to view all handles and modules associated with a process, select the check box next to the name of the process for which you want to see associated handles and modules in the Image column of the CPU tab. Selected processes move to the top of the column. Click the title bars of the Associated Handles and Associated Modules tables to expand them. An orange bar below the title bar of each table shows the processes that you have selected. Review the results in the detail tables.

If you need to identify the processes that use a handle, click the Search Handles box in the title bar of the Associated Handles table. Type the name of the handle that you want to search for, and then click Search. For example, searching for **c:\windows** returns all handles with *c:\windows* as part of the handle name. The search string is not case-sensitive, and wildcards are not supported.

Process Explorer

Process Explorer is not part of Windows Server 2008 R2, but you can download the latest version of this tool from *http://technet.microsoft.com/en-us/sysinternals/bb896653.aspx*, expand the archive into a folder (such as C:\ProcessExplorer), and start it by typing **c:\processexplorer\procexp.exe** in the Search box on the Start menu. Note that you will not be able to download Process Explorer on your isolated test network, but need to use a computer that has access to the Internet. You can save the installation files to a removeable hard disk and install the tool on VAN-DC1 if you want, but if you download it using a computer running Windows Server 2008 R2, it is easier to install the tool on that server and look at it there. Investigating Process Explorer is a Suggested Practice at the end of this chapter.

Process Explorer tells you which program has a particular file or directory open and displays information about which handles and DLLs processes have opened or loaded. You can use either Process Explorer or Resource Monitor to determine which applications are responsible for activity on your hard disk, including which files and folders are being accessed.

When it opens, Process Explorer displays a list of the currently active processes, as shown in Figure 12-20. You can toggle the lower pane on and off and select to view handles or DLLs. In Handle mode, you can see the handles that the process selected in the top window has opened. The Process Explorer search capability discovers which processes have particular handles opened or DLLs loaded.

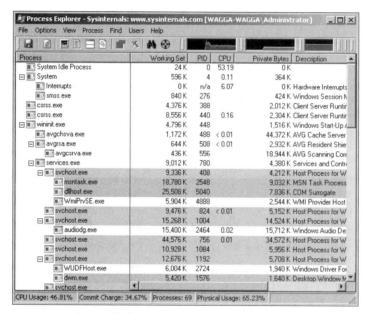

FIGURE 12-20 Process Explorer opening screen

> **MORE INFO** **ADVANCED SYSTEM TOOLS AND COMMAND-LINE UTILITIES**
>
> For more information about advanced system tools for Windows, including their corresponding command-line utilities, and for the chance to try them without needing to download and install them, see http://technet.microsoft.com/en-us/sysinternals/default.aspx.

When you click System Information on the Process Explorer opening screen, you can view the Process Explorer System Information screen. This contains a Summary tab and tabs that display mini-graphs for CPU, memory, and I/O history. The mini-graphs show the history of system activity, and pausing the mouse over a point on a graph displays the associated time and the process information as a tooltip. For example, the tooltip for the mini-CPU graph shows the process that was the largest consumer of CPU. Highlighting helps you see what items change between refreshes. Items that exit or are closed, including processes, DLLs, and handles, show in red and new items show in green. Figure 12-21 shows the Process Explorer System Information Summary screen.

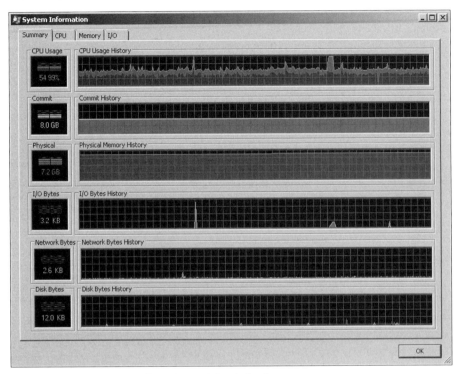

FIGURE 12-21 The Process Explorer System Information Summary screen

System Information graphs on the relevant tabs display the CPU Usage History, Committed Virtual Memory Usage, and I/O Throughput History. Red in the CPU usage graph indicates CPU usage in kernel mode, whereas green shows the sum of kernel- and user-mode execution. When Committed Virtual Memory reaches the system's Commit Limit, both applications and the system itself become unstable. The Commit Limit is the sum of most of the physical memory and the sizes of any paging files. The Memory tab displays Commit History and Physical Memory History.

The I/O tab displays I/O Bytes History, Network Bytes History, and Disk Bytes History. The blue line on each of the graphs indicates total traffic, and the pink line shows write traffic.

You can reorder columns in the Process Explorer opening screen by dragging them to their new positions. To select which columns of data you want visible in each of the tabs and the status bar, click Select Columns on the View menu or right-click a column header and click Select Columns. You can save a column configuration and its associated settings by clicking Save Column Set on the View menu.

On the Options menu, you can choose to have Process Explorer open instead of Task Manager whenever Task Manager is started, or you can ensure that the Processor Explorer window is always on top and always visible. You can specify that only one instance of Process Explorer is open at a time.

The Services Console

You can obtain a list of all the services available on a computer running Windows Server 2008 R2 by accessing the System Configuration console from the Administrative Tools menu and clicking the Services tab. This will tell you which services are running and which are stopped. However, to monitor and manage services, you should instead use the Services console, which also is available on the Administrative Tools menu. This tool lists the same services as the Services tab of the System Configuration tool, but it provides more information about each service and more service management options. For example, the Services console tells you the service startup type (not just whether or not it is running) and the logon details. You can also access the Services console by entering **services.msc** in the Search box on the Start menu, in the Run box, or in a command prompt window.

When you right-click a service in the Services console, you can start it, stop it, restart it, pause it, and resume it. You can access the Properties dialog box for the service and select the General, Log On, Recovery, and Dependencies tabs.

The General tab lets you specify the startup type. This can be Automatic, Automatic (Delayed Start) Manual, or Disabled. You should consider the following when specifying the startup type:

- If a service is configured as Automatic, it starts at boot time. Some services also stop automatically when no longer required. However, if you find that you do not need a service, configure its start type as Manual or Disabled.

- If a service is configured as Automatic (Delayed Start), it starts just after boot time. Configuring this setting can result in a faster boot, but if you need the service to be up and running when you boot, configure it as Automatic. On the other hand, if you do not need a service, configure its start type as Manual or Disabled.

- Manual mode allows Windows Server 2008 R2 to start a service when needed. In practice, some services do not start when required in Manual mode. If you find that you need a service, configure it as Automatic.

- If you configure a service as Disabled, it does not start even if it is needed. Unless you have a very good reason for disabling a service, configure its startup type as Manual instead.

The General tab also tells you whether a service is currently started, lets you start or stop it (as appropriate), and specifies the start parameters.

The Logon tab typically specifies that the service logs on with a Local System account. You can specify another account if you need to do so, typically a local Administrator account on the computer on which the service is running.

The Recovery tab specifies the actions that you take if a service fails. You can specify actions for the first failure, the second failure, and subsequent failures. The following options are available on this tab, depending on the actions that you specify and whether you want to enable actions on stops with errors:

- If you specify Run A Program as an action, you need to type the full path for the program that you want to run. Programs or scripts that you specify should not require user input.

- If you specify Restart The Computer as an action, you need to specify how long the computer waits before restarting. You can also specify when the fail count is restarted.

- If you select Enable Actions For Stops With Errors, you can trigger the recovery actions when the service stops with an error.

The Dependencies tab lists the services, system drivers, and load order groups that a service depends on. If a service is not running as you expect, you might have disabled another service that it depends on.

If you want to be informed when services fail, you can create a program that triggers an alert mechanism. You can also create programs that generate reports about the operation of services that you want to monitor. In general, however, the bulk of services are not monitored automatically, and it is a good idea to access the Services console on a regular basis to check that everything is as you expect.

Logging and Forwarding Events and Event Subscriptions

As an experienced administrator, you almost certainly have used Event Viewer, and this section discusses this tool only briefly before going on to event forwarding and event subscriptions, with which you might be less familiar.

When you are planning a monitoring strategy for a production network that includes a number of servers, you should consider collecting event logs for all the machines that you need to monitor on a single collector computer (which is typically, but not necessarily, an administrative workstation). You need to consider what events to monitor and what action to take when you observe critical, error, or warning events. If you require immediate notification when particular events occur, or if you want an event to trigger an action automatically, you need to consider attaching tasks to events. Forward planning of your event monitoring strategy requires both time and thought, but in the end, it could save you a lot of work and trouble.

Details about event subscriptions can be found in the Subscriptions tab of the event log Properties dialog box. The General tab of this dialog box gives details such as current log size, maximum log size, and the action to take when maximum log size is reached. Arguably, the easiest way to start Event Viewer is to enter **eventvwr** in the Search box of the Start menu.

Event Viewer displays event logs, which are files that record significant events on a computer—for example, when a user logs on or when a program encounters an error.

You will find the details in event logs helpful when troubleshooting problems. The events recorded fall into the following categories:

- Critical
- Error
- Warning
- Information

The security log contains two more event categories: Audit Success and Audit Failure, which are used for auditing purposes. You can also specify Verbose to obtain additional information about an event.

Event Viewer tracks information in several different logs. Windows logs include the following:

- **Application** Stores program events. Events are classified as error, warning, or information, depending on the severity of the event. The critical error classification is not used in the Application log.
- **Security** Stores security-related audit events that can be successful or failed. For example, the Security log will record an audit success if a user logs on successfully to the computer.
- **Setup** Contains events related to application setup, such as whether a setup operation required a computer restart.
- **System** Stores system events that are logged by Windows Server 2008 R2 and system services. System events are classified as critical, error, warning, or information.
- **Forwarded Events** Stores events that are forwarded by other computers.

Custom Views

You can create custom views by clicking Custom Views in the Event Viewer left pane and then clicking Create Custom View on the Action menu (or by right-clicking Custom Views and clicking Create Custom View). You then create a filter by specifying the Logs or Source Events and filter by Level, Time Logged, Event ID, Task Category, Keywords, User, or Computer. You are unlikely to specify all these criteria, but this facility enables you to refine your search to where you think a problem might be occurring rather than searching through a very large number of events. Figure 12-22 shows a filter specification.

Your next step is to save the specified filter as a custom view. A filter is not persistent. If you set up a filter to view specific information in an event log, you need to configure the same filter again the next time you want to see the same information. Custom views are persistent, which means you can access them whenever you open Event Viewer. You can save a filter as a custom view so it becomes persistent and you do not need to configure it for each use. The Action menu also allows you to import custom views from another source and to connect to another computer. You need to have an administrator-level account on that computer.

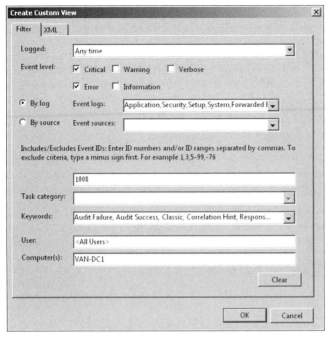

FIGURE 12-22 Specifying a filter to create a custom view

Applications And Services Logs

Event Viewer provides a number of Applications And Services Logs. These include logs for programs that run on the computer and detailed logs that store information about specific Windows services. For example, these logs can include the following:

- Hardware Events
- Internet Explorer
- Key Management Service
- Media Center
- Microsoft Office Diagnosis
- Microsoft Office Sessions
- Windows PowerShell

You can also find a number of other logs under Applications And Services Logs\Microsoft \Windows.

Attaching Tasks to Events

Sometimes you want to be notified by email if a particular event occurs, or you might want a specified program to start, such as one that activates a pager. Typically, you might want an event in the Security log—such as a failed logon (Event ID 4625) or a successful logon by a user who should not be able to log on to a particular computer—to trigger this action. To implement this functionality, you attach a task to the event so that you receive a notification.

To do this, open Event Viewer and navigate to the log that contains the event about which you want to be notified. Typically, this would be the Security log in Windows logs, but you can implement this in other Windows logs or in Applications and Services logs if you want to. Click the event, access the Action menu, and select Attach Task To This Event.

This opens the Create A Basic Task Wizard. You name and (optionally) describe the task and then click Next. The next screen summarizes the event, and you can check that you have chosen the correct event before clicking Next. The next screen gives you the option of starting a program, sending an email, or displaying a message. When you make your choice and click Next, you configure the task. For example, if you want to send an email, you would specify source address, destination address, subject, task, attachment (if required), and SMTP server, as shown in Figure 12-23. Click Next and then click Finish.

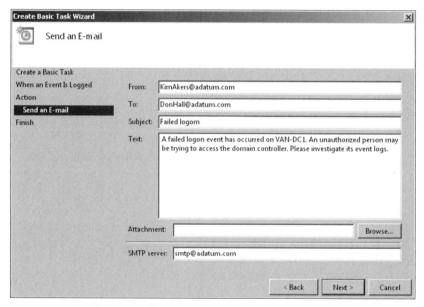

FIGURE 12-23 Specifying an action to take if an event occurs

Using Network Diagnostics with Event Viewer

When you run Windows Network Diagnostics (for example, from a browser window when a network connection fails), any problem found, along with a solution or solutions, is displayed in the Network Diagnostics dialog box. However, if more detailed information about the problem and potential solutions is available, Windows Server 2008 R2 saves it in one or more event logs. You can use the information in the event logs to analyze connectivity problems or help interpret the conclusions. You also can filter for network diagnostics and Transmission

Control Protocol/Internet Protocol (TCP/IP) events by specifying (for example) Tcpip and Tcpiv6 event sources and capturing events from these sources in a custom view.

If Network Diagnostics identifies a problem with a wireless network, it saves information in the event logs as either helper class events or informational events. Helper class events provide a summary of the diagnostics results and repeat information displayed in the Network Diagnostics dialog box. They can also provide additional information for troubleshooting, such as details about the connection that was diagnosed, diagnostics results, and the capabilities of the wireless network and the adapter being diagnosed.

Informational events can include information about the connection that was diagnosed, the wireless network settings on the computer and the network, visible networks and routers or access points in range at the time of diagnosis, the computer's preferred wireless network list, connection history, and connection statistics—for example, packet statistics and roaming history. They also summarize connection attempts, list their status, and tell you what phases of the connection failed or did not start.

Event Forwarding and Event Subscriptions

Event forwarding enables you to transfer events that match specific criteria to a collector computer. This enables you to manage events centrally. A single event log on the collector computer holds important events from computers anywhere in your organization. You do not need to connect to the local event logs on individual computers.

Event forwarding uses HTTP or, if you need to provide an additional encryption and authentication layer for greater security, HTTPS to send events from a source computer to a collector computer. Because event forwarding uses the same protocols that you use to browse websites, it works through most firewalls and proxy servers. Event forwarding traffic is encrypted whether it uses HTTP or HTTPS.

To use event forwarding, you must configure both the source and collector computers. On both computers, start the Windows Remote Management (WinRM) and the Windows Event Collector services. On the source computer, configure a Windows Firewall exception for the HTTP protocol. You might also need to create a Windows Firewall exception on the collector computer, depending on the delivery optimization technique that you choose.

You can configure collector- or source-initiated subscriptions. In collector-initiated subscriptions, the collector computer retrieves events from the computer that generated the event. You would use a collector-initiated subscription when you have a limited number of source computers and these are already identified (if, for example, you are collecting events from your servers). In this type of subscription, you configure each computer manually.

In a source-initiated subscription (sometimes termed a *source computer–initiated subscription*), the computer on which an event is generated (the source computer) sends the event to the collector computer. You would use a source-initiated subscription when you have a large number of source computers (for example, your clients) and you configure these computers through Group Policy.

In a source-initiated subscription, you can add additional source computers after the subscription is established and you do not need to know immediately which computers in your network are to be source computers. In collector-initiated subscriptions, the collector computer retrieves events from one or more source computers. Collector-initiated subscriptions are typically used in small networks or in networks where you are collecting events from a limited number of servers. In source-initiated subscriptions, the source computers forward events to the collector computer. Enterprise networks use source-initiated subscriptions.

A collector computer needs to run Windows Server 2008 R2, Windows Server 2008, Windows 7, Windows Vista, or Windows Server 2003 R2. A source computer needs to run Windows XP with SP2, Windows Server 2003 with SP1 or SP2, Windows Server 2003 R2, Windows Vista, Windows 7, Windows Server 2008, or Windows Server 2008 R2.

> **NOTE   FORWARDING COMPUTERS**
>
> Much of the literature on this subject uses the term *forwarding computer* rather than *source computer*, sometimes inaccurately. In collector-initiated subscriptions, the collector computer retrieves events from the source computer. The source computer does not forward events. Only in source-initiated subscriptions does the source computer forward events, and only then can it accurately be called a forwarding computer. To prevent confusion, the term *source computer*, rather than *forwarding computer*, is used throughout this chapter.

In a collector-initiated subscription, you first manually configure one or more source computers and the collector computer. When the source computers and the collector computer are configured, you can create an event subscription to determine what events should be transferred.

Configuring a Collector-Initiated Subscription

To configure a computer running Windows Server 2008 R2 so that a collector computer can retrieve events from it, open an elevated command prompt and use the WinRM command-line tool Winrm to configure the Windows Remote Management service by entering the following command:

```
winrm quickconfig
```

You can abbreviate this to `winrm qc`. Windows displays a message similar to that shown in Figure 12-24. This screen has been captured from domain controller VAN-DC1. The changes that must be made depend on how the operating system is configured. You enter **Y** to make these changes. Note that if any of your network connector types is set to *public*, you must set it to *private* for this command to work.

Next, add the computer account of the collector computer to the local Event Log Readers group or the local Administrators group on the source computer. You can do this by using the Local Users And Groups MMC snap-in or by entering a Net.exe command in an elevated command prompt.

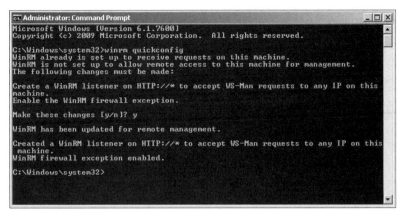

FIGURE 12-24 Configuring the Windows Remote Management service

You can add the collector computer account to the local Administrators group or the Event Log Readers group on the source computer. If you do not require the collector computer to retrieve events in Security Event logs, it is considered best practice to use the Event Log Readers group. However, if you do need to transfer Security Event log information, you must use the local Administrators group.

By default, the Local Users And Groups MMC snap-in does not permit you to add computer accounts. You must click the Object Types button in the Select Users, Computers, Or Groups dialog box and select the Computers check box. You can then add computer accounts.

Configuring a Computer to Hold Collector-Initiated Subscriptions

You cannot configure a computer to be both a source and a collector computer. If you have configured your VAN-DC1 domain controller as your source computer, you should use your VAN-SRV1 server as your collector computer. In a production network, the collector computer typically would be an administrative workstation running Windows 7.

To configure a computer running Windows Server 2008 R2 to collect events, open an elevated command prompt and enter the following command to configure the Windows Event Collector service:

`wecutil qc`

Note that you are informed that the service startup mode will be changed to Delay-Start when you enter this command. You need to enter **Y** to continue. When you have configured the source and collector computers, you next configure the event subscription by specifying what events the collector computer needs to retrieve and the event sources (specifically the source computers) from which it must retrieve them.

EXAM TIP

Distinguish between `Winrm` and `Wecutil`. `Winrm` is used to configure Windows Remote Management and is typically used on the source computer. `Wecutil` is used to configure the Windows Event Collector service and is typically used on the collector computer.

MORE INFO   **CREATING A COLLECTOR-INITIATED SUBSCRIPTION**

For more information about creating a collector-initiated subscription, see
http://msdn.microsoft.com/en-us/library/bb513652(VS.85).aspx.

Configuring a Source-Initiated Subscription

Source-initiated subscriptions typically are configured in enterprise networks in which you can use Group Policy to configure a number of source computers. To configure a source-initiated subscription, you configure the collector computer manually and then use Group Policy to configure the source computers. When the collector computer and source computers are configured, you can create an event subscription to determine which events are forwarded.

Source-initiated subscriptions (sometimes termed *source computer–initiated subscriptions*) enable you to configure a subscription on a collector computer without defining the event source computers. You can then set up multiple remote event source computers by using Group Policy to forward events to the event collector computer. By contrast, in the collector-initiated subscription model, you must define all the event sources in the event subscription.

To configure the collector computer in a source-initiated subscription, you need to use command-line commands entered in an elevated command prompt. If the collector and source computers are in the same domain, you must create an event subscription XML file (called, for example, Subscription.xml) on the collector computer, open an elevated command prompt on that computer, and configure WinRM by entering the following command:

```
winrm qc -q
```

Configure the Event Collector service on the same computer by entering the following command:

```
wecutil qc -q
```

Create a source-initiated subscription on the collector computer by entering the following command:

```
wecutil cs subscription.xml
```

You cannot configure your source computer to use a source-initiated subscription if you have already configured it to use a collector-initiated subscription. It is, therefore, necessary to plan in advance what type of subscription works best for your network. To configure a source computer to use a source-initiated subscription, you first configure WinRM on that computer by entering the following command:

```
winrm qc -q
```

You then use Group Policy to add the address of the event collector computer to the SubscriptionManager setting. From an elevated command prompt, start Group Policy by entering the following command:

```
%SYSTEMROOT%\System32\gpedit.msc
```

In Local Group Policy Editor, under Computer Configuration, expand Administrative Templates, expand Windows Components, and select Event Forwarding.

Right-click the SubscriptionManager setting and select Properties. Enable the SubscriptionManager setting and then click Show. Add at least one setting that specifies the event collector computer. The SubscriptionManager Properties window contains an Explain tab that describes the syntax for the setting.

After the SubscriptionManager setting has been added, run the following command to ensure that the policy is applied:

```
gpupdate /force
```

> **MORE INFO**   **SETTING UP AND CREATING A SOURCE-INITIATED SUBSCRIPTION**
>
> For more information about setting up a source-initiated subscription, see *http://msdn.microsoft.com/en-us/library/bb870973(VS.85).aspx*. For more information about creating such a subscription programmatically, see *http://msdn.microsoft.com/en-us/library/bb870971(VS.85).aspx*. You should be aware, however, that the exam will not ask you to write C++ programs.

Creating an Event Subscription

To receive events transferred from a source computer to a collector computer, you must create one or more event subscriptions. Before setting up a subscription, configure both the collector and source computers as previously described. To create a subscription on a collector computer, perform the following procedure:

1. In Event Viewer, right-click Subscriptions and select Create Subscription.

2. If prompted, click Yes to configure the Windows Event Collector Service to start automatically.

3. In the Subscription Properties dialog box shown in Figure 12-25, type a name for the subscription. You can also type a description if you want.

4. Select the type of subscription that you want to create—Collector Initiated or Source Computer Initiated. Specify Computers or Computer Groups.

5. Click the Select Events button in the Subscription Properties dialog box to open the Query Filter dialog box. Use this dialog box to define the criterion that forwarded events must match. Then click OK.

6. If you want, you can click the Advanced button in the Subscription Properties dialog box to open the Advanced Subscription Settings dialog box. You can configure three types of subscriptions: Normal, Minimize Bandwidth, and Minimize Latency.

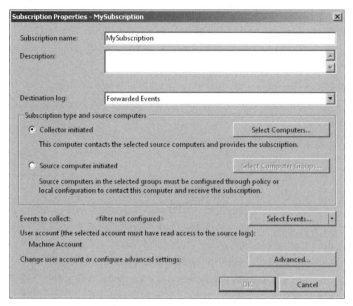

FIGURE 12-25 The Subscription Properties dialog box

NOTE   SPECIFYING THE ACCOUNT THE SUBSCRIPTION USES

Use the Advanced Subscription Settings dialog box to configure the account the subscription uses. Whether you use the default Machine Account setting or specify a user, you must ensure that the account is a member of the source computer's Event Log Readers group (or, if you are collecting Security Event log information, the local Administrators group).

7. Click OK in the Subscription Properties dialog box to create the subscription.

MORE INFO   USING THE WINDOWS EVENT COLLECTOR SOFTWARE DEVELOPMENT KIT (SDK)

If you are interested in using programmatic methods to create Event Collector solutions from a professional viewpoint, you can access *http://msdn.microsoft.com/en-us/library/ bb513659(VS.85).aspx* and follow the links. However, programming solutions are not included in the exam specification, and you will not be asked to write C++ programs under exam conditions.

Generating a Snapshot of Disk Performance Data

In this practice, you take a snapshot of performance data on your VAN-DC1 domain controller. You then view this data in graph, histogram, and report format. You will probably obtain different results from the VAN-DC1 computer in your practice network. Before you carry out this practice, connect a second storage device, such as a second hard disk or USB flash memory, to your computer. If you are using virtual computers, you can use a virtual hard disk.

EXERCISE 1   Add and Monitor Disk Counters

In this exercise, you add counters that enable you to monitor the performance of your system (C:) hard disk volume. If you have additional volumes on a single hard disk or additional hard disks on your system, you can extend the exercise to monitor them as well.

Note that you should start Exercise 2 immediately after you have completed Exercise 1, so allow enough time to do both exercises together.

> **NOTE   DISKPERF**
>
> Both logical and physical disk performance counters are enabled on demand by default on Windows Server 2008 R2. The Diskperf command still exists, and you can use it to enable or disable disk counters forcibly for older applications that use Ioctl_disk_performance to retrieve raw counters.

> **MORE INFO   IOCTL_DISK_PERFORMANCE**
>
> For more information about Ioctl_disk_performance, see *http://msdn.microsoft.com/en-us/library/ff560388(VS.85).aspx*. Note, however, that this is an older feature and is unlikely to be tested in the exam.

A bottleneck affecting disk usage and speed has a significant impact on a computer's overall performance. To add counters that monitor disk performance, perform the following procedure:

1. Log on to the VAN-DC1 computer using the Kim Akers account.
2. Open the Performance Monitor console and click Performance Monitor.
3. In Performance Monitor, click the Add button (that is, the green + symbol).
4. In the Add Counters dialog box, ensure that Local Computer is selected in the Select Counters From Computer drop-down list.
5. Select the Show Description check box.
6. Select any counters currently listed in the Added Counters pane and click Remove.
7. In the Available Counters pane, expand LogicalDisk and select % Free Space. In the Instances Of Selected Object pane, select C:, as shown in Figure 12-26. The LogicalDisk\% Free Space counter measures the percentage of free space on

the selected logical disk drive. If this falls below 15 percent, you risk running out of free space for the operating system to store critical files.

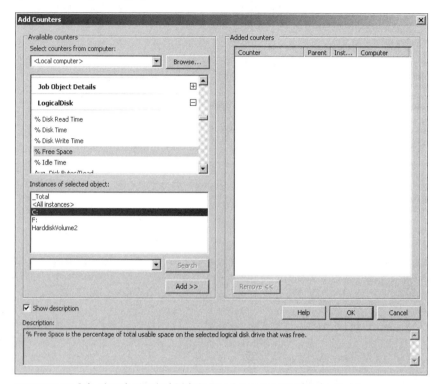

FIGURE 12-26 Selecting the Logical Disk\% Free Space Counter for the C: drive

8. Click Add to add this counter.

9. In the Select Counters From Computer pane, expand PhysicalDisk and select % Idle Time. In the Instances Of Dialog Box pane, select C:, as shown in Figure 12-27. This counter measures the percentage of time that the disk was idle during the sample interval. If this value falls below 20 percent, the disk system is said to be saturated, and you should consider installing a faster disk system.

10. Click Add to add this counter.

11. Use the same technique to add the C: instance of the PhysicalDisk\Avg. Disk Sec/Read counter. This counter measures the average time in seconds to read data from the disk. If the value is larger than 25 milliseconds (ms), the disk system is experiencing latency (delay) when reading from the disk. In this case, consider installing a faster disk system.

12. Use the same technique to add the C: instance of the PhysicalDisk\Avg. Disk Sec/Write counter. This counter measures the average time in seconds to write data to the disk. If the value is larger than 25 ms, the disk system is experiencing latency (delay) when writing to the disk. In this case, consider installing a faster disk system.

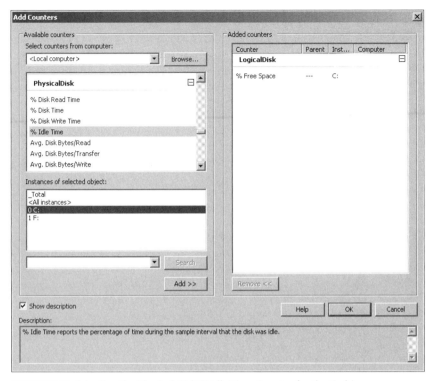

FIGURE 12-27 Selecting the Physical Disk\% Idle Time Counter for the C: drive

---

MORE INFO   PHYSICALDISK\% DISK TIME COUNTER

Because the value in the PhysicalDisk\% Disk Time counter can exceed 100 percent, many administrators prefer to use the PhysicalDisk\% Idle Time, PhysicalDisk\Avg. Disk Sec/Read, and PhysicalDisk\Avg. Disk Sec/Write counters to obtain a more accurate indication of hard disk usage. For more information about the PhysicalDisk\% Disk Time counter, see *http://support.microsoft.com/kb/310067*. This article is not specific to Windows Server 2008 R2, but it should provide the background information that you need.

---

13. Use the same technique to add the C: instance of the PhysicalDisk\Avg. Disk Queue Length counter. This counter indicates how many I/O operations are waiting for the hard drive to become available. If the value of this counter is larger than twice the number of spindles in a disk array, the physical disk itself might be the bottleneck.

14. Use the same technique to add the Memory\Cache Bytes counter. This counter indicates the amount of memory being used for the file system cache. There might be a disk bottleneck if this value is greater than 300 MB.

15. Check that the Add Counters dialog box shows the same counters and instances as in Figure 12-28. Click OK.

> **NOTE COUNTER INCLUDED BY DEFAULT**
>
> The Processor\%Processor Time counter is included by default; you do not need to add it. It does not appear in the list in Figure 12-28, but you can see it in the line graph, histogram, and report views shown in Exercise 2.

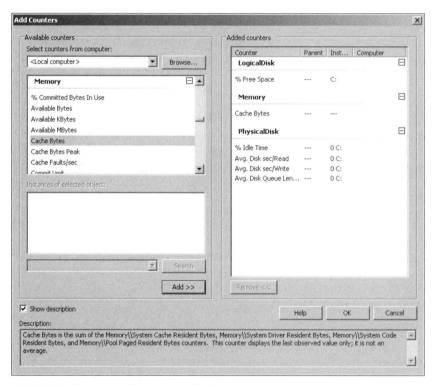

FIGURE 12-28 Counters and instances added

16. Do not close Performance Monitor. Go directly to Exercise 2.

EXERCISE 2   Set Performance Monitor Properties and Monitor Disk Performance

In this exercise, you set the sample interval and duration and read data from and write data to the disk volume you are monitoring. You view the results in line, histogram, and report formats.

1. On the Performance Monitor Action menu, click Properties.

2. On the General tab of the Performance Monitor Properties dialog box, in the Graph Elements section, change the Sample Every value to 5 and the Duration value to 300. Click OK.

3. Copy a file or folder (about 100 MB in size) from your C: drive to your attached storage device. If you are asked to provide administrative permission to do this, click Continue.

4. Copy a file or folder (about 100 MB in size) from your attached storage device to your C: drive. If you are asked to provide administrative permission to do this, click Continue.

5. View the line graph in Performance Monitor, as shown in Figure 12-29. This might not easily provide the information you want.

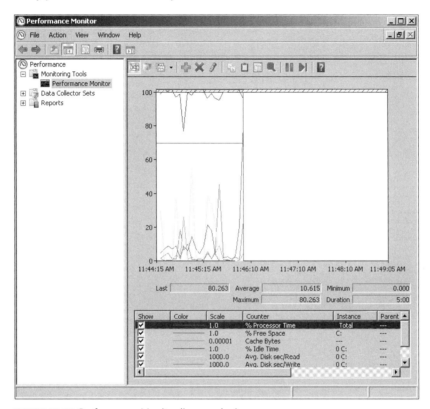

FIGURE 12-29 Performance Monitor line graph view

6. From the Change Graph drop-down list, select Histogram Bar. View the histogram in Performance Monitor, as shown in Figure 12-30.

7. From the Change Graph drop-down list, select Report. View the Report in Performance Monitor, as shown in Figure 12-31.

8. Analyze the counter values in the light of the information given about each counter in Exercise 1. The results shown in the screenshots indicate that adequate free space remains on the C: volume and no problem occurred when copying a fairly large file or folder. Cache memory usage was significant, but that is normal and acceptable in this operation. (The results that you obtain are likely to be different.)

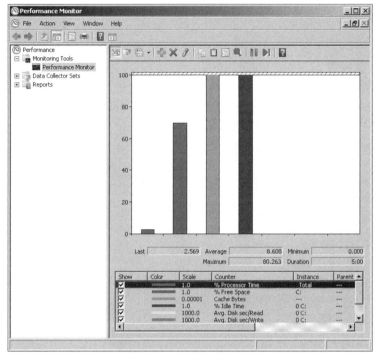

FIGURE 12-30 Performance Monitor histogram view

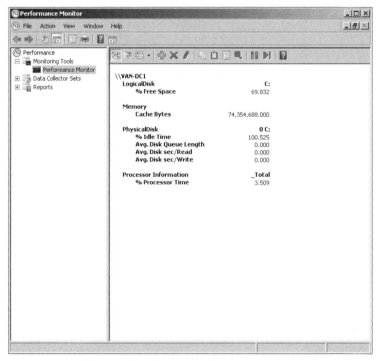

FIGURE 12-31 Performance Monitor report view

Lesson Summary

- You can use Performance Monitor to view performance data in real time or performance counter values captured in DCSs. A system diagnostics report gives you details about the status of hardware resources, system response times, and processes on the local computer, along with system information and configuration data.

- Reliability Monitor tracks a computer's stability. It can also tell you when events that could affect stability (such as the installation of a software application) occurred and whether any restarts were required after these events. Action Center monitors your computer and reports problems with security, maintenance, and related settings. The Services tool lets you check whether a service is running, configure its startup type, and specify the action to take if the service fails or stops with errors.

- Task Manager gives you a snapshot of resource usage and lets you manage applications, services, and protocols. Resource Monitor allows you to view information about hardware and software resource use in real time. Process Explorer performs the same functions as Task Manager but gives you additional controls and more detailed system information.

- Event Viewer lets you access and filter event logs and create custom views. You can attach tasks to events and configure event forwarding and event subscriptions so that a collector computer can store events generated on one or more source computers.

Lesson Review

You can use the following questions to test your knowledge of the information in Lesson 1, "Monitoring Data." The questions are also available on the companion CD if you prefer to review them in electronic form.

1. A server running Windows Server 2008 R2 is taking an unacceptable amount of time to boot. You have identified a service that takes a significant time to start, and you believe this is delaying the boot process. You do not need the service to start

immediately when the computer restarts, but you do want it to start automatically as soon as a boot is completed. How should you configure startup for this service?

A. Automatic

B. Manual

C. Automatic (Delayed Start)

D. Disabled

2. A server running Windows Server 2008 R2 is experiencing intermittent performance problems. You suspect the problems might be caused by an application that you recently installed, but you have forgotten exactly when you did this. Which tool or feature would you use to determine when the application was installed?

A. Reliability Monitor

B. Action Center

C. DCSs

D. Performance Monitor

3 Which of the following types of information are stored in Reliability Monitor? (Each correct answer presents part of the complete solution. Choose all that apply.)

A. An application failed and needs to be restarted.

B. A Windows error occurred and the system was rebooted.

C. An application was uninstalled.

D. A service was stopped.

E. A device driver failed.

4 You are configuring a server running Windows Server 2008 R2 named VAN-SRV1 to retrieve events from a domain controller running Windows Server 2008 R2 named VAN-DC1. Both computers are in the same domain. Which of the following commands would you run on the collector computer to configure the Event Collector service?

A. `wecutil qc`

B. `winrm qc`

C. `winrm qc -q`

D. `%SYSTEMROOT%\System32\gpedit.msc`

5. You want to use Performance Monitor to display performance data captured in a DCS. You open the tool and access the Performance Monitor Properties dialog box. On which tab can you choose whether to display current activity in real time or log files that you have saved using a DCS?

A. General

B. Source

C. Data

D. Graph

E. Appearance

Chapter Review

To further practice and reinforce the skills you learned in this chapter, you can perform the following tasks:

- Review the chapter summary.
- Review the list of key terms introduced in this chapter.
- Complete the case scenarios. These scenarios set up real-world situations involving the topics of this chapter and ask you to create a solution.
- Complete the suggested practices.
- Take a practice test.

Chapter Summary

- Windows Server 2008 R2 tools such as Performance Monitor, Reliability Monitor, and the Action Center let you gauge whether your computer is performing as it should, whether it needs more resources to do what you want it to do, and where performance bottlenecks are occurring.
- Tools such as Task Manager, Resource Manager, and Process Explorer give you a snapshot of how your computer is currently performing, whereas event logs can store historical events in addition to warning you when problems occur, and DCSs can hold both current and historical counter values so that you can compare a computer's performance with how it was performing at a specified time in the past.
- You need to plan what to monitor and when, and what tools to use. You need to establish baselines, track trends, and generate reports that indicate any performance deterioration before this becomes a perceived problem for the user.

Key Terms

The following terms were introduced in this chapter. Do you know what they mean?

- Data Collector Set (DCS)
- Event forwarding
- Event log
- Event subscription
- Performance counter

Case Scenarios

In the following case scenarios, you will apply what you've learned about network settings. You can find answers to these questions in the "Answers" section at the end of this book.

Case Scenario 1: Using Data Collector Sets and Event Forwarding

James Seymour is a server administrator administering the production network at Tailspin Toys. Recently, users have been experiencing intermittent performance problems when accessing a file server called DEN-FS1 running Windows Server 2008 R2. James checks resource usage on the file server by using Task Manager, but he sees no indication of excessive processor, memory, disk, or network resource usage. He needs to monitor these resources over a period of time rather than look at a real-time snapshot, and he needs to monitor resources both when the performance problems are occurring and when they are not.

James is using a server called DEN-SPARE running Windows Server 2008 R2 as his event subscriptions collector because this computer is not heavily used and his administrative workstation running Windows 7 is used extensively for other purposes. James opens Performance Monitor on DEN-SPARE and connects to the DEN-FS1 file server. With these facts in mind, answer the following questions.

1. How does James generate performance logs that help him analyze disk, network, processor, and memory resource usage on the server, both when problems are occurring and when performance is normal?

2. James knows roughly when problems started to occur. How can he check what applications were installed or upgraded at that time?

3. Recently, a number of users have had problems downloading files and email messages because the space on their local disks had reached a critical limit. James needs to create a proactive method of identifying low disk space problems on clients running Windows 7 on the Tailspin Toys network so he can ask his desktop support technicians to free disk space on clients before critical limits are reached. How does he use the DEN-SPARE server to monitor clients for low disk space events?

Case Scenario 2: Planning Monitoring on Server Computers

James is planning a monitoring strategy for the computers in the Tailspin Toys server farm. He needs to select the most appropriate tools for particular tasks. Answer the following questions.

1. On each of the servers for which he is responsible, James wants to obtain information that will help him to maximize performance and streamline system operation. He needs to obtain details about the status of hardware resources, system response times, and processes on each computer. What tool can he use to do this?

2. James needs to view information about hardware and software resource use in real time. He wants to filter the results according to the processes or services that he wants to monitor. He also wants to use the same tool to start, stop, suspend, and resume processes and services and to troubleshoot unresponsive applications. What tool should he use?

3. James has downloaded Process Explorer on all his servers and prefers to use it instead of Task Manager because it provides additional features. He wants to ensure that members of his team also use Process Explorer rather than Task Manager. How can he accomplish this?

Suggested Practices

To help you master the exam objectives presented in this chapter, complete the following tasks.

Use the Performance Monitoring Tools

- **Experiment with DCSs**   Look at the standard DCSs available and experiment with creating your own. DCSs provide a powerful method of managing current and historical performance on your computer, and the only way to become comfortable with them is to use them.

- **Look more closely at the Reports tool**   It is part of any administrator's job not only to carry out the tasks required to keep computer and network equipment performing efficiently, but also to report on these tasks to colleagues and to management. You will be judged on the clarity and relevance of your reports, and they will be a factor in your budget allocation. Learn to generate good reports.

Manage Event Logging

- **Investigate event forwarding and subscriptions**   This topic often seems complex at first, but it becomes clearer when you have practiced configuring subscriptions and forwarding events. If you did not already do this when studying the chapter, configure VAN-DC1 as a source computer and VAN-SRV1 as a collector computer on your test network. Configure the subscription type (collector-initiated is probably most appropriate), create event subscriptions, and collect events that occur on VAN-DC1 on the VAN-SRV1 server. Become proficient at event forwarding before you need to do it on a production network for real.

Investigate Process Explorer

- **Download and install Process Explorer and investigate its facilities**   Process Explorer is a sophisticated, multifunctional package that offers a wide range of facilities. You will become familiar with it only through use. Download the installation file on a computer that has access to the Internet. If this computer is running Windows Server 2008 R2, you can install Process Explorer on it and check the package out. Failing this, save the installation file to removable media and install the tool on VAN-DC1 (or VAN-SRV1).

Take a Practice Test

The practice tests on this book's companion CD offer many options. For example, you can test yourself on just one exam objective, or you can test yourself on all the 70-646 certification exam content. You can set up the test so that it closely simulates the experience of taking a certification exam, or you can set it up in study mode so that you can look at the correct answers and explanations after you answer each question.

> **MORE INFO**   **PRACTICE TESTS**
>
> For details about all the practice test options available, see the section entitled "How to Use the Practice Tests," in the Introduction to this book.

CHAPTER 13

Backup and Recovery

Backup and recovery have always been a core component of a systems administrator's job. Although more reliable hardware has meant that the amount of time that a systems administrator spends on backup and recovery has decreased, it also has meant that management's expectations about server availability have changed. Users who accepted that a file server might have been out of action for 24 hours in the late 1990s are unwilling to accept several hours of downtime a decade later. In this chapter, you will learn what is new about the process of backing up Windows Server 2008 R2 and the data and services that it hosts for your organization. You will also learn how to plan and implement the disaster recovery for your organization's Windows Server 2008 R2 environment. You will learn how to recover everything, from single Active Directory objects to files, folders, roles, volumes, and even entire servers.

Exam objective in this chapter

- Plan for backup and recovery.

Lessons in this chapter:

Before You Begin

To complete the exercises in the practices in this chapter, you need to have done the following:

- Installed a server called VAN-DC1 running Windows Server 2008 R2 Enterprise edition and configured as a domain controller in the adatum.com domain, as described in Exercise 1 of the Appendix, "Setup Instructions for End-of-Chapter Labs."

- Created a user account in the adatum.com domain with the user name Kim Akers and password Pa$$w0rd, and added this account to the Domain Admins, Enterprise Admins, and Schema Admins groups. This procedure is described in Exercise 1 of the appendix.

- Installed a server called VAN-SRV1 running Windows Server 2008 R2 Enterprise edition and configured as a member server in the adatum.com domain, as described in Exercise 2 of the appendix. This computer is not used in the practice exercises but is required if you want to complete the suggested practices.

- We recommend that you use an isolated network that is not part of your production network to do the practice exercises in this book. Internet access is not required for the exercises, and you do not need to configure a default gateway. To minimize the time and expense of configuring physical computers, we recommend that you use virtual machines. For example, you can create virtual machines using the Hyper-V server role.

- The practices in this chapter require that you have access to an extra disk that is able to store 40 GB of data and attach it to domain controller VAN-DC1. This disk can be an extra virtual disk if you are using virtual machines software, a physical disk, or an attached USB 2.0 or IEEE 1394 disk if you are using real hardware. This disk will be used to store backup data. As the practices are written, this disk is the F: drive. If the drive letter you choose is different, please amend the practices accordingly.

 REAL WORLD

Ian McLean

In my experience, the most important factor in recovering from a disaster is keeping a cool head. If you're calm and methodical, everything fits into the right place and you're smoothly back to where you were before the disaster occurred. If you're flustered, you will run into problems. People make mistakes under stress, and recovery operations can go awry because someone was nervous and rushed.

The key to staying calm is to plan your disaster recovery. Don't wait for the disaster to occur before you formulate a disaster plan. Document your plan so you know exactly how you need to proceed in any foreseeable circumstance (or at least the most likely ones). Test your plan as much as you possibly can, for example by using trial restores.

Take a few moments and a few deep breaths to clear your head. Have your plan documentation readily on hand (keeping the only copy on a hard disk is a bad idea). It's much more effective to start slowly and prepare yourself, rather than to panic and rush the job and then need to start all over again.

Lesson 1: Backing Up Data

The backup tools introduced in Windows Server 2008 and enhanced in Windows Server 2008 R2 are significantly different from those that were included in Windows Server 2003. Backup techniques that you may have been familiar with over the course of your career have changed. For example, scheduled backups can no longer be written to tape drives. In this lesson, you will learn how to use the backup utility introduced by Windows Server 2008 to back up your servers and how you can use additional options in Windows Server 2008 R2 to exclude file types and paths from your backup. You will learn how to use the Wbadmin.exe command-line backup utility and how to back up files, folders, and Active Directory. You will also learn how to configure Shadow Copies of Shared Folders, a technology that allows you to move the process of recovering deleted or corrupted shared files to the individual user rather than to the help desk.

> **After this lesson, you will be able to:**
> - Understand how to use the Wbadmin.exe utility to back up servers.
> - Perform a complete server backup.
> - Back up Active Directory and Server Role data.
> - Back up System State data.
> - Perform remote backup operations.
>
> **Estimated lesson time: 45 minutes**

Using Shadow Copies of Shared Folders

Implementing Shadow Copies of Shared Folders can reduce your restoration workload dramatically because it almost entirely eliminates the need for administrator intervention in the recovery of deleted, modified, or corrupted user files. Shadow Copies of Shared Folders work by taking snapshots of files stored in shared folders as they exist at a particular point in time, dictated by a schedule. The default schedule for Shadow Copies of Shared Folders is to make shadow copies at 7:00 A.M. and 12:00 P.M. every weekday. Multiple schedules can be applied to a volume, and the default schedule is made up of two schedules applied at the same time.

To enable Shadow Copies of Shared Folders, open Computer Management from the Administrative Tools menu, right-click the Shared Folders node, click All Tasks, and select Configure Shadow Copies. This will bring up the Shadow Copies dialog box, shown in Figure 13-1. This dialog box allows you to enable and disable Shadow Copies of Shared Folders on a per-volume basis. It allows you to edit the Shadow Copies of Shared Folders settings for a particular volume. It also allows you to create a shadow copy of a particular volume manually.

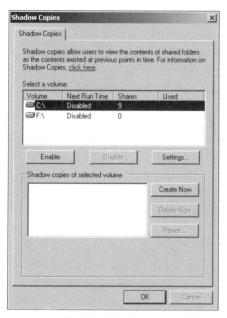

FIGURE 13-1 Enabling Shadow Copies of Shared Folders

Enabling Shadow Copies of Shared Folders on a volume will generate an initial shadow copy for that volume automatically. Clicking Settings opens the dialog box shown in Figure 13-2. From this dialog box, you can configure the storage area, the maximum size of the copy store, and the schedule at which copies are taken. Clicking Schedule allows you to configure how often shadow copies are generated. On volumes hosting file shares that contain files that are updated frequently, you would use a frequent shadow copy schedule. On a volume hosting file shares where files are updated less frequently, you should configure a less frequent shadow copy schedule.

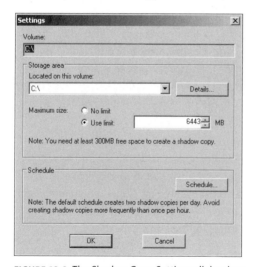

FIGURE 13-2 The Shadow Copy Settings dialog box

When a volume regularly experiences intense read and write operations, such as a commonly used file share, you can mitigate the performance impact of shadow copies of shared folders by storing the shadow copy data on a separate volume. If a volume has less space available than the set limit, Windows will remove the oldest shadow copies that it has stored as a way of freeing up space.

Finally, no matter how much free space is available, a maximum of 64 shadow copies can be stored on any one volume. This directly influences the length of shadow copy data retention. For example, where space is available, a schedule in which shadow copies are taken once every Monday, Wednesday, and Friday allows shadow copies from the previous 21 weeks to be retrieved. The default schedule allows for the retrieval of up to 6 weeks of previous shadow copies.

When planning the deployment of Shadow Copies of Shared Folders, it is important to remember that you configure settings on a per-volume basis. This means that the storage area, maximum size, and schedules for different volumes can be completely separate. If you plan shares in such a way that each volume hosts a single share, you can optimize the shadow copy settings for that share based on how the data is used, rather than trying to compromise in finding an effective schedule for very different shared folder usage patterns.

 Quick Check

1. On what basis (server, volume, share, disk, or folder) are Shadow Copies of Shared Folders enabled?

2. What happens to shadow copy data when the volume that hosts it begins to run out of space?

Quick Check Answers

1. Shadow Copies of Shared Folders are enabled on a per-volume basis.

2. The oldest shadow copy data is deleted automatically when volumes begin to run out of space.

Windows Server Backup

Windows Server Backup consists of the Windows Server Backup MMC snap-in, the Wbadmin command-line tool, and Windows PowerShell cmdlets. Windows Server Backup provides a complete solution for your backup and recovery needs. It can back up a full server (all volumes), selected volumes, the system state, or specific files or folders. You can also create a backup that you can use for bare metal recovery from a disaster such as a hard disk failure. You can recover volumes, folders, files, certain applications, and the system state. You can use Windows Server Backup to create and manage backups for the local computer or a remote computer, and you can schedule backups to run automatically.

EXAM TIP

The Windows Server Backup tool in Windows Server 2008 and Windows Server 2008 R2 is significantly different from the NTbackup.exe tool included in Windows Server 2000 and Windows Server 2003. You should study the capabilities and limitations of the Windows Server Backup utility introduced in Windows Server 2008 and the enhancements added in Windows Server 2008 R2, because many aspects of the tool's functionality have changed.

The key enhancements introduced to backup in Windows Server 2008 are the following:

- Windows Server Backup cannot write to tape drives.

- You cannot write to network locations or optical media during a scheduled backup.

- The smallest object that you can back up using Windows Server Backup is a volume.

- Only local NTFS-formatted volumes can be backed up.

- Windows Server Backup files write their output as Virtual Hard Disk (VHD) files. VHD files can be mounted with the appropriate software and read, either directly or through virtual-machine software like Hyper-V.

The key enhancements introduced to backup in Windows Server 2008 R2 are the following:

- **The ability to back up or exclude individual files and to include or exclude file types and paths from a volume** Windows Server Backup enables you to back up selected files. New options added to the Schedule Backup and Backup Once wizards enable you to choose files and folders to add to your backup (rather than only full volumes). You can also exclude files from your backups based on file type or path. In addition, the `wbadmin enable backup` and `wbadmin start backup` commands have been updated to include this functionality.

- **Improved performance and the use of incremental backups** By default, Windows Server Backup creates incremental backups that enable you to recover any item from a single backup, but that occupy only the space needed for an incremental backup. All file and folder backups (except the first one) are incremental backups where only files that have been changed since the previous backup are read and transferred to the backup storage location. In addition, Windows Server Backup does not require that you periodically delete older backups to free disk space. Older backups are deleted automatically. No user action is required to create incremental backups. However, if you are backing up full volumes, you can configure performance settings by using the Optimize Backup Performance dialog box available from the Windows Server Backup tool and shown in Figure 13-3.

- **Expanded options for backup storage** Windows Server 2008 R2 allows you to store backups created using a scheduled backup on a remote shared folder or volume. If, however, you store backups on a remote shared folder, only one version of your backup will be maintained. You can also store backups on VHDs. New options are added to the Schedule Backup Wizard that let you select a remote shared folder or volume as the backup storage location. The `wbadmin enable backup` command has been updated to include this functionality.

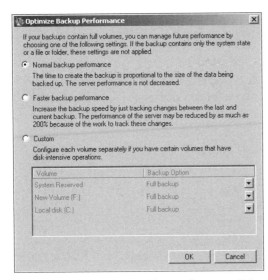

FIGURE 13-3 The Optimize Backup Performance dialog box

- **Options and improved performance for system state backup** You can use Windows Server Backup to create system state backups. You can also use a single backup to back up both the system state and other data on a server. System state backups in Windows Server 2008 R2 require less space for multiple versions because they use shadow copies for versioning rather than creating individual folders for each version. In addition, the wbadmin enable backup and wbadmin start backup commands now include the -*SystemState* parameter, which enables you to include the system state in scheduled or one-time backups.

- **Expanded command-line support** Enhancements to the wbadmin start backup and wbadmin enable backup commands provide command-line support to the enhancements to Windows Server Backup—that is, the ability to back up files instead of full volumes, the ability to exclude certain file types or paths, and the ability to store scheduled backups on remote shared folders and volumes.

> **NOTE   WBADMIN START SYSRECOVERY**
>
> Lesson 2, "Disaster Recovery," discusses enhancements to the wbadmin start sysrecovery command introduced by Windows Server 2008 R2.

- **Expanded Windows PowerShell support** Windows Server 2008 R2 has enhanced the Windows PowerShell cmdlets to automate routine tasks and to better manage backup scripts. The new Active Directory Module For Windows PowerShell (discussed in detail in Lesson 2) and enhancements to Windows PowerShell cmdlets mirror the changes to Windows Server Backup and provide the ability to back up files instead of full volumes, to exclude certain file types or paths, and to store scheduled backups on remote shared folders and volumes.

Windows Server Backup is not installed by default on Windows Server 2008 or Windows Server 2008 R2. You install it as a feature using the Add Features item under the Features node of the Server Manager console, which you will do in the practice later in this chapter. When it is installed, you can open the Windows Server Backup console from the Administrative Tools menu. The Wbadmin.exe command-line utility, also installed during this process, is covered in the section entitled "The Wbadmin Command-Line Tool," later in this lesson.

To use Windows Server Backup or Wbadmin to schedule backups, your computer typically requires an extra internal or external disk. External disks will need to be either USB 2.0– or IEEE 1394–compatible. When planning the deployment of disks to host scheduled backup data, you should ensure that the volume is capable of holding at least two and a half times the amount of data that you want to back up. When planning deployment of disks for scheduled backup, you should monitor how well this size works and what sort of data retention it allows in a trial before deciding on a disk size for wider deployment throughout your organization.

When you configure your first scheduled backup, the disk that hosts backup data is hidden from Windows Explorer. If the disk currently hosts volumes and data, these will be removed to store scheduled backup data. Note that this only applies to scheduled backups and not to manual backups. You can use a network location or external disk for a manual backup without worrying that data already stored on the device will be lost. The format and repartition happens only when a device is first used to host scheduled backup data. It does not happen when subsequent backup data is written to the same location.

If you choose to use a network share as the destination for scheduled backups, it can hold only the latest backup because data from a scheduled backup will overwrite previous backup data. If you use a volume rather than a full hard disk as a destination for scheduled backups,

Microsoft recommends that you do not store any other data on that volume because the performance of the volume may be reduced by up to 200 percent when it is being used to store backups.

It is also important to remember that a volume can store only a maximum of 512 backups. If a greater number of backups need to be stored, it will be necessary to write them to a different volume. In practice, given the amount of data on most servers, it is unlikely that you will find a disk that has the capacity to store so many backups. So that scheduled backups can always be executed, Windows Server Backup will remove the oldest backup data automatically on a volume that is the target of scheduled backups. It is not necessary for you to clean up or remove old backup data manually.

Performing a Scheduled Backup

Scheduled backups allow you to automate the backup process. Once you set the schedule, Windows Server Backup takes care of everything else. By default, scheduled backups are set to occur at 9 P.M. If your organization still has people regularly working on documents at that time, you should configure another backup time. When planning a backup schedule you should ensure that the backup occurs at a time where the most recent day's changes to data are always captured. Only members of the local Administrators group can configure and manage scheduled backups.

To configure a scheduled backup, perform the following steps:

1. Open Windows Server Backup and click Backup Schedule in the Actions pane. This starts the Backup Schedule Wizard. Click Next.

2. The Select Backup Configuration page of the wizard asks you whether you want to perform a Full Server (Recommended) or Custom backup. If you choose Custom, click Next and then click Add Items on the Select Items For Backup page, you can (if you want to) select Bare Metal Recovery, System State, one or more full volumes, or one or more folders within a volume. Do not select the volume that will hold your backup. If you click Advanced Settings on the Select Items For Backup page and click Add Exclusion on the Exclusions tab of the Advanced Settings dialog box, you can specify folders and files to exclude. On the VSS Settings tab of the same dialog box, you can specify VSS Full Backup or VSS Copy Backup. Clicking Next on the Select Items For Backup page takes you to the Specify Backup Time page.

3. If, on the other hand, you select Full Server (Recommended) on the Backup Configuration page and click Next, you go directly to the Specify Backup Time page.

4. On the Specify Backup Time page, shown in Figure 13-4, you can specify whether to schedule the backup once or several times per day. The default backup schedule is once a day at 9 P.M. You are most likely to want to configure multiple backups to be taken during each day if data on the server that you are backing up changes rapidly. On servers such as web servers, where data changes a lot less often, you would configure a daily schedule. In either case, you would choose your backup times to

coincide with periods of relatively low server activity. When you have configured your backup schedule, click Next to access the Specify Destination Type page.

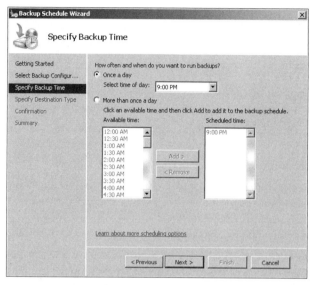

FIGURE 13-4 The Specify Backup Time page

5. On the Specify Destination Type page for scheduled backups, shown in Figure 13-5, you can choose to back up to a dedicated hard disk, a volume, or a shared network folder. Note that you do not have the options of backing up to a volume if you are carrying out a non-scheduled one-time backup. You will perform this type of backup in a practice later in this chapter.

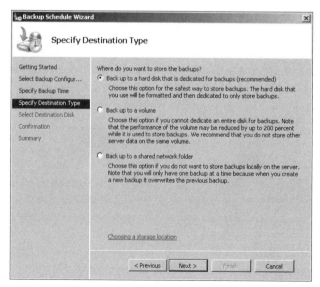

FIGURE 13-5 The Specify Destination Type page

6. On the Select Destination Disk page, shown in Figure 13-6, you select the disk to which backups are written. If multiple disks are selected, multiple copies of the backup data are written. You should note that the entire disk will be used. All existing volumes and data will be removed, and the backup utility will format and hide the disk or disks prior to writing the first backup data.

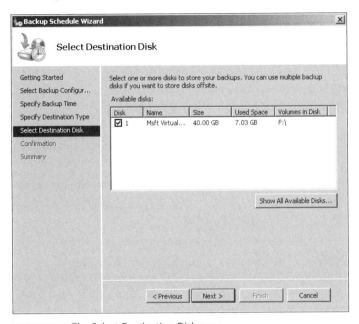

FIGURE 13-6 The Select Destination Disk page

7. When you click Next on the Select Destination Disk page, you are informed if you have specified the backup destination disk as one of the disks to be backed up (this typically happens during a Full Server backup) and are given the option of removing this disk from the backup list. You are warned that the backup destination disk or disks will be hidden and reformatted. When you accept this warning, this accesses the Confirmation page. Click Finish to close the wizard. The backups are performed as scheduled.

8. When you finish the wizard, the target destination is formatted and then the first backup will occur at the scheduled time.

An important limitation of Windows Server Backup is that you can schedule only one backup job. This means that jobs that you might be used to scheduling in earlier versions of Windows (prior to Windows Server 2008), such as a full backup on Monday night with a series of incremental backups every other day of the week, cannot be scheduled using Windows Server Backup. In Windows Server 2008 R2, Windows Server Backup automatically performs incremental backups after the first full backup has been made.

Performing an Unscheduled Single Backup

Unscheduled single backups, also known as *manual backups,* can be written to shared network locations, local and external hard disks, and local DVD media. If a backup encompasses more than the space available on a single DVD, it is possible to span the backup across multiple DVDs. Otherwise, if the calculated size of a backup exceeds the amount of free space available on the destination location, the backup will fail. You will perform a manual backup in a practice later in this chapter.

If you select Custom rather than performing a Full Server backup on either a manual backup or a scheduled backup, you can choose between two different types of Volume Shadow Copy Service (VSS) backup by clicking Advanced Options on the Select Items For Backup page of the appropriate wizard. These choices are as follows:

- **VSS Full Backup**   This option should be selected when no other products are used to back up the host computer. The option updates each file's backup attribute and clears application log files.

- **VSS Copy Backup**   This option should be selected when another product is also used to back up applications on volumes in the current backup. Application log files are retained when you perform this type of backup.

Optimizing Backup Performance

When you create a backup job using Windows Server Backup on a computer running Windows Server 2008 or Windows Server 2008 R2, you do not configure individual backups as full, differential, or incremental as you did in previous Windows Server versions. In Windows Server 2008 R2, the first backup is a full backup and all subsequent backups are incremental by default. Differential backups cannot be specified and you can implement a recovery operation from a single incremental backup. When you configure backup performance and choose the Custom option, you can configure backups as either full or incremental on a per-volume basis. The first backup image taken in a schedule is the equivalent of a full backup.

If your backups include full volumes, you can configure backup performance by clicking Configure Performance in the Actions pane of the Windows Server Backup console. When you do this, you can select from the options shown in Figure 13-7. The Custom backup option allows you to choose full or incremental backups on a per-volume basis. Selecting the Incremental Backup option will allow you to store more scheduled backups on the same media, and in general, you should use this option because it will give you a greater window from which you can restore data. You cannot configure the Backup Option on a volume if you select Normal Backup Performance or Faster Backup Performance.

A benefit of Windows Server Backup is that you will not have to hunt around for specific incremental backup sets when performing a restore. When you perform a restore, the appropriate backup images are located based on your restoration selections. Restoration is covered in more detail in Lesson 2.

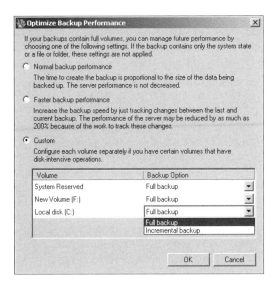

FIGURE 13-7 Configuring backup performance

The Wbadmin Command-Line Tool

The Wbadmin utility is available on both the standard and Server Core installations of Windows Server 2008 and Windows Server 2008 R2. Note that the Windows Server Backup console is not available on computers running Server Core installations, although you can use it if you connect remotely to such a computer. The command-line utility enables you to do everything that you can do with the Windows Server Backup console, and even more. Wbadmin is installed on a standard installation of Windows Server 2008 or Windows Server 2008 R2 when you install the Windows Server Backup feature and choose to install the Command-Line Tools option, as described in a practice later in this chapter. Wbadmin can be installed on a computer running in the Server Core configuration by entering the command:

```
Ocsetup WindowsServerBackup
```

The following Wbadmin.exe commands are useful for backing up Windows Server 2008 and Windows Server 2008 R2 files:

- **wbadmin enable backup**   This command allows you to create and manage scheduled backups. In Windows Server 2008 R2, the following additional parameters are introduced:
  - *include*   This parameter is supported in Windows Server 2008. However, in Windows Server 2008 R2, it is enhanced so that it can specify multiple files, folders, or volumes.
  - *nonRecurseInclude*   Specifies a non-recursive, comma-delimited list of items to include in the backup.
  - *exclude*   Specifies the comma-delimited list of items to exclude from the backup.

- **nonRecurseExclude** Specifies the non-recursive, comma-delimited list of items to exclude from the backup.

- **systemState** Creates a backup that includes the system state in addition to any other items that you specified with the -*include* parameter.

- **vssFull** and **vssCopy** Specify whether a backup is a VSS full backup or a VSS copy backup.

- **user** Specifies the user with write permission to the backup storage destination (if it is a remote shared folder).

- **password** Specifies the password for the user name provided by the *user* parameter.

MORE INFO   **WBADMIN ENABLE BACKUP**

For more information about the wbadmin enable backup **command, see** *http://technet.microsoft.com/en-us/library/cc742130(WS.10).aspx.*

- **wbadmin start systemstatebackup**   This command allows you to perform a manual system state data backup. It implements only a system state backup, and you cannot include other files, folders, or volumes. The command works only on computers running Windows Server 2008 or Windows Server 2008 R2. The command syntax in Windows Server 2008 and Windows Server 2008 R2 is the same.

MORE INFO   **WBADMIN START SYSTEMSTATEBACKUP**

For more information about the wbadmin start systemstatebackup **command, see** *http://technet.microsoft.com/en-us/library/cc742124(WS.10).aspx.*

- **wbadmin start backup**   This command allows you to start a single manual backup. If no backup parameters are specified, it uses the settings configured for scheduled backups. In Windows Server 2008 R2, the following additional parameters are introduced:

  - **include**, **exclude**, **nonRecurseInclude**, **nonRecurseExclude**, **systemState**, and **vssCopy**   These Windows Server 2008 R2 parameters work in the same way that was described for the wbadmin enable backup command. Note that for the wbadmin start backup command the −*name*, -*password*, and −*vssFull* parameters are available for both Windows Server 2008 R2 and Windows Server 2008.

MORE INFO   **WBADMIN START BACKUP**

For more information about the wbadmin start backup **command, see** *http://technet.microsoft.com/en-us/library/cc742083(WS.10).aspx.*

- **wbadmin get versions** This command enables you to view details of backups that have already been taken. The command syntax in Windows Server 2008 and Windows Server 2008 R2 is the same.

MORE INFO **WBADMIN GET VERSIONS**

For more information about the wbadmin get versions command, see *http://technet.microsoft.com/en-us/library/cc742116(WS.10).aspx.*

- **wbadmin get items** This command enables you to determine which items are contained in a specific backup image. The command syntax in Windows Server 2008 and Windows Server 2008 R2 is the same.

MORE INFO **WBADMIN GET ITEMS**

For more information about the wbadmin get items command, see *http://technet. microsoft.com/en-us/library/cc742041(WS.10).aspx.*

Windows Server 2008 administrators can use the wbadmin start backup command to perform manual backups to shared folders by using the parameter syntax –backuptarget:\\ Share\Folder, where the shared folder location is expressed as a UNC path name. (This restriction does not apply to Windows Server 2008 R2 although the command works just the same.) If you need to provide authentication credentials to write data to the shared folder, you can use the *user* and *password* parameters. For example, to back up volumes E, F, and G of a server to the shared folder Store on the domain controller VAN-DC1 using Kim Aker's credentials, you would enter the command:

```
Wbadmin start backup –backuptarget:\\VA-DC1\Store –include:E:,F:,G:
  –user:KimAkers@adatum.com –password:Pa$$w0rd
```

MORE INFO **ADDITIONAL WBADMIN COMMANDS**

The list of wbadmin commands given in this section includes (arguably) the most commonly used commands but it is not exclusive. For information about the commands not included in the list, access *http://technet.microsoft.com/en-us/library/ cc754015(WS.10).aspx?ppud=4* and follow the links.

Because Wbadmin.exe can be called from a batch file and batch files can be called from the Scheduled Tasks utility, it is possible to schedule the execution of more precisely configured backups than is possible using Windows Server Backup's scheduling options. Windows Server 2008 does not permit normal scheduled backups to network locations (but Windows Server 2008 R2 does), and you can also use this method if you need to configure scheduled backups to network locations on a computer running Windows Server 2008. For example, the following command creates a batch file named Ssbackup.bat in the C:\Scripts directory that performs a system state backup to the network share \\Server\Share using the credentials of user RemoteUser:

```
Echo wbadmin start systemstatebackup -backupTarget:\\Server\Share -user:RemoteUser
  -password:RemotePassword -quiet >> c:\scripts\ssbackup.bat
```

You can use Scheduled Tasks to configure this batch file to run according to a schedule, mimicking Windows Server Backup's backup schedule functionality. There are some points to take note of when planning backups using this method:

- The *-quiet* option is necessary in the wbadmin command because you do not want a scheduled task to halt because it is waiting for input.
- The scheduled task must be run using the local Administrator account because Wbadmin.exe must be run with elevated privileges.
- If the scheduled task is writing to a network share, it will be necessary to put user account credentials into the script called by the scheduled task. You can protect these credentials by using the Encrypting File System (EFS) to encrypt the file so that only the local Administrator account can view the script contents.

Backing Up Server Roles and Applications

In general, backing up a particular server role, such as the DHCP or DNS role, with its associated data is simply a matter of backing up system state data. You perform a system state backup in a practice exercise later in this chapter. In Windows Server 2008, the only method by which you can back up only the system state data is to use Wbadmin.exe with the start systemstatebackup option. In Windows Sever 2008 R2, however, both the Windows Server Backup console and the wbadmin start backup -systemState command also allow you to do this. Performing a system state data recovery is covered in detail in Lesson 2.

Backing Up Applications

Windows Server Backup will take special note of applications that are VSS- and Windows Server Backup–aware, allowing you to restore just the application and its associated data from a full server or volume backup. To be able to use this functionality, it is necessary for an application to be registered with Windows Server Backup, which occurs automatically during the application's installation process. This limits this functionality to applications that are designed to run on Windows Server 2008 or Windows Server 2008 R2.

You can back up and restore data related to an application even if the application does not register itself with Windows Server backup. The benefit of this feature is that it simplifies the application restoration process, ensuring that all application data, from executable files to registry settings, is packaged in such a way that you can restore just that application and its dependencies and data.

Backing Up Active Directory

Active Directory is backed up automatically whenever you back up the volumes on a domain controller that contains the system files. You can also back up Active Directory by performing a system state backup. A copy of the Active Directory Domain Services (AD DS) database is stored on all domain controllers within a domain, so in the event that if a domain controller is lost and you do not have access to backup data, you can perform a recovery by reinstalling the domain controller from scratch and replicating the database back from other domain controllers.

Although performing a system state backup backs up all Active Directory objects, the nature of Active Directory replication makes the recovery of some objects more difficult than the recovery of others. The process of performing an authoritative restore is covered in detail in Lesson 2. However, the technique for restoring a deleted Group Policy object (GPO) is significantly different from restoring a user account or OU tree. GPOs are backed up using the Group Policy Management Console (GPMC), and you should use this console, rather than Directory Services Restore Mode (DRSM), to recover deleted GPOs. Chapter 4, "Group Policy Strategies," discusses GPO backup and restore in detail.

Quick Check

1. What command is used to install Wbadmin.exe on a computer running Windows Server 2008 R2 with the Server Core configuration?

2. What happens to any volumes and data stored on a disk that you select as a target to store backup data generated by a scheduled backup configured in Windows Server Backup?

Quick Check Answers

1. `Ocsetup WindowsServerBackup`

2. All volumes and data on the target disk are removed before Windows Server Backup writes its first set of backup data. In addition, the disk is no longer visible in Windows Internet Explorer.

Backing Up Computers Remotely

The Windows Server Backup tool can be used to connect to a remote computer running Windows Server 2008 or Windows Server 2008 R2 and perform backup tasks as though the backup were being performed on the local computer. This allows users that have the Remote Server Administration Tools (RSAT) installed on workstations running Windows Vista or Windows 7 to connect to servers running Windows Server 2008 or Windows Server 2008 R2 and perform backup operations as though they were logged on locally. To perform this operation, the user making the connection must be a member of the Backup Operators or local Administrators group on the computer running Windows Server 2008 or Windows Server 2008 R2 to which they are making the connection.

The same limitations apply to remote connections using the Windows Server Backup console as apply to a locally run instance. A user that is only a member of the Backup Operators local group will be unable to schedule backups and will only be able to perform unscheduled backups. A user that is a member of the local Administrators group on the server that is the target of the remote Windows Server Backup connection will be able to perform all normal backup tasks.

Windows Server Backup does not allow you to schedule backup data generated on remote computers to be written to a local source. You can write to a local source when performing an unscheduled backup only if the computer you are attempting to write data to has a shared folder configured. You cannot use the Wbadmin.exe utility to manage backups on remote computers.

Further Considerations for Planning Backups

In Windows Server 2008, the smallest unit of backup became the volume, as opposed to the ability to back up individual files and folders in Windows Server 2003. This significantly affected how you configured servers prior to their deployment. However, Windows Server 2008 R2 offers quite a bit more flexibility, allowing you to specify folders and even individual files. You can also exclude folders and file types from a backup.

Another thing you need to consider when planning backups is how frequently particular items need to be backed up. You can use Storage Reports to gain insight as to how often files on a particular volume are altered. A folder that hosts documents that are updated only on an occasional basis does not need to be backed up nightly. You can exclude this folder from your normal scheduled backup and configure less frequent backups by using a batch file and Scheduled Tasks, as discussed earlier in this lesson. In Windows Server 2008, you needed to move this folder to its own partition to configure separate backups of its contents. However, the increased flexibility provided by Windows Server 2008 R2 means you no longer need to do this.

Alternatively, you might identify a particular folder where data is updated so frequently and is so mission-critical that you need to back it up every few hours. Again, the improved flexibility provided by Windows Server 2008 R2 lets you schedule more frequent backups for this particular folder. You can develop a backup strategy that best meets your organization's needs, rather than the limitations of the specific tools that you have to work with.

A final consideration in the planning of backups is developing an offsite strategy. Offsite backups ensure that if the building that hosts your servers is destroyed by flood, fire, or earthquake, your organization can still recover its data. When planning an offsite backup strategy, consider the following points:

- Offsite backups must be stored in secure locations. You should avoid having members of staff take backup data home because this practice is not secure.

- Ensure that if data is encrypted, the recovery keys are included in the offsite backup data set.

- Ensure that you have enough equipment at your recovery site so that you can recover your servers.

MORE INFO **WINDOWS SERVER 2008 R2 BACKUP**

For more information about Windows Server 2008 R2 backup, including a detailed step-by-step guide, see *http://technet.microsoft.com/en-us/library/ee849849(WS.10).aspx*.

System Center Data Protection Manager

System Center Data Protection Manager (DPM) 2010 delivers data protection for Windows servers such as Microsoft SQL Server, Microsoft Exchange Server, Microsoft SharePoint, Microsoft Hyper-V, and file servers. You can also use it to protect Windows clients. DPM is a backup and recovery solution for Windows environments. It supports Windows Server 2008 and Windows Server 2008 R2 and provides the following advantages:

- **Protection for Windows clients, while they are online or offline** A single DPM server can protect more than 1,000 Windows clients and enable users to restore their own data using Windows Explorer or Microsoft Office.

- **Protection of Virtualization platforms** For example, DPM 2010 can protect virtual machines created through the Hyper-V server role. It can also restore single-file items from host-based virtual machine backups.

- **Enhanced Protection for SQL Server and Exchange Server** DPM 2010 scales to more than 2,000 databases per server and offers auto-protection of new databases. DBAs can now restore their own databases through a self-service restore utility for SQL Server. Also, DPM 2010 scales to over 40 TB of email and support for Exchange 2010 Database Availability Groups.

- **Byte-level backups.** In an incremental backup, only files that have changed since the most recent backup are written to the backup. In a byte-level backup, only those bytes in the files that have changed are written to the backup, significantly reducing the amount of data that needs to be written to a backup.

- **Zero data loss restoration of Exchange, SQL Server, and SharePoint** Integrating point-in-time database backups with existing application logs ensures that application data can be restored to the point in time where the failure occurred, not just to the point where the last backup was taken.

- **Agent software installed on branch office servers** This allows backup data to be forwarded over WAN links. Agent software can also be used to forward backup data over LANs, allowing remote backups to be written to local media.

- **Supports backup to direct attached storage** You can back up to Fibre Channel SAN and iSCSI SAN. Note that this feature does not support USB and IEEE 1394 devices.

- **Comprehensive reporting** This includes protection success and failure, as well as backup media utilization.

- **Management Pack is available for System Center Operations Manager 2010** This allows centralized management of data protection and recovery for multiple DPM 2010 servers and servers with DPM 2010 agent software installed. This feature is best used in environments with many DPM 2010 servers and clients.

Lesson Summary

- Windows Server Backup is a feature that allows the creation of scheduled and manual backups on Windows Server 2008 and Windows Server 2008 R2.

- Only members of the Administrators local group can schedule backups on Windows Server 2008 and Windows Server 2008 R2, though members of the Backup Operators group can take manual backups.

- Windows Server 2008 R2 allows you to specify files and folders to include and to exclude in a backup. In Windows Server 2008, the smallest unit of backup is the volume.

- The Wbadmin.exe command-line tool provides more functionality than Windows Server Backup, but it can be used only from an elevated command prompt. All the Windows Server 2008 R2 enhanced features that you can implement from the Windows Server Backup console are also available using the command-line tool.

- In Windows Server 2008, scheduled backups can be written only to local disks or externally attached USB 2.0 or IEEE 1394 disks, although if you use a script file and the Scheduled Tasks tool, you can write scheduled backups to a network share. In Windows Server 2008 R2, you can write scheduled backups to internal or external hard disks, to a volume contained in such a disk, or to a network share. On both operating systems, manual backups can be written to local hard disks as well as network shares and local DVD writers.

- Window Server Backup can create only a single backup schedule. You can, however, create additional scheduled backups by placing a Wbadmin.exe command within a script and scheduling it using the Scheduled Tasks tool. A script that calls the Wbadmin.exe command must be run using the local Administrator account.

- A system state backup backs up Active Directory. Taking a system state backup is generally all that is required to back up Windows Server 2008 roles and role services.

Lesson Review

You can use the following questions to test your knowledge of the information in Lesson 1, "Backing Up Data." The questions are also available on the companion CD if you prefer to review them in electronic form.

1. You want to enable a user at a remote site to take manual backups of a file server once a week to a removable USB 2.0 device, which then will be transported by courier to your organization's head office. Which local group on the file server should you add this trusted staff member's domain user account to so that she can accomplish this task without being granted unnecessary administrative privileges?

   A. Power Users

   B. Backup Operators

   C. Administrators

   D. Remote Desktop Users

2. You want to back up a folder that contains frequently updated mission-critical files to a network share every three hours. You have already implemented a backup schedule that backs up your entire server running Windows Server 2008 R2 every 24 hours. Which of the following should you do to schedule the more frequent backup? (Each answer forms a part of the complete solution. Choose two.)

   A. Create a batch file that contains the wbadmin start backup command and that targets the UNC path of the network share with credentials that have access to the share. Use the *–include* parameter to specify the folder to be backed up.

   B. Create a batch file that contains the wbadmin start backup command and targets a local volume using the local Administrator account credentials.

   C. Use the scheduled tasks tool to configure a job that runs the batch file every three hours using the local Administrator account credentials.

   D. Use the scheduled tasks tool to configure a job that runs the batch file every three hours using credentials that have access to the share.

   E. Use the scheduled tasks tool to configure a job that runs the batch file once per day using the local Administrator account credentials.

3. Which of the following locations can be the target of backups scheduled with Windows Server Backup on a computer running Windows Server 2008 R2? (Each answer is a complete solution. Choose four.)

   A. A USB 2.0 external disk

   B. An IEEE 1394 external disk

   C. An IDE internal disk

   D. An iSCSI SAN

   E. A volume on an external hard disk

   F. A DVD drive

4. You are optimizing backup performance on a computer running Windows Server 2008 R2. Disk-intensive operations are carried out on the H: volume of this computer and you want to configure volumes individually. Which performance optimization option should you select?

   A. Normal Backup Performance

   B. Faster Backup Performance

   C. Custom

   D. VSS Full Backup

   E. VSS Copy Backup

5. You are developing organizational policy with respect to modifications to AD DS. You want to ensure that a system state backup is taken prior to any modifications being made to AD DS. You want to back up only system state data on your domain controller running Windows Server 2008 R2, and you will be using the Backup Once Wizard on the Windows Server Backup console. Which of the following targets can you specify? (Each answer is a complete solution. Choose three.)

   A. A network share

   B. A DVD writer

   C. An external USB 2.0 hard disk drive

   D. An iSCSI SAN

Lesson 2: Disaster Recovery

Part of the disaster recovery process is determining the cause of the original failure. If you do not deal with the cause of the original failure, it is possible that the failure will occur again. For example, if a disk drive fails because there is a problem on the motherboard and you are unable to diagnose this problem correctly, it is possible that a replacement disk will suffer the same fate as the original. In this lesson, you learn how to recover from disaster using backups that you have already taken. You learn how to recover an entire server using the bare metal recovery process, learn how to recover system state data, and learn about the process of authoritatively restoring deleted items from Active Directory.

> **After this lesson, you will be able to:**
> - Recover servers.
> - Recover roles and role services.
> - Recover data.
> - Recover Active Directory.
>
> **Estimated lesson time: 40 minutes**

Windows Server Backup Recovery Modes

If you want to perform recovery operations using Windows Server Backup, your user account must be a member of the Backup Operators or Administrators group or must have been delegated the appropriate permissions. As mentioned at the start of the chapter, backups taken with NTbackup.exe cannot be restored using Windows Server Backup or Wbadmin.exe. There is a version of NTbackup.exe that is compatible with Windows Server 2008 R2 (and another version that is compatible with Windows Server 2008). These utilities can be obtained from Microsoft and the links for them are provided in Lesson 1, "Backing Up Data."

Recovering Files and Folders

Even if you choose to back up at the volume level, you can perform recovery at the file and folder levels. As Figure 13-8 shows, you can restore a set of files and folders, or even just an individual file.

When planning to restore a file or folder, you need to know the following:

- The date that the file or folder was backed up
- The location of the file or folder
- Whether you want to restore the file's or folder's security settings
- The location to which you want to restore the file or folder
- What to do if a duplicate is found in the restoration location

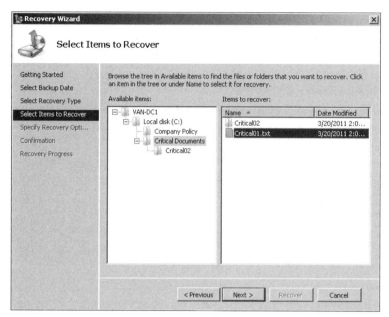

FIGURE 13-8 Selecting items to restore

If a duplicate is found in the restoration location, the options are to automatically have a copy created, to overwrite the existing files with recovered files, or to not recover those specific files where duplicates exist.

Windows Server Backup manages your existing backup files so that if backup data needs to be read from several different backup files, such as when several volumes on a folder that has been backed up incrementally need to be restored, the process occurs automatically. Previously, determining which backups were required when performing a restoration was the greatest drawback to performing a restore from incremental backups. You perform a file and folder recovery exercise in a practice later in this chapter.

Recovering Applications and Application Data

Windows Server Backup in Windows Server 2008 and Windows Server 2008 R2 can perform application-specific restorations. An application-specific restoration restores an application, its settings, and associated application data. It is possible to use Windows Server Backup to perform an application restoration if an application that been registered with Windows Server Backup. This process occurs during application installation.

When you perform an application recovery, you will be given a list of applications registered with Windows Server Backup that can be recovered based on the backup date that you have selected. If the backup from which you are performing the restore is the most recent backup taken of that application, according to the data stored in the backup catalog, you will have the option of rolling forward the application database. The default option is to allow roll-forward. You should select only the Do Not Perform A Roll-Forward Recovery Of

The Application Database if you want to block roll-forward. You would use this option if a change was made after the backup was taken—such as an important table in a SQL Server database being dropped—and you are trying to undo that change.

> **MORE INFO** **RECOVERING APPLICATIONS AND RELATED DATA**
>
> For more information about recovering Windows Server Backup–aware applications and related data, see *http://technet.microsoft.com/en-us/library/cc725726.aspx*.

Recovering Volumes

Volume recovery is a recovery of all volume contents. You can use volume recovery in situations where you have lost a volume due to the failure of a disk, but you do not want to go as far as performing a full operating system or server recovery. The important thing to remember about performing a volume recovery is that all existing data at the destination location will be lost. You can recover one or more volumes during a volume recovery.

> **MORE INFO** **VOLUME RECOVERY USING THE WBADMIN TOOL**
>
> For more information about using the Wbadmin command-line tool to recover a volume, see *http://technet.microsoft.com/en-us/library/dd364720(WS.10).aspx*.

Full Server and Operating System Recovery

Full Server Recovery is also known as Bare Metal Recovery. Full Server Recovery allows you to restore the server completely by booting from the Windows Server 2008 R2 installation media or Windows Recovery Environment. Full Server Recovery goes further than the Automated System Recovery (ASR) feature that was available before Windows Server 2008 because Full Server Recovery restores all operating system, application, and other data on a server. ASR did not provide such a complete recovery, and you needed to restore data from backup further when the ASR process was complete.

> **MORE INFO** **FULL SERVER AND OPERATING SYSTEM RECOVERY**
>
> For more information about Full server and operating system recovery (or bare metal recovery), see *http://technet.microsoft.com/en-us/library/cc755163.aspx*.

An Operating System Recovery is similar to a Full Server Recovery, except that you recover only critical volumes and do not recover volumes that do not contain critical data. For example, if you have a file server where the disks that host critical operating system volumes are separate from the disks that host shared folder volumes and the disks that host the critical operating system volumes fail, you should perform an Operating System Recovery.

When performing either a Full Server or Operating System Recovery, you must ensure that the disk you are recovering to is at least as large as the disk that contained the volumes you backed up, regardless of the size of the volumes on that disk. For example, if you performed a Full Server Backup on a server that was configured to use only a 30-GB partition on a 100-GB disk and that disk failed, when performing a Full Server or Operating System Recovery, you will need to perform the restore to a disk that is at least 100 GB in size.

Operating System and Full Server Recovery are both performed by booting from the Windows Server 2008 R2 installation media or into the recovery environment and using the computer repair options. To perform an Operating System Recovery or a Full Server Recovery of a server running Windows Server 2008 R2, perform the following steps:

1. Boot off the Windows Server 2008 R2 installation media.

2. In the dialog box for specifying language settings, click Next.

3. On the Install Windows page, click Repair Your Computer.

4. If you are recovering your computer onto new hardware, the System Recovery Options list will be empty. Otherwise, it will contain any detected operating systems on the computer, even if they are corrupted. Either way, click Next.

5. In the System Recovery Options dialog box, shown in Figure 13-9, click Windows Complete PC Restore.

FIGURE 13-9 Selecting Windows Complete PC Restore

6. When you select the Windows Complete PC Restore option, the utility will scan all local and attached storage devices for the most recent complete backup. You can choose to restore from the most recent available backup detected, or specify a different backup by choosing the Restore A Different Backup option. Figure 13-10 shows several different backups that can be restored off the same external USB 2.0 device. Clicking the Advanced option allows you to search for a backup on the network or to install a driver for a locally attached disk, such as a SCSI drive, that is not visible because the appropriate software has not been loaded.

7. On the Choose How To Restore The Backup page, select the Format And Repartition Disks option if you have not already prepared the disks for restoration. Select the Exclude Disks option if there are disks that you do not want formatted and repartitioned. The disk hosting the backup data is excluded automatically. If there are disks that do not contain critical data, you can select the Only Restore System Disks

option to perform a system-only recovery. At this point, you can also install extra drivers if the disks to which you are recovering data require extra drivers to function. Clicking Advanced allows disks to be checked for errors immediately after recovery is complete.

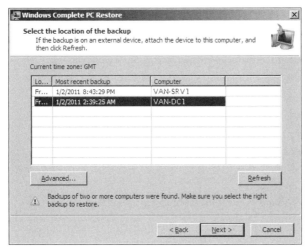

FIGURE 13-10 Selecting the backup to restore

System State Recovery

Performing a system state recovery is the most common method of recovering corrupt server role data or restoring Active Directory. It is not possible to perform a partial system state recovery; system state recovery must occur in its entirety. You perform a system state recovery in a practice later in this chapter. The high-level procedure to perform a system state recovery using the Wbadmin utility is as follows:

1. Open an administrative command prompt, type the command **wbadmin get versions**, and press Enter. This produces a list of backups, with the most recent backup shown first.

2. Make a note of the backup version identifier, which will be in the format MM/DD/YYYY-HH:MM. It is necessary to provide the entire backup version identifier when performing the restore.

3. Type the command **wbadmin Start SystemStateRecovery –version:MM/DD/YYYY-HH:MM** and press Enter. Type **Y** to accept the System State Recovery, and then press Enter to start the recovery process. When the process completes, reboot the server.

4. The server may need to reboot several times, depending on which server roles were installed on Windows Server 2008 R2 when the system state backup was taken.

Recovering Active Directory and Server Roles

Active Directory is recovered when you recover a domain controller's system state data. Recovering system state data recovers server roles (including AD DS) and role services. When you recover system state data, you are performing what is termed a *non-authoritative restore*. A non-authoritative restore brings the AD DS database on the server back to the point where it was when the backup was taken.

When you restart the domain controller at the end of the System State replication process, the domain controller replicates with other domain controllers in the domain and the Active Directory database is updated with changes that have occurred since the backup was taken. If, rather than just wanting to recover the domain controller, you want to recover specific Active Directory objects that have been deleted from the database, you need to perform what is known as an *authoritative restore*. Authoritative restores are discussed in the next section.

Authoritative Restores

When a non-authoritative restore is performed, objects deleted after the backup was taken will be deleted again when the restored domain controller replicates with other domain controllers in the domain. On every other domain controller, the object is marked as deleted, so when replication occurs, the local copy of the object also will be marked as deleted. The authoritative restore process marks the deleted object in such a way that when replication occurs, the object is restored to active status across the domain. It is important to remember that when an object is deleted, it is not removed instantly from Active Directory; rather, it gains an attribute that marks it as deleted until the tombstone lifetime is reached and the object is removed. The tombstone lifetime is the amount of time a deleted object remains in AD DS, which has a default value of 180 days.

To ensure that the AD DS database is not updated before the authoritative restore takes place, you use the Directory Services Restore Mode (DSRM) when performing the authoritative restore process. DSRM enables you to perform the necessary restorations and mark the objects as restored before rebooting the domain controller and allowing those changes to replicate to other domain controllers in the domain.

> **NOTE** **AUTHORITATIVE RESTORES ARE NOT NECESSARY ON THE ONLY DOMAIN CONTROLLER IN THE DOMAIN**
>
> Authoritative restores are not necessary if there is only one domain controller in the domain because there is no other copy of the AD DS database.

Booting into Directory Services Restore Mode

You can use one of three methods to boot into DSRM. The first method is to press F8 during the boot process, and then to select Directory Services Restore Mode from the prompt, as shown in Figure 13-11.

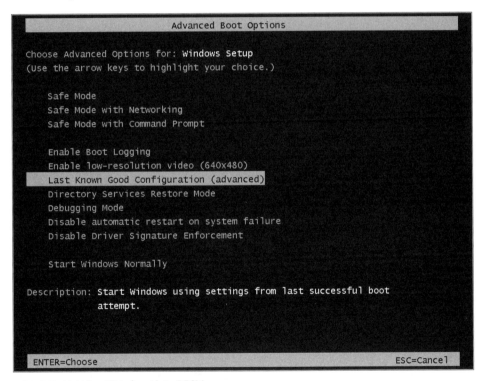

FIGURE 13-11 Using F8 to boot into DRSM

Only a small amount of time is available to you when using the F8 method, and many administrators find that they press the key too late, meaning that they have to boot all the way into Windows Server 2008 R2 normally. The second method involves opening an administrative command prompt and entering the following command:

```
Bcdedit /set safeboot dsrepair
```

This changes the boot option so that Windows Server 2008 R2 automatically boots into DSRM. This option typically is used on domain controllers that are configured to run in the Server Core configuration. To remove this boot option, open an administrative command prompt and enter the following command:

```
Bcdedit /deletevalue safeboot
```

If you do not remove this option, the server will always boot into DSRM.

The third method of starting a domain controller running Windows Server 2008 R2 in DSRM is to open the System Configuration console from the Administrative Tools menu, and to select the Active Directory Repair option under Safe Boot on the Boot tab. This setting is shown in Figure 13-23 in a practice later in the chapter.

Logging into DSRM requires that you have the DSRM password. The DSRM password is set on an individual basis for each domain controller during the domain controller promotion process. Because there can be some time between a domain controller being promoted and an administrator needing to use DSRM, this password is often forgotten. If the DSRM password has been forgotten, it is possible to reset it by performing the following actions, which are also shown in Figure 13-12:

1. Log on to the domain controller with an account that is a member of the Domain Admins group.

2. Open an administrative command prompt. Type **ntdsutil** and then press Enter.

3. At the ntdsutil: command prompt, type **set dsrm password** and then press Enter.

4. At the Reset DSRM Administrator Password: command prompt, do one of the following:

    -   If resetting the DSRM password on the local domain controller, type the command **reset password on server null** and then press Enter. Enter and confirm the new password.

    -   If resetting the DSRM password for another domain controller, type the command **reset password on server *servername***, where *servername* is the fully qualified domain name (FQDN) of the server for which you are resetting the password, and then press Enter.

5. At the Reset DSRM Administrator Password prompt, type **q** and press Enter to access the ntdsutil: command prompt, and then type **q** and press Enter to exit.

When a domain controller has been rebooted into DSRM and you have logged on using the Administrator account and the DSRM password, you need to perform a non-authoritative restore by restoring the system state data using the Wbadmin.exe utility. This process was covered in the section entitled "System State Recovery," earlier in this lesson. If it is necessary to perform an authoritative restore of SYSVOL, perform the system state recovery using the –AuthSysVOL option. You should use this option only when it is necessary to roll SYSVOL back to an earlier version than currently exists, and this option is not commonly used as a part of the authoritative restore process.

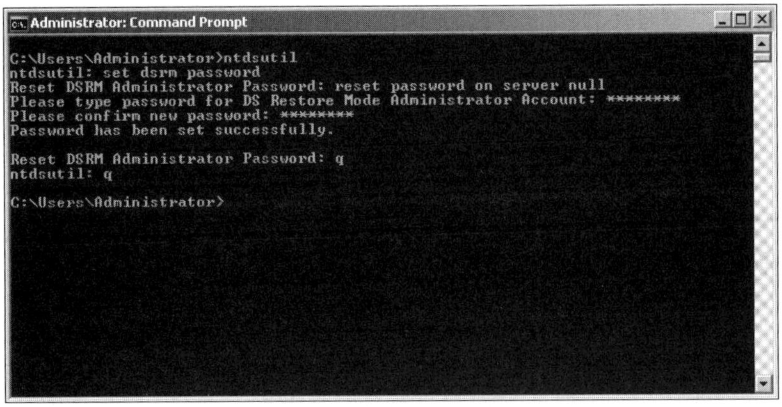

FIGURE 13-12 Resetting the DSRM password

Performing an Authoritative Restore

When the system state recovery process is complete, you need to use the ntdsutil utility to enter Authoritative Restore mode. From here, you can restore objects by making reference to their distinguished name (DN).

To restore an object, type **Restore Object** and then the object's DN. To restore a container and everything located under it, type **Restore Subtree** and then the container's DN. For example, to restore the Platapus OU and all its contents in the Tailspintoys.com domain, enter the command:

```
Restore Subtree "OU=Platapus,DC=Tailspintoys,DC=com"
```

If objects have back links, an LDAP Data Interchange Format (LDIF) file will be generated in the directory from which you have performed the authoritative restore operation. A back link includes information, such as group memberships that the restored object had, which are not included automatically when you perform the authoritative restore operation. You must run the ldif file in each domain that might have GPOs that may have included the restored object at the time of its deletion. To perform this operation, execute the following command on a domain controller in each necessary domain:

```
Ldifde -I -k ldif.filename
```

You perform the authoritative restoration of AD DS objects in a practice later in this chapter.

> **MORE INFO RECOVERING AD DS**
>
> For more information about performing an authoritative restoration of AD DS objects, see *http://technet.microsoft.com/en-us/library/cc816751(WS.10).aspx.*

Recovering Deleted GPOs

Deleted GPOs cannot be restored using an authoritative restore and must be recovered using the GPMC. To do this, open the GPMC, right-click the Group Policy Objects container, and then click Manage Backups. Browse to the location where backed-up GPOs are stored, select the GPO that you want to recover in the dialog box shown in Figure 13-13, and then click Restore.

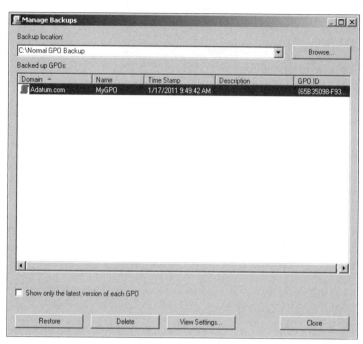

FIGURE 13-13 Restoring a GPO

Performing Full Server Recovery on a Domain Controller

When performing a Full Server Recovery of a domain controller, you automatically perform a non-authoritative restore of Active Directory. Due to the nature of the Full Server Recovery process, it is difficult to use it to perform an authoritative restore because the server will most likely reboot and replicate before you have a chance to force it into DSRM to perform the authoritative restoration process. It might be technically possible for an administrator who is quick to press F8 at the appropriate time, but performing a Full Server Recovery on a domain controller should not be considered a viable method of restoring deleted Active Directory object data. Of course, once the Full Server Recovery is complete, there is nothing stopping you from then performing a more traditional authoritative restore using the methods outlined earlier in this lesson. Performing a Full Server Recovery on a domain controller follows the steps of performing a standard Full Server Recovery outlined earlier in the lesson.

Active Directory Domain Services Database Mounting Tool

The Active Directory Domain Services Database Mounting Tool (Dsadmin.exe) enables you to create and view data stored within AD DS without needing to restart the domain controller in DSRM. The Dsadmin.exe tool can be used to compare the state of AD DS as it exists in different snapshots without needing to restore multiple backups. This can be very useful if you are trying to determine whether a particular backup of AD DS contains the objects that you want to restore.

Dsadmin.exe can also be used with both the `ntdsutil` snapshot operation and with a Windows Server 2008 R2 system state data backup. The process involves using `ntdsutil` to mount the snapshot of the directory and then using Dsadmin.exe to view and modify the snapshot. For security reasons, only members of the Domain Admins and Enterprise Admins groups are able to view these snapshots.

> **MORE INFO**   **TOMBSTONE REANIMATION**
>
> If you want in-depth information about recovering deleted objects from AD DS, you should read the article "Reanimating Active Directory Tombstone Objects," at *http://technet.microsoft.com/en-gb/magazine/2007.09.tombstones.aspx*. This is a general article and is not specific to Windows Server 2008 R2.

The Active Directory Module For Windows PowerShell in Windows Server 2008 R2 lets you use Windows PowerShell cmdlets to manage your AD DS domains, Active Directory Lightweight Directory Services (AD LDS) configuration sets, and Active Directory Database Mounting Tool instances in a single, self-contained package. The Active Directory Module For Windows PowerShell is discussed in more detail in the next section of this lesson.

The Active Directory Module For Windows PowerShell

The Active Directory Module For Windows PowerShell is installed with Windows PowerShell and Microsoft .NET Framework 3.5.1 by default. Both Windows PowerShell and .NET Framework 3.5.1 must be installed and working for the module to function correctly.

If you want to use the module to manage an AD DS domain, an AD LDS instance or configuration set, or an Active Directory Database Mounting Tool instance, the Active Directory Web Services (ADWS) service in Windows Server 2008 R2 needs to be installed on at least one domain controller in the domain or on the server that hosts your AD LDS instance.

You can access the Active Directory Module For Windows PowerShell command prompt by clicking Active Directory Module For Windows PowerShell in the Administrative Tools menu. The module provides Windows PowerShell commands that enable you to manage the following:

- Group management
- Managed service accounts

- OUs
- Password policies
- Optional features (such as the Recycle Bin feature)
- Search\modify objects
- Forest and domain management
- Domain controller and operations master management

For the purposes of this lesson, we consider the Search\modify objects option, and in particular how to use Windows PowerShell to restore a single AD DS object or to restore a container object and its children.

To restore a single object in AD DS, you use the Get-ADObject and Restore-ADObject Windows PowerShell cmdlets. The following example demonstrates how to restore the deleted OU Sales_Department in the local domain:

```
Get-ADObject -ldapFilter:"(msDS-LastKnownRDN=Sales_Department)" -IncludeDeletedObjects |
Restore-ADObject
```

As shown in Figure 13-14, this command does not generate an output on the Windows PowerShell console. If the deleted object is found, it is restored. The disadvantage is that you get no warning if the deleted object is not found.

FIGURE 13-14 Restoring a single AD DS object

To restore a container object and its children, you use the same Windows PowerShell commands as for restoring a single object, but you need to carry out a two-stage process. For example, to restore the OU HR_Department in the adatum.com domain with all its child objects, you would first restore the OU by entering the following Windows PowerShell command:

```
Get-ADObject -ldapFilter:"(msDS-LastKnownRDN=HR_Department)" -IncludeDeletedObjects |
Restore-ADObject
```

To restore the deleted child objects of the OU HR_Department, you would then enter the following command:

```
Get-ADObject -SearchBase "CN=Deleted Objects,DC=adatum,DC=com" -Filter {lastKnownParent
-eq "OU=HR_Department,DC=adatum,DC=com"} -IncludeDeletedObjects | Restore-ADObject
```

Figure 13-15 shows these commands. As with restoring a single object, the commands complete without output, and you then need to check that the object and its child objects have been restored.

FIGURE 13-15 Restoring an AD DS object and its children

> **MORE INFO** **GET-ADOBJECT AND RESTORE-ADOBJECT**
>
> For more information about the parameters that you can pass to Get-ADObject and Restore-ADObject Windows PowerShell cmdlets, open the Active Directory module command prompt, type either **Get-Help Get-ADObject –detailed or Get-Help Restore-ADObject –detailed** as appropriate, and then press Enter.

> **MORE INFO** **ACTIVE DIRECTORY ADMINISTRATION WITH WINDOWS POWERSHELL**
>
> For more information about using Windows PowerShell to manage AD DS objects, access *http://technet.microsoft.com/en-us/library/dd378937(WS.10).aspx* and follow the links.

Hyper-V and Disaster Recovery

Windows Server Backup writes backup data as image files in VHD format. Using Windows Server Backup and Wbadmin.exe, it is possible to perform an Operating System Recovery or to recover a volume or individual files and folders to the original or to a different server. Another option is to perform a recovery to a virtual machine hosted under Hyper-V.

From the perspective of disaster recovery planning, this means that you can use Windows Server 2008 R2 Datacenter edition as a recovery platform when you need to bring servers back up but do not have the available hardware because your head office site has burned down. Alternatively, if an important server's hardware fails and it will take some time before the components can be replaced, you can run the recovered server in a virtualized environment as a stopgap measure.

You can also mount the backup images as volumes on existing virtual machines by editing the virtual machine properties and adding the VHD image as a new virtualized hard disk drive. In general, though, it is easier to use Windows Server Backup's restore functionality to perform this type of operation, though this technique can be useful as a quick method of migrating a partition from a real to a virtual server without having to go through the file copy process.

Lesson Summary

- To perform a recovery, a user's account must be a member of the local Backup Operators or Administrators group.
- When performing an Operating System Recovery or a Full Server Recovery to a new hard disk, you must ensure that the disk is as big as the original disk that contained the volumes that were backed up.
- Application restore can be used only on applications that are registered with Windows Server Backup.
- Recovering the system state data restores most server roles, including AD DS.
- An authoritative restore is performed after rebooting a domain controller into DSRM. AD DS authoritative restores are used to recover deleted AD DS objects.
- You can use the Windows PowerShell Active Directory module to carry out a number of tasks, including restoring a single AD DS object or an AD DS object and its children.

Lesson Review

You can use the following questions to test your knowledge of the information in Lesson 2, "Disaster Recovery." The questions are also available on the companion CD if you prefer to review them in electronic form.

> **NOTE ANSWERS**
>
> Answers to these questions and explanations of why each answer choice is correct or incorrect are located in the "Answers" section at the end of the book.

1. You have rebooted a domain controller in the adatum.com domain into DSRM, performed a system state recovery, and put the `ntdsutil` utility into Authoritative Restore mode. Which of the following commands would you use to authoritatively restore the accidentally deleted Pluto computer account to the Solar OU?

   A. `Restore Object "cn=Solar,OU=Pluto,dc=Adatum,dc=com"`

   B. `Restore Computer "cn=Pluto,OU=Solar,dc=Adatum,dc=com"`

   C. `Restore Object "cn=Pluto,OU=Solar,dc=Adatum,dc=com"`

   D. `Restore Computer "cn=Solar,OU=Pluto, dc=Adatum,dc=com"`

2. Kim Akers is a member of the local Administrators group on a server named Glasgow that is running Windows Server 2008 R2. Glasgow hosts a network share to which Sam Abolrous, a member of the local Administrators group on a computer named Dundee that is running Windows Server 2008 R2, uses as a target location when he performs

manual backups of the data on server Dundee's volumes. Sam is attending a training course this week, and the users of server Dundee need Kim to restore some deleted folders that they cannot access through VSS. Which group membership must Kim have to use the Windows Server Backup tool from Glasgow to restore data on Dundee while adhering to the principle of least privilege?

A. The Power Users group on Glasgow

B. The Power Users local group on Dundee

C. The Backup Operators group on Dundee

D. The Administrators group on Dundee

3. You are using the Active Directory Module For Windows PowerShell to restore an accidentally deleted OU named Australia, which contains the computer account Melbourne, in the adatum.com domain. You use the Get-ADObject and Restore-ADObject cmdlets to restore the OU. What command do you then enter to restore the Melbourne computer account?

A. You do not need to enter any commands. Restoring the OU automatically restores its child objects.

B. `Get-ADObject -SearchBase "CN=Deleted Objects,DC=adatum,DC=com"`
`-Filter {lastKnownParent -eq "OU=Melbourne,DC=adatum,DC=com"}`
`-IncludeDeletedObjects | Restore-ADObject`

C. `Restore-ADObject -SearchBase "CN=Deleted Objects,DC=adatum,DC=com"`
`-Filter {lastKnownParent -eq "OU=Australia,DC=adatum,DC=com"}`
`-IncludeDeletedObjects | Get-ADObject`

D. `Get-ADObject -SearchBase "CN=Deleted Objects,DC=adatum,DC=com"`
`-Filter {lastKnownParent -eq "OU=Australia,DC=adatum,DC=com"}`
`-IncludeDeletedObjects | Restore-ADObject`

4. The motherboard of an important intranet server at one of your organization's remote branch offices has just failed. The motherboard is the only component that needs to be replaced, but because of the branch office's remote location, it will be several days before a replacement can be obtained. A full server backup was performed manually on the server 12 hours before the failure occurred. This backup was written to removable USB disk drive. A computer running Windows Server 2008 R2 Datacenter edition with the Hyper-V server role installed is also located at the site and hosts a virtualized domain controller. Which of the following steps should you take to ensure that the intranet server is available until the replacement components arrive while not disrupting existing services?

A. Perform a bare metal restore on the computer running Windows Server 2008 R2 Datacenter edition.

B. Mount the backup images on the computer running Windows Server 2008 R2 Datacenter edition as extra volumes.

    C. Perform a Full Server Recovery to a Hyper-V virtual machine.

    D. Restore the system state data from the backup images to the computer running Windows Server 2008 R2 Datacenter edition.

PRACTICE Backing Up Windows Server 2008 R2

In this practice, you perform three separate types of backup on the VAN-DC1 domain controller running Windows Server 2008 R2. The first type of backup is a normal Windows Server Backup operating system backup. The second type of backup involves using Wbadmin.exe to perform a simple volume backup. The final type of backup will be a system state only backup.

> **NOTE   EXTRA DISK**
>
> As specified in the section entitled "Before You Begin," at the beginning of this chapter, the practices in the chapter require you to have access to an extra disk attached to VAN-DC1. This disk can be an extra virtual disk if you are using virtual machines. If you are using real hardware, the disk can be an internal physical disk or an attached USB 2.0 or IEEE 1394 disk. This disk will be used to store backup data. The disk should be a minimum of 40 GB in size so that it can store all the backup data generated in these practice exercises.

EXERCISE 1   Performing a Manual Backup Using Windows Server Backup

In this exercise, you will install the Windows Server Backup feature and then perform a manual backup of server VAN-DC1. To start, you will create a set of Active Directory objects to be backed up. These objects will be removed and later restored as a part of the second practice in this chapter.

To complete this exercise, perform the following steps:

1. Log on to VAN-DC1 using the Kim Akers account. If Server Manager does not open automatically, open it from the Administrative Tools menu.

2. In the Server Manager console, click the Features node and then click Add Features. On the Features page of the Add Features Wizard, expand the Windows Server Backup Features node, and select Windows Server Backup and Command-line Tools, as shown in Figure 13-16.

3. Click Next and then click Install. When the Windows Server Backup features have been installed, click Close to exit the Add Features Wizard.

> **NOTE   WINDOWS POWERSHELL AND WINDOWS SERVER BACKUP**
>
> Depending on the current configuration of VAN-DC1, you may need to confirm the installation of the Windows PowerShell feature. In Windows Server 2008 R2, Windows Server Backup has enhanced the Windows PowerShell cmdlets to automate routine tasks and better manage backup scripts. (Note that Windows PowerShell is installed by default on Windows Server 2008 R2.)

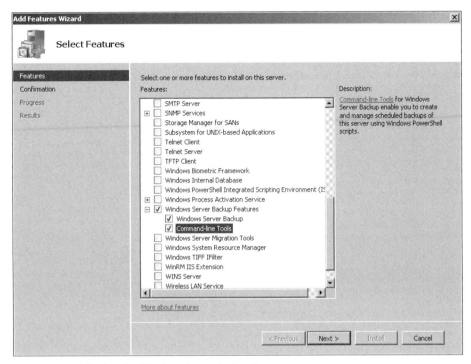

FIGURE 13-16 Selecting the Windows Server Backup features

4. From the Administrative Tools menu, open Active Directory Users And Computers. Create a new OU called Planets under the adatum.com domain. Within the Planets OU, create four computer accounts named Saturn, Jupiter, Neptune, and Uranus. Close Active Directory Users And Computers.

5. Verify that the additional disk is connected to your computer and that you know its volume name. If the disk is not formatted, format it using the NTFS file system.

NOTE NTFS AND FAT32

Although a manual backup can be written to a FAT32 file system, NTFS gives you more backup options and better performance.

---

6. From the Administrative Tools menu, open Windows Server Backup. In the Actions pane, click Backup Once. This opens the Backup Once Wizard.

7. Ensure that Different Options is selected, and then click Next.

8. On the Select Backup Configuration page, select Custom, as shown in Figure 13-17, and then click Next.

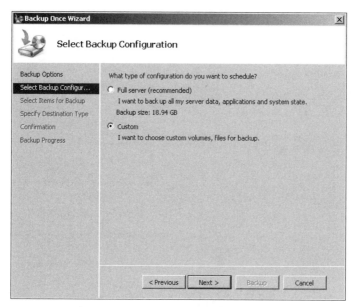

FIGURE 13-17 Choosing the Custom backup configuration

9. On the Select Items For Backup page, click Add Items. In the Select Items dialog box, shown in Figure 13-18, select Local Disk (C:). Click OK.

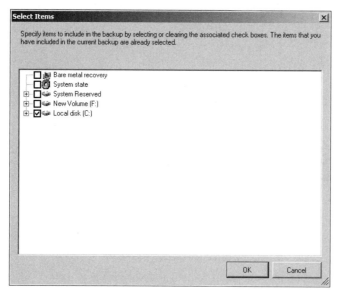

FIGURE 13-18 Selecting backup items

10. On the Select Items For Backup page, click Advanced Settings. On the Exclusions tab of the Advanced Settings dialog box, click Add Exclusion. Note the options available for excluding backup items, but do not exclude anything. Click Cancel.

11. On the VSS Settings tab of the Advanced Settings dialog box, select VSS Full Backup. Click OK. On the Select Items For Backup page, click Next.

12. On the Specify Destination Type page, ensure that Local Drives is selected and then click Next.

13. On the Select Backup Destination page, use the drop-down menu to select the new disk that you added to VAN-DC1, as shown in Figure 13-19, and then click Next.

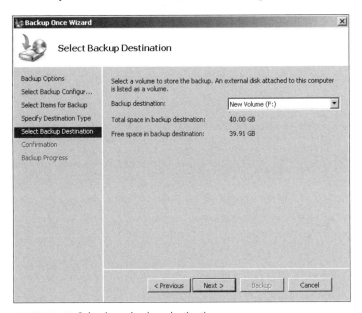

FIGURE 13-19 Selecting a backup destination

14. On the Confirmation page, click Backup. When the backup process completes, click Close. Note that the backup process can take considerable time, but you have the option of clicking Close on the Backup Progress page, and the backup will continue in the background.

EXERCISE 2 Performing a Volume and a System State Backup Using Wbadmin.exe

In this exercise, you perform a volume backup and a system state backup using the Wbadmin.exe command-line utility. To complete this exercise, perform the following steps:

1. If necessary, log on to VAN-DC1 with the Kim Akers user account.

2. Create a folder on the C: volume named Continents. Create five text files within this volume named Europe.txt, Antarctica.txt, Africa.txt, Australia.txt, and Asia.txt. The content of each text file should be its name.

3. Open a command prompt with administrative privileges. If necessary, click Yes to close the User Account Control dialog box.

4. Type the following command and then press Enter:

```
wbadmin start backup –backuptarget:f: –include:c: –vssFull –quiet
```

5. After the backup has completed, note the date and time of this backup (you will need it for the next exercise) and then delete the C:\Continents folder.

6. Type the following command and then press Enter:

```
wbadmin start systemstatebackup –backuptarget:f: -quiet
```

7. When the backup completes, type the following command and then hit Enter:

```
wbadmin get versions
```

8. Verify that three backup jobs have been created.

PRACTICE **Restoring Windows Server 2008 R2**

This practice requires that you have completed all the exercises in the previous practice. In this set of exercises, you restore files and folders that were backed up and then deleted. You boot into DSRM, perform an authoritative restore of Active Directory objects, and restore a backup catalog.

EXERCISE 1 **Restoring Files and Folders**

In this exercise, you will restore the deleted Continents directory and the files that it hosted. You will also prepare for the second exercise by deleting several Active Directory objects. To complete this practice, perform the following steps:

1. Log on to VAN-DC1 with the Kim Akers user account. Verify that the C:\Continents directory is not present.

2. From the Administrative Tools menu, start Windows Server Backup.

3. In the Actions pane, click Recover. This will start the Recovery Wizard. On the Getting Started page, shown in Figure 13-20, select This Server (VAN-DC1) and click Next.

4. On the Select Backup Date page, select the date and time that you performed the second exercise in the previous practice and then click Next.

5. On the Select Recovery Type page, select Files And Folders and then click Next.

6. On the Select Items To Recover page, expand VAN-DC1 under Available Items and select Local Disk (C:). Then, under Items To Recover, select the Continents folder, as shown in Figure 13-21, and then click Next.

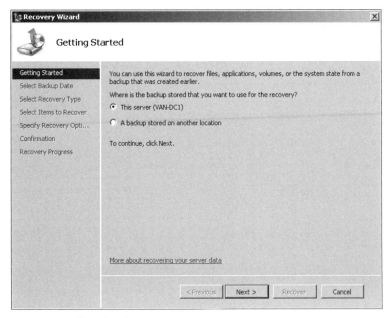

FIGURE 13-20 Choosing the server to recover

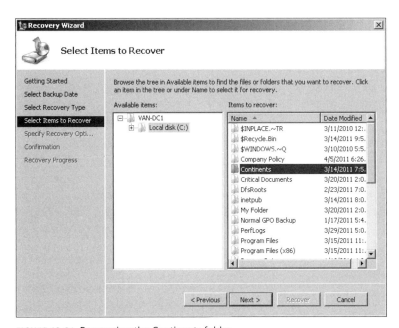

FIGURE 13-21 Recovering the Continents folder

7. On the Specify Recovery Options page, shown in Figure 13-22, set the Recovery Destination to the Original Location and ensure that the check box in the Security Settings section is selected. Click Next.

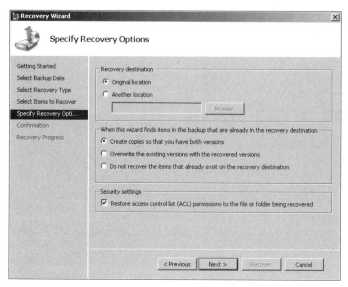

FIGURE 13-22 Recovery options

8. On the Confirmation page, click Recover. When the recovery is complete, click Close.

9. Check that the Continents folder has been recovered, with all the files it contains.

10. From the Administrative Tools menu, open Active Directory Users And Computers. From the View menu, select the Advanced Features option.

11. Right-click the Planets OU and select Properties. On the Object tab, clear the Protect Object From Accidental Deletion check box and then click OK. Right-click the Planets OU and then click Delete. Click Yes to confirm the deletion, and click Yes again to confirm that you want to delete all the objects contained within the Planets OU.

12. Close Active Directory Users And Computers.

EXERCISE 2 Performing an Authoritative Restore

In this exercise, you use the system state backup of domain controller VAN-DC1 that you took during the previous practice as the basis of an authoritative restore of specific objects within the deleted Planets OU. You will also need your DSRM password to perform this action. If you have forgotten this password, you can reset it using the instructions provided in the section entitled "Booting into Directory Services Restore Mode," earlier in this lesson.

1. If necessary, log on to VAN-DC1 with the Kim Akers user account. Open the System Configuration console from the Administrative Tools menu. If prompted, click Yes to close the User Account Control dialog box.

2. On the Boot tab, select Safe Boot and then choose the Active Directory Repair option, as shown in Figure 13-23. Click OK to close the System Configuration console.

3. When prompted, click Restart. VAN-DC1 restarts.

4. When the domain controller restarts, log on as Administrator with the DSRM password.

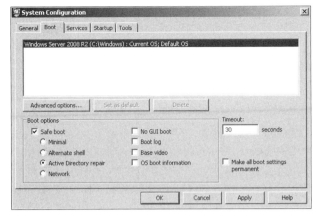

FIGURE 13-23 Selecting Active Directory repair

5. Verify that the server has rebooted into safe mode. The desktop background should become black, and the words "Safe Mode" should appear in the corners of the screen. If the computer has not rebooted into safe mode, start again from step 1.

6. Open a command prompt with elevated privileges, and then type **wbadmin get versions** and press Enter.

7. The final backup in the list should state that you can recover Application(s), System State. Make a note of the Version Identifier. In Figure 13-24, the version identifier for the System State backup is 03/14/2011-19:57.

FIGURE 13-24 Locating the backup version identifier

8. Enter the command **wbadmin Start SystemStateRecovery –version:03/14/2011-19:57 –backupTarget:f:** substituting the appropriate version identifier and backup location from your own System State backup. When prompted, type **Y** and hit Enter to start the system state recovery operation. Do this again to continue.

9. When the System State recovery process has completed, the domain controller requires a reboot. Type **Yes** and press Enter to reboot VAN-DC1.

10. When the computer reboots, log on with the Administrator account and the DSRM password.

11. The computer boots up in safe mode, and the command prompt opens. Press Enter to continue. The command prompt closes.

12. Open the command prompt with elevated privileges. Type **ntdsutil** and then press Enter.

13 Type **Activate Instance NTDS** and then press Enter.

14. Type **Authoritative Restore** and then press Enter.

15. Type **Restore Object "OU=Planets,dc=adatum,dc=com"** and then press Enter. Click Yes at the prompt to confirm that you want to perform the restore. Verify that ntdsutil reports that the Authoritative Restore Completed Successfully, as shown in Figure 13-25.

FIGURE 13-25 Successful authoritative restore

16. Type **Restore Object "cn=Saturn,OU=Planets,dc=adatum,dc=com"** and press Enter. Click **Yes** at the prompt to confirm that you want to perform the restore.

17. Type **Quit** and hit Enter twice to exit the ntdsutil tool. Type **Exit** and hit Enter to close the command prompt.

18. From the Administrative Tools menu, open System Configuration. On the Boot tab, clear the Safe Boot option and click OK. When prompted, click Restart to restart the server. The server may reboot several times as a part of the recovery process.

19. When the server completes the reboot process, log on with the Kim Akers user account and password. Press Enter in the command prompt to acknowledge that System State recovery operation has completed.

20. From the Administrative Tools menu, open Active Directory Users And Computers. Check that the Planets OU has been restored and that it contains the Saturn computer account.

EXERCISE 3 Recovering a Backup Catalog

In this exercise, you simulate the process of deleting a corrupted backup catalog and restoring a new catalog from the current set of backups. To complete this exercise, perform the following steps:

1. If necessary, log on to VAN-DC1 with the Kim Akers user account. Open an elevated command prompt. If prompted, click Yes to close the User Access Control dialog box.

2. Type **wbadmin delete catalog** and press Enter.

3. Type **Y** and hit Enter when prompted about catalog deletion. Type **wbadmin get versions** and press Enter to verify that the catalog has been deleted.

4. Type **wbadmin restore catalog –backupTarget:**_f:_**,** where _f:_ is the volume that backups are stored on. Then press Enter.

5. Enter **Y** when prompted about catalog restoration. Your command prompt entries should look similar to Figure 13-26.

FIGURE 13-26 Deleting and restoring a backup catalog

6. Enter **wbadmin get versions** to confirm the contents of the catalog, as shown in Figure 13-27.

FIGURE 13-27 Viewing the restored backup catalog

Chapter Review

To further practice and reinforce the skills you learned in this chapter, you can perform the following tasks:

- Review the chapter summary.
- Review the list of key terms introduced in this chapter.
- Complete the case scenarios. These scenarios set up real-world situations involving the topics of this chapter and ask you to create a solution.
- Complete the suggested practices.
- Take a practice test.

Chapter Summary

- In Windows Server 2008 R2, Windows Server Backup scheduled backups can be written to local internal or external disks, disk volumes, or network shares. Windows Server Backup manual backups can be written to local internal or external disks, DVD-writers, and network locations.
- You can use the Wbadmin.exe command-line utility to back up and restore Server Core, as well as standard deployments of Windows Server 2008 R2.
- To perform recoveries using Windows Server Backup, an account must be a member of the Backup Operators or Administrators group or have been delegated the appropriate authority.
- You can use Active Directory Module For Windows PowerShell to restore AD DS objects.
- When performing an Operating System Recovery or a Full Server Recovery to a new hard disk, you must ensure that the disk is as big as the original disk that contained the volumes that were backed up.

Key Terms

The following terms were introduced in this chapter. Do you know what they mean?

- Authoritative Restore
- Bare Metal Restore
- Directory Services Restore Mode
- System State Backup

Case Scenarios

In the following case scenarios, you will apply what you've learned about backup and recovery. You can find answers to these questions in the "Answers" section at the end of this book.

Case Scenario 1: Wingtip Toys Backup Infrastructure

You are planning the backup strategy for Wingtip Toys in light of their soon-to-be-completed migration from all servers running Windows 2000 Server to running Windows Server 2008 R2. The current strategy at Wingtip Toys was developed in an ad hoc manner, and part of your job is to ensure that there is some consistency to backup procedures. With that in mind, you must find answers to the following questions.

1. A total of 30 file servers that use NTbackup to write backup data to Digital Linear Tape are to be upgraded to Windows Server 2008 R2. What steps must be taken to ensure that scheduled daily backups still can be taken using the Windows Server Backup utility?

2. You are considering your organization's offsite backup strategy for scheduled backups using Windows Server Backup. What types of hardware device should you consider deploying to support this strategy?

3. Currently 23 percent of all help desk jobs involve restoring documents to shared folders that were deleted accidentally by the people working on them. What steps can you take to reduce the impact of this problem on help desk staff?

Case Scenario 2: Disaster Recovery at Fabrikam

On Saturday evening at 11:00 P.M., the Fabrikam head office building was destroyed by a massive fire. The Fabrikam head office hosted the Fabrikam.internal forest root domain domain controllers and the hq.fabrikam.internal child domain. There are 15 domains in the Fabrikam.internal forest. The following backups exist at an offsite location:

- Full server backups of the forest root domain controllers taken on Friday
- System state data backups of the hq.fabrikam.internal domain controllers taken on Wednesday
- Full server backups of the hq.fabrikam.internal domain controllers taken on Friday
- A full server backup of fileserv.hq.fabrikam.internal file server taken on Wednesday
- A manual backup of all shared folders on fileserve.hq.fabrikam.internal taken on Friday

On Thursday night, several important Active Directory objects were removed accidentally from the hq.fabrikam.internal domain during a software upgrade. These objects were restored on Saturday morning prior to the fire. You are now at the disaster recovery site and have replacement servers.

1. Which domain controllers should you restore first, and why?
2. What steps should you take to ensure that the objects that were present within Active Directory on Saturday afternoon are restored as completely as possible?
3. What steps should you take to restore shared files on fileserve.hq.fabrikam.internal as completely as possible?

Suggested Practices

To help you master the examination objectives presented in this chapter, complete the following tasks.

Remote Backup

- If you have the Member Server VAN-SRV1 installed on your network, use the Windows Server Backup console on VAN-DC1 to perform a full system backup of VAN-SRV1.

Server Restore

- Boot VAN-SRV1 using the Windows Server 2008 R2 installation media and perform Full Server Recovery. Use the full server backup data that was generated in Practice 1.
- Delete an OU that contains computer accounts on VAN-DC1. Use Active Directory Module For Windows PowerShell to restore the OU and its child objects.

Take a Practice Test

The practice tests on this book's companion CD offer many options. For example, you can test yourself on just one exam objective, or you can test yourself on all the 70-646 certification exam content. You can set up the test so that it closely simulates the experience of taking a certification exam, or you can set it up in study mode so that you can look at the correct answers and explanations after you answer each question.

> **MORE INFO** **PRACTICE TESTS**
>
> For details about all the practice test options available, see the "How to Use the Practice Tests" section in this book's Introduction.

Setup Instructions for Exercises and Labs

Setup Instructions for End-of-Chapter Labs

This set of exercises contains abbreviated instructions for setting up the VAN-DC1, VAN-SRV1, and VAN-SRV2 computers used in the practice exercises in all chapters of this training kit except Chapter 1, "Installing, Upgrading, and Deploying Windows Server 2008 R2." To perform these exercises, first install Windows Server 2008 R2 Enterprise edition using the default configuration, setting the administrator password to **Pa$$w0rd**.

EXERCISE 1 Prepare a Computer to Function as a Windows Server 2008 R2 Domain Controller

1. Log on to the first computer that you have installed Windows Server 2008 R2 on using the Administrator account and the password **Pa$$w0rd**.

2. Open an elevated command prompt and issue the following commands:

   `Netsh interface ipv4 set address "Local Area Connection" static 10.10.0.10`

3. Enter the following command:

   `netdom renamecomputer %computername% /newname:VAN-DC1`

4. Restart the computer and log back on using the Administrator account.

5. Click Start. In the Search Programs and Files text box, type the following:

   `Dcpromo`

6. When the Active Directory Domain Services Installation Wizard starts, click Next twice.

7. On the Choose A Deployment Configuration page, choose Create A New Domain In A New Forest, and then click Next.

8. On the Name The Forest Root Domain page, enter **Adatum.com**, and then click Next.

9. On the Forest Functional Level page, set the Forest Functional Level to Windows Server 2008, and then click Next.

10. On the Set Domain Functional Level page, ensure that Windows Server 2008 is set, and then click Next.

11. On the Additional Domain Controller Options page, ensure that the DNS Server option is checked, and then click Next. When presented with the warning that the delegation for the DNS server cannot be created, click Yes when asked if you want to continue.

12. Accept the default settings for the Database, Log Files, and SYSVOL locations and click Next.

13. In the Directory Services Restore Mode Administrator Password dialog box, enter the password **Pa$$w0rd** twice, and then click Next.

14. On the Summary page, click Next to begin the installation of Active Directory Domain Services (AD DS) on computer VAN-DC1. When the wizard completes, click Finish. When prompted, click Restart Now to reboot computer VAN-DC1.

EXERCISE 2 Prepare AD DS

1. Log on to server VAN-DC1 using the Administrator account.

2. Using Active Directory Users And Computers, create a user account named Kim_Akers in the Users container and assign the account the password **Pa$$w0rd**. Configure the password to never expire. Add this user account to the Enterprise Admins, Domain Admins, and Schema Admins groups.

3. Open the DNS console and create a primary reverse lookup zone for the subnet 10.10.0.x. Ensure that the zone is stored within AD DS and is replicated to all DNS servers running on domain controllers in the forest.

EXERCISE 3 Preparing a Member Server and Joining It to the Domain

1. Ensure that computer VAN-DC1 is turned on and connected to the network or virtual network to which the second computer is connected.

2. Log on to the second computer that you have installed Windows Server 2008 R2 on using the Administrator account and the password **Pa$$w0rd**.

3. Open an elevated command prompt and issue the following commands:

```
Netsh interface ipv4 set address "Local Area Connection" static 10.10.0.20

Netsh interface ipv4 set dnsservers "Local Area Connection" static 10.10.0.10
primary
```

4. Enter the following command:

```
netdom renamecomputer %computername% /newname:VAN-SRV1
```

5. Restart the computer and then log on again using the Administrator account.

6. From an elevated command prompt, issue the following command:

```
netdom join VAN-SRV1 /domain:adatum
```

7. Restart the computer. When the computer restarts, log on as adatum\Administrator and then turn off the computer.

EXERCISE 4   Preparing a Second Member Server and Joining It to the Domain

1. Ensure that computer VAN-DC1 is turned on and connected to the network or virtual network to which the second computer is connected.

2. Log on to the third computer that you have installed Windows Server 2008 R2 on using the Administrator account and the password **Pa$$w0rd**.

3. Open an elevated command prompt and issue the following commands:

   ```
   Netsh interface ipv4 set address "Local Area Connection" static 10.10.0.21
   ```

   ```
   Netsh interface ipv4 set dnsservers "Local Area Connection" static 10.10.0.10
   primary
   ```

4. Enter the following command:

   ```
   netdom renamecomputer %computername% /newname:VAN-SRV2
   ```

5. Restart the computer and then log on again using the Administrator account.

6. From an elevated command prompt, issue the following command:

   ```
   netdom join VAN-SRV2 /domain:adatum
   ```

7. Restart the computer. When the computer restarts, log on as adatum\Administrator. Turn off the computer.

EXERCISE 5   Configuring a Client Computer

1. Ensure that computer VAN-DC1 is turned on and connected to the network or virtual network to which the second computer is connected.

2. Log on to the first computer that you have installed Windows 7 Enterprise or Ultimate edition on using the Administrator account Admin and the password **Pa$$w0rd**.

3. Open an elevated command prompt and issue the following commands:

   ```
   Netsh interface ipv4 set address "Local Area Connection" static 10.10.0.31
   ```

   ```
   Netsh interface ipv4 set dnsservers "Local Area Connection" static 10.10.0.10
   primary
   ```

4. Hold down the Windows Key and the Break Key to open the System Properties dialog box. Click Advanced System Settings. On the Computer Name tab click Change. In the Computer Name textbox enter VAN-CL1. Click OK.

5. Restart the computer and log back on using the Admin account.

6. Hold down the Windows Key and the Break Key to open the System Properties dialog box. Click Advanced System Settings. On the Computer Name tab click Change. In the Domain textbox enter ADATUM. When prompted, enter the Administrator account credentials.

7. Restart the computer and log back on using the Admin account.

8. In Control Panel, click Set Up File Sharing. In the Network And Sharing Center, verify that the network is configured as a Private network and that File Sharing is enabled.

Answers

Chapter 1

Lesson 1

1. **Correct Answer: C**

    A. **Incorrect:** Only Windows Server 2003 Datacenter edition (x64) can be upgraded to Windows Server 2008 R2 Datacenter edition.

    B. **Incorrect:** Only Windows Server 2003 Web Server edition can be upgraded to Windows Web Server 2008 R2.

    C. **Correct:** Windows Server 2003 R2 Standard edition can be upgraded to Windows Server 2008 R2 Enterprise edition so long as it is the x64 version.

    D. **Incorrect:** Windows Server 2003 R2 Standard edition (x64) cannot be upgraded to Windows Server 2008 (x86) Standard edition.

    E. **Incorrect:** Although Windows Server 2003 Standard edition (x64) can be upgraded to Windows Server 2008 R2 Standard edition, it is not possible to upgrade any edition of Windows Server 2003 to a Server Core version of Windows Server 2008 R2.

2. **Correct Answer: A**

    A. **Correct:** The 32-bit version Windows Server 2003 Standard edition can be upgraded only to a 32-bit version of Windows Server 2008 Standard or Enterprise edition.

    B. **Incorrect:** It is not possible to upgrade a 32-bit version of Windows Server 2003 to Windows Server 2008 R2.

    C. **Incorrect:** It is not possible to upgrade Windows Server 2003 Standard edition to Windows Server 2008 Datacenter edition.

    D. **Incorrect:** It is not possible to upgrade a 32-bit version of Windows Server 2003 to Windows Server 2008 R2.

3. **Correct Answer: A**

    A. **Correct:** You can configure a computer running the Server Core version of Windows Server 2008 R2 Enterprise as an AD DS domain controller.

    B. **Incorrect:** You cannot configure a computer running the Server Core version of Windows Server 2008 R2 Enterprise with the Active Directory Rights Management Services role.

    C. **Incorrect:** You cannot configure a computer running the Server Core version of Windows Server 2008 R2 Enterprise with the Active Directory Federation Services role.

    D. **Incorrect:** You cannot configure a computer running the Server Core version of Windows Server 2008 R2 Enterprise edition with the WDS role.

4. **Correct Answer: C**

   A. Incorrect: The Enterprise edition of Windows Server 2008 R2 includes four virtual machine licenses.

   B. Incorrect: The Enterprise edition of Windows Server 2008 R2 includes four virtual machine licenses.

   C. Correct: The Enterprise edition of Windows Server 2008 R2 includes four virtual machine licenses.

   D. Incorrect: The Enterprise edition of Windows Server 2008 R2 includes four virtual machine licenses.

5. **Correct Answer: C**

   A. Incorrect: The failover clustering feature is supported only in the Enterprise and Datacenter editions of Windows Server 2008 R2.

   B. Incorrect: The failover clustering feature is supported only in the Enterprise and Datacenter editions of Windows Server 2008 R2.

   C. Correct: The failover clustering feature is supported only in the Enterprise and Datacenter editions of Windows Server 2008 R2.

   D. Incorrect: The failover clustering feature is supported only in the Enterprise and Datacenter editions of Windows Server 2008 R2.

Lesson 2

1. **Correct Answers: A, B, and C**

   A. Correct: A computer running Windows Server 2008 R2 must be a member of an existing AD DS domain prior to the deployment of WDS.

   B. Correct: A DHCP server that is authorized in AD DS must be present for WDS to function correctly.

   C. Correct: A properly configured DNS server must be present for WDS to function correctly.

   D. Incorrect: WDS is not dependent on the Application Server role.

2. **Correct Answer: A**

   A. Correct: An unattended installation can be initiated from the Windows PE environment.

   B. Incorrect: An unattended installation cannot be initiated from a Windows NT boot disk.

   C. Incorrect: An unattended installation cannot be initiated from an MS DOS boot disk.

   D. Incorrect: An unattended installation can be started only from the Windows PE 2.0 environment, or from within Windows Server 2003.

3. **Correct Answer: A**

   A. Correct: When co-locating DHCP and WDS, you must ensure that the WDS server is configured not to listen on port 67 and that the DHCP option 60 is set to PXEClient. This is done through the DHCP Settings tab of the WDS server Properties dialog box.

B. **Incorrect:** You cannot configure WDS to listen on an alternate port through the DHCP Server console. By default, DHCP and PXE servers listen on the same port, so if both services are co-located on the same server, you must get WDS to listen on an alternate port and update DHCP—which you can do through the WDS server Properties dialog box—to inform PXE clients to look on an alternate port through DHCP option 60.

C. **Incorrect:** The DNS server is not the problem. The problem in this situation is a conflict between the DHCP and WDS servers.

D. **Incorrect:** The client's settings are used to set up unattended installation settings. The problem in this case is that WDS cannot listen on the port that DHCP is already listening on and must be configured to use an alternative.

4. **Correct Answer: D**

A. **Incorrect:** DNS information does not need to be modified to support WDS.

B. **Incorrect:** It is not necessary to configure a special IPv6 DHCP scope for PXE clients.

C. **Incorrect:** It is not necessary to configure a special IPv4 DHCP scope for PXE clients.

D. **Correct:** Routers that support multicast transmissions are required when using WDS multicast transmission functionality. The question indicates that the WDS server and the clients are located on different subnets, which hints that the router might be the problem.

5. **Correct Answer: C**

A. **Incorrect:** Although placing an Unattended XML answer file on a shared folder could be made to work, it would require significant intervention because the servers would need to network boot into Windows PE so that the correct setup argument could be issued.

B. **Incorrect:** Unattended XML answer files are configured on a per-WDS server basis, not on a per-multicast–transmission basis.

C. **Correct:** Default unattended XML answer files can be configured on a per-WDS server basis.

D. **Incorrect:** Although placing an unattended XML answer file on a removable USB device could work, this would require significantly greater manual intervention than locating the unattended XML file on the WDS server.

Case Scenario 1: Contoso's Migration to Windows Server 2008

1. Because it is not possible to upgrade to a Server Core edition of Windows Server 2008 R2, you will need to perform a migration where data is backed up, a clean installation is performed on the existing hardware, and then the data is restored.

2. Windows Web Server 2008 R2 would be the appropriate edition of Windows Server 2008 R2 to deploy if the server's only function will be to host the company website.

3. You should deploy the Datacenter edition of Windows Server 2008 R2 because it comes with unlimited virtual machine rights.

Case Scenario 2: Tailspin Toys automates Windows Server 2008 deployment

1. It is important to check that all the older routers support multicast transmissions.

2. During WDS setup, it is important to stop WDS from listening on port 67 and to ensure that all DHCP scopes have option 60 set.

3. Create a multicast transmission that will not start until 10 clients have connected to the WDS server.

Chapter 2

Lesson 1

1. Correct Answer: B

   A. Incorrect: A site-local unicast IPv6 address identifies a node in a site or intranet. It is the equivalent of an IPv6 private address, such as 10.0.0.1.

   B. Correct: A global unicast address (or aggregatable global unicast address) is the IPv6 equivalent of an IPv4 public unicast address and is globally routable and reachable on the IPv6 Internet.

   C. Incorrect: A link-local unicast IPv6 address is autoconfigured on a local subnet. It is the equivalent of an IPv4 APIPA address, such as 169.254.10.123.

   D. Incorrect: Two special IPv6 addresses exist. The unspecified address :: indicates the absence of an address and is equivalent to the IPv4 unspecified address 0.0.0.0. The loopback address ::1 identifies a loopback interface and is equivalent to the IPv4 loopback address 127.0.0.1. Neither is the IPv6 equivalent of an IPv4 public unicast address.

2. Correct Answer: A

   A. Correct: The solicited mode address consists of the 104-bit prefix ff02::1:ff (written ff02::1:ff00:0/104) followed by the last 24 bits of the link-local address, which in this case is a7:d43a.

   B. Incorrect: Although the 104-bit prefix is written ff02::1:ff00:0/104, the /104 indicates that only the first 104 bits (ff02::1:ff) are used. Hence, the solicited mode address is ff02::1:ffa7:d43a.

   C. Incorrect: Addresses that start with *fec0* are site-local, not solicited-node.

   D. Incorrect: Addresses that start with *fec0* are site-local, not solicited-node.

3. Correct Answer: D

   A. Incorrect: ARP is a broadcast-based protocol used by IPv4 to resolve MAC addresses to IPv4 addresses. ND uses ICMPv6 messages to manage the interaction of neighboring nodes.

   B. Incorrect: EUI-64 is not a protocol. It is a standard for 64-bit hardware addresses.

C. **Incorrect:** DHCPv6 assigns stateful IPv6 configurations. ND uses ICMPv6 messages to manage the interaction of neighboring nodes.

D. **Correct:** ND uses ICMPv6 messages to manage the interaction of neighboring nodes.

4. **Correct Answer: A**

A. **Correct:** In configured tunneling, data passes through a preconfigured tunnel using encapsulation. The IPv6 packet is carried inside an IPv4 packet. The encapsulating IPv4 header is created at the tunnel entry point and removed at the tunnel exit point. The tunnel endpoint addresses are determined from configuration information.

B. **Incorrect:** Dual stack requires that hosts and routers provide support for both protocols and can send and receive both IPv4 and IPv6 packets. Tunneling is not required.

C. **Incorrect:** ISATAP connects IPv6 hosts and routers over an IPv4 network using a process that views the IPv4 network as a link layer for IPv6, and views other nodes on the network as potential IPv6 hosts or routers. This creates a host-to-host, host-to-router, or router-to-host automatic tunnel. A preconfigured tunnel is not required.

D. **Incorrect:** Teredo is an enhancement to the 6to4 method. It enables nodes that are located behind an IPv4 NAT device to obtain IPv6 connectivity by using UDP to tunnel packets. Teredo requires the use of server and relay elements to assist with path connectivity. It does not require a preconfigured tunnel.

5. **Correct Answer: D**

A. **Incorrect:** This command displays the IPv6 configuration on all interfaces. It does not configure an IPv6 address manually.

B. **Incorrect:** You can use this command to add the IPv6 address of a DNS server to an IPv6 configuration, but not to configure an IPv6 address manually. You use netsh interface ipv6 set address to configure an IPv6 address manually.

C. **Incorrect:** This command lets you change IPv6 interface properties, but not an IPv6 address. You use netsh interface ipv6 set address to configure an IPv6 address manually.

D. **Correct:** You use netsh interface ipv6 set address to configure an IPv6 address manually.

6. **Correct Answers: A, D, F, and G**

A. **Correct:** IPv4 and IPv6 are both supported by Trey's network hardware and service provider. Dual stack is the most straightforward transition strategy.

B. **Incorrect:** Trey does not need to encapsulate IPv6 packets inside IPv4 packets. Configured tunneling is typically employed if IPv6 is not currently available.

C. **Incorrect:** Trey saw no need to configure NAT and use private IPv4 addresses. The organization is unlikely to use site-local addresses, which are the IPv6 equivalent of private addresses.

D. **Correct:** Trey uses public IPv4 addresses throughout its network. It is likely to use global unicast addresses in its IPv6 network.

E. Incorrect: Trey's clients run Windows 7 Enterprise edition, and its servers run Windows Server 2008 R2 Enterprise edition. All Trey's clients and servers support IPv6, and the protocol is installed by default.

F. Correct: There is no guarantee that Trey's network projectors and network printers support IPv6, although they likely do because the company believes in investing in cutting-edge technology.

G. Correct: Network management systems need to be checked for IPv6 compatibility.

H. Incorrect: High-level applications are typically independent of the Internet protocol used.

Lesson 2

1. **Correct Answer: B**

   A. Incorrect: The zone is AS DS–integrated, so you need to use the /DsPrimary switch. You specify /Primary for file-based DNS, in which case you also need to specify a file name.

   B. Correct: This creates the correct type of zone and the address prefix is in the correct format.

   C. Incorrect: The in-addr.arpa designation is used for IPv4 Reverse Lookup zones. Also, the zone type is specified incorrectly.

   D. Incorrect: You need to use 4-bit nibbles in reverse order to specify the address prefix. You cannot use slash notation in the dnscmd command.

2. **Correct Answer: A**

   A. Correct: You cannot list DNS records by using nslookup unless you have allowed zone transfers, even when the records are on the same computer.

   B. Incorrect: You run the Command Prompt as an administrator when using configuration commands, such as dnscmd. You do not need to do so when you are displaying but not changing information.

   C. Incorrect: You can enter **nslookup ls –d adatum.internal** directly from the Command Prompt. However, you can also enter **nslookup** and then enter *ls* **–d adatum.internal** from the nslookup> prompt.

   D. Incorrect: You can perform most operations on a server, including nslookup, by logging on through a Remote Desktop connection. Logging on to servers interactively is a bad practice and should be avoided.

3. **Correct Answer: D**

   A. Incorrect: There is no problem with the host record for the web server. Other users can access the internal website.

   B. Incorrect: You do not need to flush the DNS cache on the DNS server. The problem is with the user's client.

   C. Incorrect: The client computer is registered in DNS and can access other websites.

   D. Correct: A DNS cache entry on the client has marked the website Uniform Resource Locator (URL) as not resolvable. Flushing the DNS cache solves the problem.

4. **Correct Answer: B**

   A. **Incorrect.** The centralized WINS topology uses a single, centralized, high-availability WINS server or WINS server cluster.

   B. **Correct.** The full-mesh WINS topology is a distributed WINS design with multiple WINS servers or clusters deployed across the enterprise. Each server or cluster replicates with every other server or cluster.

   C. **Incorrect.** The ring WINS topology is a distributed WINS design created by having each WINS server replicate with a specific neighboring partner, forming a circle.

   D. **Incorrect.** Hub-and-spoke WINS topology is a distributed WINS design in which a central WINS server is designated as the hub and additional WINS servers replicate only with the hub in the site where they are located.

Case Scenario 1: Implementing IPv6 Connectivity

1. Site-local IPv6 addresses are the direct equivalent of private IPv4 addresses and are routable between VLANs. These addresses can still be used, but they are deprecated. You should, therefore, consider configuring every device on your network with an aggregatable global unicast IPv6 address. NAT and CIDR were introduced to address the problem of a lack of IPv4 address space, and this is not a problem in IPv6. You cannot use only link-local IPv6 addresses in this situation because they are not routable.

2. Both IPv4 and IPv6 stacks are available. In this scenario, dual stack is the most straightforward transition strategy.

3. As with DHCP for IPv4, you should configure a dual-scope DHCPv6 server on each subnet. The scope for the local subnet on each server should include 80 percent of the full IPv6 address range for that subnet. The scope for the remote subnet on each server should include the remaining 20 percent of the full IPv6 address range for that subnet.

Case Scenario 2: Configuring DNS

1. You can configure secure dynamic updates. This ensures that only authenticated users and clients can register information in DNS.

2. You can configure zone replication to occur only with DNS servers that have NS records and are on the Name Server list. Alternatively, you can specify a list of servers and configure zone replication manually so that zone information is replicated only to these servers.

3. When a Windows Server 2008 R2 server is configured as an RODC, it replicates a read-only copy of all AD DS partitions that DNS uses, including the domain partition, ForestDNSZones, and DomainDNSZones. Therefore, DNS zone information on RODCs updates automatically.

4. Create an IPv6 Reverse Lookup zone.

Chapter 3

Lesson 1

1. **Correct Answers: B, E, F, and H**

   A. **Incorrect:** You need to set the forest functional level to Windows Server 2008 R2. Therefore you need to set the domain functional level on all three domains to Windows Server 2008 R2. To do this, you need to ensure that all domain controllers in all domains are running Windows Server 2008 R2.

   B. **Correct:** You need to ensure that all domain controllers in all domains are running Windows Server 2008 R2. This enables you to raise the domain functional levels to Windows Server 2008 R2, and this in turn enables you to raise the forest functional level to Windows Server 2008 R2.

   C. **Incorrect:** You need to set the forest functional level to Windows Server 2008 R2. Therefore, you need to set the domain functional level on all three domains to Windows Server 2008 R2. To do this, you need to ensure that all domain controllers in all domains are running Windows Server 2008 R2.

   D. **Incorrect:** You need to set the forest functional level to Windows Server 2008 R2. Therefore, you need to set the domain functional level on all three domains to Windows Server 2008 R2.

   E. **Correct:** Setting the domain functional level on all three domains to Windows Server 2008 R2 enables you to raise the forest functional level to Windows Server 2008 R2.

   F. **Correct:** You need to raise the forest functional level to Windows Server 2008 R2 on a global catalog server in the root domain.

   G. **Incorrect:** You can raise the forest functional level to Windows Server 2008 R2 only once.

   H. **Correct:** When the forest functional level is Windows Server 2008 R2, you can use the Enable-ADOptionalFeature cmdlet to enable the Active Directory Recycle Bin.

   I. **Incorrect:** The Enable-ADAccount cmdlet enables an Active Directory account. You cannot use it to enable the Active Directory Recycle Bin.

   J. **Incorrect:** When the Active Directory Recycle Bin is enabled, every non-global catalog domain controller acts like an Infrastructure Master. As a result, IM FSMO placement no longer matters.

2. **Correct Answers: A and B**

   A. **Correct:** Typically, you apply a PSO to a global security group.

   B. **Correct:** You can apply a PSO to a domain user account, although it is better practice to apply it to a global security group and place the domain user account in that group.

   C. **Incorrect:** You cannot apply a PSO directly to an OU. If you want to apply it to user accounts in an OU, you need to create a special group, which is a global distribution group that contains all the user accounts in the OU.

D. **Incorrect:** A global distribution group is used to create an Exchange Server mail list. You cannot associate a PSO with a global distribution group.

E. **Incorrect:** You cannot associate a PSO with a computer account.

3. **Correct Answer: C**

A. **Incorrect:** You can control which AD DS operations you want to audit by modifying the SACL of an object. The SACL is not a tool, and you cannot use it to view Active Directory data stored in snapshots.

B. **Incorrect:** The PSC object is created by default under the System container in the domain. It stores the PSOs for that domain. The PSC is not a tool, and you cannot use it to view Active Directory data stored in snapshots.

C. **Correct:** You can use the AS DS data mining tool to view Active Directory data stored in snapshots online, compare data in snapshots that are taken at different times, and decide which data to restore without having to restart the domain controller.

D. **Incorrect:** The AS DS Installation Wizard lets you specify whether you are installing a writable domain controller or an RODC. You cannot use it to view Active Directory data stored in snapshots.

4. **Correct Answer: B**

A. **Incorrect:** Forest trusts are between forests. Windows NT 4 does not recognize the concept of a forest.

B. **Correct:** External trusts are used when migrating resources from Windows NT domains. Windows NT does not use the concept of forests; a Windows NT 4 domain is a self-contained, autonomous unit. You would use an external trust when you plan to migrate resources from a Windows NT 4 domain into an existing Active Directory forest.

C. **Incorrect:** You use a realm trust when accessing resources in a UNIX realm. You would not use a realm trust if you plan to migrate resources from a Windows NT 4 domain into an existing Active Directory forest.

D. **Incorrect:** If users in one child domain frequently need to access resources in another child domain in another forest, you might decide to create a shortcut trust between the two domains. You would not use a shortcut trust if you plan to migrate resources from a Windows NT 4 domain into an existing Active Directory forest.

5. **Correct Answer: D**

A. **Incorrect:** Password Replication Policy is configured by connecting Active Directory Users And Computers to a writable domain controller, not an RODC. Your branch office colleague does not have the rights required to configure this policy.

B. **Incorrect:** Password Replication Policy cannot be configured in Server Manager. Also, it is very bad practice to add users who may not have the appropriate skills to the Domain Admins group.

C. **Incorrect:** Password Replication Policy cannot be configured in Server Manager.

D. **Correct:** A domain administrator can configure Password Replication Policy by opening Active Directory Users And Computers and ensuring that the tool is connected to a writable domain controller.

6. **Correct Answer: C**

   A. **Incorrect:** Windows 2000 forest functional level does not support forest trusts.

   B. **Incorrect:** Windows 2000 native is a domain functional level, not a forest functional level. It does not support forest trusts.

   C. **Correct:** Windows Server 2003 forest functional level supports forest trusts.

   D. **Incorrect:** Windows Server 2008 forest functional level supports forest trusts. However, the minimum forest functional level that supports forest trusts is Windows Server 2003.

   E. **Incorrect:** Windows Server 2008 R2 forest functional level supports forest trusts. However, the minimum forest functional level that supports forest trusts is Windows Server 2003.

7. **Correct Answer: C**

   A. **Incorrect:** Windows Server 2008 R2 domain functional level supports Netdom.exe. However, it does not support Windows Server 2003 and Windows Server 2008 domain controllers.

   B. **Incorrect:** Windows 2008 domain functional level supports Netdom.exe. However, it does not support Windows Server 2003 domain controllers.

   C. **Correct:** Windows Server 2003 domain functional level supports Windows Server 2003 domain controllers, Windows Server 2008 domain controllers, and Netdom.exe.

   D. **Incorrect:** Windows Server 2000 native domain functional level does not support Netdom.exe.

   E. **Incorrect:** Windows 2000 mixed domain functional level is not available in a domain that contains Windows Server 2008 or Windows Server 2008 R2 domain controllers. Also, it does not support Netdom.exe.

Lesson 2

1. **Correct Answer: B**

   A. **Incorrect:** You should not deploy an Enterprise Root CA because the question indicates that one has already been deployed.

   B. **Correct:** As the question indicates, there is already an Enterprise CA present in some capacity at the head office location, so you should deploy an Enterprise Subordinate CA.

   C. **Incorrect:** Because the question mentions support for autoenrollment policies, an Enterprise Subordinate CA is required.

   D. **Incorrect:** Because the question mentions support for autoenrollment policies, an Enterprise Subordinate CA is required.

2. **Correct Answers: A and B**

   A. Correct: To deploy autoenrollment, you need to enable autoenrollment within Active Directory.

   B. Correct: Autoenrollment permissions must be applied to certificate templates before certificates can be enrolled automatically.

   C. Incorrect: CRL publication settings do not need to be modified from their defaults to support the deployment of autoenrollment.

   D. Incorrect: An Online Responder is not necessary for the deployment of autoenrollment.

   E. Incorrect: Web Enrollment is not necessary for the deployment of autoenrollment.

3. **Correct Answers: B, C, and D**

   A. Incorrect: The OSCP Response Signing certificate needs to be installed on the Online Responder, not the CA.

   B. Correct: You need to configure the OCSP Response Signing certificate template on the CA.

   C. Correct: You need to install the OCSP Response Signing certificate on the server that will perform the Online Responder function.

   D. Correct: You need to configure the AIA extension on the CA with the URL of the Online Responder.

   E. Incorrect: You need to configure the AIA extension on the CA with the URL of the Online Responder rather than the URL of the CA.

4. **Correct Answer: D**

   A. Incorrect: Installing an Enterprise Subordinate CA in the branch office will not reduce problems associated with revocation checks that currently occur across WAN links.

   B. Incorrect: Although it is possible to publish CRL data to alternate locations, such as a branch office file share, by default, the deployment of an Enterprise Subordinate CA does not include CRL information of certificates issued by a CA farther up the PKI hierarchy. This task is best suited to Online Responders.

   C. Incorrect: Standalone Subordinate CAs cannot help in servicing revocation checks for certificates issued by Enterprise Root CAs.

   D. Correct: Online Responders can speed up certificate verification as they hold a copy of the CRL and can reply to requests on an individual basis about the status of specific certificates. Having a local Online Responder in the satellite office reduces traffic over WAN links.

5. **Correct Answer: C**

   A. Incorrect: The Certification Authority console can view the status of one CA at a time. The Enterprise PKI tool can be used to view the status of all CAs in an Active Directory forest at a time.

B. Incorrect: The Online Responder Management Console is used to manage Online Responders. Even though the console can be used to manage Online Responder Arrays, Online Responders do not have to be installed on servers that function as CAs.

C. Correct: The Enterprise PKI tool can be used to view the status of a network's PKI environment, including all CA hierarchies that exist within an Active Directory forest.

D. Incorrect: The Certificates snap-in allows you to view certificates for a user, computer, or service account. It cannot be used to view the status of Certificate Authorities.

Case Scenario 1: Planning an Upgrade from Windows Server 2003 to Windows Server 2008 R2

1. Windows Server 2008 introduced fine-grained password policies that enable settings other than the default to be set for specified users or security groups, and this facility is retained in Windows Server 2008 R2. In Windows 2003 domains, variations in password policy typically require additional domains.

2. There is no need to raise the forest functional level to Windows Server 2008 R2 during this upgrade because the Windows Server 2003 forest functional level supports all the new features. The eventual plan is to raise the domain functional level to Windows Server 2008 R2 to take advantage of (for example) fine-grained password policies and the Active Directory Recycle Bin, but this need not be done until all domain controllers are running Windows Server 2008 R2. Domain and forest functional levels do not affect member severs. A Windows 2000 Server member server can operate in a domain with a Windows Server 2008 R2 domain and forest functional level.

3. Windows Server 2008 R2 RODCs can be installed at branch offices, possibly on the servers that currently host the secondary DNS servers. This improves logon speed while avoiding the security and administration issues that would result from placing writable domain controllers at these locations.

Case Scenario 2: Deploying Certificate Services at Coho Vineyard.

1. Configure autoenrollment in Active Directory and on the IPsec certificate template.

2. Deploy an Online Responder.

3. You can specify that issued certificates are not stored in the CA database on enterprise CAs running any edition of Windows Server 2008 R2. However, if you specify this option, you need to keep in mind that because issued certificates are not stored in the CA, certificate revocation is not possible.

Chapter 4

Lesson 1

1. **Correct Answers: B, C, and E**

   A. **Incorrect:** If you right-click a GPO under an OU, the Manage Backups control is not available. You need to right-click the GPO in the Group Policy Objects container.

   B. **Correct:** This procedure restores MyGPO from backup.

   C. **Correct:** This procedure lets you select the MyGPO backup and restore MyGPO.

   D. **Incorrect:** The Manage Backups control in the Starter GPOs container enables you to restore a selected Starter GPO from backup. It does not let you restore a normal GPO.

   E. **Correct:** This procedure lets you select the MyGPO backup and restore MyGPO.

2. **Correct Answers: B and C**

   A. **Incorrect:** This procedure backs up all normal GPOs. It does not back up Starter GPOs.

   B. **Correct:** This procedure backs up all Starter GPOs, including MyStarterGPO.

   C. **Correct:** This procedure specifically backs up MyStarterGPO.

   D. **Incorrect:** The Manage Backups control in the Starter GPOs container enables you to restore a selected Starter GPO from backup. It does not back up a GPO.

   E. **Incorrect:** The Manage Backups control in the Group Policy Objects container enables you to restore a selected normal GPO from backup. It does not back up a GPO.

3. **Correct Answers: A, C, D, and E**

   A. **Correct:** This setting displays policy settings that have text in the Comment field.

   B. **Incorrect:** This setting does not display policy settings that have text in the Comment field. It will not therefore display settings with "Internet Explorer" in this field.

   C. **Correct:** You need to enable the Keyword filters to identify Comment fields that contain the keywords that you define.

   D. **Correct:** You need to define the text pattern for which you are searching. The Exact setting specifies that an exact pattern match needs to be detected. If, instead, you specify Any, any comment that contains the word "Internet" or the word "Explorer" would be displayed.

   E. **Correct:** This setting looks for the text pattern in the Comment field.

   F. **Incorrect:** This setting looks for the text pattern in the Policy Setting Title or the Help Text fields, but not in the Comment field. You want to detect the text pattern in the Comment field, according to the question.

4. **Correct Answer: D**

   A. **Incorrect:** The Policies element contains the individual policy setting definitions. It does not contain version numbers or encoding information.

   B. **Incorrect:** The SupportedOn element specifies references to localized text strings defining the operating systems or applications affected by a specific policy setting. It does not contain version numbers or encoding information.

   C. **Incorrect:** The PolicyNamespaces element defines the unique namespace for the ADMX file. It does not contain version numbers or encoding information.

   D. **Correct:** The XML declaration is required to validate the file as an XML-based file. It contains version numbers and encoding information.

5. **Correct Answer: B**

   A. **Incorrect:** The Categories element specifies categories under which the policy setting in the file will be displayed in the Group Policy Management Editor. It does not specify references to localized text strings defining operating systems or applications.

   B. **Correct:** The SupportedOn element specifies references to localized text strings defining the operating systems or applications affected by a specific policy setting. It does not contain version numbers or encoding information.

   C. **Incorrect:** The PolicyNamespaces element defines the unique namespace for the ADMX file. It does not specify references to localized text strings defining operating systems or applications.

   D. **Incorrect:** The Resources element specifies the requirements for the language-specific resources, such as the minimum required version of the associated .adml file. It does not specify references to localized text strings defining operating systems or applications.

Lesson 2

1. **Correct Answers: A and E**

   A. **Correct:** The Disk Diagnostic: Configure Execution Level computer-based policy setting requires that Desktop Experience be installed on a server running Windows Server 2008 or Windows Server 2008 R2. It determines the execution level for SMART-based disk diagnostics.

   B. **Incorrect:** The Do Not Allow Clipboard Redirection user-based policy setting specifies whether to prevent the sharing of Clipboard contents between a remote computer and a client during a Terminal Services or Remote Desktop Services session. It does not require that Desktop Experience be installed on a server running Windows Server 2008 or Windows Server 2008 R2.

   C. **Incorrect:** The Enforce Removal Of Remote Desktop Wallpaper user-based policy setting specifies whether desktop wallpaper is displayed on remote clients connecting via Terminal Services or Remote Desktop Services. It does not require that Desktop Experience be installed on a server running Windows Server 2008 or Windows Server 2008 R2.

D. **Incorrect:** The Set Update Interval To NIS Slaves computer-based policy setting allows you to set an update interval for pushing NIS maps to NIS subordinate servers. It does not require that Desktop Experience be installed on a server running Windows Server 2008 or Windows Server 2008 R2.

E. **Correct:** The Disk Diagnostic: Configure Custom Alert Text computer-based policy setting requires that Desktop Experience be installed on a server running Windows Server 2008 or Windows Server 2008 R2. It substitutes custom alert text in the disk diagnostic message shown to users when a disk reports a SMART fault.

2. **Correct Answers: A, C, and D**

A. **Correct:** The Allow Time Zone Redirection user-based policy setting determines whether or not the client redirects its time zone settings to the Terminal Services or Remote Desktop Services session.

B. **Incorrect:** The Disk Diagnostic: Configure Execution Level computer-based policy setting determines the execution level for SMART-based disk diagnostics. It is not associated with Terminal Services or Remote Desktop Services.

C. **Correct:** The Do Not Allow Clipboard Redirection user-based policy setting specifies whether to prevent the sharing of Clipboard contents (Clipboard redirection) between a remote computer and a client during a Terminal Services or Remote Desktop Services session.

D. **Correct:** The Enforce Removal Of Remote Desktop Wallpaper user-based policy setting specifies whether desktop wallpaper is displayed on remote clients connecting via Terminal Services or Remote Desktop Services.

E. **Incorrect:** The Turn On Extensive Logging For Domain Controllers Running Server For NIS computer-based policy setting allows you to manage the extensive logging feature for SNIS domain controllers. It is not associated with Terminal Services or Remote Desktop Services.

3. **Correct Answers: B, C, and E**

A. **Incorrect:** Although having too many GPOs (often with the same settings) is a common mistake, it is also a bad idea to have too few. If a GPO has a lot of policy settings configured in different areas, it can be difficult to understand everything it does or to give it a descriptive name. Linking GPOs to OUs across sites can slow replication and increase traffic over slow wide area network (WAN) links.

B. **Correct:** If you put ADMX files in a central store on a domain controller, they can be replicated to other domain controllers in your domain. The Group Policy Management Editor does not copy ADMX files to each edited GPO but instead reads them from a single domain-level location or central store. This speeds up the process and reduces network traffic. Also, if you decide to generate custom ADMX files, you can put them in the central store and they will be read (or consumed) by the Group Policy Management Editor.

C. **Correct:** Both GPOs and OUs should have descriptive names. You might know what GPO06 does right now, but will you remember in three months? If you had called it Kiosk

Policy (for example), its function would be much clearer. Similarly, an OU named Human Resources is more helpful than one that is named OU23.

D. Incorrect: Features such as block inheritance, no override, security filtering, and loopback policies can be useful in the situations for which they were designed. However, they add complexity and make your Group Policy design more difficult to understand. You should use these features only where you can identify a real advantage in doing so.

E. Correct: Even if changes to a GPO have been replicated across the domain, they do not take effect until the next time Group Policy is refreshed. The Gpupdate command forces a policy refresh. You can use the command on a domain controller or on any member server or client on the domain where you want Group Policy changes to take effect immediately.

4. **Correct Answer: B**

A. Incorrect: GPResult.exe verifies all policy settings in effect for a specific user or computer. It does not check GPOs for consistency on each domain controller in a domain, and it is not a resource kit utility.

B. Correct: The GPOTool.exe utility, which is part of the Windows Server 2003 Resource Kit Tools, checks GPOs for consistency on each domain controller in a domain, determines whether the policies are valid, and displays detailed information about replicated GPOs.

C. Incorrect: The GPMC report function generates GPO reports that you can examine and look for answers to questions such as whether Group Policy Results list the GPO as applied. However, it does not check GPOs for consistency on each domain controller in a domain, and it is not a resource kit utility.

D. Incorrect: When you have completed reconfiguring Group Policy settings, you should use the Gpupdate.exe tool to force a policy refresh. However, Gpupdate does not check GPOs for consistency on each domain controller in a domain, and it is not a resource kit utility.

5. **Correct Answer: A**

A. Correct: This generates the Group Policy Results or RSoP report for the logged-on user on the local domain controller.

B. Incorrect: Group Policy Modeling allows the user to simulate a policy deployment that could be applied to users and computers before actually applying the policies. The Group Policy Modeling report is sometimes known as the RSoP-Planning Mode report, but it is not the RSoP report.

C. Incorrect: Group Policy Modeling allows the user to simulate a policy deployment that could be applied to users and computers before actually applying the policies. The Group Policy Modeling report is sometimes known as the RSoP-Planning Mode report, but it is not the RSoP report.

D. Incorrect: This procedure generates and saves a GPO report rather than an RSoP report.

Case Scenario 1: Using Starter GPOs

1. If there are no configured Computer Configuration policies, it is a good idea to disable Computer Configuration on a GPO. This speeds up GPO processing.

2. Starter GPOs need to be backed up separately from normal GPOs, preferably in a separate container. Don should either right-click his Starter GPO and click Back Up or right-click the Starter GPOs container and click Back Up All.

Case Scenario 2: Planning and Documenting Troubleshooting Procedures

1. The first thing to check is whether the user should have access to the facilities. The colleagues she mentions could, for example, work in another department. The next procedure is to determine the RSoP for that user. This can be done through GPMC or by using the GPResult.exe tool. Finally, look at factors that might delay the application of policy changes to that particular user. For example, the policy change might have been applied recently and the user needs to log off and back on again, or it might be necessary to run Gpupdate on the user's computer before she can have access.

2. If problems are computer-related rather than user-related, the first thing to check is the network infrastructure. Is the computer plugged into the network? Are services running? Has the computer received the correct configuration through Dynamic Host Configuration Protocol (DHCP)? Are there Domain Name System (DNS) problems? Next, check that the computer is in the correct OU. If recent changes have been made to Group Policy settings, run Gpupdate on the computer.

3. Does Group Policy Results list the GPO as applied? Is the setting listed in Group Policy Results Report? Is the GPO listed in the Denied List?

Chapter 5

Lesson 1

1. Correct Answers: A, D, and E

   A. **Correct:** You can install RSAT on computers running Windows Vista Business, Enterprise, or Ultimate edition, Windows Server 2008, Windows Server 2008 R2, and Windows 7 Professional, Enterprise, or Ultimate edition.

   B. **Incorrect:** You cannot use RSAT with computers running Windows XP.

   C. **Incorrect:** You cannot use RSAT with editions of Windows Vista or Windows 7 that are unable to connect to an Active Directory Domain Services (AD DS) domain.

   D. **Correct:** You can install RSAT on computers running Windows Vista Business, Enterprise, or Ultimate edition, Windows Server 2008, Windows Server 2008 R2, and Windows 7 Professional, Enterprise, or Ultimate edition.

E. Correct: You can install RSAT on computers running Windows Vista Business, Enterprise, or Ultimate edition, Windows Server 2008, Windows Server 2008 R2, and Windows 7 Professional, Enterprise, or Ultimate edition.

2. **Correct Answers: A and B**

   A. Correct: By default, members of the Administrators group are able to connect to a stand-alone computer running Windows Server 2008 using Remote Desktop.

   B. Correct: Members of the Remote Desktop Users group can connect to a stand-alone computer running Windows Server 2008 or Windows Server 2008 R2, even if they are not members of the Administrators local user group.

   C. Incorrect: Members of the Power Users group are not granted the ability to log on to a stand-alone computer using Remote Desktop by default.

   D. Incorrect: Members of the Print Operators group are not granted the ability to log on to a stand-alone computer using Remote Desktop by default.

   E. Incorrect: Members of the Backup Operators group are not granted the ability to log on to a stand-alone computer using Remote Desktop by default.

3. **Correct Answer: C**

   A. Incorrect: You will be unable to connect to a computer using Remote Desktop if its network adapter has failed.

   B. Incorrect: You will be unable to connect to a computer using Telnet if its network adapter has failed.

   C. Correct: You will be able to turn off a computer through EMS even if its graphics adapter and network cards no longer function. EMS connections can be made through USB or serial ports.

   D. Incorrect: Because you are unable to see a display, you cannot use PowerShell to accomplish the task stipulated in the question.

4. **Correct Answer: A**

   A. Correct: RD Gateway servers allow Remote Desktop sessions to be tunneled through a firewall on port 443. Placing an RD Gateway server at the subsidiary office location will allow you to connect to the remote office's Windows Server 2008 servers to perform administrative tasks.

   B. Incorrect: You should not place an RD Gateway server at the local office because this will not grant you access to the remote office's servers.

   C. Incorrect: Port 25 is not used for RDP.

   D. Incorrect: Port 25 is not used for RDP, and even if you could use port 25, your head office's private IP address range would be the incorrect configuration for the firewall.

5. **Correct Answer: B**

   A. Incorrect: Filters must be created each time that they are used. Custom views are persistent and can be saved.

B. **Correct:** Custom views can be saved and will allow you to achieve the goal of automatically viewing critical events from the Forwarded Events log that have occurred within the last 24 hours.

C. **Incorrect:** Although subscriptions can be configured only to extract critical event data, the question asked for the ability to view only critical events, not to collect only critical events. The difference is that with a subscription, you can collect all types of events and then apply a custom view to show only specific events.

D. **Incorrect:** You should not configure a WSRM policy. WSRM policies are unrelated to Event Logs.

Lesson 2

1. **Correct Answer: A**

   A. **Correct:** Feature delegation at the global level is possible only when the built-in Administrator account is logged on directly or invoked through the runas command.

   B. **Incorrect:** Feature delegation at the global level is possible only with the built-in Administrator account. It is not possible to perform IIS feature delegation at the global level with an account that is a member of the local Administrators group unless that account is the built-in Administrator account.

   C. **Incorrect:** Feature delegation at the global level is possible only with the built-in Administrator account. Adding a domain account to the Domain Admins group will not resolve this problem.

   D. **Incorrect:** Adding a local account to the local Administrators group will not resolve the problem because the only way to perform feature delegation at the global level is by using the built-in Administrator account.

2. **Correct Answer: D**

   A. **Incorrect:** Delegating the ability to manage groups will not allow trusted users to change passwords.

   B. **Incorrect:** Delegating the ability to create user accounts will provide branch office users with more rights than are necessary and also will not allow them to change passwords.

   C. **Incorrect:** Allowing a trusted user at each branch office to read user information will not allow that person to change passwords.

   D. **Correct:** Delegating the Reset User Passwords And Force Password Change At Next Logon task to a trusted user at a branch office site will allow that person to perform basic password management tasks without granting other unnecessary permissions.

3. **Correct Answer: D**

   A. **Incorrect:** Although this would work technically, Hazem would be granted the ability over all groups located in the OU, not just the Interns group. This violates the principle of least privilege, which requires that you assign only those rights that are necessary.

   B. **Incorrect:** The Delegation Of Control Wizard cannot be used directly on security groups.

C. Incorrect: The Delegation Of Control Wizard cannot be used directly on security groups.

D. Correct: Using the Managed By tab to set Hazem's user account, the Group Manager also confers the ability to modify group membership.

4. **Correct Answers: A and B**

A. Correct: The dsacls command, targeted at the appropriate OU with the /resetDefaultDACL option, will reset an OU's permissions to the default state.

B. Correct: Clicking the Restore Defaults button in the Advanced Security Settings for Delegation dialog box for an OU will reset the OU's permissions to the default state.

C. Incorrect: The Managed By tab in the Properties dialog box for an OU is for information purposes, rather than administrative.

D. Incorrect: The Managed By tab in the Properties dialog box for an OU is for information purposes, rather than administrative.

E. Incorrect: The dsquery command only provides information about objects in AD DS. It cannot be used to reset an errant delegation.

Case Scenario 1: Fabrikam Event Management

1. Ensure that the Windows Event Collector service is configured to start automatically. Configure a source computer–initiated subscription on the collector computer.

2. Use Group Policy to configure the 30 servers to forward events to the computer that you have configured as a collector.

3. Attach a task to the event using the Event Log Viewer and set the task as the PowerShell script that you created.

Case Scenario 2: Delegating Rights to Trusted Users at Wingtip Toys

1. You need to separate user accounts into an OU structure that represents existing departmental organization. Once user accounts are placed into new OUs, you can use the Delegation Of Control Wizard to grant departmental administrative assistants the right to change and reset passwords.

2. Although team leaders should be able to modify group membership, they have no reason to be able to create or delete groups. To prepare for the implementation of this plan, create the specified team groups and then, by using the Managed By tab of each security group's Properties dialog box, specify the corresponding manager's user account.

Chapter 6

Lesson 1

1. **Correct Answer: A**

    A. **Correct:** The Equal_Per_User WSRM policy ensures that a user connected to an RD Session Host server with two concurrent sessions is assigned the same resources as a user connected with a single session.

    B. **Incorrect:** The Equal_Per_Session WSRM policy ensures that each session connected to an RD Session Host server is allocated equal resources. When this policy is enforced, a user connected with two sessions will be allocated more system resources than a user connected with a single session.

    C. **Incorrect:** Resource allocation cannot be configured by editing the properties of a server in the RD Session Host server's Management console. Resource allocation can be managed only using WSRM.

    D. **Incorrect:** Resource allocation cannot be configured by editing the RDP-Tcp properties. Resource allocation can be managed only using WSRM.

2. **Correct Answer: A**

    A. **Correct:** If a license server's discovery scope is set to Domain, only computers within the local domain will be able to request CALs from that server.

    B. **Incorrect:** If a license server's discovery scope is set to Forest, it is possible that clients from other domains in the forest will acquire licenses from it even if there is a server closer to them—for example, when their local server runs out of CALs.

    C. **Incorrect:** A license server located in the root domain with a scope set to Forest will provide CALs to clients in the forest, but it will not do so in a way that satisfies the location requirements of the scenario.

    D. **Incorrect:** A license server located in the root domain with a scope set to Domain will provide CALs only to clients in the root domain, not in the specific branch office locations mentioned in the question.

3. **Correct Answers: A and C**

    A. **Correct:** It is necessary to set the license server scope prior to installing CALs on an RD license server.

    B. **Incorrect:** It is not necessary to set the domain functional level to Windows Server 2008 R2 to install licenses on an RD license server.

    C. **Correct:** It is necessary to activate the RD license server prior to the installation of CALs.

    D. **Incorrect:** RD license servers can issue both per-device and per-user CALs.

4. **Correct Answer: D**

   A. **Incorrect:** Using WSRM policies will not enable capacity to be added as needed.

   B. **Incorrect:** Hyper-V would not work as a solution because there is an upper limit to the processor capacity on the virtual host. This solution requires the ability to add processor capacity as required.

   C. **Incorrect:** Although adding RD Session Host servers would meet emerging capacity needs, it would not meet the requirement that clients do not need to be reconfigured.

   D. **Correct:** Planning the deployment of an RD Session Host server farm allows you to add and remove servers from the farm as necessary without altering client configuration.

5. **Correct Answer: C**

   A. **Incorrect:** Forefront Endpoint Protection and other antivirus solutions can check for viruses and malware after a client connection has been made, but they cannot block unhealthy clients from connecting.

   B. **Incorrect:** RD Connection Broker is used to manage sessions that connect to RD Session Host server farms—you cannot use it to ensure that connecting clients pass health checks.

   C. **Correct:** A TS Gateway server can be used in conjunction with NAP to prevent computers that have not passed a heath check from connecting to the RD Session Host server.

   D. **Incorrect:** ISA Server 2006 cannot be used to block clients from connecting to an RD Session Host server if they do not pass a health check. It is possible to use NAP in conjunction with ISA Server 2006 but not specifically to block access to RDS clients.

Lesson 2

1. **Correct Answers: A, B, and C**

   A. **Correct:** It is possible to access RemoteApp applications through a Web page and to deploy Web page bookmarks through Group Policy.

   B. **Correct:** It is possible to create Windows Installer packages for RemoteApp applications and to deploy these packages through Group Policy.

   C. **Correct:** It is possible to create RDP shortcuts and to place these on accessible shared folders to allow users to access RemoteApp applications.

   D. **Incorrect:** RemoteApp does not work by executing applications on shared folders, but by executing the applications on the RD Session Host server. Applications can be deployed using RD Web Access pages, through Windows Installer Packages, and through RDP shortcuts.

2. **Correct Answer: C**

   A. **Incorrect:** You should use App-V; TS RemoteApp will not resolve the problem of applications conflicting when installed on the same RD Session Host server.

   B. **Incorrect:** You should use App-V; a TS Gateway server will not resolve the problem of applications conflicting when installed on the same RD Session Host server.

    C. Correct: App-V allows applications that would normally conflict—including different versions of the same application—to be deployed from the same RD Session Host server.

    D. Incorrect: You should use App-V; RD Web Access will not resolve the problem of applications conflicting when installed on the same RD Session Host server.

3. **Correct Answer: C**

    A. Incorrect: The problem is caused by the most recent version of the RDC software not being installed. Installing Internet Explorer 6.0 will not resolve this problem.

    B. Incorrect: Disabling the Windows XP firewall will not resolve this problem—it is necessary to install the most recent version of the RDC software, which is included in Windows XP SP3.

    C. Correct: Windows XP clients need the version of the RDC software shipped with Windows XP SP 3 to connect to RemoteApp applications using RD Web Access.

    D. Incorrect: Installing Windows Defender will not resolve this problem. It will be necessary to install the most recent version of the RDC software, which is included with Windows XP SP3.

4. **Correct Answers: B and D**

    A. Incorrect: Installing DFS would require opening ports related to the SMB protocol on the firewall between the perimeter and internal network.

    B. Correct: Although FTP 7.5 only supports basic authentication, you can secure authentication and transmissions from the internal network using SSL.

    C. Incorrect: Configuring a file share would require opening ports related to the SMB protocol on the firewall between the perimeter and internal network.

    D. Correct: WebDAV support secure authentication methods. Transmissions from the internal network can be protected using SSL.

Case Scenario 1: Planning an RDS Strategy For Wingtip Toys

1. Deploy an RD license server in each state office. Set the server to use the Domain discovery scope.

2. Create a Terminal Service farm using TS Session Broker.

3. To access RemoteApp applications through RD Web Access, it is necessary to upgrade clients running Windows Vista to SP1 and clients running Windows XP to SP3. As an alternative, you could upgrade all clients to Windows 7.

Case Scenario 2: App-V at Contoso

1. You should use App-V to allow users in the testing department to run different versions of the same application.

2. You should create Windows Installer files for the RemoteApp applications and configure the settings of the installers so that documents are associated with the RemoteApp application.

3. When preparing the installer files, you can configure RD Gateway settings. When the application is started, a check will occur to determine if the computer is on the internal or an external network. If the computer is on an external network, it will contact the RD Gateway server to make the connection.

Chapter 7

Lesson 1

1. **Correct Answer: D**

   A. **Incorrect:** You can use the Print Management console to change printer ports for a printer on a remote server. However, you could change ports on a local server previously, so this task is not new to the Print Management console.

   B. **Incorrect:** You can use the Print Management console to view the printer status for a printer on a remote server. However, you could view the printer status on a local server previously, so this task is not new to the Print Management console.

   C. **Incorrect:** You can use the Print Management console to add or modify forms for a printer on a remote server. However, you could add or modify forms on a local server previously, so this task is not new to the Print Management console.

   D. **Correct:** Custom printer filters allow you and other administrators to view and manage selected printers based on their site, rights, and roles. This task is new to the Print Management console.

2. **Correct Answer: B**

   A. **Incorrect:** The Print permission is assigned to the Everyone group by default. The user can connect to a printer and send documents but cannot pause, resume, restart, cancel, or rearrange the order of documents submitted by all other users.

   B. **Correct:** The Manage Documents permission is assigned by default to the Creator Owner security group. It allows a user to pause, resume, restart, cancel, and rearrange the order of documents submitted by all other users, but it does not permit the user to send documents to the printer or control the status of the printer.

   C. **Incorrect:** The Manage Printers permission is assigned to members of the Administrators, Print Operators, and Server Operators groups by default. The user can perform the tasks associated with the Print permission and has complete administrative control of the printer. A user with this permission can send documents to the printer and control the status of the printer.

   D. **Incorrect:** The Manage Server permission lets users create and delete print queues (with already installed drivers), add or delete ports, and add or delete forms. By default, the Administrators, Server Operators, and Print Operators groups are granted this permission. This is a server permission and does not permit a user to pause, resume, restart, cancel, or rearrange the order of documents submitted by all other users.

3. **Correct Answer: A**

   A. Correct: The Manage Server permission lets users create and delete print queues (with already installed drivers), add or delete ports, and add or delete forms. A standard user who is granted this permission is called a *delegated print administrator*.

   B. Incorrect: The View Server permission allows a user to view the print server. Without the View Server permission, a user cannot see printers that are managed by the server, and for this reason, this permission is given to members of the Everyone group. Granting this permission does not make a standard user a delegated print administrator.

   C. Incorrect: The Manage Documents permission allows a user to pause, resume, restart, cancel, and rearrange the order of documents submitted by all other users. It does not permit the user to administer ports or forms, and granting this permission does not make a standard user a delegated print administrator.

   D. Incorrect: The Manage Printers permission allows the user to perform the tasks associated with the Print permission and grants the user complete administrative control of the printer. This permission should not be granted to a standard user.

4. **Correct Answers: C and E**

   A. Incorrect: The Group Policy setting called Disallow Installation Of Printers Using Kernel Mode Drivers determines whether printers using kernel-mode drivers may be installed on the local computer. It does not affect whether a shared printer is published automatically.

   B. Incorrect: The Group Policy setting called Always Render Print Jobs On The Server applies when printing is through a print server. This setting determines whether the spooler on the print client will process print jobs itself or pass them on to the server. The setting does not affect whether a shared printer is published automatically.

   C. Correct: If enabled, the Group Policy setting called Automatically Publish New Printers In Active Directory ensures that a printer is published automatically in Active Directory when it is shared—provided that printer publishing is enabled.

   D. Incorrect: The Group Policy setting called Pre-Populate Printer Search Location Text enables the physical Location Tracking setting for Windows printers. It does not affect whether a shared printer is published automatically.

   E. Correct: The Group Policy setting called Allow Printers To Be Published enables printer publishing. When printer publishing is enabled, the Group Policy setting called Automatically Publish New Printers In Active Directory ensures that a printer is published automatically in Active Directory when it is shared.

Lesson 2

1. **Correct Answer: A**

   A. Correct: You can access the Provision A Shared Folder Wizard from the Share And Storage Management console.

   B. Incorrect: You access the New Namespace Wizard from Namespaces in the DFS Management console.

C. Incorrect: You do not use a wizard to create quotas. You can access the Create Quota dialog box from Quotas in the FSRM console.

D. Incorrect: You do not use a wizard to create file screens. You can access the Create File Screen dialog box from File Screens in the File Server Resource Manager console.

2. **Correct Answers: A, B, and D**

A. Correct: You can use the Provision A Shared Folder Wizard to share an existing folder.

B. Correct: You can use the Provision A Shared Folder Wizard to create and share a folder.

C. Incorrect: You have not installed the Services For NFS role service. Therefore, SMB is the only network sharing protocol available, and you cannot change it.

D. Correct: Provided that the shared resource is on (or is) an NTFS-formatted volume, you can configure local NTFS permissions with the Provision A Shared Folder Wizard.

E. Incorrect: You have not installed the DFS server role. Therefore, you cannot publish the shared resource to a DFS namespace.

3. **Correct Answer: C**

A. Incorrect: In Windows Server 2008 and Windows Server 2008 R2, quotas typically can be applied to both volumes and shared folders. In previous versions of Windows Server, they could be applied only to volumes. The 100 MB Limit template creates a hard quota (which cannot be exceeded) that can be applied to both volumes and shared folders.

B. Incorrect: In Windows Server 2008 and Windows Server 2008 R2, quotas typically can be applied to both volumes and shared folders. In previous versions of Windows Server, they could be applied only to volumes. The 200 MB Limit Reports To User template creates a hard quota (which cannot be exceeded) that can be applied to both volumes and shared folders.

C. Correct: In Windows Server 2008 and Windows Server 2008 R2, quotas typically can be applied to both volumes and shared folders. In previous versions of Windows Server, they could be applied only to volumes. However, the Monitor 200 GB Volume Usage template creates a soft quota (which can be exceeded and is used for monitoring) that can be applied to volumes only.

D. Incorrect: In Windows Server 2008 and Windows Server 2008 R2, quotas typically can be applied to both volumes and shared folders. In previous versions of Windows Server, they could be applied only to volumes. However, the Monitor 50 MB Share Usage template creates a soft quota (which can be exceeded and is used for monitoring) that can be applied to shared folders only.

4. **Correct Answer: D**

A. Incorrect: The FSRM role service manages quotas, file screening, and storage reports. It does not implement file storage at branch offices, and it does not have a Hosted Cache mode.

B. Incorrect: The FSRM role service manages quotas, file screening, and storage reports. It does not implement file storage at branch offices, and it does not have a Distributed Cache mode.

C. Incorrect: The Distributed Cache mode of the BranchCache For Network Files feature in Windows 7 typically is used in branch offices with fewer than 50 users. In Distributed Cache mode, a local client running Windows 7 keeps a copy of the content and makes it available to other authorized clients.

D. Correct: The Hosted Cache mode of BranchCache For Network Files deploys a computer running Windows Server 2008 R2 as a host in the branch office.

Case Scenario: Planning a Windows Server 2008 R2 Upgrade

1. You can install the BranchCache For Network Files role service as part of the File Server server role on a computer running Windows Server 2008 R2. This role service caches, within a branch office, a copy of the content that is retrieved from a web server or file server at a central location. If another client in the branch requests the same content, that client can download it directly from the local branch network without needing to retrieve the content over the WAN.

2. If the BranchCache For Network Files role service is installed and enabled on the source server at the central office, you can use this feature In Distributed Cache mode. In this mode, a local client running Windows 7 keeps a copy of the content and makes it available to other authorized clients. This eliminates the need for a server running Windows Server 2008 R2 in the branch office. Distributed Cache mode is best suited to small branch offices where all the computers are on a single subnet.

3. The FCI in Windows Server 2008 R2 provides a built-in solution for file classification that automates manual processes with predefined policies based on the business value of the data. You can use the functionality built into the FSRM role service in Windows Server 2008 R2 to classify files based on content and location so that the files can be protected and managed more effectively depending upon their business value.

4. The enhanced Windows Server 2008 R2 Print Management console features an improved Network Printer Installation Wizard, which reduces the number of steps that are required to add a network printer. The wizard automatically locates printers and installs the appropriate printer driver if this is available.

Chapter 8

Lesson 1

1. **Correct Answer: A**

   A. Correct: The Audit Account Logon Events policy records logon events authenticated by a domain controller. Forwarding these events to the server SRV-Records from all domain controllers will allow you to get a full picture of account logon activity at the site.

   B. Incorrect: Account management relates to the creation or modification of user accounts or groups. It does not relate to recording domain authentication events.

C. Incorrect: Audit Logon Events writes only local logon events to the event log. If instituted, it would provide data about people logging on to the domain controller, rather than logon events authenticated by the domain controller when they log on using another computer in the domain.

D. Incorrect: The Audit Directory Service Access policy is used to enable auditing on the access to Active Directory objects that have SACLs applied.

2. **Correct Answer: C**

   A. Incorrect: Although shared folders can be protected using BitLocker, BitLocker works on a per-volume basis and cannot be used to restrict access on a per-user account basis.

   B. Incorrect: EFS works only with user accounts. Group accounts cannot be assigned EFS certificates.

   C. Correct: Using EFS to encrypt the confidential data to each accountant's EFS certificate will meet this goal.

   D. Incorrect: Although shared folders can be protected using BitLocker, BitLocker works on a per-volume basis and cannot be used to restrict access on a per–user account basis.

3. **Correct Answers: B, C, E, and F**

   A. Incorrect: While it is always useful to know who is mounting an attack, this information is seldom readily discoverable. The purpose of forensic analysis is to track the timing, severity, and consequences of a security breach and to identify the systems that attackers have compromised. A forensic analysis typically does not record the identity of the attacker.

   B. Correct: The purpose of forensic analysis is to track the timing, severity, and consequences of a security breach and to identify the systems that attackers have compromised. Therefore, it should record the time of the attack.

   C. Correct: The purpose of forensic analysis is to track the timing, severity, and consequences of a security breach and to identify the systems that attackers have compromised. Therefore, it should record the duration of the attack.

   D. Incorrect: While it is always useful to know the computer from which the attack originated, this cannot always be determined. If the attack is external, the identity of the network from which it originates can be difficult to discover and the actual source computer is almost impossible to identify. The purpose of forensic analysis is to track the timing, severity, and consequences of a security breach and to identify the systems that attackers have compromised. A forensic analysis typically does not record the identity of the computer from which the attack originates.

   E. Correct: The purpose of forensic analysis is to track the timing, severity, and consequences of a security breach and to identify the systems that attackers have compromised. Therefore, it should record the identities of the computers that were affected by the attack.

F. Correct: The purpose of forensic analysis is to track the timing, severity, and consequences of a security breach and to identify the systems that attackers have compromised. Therefore, it should record the changes to the network that occurred because of the attack.

4. **Correct Answer: D**

A. Incorrect: The DS Access category allows you to audit events related to DS access, DS replication, and modifications to AD DS objects. It does not enable you to track the creation and deletion of security groups.

B. Incorrect: The Detailed Tracking category allows you to audit events generated when encryption or decryption requests are made to the DPAPI, when a process is created, starts, or ends, and when inbound RPC connections are made. It does not enable you to track the creation and deletion of security groups.

C. Incorrect: The Object Access category lets you audit a wide range of access events and events related to operations. Access events include access to the registry, to a network share and the files and folders that it contains, to file system objects, to COM+ objects, to SAM objects, and to kernel objects. This category does not enable you to track the creation and deletion of security groups.

D. Correct: The Account Management category lets you audit the creation, deletion, or alteration of application, distribution, and security groups and computer and user accounts.

5. **Correct Answer: C**

A. Incorrect: 21 days is a typical storage limit for online data storage in a database. This provides rapid access to recent events.

B. Incorrect: 180 days is a typical storage limit for offline data storage on backup media. Most organizations consider this to be a reasonable limit.

C. Correct: Typically, regulatory agencies require data to be retained for 7 years.

D. Incorrect: If data impacts on national security you must retain it permanently and never delete it. However this is not a requirement for normal regulatory data.

Lesson 2

1. **Correct Answers: B and C**

A. Incorrect: NLB is used only to balance traffic between WSUS servers; it will not help ensure that clients connecting at any office will use the local WSUS server.

B. Correct: Enabling DNS Round Robin and netmask ordering ensures that clients are provided with the IP address of their closest WSUS server.

C. Correct: For the DNS Round Robin and netmask ordering method to work, all clients need to access the WSUS server using the same FQDN. This allows the DNS server to return the "closest" result to the querying DNS client.

D. Incorrect: BIND secondaries allow non-Windows DNS servers to host zone data from Windows DNS servers. This setting is not related to WSUS deployment.

E. Incorrect: Configuring a large host file will not solve the problem. Queries to host files do not return results based on the querying host's IP address.

2. **Correct Answer: C**

A. Incorrect: Because each faculty's IT department needs the ability to approve updates, you should not configure downstream servers as replicas.

B. Incorrect: Replica servers do not allow for local administrators to approve updates.

C. Correct: Configuring one upstream server to retrieve updates from the Internet and five downstream autonomous servers, one for each faculty, meets the question objectives of minimizing bandwidth use and allowing each faculty's IT department to approve or disapprove updates.

D. Incorrect: Although five autonomous servers would allow faculty IT departments to approve updates, it would not minimize the amount of traffic between the University and Microsoft Update.

3. **Correct Answers: A and C**

A. Correct: You need to create computer groups on the WSUS server and then assign clients to these computer groups using Group Policies applied to departmental OUs.

B. Incorrect: The GPOs need to be assigned to OUs rather than to the domain.

C. Correct: You need to create computer groups on the WSUS server and then assign clients to these computer groups using Group Policies applied to departmental OUs.

D. Incorrect: There is no need to create a security group. You need to create a WSUS computer group.

E. Incorrect: There is no need to create a security group. You need to create a WSUS computer group.

4. **Correct Answer: C**

A. Incorrect: Although this may be possible with a significant amount of administrative effort, creating a scheduled task is not the best way to deploy updates using WSUS. You should create an Automatic Approval rule that uses the PatchTest WSUS computer group as a target.

B. Incorrect: An Automatic Approval rule that deploys updates to the All Computers group will deploy updates to all computers, not the PatchTest WSUS group as specified in the question.

C. Correct: Automatic Approval rules use WSUS computer groups as targets for update deployment.

D. Incorrect: Automatic Approval rules do not use security groups as targets for update deployment.

5. **Correct Answer: C**

   A. **Incorrect:** Update Status Summary provides information about the number of computers on which the update did not install, but it does not provide detailed information about specific computers.

   B. **Incorrect:** Computer Status Summary provides summary information about computers and updates, but it does not provide detailed information about specific computers.

   C. **Correct:** The Update Detailed Status report provides a per-update report with a list of computers and update status. Navigating to the page that holds information about the problematic update will allow you to locate the relevant computers quickly.

   D. **Incorrect:** A Computer Detailed Status report will give you one computer per-page information about the status of particular updates. Although it would be possible to check every page of such a report, the Update Detailed Status report more easily provides the information that you require to find information about the problematic update and to enable you to locate the relevant computers quickly.

Case Scenario 1: Implementing a Security Plan for the Adatum Corporation

1. You need to configure Audit Policies under Advanced Audit Policy Configuration in Security Settings under Windows Settings in Group Policy Computer Settings. You use the Group Policy Management Editor to configure the auditing of these policies and Event Viewer to view the results of this audit.

2. The Adatum Corporation needs to store any data that affects national security permanently and cannot delete it. This includes forensic information about attacks that attempt to access such data.

3. Web servers on a peripheral network are the most likely to be the target for DoS attacks and need to be protected against such attacks by, for example, the use of IP Filtering and Black Lists.

Case Scenario 2: Deploying WSUS 3.0 SP2 at Fabrikam

1. You should add the CIO's account to the WSUS Reporters local group. This will allow the CIO to run reports without being assigned unnecessary administrative privileges.

2. You should configure the downstream WSUS servers at the Fabrikam satellite offices as WSUS replicas. This way, the update approvals and the computer group configuration at the head office WSUS server will be inherited automatically by the downstream servers.

3. You should generate an Update Detailed Status report. This will allow you to bring up an update's report page, which will list the specific computers that the update failed to install on.

Chapter 9

Lesson 1

1. **Correct Answer: B**

    A. **Incorrect:** L2TP over IPsec uses port 1701 and would be blocked by the firewall configuration outlined in the question.

    B. **Correct:** SSTP uses port 443 and would be able to traverse the firewall configuration outlined in the question.

    C. **Incorrect:** PPTP uses port 1723 and would be unable to traverse the firewall configuration outlined in the question.

    D. **Incorrect:** IKEv2 runs across UDP Port 500 and would be unable to traverse the firewall configuration outlined in the question.

2. **Correct Answer: D**

    A. **Incorrect:** The L2TP/IPsec protocol does not support automatic reconnection after a computer is woken from hibernation. It would be necessary to reauthenticate when reestablishing a VPN connection using this protocol.

    B. **Incorrect:** The SSTP protocol does not support automatic reconnection after a computer is woken from hibernation. It would be necessary to reauthenticate when reestablishing a VPN connection using this protocol.

    C. **Incorrect:** The PPTP protocol does not support automatic reconnection after a computer is woken from hibernation. It would be necessary to reauthenticate when reestablishing a VPN connection using this protocol.

    D. **Correct:** The IKEv2 protocol supports automatic reconnection up to 8 hours after the initial connection was established.

3. **Correct Answers: A and B**

    A. **Correct:** Computers running Windows Vista with SP1 or Windows 7 can connect to an SSTP VPN server running Windows Server 2008 R2.

    B. **Correct:** Computers running Windows Vista with SP1 or Windows 7 can connect to an SSTP VPN server running Windows Server 2008 R2.

    C. **Incorrect:** Computers running Windows XP Professional cannot connect to an SSTP VPN server running Windows Server 2008 R2.

    D. **Incorrect:** Computers running Windows 2000 Professional with SP2 cannot connect to an SSTP VPN server running Windows Server 2008 R2.

4. **Correct Answer: D**

    A. **Incorrect:** NPS accounting data is generated on the NPS server, which is also the RADIUS server, rather than on the RADIUS client.

    B. **Incorrect:** NPS accounting data is generated on the NPS server, which is also the RADIUS server, rather than on the RADIUS client.

C. **Incorrect:** The computer running SQL Server will not be forwarding RADIUS accounting data to the NPS server; the NPS server will be forwarding RADIUS accounting data to the computer running SQL Server.

D. **Correct:** It is possible, using the accounting node in the NPS console, to configure all NPS accounting data to be written to a database in SQL Server rather than the local log files.

5. **Correct Answer: C**

A. **Incorrect:** DirectAccess is only available to clients running the Enterprise and Ultimate editions of the Windows 7 operating system.

B. **Incorrect:** You cannot use DirectAccess with the Windows Vista Enterprise operating system. DirectAccess is only available to clients running the Enterprise and Ultimate editions of the Windows 7 operating system.

C. **Correct:** DirectAccess is only available to clients running the Enterprise and Ultimate editions of the Windows 7 operating system.

D. **Incorrect:** You cannot use DirectAccess with the Windows 7 Home Premium operating system. DirectAccess is only available to clients running the Enterprise and Ultimate editions of the Windows 7 operating system.

Lesson 2

1. **Correct Answer: A**

A. **Correct:** IPsec enforcement can be configured to allow and deny access on a port-by-port basis. This means that you can allow access only to computers with valid health certificates on the RDP port while allowing access to HTTP and HTTPS for computers without valid health certificates.

B. **Incorrect:** 802.1X places clients on VLANs according to their health. A healthy client will be placed on a different VLAN from an unhealthy one. Although it may change in future, as OSI Layer 2 devices, switches cannot be configured to block specific TCP/UDP ports (although some switches can prioritize particular traffic). In general, the term *port* on a switch refers to an interface.

C. **Incorrect:** DHCP enforcement places clients on different IP networks based on their health and cannot be configured to allow traffic on one port and block it on another.

D. **Incorrect:** VPN enforcement works on remote clients and is not appropriate in an intranet scenario because it will not influence non-remote clients.

2. **Correct Answers: A and D**

A. **Correct:** Using the operating system as a condition allows you to apply different rules to clients running Windows XP and Windows Vista.

B. **Incorrect:** You should not create a VLAN; you should create a conditional policy based on the client operating system.

C. Incorrect: You should configure the policy to allow Windows XP, not Windows Vista, to bypass the health check.

D. Correct: Configuring a policy that allows computers running Windows XP to bypass the health check means that computers running Windows Vista will still be checked.

3. **Correct Answer: C**

A. Incorrect: The domain controller running Windows Server 2003 does not need to be upgraded to support DHCP NAP enforcement.

B. Incorrect: The DNS server does not need to be upgraded to support DHCP NAP enforcement.

C. Correct: The DHCP ES is available only on Windows Server 2008 and Windows Server 2008 R2. The existing computer running Windows Server 2003 must be upgraded to Windows Server 2008 or Windows Server 2008 R2 to use DHCP NAP enforcement.

D. Incorrect: The NPS server does not need to be upgraded to support DHCP NAP enforcement.

4. **Correct Answers: A and B**

A. Correct: IPsec enforcement requires an HRA and a Windows Server 2008 CA.

B. Correct: IPsec enforcement requires an HRA and a Windows Server 2008 CA.

C. Incorrect: A DHCP server running Windows Server 2008 is not necessary for IPsec enforcement because statically configured addresses can be used.

D. Incorrect: HCAP servers are used in conjunction with Cisco Network Access Control and is not implemented as a part of the IPsec enforcement program.

5. **Correct Answers: A and C**

A. Correct: A computer running Windows Server 2008 must host the NPS Server role in an environment where 802.1X NAP enforcement is to be deployed.

B. Incorrect: A RADIUS proxy server is not necessary to implement 802.1X NAP enforcement.

C. Correct: Clients must have the EAPHost EC for 802.1X NAP enforcement to be deployed.

D. Incorrect: HCAP is only necessary when you are using Cisco Network Access Control clients. Although you might use Cisco switches, 802.1X NAP enforcement does not require the HCAP server role be installed.

Case Scenario 1: Remote Access at Wingtip Toys.

1. At the Sydney site, you would use an RD-CAP.

2. SSTP should be used because port 443, which SSTP uses, is already open.

3. You should use VPN enforcement in the Melbourne location.

Case Scenario 2: Coho Vineyard NAP

1. Given that several of Coho's legacy servers don't support IPsec, you should use the DHCP enforcement method until the pilot program is deemed successful.

2. When the pilot program is deemed successful, you should deploy the 802.1x enforcement method. This will meet your goal of limiting access at the switch level to computers that are not compliant with your organization's health policies.

3. Create a remediation group. When the 802.1x NAP enforcement method is deployed, create a separate VLAN that allows access to the remediation servers but blocks access to the production network.

Chapter 10

Lesson 1

1. **Correct Answer: B**

   A. **Incorrect:** A RAID 0 array, also known as disk striping, does not provide fault tolerance.

   B. **Correct:** If you have two disks and you want to prioritize fault tolerance over performance, you would create a RAID 1 array (also known as disk mirroring).

   C. **Incorrect:** A RAID 5 array requires a minimum of three disks. The question states that only two disks are available.

   D. **Incorrect:** You cannot create a RAID 1+0 volume using Windows Server 2008 R2.

2. **Correct Answer: B**

   A. **Incorrect:** Domain-based namespaces are accessed using the format *domain**namespace*.

   B. **Correct:** Domain-based namespaces are accessed using the format *domain**namespace*.

   C. **Incorrect:** Domain-based namespaces are accessed using the format *domain**namespace*.

   D. **Incorrect:** Domain-based namespaces are accessed using the format *domain**namespace*.

3. **Correct Answer: D**

   A. **Incorrect:** File Server Resource Manager provides functionality such as file screens, quotas, and file expiration. File Server Resource Manager does not provide any versioning or collaboration functionality.

   B. **Incorrect:** DFS, whether domain-based or standalone, does not provide versioning functionality.

   C. **Incorrect:** DFS, whether domain-based or standalone, does not provide versioning functionality.

   D. **Correct:** SharePoint Foundation 2010 provides both file versioning and collaboration functionality.

4. **Correct Answer: D**

   A. **Incorrect:** Override referral ordering is a way to get one target preferred over another. It will not limit users so that they can see only the files to which they have access.

   B. **Incorrect:** Offline files allows files on specially configured shares to be available offline. It will not limit users so that they can see only the files to which they have access.

   C. **Incorrect:** BranchCache increases the availability of files in branch offices. It will not limit users so that they can see only the files to which they have access.

   D. **Correct:** Access-based Enumeration means that users see only the files and folders to which they have access.

5. **Correct Answers: C and D**

   A. **Incorrect:** This option specifies that the user chooses the files that are synchronized and available offline. This will not ensure that the next time the user runs the executable, the file will be accessed from the cache rather than the share.

   B. **Incorrect:** This option prevents files from being cached offline.

   C. **Correct:** You need to enable the Select All Files and Programs That Users Open From The Share Are Automatically Available Offline option and then select the Select Optimize For Performance check box to ensure that the next time clients run an executable file, it will run from the cache instead of the shared resource on the server.

   D. **Correct:** You need to enable the Select All Files and Programs That Users Open From The Share Are Automatically Available Offline option and the Select Optimize For Performance check box to ensure that the next time clients run an executable file, it will run from the cache instead of the shared resource on the server.

Lesson 2

1. **Correct Answer: C**

   A. **Incorrect:** Remote Differential Compression is related to the transfer of data using minimal bandwidth. It is not directly related to Fibre Channel storage devices.

   B. **Incorrect:** UDDI is used by web services and is not related to Fibre Channel storage devices.

   C. **Correct:** MPIO must be installed on a server if it will access a LUN through multiple Fibre Channel ports or iSCSI initiator adapters.

   D. **Incorrect:** RPC over HTTP Proxy is not directly related to Fibre Channel storage devices.

2. **Correct Answer: D**

   A. **Incorrect:** The spanned LUN type does not provide improved I/O performance and is not fault-tolerant.

   B. **Incorrect:** The striped LUN type provides improved I/O performance over the simple type but is not fault-tolerant.

C. **Incorrect:** The simple LUN type does not provide I/O improvements and is not fault-tolerant.

D. **Correct:** The Striped with Parity LUN type (also known as RAID-5) provides improved I/O performance over the simple, spanned, and mirrored LUN types and also is fault-tolerant.

3. **Correct Answer: B**

A. **Incorrect:** The Failback MPIO policy uses a preferred path, only shifting I/O to an alternate path when the preferred path fails.

B. **Correct:** The round-robin MPIO policy uses all available paths between the server and the SAN array.

C. **Incorrect:** The Weighted Path MPIO policy directs I/O to the path that has been assigned the least weight by the administrator that configured it.

D. **Incorrect:** The Dynamic Least Queue Depth MPIO policy directs I/O to the path with the least number of outstanding requests. It does not distribute requests equally across all paths but directs requests taking into account a path's current load.

4. Correct Answer: A

A. **Correct:** Storage Manager for SANs is used to create LUNs.

B. **Incorrect:** Storage Explorer is used to manage Fibre Channel and iSCSI fabrics. It cannot be used to create LUNs on storage arrays.

C. **Incorrect:** Device Manager cannot be used to create LUNs on a Fibre Channel Array.

D. **Incorrect:** Disk Management cannot be used to create LUNs on a Fibre Channel array.

Case Scenario 1: DFS at Wingtip Toys

1. You need to install the DFSR service on all servers that host a replica.
2. Configure a server at each site to host a copy of the DFS namespace.
3. Configure replication to use the full mesh topology.

Case Scenario 2: Provision Data at Contoso

1. SharePoint Foundation 2010 or SharePoint Server 2010.
2. You should enable Offline Files to ensure that users are able to access shared folders when they return home.
3. Either RAID 1 or RAID 5 meets your redundancy objective.

Chapter 11

Lesson 1

1. **Correct Answer: A**

   A. **Correct:** Netmask ordering ensures that when a client requests a host name that is associated with multiple IP addresses, a check will be performed to determine if a record exists within the zone that is associated with the requesting client's subnet.

   B. **Incorrect:** Configuring a DNS secondary zone will not ensure that a client receives a host address on its subnet if one is available through DNS Round Robin.

   C. **Incorrect:** Configuring a DNS secondary zone will not ensure that a client receives a host address on their subnet if one is available through DNS Round Robin.

   D. **Incorrect:** Configuring a DNS stub zone will not ensure that a client receives a host address on their subnet if one is available through DNS Round Robin.

2. **Correct Answer: A**

   A. **Correct:** You should configure the Single Host filtering mode and ensure that all port 25 traffic is directed to the host with the SMTP server installed.

   B. **Incorrect:** You should not configure a port filtering rule with the Disable Port Range option. You need to configure a port rule with the Single Host filtering mode option.

   C. **Incorrect:** You should not configure the Multiple Host Filtering mode because you want all traffic to go to a single NLB node.

   D. **Incorrect:** You should not configure the Multiple Host Filtering mode because you want all traffic to go to a single NLB node.

3. **Correct Answer: C**

   A. **Incorrect:** You should not configure the Single Host, no affinity setting because this will direct clients to a specific host rather than the NLB node on their local subnet.

   B. **Incorrect:** You should not configure the Multiple Host Filtering, no affinity setting because this will not direct clients to the NLB node on their local subnet.

   C. **Correct:** You need to configure the Multiple Host Filtering, network affinity setting in the port rule because this will ensure that clients are redirected to the NLB cluster node on their local subnet.

   D. **Incorrect:** You should not configure the Multiple Host Filtering, single affinity setting because this will not direct clients to the NLB node on their local subnet.

4. **Correct Answer: C**

   A. **Incorrect:** The Stop option will terminate existing sessions as well as blocking new sessions.

   B. **Incorrect:** You use the Start option to resume the node after it has been stopped. You cannot use it to block new sessions from being created.

C. Correct: The Drainstop option will block new sessions from being created without blocking existing sessions.

D. Incorrect: You use the Pause option to suspend the cluster node. This terminates existing sessions, as well as blocking new sessions.

Lesson 2

1. **Correct Answers: B and C**

   A. Incorrect: Node and File Share Majority is appropriate for clusters with an even number of nodes.

   B. Correct: The Node Majority quorum model is appropriate for clusters with an odd number of nodes.

   C. Correct: Although Microsoft does not recommend that you use this model, this model is appropriate for clusters with an odd number of nodes.

   D. Incorrect: Node and Disk Majority is appropriate for clusters with an even number of nodes.

2. **Correct Answer: A**

   A. Correct: The Node and File Share Majority uses a file share to store the configuration data and can continue if half of the nodes fail.

   B. Incorrect: The witness disk is stored on a file share.

   C. Incorrect: The use of a file share means that the cluster resource remains available on the file share, thus making this answer incorrect.

   D. Incorrect: This quorum model allows half of the nodes to fail and it will still run.

3. **Correct Answers: C and D**

   A. Incorrect: Windows Server 2008 R2 Foundation edition does not support failover clustering. Failover clustering is supported only on the Enterprise and Datacenter editions of Windows Server 2008 R2.

   B. Incorrect: Windows Server 2008 R2 Standard edition does not support failover clustering. Failover clustering is supported only on the Enterprise and Datacenter editions of Windows Server 2008 R2.

   C. Correct: Failover clustering is supported only on the Enterprise and Datacenter editions of Windows Server 2008 R2.

   D. Correct: Failover clustering is supported only on the Enterprise and Datacenter editions of Windows Server 2008 R2.

4. **Correct Answer: D**

   A. Incorrect: Node and Disk Majority remains online when half or more of its nodes are available. This means that five nodes must fail if the shared disk remains online for the cluster to fail.

   B. Incorrect: Node and Disk Majority remains online when half or more of its nodes are available. This means that five nodes must fail if the shared disk remains online for the cluster to fail.

C. Incorrect: Node and Disk Majority remains online when half or more of its nodes are available. This means that five nodes must fail if the shared disk remains online for the cluster to fail.

D. Correct: Node and Disk Majority remains online when half or more of its nodes are available. This means that five nodes must fail if the shared disk remains online for the cluster to fail.

Case Scenario: Choose the Appropriate Availability Strategy

1. You could improve the availability of the SQL Server database by using failover clustering. SQL Server 2008 R2 is cluster-aware and the only way to ensure that it remains available in the event of server failure is by implementing failover clustering. Based on the information given, the company's main website appears to run from one server. You should add an additional server and then implement NLB to ensure that the web application can survive server failure. The web application running on the Linux server should use DNS Round Robin because you cannot use Windows NLB.

2. You need to configure a failover cluster that uses shared storage on the SAN. Once you had created the failover cluster, you could install SQL Server on the cluster and then migrate the database across to this server.

3. The most likely quorum model would be Node and File Share Majority because it enables the witness disk to be on a file share. Because there are only two servers in this scenario, it would be best to store witness disk information in a separate location.

Chapter 12

Lesson 1

1. **Correct Answer: C**

   A. Incorrect: If a service is configured as Automatic, it starts at boot time. It is very likely that the service in question is configured as Automatic and this is causing boot delays. You do not need the service to start immediately when the computer restarts, and a setting of Automatic is not required.

   B. Incorrect: Manual startup mode allows Windows Server 2008 R2 to start a service when needed. The service can also be started manually by an administrator or server operator. However, you want the service to start automatically as soon as a boot has completed, and Manual startup mode does not do this.

   C. Correct: If a service is configured as Automatic (Delayed Start), it starts just after boot time. Configuring this setting for the service described should result in a faster boot, and the service will start automatically as soon as the boot has completed.

   D. Incorrect: If you configure a service as Disabled, it does not start even if needed. This is not what is required for this service.

2. **Correct Answer: A**

   A. **Correct:** Reliability Monitor tracks application installations. It enables you to determine whether applications have been installed and exactly when the installations occurred.

   B. **Incorrect:** Action Center can tell you if an application or device driver is not working properly. It cannot tell you when an application was installed.

   C. **Incorrect:** DCSs capture current performance and configuration data. They cannot tell you when an application was installed.

   D. **Incorrect:** You can use Performance Monitor to view performance counters in real time or analyze performance data in a DCS. However, Performance Monitor does not record when an application was installed.

3. **Correct Answers: A, B, C, and E**

   A. **Correct:** Application failures are recorded in Reliability Monitor.

   B. **Correct.** Windows errors are recorded in Reliability Monitor.

   C. **Correct:** Application installs and uninstalls are recorded in Reliability Monitor.

   D. **Incorrect:** A service starting or stopping typically is recorded in the event log, not Reliability Monitor.

   E. **Correct:** Device driver failures are recorded in Reliability Monitor.

4. **Correct Answer: A**

   A. **Correct:** You can use the Wecutil command to configure the Event Collector service.

   B. **Incorrect:** The Winrm command configures WinRM. Typically, you run it on a source computer. You can run it on the collector computer if you are configuring a source-initiated conscription, but this is not relevant to this scenario because VAN-SRV1 is retrieving events from VAN-DC1. In any case, this command does not configure the Event Collector service.

   C. **Incorrect:** The Winrm command configures WinRM. Here, you are running it in quiet mode. Whether you use the -q switch or not, the command does not configure the Event Collector service.

   D. **Incorrect:** This command starts the Group Policy MMC snap-in. You can use Group Policy to add source computers to a source-initiated conscription, but this is not relevant to this scenario. In any case, the command does not configure the Event Collector service.

4. **Correct Answer: B**

   A. **Incorrect:** On the General tab, you can specify how frequently the graph updates and how much data is displayed in the graph before Performance Monitor begins overwriting the graph on the left portion of the chart. You can also specify whether Legend, Value Bar, and Toolbar are displayed and whether the Report and Histogram views show Default, Maximum, Minimum, Average, or Current values. You cannot choose whether to display current activity in real time or show log files saved using a DCS.

B. **Correct:** On the Source tab, you can choose whether to display current activity in real time or log files saved using a DCS. If you display a log file, you can use this tab to control the time range that is displayed in the Performance Monitor window.

C. **Incorrect:** You can use the Data tab to configure the display of specific counters. In the Counters list, you can select the counter that you want to configure and adjust Color, Width, and Style. You can increase or decrease the Scale value. You cannot choose whether to display current activity in real time or log files saved using a DCS.

D. **Incorrect:** You can use the Graph tab to select the scroll style and the type of graph to display. You cannot choose whether to display current activity in real time or log files saved using a DCS.

E. **Incorrect:** If you keep multiple Performance Monitor windows open simultaneously, you can use the Appearance tab to change the color of the background or other elements. This makes it easier to distinguish between the windows. You cannot choose whether to display current activity in real time or log files saved using a DCS.

Case Scenario 1: Using Data Collector Sets and Event Forwarding

1. James uses DCSs to record a performance baseline when the server is performing normally. He then runs the same DCSs manually when a performance problem occurs. If the performance problems occur at a certain time of day, he can schedule the performance data sets to record data at that time over an extended period. He uses Performance Monitor to analyze the results, compare them with the baseline, and identify the factors that could be causing the problems.

2. James accesses the DEN_FS1 server from DEN_SPARE through Remote Desktop and runs Reliability Monitor. This shows the applications that were installed or updated on the server at about the time that problems began to occur.

3. James uses event forwarding to transfer low disk space events to the DEN_SPARE server, which has been configured as a collector computer. He then monitors the DEN_SPARE event log to identify computers with low disk space by attaching a task that informs him that a low-disk-space event has been logged.

Case Scenario 2: Planning Monitoring on Server Computers

1. James should use the Reports tool in the Performance Tools console to generate regular system diagnostic reports on each server. A system diagnostics report provides details about the status of hardware resources, system response times, and processes on the local computer, along with system information and configuration data.

2. James should use Resource Monitor. This tool allows him to view the information that he requires in real time, to filter the results, and to start, stop, suspend, and resume processes and services and troubleshoot unresponsive applications.

3. James can configure Process Explorer so that it loads instead of Task Manager whenever anyone tries to open the Task Manager tool.

Chapter 13

Lesson 1

1. **Correct Answer: B**

    A. **Incorrect:** Members of the Power Users group cannot perform manual backups.

    B. **Correct:** Members of the Backup Operators group cannot configure Windows Server Backup schedules, but they can perform manual backups on computers running Windows Server 2008.

    C. **Incorrect:** Although members of the Administrators group can perform manual backups, adding the trusted staff member to this group will provide unnecessary administrative privileges because this task also can be accomplished by members of the Backup Operators group.

    D. **Incorrect:** Members of the Remote Desktop Users group cannot perform manual backups.

2. **Correct Answers: A and C**

    A. **Correct:** The script will run with the local administrator account credentials; therefore, it is necessary to place extra credentials for the remote share in the script. The *–include* parameter lets you specify the folder you want to back up.

    B. **Incorrect:** Local administrator account credentials will not enable access to a remote shared folder (unless the remote computer uses the same Administrator password).

    C. **Correct:** It is necessary to run the script using the local Administrator account because Wbadmin.exe can be executed only with elevated privileges.

    D. **Incorrect:** It is necessary to run the script using the local Administrator account credentials because Wbadmin.exe can be executed only with elevated privileges.

    E. **Incorrect:** The question specifies that the task must run every three hours.

3. **Correct Answers: A, B, C, and E**

    A. **Correct:** Windows Server Backup can write scheduled backups to local external USB 2.0 disks.

    B. **Correct:** Windows Server Backup can write scheduled backups to local external IEEE 1394 disks.

    C. **Correct:** Windows Server Backup can write scheduled backups to IDE internal disks.

    D. **Incorrect:** Windows Server Backup cannot be used to write scheduled backups to iSCSI SANs.

    E. **Correct:** Windows Server Backup can write scheduled backups to a volume on an external disk on a server running Windows Server 2008 R2.

    F. **Incorrect:** Windows Server Backup cannot be used to write scheduled backups to DVD drives.

4. **Correct Answer: C**

   A. Incorrect: If you select Normal Backup Performance, the backup time is directly proportional to the amount of data that is backed up. The server performance is not decreased. You cannot configure volumes separately to hold full or incremental backups.

   B. Incorrect: If you select Faster Backup Performance, you can increase the backup speed by tracking changes between the last and the current backup. The server performance can decrease significantly during backup. You cannot configure volumes individually to hold full or incremental backups.

   C. Correct: Where certain volumes have disk-intensive operations, you can choose the Custom option. This enables you to configure volumes individually to hold full or incremental backups.

   D. Incorrect: You should select VSS Full Backup when no other backup products are used to back up the host computer. The option updates each file's backup attribute and clears application log files. VSS Full Backup is not a performance optimization setting but is instead a backup configuration option.

   E. Incorrect: You should select VSS Copy Backup when another product is also used to back up applications on volumes in the current backup. Application log files are retained when you perform this type of backup. VSS Copy Backup is not a performance optimization setting but is instead a backup configuration option.

5. **Correct Answers: A, B, and C**

   A. Correct: When performing a manual backup of system state data on a domain controller running Windows Server 2008 R2, you can write backup data to a network share.

   B. Correct: When performing a manual backup of system state data on a domain controller running Windows Server 2008 R2, you can write backup data to a DVD writer. If the size of the backup requires more than one DVD, you will be prompted to insert additional DVDs as required.

   C. Correct: You can write a manual system state backup to an external USB 2.0 hard disk drive.

   D. Incorrect: You cannot write a manual system state to an iSCSI SAN.

Lesson 2

1. **Correct Answer: C**

   A. Incorrect: This command recovers the object named Solar located in the Pluto OU.

   B. Incorrect: You must use the Restore Object command to restore an object, whether it is a user or computer account.

C. **Correct:** You need to issue the command Restore Object "cn=Pluto,OU=Solar, dc=Contoso,dc=internal" to restore the Pluto computer account to the Solar OU in the domain Contoso.internal.

D. **Incorrect:** You must use the Restore Object command to restore an object, whether it is a user or computer account.

2. **Correct Answer: C**

A. **Incorrect:** Members of the Power Users local groups cannot restore backup data.

B. **Incorrect:** Members of the Power Users local groups cannot restore backup data.

C. **Correct:** To perform a restoration, it is necessary to be a member of the Backup Operators or local Administrators group on the server that the restoration is being performed on. Because user accounts that are members of the Backup Operators group have fewer privileges than user accounts that are members of the local Administrators group, you should use the former if you want to follow the principle of least privilege.

D. **Incorrect:** Although membership of the local Administrators group will allow for restoration of files and folders to be performed, this task also can be performed by members of the Backup Operators group. The Backup Operators group is assigned fewer privileges than the local Administrators group, so you should use the former if you want to follow the principle of least privilege.

3. **Correct Answer: D**

A. **Incorrect:** You first need to restore the AD DS container object, and then you need a second command to restore its contents.

B. **Incorrect:** The OU is named Australia, not Melbourne, so the code is in error.

C. **Incorrect:** You need to pipe the output of the Get-ADObject cmdlet into the Restore-ADObject cmdlet, not the other way round.

D. **Correct:** This restores the Melbourne computer account (and any other child objects contained in the Australia OU).

4. **Correct Answer: C**

A. **Incorrect:** You should not perform a bare metal recovery because this will remove the existing operating system and applications from the server.

B. **Incorrect:** You should not mount the backup images as volumes because this will not restore the intranet server's functionality without further intervention.

C. **Correct:** In this case, mounting the backup images as a virtual machine under Hyper-V will work as an effective stopgap measure until the replacement component arrives and the server can be restored normally.

D. **Incorrect:** Restoring the system state data from one server to another will not resolve this problem and may cause stability problems.

Case Scenario 1: Wingtip Toys Backup Infrastructure

1. An internal or external USB 2.0 or IEEE 1394 storage device must be attached to the servers so that scheduled backup data can be written. You also can write scheduled backups to volumes on hard disks or to network shares, but you are more likely to use hard disks for organizational backups.

2. Windows Server Backup can write scheduled backups only to local or externally connected hard disks, volumes, and network shares. Offsite backup requires that backup media be moved to an offsite location. This means that removable external devices, such as USB 2.0 or IEEE 1394 storage devices, must be used because these devices can be transported easily to offsite locations.

3. Configure Shadow Copies of Shared Folders on each shared folder and instruct users how to access it. This allows users to recover their own files and reduce the amount of time that help desk staff must spend on this task.

Case Scenario 2: Disaster Recovery at Fabrikam

1. You should restore the forest root domain controllers first because they must be in place to perform some operations on the domains comprising the rest of the forest.

2. Recover the domain controllers using the Friday full server backups. Perform an authoritative restore of the objects that were deleted on Thursday using the Wednesday system state backups.

3. To restore fileserve.hq.fabrikam.com as completely as possible, restore the full server backup and then restore the manual backup of the shared folders.

Index

About the Authors

IAN MCLEAN, MCSE, MCTS, MCITP, MCT, has over 40 years experience in industry, commerce, and education. He started his career as an electronics engineer before going into distance learning and then education as a university professor. Currently he runs his own consultancy company. Ian has written over 20 books plus many papers and technical articles. He has been working with Microsoft Server operating systems since 1997.

ORIN THOMAS, MCITP, MCT, MVP is an author, trainer and regular public speaker who has authored more than a dozen books for Microsoft Press. He holds the MCITP Server Administrator and Enterprise Administrator certifications. He is the convener of the Melbourne Security and Infrastructure Group and a Microsoft vTSP. His most recent books are on Windows 7 and Exchange Server 2010. You can follow him on Twitter @orinthomas.

Windows Server 2008 Resource Kit—
Your Definitive Resource!

**Windows Server® 2008
Resource Kit**

Microsoft® MVPs with
Microsoft Windows Server Team

ISBN 9780735623613

Your definitive reference for deployment and operations—from the experts who
know the technology best. Get in-depth technical information on Active Directory®,
Windows PowerShell® scripting, advanced administration, networking and network
accessprotection, security administration, IIS, and other critical topics—plus an
essential toolkit of resources on CD.

ALSO AVAILABLE AS SINGLE VOLUMES

**Windows Server 2008
Security Resource Kit**

Jesper M. Johansson et al. with
Microsoft Security Team

ISBN 9780735625044

**Windows Server 2008
Networking and Network
Access Protection (NAP)**

Joseph Davies, Tony Northrup,
Microsoft Networking Team

ISBN 9780735624221

**Windows Server 2008
Active Directory Resource Kit**

Stan Reimer et al. with
Microsoft Active Directory Team

ISBN 9780735625150

**Windows® Administration
Resource Kit: Productivity
Solutions for IT Professionals**

Dan Holme

ISBN 9780735624313

**Windows Powershell
Scripting Guide**

Ed Wilson

ISBN 9780735622791

**Internet Information
Services (IIS) 7.0
Resource Kit**

Mike Volodarsky et al.
with Microsoft IIS Team

ISBN 9780735624412

Windows Server 2008— Resources for Administrators

Windows Server® 2008 Administrator's Companion

Charlie Russel and Sharon Crawford

ISBN 9780735625051

Your comprehensive, one-volume guide to deployment, administration, and support. Delve into core system capabilities and administration topics, including Active Directory®, security issues, disaster planning/ recovery, interoperability, IIS 7.0, virtualization, clustering, and performance tuning.

Windows Server 2008 Administrator's Pocket Consultant, Second Edition

William R. Stanek

ISBN 9780735627116

Portable and precise—with the focused information you need for administering server roles, Active Directory, user/group accounts, rights and permissions, file-system management, TCP/IP, DHCP, DNS, printers, network performance, backup, and restoration.

Windows Server 2008 Resource Kit

Microsoft MVPs with Microsoft Windows Server Team

ISBN 9780735623613

Six volumes! Your definitive resource for deployment and operations—from the experts who know the technology best. Get in-depth technical information on Active Directory, Windows PowerShell® scripting, advanced administration, networking and network access protection, security administration, IIS, and more—plus an essential toolkit of resources on CD.

Internet Information Services (IIS) 7.0 Administrator's Pocket Consultant

William R. Stanek

ISBN 9780735623644

This pocket-sized guide delivers immediate answers for administering IIS 7.0. Topics include customizing installation; configuration and XML schema; application management; user access and security; Web sites, directories, and content; and performance, backup, and recovery.

Windows PowerShell 2.0 Administrator's Pocket Consultant

William R. Stanek

ISBN 9780735625952

The practical, portable guide to using *cmdlets* and scripts to automate everyday system administration—including configuring server roles, services, features, and security settings; managing TCP/IP networking; monitoring and tuning performance; and other essential tasks.

ALSO SEE

Windows PowerShell 2.0 Best Practices
ISBN 9780735626461

Windows® Administration Resource Kit: Productivity Solutions for IT Professionals
ISBN 9780735624313

Windows Server 2008 Hyper-V™ Resource Kit
ISBN 9780735625174

Windows Server 2008 Security Resource Kit
ISBN 9780735625044

mIcrosoft.com/mspress

Get Certified—Windows® 7

Desktop support technicians and administrators—demonstrate your expertise with Windows 7 by earning a Microsoft® Certification focusing on core technical (MCTS) or professional (MCITP) skills. With our 2-in-1 *Self-Paced Training Kits*, you get a comprehensive, cost-effective way to prepare for the certification exams. Combining official exam-prep guides + practice tests, these kits are designed to maximize the impact of your study time.

EXAM 70-680
MCTS Self-Paced Training Kit: Configuring Windows 7
Ian McLean and Orin Thomas
ISBN 9780735627086

EXAM 70-685
MCITP Self-Paced Training Kit: Windows 7 Enterprise Desktop Support Technician
Tony Northrup and J.C. Mackin
ISBN 9780735627093

EXAM 70-686
MCITP Self-Paced Training Kit: Windows 7, Enterprise Desktop Administrator
Craig Zacker and Orin Thomas
ISBN 9780735627178

GREAT FOR ON THE JOB

Windows 7 Resource Kit
Mitch Tulloch, Tony Northrup, Jerry Honeycutt, Ed Wilson, and the Windows 7 Team at Microsoft
ISBN 9780735627000

Windows 7 Inside Out
Ed Bott, Carl Siechert, Craig Stinson
ISBN 9780735626652

Windows 7 Administrator's Pocket Consultant
William R. Stanek
ISBN 9780735626997

Get Certified—Windows Server 2008

Ace your preparation for the skills measured by the Microsoft® certification exams—and on the job. With 2-in-1 *Self-Paced Training Kits*, you get an official exam-prep guide + practice tests. Work at your own pace through lessons and real-world case scenarios that cover the exam objectives. Then, assess your skills using practice tests with multiple testing modes—and get a customized learning plan based on your results.

EXAMS 70-640, 70-642, 70-646

MCITP Self-Paced Training Kit: Windows Server® 2008 Server Administrator Core Requirements

ISBN 9780735625082

EXAMS 70-640, 70-642, 70-643, 70-647

MCITP Self-Paced Training Kit: Windows Server 2008 Enterprise Administrator Core Requirements

ISBN 9780735625723

EXAM 70-640

MCTS Self-Paced Training Kit: Configuring Windows Server® 2008 Active Directory®

Dan Holme, Nelson Ruest, and Danielle Ruest

ISBN 9780735625136

EXAM 70-647

MCITP Self-Paced Training Kit: Windows® Enterprise Administration

Orin Thomas, et al.

ISBN 9780735625099

EXAM 70-642

MCTS Self-Paced Training Kit: Configuring Windows Server 2008 Network Infrastructure

Tony Northrup, J.C. Mackin

ISBN 9780735625129

ALSO SEE

Windows Server 2008, Administrator's Pocket Consultant, Second Edition

William R. Stanek

ISBN 9780735627116

EXAM 70-643

MCTS Self-Paced Training Kit: Configuring Windows Server 2008 Applications Infrastructure

J.C. Mackin, Anil Desai

ISBN 9780735625112

Windows Server 2008 Administrator's Companion

Charlie Russel, Sharon Crawford

ISBN 9780735625051

Windows Server 2008 Resource Kit

Microsoft MVPs with Windows Server Team

ISBN 9780735623613

EXAM 70-646

MCITP Self-Paced Training Kit: Windows Server Administration

Ian McLean, Orin Thomas

ISBN 9780735625105

Microsoft®
Press

microsoft.com/mspress